Public Sector Transformation Processes and Internet Public Procurement: Decision Support Systems

Nataša Pomazalová
University of Defense, Czech Republic

Information Science
REFERENCE

Managing Director:	Lindsay Johnston
Editorial Director:	Joel Gamon
Book Production Manager:	Jennifer Yoder
Publishing Systems Analyst:	Adrienne Freeland
Development Editor:	Monica Speca
Assistant Acquisitions Editor:	Kayla Wolfe
Typesetter:	Alyson Zerbe
Cover Design:	Nick Newcomer

Published in the United States of America by
Information Science Reference (an imprint of IGI Global)
701 E. Chocolate Avenue
Hershey PA 17033
Tel: 717-533-8845
Fax: 717-533-8661
E-mail: cust@igi-global.com
Web site: http://www.igi-global.com

Library of Congress Cataloging-in-Publication Data

Public sector transformation processes and internet public procurement : decision support systems / Natasa Pomazalova, editor.
    p. cm.
 Includes bibliographical references and index.
 Summary: "This book presents the methods, theories and practices involved in the growth and expansion of decision support systems as they relates to the public sector transformation process as well as internet public procurement"--Provided by publisher.
 ISBN 978-1-4666-2665-2 (hardcover) -- ISBN 978-1-4666-2696-6 (ebook) -- ISBN 978-1-4666-2727-7 (print & perpetual access) 1. Government purchasing. I. Pomazalova, Natasa, 1977-
 JF1525.P85P85 2013
 352.5'302854678--dc23
                          2012029184

British Cataloguing in Publication Data
A Cataloguing in Publication record for this book is available from the British Library.

All work contributed to this book is new, previously-unpublished material. The views expressed in this book are those of the authors, but not necessarily of the publisher.

This book is dedicated to the memory of Rudolf Pomazal, whose inspiration and whose approach is a reminder that ideas and dreams undergo development.

Editorial Advisory Board

Table of Contents

Detailed Table of Contents

This chapter suggests an original perspective for delineating the role played by procurement specialists
within the context of the efforts to redefine digital public procurement as a major pylon in the transformation of governance. Although in the last two decades scholars have provided an abundance of quality
academic accounts addressing the possible transformative benefits of e-procurement, more often than
not, public procurement specialists remain a mere afterthought within such discussions. In this chapter,
it is argued that the digitalization of public procurement will sustain the desired transformative returns
only if these efforts are accompanied by a reformative evolution of public procurement professionals.
Paradoxically, transformation at the individual level is found to be the key element for instituting genuine changes and effectively employing digital decision-making support systems in public procurement.

Chapter 2

The Kingdom of Saudi Arabia has embarked on the privatization of its public enterprises with the main
objectives of improving the efficiency of the national economy, enlarging Saudi citizens' ownership of
productive assets, and encouraging local and foreign capital investment in the Kingdom. Subsequently,
in 2003, the Saudi Council of Ministers approved a list of twenty-two targeted economic activities
and government services to be privatized and the private sector is being invited to participate in many
economic activities and services. As such, the aim of this chapter is to present the historical context and
rationale for privatization in Saudi Arabia. The objectives and implementation process taken by the Saudi
government to create a suitable environment for private sector investment and the issues and problems
associated with privatization initiatives are also discussed in this chapter.

Chapter 3

The current situation of taxation of electronic commerce is still in its infancy in regard to its actual implementation as well as in the existence of doctrinal principles and generally accepted guidelines on the characteristics and implementation of taxation. This chapter uses the concepts, analytical tools, and appropriate models of economic analysis to understand and explain the economic phenomena observed in the New Economy and how the public sector can adapt to the new challenges. Thus, the chapter analyzes the optimal design of tax policy for electronic markets, in particular electronic commerce, and the guidelines of antitrust policy in electronic markets. This chapter also analyzes the strategies that can be adopted by firms in the New Economy to avoid or minimize the risk of intervention by antitrust authorities.

Persuasion happens when somebody tries to change someone else's attitudes or behavior without using coercion or force. In different cultures, different persuasion principles seem to work better than others. This has to be taken into account in marketing and design. It is especially true when developing persuasive systems, i.e. systems that aim at changing the user. In this chapter, the authors study the role of culture in the context of authority and social proof. This was examined through positivist survey conducted by South Korean and Finnish College Students. The received results suggest that authority plays a bigger role in the Republic of Korea than in Finland. Ergo, the authors conclude that the implications of culture should be regarded when designing systems that aim at any kind of change.

Chapter 5

E-procurement has had a tremendous impact on the modernization of government and administration. In the U.S., the relationship between technology and e-procurement is central in determining the ability to adopt successful e-procurement. Significant investment in technology and human capital is required for the implementation of e-procurement systems. Despite widespread efforts to initialize e-procurement through direct investment in information and component technologies, a substantial portion of administrations' efforts at achieving e-governance have failed. The need for customized solutions and managerial intervention has challenged government at all levels. Furthermore, technological advancement has not been welcomed by all administrations. Nonetheless, the advantages of e-procurement typically justify the effort required to implement and maintain such systems. Reductions in transaction costs, increased transparency, and improved relationships between government and businesses are all advantages of e-procurement. While there are significant challenges to e-procurement not limited to corruption, the benefits of e-procurement far outweigh the costs.

This chapter focuses on the effective implementation of new electronic tools for Public e-Procurement in
public sector organizations. While an analysis of the characteristics of transformation processes necessary
for the development of e-Government and the choice between Public e-Procurement tools is theoretically already well developed, there are still a number of ambiguities in the approaches of rationalization implementation of these. A deeper understanding of the decision-making phenomenon in general
is provided. Flexibly adjusting the e-Government strategy on dynamics of the development of Public
e-Procurement tool ex ante or leading in an effort to change the organizational structures, information
flows, and constraints in which public sector organizations operate in the area of Public e-Procurement.
Public e-Procurement tools are selected for the analysis, because interesting progress is expected here.
Results from the nature of the dynamic transformation processes and decision-making show the need to
support changes in the environment arising from the development of e-Government.

Chapter 7

The benefits of e-business have been widely promoted but the Architecture, Engineering, and Construction (AEC) sector has lagged behind other sectors in the adoption of e-procurement. The prospective
benefits for the AEC sector are suggested by the proven advantages of general e-procurement where
adoption has been faster and deeper. However, several studies indicated that barely 20% of documentation is tendered electronically, suggesting there are barriers to e-procurement. In order to promote
adoption of e-procurement in the AEC sector, it is important to establish the status of the industry and
identify the drivers as well as barriers to e-procurement. This chapter provides a detailed discussion of
the state of the industry and its drivers and barriers while ranking these according to its importance. It
acts as a reference guide to allow those implementing e-procurement in construction to make informed
decisions as to where to focus their efforts to achieve successful realisation incorporating the benefits
and avoiding the pitfalls in the process. The chapter also provides some insight into the current state,
trends, and future directions of e-procurement in the construction industry.

Chapter 8

The chapter explores the Nordic statutory EU-based remedy regimes. Due to the European Economic Area
(EEA) agreement, the EU commitments do not vary between EU member states, Denmark, Finland, and
Sweden and (non-members) Norway and Iceland. The legislation on procurement remedies is assumed
to be EU/EEA compliant. There are however material differences in the set up for handling disputes
and complaints—also subsequent to the 2010-2012 Nordic adaptation of EU Directive 2007/66/EC on
enhanced procurement remedies. The pending issue is whether the EU "sufficiently serious breach"
principle on treaty infringements applies on liability for procurement flaws. Loss of contract damage

has been awarded in all Nordic countries, whereas cases on negative interest (costs in preparing futile tender bids) seem more favorable to plaintiffs. Per mid-2012, there are no Nordic rulings on the effect of the recent somewhat ambiguous EU Court of Justice Strabag and Spijkers 2010 rulings.

Chapter 9

The dynamic global environment has necessitated governments to adopt a systems approach of integrating suppliers, customers, and information linkages in an endeavor to create and sustain value for public services. The evolution of the concept "the customer is king" has placed the customer foremost in public management thinking. As a result, optimizing customer value in the public domain has become a focal point in managing procurement. The large quantity of public resources used for service delivery points to the importance of efficiency and effectiveness in expenditures as well as accountability. E-Procurement systems provide mechanisms for controlling, simplifying, and automating goods and services from different suppliers. While benefits like stricter control over spending authorization, easier transaction processing and elimination of redundant stock are achieved through automated procurement processes; the viability and success of e-procurement for the public sector is determined by various conditions. The conditions for successful implementation of an e-procurement system are explored as every government activity involves the spending of public monies on goods and services. Any failings in e-procurement practices can create possibilities for large-scale losses through incompetence, waste, and fraud, which directly impact the public.

Relations between public procurement, regional development, and e-procurement are discussed in this chapter. First, main themes of the debate are reviewed. Subsequently, some relations between public procurement, regional development, and e-procurement are discussed. The Czech Republic is used as a case study in this regard. The authors' findings confirm the potential of public procurement to stimulate development of Czech regions. Spatially, public procurement may not be regarded as a suitable tool for reduction of regional disparities. However, there seems to be an important impact of public procurement on the development of local small and medium enterprises. In addition, the authors' findings point at some links between public procurement and the concepts of sustainable development and competitiveness. Nevertheless, the dominant position of price as evaluation criterion indicates that the linkages are rather weak. Finally, the increasing interest of the Czech Republic in e-procurement was documented.

Chapter 11

Oana Gherghinescu, University of Craiova, Romania
Paul Rinderu, University of Craiova, Romania
Demetra Lupu-Visanescu, University of Craiova, Romania

The present chapter, after a short introduction presenting basic information about the European Union cohesion policy, presents the seven operational programmes that have been negotiated by Romania with the European Commission for the current programming period. The difficulties deriving from public procurement-acquisition procedures in Romania are identified; such difficulties are encountered during the implementation of European projects, thus questioning the effectiveness of the Electronic Public Procurement-Acquisition System. Although it was created with a view to securing the transparency of public funds distribution, it does not allow for tracking the concluded contracts compliance with procurement-acquisition terms. It is at this stage that the most serious problems related to public funds effective use arise. Emphasis is also placed on innovative tools used for submitting, evaluating, and monitoring projects, emphasizing the role of Management Authorities, as public bodies for managing this process. For each operational programme, an econometric model GARCH-like has been developed and applied for realizing this analysis at the level of NUTS2. Bucharest-Ilfov region has been chosen as a case study. Conclusions emphasize the beneficial role of such models especially for assessing the current status of absorbing the structural funds as well as for formulating suggestions for improvement as regards the next programming period. The chapter also pays special attention to the potential use of innovative tools in the application and implementing process as drivers for increasing the efficiency and effectiveness of the process.

Chapter 12

Karunanidhi Reddy, Durban University of Technology, South Africa
Renitha Rampersad, Durban University of Technology, South Africa

Broad-based black economic empowerment has been a central part of the South African government's economic transformation strategy. The main purpose of BEE is to increase the number of black people that manage, own, and control the country's economy, and as a result, to reduce income inequalities and to contribute to economic transformation in South Africa. During apartheid in South Africa, the government procurement system favoured large, established businesses and made it difficult for newly established businesses to participate in the procurement system. This chapter gives an overview of the Black Economic Empowerment policy as a means to achieve socio-economic transformation in South Africa by providing preferences for Historically Disadvantaged Individuals (HDIs) and small businesses, when making procurement decisions. It also examines how procurement is used as a policy tool by government while simultaneously ensuring that it does not contradict the constitutional right to equality. The chapter also explores the implications of the Preferential Public Procurement Framework Act (Act 5 of 2000) and the latest procurement regulations. Finally, it discusses the use of ICT and the vital role it plays in preferential procurement in South Africa.

Public sector governance relates to accountability, transparency, inclusiveness, and also effectiveness and efficiency of governmental organizations. Such objectives have been the intended outcome of some of the public transformation and reformation programs in Malaysia. However, even after the various improvement initiatives, there are still complaints made against public organizations, especially against local authorities regarding their lack of good governance and accountability. Thus, the question that needs to be answered is why local governance is still a problematic issue even after all the initiatives that have been implemented over the years. As such, the various challenges facing local authorities that constrains them from achieving the intended outcomes of transformation programs is discussed in this chapter. In so doing, a contextual description of the local governmental system and the contemporary reformation programs of public organizations, specifically the local authorities, are explained. In addition, the recommendations to overcome those challenges and to achieve good governance are explained in this chapter as well.

Foreword

The central theme of the book is electronic public procurement. The book pulls together a number of major issues facing the public sector, dealing with e-procurement and related areas. It is both an introduction to public procurement issues and a comprehensive guide to more detailed processes of development, transformation, and redefining matters associated with changes of the public sector's institutions and principles of authority. In particular, the following key areas are addressed with specific reference to public sector. The underlying conceptual issues are associated with running a public procurement and transformation of government policy. Further, it covers the underlying technology challenges and systems supporting the e-business. The action items for management concepts in an electronically-enabled world such as decision-making, e-governance, e-commerce, e-procurement, privatization, etc., are explained. The editor's purpose is to provide advanced research findings from the most significant experts and authors in public procurement domain.

This book begins with basic issues that arise at the front end of public procurement engagement. Next, the basic theory is discussed, and then insight into the specific applications of those established theories in various public procurements and under various contexts is observed. There are thirteen chapters—each addressing key concepts and assuming subject knowledge of subject matter to start with and subsequently progressing quickly into more detailed research findings. Each chapter is illustrated with qualitative and quantitative results and also contains a few core ideas with more detailed description. Finally, concluding remarks and future research directions are provided in each chapter. A references part and useful additional readings section along with key terms and definitions are enclosed.

As background, the transformation framework is mainly improving service quality delivery, reducing costs, and renewing administrative processes, or gained from the needs of government as re-examining the functioning of democratic practices and processes. In this regard, transformation is regarded as the cornerstone of theoretical concepts and innovative milieu. Moreover, there are close links between transformation on one hand and change on the other. Naturally, it is supposed that a change is beneficial for development. Changes are accomplished by projects and programs for redesigning the organization and strengthening core competencies during identity change of any organization, but transformation is a very complex process; therefore, there exists a high rate of failures related to changes. This state is based on lack of experience, hence, knowledge or incompetence, but tolerance to failures has a positive effect on the knowledge culture of the organization. Transformational change is driven by a combination of opportunities caused by new transformation policy, strategy, technology, ICT, etc. The change approach for transformation as combination of radical and incremental changes is based on moving from one stage to another.

Making use of e-Government, the public administration may achieve:

- **Financial Terms:** Cost reduction and better management of public budgets as required by the principles of cost-effectiveness and efficiency when administering task-related public resources.
- **Business Terms:** Concentration of public administration capabilities on objectives stipulated by the legislation.
- **Organizational Terms:** Trimming down of the organizational structure of the public administration and its more effective functioning actually mean better controllability, transparency, and subsequently, also better public administration management. Effective employment of personnel enables the public administration to maintain the optimal amount of employees.
- **Terms of Cooperation:** Links to other entities of the public sector when implementing the e-Government and acquiring new experience.

The e-Government implementation is usually brought into practice by the means of a project. An e-Government project depends on the public administration functional area and on the existing arrangement of a given area. Its progress is always very specific because of particular terms and conditions. A general structure is composed of the following activities:

- Strategic analysis of public administration functional areas.
- Specification of functional areas that will be subject to e-Government.
- Specification of e-Government implementation providers for different public administration areas.
- Specification of work share of different public administration areas when implementing e-Government.
- Transformation of the public administration for the purpose of e-Government implementation.
- Management of relations during e-Government implementation.

Individual activities are mutually interconnected, and therefore, it is difficult to exclude any particular activity. Everything must proceed in line with a project plan, which has been clearly defined in advance.

However, the formation of the e-Government accepts the characteristic of the establishment of this new face of governments, which together with new forms of technology and the growing interest and involvement of citizens and companies in what and how e-Public procurement is realized establish the future direction of the e-Public procurement in the e-government.

Their influence not only shapes the essence of an e-Government environment while limiting ways to reorganize the internal resources so that the pressure changes caused by these forces respond effectively and the possibility to compete successfully in a wide range of newly forming government is excluded, but creates conditions for sustainable development of entire public procurement.

E-Public procurement is serviced by a number of companies supplying products and services, including application of new knowledge of science and technology and information technology. The entirely new principles are beginning to build relationships with private suppliers of goods and services.

Changes in demographic structure in the administrative procedures fundamentally transform the nature of public procurement. There is also a further shift in the assessment of the role of e-Public procurement in their understanding as a prerequisite for effectiveness, transparency, and overall support for public sector. In the public sector, there are significant changes in increasing demand on product quality, production technology, the origin and safety of goods and services. This transformation is significantly subjected by economy in given country. There is a structural change at the national economies, and multinational power.

Overall, the governmental environment determined by the rules and principles conduct of e-Public procurement and other operating ongoing processes of e-Government and e-Public procurement, which is reflected generally in strengthening the position of subjects related to e-Public procurement, to find other ways to increase efficiency, including acquisitions, to reducing transaction costs, application of scientific and technological approaches in practice, which fundamentally change processing, competition, decision-making, and contracting in the new conditions. Another significant factor influencing e-Public procurement is the previously mentioned effect of cultural and economic development. Not only in the aforementioned aspects of these changes, but also in terms of current knowledge based e-Public procurement formation, it is clear that changes in e-Public procurement are influenced by the conditions of transmission of information, financial flows, and forming e-market structures. The process of choosing a governance structure is dynamic and the ability to understand these trends, in context with transformation across the whole society, becomes a crucial issue to find opportunity for the e-Public procurement.

What emerges is that to work effectively in public procurement in the 21st century we not only need to understand and be familiar with our own specialty in the public sector, but we also need to be aware of interdependencies between the public and private sector, the technologies that have evolved to facilitate doing business, innovative strategies and processes, cross-cultural and socio-economic challenges, and the law associated with the electronic environment. This book offers us excellence in all these fields.

Mojmír Sabolovič
Mendel University in Brno, Czech Republic

Mojmír Sabolovič *is Vice Dean of the Faculty of Regional Development and International Studies at Mendel University in Brno, Czech Republic. He was a Research Assistant in the Department of Regional and Business Economics, an Organization Worker in the Department of Languages, a Coordinator of the FRRMS project in the Dean's Office of the Faculty of Regional Development and International Studies, and Deputy Head of the Department of Languages. He has taught courses in Business Validation, English for Genetics, Financial Management, Investment Decision, and Valuation of Intangible Assets.*

Preface

The following list summarizes the topics covered in each chapter of this book. Although, it should be noted that each chapter has its own introduction and set of chapter objectives, methods, research findings, and conclusions.

Chapter 1, "The 'Mental Revolution' of the Public Procurement Specialist: Achieving Transformative Impacts within the Context of e-Procurement," covers an original perspective of the key role of procurement specialists for success in e-procurement implementation. The soft skills in accordance with Resourced-Based Theory are discussed as a cornerstone of significant change in the nature and dynamics of the procurement process. Traditionally, public procurement relied on standardized decision-making structures and has been an administrative area satiated with politics. E-procurement platforms can easily amplify this bureaucratization by supposedly shifting the responsibility for the decision from the specialists to the virtual environment. Digital procurement platforms provide the capacity for network-collaborative-type procurement. The nine core challenges for overcoming the barriers in e-procurement initiatives are described hand-in-hand with technical and political aspects. The core challenges are a fragmented understanding of technological dynamics, implementation, and spotty legislative support; technology's "halo" effect, lack of technological "know how" and financial constraints and waste; incompatibility of platforms or managerial/philosophical strategies; interrupted (punctuated) implementation: or the need for maintaining dedication and learning beyond first stage adoption; internal customer satisfaction and maverick purchasing; resistance to technology and cooptation; complexity, uncertainty, ambiguity, and network-driven contractual instability; biased data or "dead end" collection; and software developers are not "public" ready, oriented, or reasonably priced. A theoretical case study on the decision-making process within digital procurement processes leads to the conclusions that specialists accept adoption of digital platform, decides to use only the features of the system, which are not in conflicts with their goals, or decides to contact the software developers to customized particular features. Finally, the recommendations for adoption of e-procurement systems are to redefine the roles of procurement specialists and enable the reinterpretation of their professional perspectives and assume personally entrepreneur-type approaches in using the digital platform.

Chapter 2, "Public Sector Transformation: Privatization in Saudi Arabia," focuses on the historical context and rationale for privatization in Saudi Arabia. The first issue explores an economic and political situation in Saudi Arabia. The background of the Saudi Arabian governmental system presents a number of established agencies implementing economic reforms such as the Supreme Economic Council (SEC), the Supreme Council for Petroleum and Minerals (SCPM), the General Commission for Tourism and Antiquities (GCTA), the Saudi Arabian General Investment Authority (SAGIA), the Food and Drugs Authority (FDA), and the Council of Saudi Chambers of Commerce and Industry. The results of the extended literature survey leads to the general recommendation of the privatization policy. Namely, shortening the entire privatization process establishes independent joint ventures and sets up appropriate regulatory authorities. The objectives of privatization strategy can be summarized in the following crucial points: to elevate the competence of the national economy (through subjecting the public sector projects to market forces) and increase its competitive ability (through creating proper investment environment, i.e. capital market); to face the challenges in regional and international competition, and to encourage private sector investment and effective participation in the national economy through privatizing public enterprises and services and operating those on commercial bases (this will ultimately provide the opportunity to diversify the Saudi economic base away from the dependence on oil); to increase partnership of citizens in productive government assets through using a general subscription system, as a so-called Initial Public Offering "IPO"; to encourage national and foreign capital for local investments through partial owning of productive projects; to continue to develop the capital market to give a chance to increase local and foreign investments; to provide additional channels to attract savings; to increase the Saudi employment opportunities, optimize the use of national labor, and ensure the continued equitable increase of individual income; to provide all necessary services for citizens and investors at suitable time; to place regulatory measures (i.e., good quality services with reasonable costs, through establishing regulatory authority to regulate the service tariff and monitor the services); to rationalize government spending and reduce the government budget by providing opportunity to the private sector to finance, operate, and maintain some of the service sectors that they are capable of doing; to increase government revenues from the returns of privatization to be transferred to the private sector, i.e. from granting concessions or sale of government properties. The future challenges are focused on examine the cost effectiveness of used procurement systems and evaluation of the pros and cons of opening up key sectors to foreign investors, especially with respect to religious and cultural activities.

Chapter 3, "Public Sector Transformation and the Design of Public Policies for Electronic Commerce and the New Economy: Tax and Antitrust Policies," summarizes the appropriate models and techniques of economic analysis for understanding how the public sector absorbs the philosophy and tools of the New Economy. The crucial factor of success is human capital. The chapter deals with optimal design of tax policy in electronic markets and the guidelines of antitrust policy in electronic markets. Consequences to mainstream economics are observed firstly. Subsequently, the case study on taxation of electronic commerce is explained. The dominant position and barriers to entry to the New Economy according to the Schumpeterian vision are discussed. New Economy leads to both a high concentration of production and to a wide range of strategies used by enterprises (protection of intellectual property, price differentiation, bundling, etc.) as well as greater cooperation between them. Hence, antitrust authorities should reformulate the traditional analysis of barriers to entry to take into account that the benefits associated with entry in the New Economy markets are high when it is possible to replace the leader and dominate the market. Research findings pass noteworthy results in taxation of e-commerce. As is mentioned in future research directions, the growth strategy is essential for companies operating on the supply side in economies of scale, scope economies, economies of experience, and network economies on the demand side. The huge challenge is the reevaluation and measurement of business strategies in the public sector transformation process.

Chapter 4, "Persuading for Change: The Impact of Culture on the Principles of Authority and Social Proof," offers insight to persuasive technologies as a tool to change our behavior or attitude without using coercion or deception. The brand new meaning is especially evident in special markets like Web 2.0, e-business, and mobile domain. The need of understanding information systems in cultural context plays a significant role in increasing competitive advantages. Comparison of Korean and Finland societies are population for hypothesis verification. The Korean society represents Confucianism through five human relationships and the development of Neo-Confucianism. The hypothesis on the principles of authority in the Korean group and principles of social proof in the Finnish group are tested. The six principles of persuasion are reciprocation, commitment and consistency, social proof, authority, liking, and scarcity. The methodology is built on positive approach. The selected samples of Korean and Finnish students were asked six questions to understand the role of social proof and authority differing in a cultural context. Research findings show that designing information systems culture should be taken into account. The results can help managers to identify new challenges raised in persuasive systems development. In particular, the utility persuasive technology features, e.g. for internet public procurement, culture should be considered carefully. The future research directions aim to analyze how to cope with differing cultural issues within behavioral patterns in the light of Information Systems Development.

Chapter 5, "Technology Advancement and E-Procurement in the US," is focused on the analysis of modernization of government and administration and the relationship between technology and e-procurement systems. Development of technologies and economic overview is discussed firstly. The e-procurement is a relatively new phenomenon. Perhaps the greatest challenge is that the adoption of e-procurement has spurred a new wave of corruption. The growth of private sector suppliers of technology is emphasized. Current state of the art of implementation of e-procurement reflexes customer effectiveness by providing multimedia capabilities such as sound, image, text, and other visual tools that aid to develop customer learning and assist in the product selection process, with the goal of optimally fulfilling customer demands. E-procurement is difficult to implement, and sustainability of effective e-purchasing systems is equally as challenging. Among all the components of e-procurement, e-purchasing requires the largest number of legal provisions. The publication of rules, deadlines, data, and information, the announcement of a tender, data about previous tenders, bidders, and winners should be made accessible to the marketplace and related public sphere. Nevertheless, the reduction of errors is a crucial part for the cost reduction and economic rationality. Nowadays, customized challenges and the intellectual prowess of public procurement managers are needed. The systems tend to outsource technological expertise. Further directions require established methods and techniques of optimizing e-procurement connectivity between administration, government agencies, businesses, and the public. Another research area to be addressed is related to public policy considerations. The swift advancement of technology creates a need for better understanding regarding the rights of purchasers and suppliers when dealing in a highly communicative environment.

Chapter 6, "Rationale behind Implementation of New Electronic Tools for e-Public Procurement," is focused on the effective implementation of new electronic tools for e-public procurement in public sector organizations. The current acceleration of the e-government is driven by an effort to achieve the highest and best use of the decision-making process. Political (more effective cooperation of the public and private sectors), social (potential exploitation of knowledge and experience of experts working within the private sector), economic (envisaged long-term cost savings, quality improvements in any given area, better services, and more flexibility when providing them, stimulation of electronic tools development by the private sector), and public administration reasons (after implementation of the electronic administration, it will be possible, based on the increased labor productivity, to reduce the number of public sector employees in a socially sensitive way) are taken into account in transformation processes. EU legislation as a direction indicator is discussed with emphasis on the military sector. Pan-European Public e-Procurement On-Line Project (PEPPOL) according to European Commission is explored and standardization, codification, and classification in the e-government are surveyed. Case studies in Germany and the Czech Republic are analyzed. Further, the evaluation criteria of new electronic tools are stipulated and the mathematical model of decision-making process within the public administration is articulated. The basis model's principles are automatic methods of variant evaluation and component criteria based on individual views of expert team members. The key step in the future direction of procurement service evolvement is rationalization of procedures. Future research directions follow practical e-public procurement and electronization of purchase processes—online use of online means of mathematical decision-making support, use of mathematical modeling methods enabling not just accelerated but also more objective decision-making especially when selecting the most convenient offer, use of modern information and communication technologies, significant reduction of potentially negative effects of subjective factors in such award procedures when provisional bids of suppliers and bidders are being evaluated, savings in transaction cost because of decreased administrative labor intensity of public procurement, increased price transparency of public contracts, and using a standardized description of purchased commodities to acquire data for statistical evaluation of public contract market including the commodity aspect and to perform more efficient audits, and monitoring of the public procurement market.

Chapter 7, "Electronic Procurement in the Construction Industry," covers the current state, trends, and future directions of e-procurement in the construction industry in public and private sector. The basic rules and directions in the hierarchy of World Procurement Law, European Procurement Law, and UK Procurement Law are discussed. Indisputable role plays the use of electronic auctions as negotiation mechanism for construction procurement. There had been a substantial number of government led initiatives to improve the uptake of e-procurement in the UK, commencing with the Modernizing Government White Paper. The use of electronic auctions in construction proved controversial, yet was adopted by some building clients. Quantitative analyses of e-procurement implementation, drivers, and barriers in the UK are explored. The important fields concerning convenience of archiving completed work, increasing quality through increased accuracy and efficiency, and reduction in time and procurement staff are assigned as the crucial drive factors. The UK government emphasizes the e-business as a priority growth area and actively support them. The two most important drivers for UK construction organizations (both public and private) are "Process, Transaction, and Administration Cost Savings" and "Convenience of Archiving Completed Work." It was revealed that the cost savings from adoption of e-procurement has been widely documented. The new challenge is cloud computing and advancement in IT technologies resulting in reducing expenditures and increasing effectiveness. There is significant pressure developing from the rapid advancement of large-scale construction companies and the rate of development of technology. Current research into BIM indicates the possibility of BIM enabled e-procurement becoming mainstream within the next decade. This will further drive down procurement costs, but the cost effectiveness of BIM remains a concern. The UNCITRAL Working Group on the Model Law on Electronic Signatures needs to address some of the security, proof of intent, validity, and confidentiality-related issues identified as barriers for e-procurement in this chapter.

Chapter 8, "EU Public Procurement Remedies Regimes: The Nordic Experience," deals with the Nordic statutory EU-based remedy regimes. EU commitment does not differ between EU Member states, Sweden, Denmark, Finland, and non-member states, Norway and Iceland. The EU regime on public procurement law is effective in all member states and relevant guidelines and directives are extended to non-member states. The legislation on procurement remedies is EU/EEA compliant. The general overview of the domain covers the UNITRAL 2011 Model Law on Public Procurement for state legislation.

On the basis of free trade transparency in relation to laws, regulations, and procurement practice, enable international competition on deliveries to states and local authorities and reduce corruption and other unfair business practice. The World Bank (IBRD) sets guidelines (2011) on Procurement Loans and IDA Credits as the primary remedy a withdrawal of financial resources from the recipient. A great number of cases deal with procurement remedies for the European Court of Justice. Nordic law can be classified as a separate legal branch different from common law and civil law codifications, such as Germany, France, and the Mediterranean countries. Historically, the Nordic countries have cooperated on major legislative projects in private law. Norwegian public procurement law consists of a short 1999-07-16 No 69 framework statute. Danish EU procurement law on procedures is the black letter procurement directive with some supplementary regulations outside the scope of the directives themselves (sub-threshold and B-services). Remedies are addressed in the 2010-05-12 No. 492 Act on remedies. The Finish legislation on procurement consists of two comprehensive statutes on public and utilities procurement—with provisions on remedies in the statute on public procurement 30.3.2007/348 (with later amendments). Selected 2010/2012 law reform issues are discussed in the chapter. The future research directions are an econometric factor analysis on the efficiency of implementation of the changes in law environment.

Chapter 9, "Conditions Determining the Success of Public E-Procurement," is focused on e-procurement as a component of supply chain management. E-procurement, as a subset of supply chain management, contributes to the controlling, simplifying, and automating of the purchase of goods and services from several suppliers. The main tasks of e-procurement concern support of basic transactions like requisitioning, ordering, and payment, facilitating processes like supplier selection, value analysis, and performance evaluation, enhancing advanced applications such as cross-functional and cross-organizational co-operation and integration; and assisting in relationship management. E-procurement can be considered an "evolutionary shift" from poor planning, inconsistent quality of goods and services. Legislative and regulatory framework is discussed and notable reforms (shifting authority and responsibility to individual government departments and their accounting officers, compulsory expenditure planning and budgetary control across all operations in each government department, application of the principle of value for money for performance budgeting, whereby managers strive to achieve more than what the budget and costs specified, decentralized procurement systems which are less prescriptive, thereby according greater managerial responsibility, minimizing risk through increased internal control within government departments, monitoring mechanisms to identify unauthorized, wasteful, and irregular expenditure as determined by regulations) are explored. Research findings lead to significant recommendations in the implementation process. Government has to absorb sensitivity to local socio-economic imbalances within the context of a global economy. Institutionalization of a code of ethics for all e-procurement users within government, underpinned by regular education and training supporting e-procurement implementation management has to be taking into account. The regulatory framework that addresses national policy imperatives should lead to coherent and comprehensively resourced e-procurement. Human resources have to be developed adequately to operate within an e-procurement environment. Technological capacity has to be developed enough for manage e-procurement managing. Local and international participation should be managed in developing policies and systems process to support e-procurement. Investigating public sector incentives covers statistical sample for modeling e-procurement compatibility with suppliers. Future research directions tend to "enterprise-wide" initiative within government gives the overlapping and competing power interests. Provision of government technology supports structures to assist businesses in providing trading portals and exchange services.

Research into horizontal processes can integrate the supplier-buyer interface, rather than only sharing critical inventory information with suppliers.

Chapter 10, "Public Procurement in the Czech Republic: Focused on Regional Development and E-Procurement," covers relations between public procurement, regional development, and e-procurement. The transformation and advancement of e-procurement is explored on case study focused on the Czech Republic. The huge steps were forced by EU directives in 2008. Preliminary research shows a close relationship between location of contractor and supplier headquarters. Research findings show public procurement as an important source of funds for stimulation of endogenous development based on SMEs. As results of empirical research public procurement is not a suitable tool for the reduction of regional disparities. The significant ratio of public procurement on HDP ensures important position as a source of funds for the financing of regional development, and there is an increasing interest in e-procurement procedures in the Czech Republic. E-procurement may increase competition for public procurement because spatial barriers are reduced. E-procurement may substantially reduce administration costs and speed up the public procurement procedures. There are various forms of e-procurement tools, including e-tendering, e-auctions, or transmission of invoices online. It is noteworthy that e-auctions may represent an interesting tool to reduce not only transaction costs but also the final price of public procurement contracts. Future research directions are whether differences between anticipated and real prices of public procurement can be modeled with strong correlation. Thus, the research question is whether public procurement tenders reduce the real prices may be answered. Subsequently, the factors, which explain the differences, may be surveyed. The role of e-auctions may be considered in this regard.

Chapter 11, "The Architecture of the EU Structural Instruments in Romania: Public Administration Bodies' Functioning, Econometric Modeling, and E-Solutions," is aimed to EU cohesion policy with special emphasis on seven ongoing operational programs successfully negotiated by Romania. The three following aspects are analyzed: the use of structural funds via the operational programs at country/regional level represents the most important tool for sustainable development and socio-economic progress; the proposed models for analyzing the absorption of these funds are highly original and might constitute a precise tool for further programming exercises and assessment of their efficiency and effectiveness; the proposed models could be used for performing the same type of analysis for the other seven NUTS2 development regions in Romania and, further on, a global model at country level could be used. The question on effectiveness and transparency of public funds distribution via Electronic Public Procurement-Acquisition System is explored. Emphasis is also placed on innovative tools used for submitting, evaluating, and monitoring projects, emphasizing the role of Management Authorities, as public bodies, for managing this process. For each operational program, an econometric model GARCH-like has been developed and used at the level of NUTS2. Operational program architecture is discussed and six priority axes are elaborated. In Romania, the Electronic Public Procurement System (SEAP) allows performing operations such as transmission of awarding documentation and of explanatory notes to be validated by the National Authority for the Regulation and Monitoring of Public Procurement, Publication of Contract Notices, carrying out the initial phase of electronic bidding, and performing the entire procurement procedure online, publication of contract award notices. A key point of interest in this phase of the implementation of operational programs in Romania is to understand how absorption is ensured as a prerequisite for the N+3/N+2 rule compliance in the short run but also as a pre-requisite for ensuring the expected impact in the medium and long run. For performing the analysis, an Autoregressive Conditional Heteroskedasticity (ARCH) model has been developed and generalized as GARCH. Finally, research findings express that online tools cannot support big steps forward when it comes to absorption if they are not complemented by strong monitoring arrangements for incentivizing projects to spend and report regularly, administrative measures to allow the MA and IB to process reimbursements faster, favoring projects which are resorting to simple implementation procedures and therefore can spend faster.

Chapter 12, "Black Economic Empowerment, ICT, and Preferential Public Procurement in South Africa," examines government policy using procurement in conjunction with constitutional right to equality. The Black Economic Empowerment policy provides preferences for Historically Disadvantaged Individuals and small business in the procurement decision-making process. The survey is conducted in accordance with Preferential Public Procurement Framework Act (Act 5 of 2000) and the role of ICT is discussed. South Africa and the role of procurement during apartheid are explored. The focus of public procurement is on construction and the mainlining of infrastructure and services delivering. The preferential procurement system in South Africa requires that the contracts must be awarded to the tenderer who scores the highest points in terms of the preference system according to the Procurement Act. Government support e-procurement as the process of electronically purchasing the goods and services needed for an organization's operation in South Africa. The purpose is to maintain the advantages of e-governance concerning cost effectiveness, transparency, curbing corruption, improving access to information, improving efficiency and the ability to reach wider section of citizens. The challenges of the delivery of e-government services in Southern Africa are a lack of ICT skills, limited public access to Internet and other ICT technologies, and the know-how to operate them efficiently. From the international perspective, the implications for future research directions are free trade measures for preferential procurement systems, including the regulations. Public procurement in South Africa is used as a policy instrument for socio-economic transformation, which completely differs from other countries.

Chapter 13, "Public Sector Transformation in Malaysia: Improving Local Governance and Accountability," discusses various public sector reformation programs in Malaysia initiated with the focus on ensuring good governance and better accountability of public agencies. The research problem is challenges faced by local government that has impact on governance of local authorities. The overview of local government is surveyed in Malaysia. Government transformation programs were introduced, such as the use of the Key Performance Indicators system in 2005. The more outcome-oriented approach Government Transformation Program is in force since 2009. Short-term and long-term priorities combine Six National Key Result Areas program. For measuring management, compliance was elaborated in the accountability index, and for improvement in service delivery, the Star Rating System for Local Authorities concerning 354 indicators was derived. Stakeholder participation and consensus-oriented decision-making has been undertaken in the Local Agenda 21 program. Essential criticism concerning public sector leadership is the lack of rudimental principles of public service. The government faces the ineffectiveness in terms of funds, staff capacities, office facilities, and IT infrastructure. The prevailing part of the work is done manually. Future research directions concerning the research agenda on the methods of incorporate stakeholder participation in the decision-making process of local Malaysian council. Other relevant research issues are covered.

Enjoy reading this book.

Nataša Pomazalová
University of Defense, Czech Republic

Acknowledgment

My thanks go to the contributing authors who have participated and completed their chapters and the anonymous reviewers who have provided valuable comments. Thanks go to the editorial board, which helped in the final editing of this book.

I want to especially express gratitude to the publisher, IGI Global, for funding this project.

Nataša Pomazalová
University of Defense, Czech Republic

Chapter 1

The "Mental Revolution" of the Public Procurement Specialist:
Achieving Transformative Impacts within the Context of E–Procurement

Alexandru V. Roman
Florida Atlantic University, USA

ABSTRACT

This chapter suggests an original perspective for delineating the role played by procurement specialists within the context of the efforts to redefine digital public procurement as a major pylon in the transformation of governance. Although in the last two decades scholars have provided an abundance of quality academic accounts addressing the possible transformative benefits of e-procurement, more often than not, public procurement specialists remain a mere afterthought within such discussions. In this chapter, it is argued that the digitalization of public procurement will sustain the desired transformative returns only if these efforts are accompanied by a reformative evolution of public procurement professionals. Paradoxically, transformation at the individual level is found to be the key element for instituting genuine changes and effectively employing digital decision-making support systems in public procurement.

INTRODUCTION

The nature of modern governance has emphasized at least four interrelated and mutually enforcing dynamics. First, the evolving complexity of administrative challenges and the financial and economic hypersensitivity induced by global interdependence have rendered many of the traditional governance perspectives by in large obsolete. Scholars argue that wicked social and economic problems, issues that adapt and resist imposed solutions, will become the norm rather than the exception in governance (Clarke & Stewart, 1997; Fountain, 2001). Second, advancements in Information Communication Technologies (ICTs) give credence to the idea that in spite of the increasing complexity and financial constraints, it is possible to improve administrative practices, mainly by reliance on digital decision-making support systems (Fountain, 2001; West, 2005;

DOI: 10.4018/978-1-4666-2665-2.ch001

Milakovich, 2012). Whilst, it is still relatively early to conclusively review whether ICTs can indeed lead towards more effective, legitimate and democratic governance constructs—governments at all levels have already hedged their financial health and governance stability in technology's capacity to deliver such results (Kamarck & Nye, 2002; West, 2005). Third, what forms the proper scope and means of governmental action has become rather fuzzy (Kettl, 2002). Finally, network structures have become an inexorable condition of the art of government. Agencies no longer posses the capabilities or knowledge to fulfill citizens' demands and expectations solely relying on own structures (Fountain, 2001; Milakovich, 2012).

E-procurement encompasses all four of the above-mentioned dynamics. On the one hand, public procurement is probably one of the most complex administrative dimensions of governance (Leukel & Maniatopoulos, 2005; Bof & Previtali, 2007). Ambiguity and knowledge asymmetries are omnipresent throughout the procurement process. On the other hand, the impacts of digital procurement are not yet adequately understood and the realities within e-procurement implementation often fall short of touted benefits (Somasundaram & Damsgaard, 2005; Bof & Previtali, 2007; Mota & Filho, 2011; Peck & Cabras, 2011; Hoque, et al., 2011). Furthermore, discretionary decision-making and professional relationships based on network structures are now accepted as important characteristics of digital public procurement.

The main objective of this chapter is to argue and provide support for the idea that procurement specialists represent the key for the success in e-procurement implementation. It is difficult to envision the realization of e-procurement-induced transformation outside a fundamental acceptance and shift within value constructs of procurement specialists. Here, by transformative it is meant a significant change in the nature and dynamic of the procurement process (e.g. more democratic, increasing policy, or financial management impacts). In short, the technologically driven trans-

formation of governance is almost impossible if it is not preceded and continuously supported by an equally important "evolution" at the individual level. Ironically, in order to realize the benefits of digital procurement or e-government initiatives in general, redefining and reemphasizing "people" skills are probably more important than learning software applications. In bland terms, transformative e-procurement calls for a special "state of mind" on the part of procurement specialists.

In what follows, the argument will be constructed within the contingency of three logically co-dependent sections. The first part will trace the implications of "governance by contract" (Van Slyke, 2007). The discussion will then turn to the delineation of the current status of e-procurement implementation. The final section will address the shortcomings in terms of transformative impacts and will suggest emphasizing public procurement specialist as the agents of technological transformation in public procurement.

GOVERNANCE BY CONTRACT

Scholars have suggested that current governance dynamics promote administrative constructs that are significantly different from long-established bureaucratically driven frameworks. The devolution of governance and the reliance on networks and contracts to fulfill what habitually have been government's responsibilities, have led some to describe the created condition as the hollow, contract or transformed state (Milward & Provan, 2000; Savas, 2000; Sclar, 2000; Kettl, 2002; Cooper, 2003). Within the framework imposed by the latter, traditional governance has evolved into one by contract (Van Slyke, 2007). On many occasions, hierarchical structures are supplemented or even replaced with inter-agency and inter-sector collaborative relationships.

Until recently, network type structures and public-private partnerships were perceived as a rather peripheral part of what it meant to govern.

While fairly blurry, one could have made the case that theoretical dichotomies between public and private sectors were still appropriate. This is no longer the case. Currently, in certain areas, the governance role played by private, nongovernmental organizations and not-for-profit entities frequently overshadows and might even compete for legitimacy with public agencies. The different managerial make-up demanded of administrators within the contexts of networks is also often at odds with the skill sets emphasized in the bureaucratic state. In essence, while not completely dissimilar, network and contract-driven governance requires new administrative approaches, thinking and even management constructs (Mintrom, 2003; Agranoff, 2007; McGuire & Agranoff, 2011).

One could look at any aspect or level of administration and easily distinguish the above-mentioned contractual dynamics. For example, in the Unites States within the provision of social services at state levels, administrative decision-making patterns have evolved past hierarchical constructs or simplistic principal-agent delimitations (Johnston & Romzek, 2008). Numerous governmental agencies and nongovernmental organizations, bound by evolving and often fragile links, collaborate in order to provide the expected degree of service. Every so often governmental agencies are reduced to the role of network managers rather than providers, and public servants become "separated" from the citizens by layers of contractual agreements (Johnston & Romzek, 2008). Due to the latter, administrators are expected to focus on defining terms of contracts and negotiating conditions and performance measurements, whereas nongovernmental parties assume "street-level" roles. Rather than eliminating bureaucratic agencies, the working instruments of governing have to be understood as an emergent 'transactional DNA' of government and its interlocutors. These tools include not only grants, contracts, regulations, and standard procurement of goods and services, but also services partnerships, joint ventures, loans, loan guarantees, insurance, tax sharing and tax

expenditures, vouchers, and cost reimbursements. Some of these tools operate through the network vehicle whereas many provide linkages between government and nongovernmental organizations completely outside of networks (McGuire & Agranoff, 2011, p. 275).

Although some might challenge the ethical implications of these emerging conditions, for the purpose of this chapter it is important to note that these transformations imply fundamental shifts within the roles of public servants. For administrators, the need for network management skills starts to rival the importance of interacting and understanding citizens. The new administrative constructs do not completely replace old ones, but simply expand the set of skills demanded of public servants. Intrinsically, administrators are asked to do more within the context of a significantly diminished capacity to control or monitor. Hence, while networks might increase administrative responsiveness and effectiveness, they also make upholding accountability demands increasingly challenging.

Under these conditions, ICT is expected to provide the means to meet the operational needs for increased effectiveness in the short run and ultimately to lead to transformation in the long run (Kamarck & Nye, 2002; West, 2005; Milakovich, 2012). At least in theory, technology can significantly reduce the cost of communication and information processing; as the capacity of technology to process and store information has long surpassed that of humans. In addition, technology can minimize some of the administrative rigidness characteristic to brick-and-mortar administration. The provision of public service no longer necessitates a direct contact between public servants and citizens. Generally, it is expected that the benefits from a more efficient administration will be sufficiently large to compensate for the diminished human interaction between citizens and public servants.

Holistically, however, there are two major issues with such expectations. First and foremost, the mere implementation of technology does not guarantee transformative-type outcomes or success. Technology's transformative capacity is deterministic only in a limited sense (Orlikowski, 1992, 2000). For example, West (2005), after evaluating 17,077 government websites over the period of 2000-2003, finds minimum transformative dynamics. According to West (2005), the shifts motivated by ICT implementation are incremental in character. It is important to note that scholars in the field appear to agree that regardless of a given technology's transformative capacity, its actual impacts during implementation are primarily shaped by institutional characteristics. Thus, transformation is not a direct outcome of technology's technical design or objective capacity (Fountain, 2001).

Second, the global discourse supporting the early push for the digitalization of governance was importantly informed by the tenets of new public management (Osborne, 2006; Dunleavy, et al., 2006). The latter lens primarily focused on redesigning process flows rather than substantially influencing structural reorganizations (Fountain, 2001). Thus, while it was believed that technology can motivate transformation, in practice the global implementation processes were designed in a manner that made transformative considerations secondary to operational efficiency. Therefore, perhaps somewhat incongruously with e-government discourse, implementation initiatives have been framed on the grounds provided by perspectives that enforced old public administration constructs. One could argue that if ICT is to be successful in re-constructing current administration it might do so more by chance than as a result of original legislative and policy designs.

In sum, the virtual state is inexorably a networked one (Fountain, 2001), where the networks are constructed on mutual trust, need and contractual agreements (Van Slyke, 2007). In many ways, the scope and informational demands within governance by contract make it realistic only by the means provided by the processing speed and technological capacity of digital platforms. By some accounts, the digitalization of governance is a foregone conclusion, both on instrumental and philosophical grounds. According to World Bank (2004), for instance, it is now common for governments around the globe to spend more on ICT projects than on traditional capital investments.

The fact that governance has become far too complex and surpassed any agency's own capacity to handle such density has made public procurement a central and perhaps unexpected focus of transformative dynamics (Hardy & Williams, 2008). Within the contexts of the increased need to design, bid and monitor contractual performance, the administrative role played by procurement specialists is only expected to grow. Consequently, e-procurement, which is typically defined as the use of ICT to automate and increase the effectiveness, and responsiveness of the procurement frameworks (Coulthard & Castleman, 2001; Bof & Previtali, 2007; Andersen, et al., 2009) has emerged as an important part of the solution for improving public procurement processes and consequently public administration.

CURRENT STATUS AND CHALLENGES OF E-PROCUREMENT IMPLEMENTATION

The Status of E-Procurement Implementation

Governments at all levels are making significant investments in digital procurement platforms (Coulthard & Castleman, 2001; Somasundaram & Damsgaard, 2005; Hardy & Williams, 2008; Mota & Filho, 2011) and in the diffusion and support for the use of e-procurement (OECD, 2011). A 2010 survey of 34 OECD members as well as Brazil, Egypt, and Ukraine indicates that 90% of the countries use websites to provide tender announcements and procurement related information, while more than half provide contract management tools (OECD, 2011). The intrinsic difficulty of measuring e-procurement investments and the fragmented nature of the implementation process make qualifying the size of the investments difficult; nevertheless, such outlays are notable. Although, it is still early to argue for success or failure of such initiatives, it becomes evident that the trend towards digital procurement is enjoying important political support and it is perhaps already irreversible.

On the operational level, scholars suggest that digitalizing the public procurement process will lead to more transparent, responsive, responsible, legislatively compliant, and accountable procurement practices (Henriksen & Mahnke, 2005; Varney, 2011). On a structural level, it is expected for e-procurement to motivate substantive growth in professionalism (Croom & Johnston, 2003; Brandon-Jones & Carey, 2009) and improved policy outcomes (Varney, 2011). It is the latter dimension that promises the bulk of transformative benefits. Overall, it is believed that e-procurement platforms can support a decision-making environment that would minimize the tradeoffs between democratic prerogatives and administrative efficiency in the context of public purchasing choices.

Despite the significant investments in digital procurement and the support from global governance organizations, the early results have not necessarily been encouraging (Leukel & Maniatopoulos, 2005; Bof & Previtali, 2007). In many instances procurement platforms failed to reach any type of transformative effects and simply automated extant processes and enforced existing organizational power structures (Andersen, 2004; Mota & Filho, 2011; Roman, 2012a). Furthermore, e-procurement implementation projects regularly degenerated into unproductive systems and structures that led to financial waste (Somasundaram & Damsgaard, 2005).

At the individual level, public procurement specialists regularly argue that systems designed by and for the private sector are not fit for public needs

and as a result they would be inclined to engage in "maverick purchasing [finding ways of 'going around' the system]" (Croom & Johnston, 2003; Brandon-Jones & Carey, 2010). For instance, Mota and Filho (2011) find that e-procurement implementation in Brazil is heavily satiated by contradictions, competing interpretations of goals and habitual reinforcement of status quo. Similar findings were delimited in Australia, New Zealand, Scotland (Hardy & Williams, 2008), and Italy (Bof & Previtali, 2007; Hardy & Williams, 2008).

What e-procurement is understood to be and how to reach transformative changes is contingent on institutional contexts and the interpretations of the implementers. The results from a 2010 survey of American and Canadian procurement specialists suggest that despite recent legislative emphasis, e-procurement has yet to achieve any notable changes. A total of 45% of the 499 respondents indicated that their agencies did not use any of the staple e-procurement systems (McCue & Roman, 2012). The same study finds that only 20% of the agencies that use e-procurement platforms have adopted them within the frame of previous five years. Approximately 55% of the agencies that stated that they used e-procurement systems have instituted the platforms in the 1990s. It should be noted here that all respondents claimed very low levels of integration between e-procurement and financial platforms, with no statistically significant difference between early and late adopters (McCue & Roman, 2012). It can take decades for technology to lead to structural changes (Fountain, 2001) and it appears that in the case of e-procurement platforms that has yet to happen.

Indentifying the Individual within the Core Challenges

What then stops e-procurement from achieving a transformative reshaping of public procurement? As it is the case with most administrative dimensions, a simple or unique answer does not exist. Some reasons for the initial scarcity of transformative impacts induced by e-procurement are common to all technological endeavors, whereas others are somewhat specific to public procurement. An extensive review of current literature suggests that there are at least nine major barriers that stymie e-procurement initiatives from achieving encompassing and meaningful administrative impacts in Table 1 (Roman, 2012a).

Technical and political aspects notwithstanding, it becomes obvious that the procurement specialists, especially those with managerial type roles, are the common denominator along the

main challenges and possible solutions for achieving transformative impacts through e-procurement. Scholars have regularly noted that transformational leadership is critical for supporting public service motivation and alignment of individual perceptions with organizational goals (Wright, et al., 2011). As a whole, one can argue that transformation is a function of leadership and the acceptance of the need for transformation.

For example, in the context of the first challenge, public procurement specialists can play a key corrective part by undertaking on policy-

Table 1. Challenge or barrier type

	Challenge/Barrier Type	Description
1	Fragmented understanding of technological dynamics, implementation and spotty legislative support	E-procurement means different things to different stakeholders. Systems are implemented in a localized manner. There is limited organizational or national integration or legislative coordination.
2	Technology's "halo" effect, lack of technological "know how," and financial constraints and waste	The expectation that it is sufficient to implement the technology and the benefits "will come." Implementing e-procurement without providing the supportive context is unlikely to lead to desired outcomes. Limited understanding of technological effects coupled with lack of experience in the matter cause great financial waste and strategic disappointments.
3	Incompatibility of platforms or managerial/philosophical strategies	E-procurement systems are often incompatible with other digital platforms used by organizations or with traditional procurement practices.
4	Interrupted (punctuated) implementation: Or the need for maintaining dedication and learning beyond first stage adoption	As it is the case with the majority of ICT uses in government, e-procurement adoption is undertaken in spurts. At this point in time, there is an obvious shortcoming in continuous support and dedication to the idea. Early failures stymie future investments or transformational changes.
5	Internal customer satisfaction and maverick purchasing	If e-procurement software is found to be inadequate for organizational needs and not representative of the decision-making dynamics within the agency - procurement specialists will "go around" the system. Thus, any benefit from e-procurement will be lost since the system's use becomes trivial.
6	Resistance to technology and cooptation	Organizations often resist the changes associated with e-procurement adoption. Without a proper approach and managerial support, the system will be resisted and sabotaged or co-opted within existing power constructs.
7	Complexity, uncertainty, ambiguity and network-driven contractual instability	Public procurement is probably one of the most complex areas of public administration. Within the context of increasing reliance on contracts and network matters become even more complicated. The governance complexity and instability make effective e-procurement (transformative procurement in general) challenging and at times even technologically prohibitive.
8	Biased data or "dead end" collection	Either due to financial and knowledge constraints, strategic focus or organizational and legislative designs - the data and insights garnered by employing e-procurement are not used. When such data are considered, it is often the case that it is done in a biased manner.
9	Software developers are not "public" ready, oriented or reasonably priced	The platforms available on the market are either primarily oriented for the private sector or are not sufficiently sophisticated to address the complexity and network-driven needs of a public entity. Public procurement specialists are not active participants in the design of the procurement software.

Source: Roman (2012a)

entrepreneur-type roles in order to develop a common understanding of e-procurement across agencies. Whereas, the second challenge would be addressed by means of public procurement specialists making ICT usage for procurement purposes a matter of professional and personal interests. Similar fundamental roles for procurement specialists can be identified within the other seven types of challenges.

The ninth challenge, however, merits particular attention, especially in the milieu of attempting to transform public procurement. The literature on public procurement often neglects or underestimates the consequential ramifications of the choices made within the design of procurement platforms. The majority of private developers do not discern between the needs of the public and private sector. On most occasions, the platforms offered to public agencies represent slight modifications of identical systems employed by private enterprises. But since democratic and policy consideration are not necessarily a priority for the private sector, procurement platforms are designed and perfected in manner that empathizes efficiency and cost reduction. Once employed by public agencies these systems would "require" the public procurement specialists to adapt their administrative habits to fit the dynamics imposed by the digital platforms. Given that, the communication between software designers and public agencies is rather one dimensional; this sets a somewhat risky pattern of private developers constructing the meaning of e-procurement for the public sector. Within this context, there is a substantial need for high levels of interpretive flexibility (Orlikowski, 1992), with the latter referring to the degree of participation of institutional actors and technology users in shaping technology during implementation and use.

In sum, it becomes clear that in order for e-procurement to yield the desired outcomes in terms of policy and democratic imperatives, public procurement specialists need to embrace their roles and new capacities as redefined by e-procurement

systems. Digital procurement can provide the data to support improved decision-making, but if such data goes unused or even misused it defies the purpose of the efforts and the costs that were undertaken during implementation. Though it might be easy to theoretically argue for the need for an increased policy implication on the part of public procurement specialists, the structures and habits of the administrative state make such a fundamental shift rather difficult.

Historically, public procurement has been considered for the most part a clerical-type activity. Understanding and improving the procurement processes were often less important than insuring that the imposed mechanical procedures are closely followed. It was not until relatively recently that there has been a considerable push for the professionalization of the field (Thai, 2001). Hence, for public procurement specialists compliance and enforcement of a procurement process, regardless of how representative or efficient the process might be, represented the core of their job responsibilities. In several ways, this is still the case for many procurement specialists who activate in highly political and unstable environments (Diggs & Roman, 2012).

THE NEED FOR A "MENTAL REVOLUTION"

There are two important matters that merit considerable attention when addressing transformative effects of e-procurement within the realm of public administration. First, the structurational model of technology (Orlikowski, 1992, 2000; Walshman, 1993; DeSanctis & Poole, 1994) provides what could be considered the most comprehensive perspective for discussing technology within an organizational context. Orlikowski (1992) argues that traditionally research has treated technology either as an objective external force or as a product of social action. Under the former perspective, technology is believed to be objective by nature and its impacts are primarily deterministic. Under the latter, technology is treated as a product of the social context. Structurational model of technology suggests that technology does have objective characteristics; yet it is simultaneously a construct shaped by the social interaction. For Orlikowski (1992), technology shapes organizational and institutional structures. At the same time, however, human actors through their interpretations and use of the technology might be able to redefine and transform institutional constructs. Focusing attention on how structures are constituted and reconstituted in recurrent social practices acknowledges that while users can and do use technologies as they were designed, they also can and do circumvent inscribed ways of using the technologies—either ignoring certain properties of the technology, working around them, or inventing new ones that may go beyond or even contradict designer's expectations and inscriptions (Orlikowski, 2000, p. 407). Figure 1 provides a visual interpretation of the model.

Second, public administration suffers from what could be called a *schizophrenic re-identification*—a habitual predisposition of answering the field's hardest questions by falling into a theory or practice frenzy of repackaging old concepts into new shiny boxes; a general tendency to easily fall for an administrative fad and "forget and abandon" tested knowledge. It is often the case that the majority of the "revolutionary" ideas that are pitched by outside consultants are nothing more than a restatement of an old beliefs or practices.

Somehow, in the drive to improve government, previous valuable and useful knowledge seems easily disposed off. For instance, scholars at least as far back as Taylor (1967) have suggested that technology and administrative processes by their nature can rarely impose substantive structural changes if not accompanied by a psychological shift of acceptance on the part of users. Taylor, who is commonly associated with providing the basis for rationalization of bureaucracy in modern

Figure 1. Structurational model of technology

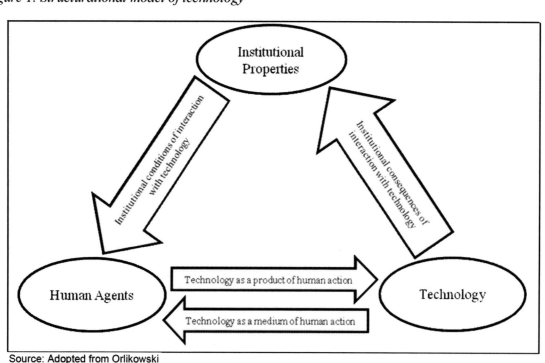

Source: Adopted from Orlikowski

governance, also supported a mental revolution on the part of managers (Fry & Raadschelders, 2008). Some, however, appear to overlook this critical vector within Taylor's ideas. Despite the fact that many of Taylor's principles have been rightfully discredited, he was accurate in delineating the end user of technology as the key to the success of any process or technological adoption. In this sense, this chapter emphasizes that regardless of the apparently limitless capacity provided by ICTs, a great deal still depends on the individual. Moreover, it can even be argued that historically, none of the other forms of technological advancements have been simultaneously as intrusive and as sensitive to individual and institutional constructs as ICTs (Fountain, 2001).

Technology has been shown to have dehumanizing and deskilling effects. Systems that are built to support decision-making can turn into data dumping grounds with the end user's job reduced to data collection, devoid of an understanding of the process or the meaning associated with such data (Fountain, 2001). Aside from instrumental purposes, administrative processes are also mechanisms for meaning creation; their digitalization can lead to the loss of learning patterns as well as extant knowledge. There are certain decision-making dynamics and skills that cannot be copied or understood outside the realm of professional experience (Mintrom, 2003) and no software would be able to duplicate it. At least at this point in time, human is still the one thing that technology cannot "be." The same can be stated about the inability of ICT to capture the relationships and social constructs present within networks (Agranoff, 2007). Although ICT is able to assist in speeding, developing and maintaining relationships, it simply cannot substitute for the human dimension, which is critical in any successful network. It is within these personal and social contexts that public procurement specialists have to evolve.

Traditionally, public procurement relied on standardized decision-making structures and has been an administrative area satiated with politics. When faced with the ambiguity an instability caused by political pressure, public procurement specialists will use bureaucratic structures as a buffer against perceived hostile environments (Diggs & Roman, 2012). E-procurement platforms can easily amplify this bureaucratization by supposedly shifting the responsibility for the decision from the specialists to the virtual logarithm (Roman, 2012b). In this sense, e-procurement reduces the individual accountability to the satisfaction of software demands. Hence, if specialists use only the features they are comfortable with, it becomes easy for them to lose their professional associations and regress to data entry-type decision-making.

A simplified hypothetical example will help clarify the condition. Assume that in order to improve efficiency and responsiveness, the procurement process of a medium size municipality is being digitalized. The hypothesized municipality is known for the fact that it provides a friendly framework for bid participation for local small businesses, which relies heavily on historical performance, mutual trust, and networks. The austere budgetary constraints have motivated the municipality to look into e-procurement as a possible source for savings. The adoption of e-procurement, however, could strain the relationship between the municipality and its local vendors, since the software was not designed with room for structures that the municipality traditionally employs. In addition, the transition to a digital procurement process might impose some costs on vendors. In this context, the procurement specialist could make any one of three distinct decisions:

1. The specialist accepts that the adoption of the digital platform represents and institutional preference and he or she advises the local vendors that they have to adapt to the new conditions.
2. The specialist decides that the e-procurement system does not fully reflect his or her needs.

He or she decides to use only the features of the system that do not conflict with the purchasing relationships, which, after all, were established and legitimated under the operating legislative framework.

3. The specialist acknowledges both the value of an e-procurement system and the institutional motivation for a preferential treatment of local small businesses. He or she decides to contact the software developers to customize some of the features and to provide assistance to local vendors.

Depending on one's perspective, any of the three hypothetical actions can be defended as the correct decision. However, it becomes rather evident that third option offers the greatest probability of achieving transformative outcomes. In this theoretical scenario, the probability of success is greatly diminished if the procurement specialist does not concurrently embrace both the benefits of the technological change and the value of established relations.

The simplicity of the above hypothetical case notwithstanding, the example is employed in order to suggest that the procurement specialists play a critical role in achieving transformative impacts. Whether the procurement specialists opt for the first, second or third choice is conditional on their view of their professional role within the e-government framework. Opting for the third choice, nonetheless, would require them to step outside what has traditionally been delineated as the role of a procurement specialist. In certain ways, the latter would represent an important change, and within organizational contexts, individuals often resist such shifts (Morgan, 2006). The decision on whether to oppose or embrace change is a choice that would primarily have to be made at the individual level, and not necessarily within the institutional context.

Solutions and Recommendations

Digital procurement platforms provide the capacity for network-collaborative-type procurement. Yet, employing such features is riskier than traditional purchasing patterns. In order to maximize the benefits from a specific software the users have to assume more risk, to "build a little, test a little" (Fountain, 2001, p. 43)—in essence becoming technological entrepreneurs. The specialists have to become an important part of the knowledge creation process (Hardy & Williams, 2008) and not restrain their efforts to data collection. Databases on their own are of little use, as outcomes are not functions of data size. Unused or misused data are probably as undesirable as no data. E-procurement systems do indeed have the potential to provide processing speeds and the information that would support broader policy decision-making. The latter, however, is a realistic outcome only in the case when procurement specialists embrace the capacity offered by digital procurement and use the technology in transformative ways, rather than adapt the technology use to existing structures.

FUTURE RESEARCH DIRECTIONS

The extant literature suggests that e-procurement implementation has achieved modest integration with other administrative platforms and few transformative impacts (Varney, 2011; McCue & Roman, 2012). It is suggested here, that transformation within public procurement perhaps should start with redefining the roles of procurement specialists, in a manner in which the individuals understand, believe, and are personally involved in reconstructing the process. Procurement specialists might have to reinterpret their professional perspectives and assume entrepreneur-type approaches in using the data and the network capacity offered by digital platforms. Although, e-procurement allows for procurement to be much more than "just purchasing," it will not be transformed until procurement specialists start thinking of themselves as much more than "buyers."

CONCLUSION

As means of bringing together separate themes regarding governance transformation and ICTs, and drawing practical conclusions based on e-procurement, this chapter argued that technological transformation of governance starts with the individual. It is important to note that by its nature technology is not satiated with normative connotations. Most of the time, ICT is neither good nor bad. Along the same lines, digitalization of administrative processes does not automatically lead to transformative changes, nor does it necessarily motivate the outcomes expected by design. It is the manner in which technology's implementation is undertaken and nurtured in the long run, rather than the design of the digital structure, that most of the time defines success. The involvement and acceptance by specialists of transformative roles within the use the digital platforms are critical in obtaining desired outcomes.

There is a multitude of questions regarding e-procurement that remain to be addressed. For instance, it is not yet fully clear whether digital procurement actually leads to significant administrative cost savings or simply cost shifting. Research addressing the effects of e-procurement platforms on small to medium size markets is another area that has yet to receive sufficient scholarly attention. The education and training of public procurement specialists is a further research dimension that can add significantly to our knowledge in terms of motivating transformative changes.

As it has been shown in this chapter, the implications of e-procurement cannot be localized or studied outside the broader set of dynamics that it motivates. Thus, while questions of scale impacts can be answered by employing quantitative techniques, the majority of issues related to transformation can be addressed only by employing a combination of quantitative and qualitative methodologies. The implications of a digitalized procurement can rarely be numerically qualified; hence, scholars should maintain a research sensitivity that goes past the operational demands. Methodological questions aside, understanding e-procurement necessitates transdisciplinary research efforts. In describing their research in e-procurement, Hardy and Williams (2011) stated, "... researching e-procurement did not simply involve a pragmatic alliance of disciplines, theories, and practice but also transdisciplinary and interactive research designs. Incorporating such aspects into e-government research involves the coproduction of knowledge at different levels (e.g., theoretical and practical), involving different interests (e.g., economic, social, technical), stakeholders, and disciplinary fields" (pp. 411-412).

In time, network structures and technology will probably become a dominant aspect within governance by contract. Under these conditions, public procurement might be associated with both growing expectations and scrutiny. Currently, similar to the manner in which agencies have to rely on other nongovernmental actors to complete their administrative tasks, public procurement specialists have to adopt skills and perspectives that might not have been previously emphasized. As scholars have suggested, regardless of the transformative nature of any digital platform, technology adoption will be shaped by interpretations at the individual and institutional levels. Hence, procurement specialists need to be simultaneously educated and involved in the implementation processes. As practitioners, they possess a great deal of knowledge that rarely can be reprogrammed within the coding language of specific software package. Digitally induced process transformation has to start with "revolutionary mental transformation" of public procurement specialists.

REFERENCES

Agranoff, R. (2007). *Managing within networks: Adding value to public organizations.* Washington, DC: Georgetown University Press.

Andersen, K. V. (2004). *E-government and public sector process rebuilding (PPR): Dilettantes, wheelbarrows, and diamonds.* Boston, MA: Kluwever Academic Publishers.

Bof, F., & Previtali, P. (2007). Organisational pre-conditions for e-procurement in governments: The Italian experience in the public health care sector. *The Electronic. Journal of E-Government, 5*(1), 1–10.

Brandon-Jones, A., & Carey, S. (2010). The impact of user-perceived e-procurement quality on system and contract compliance. *International Journal of Operations & Production Management, 31*(3), 374–396.

Clarke, M., & Stewart, J. (1997). *Handling the wicked issues: A challenge for government.* Birmingham, UK: University of Birmingham.

Cooper, P. J. (2003). *Governing by contract: Challenges and opportunities for public managers.* Washington, DC: CQ Press.

Coulthard, D., & Castleman, T. (2001). Electronic procurement in government: More complicated than just good business. In *Proceedings of the 9th European Conference on Information Systems,* (pp. 999-1009). IEEE.

Croom, S., & Johnston, R. (2003). E-service: Enhancing internal customer service through e-procurement. *International Journal of Service Industry Management, 14*(5), 539–555. doi:10.1108/09564230310500219

DeSanctis, G., & Poole, M. S. (1994). Capturing the complexity in advanced technology use: Adaptive structuration theory. *Organization Science, 5*(2), 121–147. doi:10.1287/orsc.5.2.121

Diggs, S. N., & Roman, A. V. (2012). *Understanding and tracing accountability within the public procurement process: Interpretations, performance measurements and the possibility of developing public-private partnerships.* Public Performance & Management Review. *36*(2), 289-314. doi:10.2753/PMR 1530-9576360207

Dunleavy, P., Margetts, H., Bastow, S., & Tinkler, J. (2006). New public management is dead: Long live digital-era governance. *Journal of Public Administration: Research and Theory, 16*(3), 467–494. doi:10.1093/jopart/mui057

Fountain, J. E. (2001). *Building the virtual state: Information technology and institutional change.* Washington, DC: Brookings Institution Press.

Fry, B. R., & Raadschelders, J. C. N. (2008). *Mastering public administration: From Max Weber to Dwight Waldo.* Washington, DC: CQ Press.

Hardy, C. A., & Williams, S. P. (2008). E-government policy and practice: A theoretical and empirical exploration of public e-procurement. *Government Information Quarterly, 25,* 155–180. doi:10.1016/j.giq.2007.02.003

Hardy, C. A., & Williams, S. P. (2011). Assembling e-government research designs: A transdisciplinary view and interactive approach. *Public Administration Review, 71*(3), 405–413. doi:10.1111/j.1540-6210.2011.02361.x

Henriksen, H. Z., & Mahnke, V. (2005). E-procurement adoption in the Danish public sector: The influence of economic and political rationality. *Scandinavian Journal of Information Systems, 17*(2), 85–106.

Hoque, K., Kirkpatrick, I., Londsdale, C., & De Ruyter, A. (2011). Outsourcing the procurement of agency workers: The impact of vendor managed services in English social care. *Work, Employment and Society, 25*(3), 522–539. doi:10.1177/0950017011407971

Johnston, J. M., & Romzek, B. S. (2008). Social welfare contracts as networks: The impact of network stability on management and performance. *Administration & Society, 40*(2), 115–146. doi:10.1177/0095399707312826

Kamarck, E. C., & Nye, J. S. (Eds.). (2002). *Governance.com: Democracy in the information age.* Washington, DC: Brookings Institution Press.

Kettl, D. F. (2002). *The transformation of governance.* Baltimore, MD: Johns Hopkins University Press.

Leukel, J., & Maniatopoulos, G. (2005). A comparative analysis of product classification in public vs. private e-procurement. *The Electronic. Journal of E-Government, 3*(4), 201–212.

McCue, C., & Roman, A. V. (2012). E-procurement: myth or reality? *Journal of Public Procurement, 12*(2), 212-238.

McGuire, M., & Agranoff, R. (2011). The limitations of public management networks. *Public Administration, 89*(2), 265–284. doi:10.1111/j.1467-9299.2011.01917.x

Milakovich, M. E. (2012). *Digital governance: New technologies for improving public service and participation.* New York, NY: Routledge.

Milward, B., & Provan, K. (2000). Governing the hollow state. *Journal of Public Administration: Research and Theory, 10*(2), 359–379. doi:10.1093/oxfordjournals.jpart.a024273

Mintrom, M. (2003). *People skills for policy analysts.* Washington, DC: Georgetown University Press.

Mota, F. P. B., & Filho, R. J. (2011). Public e-procurement and the duality of technology: A comparative study in the context of Brazil and of the state of Paraiba. *Journal of Information Systems and Technology Management, 8*(2), 315–330. doi:10.4301/S1807-17752011000200003

OECD. (2011). E-procurement. *Proceedings of Government at a Glance, 2011*, 152–153. OECD Publishing.

Orlikowski, W. J. (1992). The duality of technology: Rethinking the concept of technology in organizations. *Organization Science, 3*(3), 398–427. doi:10.1287/orsc.3.3.398

Orlikowski, W. J. (2000). Using technology and constituting structures: A practice lens for studying technology in organizations. *Organization Science, 11*(4), 404–428. doi:10.1287/orsc.11.4.404.14600

Osborne, S. (2006). The new public governance: 1. *Public Management Review, 8*(3), 377–387. doi:10.1080/14719030600853022

Peck, F., & Cabras, I. (2011). The impact of local authority procurement on local economies: The case of Cumbria, North West London. *Public Policy and Administration, 26*(3), 307–331. doi:10.1177/0952076709356859

Roman, A. V. (2012a). *Maximizing transformative impacts: Public policy and financial management through e-procurement.* Working Paper. Boca Raton, FL: Florida Atlantic University.

Roman, A. V. (2012b). *The politics of bounded procurement: Purists, brokers and the politics-procurement dichotomy.* Working Paper. Boca Raton, FL: Florida Atlantic University.

Savas, E. S. (2000). *Privatization and public-private partnerships.* New York, NY: Chatham House.

Sclar, E. D. (2000). *You don't always get what you pay for: The economics of privatization.* Ithaca, NY: Cornell University Press.

Somasundaram, R., & Damsgaard, J. (2005). Policy recommendations for electronic public procurement. *The Electronic. Journal of E-Government, 3*(3), 147–156.

Taylor, F. W. (1967). *The principles of scientific management*. New York, NY: Norton.

Thai, K. V. (2001). Public procurement re-examined. *Journal of Public Procurement, 1*(1), 9–50.

Van Slyke, D. M. (2007). Agents or stewards: Using theory to understand the government-nonprofit social service contracting relationship. *Journal of Public Administration: Research and Theory, 17*(2), 157–187. doi:10.1093/jopart/mul012

Varney, M. (2011). E-procurement—Current law and future challenges. *ERA-Forum, 12*(2), 185-204.

Walsham, G. (1993). *Interpreting information systems in organization*. New York, NY: John Wiley.

West, D. M. (2005). *Digital government: Technology and public sector performance*. Princeton, NJ: Princeton University Press.

World Bank. (2004). *Strategic electronic government procurement – Strategic overview an introduction for executives*. New York, NY: World Bank Institute.

Wright, B. E., Moynihan, D. P., & Pandey, S. K. (2011). Pulling the levers: Transformational leadership, public service motivation, and mission valence. *Public Administration Review, 72*(2).

ADDITIONAL READING

Bekkers, V., & Homburg, V. (2007). The myths of e-government: Looking beyond the assumptions of new and better government. *The Information Society, 23*(5), 373–382. doi:10.1080/01972240701572913

Brainard, L., & McNutt, J. (2010). Virtual government-citizen relations: Informational, transactional, or collaborative? *Administration & Society, 42*(7), 836–858. doi:10.1177/0095399710386308

Brown, M. (2007). Understanding e-government benefits. *American Review of Public Administration, 37*(2), 178–197. doi:10.1177/0275074006291635

Brown, T. L., Potoski, M., & Van Slyke, D. M. (2006). Managing public service contracts: Aligning values, institutions and markets. *Public Administration Review, 66*(3), 53–67. doi:10.1111/j.1540-6210.2006.00590.x

Coursey, D., & Norris, D. F. (2008). Models of e-government: Are they correct? An empirical assessment. *Public Administration Review, 68*(3), 523–536. doi:10.1111/j.1540-6210.2008.00888.x

Croom, S. (2000). The impact of web-based procurement on the management of operating resources supply. *The Journal of Supply chain Management, 36*(1), 4-13.

Dalcher, D., & Genus, A. (2003). Introduction: Avoiding IS/IT implementation failure. *Technology Analysis and Strategic Management, 15*(4), 403–407. doi:10.1080/095373203000136006

Dawes, S. S. (2008). The evolution and continuing challenges of e-governance. *Public Administration Review, 68*, S86–S102. doi:10.1111/j.1540-6210.2008.00981.x

De Boer, L., Harink, J., & Heijboer, G. (2002). A conceptual model for assessing the impact of electronic procurement. *European Journal of Purchasing and Supply Management, 8*(1), 25–33. doi:10.1016/S0969-7012(01)00015-6

Edmiston, K. (2003). State and local e-government: Prospects and challenges. *American Review of Public Administration, 33*(1), 20–45. doi:10.1177/0275074002250255

Enquist, B., Camén, C., & Johnson, M. (2011). Contractual governance for public service value networks. *Journal of Service Management, 22*(2), 217–240. doi:10.1108/09564231111124235

Enquist, B., Johnson, M., & Camén, C. (2005). Contractual governance for sustainable service. *Qualitative Research in Accounting & Management, 2*(1), 29–53. doi:10.1108/11766090510635370

Ganapati, S. (2011). Uses of public participation geographic information systems applications in e-government. *Public Administration Review, 71*(3), 425–434. doi:10.1111/j.1540-6210.2011.02226.x

Gichoya, D. (2005). Factors affecting the successful implementation of ICT projects in government. *The Electronic. Journal of E-Government, 3*(4), 175–184.

Hanberger, A. (2003). Democratic implications of public organizations. *Public Organization Review, 3*(1), 29–54. doi:10.1023/A:1023095927266

Hawking, P., Stein, A., Wyld, D. C., & Foster, S. (2004). E-procurement: Is the ugly duckling actually a swan down under? *Asia Pacific Journal of Marketing and Logistics, 16*(1), 3–26. doi:10.1108/13555850410765140

Ho, A. T. K. (2002). Reinventing local governments and the e-government initiative. *Public Administration Review, 62*(4), 434–444. doi:10.1111/0033-3352.00197

Hui, W. S., Othman, R., Omar, N. H., Rahman, R. A., & Haron, N. H. (2011). Procurement issues in Malaysia. *International Journal of Public Sector Management, 24*(6), 567–593. doi:10.1108/09513551111163666

Lenk, K., & Traunmüller, R. (2002). Electronic government: Where are we heading? In R. Lenk & B. Traunmüller (Eds.), *Electronic Government: First International Conference, EGOV 2002,* (173–199). New York, NY: Springer.

Mishra, A. N., Prabhudev, K., & Barua, A. (2007). Antecedents and consequences of internet use in procurement: An empirical investigation of U.S. manufacturing firms. *Information Systems Research, 18*(1), 103–120. doi:10.1287/isre.1070.0115

Moon, J. M. (2002). The evolution of e-government among municipalities: Rhetoric or reality? *Public Administration Review, 62*(4), 424–433. doi:10.1111/0033-3352.00196

Morgan, G. (2006). *Images of organization.* Thousand Oaks, CA: Sage.

Preuss, L. (2007). Buying into the future: Sustainability initiatives in local government procurement. *Business Strategy and the Environment, 16*(5), 354–365. doi:10.1002/bse.578

Sun, S. X., Zhao, J., & Wang, H. (2012). An agent based approach for exception handling in e-procurement management. *Expert Systems with Applications, 39*(1), 1174–1182. doi:10.1016/j.eswa.2011.07.121

Van Slyke, D. M. (2003). The mythology of privatization in contracting for social services. *Public Administration Review, 63*(3), 296–315. doi:10.1111/1540-6210.00291

Zsidisin, G. A., & Ellram, L. M. (2001). Activities related to purchasing and supply management involvement in supplier alliances. *International Journal of Physical Distribution & Logistic Management, 31*(9), 629–646. doi:10.1108/09600030110408143

KEY TERMS AND DEFINITIONS

E-Procurement (Digital Procurement): The use of information communication technology for purposes of public purchasing.

Information Communication Technology (ICT): Storage and communication technology used for information collection, storage, transmission, processing, and decision-making.

Interpretive Flexibility: The degree to which users shape technology during implementation or use.

Network Structures: Long term sustainable interdependency and relationship constructs among discrete entities that share resources and knowledge while working towards a common goal.

Schizophrenic Re-Identification: An original term used to describe the historical tendency of public administration literature to constantly question its own knowledge base and be captured by passing fads.

Structuration Model of Technology: Perspective that suggests that technology is objective in some regards by also socially constructed.

Transformation: A substantial change in pattern, condition, or nature.

Transformational Leadership: Ability to influence motivations and perceptions of goals within the contexts of individual roles, social responsibilities, and values.

Chapter 2
Public Sector Transformation:
Privatization in Saudi Arabia

Fareed Alyagout
National Power Company, Saudi Arabia

A.K. Siti-Nabiha
Universiti Sains Malaysia, Malaysia

ABSTRACT

The Kingdom of Saudi Arabia has embarked on the privatization of its public enterprises with the main objectives of improving the efficiency of the national economy, enlarging Saudi citizens' ownership of productive assets, and encouraging local and foreign capital investment in the Kingdom. Subsequently, in 2003, the Saudi Council of Ministries approved a list of twenty-two targeted economic activities and government services to be privatized and the private sector is being invited to participate in many economic activities and services. As such, the aim of this chapter is to present the historical context and rationale for privatization in Saudi Arabia. The objectives and implementation process taken by the Saudi government to create a suitable environment for private sector investment and the issues and problems associated with privatization initiatives are also discussed in this chapter.

INTRODUCTION

It has been argued that government bureaucracy is slow in its actions and inefficient in its performance and private enterprises are managed more efficiently. Consequently, the fundamental principle of offloading government-run industries and services to the private sector has been the subject of an ongoing debate in the Western world over the last three decades. Adoption of this policy has moved eastwards since the 1990s and is being implemented in North Africa, the Middle East, India, Pakistan and other Asian countries since its perceived that healthy economic development is achieved if privatization is well implemented (Dinavo, et al., 1995).

DOI: 10.4018/978-1-4666-2665-2.ch002

Subsequently, during the late 1990s and early 2000s, the Saudi government, after considerable deliberations and studies, decided to follow the route of privatization that has been implemented in the western world. Prior to that, the government of Saudi Arabia was directly managing all infrastructure facilities and services, which were heavily subsidized by the government. Since the national economy was heavily dependent on oil, the fluctuation in oil prices and the two gulf wars had taken a heavy toll on government expenditure, resulting in a spending deficit in spite of Saudi Arabia's status as the world's largest oil producer.

At the time, the domestic private sector was very weak in comparison with its counterparts in other nations, and was not in a position to contribute substantially to the national economy. The government realized that drastic measures were needed to improve the efficiency and productivity of infrastructure facilities such as water, electricity, seaports, telecommunications, postal and health services that provide services at subsidized rates. It was also necessary to adopt state of the art technology and the latest management techniques to introduce a sense of accountability in the departments providing these services.

Thus, the Saudi economic reform was initiated under the Sixth Development Plan covering the period from 1995 to 2000. The strategic basis of the development plan emphasized the need to continue adopting polices that help the private sector to undertake many of the economic tasks of the government, rationalizing the systems of direct and indirect subsidies provided by the government for services. Thus, the private sector was to take the role as the engine of the economic recovery and growth. In addition, the development plan emphasized the need to continue the Saudization policy and the development of the Saudi labour force, to accelerate the replacement of the non-Saudi workforce (www.mop.gov.sa). The plan also specifically called for the "stabilization of the internal and external value of

the Saudi currency with the development of the country's capital market as catalysts for private sector expansion" (Al-Salloum, 1999, p. 232). The sectors that were initially marked for privatization include: telecommunications, power generation and sea water desalination, seaports operations, education services, municipal, and health services. However, there are several fundamental issues that impede on the success of privatization in Saudi Arabia as discussed in this chapter. The next section presents the background of Saudi governmental system. This is followed by the contextual descriptions of the path towards and implementation of privatization in Saudi Arabia. The issues problems and recommended solutions are then provided in this chapter.

BACKGROUND OF THE SAUDI ARABIAN GOVERNMENTAL SYSTEM

Modern Saudi Arabia was founded in 1932 by the late King Abdulaziz bin Abdulrahman Al-Saud. Saudi Arabia is a monarchy in which the power rests in the hands of the King and the Crown Prince. From the Kingdom's foundation in 1932 until 1992, Saudi Arabia was ruled without a formal, written Constitution. It was only in March 1992 that King Fahad promulgated several Royal Decrees, which constituted a package of constitutional and administrative reforms.

The Basic Law, adopted in 1992, declared that Saudi Arabia is an independent Islamic monarchy ruled by the sons and grandsons of King Abdul Aziz Al Saud, and that the Holy Qur'an is the constitution of the country, which is governed on the basis of Islamic law (Shari'a). There are no political parties or national elections. The King must observe the Shari'a and retain a consensus of the Saudi royal family, religious scholars (Ulama), and other important elements in Saudi traditions and society. The Basic Law stipulates that the King alone chooses his successor, the Crown

Prince. However, his choice must meet with the approval of a royal family council comprising leading members of the royal family.

The Council of Ministers is the Saudi Arabian Cabinet that is appointed by and accountable to the King. The role of the Cabinet is to advise on general policy, to manage government departments and to pass legislation, which is then ratified by royal decree. The Council of Ministers is headed by the King. During late 1992, King Fahad bin Abdul Aziz Al Saud issued three additional decrees, which established a formal framework for the government.

The Basic Law of Government was issued pursuant to Royal Decree A/90 dated March 1st, 1992. This law confirmed among other things Saudi Arabia's monarchical structure and its adherence to Islam and Shari'a, and addressed the independence of the judiciary and certain fundamental rights of its citizens and residents. The second decree established and empowered the Consultative Council (Majlis Al-Shoura) to express opinions on certain matters (such as general policy of state, interpretation of laws, and adoption of international treaties) and is referred to as the President of the Council of Ministers. The Consultative Council also has the right to propose laws to be promulgated by the King. The third decree covered the internal governance of the various regions of Saudi Arabia and provided among other things for establishment of a provincial council for each province.

In 1993, another royal decree was issued, establishing new rules governing the Council of Ministers under which the Council of Ministers recommends legislation to be issued by the King. The word "law" in Saudi Arabia is understood to refer to Islamic law (in Arabic, Shari'a). All secular rules and regulations are subject to and interpreted in accordance with Shari'a precepts.

The Consultative Council, or Majlis Ashura, is the legislature of the country. The Council has 150 members that are appointed by the king; currently six of them are women. The modernization of the Majlis Ashura was considered to be an update to the enhancement of the council's framework and organisation, designed to improve efficiency. This modernization was a measure designed to equip the Council to deal with the rapid economic development that has taken place in Saudi Arabia in recent years. The Majlis consists of a Chairman, Vice-Chairman, Secretary General, General Panel, Standing Committees (which include 12 specialized committees, ad-hoc committee, sub-committees, and joint committees), and Support Administration. The specialized committees are designed to cover all political and social affairs in the country.

The Saudi government has established a number of agencies to help implement economic reforms. These agencies are: the Supreme Economic Council (SEC), the Supreme Council for Petroleum and Minerals (SCPM), the General Commission for Tourism and Antiquities (GCTA), the Saudi Arabian General Investment Authority (SAGIA), the Food and Drugs Authority (FDA) and the Council of Saudi Chambers of Commerce and Industry. The only council that has direct relevance to privatization in Saudi Arabia is the Supreme Economical Council (SEC).

THE PATH TOWARDS PRIVATIZATION

The foundation of the modern Saudi economic policy was laid by King Faisal when he ascended to the throne in 1964. The key points of the policy were Saudi control of its own natural resources, better utilization of these resources for the benefit of the country and the encouragement of private sector participation (Wright, 1996). In line with this vision, King Faisal initiated the first five-year plan; all subsequent five-year development plans have been—and still are—based on these core concepts. These concepts serve to guide the Kingdom's long term development objectives while also providing scope for each five-year plan to mitigate the particular difficulties and challenges of the targeted period, and to offer opportunities both in terms of domestic and international socioeconomic conditions (6th Development Plan, 1995, p. 15).

During the 1970s and early 1980s, a sharp increase in oil prices relieved Saudi Arabia from the economic and financial constraints of the previous decades. Massive oil revenues, combined with the limited capacity of the Saudi economy to absorb these funds, created large financial surpluses in both the private and government sectors. However, with the downturn in oil prices that began in 1982, oil revenues in the Kingdom began to shrink. The government had to revise its economic policy, from managing surpluses to coping with growing budgetary and balance-of-payments shortfalls. It had significant spending commitments, which forced the government to sell off some foreign assets in order to finance large budget, current account and balance of payments deficits (Metz, 1992).

During the 1980s, the UK and other governments opted to follow privatization or public private partnership as a strategy to solve their economic problems, by licensing private firms to carry out services that were previously provided by the government. This idea was invented and applied in the Western World and earned the enthusiasm, trust and the full support of international financial institutions such as the World Bank. Saudi Arabia and other Middle Eastern countries considered this initiative seriously when the economic situation deteriorated in the 1980s, when oil prices plummeted. Since oil was the only source of revenue for Saudi Arabia, the dramatic change in oil prices seriously affected government revenues and commitments. In fact, the Saudi Third Five-Year Development plan (1980-1985) which was ratified during the late 1970s emphasized the need for output-oriented public sector investment through economic diversification, for example through the development of petrochemical, agriculture and other industries.

As indicated by Salloum (1999) the plan stated that, "...the private sector should take the lead in the agriculture and industrial sectors in order to contribute to economic diversification" (p. 225).

During its third five-year development plan, the government started encouraging the development of the private sector by issuing directives requiring international contractors to maximize the use of locally manufactured materials and to subcontract at least 30% of their contracts to local service providers or contractors. The continued depreciation of oil prices during the mid-1980s due to the international oil supply surplus led to an OPEC decision to cut output, with the main burden of this reduction falling on Saudi Arabia. The OPEC decision coincided with the devaluation of the US dollar, the currency in which oil is sold on the international markets. This combination of price falls and reduced oil exports inevitably resulted in lower revenues and growth rate for Saudi Arabia (Metz, 1992). This new economic reality obliged the government in the Saudi Fourth Development Plan (1985-1990) to emphasize economic diversification as a priority and identifying privatization as one of its objectives to encourage the private sector to take a leading role in the development of the non-oil industries (www.mop.gov.sa). Moreover, to overcome some of the financial constraints of this period, the Saudi government offered its citizens 20% of the shares, worth US$10 bn, in its leading petrochemical entity, Saudi Arabian Basic Industries Corporation (SABIC) through an Initial Public Offering (IPO) (Chaudhry, et al., 1992).

As a continuation of the mitigation measures taken to stabilize the economy, the Saudi Fifth Development plan (1990-1995) was focused on the reduction of the effects of international economic fluctuations on the Saudi economy and the availability of essential public services. The Fifth plan put an emphasis on improving efficiency through being flexible in its resource allocations and creating an environment to facilitate the development of a stronger and more diversified private sector, by establishing a wide range of policies, incentives, and new institutional mechanisms. The plan also endorsed the initiatives to privatize some public services and lease the management of certain public enterprises to the private sector (Salloum, 1999; www.mop.gov.sa). This shift in focus was about placing a higher priority on the role of the private sector and adopting free market economic policies, to ensure that the pattern of growth and shape of the economy is influenced by the extent and direction of private sector investment rather than the size and distribution of government expenditure.

During the fifth development plan, period the Saudi government faced a heavy budgetary and trade deficit due to the expensive 1990 to 1991 war with Iraq. Total government debt reached three quarters of Saudi Gross Domestic Product (GDP). One of the most prominent challenges faced by Saudi Arabia during this time was the trend toward globalization in the world economy, where the IMF and other international organisations urged Saudi Arabia to undertake economic reforms (Akoum, 2009).

Furthermore, due to the country's status as the world's largest oil exporter, international powers have traditionally seen the Kingdom's internal stability as being in their own interest, (BMI, 2010). This pushed Saudi Arabia toward joining the World Trade Organization (WTO) and making structural changes to its economic and legal regimes and committing to economic diversification and privatization (Pauerstein, 2006).

Thus, the concept of privatization had been discussed and incorporated as an important issue in several development plans since the 1980s, by detailing various steps for privatization including objectives, policies and the development of an effective private sector. However, Saudi Arabia experienced various political crises in the Gulf region such as the Iran-Iraq war and the invasion of Kuwait and its subsequent liberation. Because of these events and the consequential financial constraints, the concept of privatization was not

a priority. It was only in 1997 the government was in a position to make privatization a reality and cautiously selected Saudi seaports to be the first sector marked for privatization. A plan for seaport privatization was introduced, involving a profit share between the government and private sector, provided that the private sector upgrade, manage, and operate the seaport terminals. Later on, other sectors were also privatized as explained in the next section.

IMPLEMENTING PRIVATIZATION PROGRAMS

Cheuing (1997) explained that the rationales for privatization around the world vary, depending on external factors derived from international pressures, and internal factors derived from local, political, social, and economic considerations. However, the motives that prompted the Saudi government to adopt a privatization policy are relatively different since, unlike other countries, the Kingdom was always a free trade economy and was not susceptible to direct external pressure or internal demand. As stated by Al-Ajmi (2003), in Saudi Arabia, the motivation to privatize state-owned enterprises has come about as a natural evolutionary process of gradual transformation in social, economic, and political spheres; it was not due to external pressures as observed in other countries.

There are also the arguments that fiscal consideration is the primary driving force for privatization in Saudi Arabia. For example, Ramady (2006) pointed out that the country would need about US\$800 bn in capital expenditure for the next 20 years and the government had compelling reasons to invite private sector participation in order to share the debt burden. The need for privatization was also highlighted in conclusions of several studies (see for example Al-Homeadan, 1996; Al-Salloum, 1999; Al-Sarhan & Persly, 2001). Privatization was required due to both dissatisfactions in public bureaucracy and the need to create new economic opportunities in order to develop the local market. The general belief is that the performance of state-owned enterprises is not satisfactory, whereas the private sector generally boasts superior managerial practices and confidence that will bring better productivity and performance, resulting in greater financial and managerial flexibility for the market.

Nonetheless, the IMF in its 2001 report urged the Saudi government to restructure state enterprises and improve resource allocation in order to overcome fiscal constraints after the oil price fluctuations of the 1990s. Saudi Arabia's accession to the WTO in 2005 has committed the Kingdom to free trade practices and an acceleration of the liberalization process in key sectors such as telecommunication, electricity, and financial services (Akoum, 2009).

Thus, privatization in Saudi Arabia started from being an important strategy for achieving economic ambitious plans, a faster pace of development and economic prosperity for the Saudi society, through to an expansion of the involvement of local private companies in all economic activities. The cornerstone of such a policy was the involvement of Saudi citizens in key economic and social decisions, to complement the process of the political system, which included the "Shura Council."

The privatization policy was also aimed at introducing a new spirit in the economic structure of public enterprises by improving their performance and production efficiency through the involvement of the private sector that manages and operates public services on a commercial basis. The policy was also aimed at attracting Saudi capital held overseas by providing an opportunity for investment in the national economy while also reducing the government financial burden. In doing so the government can focus its investment in projects that the private sector are reluctant to invest in, as well as allowing it to concentrate on strategic political and social projects.

Prior to embarking on privatization program, the Saudi government conducted studies to obtain reliable information on strategic issues related to public sector policies and performance that influence private sector activities. For example during 1990, an independent study was commissioned by the Chamber of Commerce and Industry. The field survey polled 140 businessmen of whom 91% were in favour of privatization. In 1991 another series of structured interviews were conducted in the western region of Saudi Arabia, surveying 50 chief executives from the industrial sector who were selected at random. The study concluded that 76% of those interviewed highlighted the need to change the laws and regulations, as they do not protect the interests of industrial companies. However, eighty two percent said the laws and regulations are perceived to be counter-productive in encouraging businessmen to invest in industrial projects, (Al-Sarhan & Presly, 2001; Sofi & Mayer 1991).

The results of the survey which included structured interviews with the department heads of the public sector highlighted the dissatisfaction of public bureaucracy, the desire to limit government interventions in the market place, the need to increase the capabilities of the private sector through creating new economic opportunities and collaborations with international investors (Al-Homeadan, 1996).

As a result, the Saudi government undertook the establishment of a stock market, provided incentives for the development of new listed companies, as well as more credit and loans to private enterprises from commercial banks. In order to attract foreign capital, the government removed capital flow controls, including restrictions on repatriation of capital and profits, in addition to providing tax holidays and soft loans to potential investors, (www.mop.gov.sa; Salloum, 1999).

Subsequently, in 1997, the Saudi Council of Ministers issued Decree number 60, to ensure a continued increase in the share of the private sector and to expand its participation in the national economy. The decree established privatization strategies which comprised eight objectives and the recommended policies and measures to achieve these objectives. The objectives can be summarized as follows (www.sec.gov.sa):

1. To elevate the competence of the national economy (through subjecting the public sector projects to market forces), and increase its competitive ability (through creating proper investment environment i.e. capital market) to face the challenges in regional and international competition.

2. To encourage private sector investment and effective participation in the national economy through privatizing public enterprises and services and operating those on commercial bases This will ultimately provide the opportunity to diversify the Saudi economic base away from the dependence on oil.

3. To increase partnership of citizens in productive government assets through using general subscription system, as so called Initial Public Offering (IPO).

4. To encourage national and foreign capital for local investments through partial owning of productive projects, and to continue to develop the capital market to give a chance to increase local and foreign investments, and to provide additional channels to attract savings.

5. To increase the Saudi employment opportunities, optimize the use of national labour and ensure the continued equitable increase of individual income.

6. To provide all necessary services for citizens and investors at suitable time and to place regulatory measures (i.e. good quality services with reasonable costs, through establishing regulatory authority to regulate the service tariff and monitor the services).

7. To rationalize government spending and reduce the government budget by provid-

ing the opportunity to the private sector to finance, operate and maintain some of the service sectors that they are capable to do.

8. To increase government revenues from the returns of privatization to be transferred to the private sector i.e. from granting concessions or sale of government properties.

The sharp fall in oil prices in 1998 affected Saudi government revenues, leading to public domestic debt equivalent to 118% of GDP. This put heavy "fiscal pressure" on the government, which prompted the urgency of further economic reforms (Akoum, 2009). Accordingly, in August 30th 1999, a Royal Decree was issued announcing the establishment of the Supreme Economic Council (SEC) chaired by the Crown Prince, to formulate and better coordinate Saudi economic development policies in order to accelerate institutional and industrial reform. Further role of SEC were formalized in 2001 through the issuance of Decision No. 257 of the council of Minister giving SEC the responsibility of supervising the privatization programme and monitoring its implementation in coordination with the relevant government agencies. The SEC was also authorized to develop a strategic plan and timetable identifying the sectors that are to be privatized, with an appropriate regulatory framework for each sector. The Council of Ministers decision also specified that any comments or suggestions related to the privatization programme by government agencies or non-government sources shall be submitted for study and review by the Supreme Economic Council (SEC), which will submit its recommendations in the matter for approval by the Cabinet for necessary action and implementation.

The privatization policy continued to be focused under the Seventh development plan (2000-2005) through the intensification of private sector involvement in activities related to the economy and social development), and investing in Saudi citizens' skills through higher education and vocational or on-the-job training (Cordesman,

2006). Hence, in 2000, the Saudi government announced privatization would start in other key economic sectors. It started with education (late 1999 and early 2000) where, the schools cafeterias, female schools transportation and waste paper disposal services were privatized. Later on, the establishment of private schools, kindergartens and foreign schools was permitted, and by 2007, a new strategy were adopted allowing the private sector to finance, build and then transfer the new schools to the government.

In 2002, the government decided to partially privatize the Saudi Public Investment Fund Organisation by selling shares to the public through an IPO, as well as part of the government's shares in the companies that are listed in the Saudi stock market i.e. Saudi Telecommunication Company (STC) and the National Council on Compensation Insurance Inc. (NCCI). By 2003, the government had announced the establishment of a financial regulatory body, the Capital Market Authority (CMA). The establishment of this Financial Regulatory Authority provided an impetus to the private sector to undertake infrastructure projects, including power and water projects. It also cleared the way for the private sector to directly negotiate providing captive utilities to industrial complexes. In the same year, the Council of Ministers approved the privatization of the Saudi Post Corporation which allowed the private sector to operate postal facilities on a commercial basis.

Furthermore, the government acknowledged that privatization is considered to be one of the most significant strategies of the Eighth Development plan (2005-2010). In 2005, the Secretary General of the Supreme Economic Council had stated: "Privatization in Saudi Arabia remains a corner stone of the Saudi economic reform program" (www.sec.gov.sa). The plan placed an emphasis on providing job opportunities to all Saudi citizens, and supporting public-private-partnerships in order for the private sector to play an important and efficient role in economic and social development. In addition, the plan stressed the need to privatize

more activities, facilities, public services and to accelerate the pace of privatization. Moreover, the plan also called for the continued development of laws, rules, and regulations on investments and financial services which will help the acceleration and implementation of the privatization strategy (Saudi Arabian Monitory Agency, annual report 2006).

Accordingly, during 2006 and 2007, the government publicized a major privatization plan for most service sectors including: the Saudi Railways Organisation; different social services provided by the Ministry of Social Affairs (i.e. diabetes and handicapped rehabilitation centers etc.); municipal services including sewage treatment plants; inviting the private sector to participate in the development of industrial estates, and providing the necessary utilities for the factories and operating and managing the sport cities and running them on a commercial basis. The government went further and announced that its privatization policy aimed to expand public participation in the ownership of government companies, i.e. Saudi Arabian Mining Company, Saudi Arabian Airlines etc., through public subscription (IPO),

In addition, a decision was taken by the Capital Market Authority (CMA) to partially liberalize the Saudi IPO market by allowing foreigners to invest through mutual funds and also by allowing GCC nationals to enter the Saudi equity market (Akoum, 2009).

MAIN PROBLEMS EXPERIENCED IN PRIVATIZING DIFFERENT SECTORS IN SAUDI ARABIA

The key issues for privatization of the public sector enterprises can be identified as public sector with high bureaucratic procedures and lack of transparency, weak private sector that depends of heavily low expatriate labor, and failure of government authority to carry proper studies and evaluations prior to implementing privatization policy.

Public Sector Conditions

All over the world the main function of the governments are politically biased with the main aim of satisfying the general public that their interests are being protected. In the process, the efficiency of the government's departments does not get any priority. The governments try to provide employments to as many people as possible in order to keep general satisfaction and nation stability regardless of the deficit budgets. While this approach can be tolerated for governing function, it harms the public undertakings in infrastructure sectors that provide essential services such as electricity, water, roads, airports, seaports, communications etc. when these undertakings are under public sector there is limited accountability and no profit and loss accounts which create total lethargy in the management and employment resulting low productivity and general dissatisfaction.

When the Saudi government decided to privatize these undertakings, it becomes very difficult to absorb the spirit of accountability and efficiency in the existing management and employees of these undertakings due to the nature of employment which depend on partiality and nepotism, etc. It is neither possible to dispense with their services nor easy to carry them in the privatized enterprises that need efficiency and accountability as criterion of its functioning.

Weak Private Sector

For privatization to be successful and for Saudi Arabia to achieve economic diversification, several fundamentals such as the existence of a strong banking system, business law and regulations, and a technically capable and efficient private sector are required. While the existence of these fundamentals can be taken for granted in the developed countries, it is difficult to find such comprehensive systems and capabilities in developing countries like Saudi Arabia (Al-Sarhan & Presly, 2001).

The Saudi privatization programme is a means to limit government intervention in the economy and to increase the capabilities of the local private sector. The Saudi government realized that there is a need to encourage growth in the domestic private sector and invest in the Saudi workforce's skills. Furthermore, the privatization of services provided by the public sector was the most appropriate step to encourage the domestic private sector to actively participate in building the fast-growing national economy. Encouraging growth in the private sector was also intended to involve Saudi nationals, directly or indirectly, in the government decision-making process in social, economic, and political matters for which entities such as the Shura Council and the Supreme Economic Council were formed.

While privatization was expected to increase the efficiency and productivity of services, it was also aimed at ensuring the active involvement of Saudi citizens in the ownership and management of these newly privatized sectors, many of whom were otherwise content to sponsor businesses owned and handled by expatriates. The major benefit of privatization was the advantage of creativity and a commercially competitive approach that is typically missing in the public sectors.

However, the weak private sector in Saudi Arabia was an impediment to the successful attainment of the objectives of privatization. Given that the domestic private sector was not mature enough to shoulder the burden of privatization, the doors were opened up for international private investors by offering many incentives. The involvement of foreign investors would serve as both a model to replicate, and to inject competition in the private sector, to encourage growth and maturity. However, the legal system has to be improved so as to attract FDI as indicated by Business Monitoring Intelligence report:

...There is little overall protection for foreign investors within the legal system, although non-Saudi firms are due to be granted the right to

buy real estate, according to the new foreign investment code. However, the new code has not yet been implemented by the government (BMI, 2009, p. 46).

The Saudi private sector has one more weakness. Historically, when the private sector started taking its roots in Saudi Arabia, there was lack of trained, educated, and experienced nationals within Saudi Arabia. Out of this compulsion, the private sector imported skilled and experienced manpower from all over the World and started producing profitable results for themselves as well as for the country. As the availability of Saudi nationals increased, most of them opted for jobs with Government or large organisations like Aramco, SEC, SABIC, SWCC, etc. who offered very good benefits and were not hard taskmasters like the general private sector. The private sector had therefore to rely heavily on expatriates whose benefits were low but efficiency and performance was better.

Government Failure to Carry out Proper Study and Evaluation before Privatization

The concept of privatization was initially implemented in the Western World as its economy was based on Capitalism and they had strong private sectors who had exulted in strong profit-based flourishing economy.

Most of the third world economies were weak and were heavily financed by World Bank and IMF. These financial institutes realized that the public sector enterprises in third world countries in Asia, Africa, and Latin America were running into losses. They enforced the privatization on all these third world countries compulsorily as a part of their financial aid packages. Some of these attempts failed but many succeeded. Citing these successful examples, Western World strongly recommended and virtually dictated Saudi Arabia and GCC to follow the same path.

While there was no harm to follow the privatization route, the government of Saudi Arabia should have studied in depth the implications of privatization carefully before its implementation. The culture and historical background of Saudi Arabia differed very widely with western world. Saudi Arabian private sector did not have strong foundation and experience like private sector in other countries both in West and East. Saudi Private sector is dependent heavily on expatriate manpower and does not enough profit margins to be able to absorb Saudi manpower that is very costly in comparison with expatriate manpower. Most of the employed Saudi nationals work government or very large companies drawing fat salaries with relatively less workload.

Saudi private sector is very weak in comparison with its counterparts elsewhere in the world. The government should have taken these factors into considerations before embarking on the privatization program. Nevertheless, due to these drawbacks, the government decided to opt for at least a middle path and adopted the concept of partial privatization instead of totally free privatization.

Partial Privatization Program

Many countries were in a position to opt for total privatization depending on the strength of their domestic private sector maturity and eligibility to manage and operate mega size enterprises without harming overall interests of the parent nation. In case of Saudi Arabia, it was not possible for the domestic private sector to shoulder such total privatization.

As explained earlier the domestic private sector was very weak with no previous experience to manage such large and strategically important assets and hence international private sector players were permitted to enter the privatization field with a mandatory requirement of the local private sector as a partner. The infrastructure projects of Greenfield nature or Greyfield nature that were to be privatized were the backbones of national economy. It would not have been prudent to hand over management of such key national assets to international operators bereaved of strong national supervision, in the face of weakness of the associate domestic partner.

The failure of any of these entities would have resulted in serious damages to the national economy and political and social embarrassment to the government. It was therefore appropriate for the government of Saudi Arabia to adopt the middle path of partial privatization, whereby the government was able to have a close association and watch over the day to day operations and management by international and domestic private sectors with necessary expertise they have in the subject. This way the nation was in a position to reap the benefits of professional expertise as well as security and protection of national interests.

With partial privatization, the private sector does not have direct dealing with the customers. The private sector builds, operates and maintains these services and receives its dues from the government. The government purchases from private sector and in turn provides these services to the customers at subsidized rates that are lesser than the costs paid by the government to the private sector. Because of this arrangement, the privatization of these sectors did not have any impact on the procurement of services by the public. As mid-2010, the government had not offered any state asset to be wholly owned by the private sector. Privatization activity has been primarily limited to some green field projects in power and water sectors, and in other sectors, private investors have been delegated the management, operations and service functions under limited partnerships without transferring any asset ownership.

Other Problems

The success of privatization largely depends upon the approach adopted by the government and the response it gets from the private sector as well as the public who are affected by the process of privatization. It is generally observed that the implementation of such privatization is done based upon the recommendations of outsiders and the experiences gained in other countries or other sectors without doing proper studies and evaluations of the ground realities as existing at the place of proposed implementation. It is necessary to conduct in-depth studies and also to consult and interact with all the stakeholders before finalizing the policy and process of privatization.

Saudi Arabia, as well as other GCC countries, has a unique problem of very high level of unemployment for national citizens on one side against non-availability of competent national workforce. This is mainly due to lack of appropriate training and education as well as the reluctance of the citizens to put in hard work needed for education and for mastering the skills of trade, be it a low standard job or high-class job. This is a very serious handicap and needs to be tackled with utmost priority not only by the governments but also by private sectors and the social scientists as well as community leaders and responsible citizens.

GENERAL RECOMMENDATIONS FOR THE KINGDOM'S PRIVATIZATION POLICY

The success of privatization in Saudi Arabia depends upon how effectively the Government of Saudi Arabia ensures that there is total impartiality and transparency at all levels of the participants in the process of privatization. As stated by Salloum (1999, p. 315), "The state must take an overall view of the country's interests in making its decisions with regard to fostering private enterprise development. This could limit nepotism and favoritism."

This is particularly important because Arab countries tend to favor private interests, due to their close ties with the elite. The international experience shows that privatization cannot be beneficial to the nation unless there are clearly defined rules, regulations and criteria that apply to all and that are strictly and fairly implemented by the state. In this connection, the existing Shura Council and Supreme Economical Council of the Kingdom should be given more powers, which enable them to take punitive actions whenever necessary.

The privatization of various sectors such as ports, electricity, communications, and postal services are completely different, in many respects. What is applicable for one sector is not necessarily suitable for the other sector. Moreover, most of these sectors have been privatized in different parts of the world at different times. It was necessary for the concerned Saudi Authorities to carry out an in-depth study of similar sectors in different nations with different backgrounds and cultures, and evaluate the successes and failures and to devise a policy suitable for Saudi conditions. Based on such a study, a visionary and farsighted planning approach should have been adopted to develop the rationales and objectives of privatization and to formulate rules and regulations for different sectors. This has been missing. Instead, privatization was started with half-baked theories; general rules and regulations are being rewritten at every step which is harming privatization. This approach needs radical revision.

The bureaucratic labyrinth of the multiple tasks involved in privatization must be simplified by eliminating and/or shortening the entire process of private sector participation, be it domestic private sector or international private sector. It is better to establish an independent joint venture between the government and the private sector or to transfer the ownership of non-performing or loss making assets to the private sector, rather than offering only management concessions, because management concessions still suffer from government and political influence that act as a hindrance to produce the desired efficiency and productivity.

The government must also set up appropriate regulatory authorities, with the responsibility of ensuring that the local private enterprises attain the level of competency and competitiveness at international standards, in order to participate in the privatization activities. This will ensure that there are sufficiently qualified private sector players to avoid any monopoly.

In view of the recent collapse in some of the stocks on the Saudi stock market, causing losses to the general public, the authorities are required to improve the efficiency and transparency of the capital markets, so that the benefits of privatization will reach the common people through a well regulated and transparent stock market. Such a step will encourage individual Saudis to own shares in privatized firms in place of the current government cash subsidy. Such a strategy will also help to dilute family holdings of private businesses in Saudi Arabia by ensuring a wider spread of business ownership in the Saudi private sector. With private sector ownership in the hands of Saudis, the threat of favoring expatriate workers is mitigated.

Extensive efforts are also required by the government agencies at various levels to build up managerial, entrepreneurial, and technical know-how, as well as shop floor experience among the younger generation by setting examples. This is necessary for the total benefit of Saudi society as a whole.

In addition, to increase the success of the privatization policy or at least to minimize any negative effects and gain the support of employees in the implementation process, the government may consider encouraging a remuneration package in the private sector that matches or surpasses the public sector in order to make the private sector more attractive to the Saudi employees. It is also needed to implement a "no-layoff" agreement with private companies for a reasonable period of time, to allay the fear of job losses, and to train and equip those who might lose their jobs due to privatization for re-employment into some other public jobs or in the private sector (Al-Homoud, 1995).

The importance of human assets is emphasized through some organisational change literature, which suggests that for successful change to occur within an organisation, management must focus on empowering their employees to become successful change agents. Employees must be given the opportunity to increase their skills and the authority to respond to changing needs (Carter, Giber, & Goldsmith, 2001).

FUTURE RESEARCH DIRECTIONS

There is no doubt that the rationale of privatization has lofty principles and has shown fruitful results in many countries. However, since Saudi Arabia has recently introduced a privatization policy for public utilities and other service sectors, and improving productivity has become a government priority, a closer analysis and assessment are needed. Since with partial privatization, the government purchases from private sector and in turn provides these services to the customers, there is also the need to examine the cost effectiveness of this type of procurement system.

In addition, there is a need to prove that privatizing different service sectors such as telecommunication, electricity, seaports, and airlines will not affect oil production and export. The privatization of key sectors is being done by opening up these sectors to locals as well as foreign investors, without discrimination. There is a need to evaluate the pros and cons of opening up key sectors to foreign investors, especially with respect to religious and cultural activities in Saudi Arabia, given its responsibility of maintaining the holy sites of Mecca and Medina. Given that the Kingdom of Saudi Arabia is embarking on a large-scale privatization, there is a great need to conduct investigative research to evaluate whether the intended benefits of privatization have been achieved and how. Moreover, what factors have contributed to attain these achievements and what were the hurdles faced in the process?

CONCLUSION

It is very clear that Saudi Arabia has moved towards privatization very slowly and cautiously, unlike other countries. These are the benefits that the national economy of Saudi Arabia can reap, when the privatization is successfully implemented. There is no doubt that these benefits outweigh the disadvantages of privatization to the national economy, ensuring the welfare of the Saudi people as a whole and countering any disadvantages that may become apparent during the privatization process. For this reason, some experts have gone further and said that privatization itself can be a strategic goal for any country aiming at the efficient delivery of services as well as ensuring the welfare of its people (Al-Akhdar, 1994). However, for privatization to be successful, the Saudi Government should clearly defined rules, regulations and criteria that apply to all and that are strictly and fairly implemented, it is also necessary for the concerned Saudi Authorities to carry out an in-depth study of each similar sectors that desired to be privatized in different nations with different backgrounds and cultures, and evaluate the successes and failures and to devise a policy suitable for Saudi conditions. Moreover, the government must also set up appropriate regulatory authorities, with the responsibility of ensuring that the local private enterprises attain the level of competency and competitiveness at international standards, in order to participate in the privatization activities.

REFERENCES

Akhdar, F. (1994). *Privatizing Saudi economy: Theory and application*. Jeddah, Saudi Arabia: Saudi Research and Publishing Co.

Akoum, I. (2009). Privatization in Saudi Arabia: Is slow beautiful? *Wiley Periodicals Inc*. Retrieved April 13, 2010, from http://www.intersince.wiley.com

Al-Ajmi, N. (2003, May 5). Saudi Arabia: The opening of a kingdom. *Arab Times Magazine.*

Al-Homeadan, A. (1996). *Factors that shape attitudes towards privatization: The case of Saudi Arabia.* (Unpublished Doctoral Dissertation). Florida Atlantic University. Boca Raton, FL.

Al-Homoud, M., & Abdalla, I. (1995). A survey of management training and development practices in the state of Kuwait. *Journal of Management Development, 14*(3), 14–25. doi:10.1108/02621719510078939

Al-Salloum, T. (1999). *Policy choice in developing countries: The case of privatization in Saudi Arabia.* (Unpublished Doctoral Dissertation). George Mason University. Fairfax, VA.

Al-Sarhan & Presly. (2001). Privatization in Saudi Arabia: An attitude survey. *Managerial Finance, 27*(10/11), 114–122. doi:10.1108/03074350110767600

BMI. (2009). *The Saudi Arabia business forecast report. Business Monitor International.* BMI.

BMI. (2010). *The Saudi Arabia business forecast report. Business Monitor International.* BMI.

Carter, L., Giber, D., & Goldsmith, M. (2001). Best practices in organisation development and change: Culture, leadership, retention, performance, coaching. *Pfeiffer.* Retrieved April 8, 2010, from http://library.books24x7.com.proxy.lib.chalmers.se/

Chaudhry, M. A. (1992). Cauchy representation of distributions and applications to probability II. In *Proceedings of the International Symposium on Generalized Functions and their Applications,* (pp. 29-35). New York, NY: Plenum Publishing Corporation.

Cheung, A. (1997). The rise of privatization policies: Similar faces, diverse motives. *International Journal of Public Administration, 20*(12), 2213–2245. doi:10.1080/01900699708525293

Cordesman, A. (2003). Saudi Arabia enters the twenty first century: The political, foreign policy, economic and energy dimensions. *Journal of Third World Studies, 23*(2), 248–249.

Dinavo, J. (1995). *Privatization in developing countries: It's impact on economic development and democracy.* London, UK: Praeger Publishers.

Loeffner Tuggey Pauerstein Rosenthal, L. L. P. (2006). Terms of Saudi Arabia's accession to the WTO. *Middle East Policy, 13*(1), 24. doi:10.1111/j.1475-4967.2006.00235.x

Metz, H. (1992). Saudi Arabia: A country study. *Library of Congress.* Retrieved April 15, 2010, from http://countrystudies.us/saudi-arabia/

Ramady, M. (2006, September 11). Foreign direct investment: A Saudi score sheet. *Arab News.*

Soufi, W. A., & Mayer, R. T. (1991). *Saudi Arabian industrial investment.* London, UK: Quorum Books.

Wright, J. N. (1996). Creating a quality culture. *Journal of General Management, 21*(3), 19–29.

ADDITIONAL READING

Barrak, A. (1998). *Privatization and Saudi public hospitals: The impact of contracting on the quality of services.* (Unpublished Doctoral Dissertation). Mississippi State University. Starkville, MS.

Hanke, S. (1986). The privatization option: An analysis. *Economic Impact, 3*(55), 14–20.

Kikeri, S., & Kolo, F. (2005). *Privatization trends and recent development.* Washington, DC: The World Bank. doi:10.1596/1813-9450-3765

Morgan, P. (1995). *Privatization and the welfare state: The implication for consumers and the workforce.* Aldershot, UK: Dartmouth Publishing Company Limited.

Muir, R., & Saba, J. (1995). *Improving state enterprise performance: The role of internal and external incentives.* World Bank Technical Paper no 306. Washington, DC: World Bank.

Mweisher, N. (1995). *The feasibility of privatization in Saudi Arabia.* (Unpublished Doctoral Dissertation). Temple University. Philadelphia, PA.

Nafaieh, D. (1990). *Privatization for development: An analysis for potential private sector participation in Saudi Arabia.* (Unpublished Doctoral Dissertation). University of Pittsburgh. Pittsburgh, PA.

Nellis, J., & Shirley, M. (1991). *Public enterprise reform: The lesson of experience.* Washington, DC: World Bank.

Quiggin, J. (2002). Privatization and nationalization in the 21st century. *Growth, 50,* 66–73.

Shirley, M., & Walsh, P. (2000). *Public versus private ownership: The current state of the debate.* World Bank Research working paper 2420. Washington, DC: World Bank.

Younis, T. (1996). Privatization overview of policy and implementation in selected Arab countries. *International of Public Sector Management, 9*(3), 18–25. doi:10.1108/09513559610124450

KEY TERMS AND DEFINITIONS

Consultative Council (Majlis Al-Shoura): Legislative body in Saudi Arabia whose members are appointed by the King.

Council of Ministers: Saudi Arabian Cabinet that is appointed by and accountable to the King. The role of the Cabinet is to advise on general policy, to manage government departments and to pass legislation, which is then ratified by royal decree.

Economic Reform: The reform program in Saudi Arabia whereby the private sector is to become the engine of economic growth and also concerning rationalizing the systems of direct and indirect subsidies provided by the government for services.

Restrained Privatization Program: The partial privatization program where the private sector has the responsibility to create, operate, and maintain these services, whereby the government purchases these from the private sector and in turn provides these services to the end customers.

Saudi Arabia Privatization Policy: The privatization policy in Saudi Arabia with the objectives of improving the efficiency of the national economy, enlarging Saudi citizens' ownership of productive assets and encouraging local and foreign capital investment.

Saudization Policy: The policy to achieve active involvement of Saudi citizens in the ownership and management of the privatized sector.

Supreme Economic Council (SEC): One of the agencies established to help implement economic reforms whose duties is to assist the Council of Ministers in carrying out its duties and to suggest solutions regarding economic issues. It is the only council that has direct relevance to privatization in Saudi Arabia.

Chapter 3

Public Sector Transformation and the Design of Public Policies for Electronic Commerce and the New Economy:
Tax and Antitrust Policies

Modest Fluvià
Universitat de Girona, Spain

Ricard Rigall-I-Torrent
Universitat de Girona, Spain

ABSTRACT

The current situation of taxation of electronic commerce is still in its infancy in regard to its actual implementation as well as in the existence of doctrinal principles and generally accepted guidelines on the characteristics and implementation of taxation. This chapter uses the concepts, analytical tools, and appropriate models of economic analysis to understand and explain the economic phenomena observed in the New Economy and how the public sector can adapt to the new challenges. Thus, the chapter analyzes the optimal design of tax policy for electronic markets, in particular electronic commerce, and the guidelines of antitrust policy in electronic markets. This chapter also analyzes the strategies that can be adopted by firms in the New Economy to avoid or minimize the risk of intervention by antitrust authorities.

DOI: 10.4018/978-1-4666-2665-2.ch003

Public Sector Transformation and the Design of Public Policies for Electronic Commerce

INTRODUCTION

The markets of the New Economy include those sectors associated with technological changes, which result from heavy investment in R&D. Therefore, innovation is the main characteristic of the New Economy sectors. The public sector must transform itself to adapt to a changing environment. Thus, the basic factor in these industries is human capital, since R&D activities are intensive in highly skilled labor. Although there is an agreement that innovation is very important in the New Economy sectors, there is no consensus in determining the role of innovation in these markets.

Some authors argue that innovation determines the degree of competition in these sectors. Unlike other markets of the economy, where competition is primarily via prices, in the New Economy competition takes place via innovative efforts (measured, for example, through the level of spending on R&D). From this point of view, innovations in these industries are, mostly, drastic, which often implies the replacement of the leading firm in the market. This does not happen in traditional sectors, characterized by being capital intensive and whose innovations involve, usually, product enhancements or reduction of production costs. This means that the market leader can maintain its leadership position in perpetuity. However, other authors argue that the level of innovation does not need to determine the degree of competition, but rather the opposite. From this point of view, companies in the New Economy with a dominant position in the market can use innovation as a means of barrier to entry in order to continue to maintain its dominant position, which obviously is an anticompetitive practice.

In this chapter, we draw a stylized profile of the New Economy and the implications regarding public sector transformation. This chapter's goals are essentially limited to two areas. First, the optimal design of tax policy in electronic markets, in particular electronic commerce is stated. Second, the guidelines of antitrust policy in electronic markets are introduced.

The optimal design of tax regulations for electronic markets requires a detailed analysis by the public sector of the strategies of firms operating in them. In particular, the analysis of price and marketing strategies of companies is one of the most important, although not the only one. This chapter will make an initial contribution in the form of a state-of-the-art survey on pricing and marketing strategies by firms operating in e-commerce.

After analyzing business strategies, the chapter will reflect on the inherent difficulties that e-commerce poses to tax authorities. With this background, the chapter will move on to critically analyze the main initiatives in the taxation of electronic commerce, by highlighting those principles that generate greater consensus.

The second goal of this study involves analyzing antitrust policy in e-commerce. This chapter offers insights and guidance on the likely and/or desirable paths of antitrust policy applied to electronic markets. The intrinsic difficulty of this policy has increased significantly recently. The overall objective of "protecting competition" involves subtle concepts and public officials face both enormous complexities and enormous possibilities of welfare gains and huge social losses in case of errors in policy. The chapter offers an annotated guide including the most important cases and the arguments by both sides, as well as an interpretation of the consequences of failure and a summary of the principles that can be derived from the analysis.

BACKGROUND

The rise of electronic commerce represents a new and important challenge for the public sector. Markets usually change faster than the public sector structures. Firms are usually eager to adopt new technologies in order to obtain higher profits. In this setting, the public sector needs to transform itself to deal successfully with the changes that occur in markets.

Although the literature on electronic commerce is already huge, as one could expect of such a topical issue, relevant contributions from an analytical point of view are still scarce. A notable exception is the excellent text by Shapiro and Varian (1999). Reflections on the challenges that electronic commerce poses to public policy are even rarer. Indeed, the usual approach in the literature adopts the point of view of firms. Thus, it considers the changes in business strategies that e-commerce (or, more generally, the so-called information economy) requires.

Certainly, the private and public perspectives cannot be separated analytically. In simple terms, we need to substitute social welfare functions for private goals. In other words, it is not possible to address issues of optimal design of public policies for electronic commerce without first studying its economic foundations and understanding the strategies of companies operating in this new environment. Otherwise, the exercise would be fruitless.

The thesis of Shapiro and Varian (1999) is attractive and, in our own opinion, fundamentally right. We should not underestimate the changes that Information and Communications Technology (ICTs) has brought in terms of both generating new economic activities (electronic commerce) and substantially transforming both traditional sectors and the public sector itself. We should not magnify these changes either. It has been said, for example, that economic analysis does not have much to contribute to understanding and explaining the New Economy or, in other words, that the New Economy also requires a new type of economic analysis.

Shapiro and Varian (1999) argue, however, that we already have the concepts, analytical tools, and appropriate models to understand and explain the new economic phenomena that we observe. It is not, therefore, time to "burn the manuals," but to use them with wit and sensitivity to changes. We need to introduce into the body of knowledge of economists, including future economists, a set of contributions that research in economics has generated recently. Ultimately, and against what it is often cheerfully asserted, we have some appropriate analytical foundations for understanding crucial aspects of the New Economy without falling into complacency.

What concepts and models can we use for this purpose? First, economies of scale are ubiquitous in the New Economy: both the "old" forms of supply-side economies of scale as well as more modern forms of demand-side economies of scale.

On the supply side, the cost structure of information goods is characterized by high initial fixed costs, often sunk, and small variable costs. That is, typical returns to scale and also without significant capacity constraints. There are also "scope economies," that is, joint production of various goods is more efficient than producing them separately. And finally, there are economies of experience. Overall, there is every reason to "be big" to embark in "large-scale production" and, we should not forget, this is also socially desirable.

There are also economies of scale on the demand side or "network economies." That is, the value of certain goods for consumers increases with the size of the network. A larger network is always more attractive (see Economides, 1996; Katz & Shapiro, 1994). This is for true for goods with "real" networks (telephones, faxes, railways, etc.) as well as for "virtual" networks (Internet, for example).

In addition, we could finally talk of a third source of benefits of "being big," of operating at large scale. This is what might be called "economies of aggregation" (Nalebuff, 2000): attractiveness to consumers is higher when products are offered in "packages" than when they are offered individually. This tendency to bid on "packages" may be relevant to the design of tax policy.

MARKET STRUCTURE IN THE NEW ECONOMY

All these features described in the previous section, and which are common to the sectors that are part of the New Economy, lead to both a high concentration of production and to a wide range of strategies used by enterprises (protection of intellectual property, price differentiation, bundling...), as well as greater cooperation between them. However, such properties are not unique to the markets of the New Economy. Other sectors, such as, for example, electric power or the railroad share the same characteristics. Therefore, the economic analysis of these new markets should not differ from the study undergone by other more traditional sectors. Here, we present in detail how these features lead to this market structure.

Economies of scale on the production side lead, on the one hand, to a highly concentrated market supplied by one or a few firms and, on the other hand, to various strategies for protecting intellectual property and pricing above marginal cost. Otherwise, they could never recover fixed costs (R&D). Similarly, network economies lead to market concentration, as well as to the establishment of standards or to the possibility of interconnection between different technologies (or product compatibility), resulting in cooperation between firms. Such collaboration can favor consumers, because it significantly reduces both the lock-in effect and economies of scale on the consumption side. It is true that the latter, in turn, also imply market concentration. Finally, as seen before, the durability of the assets of the New Economy requires firms to continually innovate. Thus, by giving consumers new product releases firms expand their installed base without having to lower the price of their products.

In short, the market structure of the New Economy is characterized by the presence of high market concentration, prices above marginal cost, intellectual property protection, cooperation between firms and other strategies such as product differentiation and bundling. It is no surprise that this market structure brings very high profits for firms operating in it. However, all these elements, both individually and jointly, are opposed to a scenario of perfect competition. They seem, however, to favor the presence of anticompetitive practices. Indeed, perfectly competitive markets are characterized by multiple firms (identical), which can freely enter and exit the market and a homogeneous product, so that firms must compete in price. The final result is that, in equilibrium, firms set price equal to marginal cost. Thus, any price above this cost should reflect the presence of anti-competitive practices. However, in the New Economy the market price is above marginal cost as a result of the particular characteristics of these markets, and not as a reflection of any anti-competitive behavior.

Given these characteristics of the New Economy sectors, it is true that in a market characterized by high concentrations, where there is a single firm or few firms, it may seem that competition is absent. However, this statement is not quite true. Competition in these markets is dynamic in the sense that competition does not come from established firms, but from potential rivals, that is, firms which are not yet in the market and whose only possibility to enter it is to offer a product of high quality or a new product far superior to the existing (see, for instance, Gifford & Kudrle, 2011; Gregory, Sidak, & Teece, 2009). Therefore, potential rivals in their attempt to enter the market and established firms in their attempt to maintain their position are, ultimately, competing. It is at this point that the role of innovation in these markets differs significantly.

For some, the degree of competition in these sectors is reflected in the level of expenditure on R&D and innovation performance. This reasoning is consistent with the Schumpeterian view of competition, where the dynamism of markets, through innovation, leads to competition, which is reflected in the replacement of old monopolies by new monopolies with a far superior product. From this point of view, innovation plays therefore a key role in determining whether competition exists in a market of the New Economy any. Therefore, the higher the expenditure in R&D is the greater the competition in that sector. Thus, proponents of this view point out that in order to ascertain the level of effective competition in these sectors, we need data such as evidence of innovative activity, fluctuations in market shares of competitors in the industry, and introduction of new products and versions. These constitute the most reliable evidence of the fact that there is a high degree of competition in the market.

However, for others innovation is just another instrument, in the hands of the company with a dominant position in the market, which serves to maintain that position. This idea of innovation as a barrier to entry is more closely linked to the vision of competition held by Arrow. From this perspective, we should fall into the trap of linking higher spending on R&D with a higher degree of competition in the sector. That would be wrong. What can be said without doubt is what follows. Competition arising from the possible entry of new firms favors spending on R&D by established firms. Often firms with a dominant position in the market tend to increase their spending in R&D, not only with the goal of improving and providing a product of higher quality to consumers, but in order to prevent entry by potential competitors. The proof is the existence of the so-called sleeping patents, which correspond to innovations that will never have commercial use, and that many firms use as a barrier to entry.

In short, unlike Schumpeter, for whom the monopoly is superior to perfect competition, since it promotes technological progress and economic development, Arrow defends the superiority of perfect competition versus monopoly also in this respect. These two views are appreciated in the work of Reinganum (1983) and Gilbert and Newbery (1982), respectively.

According to Reinganum (1983), the result of competition between two firms, a monopolist

and a potential entrant, who fight each other, the former to maintain its dominant position in the market and the latter to snatch the monopoly of its privileged position, will always be a monopoly. Of course, with a product in the market is significantly superior to initially. Furthermore, it is noted that the winner of that race will always be the potential entrant and never the incumbent monopoly. That is, the market structure is always a monopoly, although it is characterized by temporary monopolies where new monopolies snatch the position of a former monopoly, because the product they offer is clearly superior. The reasoning behind this solution is as follows. While the race between the two firms to achieve a superior product is on the go, the monopolist continues to obtain profits from the sale of its current product in the market. However, the entrant does not get any revenue. As the monopolist has less to lose than the potential entrant if it does not win the race, its willingness to invest will also be lower and this will mean the loss of the monopoly in favor of its rival.

However, Gilbert and Newbery (1982) in a scenario identical to the previous one, i.e., with two firms, a monopolist and a potential entrant struggling for the market, get totally opposite results. In this case, the firm with monopoly power has an incentive to keep that power, winning the race in the innovation process, or what is the same, before its opponent gets the new product (or new technology). This allows it to maintain its dominant position in perpetuity. The reason lies in the fact that the monopolist has more to lose than its opponent. Thus, if the potential entrant wins the race and, therefore, enters the market, now the monopoly would cease to be a monopoly to become an oligopoly. It is well known that oligopoly profits are smaller than those of monopoly. Therefore, the loss bore by the monopolist in terms of benefits, if the rival wins the race, would exceed the benefits of the rival once installed in the market. If this is so, the willingness of the monopoly to invest in R&D will exceed clearly that of the potential entrant. For this reason, the monopolist will always win the race, which will perpetuate its dominant position in the market. In short, the monopolist seeks to eliminate, through innovation, an important part of the producer surplus of potential entrants in order to maintain its dominant position.

These two opposing views regarding the role of innovation in the New Economy sectors carry different implications in terms of antitrust policy. Obviously, from a Schumpeterian point of view competition exists in these markets and it is "fierce." Needless to say that the reward obtained by the monopoly is not negligible: the winner of the race gets the whole market. But from the point of view of Arrow, competition in these markets is virtually nonexistent. Thus, it seems quite likely that some basic rules of competition are being violated. In this sense, Shapiro and Varian (1999) note that the authorities of competition should not investigate firms that have recently managed to become a market leader, but those which have been in that position for a certain period of time.

However, innovation is not the only instrument that a monopolist can use as a barrier to entry. Other instruments exist in the New Economy sectors, which may accomplish the same task.

PUBLIC SECTOR TRANSFORMATION AND ELECTRONIC COMMERCE

According to the OECD, electronic commerce refers to commercial transactions occurring over open networks, such as the Internet. Electronic commerce includes both business-to-business (B2B) and business-to-consumer (B2C) transactions. It is clear that electronic commerce promotes the cross-border delivery of goods and services. Indeed, e-commerce can be at the origin of increased economic growth worldwide. The OECD (2009) acknowledges that the Internet is proving to be a powerful platform for consumers, help-

ing to slash search costs and boost competition. Specifically (OECD, 2009):

Online buying helped to put downward pressures on prices, while providing consumers with more choice for an ever-expanding range of products and services that can be purchased from vendors located around the world, from anywhere and at any time. While growth in e-commerce is brisk, the potential to benefit consumers further remains great as online transactions still account for less than 5% of retail trade in many countries, The financial and economic crisis appears to be spurring growth, however; while the retail sector has been hit hard, e-commerce has grown, generating new income streams for small and larger online merchants, as consumers have become more cost-conscious and are increasingly going online to compare products and save money.

As mentioned above, the rise of electronic commerce represents a challenge for the public sector. This is a consequence of the fact that markets usually change faster than the public sector structures, since firms are usually eager to adopt new technologies in order to obtain higher profits. Because of its own nature, it takes time for the public sector to adapt to a new environment. This may threaten the development of e-commerce. As remarked by the OECD (2009):

(...) the speed at which e-commerce grows will depend on the extent to which consumer confidence can be enhanced and obstacles, particularly those affecting cross-border transactions, can be removed. Improving transparency, combating fraud, as well as protecting privacy and personal information more effectively are key in this regard.

The public sector must adapt itself to these new economic circumstances to ensure that both e-commerce and economic growth are not hindered by those potential threats. As noticed by the OECD (2009), the different challenges that the public sector must address in this respect relate to the "field of mobile commerce, digital content products, protection of children, dispute resolution, payment security, protection of personal information and privacy, and the challenges of operating borderless business models in a world yet governed by domestic laws and regulations."

The remaining of this chapter deals with the specific issues raised by e-commerce with regard to public sector transformation and tax and anti-trust policies.

ELECTRONIC COMMERCE AND PUBLIC SECTOR TRANSFORMATION: TAX POLICIES

Despite the many initiatives and works by both tax administrations and economic research, taxation of electronic commerce is still in its infancy, both in the field of the principles and fundamentals that should guide taxation and, even more notoriously, in the field of real applications (see, for instance, McLure, 2003; Reddick & Coggburn, 2007; Scanlan, 2007).

The foundations and principles that inspire the imposition of electronic commerce must be based, at least in part, on new strategies that characterize firms in the New Economy. In particular, they should pay adequate attention to new pricing and marketing strategies, areas in which competition in the New Economy differs substantially. Therefore, the first subsection presents the pricing and marketing strategies by companies in the New Economy, emphasizing those aspects relevant to taxation.

Taxation of electronic commerce raises obvious difficulties, largely as a consequence of its own nature. These difficulties are analyzed and discussed in the second subsection. Besides the inherent difficulties, the current situation of non-taxation of electronic commerce is also due to its still limited economic importance. Thus, the Report of the Commission to Study Impact of Elec-

tronic Commerce in Spanish Taxation (October 2000) underlines that "the current importance in the media does not correspond to economic reality in quantitative terms, with only their growth rates being remarkable" (p. 9).

Finally, the third subsection reviews and analyzes the major initiatives and works on taxation of electronic commerce. We provide a critical and up-to-date survey on the state of affairs and major initiatives.

Pricing and Marketing Strategies by Firms in the New Economy

A revalued business strategy in new markets is the pricing strategy. Proper pricing is critical to the bottom line of firms in e-commerce. Concepts and models of price discrimination enlighten our understanding of the strategies pursued by companies. They should also enlighten the study of the optimal design of tax figures.

Pricing policy is quite complex in the New Economy. On the one hand, there are abundant economies of scale, with very low marginal costs, which justify low prices. However, there are also very high initial fixed costs, often sunk. Discrimination may be, under these conditions, a policy which is both privately and socially desirable (Varian, 1985). On the other hand, new technologies allow access, storage, and processing capacity of massive amounts of relevant information about the tastes and willingness to pay of consumers, offering great opportunities for clever pricing policies. Bundling and tying strategies, together with, in part, price discrimination policies, are favored by economies of aggregation. Ultimately, pricing in e-commerce is critical to the economic success of firms and relevant to the design of taxes. It is also complex and subtle, and it is difficult to decide whether it threatens competition (predatory pricing) or, conversely, it is necessary in order to maintain the activity.

In what follows, we will refer to various pricing and marketing strategies relevant to the New

Economy. This is a first taxonomy, not exhaustive, of the main business practices. However, it can provide some ideas about the possibilities of taxation.

A first advantage is that ICT allows easy storing and processing of huge amounts of relevant information of consumers. Companies operating in the B2C can, indeed, gather relevant information about the tastes and willingness to pay of each consumer. This information allows firms to design almost "individualized" pricing and quality strategies, extracting as much consumer surplus as possible. This is of course optimal for companies and makes pricing decisions complex in many e-commerce operations, since there are many prices rather than a single price for each type of transaction.

A particularly interesting example of the use of the available information is the practice known as "yield management." This practice is widespread among airlines and hotel chains, which rely increasingly on electronic commerce. In short, yield management is a clever pricing policy rather than a method of forecasting demand. The practice is supported by efficient use of the huge flow of information on consumers which is intrinsic to new information technologies. The most obvious result of this is the great disparity in prices paid by different consumers for the same product, whether a flight or a hotel room. Of course, firms' profits increase with this practice.

With the introduction of consumer durable products, pricing strategies used to consist of inter-temporal discrimination: high prices at first, to extract surplus from consumers eager for the product and greater willingness to pay, and lower prices subsequently to make the products accessible to the general public. This pricing strategy does not seem appropriate for the New Economy, which is characterized by network economies. The opposite prevails: low introductory prices,

or even free offers, to rapidly achieve a sufficient initial critical size that allows demand feedback.

The wide range of practices known as "peak load pricing" are also applicable when two features concur: fluctuating demand, with peak and trough periods, and non-storability. For example, airplane tickets and hotel rooms, two of the most prevalent in e-commerce, display these two features. In short, these practices consist of setting different prices in different time periods, higher in peak demand periods and lower in trough periods.

Two-part tariffs—a fixed amount or entry fee and a variable part depending on the amount consumed—are also very common. They are favored by two factors of the New Economy: The information companies can collect about consumers and the pervasiveness of economies of scale, both on the supply and demand sides. It is important to note that these practices are not only suitable as a business strategy, but that they may be socially desirable.

Finally, bundling and tying are also present. As always with these practices, there is the added difficulty of assessing the possible anticompetitive effects.

Difficulties in the Taxation of E-Commerce

The taxation of electronic commerce involves difficulties in at least three important ways:

1. The very nature of e-commerce transactions makes it is easier for firms and consumers to avoid paying taxes. If a consumer buys a book at a traditional bookstore, she pays VAT, but if she purchases at a virtual store, then not paying becomes easier. It is even easier to escape taxes if the product is directly downloaded over the Internet, such as music, software, personal services, videos, etc.

2. Internet allows greater mobility of businesses and professionals, so that they can move, often virtually, to countries with lower taxes. It is therefore more difficult to identify potential taxpayers.

3. Internet has diminished the relevance of many intermediaries (travel agencies, retailers, banks, for example) that played an important role in collecting taxes or providing relevant information to collect them.

Certainly, the current size of e-commerce poses a serious threat to tax revenues, but could represent increased erosion in the future. It involves more danger for European countries, since EU taxation is more dependent than the U.S. on taxes on consumption. It is not, therefore, surprising that the European authorities have been more active in this respect.

Some Experiences in Taxing E-Commerce

The first initiative corresponds to the OECD (1999), particularly the "Emerging Market Economy Forum on Electronic Commerce." In what follows, we summarize the main ideas discussed.

The tax authorities have an important role to play in the potential development of electronic commerce. Its main objectives in this regard should be to provide a fiscal environment where e-commerce continues to develop, but, and this is the second objective, without compromising the ability of government to raise the revenue needed to finance public services for its citizens.

There are very different proposals on what stance should be taken by governments with regard to the taxation of electronic commerce. At one extreme, it is suggested that electronic commerce (either with specific legislation or with continuing non-intervention) should remain tax-free. However, this would imply, on the one hand, tax distortions in the structure of commerce, and on the other, to ignore the demands of citizens

regarding public services. At the other extreme, there is the introduction of a new tax specifically designed for electronic commerce (e.g. bit tax). However, this would harm the development of electronic commerce.

The generic principle that enjoys greater acceptance within the OECD is that, in order to achieve the two objectives above, there must be an international consensus on how to apply traditional tax instruments, at both national and international levels, to electronic commerce, rather than creating a new tax policy. Therefore, the main change for the tax collecting authorities should be to adapt the legislation, procedures, and practices to address any deficiencies that may arise as a result of new media and the delivery of products through electronic commerce.

In addition, an agreement has been reached on the need to develop an international consensus in the taxation of electronic commerce. Moreover, it has been pointed out that the implementation of international agreements on taxation should: 1) Help maintain fiscal sovereignty of individual countries, 2) Share the tax base of e-commerce equitably between countries, and 3) Minimize the risk of double taxation or absence of taxation.

In addition, the Forum (1999) formulated the tax principles to be applied to electronic commerce: neutrality, efficiency, security, simplicity, efficiency, fairness, and flexibility. Further progress has been made in different types of taxes.

As for the taxation of consumption, the proposal that has achieved greater consensus is that in international transactions the principle of taxation should apply at the place of consumption. Similarly, in terms of tax collection mechanisms, an approach to auto-calculate the taxable value for B2B transactions has been confirmed as the most viable. For B2C transactions, if the product is delivered online, it is acknowledged that one should evaluate how technology-based mechanisms could perform in tax collection.

Apparently, the strongest proposal is that in most cases neither websites nor Internet Service

Providers (ISPs) constitute permanent establishments. In contrast, websites servers constitute permanent establishments only under certain circumstances. With respect to income tax, the consensus is that downloading digital products does not give rise to royalties. Digital goods will be considered as services and not goods from the point of view of taxation.

Tax authorities need to improve their coordination and cooperation internationally. Many of the proposals from these bodies are designed to adapt the website identifiers of firms, the authentication information and the deductions related to business practices used by many international companies. Regarding tax revenues, experimenting is in place with software that calculates taxes on consumption across countries. The main objective is to achieve a situation of "win-win": easier compliance for businesses and easier collection for the government.

Wiseman (2000) provides a brief historical summary of the debate on Internet taxation in the US. Wiseman suggests that the current debate on Internet taxation has many parallels with that which emerged in the 60s when discussing the possibility of establishing a tax on mail order sales. Internet, as well as mail order products, is a distribution channel different from the traditional channels that require a physical establishment.

The US Supreme Court ruled twice on the question of whether distance vendors were required to collect sales tax from buyers in another state. The decision finally was that companies were not required to collect sales taxes on transactions that took place in a state where they had no geographical presence. At this point, it should be noticed that the same treatment is given to the Internet.

As a result, in many states the responsibility for paying the tax fell on consumers. However, because they either did not know that the purchase of these products was subject to tax or, if they knew they did not meet their tax obligations, the fact is that local governments did not collect revenue from this tax, so they began to consider passing legislation to regulate taxation on the Internet. Their stance was reinforced by small offline traders who saw their position in the market erode, as online retailers could offer the same product at a lower price because of the tax advantage they enjoyed.

There is an open debate as to whether or not to introduce taxes on the Internet. McLure (1999) argues that electronic commerce should be taxed, since there are implications of horizontal and vertical equity, as well as of misallocation of resources. Not taxing the Internet causes an indirect transfer of wealth to the rich (who use e-commerce). It also leads to serious disadvantages for offline retailers, which face unfair competition from online vendors not paying taxes. This distorts the economic decisions of the agents involved. It has been shown that this problem is greater in states with higher tax rates on consumption.

Lukas (1999) concludes that the tax differential will cause a migration of offline merchants to trade online, but if the problem to be solved by governments is that of equity, the best we can do is to harmonize tax rates by reducing those faced by offline merchants, instead of creating new taxes on the Internet.

Goolsbee (2001) presents an empirical work that attempts to determine the price elasticity of demand associated with Internet sales, in order to predict the effects on sales and consumption decisions (online/offline) of the introduction of a tax on e-commerce. His conclusions are that a tax on the Internet would reduce the number of buyers and the sales volume. He therefore recommends that in the short run the tax is not introduced.

Goolsbee and Zittrain (1999), on the one hand, and Cline and Neubig (1999), on the other, perform two different empirical exercises that have the same goal: to determine the magnitude of the losses by local governments for not collecting tax revenue on Internet sales. Both studies conclude that losses are not too important, so that the government has time to design an efficient model of taxation applicable to electronic commerce.

Finally, another topic of interest is that of compliance costs associated with the introduction of different fiscal policies in different states. One approach to these costs is provided by a study by the Washington State Department of Revenue, and later discussed by Cline and Neubig (1999), which shows the complexities that surround this scenario.

ELECTRONIC COMMERCE AND PUBLIC SECTOR TRANSFORMATION: ANTITRUST POLICIES

Following Shapiro and Varian (1999), the basic principle underlying antitrust laws is to protect competition as a process. That is, if the monopolist obtains its position thanks to low prices and high product quality, the competitive process has worked perfectly, since the final goal of this process is to protect the interests of consumers and stimulate economic growth. Thus, the main objective of antitrust policy is to establish whether a particular firm's conduct is anticompetitive or not, in other words, if it abuses its dominant market position, and thus harms consumers (who may be harmed either because they pay a high price or because the product is of low quality) and economic growth.

With this goal, the decisions to be taken by the authorities of competition should be based on economic principles that explain the behavior of different firms. Thus, over time these authorities have based much of their decisions by referring to the economic model of perfect competition, because the traditional market structure is "similar" to it and also because competitive markets are efficient in two ways. First, the allocation of resources is efficient, because the goods are purchased by the consumers who value them

the most. Second, the level of production is also efficient because production costs are minimal.

However, the features that characterize New Economy sectors do not correspond to those of perfect competition. It is then appropriate to analyze what should the actions of antitrust authorities in this new market structure be. In the case of the New Economy, as seen earlier, the competitive threat does not come often from firms established in the market, but from potential entrants that can offer products which are more innovative or of higher quality. Therefore, everything depends on the stance adopted with respect to the role of innovation in these sectors. Thus, if one accepts the Schumpeterian vision and the level of investment in R&D is indicative of the degree of competition, those sectors with a high level of expenditure in R&D should avoid any intervention from antitrust authorities. However, if the vision is that of Arrow, then the markets of the New Economy must be examined by antitrust authorities, as it happens with other sectors of the economy, but taking into account their particular market structure. At this point, the views on the type of intervention by antitrust authorities in the sectors of the New Economy differ substantially.

The views on the role of antitrust authorities in the New Economy sectors are diverse, and are reflected, for instance, in Cañizares et al. (2001). They are described below. First, there are those whose opinion is that antitrust authorities should not interfere with the performance of firms in the New Economy. This point of view encompasses the visions "skeptical" and "revolutionary." While the former argues that we should not worry about New Economy firms because their future is uncertain and their relevance is minimal, the latter highlights the dynamism of these markets, which ensures competition and, therefore, there is no need of intervention regarding competition. The revolutionary vision corresponds to the Schumpeterian vision about the fact that monopoly market structures are better than perfect competition with respect to innovation and economic growth. Therefore, the process should not be hampered. Second, one discovers the "official" position of antitrust authorities, which seek to maintain a significant degree of intervention, since the characteristics of these markets increase the likelihood of violations of competition. Finally, and thirdly, there is the vision of "composition," which as its name suggests, tries to reconcile the previous visions. The latter does not question the intervention of antitrust authorities in the sectors of the New Economy, nor the validity of the general principles governing it. However, it does say that the application of these principles in the New Economy sectors should be done by acknowledging their special characteristics, so that some of the traditional instruments of antitrust policy must be modified. This vision therefore suggests adopting ex ante criteria tailored to the characteristics of the New Economy.

The conciliatory approach appears best suited to the market structure of the New Economy. First, because, for example, it would be wrong to consider pricing above marginal cost as anticompetitive. Second, because the characteristics of these potential markets facilitate anticompetitive practices. Surely, this vision is closer to Arrow.

Antitrust authorities should take different steps when determining whether the conduct of a firm of the New Economy is anticompetitive or not. First, the relevant market must be defined and then whether the analyzed firm has market power or not must be determined. In this sense, there are different methods to evaluate the competitive position of a firm in the market. Among them, we can highlight the analysis of market shares. After reaching the conclusion that the firm under study has a dominant position in the market, it must be determined whether or not it abuses that position. Authorities should investigate other anti-competitive practices such as collusion or mergers between firms.

The Relevant Market

The relevant market is defined as that which contains all the goods that if they were in the hands of a monopoly firm they would provide it with the power to raise prices profitably. In practice, the definition of relevant market corresponds to the answer to the question: are the consumers of the products and/or services investigated able to shift their demand either to substitute products or to other providers in response to a permanent increase of 5%-10% in the relative prices of the products in the areas considered? If substitution is enough to make the price increase unprofitable, then the new products and their producers must be included in the relevant market. This test is known as the Small but Significant Non-Transitory Increase in Price (SSNIP) test. However, the use of this test and of other instruments usually employed by antitrust authorities to identify relevant markets has a number of major problems if applied to firms in the New Economy. This is because these indicators are based on the principles of perfect competition. In contrast, New Economy sectors are not characterized by this market structure but by another structure, which is very different.

In any case, since the definition of the relevant market is a key element when considering the effects on competition resulting from possible anticompetitive practices, the definition used by antitrust authorities must take into account that competition in markets in the New Economy may arise from three different ways. The first way is competition coming from the demand side. In this case, when consumers can respond to a price increase by demanding goods from a firm outside the market, the firm, and its products should be included in the relevant market. This kind of competition usually takes place in traditional markets. Therefore, antitrust authorities tend to define the relevant market by taking into account this sole means of competition. Thus, tools such as the SSNIP test are addressed to this type of competition.

The second mechanism of competition in the New Economy comes from the supply side. Thus, if producers of other goods may change their production processes to manufacture a substitute for the good whose price has increased, then these producers must be included in the relevant market. However, this type of competition is not taken into account most of the time by antitrust authorities. But if in the sectors of the New Economy the market-leading firms are not generally limited by the demand side (since there are no close substitutes, because a single firm tends to dominate the market and the competitive threat comes from of potential entrants), then there is the danger of defining a relevant market which is too narrow, hence arriving at a wrong conclusion, since one would be overstating the market power of firms. It is therefore necessary to consider markets whose products are not viewed as substitutes by consumers, but which are substitutes on the side of producers.

Although this statement seems, in principle, to contradict the very definition of relevant market, according to which the products, which are part of the market, are only substitutes from the consumer point of view, this is not the case. For example, if we only take into account competition from the demand side, we should define as separate markets those including dresses of different sizes or dresses made of different fabrics. Therefore, considering competition from the supply side leads to wider and better-defined markets. In this sense, the hardest part involves knowing how and when to add markets when considering competition from the supply side. The answer lies in the US Horizontal Merger Guidelines that take into account the idea of universality in competition from the supply side. Universality means that producers need to own assets, which after a simple adjustment aid design either the product or a substitute for it. In this case, firms are able to respond to the increase in the price of a good, so that consumers are protected from potentially abusive prices. It should be noted that it is not only essential to have the assets which are necessary for production, but that they must be adjusted without incurring in big investments and, at the same time, one must possess the assets for marketing and distributing the product after manufacturing it. In short, competition on the supply side requires that producers be able to produce and market substitutes goods in a relatively short period of time.

In short, in the markets of the New Economy, competition from the demand side is not effective, because the consumers of these products (when there are no substitutes), are not able to switch suppliers in response to a change in prices. At the same time, competition from the supply side is important, because producers can respond to these changes. In this sense, there seems to be unanimity with respect to the role played by this type of competition in the markets of the New Economy as a mechanism of competitive discipline, although for some authors it is not so evident that one must take it into account when defining the relevant market.

Finally, the third and final type of competition is derived from potential competition. It must be emphasized that the possibility of entry of new producers in the market, in response to increased prices, is not normally taken into account when defining the relevant market. However, the New Economy markets are characterized by the fact that competition arises precisely from potential competitors. Thus, it is not possible to ignore it and it must therefore be taken into account when defining the relevant market. However, it is very difficult for antitrust authorities to identify potential entrants and accurately assess the production capacities of them. For this reason, some authors argue that this type of competition should not be taken into account when defining the relevant market.

On the other hand, in the New Economy sectors it is very complicated to distinguish between competition from the supply side and potential competition. The latter is considered after the position of the firms operating in the relevant market has been defined, and when its dominant position from the perspective of antitrust policy has been defined. To distinguish the two concepts we should use criteria such as the time elapsed between the increase in prices and the beginning of the supply by the new producer, as well as cost-related criteria. In the first case, substitutes on the supply side respond immediately to increases in prices while potential entrants take a year or longer to start producing. In the second case, competition from the supply side involves low-cost entry and without the need to incur in irreversible investments, while potential entry implies the assumption of significant sunk costs. Moreover, competition which arises from the presence of substitutes on the supply side has a significant negative impact on prices before and after entry, whereas potential entry occurs through lower prices after entry.

To conclude this subsection, it is important to note that there are alternative approaches to defining the relevant market as a means of determining the degree of competition in the market. An alternative approach would involve, for example, studying the innovation process. This is based on the idea of Schumpeterian competition, where innovation is the main mechanism of competition in the markets of the New Economy. It should be noted that this alternative approach must be taken into account, especially when the European Commission itself has already implemented it. The EC has addressed the problem by defining the so-called "innovation markets." That is, one must analyze investment in R&D, the leading innovation-driven activity by firms, focusing on the study of current competition in R&D and potential competition in innovation. However, this alternative has been widely criticized, since it is very likely that innovation is not, in many cases, a mechanism of competition, but rather the opposite, a mechanism that acts as a barrier to entry for new competitors. This latter point of view is close to Arrow's concept of competition.

Dominant Position and Market Shares

The definition commonly used to determine the position of market dominance by a monopoly firm is as follows. A firm holds a dominant position when it has the ability to increase its prices above marginal cost for an extended period of time without a significant reduction in market share. Although antitrust authorities use several tests along the lines of this definition, market share stands out as one of the main instruments. In addition, experience suggests that market shares or other similar indexes of concentration influence the decisions taken by these authorities. Usually, a high market share is considered an indicator of the existence of market power. However, a high market share is not indicative of market power by itself. This requires that the firm abuses its position, that is, that it increases the prices of its product without losing market share. Despite this dominance, the firm may choose not to abuse its market power. Therefore, it is appropriate to distinguish between market power and abuse of it. In addition, other tests such as the presence of barriers to entry or price discrimination can be used to explain the existence of market power by one firm.

Likewise, it is important to note that the use of market shares as an instrument for determining the dominant position of a firm in the markets of the New Economy has a number of problems. The main one is its static nature. Some authors suggest that a possible answer to this problem, in a scenario where effective competition depends on potential entrants, is to adjust the calculation of market shares of the firms involved in order to give a greater role to potential entrants. This, however, is too complex. It therefore seems advisable to focus the study of the degree of competition in these markets on assessing whether established firms operate conditioned or not by the entry of competitors.

The Abuse of Dominant Position

Having established that a firm enjoys a dominant position, one must analyze whether or not that position is abused. Abuse of power is defined as all those practices that do not correspond to the behavior of a competitive firm, which takes the market structure as given and sets its prices with respect to marginal cost. Given this definition of abuse of dominant position, practices such as excessive pricing, bundling, price discrimination, predation, and refusals to provide access to an essential asset would be considered violations of antitrust laws. However, it is important to remember that given the market structure of the New Economy, many of these practices are common, and often they do not involve anti-competitive practices, such as in the case of excessive pricing, price discrimination and bundling.

The Barriers to Entry in the New Economy

Antitrust authorities have usually used the analysis of barriers to entry into traditional markets to investigate possible anti-competitive practices by a company that enjoys a dominant position in the market. However, as noted above, the market structure that characterizes the New Economy entails the presence of "natural" barriers to entry. Thus, fixed costs, usually sunk, associated with the development of new products or technologies that a potential entrant must incur are very important, which is itself a barrier to entry. Similarly, the period of time elapsed from the moment a company decides to participate in a market until actually enters it is usually longer than the dateline set by antitrust authorities. Therefore, it seems inappropriate to apply this analysis to the New Economy industries, since antitrust authorities traditionally have considered that only those entries that occur with immediacy and at low cost effectively limit the behavior of firms in a particular industry.

There are two points of view with respect to how to carry out the analysis of barriers to entry in the New Economy by antitrust authorities. According to the Schumpeterian vision, the processes of entry in the New Economy markets are relevant, i.e., the effects of the entry of new firms tend to be far more dramatic in innovative industries than in other more traditional sectors. These are common in these industries despite the presence of high fixed costs resulting from the process of innovation. Consequently, antitrust authorities should reformulate the traditional analysis of barriers to entry to take into account that the benefits associated with entry in the New Economy markets are high when it possible to replace the leader and dominate the market. When entry into these markets is fast, the succession of leaders is common, so that the dominance is fragile and temporary. Most firms operating in these markets allocate an important flow of resources to innovation and to improving their products to successfully tackle the possibility of a competitive attack by a new entrant with a superior product. After all, even if entry is slow, it can happen at any time, causing the anticipated reaction of incumbents. Therefore, it is true that in the New Economy there are barriers to entry, but the key to analyze them is the pace of innovation in the markets.

Instead, the points of view linked to Arrow believe that in the New Economy, innovation processes by themselves do not guarantee the presence of competition, because firms with a dominant market position can often use innovation as a barrier to entry, thus preventing the entry of potential competitors. Therefore, they can maintain their position by using a practice that should be considered anticompetitive. In this regard, antitrust authorities must take into account factors such as for how long a firm has been the market leader and whether its expenditure on R&D is reflected in a greater number of new products brought to the market or in a significant improvement in the quality of the existing products (new versions).

In some ways, it is sure that a significant portion of R&D spending does not end in the form of dormant patents. Similarly, tying, which will be discussed in a later section, can also be used as a barrier to entry. Therefore, antitrust policy must take into consideration all these issues and incorporate them into its analysis.

Treatment of Essential Assets

An essential asset is defined as one whose degree of competition in the market depends on its accessibility. For the antitrust authorities problems arise when one firms dominates this type of asset. This is common in highly concentrated markets or markets with a small number of companies that control most of the assets necessary for the development of productive activities, which happens quite often in the New Economy.

In principle, the solution may be to facilitate open access. However, this involves a serious problem. Since the firm that holds the key asset has to incur in a high cost to get the asset, free access would prevent recovering the significant investment, which will ultimately discourage the process of innovation. However, investment incentives can be protected if access is granted by paying an access fee. This fee should be set at a level that compensates the investor and that allows it to finance the high costs associated with innovation. Another possible solution would be to replicate the asset, but from an economic standpoint, this investment would not be justified if the cost of replicating the asset is so high that the investment becomes unprofitable. Otherwise, when the benefit exceeds the cost of replication, the asset would be erroneously declared essential. The underlying problem is therefore cost-benefit analysis, which should take into account both the high costs and high profits expected after the asset has been replicated. Since the calculation of the expected return on investments of this type is very complex, antitrust authorities do not use this method in practice.

Technology Integration and Bundling of Goods and Services

Some of the sectors that comprise the New Economy are characterized by complementarity of the goods they produce. For example, in the case of the computer software industry a word processing program, a spreadsheet and a database can be viewed by a user as complementary. Similarly, if we consider the hardware of a computer CPU, monitor, keyboard, and mouse are complementary goods from the point of view of consumption. As a result, companies in these sectors have strong incentives to offer these complementary products together. In this sense, companies have three options. The first is that each company engages in the production of one of the complementary goods and establishes an agreement with other companies that produce a complementary product to offer them together to consumers. The second possibility is that the firm develops separate different complementary products and sells them together. The last possibility is that the company offers an integrated product.

Antitrust authorities traditionally have considered such practices anti-competitive. This consideration is based on the fact that the use of these strategies increases the risk of either market monopolies or restrictive practices. The fact is that the firm (or firms) that rely on these practices indirectly can extend its dominant position in the market, because other established firms find it more difficult to compete with a firm that offers two complementary goods. In this sense, Nalebuff (2000) shows that the firm that first uses a bundling strategy wins a dominant market position, getting a bigger market share and bigger profits if the bundle includes 4 or more goods. Likewise, this dominant position is maintained in the long run because the competitor firm would harm itself if competing with the monopolist by using an identical strategy. In contrast, the competitor finds it cheaper to compete with one of the goods in the bundle. Therefore, this practice allows the first firm to use it to lead the market and maintain its dominant position in it. Consequently, bundling strategies appear as anticompetitive. Probably, the prices of the products sold separately are superior, which is clearly a disservice to both the consumers and the growth of the economy. These anticompetitive effects may be larger if they lead to the exclusion of some of the established competitors. This is more likely when the firm that bundles several products together enjoys market power in one of them, and when markets are prone to exclusion, as it is the case of the New Economy industries.

Moreover, these strategies can often be used as instruments of barrier to entry, because any potential entrant should provide two or more goods rather than just one, i.e. it should double its expenditure on R&D. This is shown, for example, by Nalebuff (2004), who shows that in an oligopoly, with a monopolist and a potential entrant, if the products are part of the a bundle are positively correlated in value, that is, they are complementary goods, then this strategy is effective as a barrier to entry of potential rivals. Therefore, bundling and tying can be justified not as an initiative to recover fixed costs, but as an anticompetitive practice which prevents the entry of a potential entrant, because the position of market dominance is threatened. In this sense, Bakos and Brynjolfsson (1999) also point out, too, that bundling prevents the entry of potential competitors. In fact, if the monopolist does not use this strategy, potential entrants will enter the market. Although the same authors suggest that this result is not derived from a predatory practice, by artificially reducing prices, but rather that the monopolist (when determining the price that maximizes its profits), makes it indirectly unattractive the entry of competitors. In the end, it takes advantage of absence of competition.

Likewise, these strategies can lead to significant pro-competitive effects. In general terms, they facilitate the reduction of transaction costs by enabling joint distribution of two or more goods. In addition, they simplify the purchasing process

of consumers, because they need not worry about the compatibility of different components and their proper functioning. Similarly, given the economies of scope and scale on the production side, bundling can lead to a sharp reduction in costs, and therefore a lower price for the consumer.

Moreover, in the case of the New Economy industries such benefits can be much more important. Bundling makes it easier for firms to undertake strategies of price discrimination, which may be optimal if the willingness to pay for a particular component depends on the use made of other complementary technology. In this context, bundling is a solution to the problem known in the economic literature as double marginalization. When two firms that offer complementary products merge, one can observe that the prices of both products tend to fall. The reason lies in the fact that the merged firm internalizes the negative effect of increasing the price of a product on the demand of the complementary product. It is also important to note that when the technology is characterized by high fixed costs and low marginal costs, the most efficient way to generate the revenue needed to finance fixed costs is price discrimination. Thus, bundling is a strategy of price discrimination, allowing businesses in the New Economy to recover fixed costs associated with investments in R&D. Therefore, there need not be any violation of the rules of competition. Thus, Nalebuff (2004) concludes that in an oligopoly, with a monopolist and a potential entrant, the strategy of bundling as an instrument of price discrimination by the monopolist works when the goods included in the bundle are negatively correlated in value, i.e., when they are substitutes.

This is not, however, the only positive effect from the use of this strategy. Three additional positive effects must be considered. First, investments in R&D related to a product can improve its own quality and the quality of other complementary products, thus increasing the value of the latter. Second, since coordination is costly, especially if it requires sharing information on technologies owned by different competitors, the use of these practices facilitates the coordination of R&D activities, which is more necessary when the quality of a product depends on the quality of the components and their interoperability. Third, since the New Economy markets are characterized by the presence of network economies, a stable standard is of great value to consumers, and the possibility to keep it increases when the system or network is the hands of one or a few companies.

In conclusion, the impact of integration and bundling on competition may be described as ambiguous. It requires a careful analysis of the effect on consumer welfare in each case and the possible negative effect of these practices on competitors should not be the only factor to consider in the decision taken by antitrust authorities.

Predation

Predation is the use of a series of anti-competitive strategies designed to drive competitors out of the market. These practices can consist of either too aggressive pricing or other practices also classified as predatory. In this regard, antitrust authorities investigating possible strategies of this type focus their analysis on a set of evidence in order to determine whether the firm under investigation uses these anti-competitive practices.

The first evidence involves finding out whether the firm under investigation sets prices below cost and incurs in losses. However, this way of dealing with cases of predation is not very appropriate in the markets of the New Economy. First, setting a reduced price, even zero, does not imply setting a price lower than marginal cost, since marginal cost is low and even very close to zero. It is true is that, given the characteristics of the New Economy sectors, very low prices equal to marginal cost would not allow to recover the significant investments in R&D. Therefore, very low prices do not seem to make any sense. However, this is not entirely true. There are a number of reasonable justifications that explain why firms in the New Economy

may be in some way, forced to set prices too low and thus promote competition.

Such justifications are based on the characteristics that make up the different markets in the New Economy. First, the presence of economies of scope, where the sale of one product favors the sale of another, may entail the establishment of a low price for a particular good in order to stimulate demand for the complementary good. This argument would justify even offering free goods, those whose marginal cost is close to zero, even if the intention of the firm is not to behave in a predatory way. Second, the presence of indirect network economies is a strong incentive to pursue a policy of low prices, since the widespread use of technology, for example, a particular software platform, leads to the designers of applications to adhere to the platform, increasing its value, and consequently, increasing the volume of the installed base of customers. Third, the existence of economies of learning, or economies of scale on the consumption side, associated with repeated use of a good involve a high probability that consumption brings habit, which induces firms to set a low initial price to stimulate not only present consumption but also the future consumption. Fourth, the presence of network economies along with lock-in, or switching costs, is an incentive for a low-price policy at least initially. In this case, when a good (or technology) achieves a critical mass of consumers and it becomes the market leader, firms are interested in achieving a critical mass as soon as possible and they encourage consumers to buy their good (or use their technology) by means of low prices. This is reflected in Varian (2001) where the presence of network economies contributes to lock-in and price discrimination. In other words, the first consumers value the good less than the following, so that sellers offer the good to the first at a lower price, a practice known as "penetration pricing." Finally, the reduced pricing does not necessarily implies losses if there are alternative sources of revenue for the product, such as, for example, advertising.

The second evidence to be examined by antitrust authorities involves determining if the analyzed firm intends to drive competitors out of the market or to reduce competitive pressure from other companies established in the market. In this sense, if the reduced price responds to any of the justifications outlined above, which do not involve anti-competitive practices, then it is clear that the intention of the firms setting reduced prices is not, at least in the first instance, to reduce or eliminate competition.

Finally, the latest evidence which antitrust authorities need to analyze is whether the firm under study has the ability to recover, through the setting of prices above competitive level, losses incurred during the predatory period. However, the sectors of the New Economy, as seen in this section, may initially set low prices in order to get established in the market, even at the cost of expulsion of rival firms. After achieving this, they can seek to recover the investments that were necessary to develop product, which is now the market leader by setting higher prices.

In any case, if setting a price too low may mean an anticompetitive practice, then antitrust authorities should specify the reference price in these markets. However, this is a really complicated task. Thus, some authors note that "competitive" prices in this industry should cover avoidable costs, defined as costs that could be avoided if the firm decides not to produce an additional unit of good. Furthermore, considering that innovation can be a source of competition, prices below incremental costs in the long run would be considered predatory because they would discourage investment and thus expel (potential) competitors out of the market, which would jeopardize the future of the industry.

Mergers, Acquisitions, and Strategic Alliances

Antitrust authorities do not content themselves to study firms, which may violate antitrust laws. They also analyze those cases of collaboration between companies or mergers or acquisitions that could lead to lack of competition to the detriment of consumers and the growth of the economy. This section shows what elements should be taken into account by antitrust authorities when investigating such strategies in the New Economy sectors.

The collaboration between companies in the sectors of the New Economy is usually in the form of strategic alliances. This is because strategic agreements involve a lesser degree of integration than mergers or acquisitions and they also have the advantage of rapidly returning to the status quo at low cost. These partnerships are essential in the dynamic markets of the New Economy, where the landscape is constantly changing and these strategies allow firms to gain the flexibility to compete. In this sense, the importance of agreements between firms, can be seen in Varian (2001), who shows that when network economies are very important in the New Economy sectors, and the value of the network depends on their size, then the decision of interconnection between different networks or standardization of technology are key strategic decisions. In other words, in a scenario with network economies cooperation between firms is a strategic variable to consider, whether this collaboration takes the form of interconnection between firms (or compatible products) or if it takes the form of a common standard.

For example, the adoption of a standard reduces the risk for consumers in two ways, since it facilitates that a number of competitors offer the same technology. First, because consumers are not afraid of being tied to a technology, now lock-in is not important, and they can change providers without problems. Second, because it reduces the risk to be attached to a technology that may lose the battle of the standards, i.e., that may never be the market leader and may be quickly replaced by another. This is the case, for example, of the battle for the standards of video Beta or VHS. Those who bet on the Beta system had to bear high switching costs. Following this same idea, Shapiro and Varian (1999) indicate that the New Economy firms are constantly developing joint standards, ensuring the compatibility of their products within a system, signing licenses and cross licensing, and cooperating, so that open standards promote competition on price and not on product features. In short, cooperation leads to significant efficiencies, encouraging consumers through lower prices. Products appear in the market which otherwise would not be developed because they depend on each other, and because the collaboration between firms that offer complementary products promotes a superior final product. That is, for example, the case of cooperation between Intel and Microsoft, which design new products and versions with the assurance that they work properly together, allowing both firms to save on costs.

However, these agreements involve risks from the standpoint of antitrust policy for three main reasons. First, they can conceal collusive agreements. Moreover, because they can reduce the number of technological options available to consumers. Finally, they can monopolize the market, especially if the agreement excludes or eliminates potential competitors. As for anti-competitive collusive agreements, antitrust authorities define them as the agreements, explicit or implicit, which restrict or distort competition between firms. They may be vertical (suppliers/customers) or horizontal (suppliers operating in the same relevant market). In addition, these agreements may include joint pricing, coordinated or joint setting of maximum production quotas, division of markets in a coordinated manner, sharing relevant information, etc.

However, some authors argue that given the characteristics of the markets of the New Economy collusive agreements are less likely than in traditional industries. One of the reasons given is that

in these industries innovation and not price is the key variable of competition. If that were true, it would make sense to coordinate the pricing of rivals because price would not be the variable that determines consumer choice. From this perspective it is difficult to see whether a firm competes aggressively by means of its pace of innovation. This point is based on a Schumpeterian view of competition, where innovation is the variable that determines the degree of competition in any sector of the New Economy. However, following Arrow's concept of competition, innovation becomes an instrument to create barriers to entry to potential competitors. Then it may make sense to reach collusive agreements in order to prevent entry by potential competitors. Alternatively, if the scenario described is that where a standard technology is adopted, then it is clear that competition is in prices and never through innovation since the latter is standard.

Regarding the possible reduction in the number of technological options, it is true that if economies of scale and scope are important then the optimal number of standards is reduced. However, what is really significant in this sense is not so much the number of technologies available to consumers but the fact that there is a lower risk of adopting technologies with negative effects for consumers and for the growth of the economy.

With respect to mergers, it is important to note that there are differences between horizontal mergers and vertical mergers. The former are carried out between firms competing in the same market, i.e., between firms producing substitute goods, while the latter are carried out by firms operating in different markets, or among companies that offer complementary goods or have a relationship of supplier and customer. Clearly, the impact on competition of such mergers is different. Thus, in the case of horizontal mergers there is the risk that the merged firm achieves a dominant position in the market and increases its prices to increase its profits, which is a clearly anti-competitive practice. In addition, in vertical mergers it should be stressed that the merger of two companies with complementary assets makes entry difficult for a new firm, because the potential entrant requires the development of two goods at a time to compete in the market. Therefore, in the case of complementary goods, in order to favor competition, it seems much better to promote agreements between firms rather than mergers. However, after the merger efficiencies can also be obtained, such as cost savings in product development as a result of maintaining only one research team.

Finally, it should be noted that agreements and mergers between firms in the New Economy need not be due to anti-competitive strategies. For example, De Santis (2000) states that joint selling arrangements between firms can be pro-competitive when one wants that products reach the market more efficiently and faster. In addition, cooperation between several firms in the purchase of supplies may be due to a need to reduce transaction costs and achieve economies of scale. Although it should be noted, that the increase of efficiency cannot justify or defend other anticompetitive practices.

Solutions and Recommendations

After analyzing the characteristics of the market structure of the New Economy sectors and the implications for antitrust policy, this section analyzes the strategies that can be adopted by firms in these sectors to avoid or minimize the risk the possible intervention by antitrust authorities.

This chapter began by noting that the interventions by antitrust authorities in firms in the New Economy have increased in recent years, due to the reversal of economic policy pursued by developed countries. Needless to say, such interventions entail very important costs to firms. These can be in terms of public image and reputation with customers, which can imply a significant loss of market share. Moreover, they can take the form of penalty, or change of initial business plans,

because they do not comply with the law. More serious, they may involve cessation of business activity. Consequently, to avoid or minimize these costs where possible, firms should anticipate these actions by taking into account an business strategy: antitrust policy. This requires knowledge of the legislation on antitrust and to take it into account in taking any business decisions. That is, it is necessary to take a proactive approach in terms of antitrust. However, developing this strategy also implies a cost. However, it is likely that the cost of implementing this proactive strategy is lower than the costs saved by the firm by avoiding intervention.

Proactive strategies, as opposed to reactive strategies, have thus as its main objective anticipating the possible actions of antitrust authorities and designing optimal plans and responses for the firm or, in other words, a logical and coherent line of reasoning. In this sense, the lines to adopt a proactive strategy involve, first, improving the public image of the firm with regard to both antitrust authorities and society in general, by developing a communication plan with antitrust authorities, other regulatory agencies, and the media. The idea can be summarized as giving accurate information on the realities of the sector in which it operates and the pro-competitive nature of the actions of the firm. The second involves minimizing the chances of being under investigation. To that end, firms must identify the limitations resulting from antitrust laws in the design of business strategies and everyday business activities and, therefore, design a regulatory mechanism for internal audit that takes such constraints into account. The company must also identify alternatives in the design of commercial and business strategies that are feasible from the point of view of antitrust policy. Third, the company must identify the potential charges against it and develop a coherent defense strategy. It must also develop a plan to anticipate negotiations with antitrust authorities to reduce proceedings, minimize the loss of reputation and the costs of the restrictions established. Finally, the firm should design a protocol that allows it to be ready to face investigations by antitrust authorities.

In short, firms in the New Economy are strongly encouraged to take a proactive approach in terms of antitrust. The basic idea is that if the firm's business strategy is sufficiently transparent at all levels; it has a good chance to avoid being taken over by antitrust authorities. With this, the firm saves the costs that would arise with the takeover. In addition, if it is taken over, the probability of avoiding being guilty of anticompetitive practices charges is very high.

FUTURE RESEARCH DIRECTIONS

As argued by Shapiro and Varian (1999), we already have the concepts, analytical tools, and appropriate models to understand and explain the new economic phenomena observed. However, we need to introduce into the body of knowledge of economists, including future economists, a set of contributions that research in economics has generated recently.

Because of economies of scale, scope economies, and economies of experience on the supply side, and network economies on the demand side, growth strategies are essential for companies operating in these markets. A revalued business strategy in new markets is the pricing strategy. All these strategies deserve more attention from researchers.

CONCLUSION

Innovation is the main feature of the New Economy firms. From a Schumpeterian perspective of competition, firms are forced to innovate in order to maintain its position in the market. This innovation is the result of a strong expenditure in R&D, which represents a major fixed cost within the cost structure of firms. Of course, firms hope

to recoup these investments later by selling new products, the result of innovation. To recoup that investment, companies cannot act as if under perfect competition by pricing at marginal cost, because this would not allow them to cover fixed costs. Therefore, in order to recover their investments firms in the New Economy can choose, on the one hand, to set prices above marginal costs or strategies such as tying or price discrimination, while, on the other hand, they use patents to protect their investment results. But from Arrow's point of view of competition, innovation is not a source of competition, and the use of these other strategies not only responds to the need to recover the heavy investment in R & D, but also to an attempt by monopoly firms, to reduce or even eliminate competition. In other words, such strategies are used as barriers of entry to potential rivals or other forms of abuse of power.

Therefore, the intervention of antitrust authorities is required in these markets. However, given the peculiarities of the market structure of these sectors, the traditional tools of antitrust policy are inadequate in these markets. In this sense, the definition of the relevant market should include competition coming from both established firms and potential entrants, because both routes are the main sources of competition in the markets of the New Economy, to the detriment of competition via demand. Failure to incorporate these two ways to the definition of relevant market, defined markets would be too narrow and one would overestimate the market power of firms.

It is also important to distinguish between market power and abuse market power. While market power simply indicates the dominance of a firm in the market, abuse is an anticompetitive practice. Alternatively, in other words, the actions of the dominant firm are harming consumers by offering low quality goods or prices that are too high. They are also harming economic growth by interfering negatively in the process of technological innovation and, therefore, the potential for economic development.

Moreover, the abuse of market power can take several forms. Thus, barriers to entry, setting "abusive" prices, the presence of impediments to access essential goods, predatory and anticompetitive agreements, among others, are strategies that are traditionally anti-competitive practices. However, these strategies may also result from the characteristics of markets of the New Economy, generate pro-competitive effects and, therefore, should not be declared anti-competitive.

REFERENCES

Bakos, Y., & Brynjolfsson, E. (1999). Bundling information goods: Pricing, profits, and efficiency. *Management Science, 45*(12), 1613–1630. doi:10.1287/mnsc.45.12.1613

Cañizares, E., Fernández, D., Padilla, A. J., & Ramos, A. (2001). *Competència i innovació en la nova economia*. Departament d'Indústria, Comerç i Turisme, Direcció General d'Indústria.

Cline, R. J., & Neubig, T. S. (1999). *The sky is not falling: Why state and local revenues were not significantly impacted by the internet in 1998*. New York, NY: Ernst & Young Economics Consulting and Quantitative Analysis.

De Santis, R. A. (2000). Optimal export taxes, welfare, industry concentration, and firm size: A general equilibrium analysis. *Review of International Economics, 8*(2), 319–335. doi:10.1111/1467-9396.00224

Economides, N. (1996). The economics of networks. *International Journal of Industrial Organization, 14*(6), 673–699. doi:10.1016/0167-7187(96)01015-6

Gifford, D. J., & Kudrle, R. T. (2011). Antitrust approaches to dynamically competitive industries in the United States and the European Union. *Journal of Competition Law & Economics, 7*(3), 695–731. doi:10.1093/joclec/nhr011

Gilbert, R. J., & Newbery, D. M. G. (1982). Preemptive patenting and the persistence of monopoly. *The American Economic Review, 72*(3), 514–526.

Goolsbee, A. (2001). The implications of electronic commerce for fiscal policy (and vice versa). *The Journal of Economic Perspectives, 15*(1), 13–24. doi:10.1257/jep.15.1.13

Goolsbee, A., & Zittrain, J. (1999). Evaluating the costs and benefits of taxing internet commerce. *National Tax Journal, 52*(3), 413–428.

Gregory, , Sidak, J., & Teece, D. J. (2009). Dynamic competition in antitrust law. *Journal of Competition Law & Economics, 5*(4), 581–631. doi:10.1093/joclec/nhp024

Katz, M. L., & Shapiro, C. (1994). Systems competition and network effects. *The Journal of Economic Perspectives, 8*(2), 93–115. doi:10.1257/jep.8.2.93

Lukas, A. (1999). Tax bytes: A primer on the taxation of electronic commerce. *Trade Policy Analysis, 9*.

McLure, C. E. (1999). *The taxation of electronic commerce: Background and proposal*. Paper presented at the Public Policy and the Internet: Taxation and Privacy. New York, NY.

McLure, C. E. (2003). The value added tax on electronic commerce in the European Union. *International Tax and Public Finance, 10*(6), 753–762. doi:10.1023/A:1026394207651

Nalebuff, B. (2000). Competing against bundles. *SSRN eLibrary*. doi: 10.2139/ssrn.239684

Nalebuff, B. (2004). Bundling as an entry barrier. *The Quarterly Journal of Economics, 119*(1), 159–187. doi:10.1162/003355304772839551

OECD. (1999). *Defining and measuring e-commerce: A status report*. Geneva, Switzerland: OECD.

OECD. (2009). *OECD conference on empowering e-consumers strengthening consumer protection in the internet economy: Background report.* Geneva, Switzerland: OECD.

Reddick, C. G., & Coggburn, J. D. (2007). E-commerce and the future of the state sales tax system: Critical issues and policy recommendations. *International Journal of Public Administration, 30*(10), 1021–1043. doi:10.1080/01900690701221373

Reinganum, J. F. (1983). Uncertain Innovation and the persistence of monopoly. *The American Economic Review, 73*(4), 741–748.

Scanlan, M. A. (2007). Tax sensitivity in electronic commerce. *Fiscal Studies, 28*(4), 417–436. doi:10.1111/j.1475-5890.2007.00062.x

Shapiro, C., & Varian, H. R. (1999). *Information rules: A strategic guide to the network economy.* Boston, MA: Harvard Business Press.

Varian, H. R. (1985). Price discrimination and social welfare. *The American Economic Review, 75*(4), 870–875.

Varian, H. R. (2001). High-technology industries and market structure. In *Proceedings* (pp. 65–101). Kansas City, MO: Federal Reserve Bank of Kansas City.

Wiseman, A. E. (2000). *The internet economy: Access, taxes, and market structure.* Washington, DC: Brookings Institution Press.

ADDITIONAL READING

Alm, J., & Melnik, M. I. (2005). Sales taxes and the decision to purchase online. *Public Finance Review, 33*(2), 184–212. doi:10.1177/1091142104267929

Ancarani, F. (2002). Pricing and the internet: Frictionless commerce or pricer's paradise? *European Management Journal, 20*(6), 680–687. doi:10.1016/S0263-2373(02)00117-2

Balto, D. A. (2000). Emerging antitrust issues in electronic commerce. *Journal of Public Policy & Marketing, 19*(2), 277–286. doi:10.1509/jppm.19.2.277.17130

Barnes, D., Hinton, M., & Mieczkowska, S. (2004). E-commerce in the old economy: Three case study examples. *Journal of Manufacturing Technology Management, 15*(7), 607–617. doi:10.1108/17410380410555853

Bruce, D., Fox, W., & Murray, M. (2003). To tax or not to tax? The case of electronic commerce. *Contemporary Economic Policy, 21*(1), 25–40. doi:10.1093/cep/21.1.25

Carlton, D. W., & Perloff, J. M. (2005). *Modern industrial organization* (4th ed.). Boston, MA: Pearson Addison-Wesley.

Coase, R. H. (1972). Durable goods monopolists. *The Journal of Law & Economics, 15,* 143–150. doi:10.1086/466731

David, P. A. (1985). Clio and the economics of QWERTY. *The American Economic Review, 75*(2), 332–337.

de Streel, A. (2003). Market definitions in the new European regulatory framework for electronic communications. *Info, 5*(3), 27–47. doi:10.1108/14636690310487237

Foer, A. A. (2001). E-commerce meets antitrust: A primer. *Journal of Public Policy & Marketing, 20*(1), 51–63. doi:10.1509/jppm.20.1.51.17284

Frazer, T., & Waterson, M. (1994). *Competition law and policy: Cases, materials and commentary.* Upper Saddle River, NJ: Prentice-Hall.

Fudenberg, D., & Tirole, J. (2000). Pricing a network good to deter entry. *The Journal of Industrial Economics, 48*(4), 373–390. doi:10.1111/1467-6451.00129

Klemperer, P. (1987). Markets with consumer switching costs. *The Quarterly Journal of Economics, 102*(2), 375–394. doi:10.2307/1885068

Klemperer, P. (1989). Price wars caused by switching costs. *The Review of Economic Studies, 56*(3), 405–420. doi:10.2307/2297555

Klemperer, P. (1995). Competition when consumers have switching costs: An overview with applications to industrial organization, macroeconomics and international trade. *The Review of Economic Studies, 62*(4), 515–539. doi:10.2307/2298075

Koyuncu, C., & Lien, D. (2003). E-commerce and consumer's purchasing behaviour. *Applied Economics, 35*(6), 721–726. doi:10.1080/0003684022000020850

Mas-Colell, A., Whinston, M. D., & Green, J. R. (1995). *Microeconomic theory*. Oxford, UK: Oxford University Press.

Owen, B. M. (2011). Antitrust and vertical integration in "new economy" industries with application to broadband access. *Review of Industrial Organization, 38*(4), 363–386. doi:10.1007/s11151-011-9291-y

Palon, D., Siegel, D. S., & Vaughan Williams, L. (2002). A policy response to the e-commerce revolution: The case of betting taxation in the UK. *The Economic Journal, 112*(480), F296–F314. doi:10.1111/1468-0297.00045

Perloff, J. M. (2008). *Microeconomics: Theory and applications with calculus*. Boston, MA: Pearson Addison Wesley.

Pindyck, R. S., & Rubinfeld, D. L. (2005). *Microeconomics* (6th ed.). Upper Saddle River, NJ: Pearson Education International.

Pitofsky, R. (2001). Challenges of the new economy: Issues at the intersection of antitrust and intellectual property. *Antitrust Law Journal, 68*(3), 913–923.

Posner, R. A. (2001). Antitrust in the new economy. *Antitrust Law Journal, 68*(3), 925–942.

Prasad, A., Venkatesh, R., & Mahajan, V. (2010). Optimal bundling of technological products with network externality. *Management Science, 56*(12), 2224–2236. doi:10.1287/mnsc.1100.1259

Schmalensee, R. (2000). Antitrust issues in Schumpeterian industries. *The American Economic Review, 90*(2), 192–196. doi:10.1257/aer.90.2.192

Schoenherr, T., & Mabert, V. A. (2006). Bundling for B2B procurement auctions: Current state and best practices. *International Journal of Integrated Supply Management, 2*(3), 189–213. doi:10.1504/IJISM.2006.008593

Segal, I., & Whinston, M. D. (2007). Antitrust in innovative industries. *The American Economic Review, 97*(5), 1703–1730. doi:10.1257/aer.97.5.1703

Shy, O. (1995). *Industrial organization: Theory and applications*. Cambridge, MA: Massachusetts Institute of Technology.

Shy, O. (2001). *The economics of network industries*. Cambridge, UK: Cambridge University Press. doi:10.1017/CBO9780511754401

Shy, O. (2008). *How to price: A guide to pricing techniques and yield management*. Cambridge, UK: Cambridge University Press.

Tirole, J. (1988). *The theory of industrial organization*. Cambridge, MA: MIT Press.

Varian, H. R. (1992). *Microeconomic analysis*. New York, NY: W.W. Norton.

Varian, H. R. (2000). Buying, sharing and renting information goods. *The Journal of Industrial Economics*, *48*(4), 473–488. doi:10.1111/1467-6451.00133

Varian, H. R. (2006). *Intermediate microeconomics* (7th ed.). New York, NY: W. W. Norton & Company.

Zodrow, G. R. (2003). Network externalities and indirect tax preferences for electronic commerce. *International Tax and Public Finance*, *10*(1), 79–97. doi:10.1023/A:1022281013965

KEY TERMS AND DEFINITIONS

Abuse of Dominant Position: Abuse of power is defined as all those practices that do not correspond to the behavior of a competitive firm, which takes the market structure as given and sets its prices with respect to marginal cost.

Barriers to Entry in the New Economy: The market structure that characterizes the New Economy entails the presence of "natural" barriers to entry. Fixed costs, usually sunk, associated with the development of new products or technologies that a potential entrant must incur.

Dominant Position and Market Shares: A firm holds a dominant position when it has the ability to increase its prices above marginal cost for an extended period of time without a significant reduction in market share.

Essential Asset: An asset whose degree of competition in the market depends on its accessibility.

New Economy: Business industries resulting from the economic development of information and communications, where information can be defined as (Shapiro & Varian, 1999): "... anything that can be digitized, encoded as a set of bits, such as books, music, movies, databases,...."

Predation: The use of a series of anti-competitive strategies designed to drive competitors out of the market.

Price Differentiation: Strategy consisting of charging different prices to different customers according to their willingness to pay for a good or service.

Relevant Market: Market that contains all the goods that if they were in the hands of a monopoly firm would provide it with the power to raise prices profitably.

Chapter 4
Persuading for Change:
The Impact of Culture on the Principles of Authority and Social Proof

Sean Watts
Yonsei University, Korea

Teppo Räisänen
Oulu University of Applied Sciences, Finland

Sami Halonen
University of Oulu, Finland

ABSTRACT

Persuasion happens when somebody tries to change someone else's attitudes or behavior without using coercion or force. In different cultures, different persuasion principles seem to work better than others. This has to be taken into account in marketing and design. It is especially true when developing persuasive systems, i.e. systems that aim at changing the user. In this chapter, the authors study the role of culture in the context of authority and social proof. This was examined through positivist survey conducted by South Korean and Finnish College Students. The received results suggest that authority plays a bigger role in the Republic of Korea than in Finland. Ergo, the authors conclude that the implications of culture should be regarded when designing systems that aim at any kind of change.

INTRODUCTION

Persuasive technology has been defined as using technology to change our behavior or attitudes without using coercion or deception (Fogg, 2002). Examples of such technology are hearth rate monitors and smoking cessation websites. In its basic form, technology can persuade users in three ways: 1) as a tool, 2) as a media, and 3) as a social actor. As a tool, technology makes target behavior easier to perform. As a media technology provides motivational experiences and helps rehearse behavior. In addition, as a social actor technology can cue social responses and take a social role in interaction (Fogg, 2002). Persuasive systems are such information systems that have

DOI: 10.4018/978-1-4666-2665-2.ch004

emphasis on supporting intended behavior or attitude change.

As our understanding of the field of persuasive technology has increased, the expectations for persuasive designs have also increased. This is especially evident in competitive markets such as Web 2.0, e-business and the mobile domain. When designing solutions for these kinds of environments, the designers must have a thorough understanding of the various persuasion, motivation, and influence strategies to gain competitive advantage. Various persuasive principles could be used in public sector transformation processes to improve the changes of achieving the desired goals.

In this chapter, globalization is defined as the major social transformations caused by the enhancement of global consciousness and increased interconnectedness of different societies (Walsham, 2002). Leidner (2010, p. 69) points out how globalization "encompasses the exchange of production materials, the substitution of production processes, the relocation of services, the redistribution of resources, and the diffusion and infusion of cultural norms, artifacts, and values." Today organizations share their processes with other organizations in order to operate more efficiently. Consequently, companies sharing their processes have become increasingly intertwined. Thus, their respective cultural levels have become more convergent and act as catalysts for change. This is where Information and Communication Technology (ICT) and culture play a pivotal role. ICT can be seen as the enabler of concurrency in organizations communication. Culture can be considered as the restraint for ascertaining seamless supply chain. The difficulty in implementing global systems is that it includes an assumption that the best for one business location automatically equates well to all other business locations as well (Leidner, 2010).

The need to understand Information Systems (IS) in cultural context have been increasing for many IS scholars (see e.g. Myers & Tan, 2003;

Leidner, 2010; Walsham, 2002). In different cultures, the relationship between behaviour and interpretation vary. Therefore, individuals reason to make sense of their realities (Adler, 1986). Hence, when an information system developer is not familiar with the end users' focal culture it is not apparent how the focal culture should be considered in IS development. If the developer does not know his own culture, it is not possible to acknowledge what is typical for developer's own behaviour regarding to the developed system's requirements in the light of cultural context.

There are various information system development issues, which are seemingly connected to persuasive systems and where cultural context appears to have an impact. These issues include perceptions of IS design techniques (Kumar, et al., 1990), user experience (Dey & Abowd, 2000; Orlikowski, et al., 1995; Kettinger, et al., 1995), user requirements (Tuunanen, et al., 2006), and system use (Myers & Tan, 2003). According to Leidner and Kayworth (2006), studies concerning information systems design and culture are affected by variations in cultural values. Differing values lead to different approaches for developing information systems in varying cultures. In this chapter, we argue that culture plays a major role in persuasive system design as well.

BACKGROUND

Anthropologist Kahn (1989, p. 13) writes that "culture is contested, temporal and emergent." Thus, culture is seen as a dynamic construct. Consequently, culture is a very intricate construct and there are numerous attempts to define it. One widely referred definition has been set by sociologists Namenwirth and Weber (1987, pp. 8), who view culture as "a system of ideas," which constitutes "a design for living." In this research, culture is understood as a system of values and norms that are shared among a group of people. According to Hill (2008) values are abstract ideas about what group believes to be good, right, and desirable, whereas norms are social rules and principles that predispose the proper behavior toward others. Fan (2000) suggests that culture can be studied at international level, national culture level, regional culture level, subculture level, business culture level, and organizational culture level. Myers and Tan (2002) invite scholars to use Fan's (2000) categorization in global information systems research as a method for a more elaborate research design. Due to its scope and focus, this study is limited to the national culture level. Even though a more through capture of the phenomenon would be called to better grasp the cultural context in as many levels as possible.

Hofstede and Bond (1988) note that inflict of the Confucian values clearly manifest themselves in the Korean organizations. Thus, in Korean organizations, the social mutuality is important, the division to inner and outer circle is apparent, personal relationships are particularist, rituals are respected, personal, and public relationships overlap. Yum (1988) regards Confucianism as a factor that has deeply persisted to the Korean society. Often Confucianism is not considered as a real religion but world-view, doctrine, or social philosophy based on moral lessons. The ideal for Confucianism is society structured as much as possible, in which people of certain positions deal with the responsibilities given to them for sense of mutuality (De Mente, 2004; Kim, 2007). The goal is to raise persons as good members of a good community. Therefore, Confucianism includes moral principles rather than conceptions of the God and the Afterlife. Moral principles regard interpersonal relationships as personal relationships. Especially family relationships are the foundation for the society according the Confucian philosophy (Yum, 1988; Hofstede, 2001).

The principles of Confucianism describe the five human relationships, which are regarded as the foundation for the society. Following these relationships is seen to be promoting concord and harmony in homes, towns, and cities nation-wide. These relationships regard the ruler and the subordinate, the father and the son, the husband and the wife, elder and the younger brothers and additionally elder and the younger friend. There is a definite hierarchy relating to these relationships in which the younger shall respect the elder, the servants respect the rulers and the women respect men. According to the Confucian perceptions, the stability of the society is based on inequality. Thus, the one with lower position shall respect the ones with higher positions, while the ones with higher positions shall take care of the ones with lower positions. Therefore, in ideal level hierarchy does not equal to domination but instead it is the basis to the request for mutuality; the servant shows loyalty and the ruler shows good will, the son shows respect and the father love, the wife is obedient and the husband is righteous, younger brother is humble and the older brother is noble; the younger friend shows trust and the older friend shows loyalty (Crane, 1999; Yum, 1988; Kim, 2007).

In Finnish culture, hard work has been highly valued not only to earn a living but rather to measure one's worth in the society (Virtanen, 1994). According to Virtanen (1994), this modern ethos has its roots in the 17th century protestant ethics where ascetic life and sedulousness were highly valued. Finland is a country with harsh climate and scarce resources. Consequently, survival in agrarian communities required individuals to help each other. However, in the end everyone was alone responsible for his/her survival (Virtanen, 1994). To some end, individualism in Finland can be considered as an opposite to Korean society where utmost objective is to strongly bind one to groups by reaching feeling of togetherness through harmony and hierarchy. Individual are not important before they have found their places in the hierarchy (Kim, 2007).

Indeed, one of the most dominant features of Neo-Confucian Korean culture is hierarchy. It penetrates all levels of society and manifests itself equally in friend relationships as in organizations and the language. Basic definition for hierarchical personal relationships is that the other side is ranked higher in the ranking. Hofstede (2001) designates the cultural dimension relating to hierarchy as power distance. It describes how big differences are accepted in people's positions. Ergo, how people accept unequal distribution of power, appreciation and wealth. In cultures of high power distance, power is often concentrated to few and its benefits are easily abused. In cultures of low power distances, power is based on expertise and it should only be used within the limits set by legislation (Hofstede, 2001, 2003). According to Hofstede's study, Korea is a culture of high power distance, whereas Finland is a culture of moderate power distance.

In the countries of high power distance the hierarchical pyramid is strict and elders are always respected more than the younger ones. Hierarchical relationship between subordinate and superior always manifests as great emotional distance so that subordinates will not approach their superiors but the superior is presumed to contact his subordinates when needed. Subordinates will not criticize decisions or opinions of their superiors, not to even talk about getting into an argument or conflict with him. In low power distance, it is normal that subordinates take part into the decision-making and impugn the situation if they feel it is unreasonable. In the countries of high power distance, managers and superiors are clearly unequal. This can be seen in the decision-making process where higher ranked simply dictate the course of action (Hofstede, 2001; Merkin, 2006).

Regarding to persuasion, Cialdini (2003) has presented six methods of how individuals influence one another. The six principles are reciprocation, commitment and consistency, social proof, authority, liking and scarcity. Previous studies (Kaptein & Eckles, 2010) have shown that users react differently to different persuasive principles. Reciprocation works better for some users while commitment and consistency works better for others. In this chapter, we will focus on the principles of authority and social proof.

The principle of authority states that people defer to experts (Cialdini, 2003). When people do not know what to do, they are likely to comply and follow the lead of a renowned expert. The principle of authority works as a shortcut in many situations: an expert is supposed to know what to do and following his/her advice should be correct in most cases.

Similarly, the principle of social proof states that people rely on other people around them for cues on how to act or think (Cialdini, 2003). It also works as a shortcut as we generally make fewer mistakes by acting similarly as everybody else is acting. The social proof is especially effective when it comes from peers.

METHODOLOGY

The hypotheses of this study are as follows. The principle of authority stated that people defer to experts. People obey authority figures even if they are asked to perform questionable tasks. We assume that in Korean culture authority plays a bigger role than in Finland. Thus we hypothesize the following:

H1: The principle of authority works better with the Korean group.

The principle of social proof stated that people rely on other people around them for cues on how to behave. We assume that culture affects how people perceive the value of social proof. According to the theory this value is should be greater in Finland, whereas power based on expertise is greater and lesser in Korea where power is based on society's hierarchy. Thus we hypothesize the following:

H2: The principle of social proof works better with the Finnish group.

The research model of this study is in Figure 1. This research was built on positivistic approach. Positivism generally assumes that reality is objectively given and that it can be described by measurable properties, which are independent of the researcher. In addition, positivistic studies usually attempt to test a theory or hypotheses in order to increase the predictive understanding of the phenomena (Myers, 1997). We used survey to collect the data from the research subjects. We collected the data from 15.3.2011 until 23.3.2011. The data set was 108 answers consisting of 57 Finnish answers and 51 Korean answers.

Finnish answers came from the students of Oulu University of Applied Sciences and Korean answers came from the students of Yonsei University's East Asia International College. We calculated independent samples t-tests to compare Korean and Finnish students. The five statements evaluated for authority in this study were: I appreciate my parents' opinions, My grandparents have an effect on my behavior, I do not often question the opinions of my senior students, I always follow my teachers instructions and I obey older people. The five statements evaluated for social proof were I like to act in the same way I see other people acting, In unclear situations I follow carefully what other people do before deciding what I'm going to do, I follow trends, I usually watch popular movies, I'd like to be friends with the popular students in my university/college. The statements were part of bigger a set of statements and questions; however the other statements and questions were omitted, because they are outside the scope of this chapter.

The reason Finland and Korea were chosen as research subjects is because the countries' cultures differ considerably (see e.g. Hofstede, 2001). In addition, authors were familiar with them and had access to carry out data gathering in both countries.

The questions were answered by using a Likert scale of 1 (completely disagree) to 5 (completely agree) with a "not applicable" option as a sixth choice. The not applicable option could be chosen e.g. with questions asking about students grandparents if they were deceased. The missing answers and answers to "not applicable" were omitted while analyzing the data. The questions were formulated based on Cialdini's principles and the ones evaluated in this study were based on authority and social proof, furthermore the previously stated viewpoints how culture differs in Finnish and Korean cultures were taken into consideration.

Figure 1. Research model

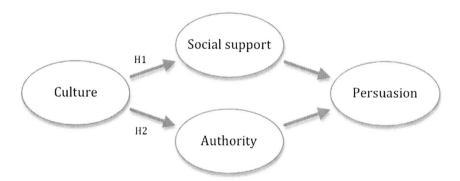

Results

The demographic data and age distribution for Korean and Finnish participants are displayed in Table 1 and Table 2. As can be seen from Table 1, both genders are represented in each group. The age distribution of Korea group is little bit more homogeneous than in the Finish group. It would seem that the classes in Finland contain more students who are little bit older than the classes in Korea where most of the students are around the same age.

We utilized independent samples t-tests to compare the means between Finnish and Korean students. With the first question, it appears that there is no difference in how Finnish and Korean students respect their parents. This is interesting and it should be studied more.

With the second question, there is no significance difference. With this question, there is always the possibility that not all students had

Table 1. Demographic data

Culture	N	Sex	
Finland	57	Male	34
		Female	23
Korea	51	Male	27
		Female	24

Table 2. Age distribution

Culture	Age	N
Finland	under 20	13
	21-25	29
	26-30	11
	over 31	4
Korea	under 20	28
	21-25	24
	26-30	-
	over 31	-

their grandparents alive or interacted with their grandchildren.

The third question implicates that Korean students respect senior students more than Finns do. This is according to the hypothesis set. Indeed, in school environment together with the teachers elder students command some respect.

With the fourth question, it seems that Koreans obey teachers much more than the Finns do ($p<0.001$). This matches the hypothesis of this study. Indeed, teacher is in a position where he has authority over students.

In the fifth question it appears that the hypothesis of this study are supported again. Korean students do seem to obey elderly people much more than Finnish students do. This is quite interesting.

With the five questions regarding authority, it would seem that in three of them the Koreans are more prone to the principle of authority than the Finns are. In the other two, there is no significant difference one-way or the other. See Table 3. Overall, this would indicate that the hypothesis is correct—Korean students are more likely to be affected by the principle of authority that the Finnish students are.

The results regarding social proof are little bit more inconclusive. There does not seem to be a big difference in how Finnish and Korean students are affected by social proof. In the sixth question, the Finns seem to be little bit more prone to social proof. The difference is not big and it is barely significant ($p=0.045$). This is according to our hypotheses.

In the seventh question there seems to be no difference between the Finns and the Korean. Maybe this question was not formulated the best possible way. In unclear situations social proof is usually a good shortcut when we a deciding what to do. Indeed this might be so independent of the culture.

In the eight questions, we asked whether or not the students follow trends. Here the Finns and the Korean alike answered exactly the same. The ninth question asked whether or not the students

Table 3. The results regarding authority

Question	Culture	N	T-Test	Sig.
1. I appreciate my parents' opinions.	Finnish	57	3.84	0.19
	Korean	51	3.63	
2. My grandparents have an effect on my behavior.	Finnish	55	2.58	0.15
	Korean	49	2.20	
3. I often question the opinions of my senior students.	Finnish	55	3.22	0.006**
	Korean	51	2.61	
4. I always follow teacher's instructions.	Finnish	56	2.98	0.000**
	Korean	51	3.65	
5. I obey elder people.	Finnish	57	3.09	0.000**
	Korean	45	3.78	

watch popular movies. Again, the differences in the answer were minimal.

With the final question, we wanted to know if the students hoped to be friends with the popular students of their schools. With this question, the results were the opposite of what was hypothesized. It seems that Korean students are much more inclined to be friends with the popular students. The Finns were much less inclined to do. This is interesting and no clear answer to why this is can be found.

With the five questions regarding social proof the Finns were more likely to act similarly as they see other people acting while the Koreans would be more willing to be friends with the popular students. In the other questions, no significant differences were found (see Table 4).

Solutions and Recommendations

The results suggest that when designing information systems culture should be taken into account. We argue that this is especially true when we are dealing with persuasive systems as different persuasive strategies work better in one culture than in the other. For example if we look at the results of this chapter, the principle of authority works better in Korea than in Finland. Similarly,

Table 4. The results regarding social proof

Question	Culture	N	T-Test	Sig.
6. I like to act in the same way I see other people acting.	Finnish	56	2.84	0.045*
	Korean	51	2.47	
7. In unclear situations I follow carefully what other people do before deciding what I'm going to do.	Finnish	57	3.40	0.43
	Korean	51	3.57	
8. I follow trends.	Finnish	57	2.04	0.98
	Korean	51	2.04	
9. I usually watch popular movies.	Finnish	56	3.54	0.69
	Korean	51	3.45	
10. I'd like to be friends with the popular students in my university/college.	Finnish	55	1.89	0.001**
	Korean	47	2.62	

how other principles and persuasive techniques work relates to the context where the information system will be used. In highly competitive markets, organizations need all the support they need to gain competitive advantage. When we are designing solutions that affect users' behaviors understanding culture helps us tailor our solutions to fit into the needs of local customers.

In addition, the results also suggest that the research topic is intricate and more research is called for. It seems like the statements we used were open to more interpretations than meant by the authors. For example, parents may be obeyed, but it does not necessitate that their opinions are appreciated. It seems that it would be worthwhile to redo the survey by first formulating and testing the statements on test audience.

FUTURE RESEARCH DIRECTIONS

As a future research, validating that the questions measure what they are meant to measure should bring better insight into the intended research aspect. We suggest that conducting qualitative research could be suitable approach for understanding pivotal concepts. Choosing different countries for the research seems also an interesting way to develop further understanding of the issue. Recently there has been an increasing amount of research stating that Hofstede's cultural dimensions might not always be valid. Thus, selecting a different method for evaluating the focal cultural context could be a valuable development for further research.

These results can help IS managers to identify some of the challenges risen in persuasive systems development. Understanding users' behavioral patterns is important for developing systems that persuade the users. Thus, considering culture is pivotal when aspiring to understand what are users behavioral patterns and how can they be affected through persuasive design. However, the challenge

of how to cope with differing cultural issues still persists. We regard future research on this issue important, especially in the light of Information Systems Development.

CONCLUSION

The results were interesting and somewhat surprising. In the questions regarding authority there were three statements where our hypothesis were supported. In addition, there were two statements where our hypothesis was not supported. The results imply that authority does play bigger role in Korea than in Finland. However, this is not totally apparent; thus, further research on the topic is called for.

With the questions regarding social proof, no differences were found. The Finns and Koreans are as likely to be affected by it. Our idea was that because authority plays a bigger role in Korea the impact of other persuasion principles would be lessened. Clearly, this does not appear to be the case with social proof. We did ask questions regarding liking as well but found no significant differences with that aspect either.

In this chapter, we studied whether culture has implications to persuasive systems design. We conducted a survey with Finnish and Korean students to understand the role of social proof and authority in differing cultural contexts. We concluded, that regarding to the principle of social proof there were no statistical difference and in context of principle of authority, indeed, has a statistically meaningful difference. However, more research is needed to reach a more thorough understanding. We suggest that when designing solutions that utilize persuasive technology features e.g. for Internet public procurement culture should be considered carefully. This might help developers in designing systems to better achieve desired goals.

REFERENCES

Adler, N. (1986). *International dimensions of organizational behavior*. Boston, MA: Kent Publishing Company.

Cialdini, R. B. (1993). *Influence: Science and practice* (3rd ed.). New York, NY: HarperCollins.

Crane, P. S. (1999). *Korean patterns – A royal Asiatic society-Korea*. Seoul, South Korea: Seoul Press.

De Mente, B. (2004). *Korean business etiquette*. Singapore, Singapore: Tuttle Publishing.

Dey, A., & Abowd, G. (2000). Towards a better understanding of context and context awareness. In *Proceedings of HUC*, (pp. 304-307). ACM Press.

Fan, Y. (2000). A classification of Chinese culture. *Cross Cultural Management, 7*(2), 3–10. doi:10.1108/13527600010797057

Fogg, B. J. (1998). Persuasive computers: Perspectives and research directions. In *Proceedings of the CHI 1998 Conference on Human Factors in Computing Systems*, (pp. 225-232). Los Angeles, CA: ACM Press.

Fogg, B. J. (2002). *Persuasive technology: Using computers to change what we think and do*. San Francisco, CA: Morgan Kaufmann.

Fogg, B. J., & Nass, C. I. (1997). Silicon sycophants: The effects of computers that flatter. *International Journal of Human-Computer Studies, 5*(46), 551–561. doi:10.1006/ijhc.1996.0104

Harjumaa, M., & Oinas-Kukkonen, H. (2007). An analysis of the persuasiveness of smoking cessation web sites. In *Proceedings of the Second International Symposium on Medical Information and Communication Technology*. Oulu, Finland: University of Oulu.

Hill, C. (2008). *International business – Competing in the global marketplace* (7th ed.). London, UK: McGraw-Hill.

Hofstede, G. F. (2001). *Culture's consequences: Comparing values, behaviours, institutions, and organizations across the nations* (2nd ed.). Thousand Oaks, CA: Sage.

Hofstede, G. F. (2003). *Cultural dimensions*. Retrieved from http://www.geert-hofstede.com/

Hofstede, G. F., & Bond, M. H. (1988). The Confucius connection: From cultural roots to economic growth. *Organizational Dynamics, 16*, 4–21. doi:10.1016/0090-2616(88)90009-5

Kahn, J. S. (1989). Culture: Demise or resurrection? *Critique of Anthropology, 9*(2), 5–25. doi:10.1177/0308275X8900900202

Kaptein, M., & Eckles, D. (2010). Selecting effective means to any end: Futures and ethics of persuasion profiling. *Lecture Notes in Computer Science, 6137*, 82–93. doi:10.1007/978-3-642-13226-1_10

Kettinger, W., & Lee, C. C. (1995). Global measures of information service quality: A crossnational study. *Decision Sciences, 26*(5), 569–588. doi:10.1111/j.1540-5915.1995.tb01441.x

Kim, C. S. (2007). *Kimchi and IT*. Seoul, South Korea: Ilchokak.

Kumar, K., Bjorn-Anderson, N., & King, R. (1990). A cross-cultural comparison of IS designer values. *Communications of the ACM, 33*(5), 528–538. doi:10.1145/78607.78613

Leidner, D. E. (2010). Globalization, culture and information: Towards global knowledge transparency. *The Journal of Strategic Information Systems, 19*, 69–77. doi:10.1016/j.jsis.2010.02.006

Leidner, D. E., & Kayworth, T. (2006). Review: A review of culture in information systems research: Toward a theory of information technology culture conflict. *Management Information Systems Quarterly, 30*(2), 357–399.

Merkin, R. (2006). Power distance and face-work strategies. *Journal of Intercultural Communication Research, 35*, 139–160. doi:10.1080/17475750600909303

Myers, M., & Tan, F. (2003). Beyond models of national culture in information systems research. *Advanced Topics in Global Information Management, 10*(2), 1–19.

Myers, M. D. (1997). Qualitative research in information systems. *Management Information Systems Quarterly, 21*(2), 241–242. doi:10.2307/249422

Namenwirth, J. Z., & Weber, R. B. (1987). *Dynamics of culture*. Boston, MA: Allen & Unwin.

Nass, C. I., Steuer, J., & Tauber, E. R. (1994). Computers are social actors. In *Proceedings of the SIGCHI Conference on Human Factors in Computing Systems: Celebrating Interdependence*, (pp. 72-78). New York, NY: ACM Press.

Orlikowski, W., Yates, J., Okamura, K., & Fujimoto, M. (1995). Shaping electronic communication: The metastructuring of technology in the context of use. *Organization Science, 6*(4), 423–444. doi:10.1287/orsc.6.4.423

Tuunanen, T., Peffers, K., Gengler, C., Hui, W., & Virtanen, V. (2006). Developing feature sets for geographically diverse external end users: A call for value-based preference modelling. *Journal of Information Technology Theory & Application, 8*(2), 42–51.

Walsham, G. (2002). Cross-cultural software production and use: a structurational analysis. *Management Information Systems Quarterly, 26*(4), 359–380. doi:10.2307/4132313

Yum, J. O. (1988). The impact of Confucianism on interpersonal relationships and communication patterns in East Asia. *Communication Monographs, 55*(4), 374–388. doi:10.1080/03637758809376178

KEY TERMS AND DEFINITIONS

Authority: Legally or socially approved use of power.

Culture: A system of ideas, which constitutes a design for living.

Information System (IS): A system implemented within an organization for the purpose of improving the effectiveness and efficiency of that organization.

Persuasion: An attempt to change attitudes or behaviors.

Persuasive Systems: Interactive technology solutions aimed at supporting wanted attitude or behavior change.

Social Proof: People will do things that they see other people are doing.

Chapter 5
Technology Advancement and E-Procurement in the US

Joshua M. Steinfeld
Florida Atlantic University, USA

Khi V. Thai
Florida Atlantic University, USA

ABSTRACT

E-procurement has had a tremendous impact on the modernization of government and administration. In the U.S., the relationship between technology and e-procurement is central in determining the ability to adopt successful e-procurement. Significant investment in technology and human capital is required for the implementation of e-procurement systems. Despite widespread efforts to initialize e-procurement through direct investment in information and component technologies, a substantial portion of administrations' efforts at achieving e-governance have failed. The need for customized solutions and managerial intervention has challenged government at all levels. Furthermore, technological advancement has not been welcomed by all administrations. Nonetheless, the advantages of e-procurement typically justify the effort required to implement and maintain such systems. Reductions in transaction costs, increased transparency, and improved relationships between government and businesses are all advantages of e-procurement. While there are significant challenges to e-procurement not limited to corruption, the benefits of e-procurement far outweigh the costs.

INTRODUCTION

Technological advancements since the 1960s have had a profound effect on public procurement in the U.S. The emergence of e-procurement has been one of the most impactful facets of modern government and administration. By using information technology, procurement approaches to the market can be aggregated and decision-making devolved. However, best practices frameworks for the implementation and sustainability of e-procurement that can be applied to all levels of government are yet to be established. Furthermore, challenges related to implementation, sustainability, and corruption present obstacles to the effective adoption of e-procurement.

DOI: 10.4018/978-1-4666-2665-2.ch005

The main purpose of this chapter is to demonstrate the important relationship between technology and e-procurement in the U.S. While numerous local, state, and federal governments have invested in new technologies that enable the initial implementation of e-procurement, successful adoption is often overstated. E-procurement has a humanistic element involving public procurement managers, senior officials, and the bureaucracy. Transparency and accessibility to the marketplace are two key elements provided by effective utilization of e-procurement systems. Conversely, corruption is a major challenge that threatens administrations attempting to incorporate e-government. While the third sector, consisting mostly of non-governmental organizations, has appeared as a facilitator to transactions taking place in the public sector, the involvement of non-government organizations is understudied and requires more research.

E-procurement improves customer effectiveness, sharing of data, and overall quality of public procurement. The reduction of transaction costs and other economic benefits are additional advantages to implementing e-procurement. However, successful implementation of e-procurement systems requires significant financial investment and managerial attention. Investment in e-procurement technologies alone is not sufficient to develop an e-procurement system.

The continually developing synthesis between technology and the public sector indicates that e-procurement processes are of a reflexive nature. E-procurement systems have the potential to improve relationships between government and business by providing market participants with transparency and accessibility. However, the ability to successfully utilize e-procurement systems largely depends on the maturity level of the e-procurement system and the underlying administration using the system. The development of information, communications, and component technologies can help public procurement manag-

ers implement customized solutions that may serve to address the complexities inherent to the public sector. Nonetheless, investment in human capital is paramount; significant managerial efforts are required to alleviate any technological constraints.

TECHNOLOGY ADVANCEMENT

Over the last 40 years, public sector organizations have been utilizing Information Technology (IT) systems to streamline and automate purchasing and related processes, but it is only in the past decade that e-procurement systems have been of focus. Developing e-procurement processes is difficult and still in its early stages of technological development (Pooler, Pooler, & Farney, 2004). There is certainly debate regarding exactly when e-procurement came into being, but there is no question as to the many advantages that e-procurement provides over previously implemented inter-organizational tools. For example, electronic data interchange has been used to support transactions involving suppliers and buyers since the 1960s. In the 1970s, enterprise resource planning dominated e-procurement strategy and with it came the first commercial use of the Internet. However, it was not until the late 1990s that the World Wide Web and its multimedia capabilities became a globally enabled resource for the execution of public procurement activities (Office of Government Commerce, 2002). The U.S. is regarded to be the first nation to adopt e-procurement in the late 1980s and early 1990s. The first use of e-procurement in the public sector can be attributed to U.S. innovation that led to "dual use" technologies and "conversion" of military technologies into civilian applications in strategic high technology sectors (Mowery, 2001). Although "dual use" programs and "cooperative" technology development policies were mostly dissolved by the late 1990s, they serve as a foundation for experimentation related to the multiple trajectories that e-procurement systems are designed to manage (Bozeman & Dietz, 2001).

By 1983, about 41 percent of the American federal government's data processing budget was allocated to personnel (Grace Commission, 1983, p. ii). Ten years later the federal government employed 113,300 IT staff, at a cost of US$5.5 billion (OMB, 1994, p. 15). Although, "if we examine the kinds of information that executives use we find that a large proportion of it is simply natural language text—the pages of newspapers, trade magazines, technical journals, and so on" (Simon, 1973, p. 496). If this could be delivered electronically the capacity of business and political decision-making could be expanded hugely.

Government has attached itself to technology in order to alleviate the demands of management and provide for market participants who come from a wide geographic area. With technological advancement comes the need to establish bodies of knowledge and specific norms of technical expertise that are devised with the type of flexibility necessary to keep up with technology. Technology also requires the inculcation of a form of life, the reshaping of various roles for human practices, the mental techniques required in terms of certain practices of communication, the practices of the self orientated around the mobile telephone, the word processor, the World Wide Web, and so forth (Rose, 1999, pp. 51-52). Thus, technologies require the synthesis and connectivity of knowledge, capacities, skills, and judgments that are inherent to humans, not machines. Therefore, in order to govern, one needs some "intellectual technology" for trying to work out what on earth one should do next—which involves criteria as to what one wants to do, what has worked in the past, and what is the main issue to be addressed (Rose, 1999, pp. 26-27). Much of the expertise in local governments and administrations remained largely uninfluenced by movements toward computerization, office automation, and even the financial IT waves (Dunleavy, Margetts, Bastow, & Tinkler,

2006). The fields of law, public health, social work, and education were even slow to respond to technological advancements that could facilitate procurement objectives (Dunleavy, et al., 2006). This process began to change rapidly from the mid-1990s onwards, first with the high-expertise sectors catching up with the general trend towards integrated computing in everyday organizational activities, and later adopting an accounting and management information toolkit (Kurunmaki, 1999a, 1999b).

At first, there were no central agencies responsible for the adoption of e-procurement in public sector organizations, for encouraging or coordinating the processing of Internet-based information on government services, or for ensuring that issues of IT-literacy and other privacy and security issues were discussed in schools and universities (Dunleavy, et al., 2006). However, the Internet spurred immediate interest in the scientific and business communities where e-procurement began to thrive. There was also widespread interest in the government. For example, in the early 1990s, electronic messaging using internal mainframes and networks was taking place by some administrators. In 1994, National Performance Review (NPR) leader Al Gore, through his Access America initiative, promised to provide all citizens with electronic access to government by 2000 through the proposed establishment of a national information infrastructure. The NPR established the Government Information Technology Services Board, which served to promote cross-agency integration in regards to new policies and rulemaking (Kerwin & Furlong, 2011). The General Services Administration (GSA) played a role in digital security. Within the GSA, the Federal Technology Service offered agencies numerous services through its "connected government" and "smart government" initiative, which included systems integration support and outsourcing advice (Johnson, 2002; Dunleavy, et al., 2006). The Office of Management and Budget (OMB) played a role in encouraging e-governance by requiring agencies to offer all government services electronically by 2003, as part of legislation set forth in the Government Paper Reduction Act (1995) (Kerwin & Furlong, 2011). OMB and General Accountability Office (GAO) decided that information would be shared electronically. Publication of the famed blue-cover reports would no longer be distributed on Capitol Hill (Barr, 2008). OMB was also responsible for overseeing implementation of a CIO initiative (part of the Clinger-Cohen Act of 1996) across the federal government, in which Cabinet agencies were mandated to appoint a CIO who reported directly to the agency head. The CIO was given primary responsibility for all IT activities including responsibilities related to purchasing (Information Technology Management Reform Act, 1996).

The growth of private sector suppliers of technology was necessary in promoting the evolution of e-procurement in government and fulfilling the needs of the public sector. Each organization should evaluate every service activity in its value chain, determine if it is 'best in world' at that activity, and if not, consider outsourcing the activity to the best-in-world provider (Quinn, 1992). Companies such as EDS, CSC, and Unisys aimed to provide such technological solutions to government and continued to grow rapidly through a series of mergers and acquisitions. Many firms specializing in e-procurement related solutions were spin-offs from large accountancy and management consultancy firms such as Accenture and Ernst & Young. Rapid growth in regards to technology outsourcing was evident from 1992-2002 in which IBM's services revenue increased from US$7.4 billion to US$36.4 billion, a 392% increase (OECD, 2004).

Garvey's (1993) recount of the Beltway Bandits demonstrated the power of computer services development. Beginning in the 1970s computer companies clustered around the federal government agencies in Washington, D.C. forming part of the Beltway Bandits. By 1990, the U.S. federal government accounted for 38 percent of the total revenue of US-based vendors, as opposed to 35 percent for U.S. commercial operations and 7 percent for state and local governments (International Digital Communications, 1993, section 3.8). By 2001, EDS held contracts totaling over US$10.3 billion with the Department of Transportation, the Immigration and Naturalization Service, the Department of Veterans Affairs, the Department of Justice, the U.S. Census, and the U.S. Postal Service (Dunleavy, et al., 2006). In addition, $600 million of CSC's $6 billion in revenue came from government contracts (Dunleavy, et al., 2006).

E-PROCUREMENT IN THE UNITED STATES

Technology, the Public Sector, and Adoption of E-Procurement

The current state of public procurement reflects tensions involving the public's expectation regarding governance, performance, and political influence in the public sector (Kettle, 2005). Dunleavy et al. (2006) examines the synthesis between information technology, the public sector, and the eventual digitizing of government. Beginning in the 1980s and 1990s, a trend towards public-private partnerships established the need to consider stakeholder interests such as business private investors (Kettle, 2002; Cooper, 2003; Xu, 2007). However, best practices have not been established to address the varying dynamics unique to each level of government. On one hand, there are prescriptive and regulated structures, where executives or directors are closely involved in most phases of the procurement process. On the other hand, there are more loosely guided approaches where responsibilities are devolved and procurement is viewed as one of several managerial functions (National Performance Review, 1993; Peters, 1996). The differences in procurement arrangements vary based upon the political party and administration in place.

Not only are best practices frameworks yet to be established that can be applied to public sectors at all levels of government and across states, but the scope of public procurement processes is not well defined. Devolved decision-making and deregulation that occurs through improved managerial freedoms do not always result in improved performance and outcomes (Simon, 1965; Corini, 2000; Schapper & Veiga Malta, 2004). The 21st century has brought with it the advent of new technologies of great significance such as Internet-based information, purchasing, and all-encompassing e-procurement systems. The information-sharing capabilities of new technologies lead to the centralization of processes and diminishing need for continually applied decision-making (MacManus, 2002). In this manner, technology can centralize the aggregated procurement approaches to the market, including the bidding and evaluation phases of public procurement. Although adoption of Internet-based technologies seems like a simple solution to addressing complexities of the public sector, few state and local level governments have effectively adopted e-procurement systems. Numerous governments have set forth initiatives to adopt e-procurement but find themselves inept and unprepared for the level of reform necessary for e-procurement adoption. Governmental use of e-procurement often leads to improved analysis and control of expenditures, but demands that the purchasing cycle be re-crafted along with management reform. Simply grafting technology onto existing manual processes will not result in effective adoption of e-procurement (Schapper & Veiga Malta, 2004). In general, senior managers have been inept at adjusting to new technologies. Additionally, Patton and McKenna (2005) and Sauter (2005) contend that data and information gathering processes have not been amply developed to make use of what Chen, Chau, and Zeng (2002) claimed to be the solution to expediting process development; advancements in Web-based information search systems.

There is a common misconception that because technology has the potential to yield significantly positive results then adoption is easy; or in cases where positive outcomes do not result easily then the potential for technology to have significant impacts is not substantial. Large amounts of governmental resources can be allocated to e-procurement systems and related technologies without impacting progress toward achieving objectives. The complexity of the public sector underlying the public procurement environment, the nature of the political system, and the interaction of workers associated with the public procurement system of a given public sector determine the ability for successful adoption of e-procurement (MacManus, 2002).

Although many public sector agencies are fiercely pursuing adoption of e-procurement, evidence demonstrates that adoption efforts are not meeting expectations. The implementation rate of e-procurement systems has been slow. Additionally, governmental agencies have a tendency to overstate the degree to which e-procurement has been implemented (MacManus, 2002). E-procurement projects have a greater reach and scope than traditional information technology development projects. The appropriate calibration of security, control of variables, operating standards, and design of interfaces have emerged as success factors more critical to e-procurement projects than traditional information technology projects. In addition, the support of upper management and unbiased performance measurement were also found to be critical to e-procurement projects (Vaidya, Sajeev, & Callender, 2006).

Today in the U.S. alone, government purchasing volume exceeds $1.4 Trillion annually and is managed by more than 500,000 purchasing professionals. As of February 2001, in the United States Department of Defense, there were 135,014 civilian and military employees dedicated to technology acquisition and e-procurement systems utilization (Carter & Grimm, 2001, p. 3). By 2006, e-procurement fueled government public procurement to a proportion representing 18.42% of world Gross Domestic Product (Auriol, 2006). In fact, numerous countries have formed specialized agencies to develop and manage e-procurement systems. The purpose of e-procurement systems has been to: 1) promote the use of the Internet across different industries; 2) provide elements of *transparency* to transactions that involve either contractors or bureaucratic participants; 3) reduce administrative cost by improving the procurement process; and 4) reduce purchasing prices due to increased efficiency and improved accessibility, especially in the bidding process (Singer, et al., 2009, pp. 58-59).

Public sector transformation toward accessibility and transparency facilitated the initial adoption of e-procurement by the United States. Not only have increased trust, accessibility, and transparency in the public sector contributed to the innovation and creativity of the administration, which is necessary in the design and implementation of e-procurement systems, in turn, e-procurement systems have been specifically adopted by local, state, and federal governments to increase levels of accessibility and transparency in the utilization of public procurement systems. Managing freely, fairly, and transparently has been a major concern of public procurement professionals (Carter & Grimm, 2001, p. 3; Neupane, Soar, & Yong, 2012). If managed effectively, e-procurement provides numerous advantages to systems users and the respective allocation of resources.

Perhaps the greatest challenge is that the adoption of e-procurement has spurred a new wave of corruption. The third sector has emerged to reduce corruption and improve the e-procurement process for all users. However, corruption related to e-procurement is as new a phenomenon as e-procurement itself, and the emergence of the third sector in the form of non-governmental organizations has yet to fully take shape. Corruption, especially as it relates to e-procurement

adoption and the third sector are two areas that require further research. Corruption counteracts the successes of e-procurement systems by creating inefficiencies and reducing competitiveness. Corruption limits the number of bidders, favors selection bias, and limits the free flow of information. Market participants that are not affiliated with corruption are effectively penalized through increases in transaction costs. Evidence suggests that reduced competition results in public procurement deficiency (Falvey, Greenaway, & Yu, 2007). It is the competitive sourcing in public procurement that encouraged the innovation and performance incentives that fueled the creation and adoption of e-procurement to begin with (United States Government Accountability Office, 2005).

Corruption is most widespread where workers are paid meager salaries, have numerous opportunities to take place in corruption and fraud, and are not likely to be discovered or reprimanded (Quah, 1999). Other factors of corruption include high degrees of control exercised by the state on the economy, weak democratic norms and institutions, and low degrees of integration into the global economy (Heilbrunn, 2004). In developing countries especially, corruption is a critical factor that prohibits the effective adoption of e-procurement (Basheka, 2009). As much as 20-25 percent of spending associated with the public procurement process is lost due to leakages and frauds in developing countries (Falvey, Greenaway, & Yu, 2007). Even in jurisdictions with democratically based administrations, as is predominate in the U.S., the issues of corruption are rarely attended to which increases susceptibility to systemic failure and lapses in accountability (Peachment, 1992). Common forms of corruption include failures to realize the existence of a contractual relationship or when information sharing involves breaches of trust and confidentiality.

Reforms have recently been made which strive to reduce the instance and curb the impact of corruption on public procurement systems, especially those procurement systems reliant on e-procurement. The call for reform has prompted the establishment of the Civil Society Organization (CSO) and non-governmental organizations that attempt to improve the way public procurement systems serve the public and allocate national resources. While the market provides goods and services and the state establishes the rules and regulations guiding participation, the third sector (CSO's and NGO's) is based upon shared public interests with concentrated purposes that are implemented by voluntary initiatives.

The sensitivity of government data and the legalities underlying orders and payments indicate that the security of data and information is critical to successful e-procurement and e-procurement deployment. E-procurement systems must have mechanisms for identifying and authenticating system users so that buyers and suppliers can proceed to fulfilling responsibilities associated with the execution of orders. These mechanisms should be related to security considerations from the e-tendering stage to authentication of bidding and eventually be applied to ensuring safe transfer of funds (Birks, Bond, & Radford, 2001). In order to encourage participation in e-procurement, all parties involved must have total trust in the security that underlies the public procurement environment.

Corruption has the ability to intrude upon the public sector at all levels of agency and government (Bardhan, 1997). Empirical evidence across countries concludes that fiscal decentralization and excessively tiered governments contribute to corruption, especially at the lower levels of government. In addition, the legal and political systems governing the public sector dictate the extent to which decentralization exists (Fisman & Gatti, 2002). However, for centralization of public procurement functions to take place through e-procurement and e-procurement systems, then trust, accessibility, and transparency must be evident within the central government, corresponding

agencies, labor market participants, and other public and private stakeholders. Management of the interaction between technology and market participants is the perhaps the best way to institute e-procurement.

Implementation of E-Procurement and Related Solutions

While successful adoption and implementation of e-procurement systems has varied in the U.S., without continued financial investment there would be no hope for improvement; and there have been numerous occasions where substantial return on investments were yielded (Batchelor, 1999; Vernon, 1999; Nairn, 2000; Neef, 2001). Despite overall mixed results, there has been significant financial investment in e-procurement systems at all levels of government that continues to increase over time (Hardy & Williams, 2008; Varney, 2011). The rapid expansion of governmental e-commerce has resulted from the conveniences offered by e-procurement in regards to consumers' ability to search information and evaluate, purchase, and use products more effectively than ever before. E-procurement increases consumer efficiency by improving consumers' access to consumption related information more quickly, thus saving time, effort, and money. E-procurement also improves customer effectiveness by providing multimedia capabilities such as sound, image, text, and other visual tools that aid to develop customer learning and assist in the product selection process, with the goal of optimally fulfilling customer demands. E-procurement has replaced traditional communication and distribution channels and continues to matriculate into a driving economic force (Moon, 2004, p. 105). Overall, the implementation of e-procurement initiatives should be viewed as an agency's desire to provide real time access to information or real time bidding (Ndou, 2004; Neupane, Soar, & Yong, 2012), increase competition among the bidders or suppliers (Hanna, 2010; International Monetary Fund, 2010; Mahmood, 2010; Neupane, Soar, & Yong, 2012; Thai, 2001), reduce human intervention in bidding process (Khanapuri, et al., 2011; Magrini, 2006; Neupane, Soar, & Yong, 2012), facilitate monitoring and tracking (Achterstraat, 2011; Asian Development Bank, 2010; Neupane, Soar, & Yong, 2012; Organization for Economic and Cooperation Developemnt, 2011), improve document transmissions efficiency and security (Attorney-General's Department, 2005; Chang, 2011; Hanna, 2010; Neupane, Soar, & Yong, 2012; Zhang & Yang, 2011), make procurement process transparent and accountable (Croom & Brandon-Jones, 2005; Neupane, Soar, & Yong, 2012; Panda,Sahu, & Gupta, 2010; Pathak, et al., 2009; Vaidya, et al., 2006), and faster and easier (Hanna, 2010; Neupane, Soar, & Yong, 2012).

Indeed, the effects of technology and e-procurement on the public procurement environment can be assessed using three broad objectives including transparency of process, efficiency, and policy coherence. There is a significant ability for e-procurement-based technology to improve governance and transparency. At a very low cost, technology can transform fraud prevention in public procurement from a process that relies on chance and windows of opportunity to a process based on comprehensive audit sampling. Not only can audits be improved in terms of comprehensive coverage but also by profiling buyer behavior, purchasing activities, and sourcing decisions according to individual agents within a procurement facility. When complex procurement systems are involved, key transparency features of e-procurement include enhanced public access to current policies, information on bidding, progress of tender evaluation, and presentation of outcomes (Schapper, Veiga Malta, & Gilbert, 2006).

Regarding public procurement system efficiency, there are many ways in which e-procurement streamlines procurement processes. E-procurement improves efficiency at many levels for suppliers and purchasers in the payment cycle,

management integration, reporting, and evaluation processes. Supply chain processing such as search, requests for quotations, authorizations, and financial reconciliations can be streamlined with a well-designed and functional government e-procurement system (Schapper, Veiga Malta, & Gilbert, 2006). For more complicated public procurement initiatives, the factors that are determinant of efficiency are most closely related to the quality and availability of management information. Return on investment and performance improvements are facilitated by the technology inherent to e-procurement systems, but the benefits can only be experienced when the application of e-procurement systems is combined with skilled procurement managers.

Public procurement managers are needed to reduce the impact of technological errors and alleviate the system constraints that result from such failures (Mota & Filho, 2011; Sun, Zhao, & Wang, 2012). Technological advancements, especially the use of Information Communication Technology (ICT) would make e-procurement initiatives more effective and positively impact the governments that properly design, implement, and use these systems (Lee, Tan, & Trimi, 2005; Dunelavy, et al., 2006; United Nations, 2010).

The greatest advantages and value attributed to e-procurement are the cost reductions, economic rationality, and positive relationships created amongst procurement managers and private suppliers. Malone, Yate, and Benjamin (1987) and Henriksen and Mahnke (2005) argue that electronic interconnectedness between public and private interests is considered to reduce work-load, at a minimum, and may be contingent on three conditions: (1) timely and accurate electronic communication; (2) the establishment of electronic markets where buyers and sellers conduct transactions through a central brokerage system; and (3) seamless integration of IT, data management, and business processes. The outcome of fulfilling all three conditions is a reduction in transaction costs and unit cost of coordination in markets (Lee,

2010). Cost-savings related to transaction costs lead to increases in capital investment.

E-procurement systems may be viewed as a continuum of the relationship between government and business, indicating that e-procurement participants should consider the political rationality of their decisions. For example, e-procurement processes are of a reflexive nature in which major functions such as tendering, proposal writing, evaluation, contracting, delivery, and follow-up are executed on an on-going basis for each component of service. Thus, the main function of e-procurement systems is to provide proper and differentiated brokerage services to the government, agencies, and businesses (Lee, 2010).

During the global financial crisis that began in late 2007, financial markets including some electronic public procurement systems froze or stopped working normally. One major criterion for the sustainability of successful e-procurement systems is the maturity level of the e-procurement system and the underlying administration utilizing the system (McHenry & Pryamonosov, 2010). The growth and maturity of e-governance systems depends on IT development and the identification of opportunities to pursue economic rationality. Williams and Hardy (2006) classify the levels of maturity as readiness, intensity, and impact, with the consideration that the growth of e-procurement is congruent with the growth of e-government and the administration as a whole. In the readiness step of e-procurement, the hardware and software components are built into the e-procurement system with a goal of informing citizens of notices of tender, product information, assessment of goods and services, and to provide accessibility to proposal documents. During the intensity level, the e-procurement portal has been synchronized to interact with government agencies and private vendors through electronic exchange, the bidding process, contractual exchange, and online orders and payments. Finally, in the impact phase, the e-procurement system is further customized through the use of external devices, software upgrades, and information security (Williams & Hardy, 2006).

E-procurement is difficult to implement, and sustainability of effective e-purchasing systems is equally as challenging. Among all the components of e-procurement, e-purchasing requires the largest number of legal provisions. The e-auction mode facilitates direct online competition between buyers (e-bidding) and suppliers (e-reverse bidding) (Talero, 2001). In this mode, final prices are set during the bidding process. E-purchasing processes entail the coordination of numerous functions such as registration of buyers and sellers, aggregation of supply and demand, bidding, transactions, and other purchasing functions (McHenry & Pryamonosov, 2010). To fulfill these objectives, an e-procurement system should have three major components: an information and registration component, an electronic tendering component, and an electronic purchasing component (Talero, 2001). Full disclosure of similar public procurement opportunities, clarifications related to the marketplace, and the contract awarding process should be clearly presented (McHenry & Pryamonosov, 2010). The publication of rules, deadlines, data, and information, the announcement of a tender, data about previous tenders, bidders, and winners should be made accessible to the marketplace and related public sphere.

FUTURE RESEARCH DIRECTIONS

E-procurement is a relatively new phenomenon that has only begun to take shape with the recent emergence of the Internet in the 1990s. Therefore, it can be assumed that the development of e-procurement technologies is in its infancy. Additionally, areas for further research are continually being explored. The interaction between humans and technology has been of focus as information, communications, and component technologies continue to advance to provide transparency, clarity, and synthesis among users. Managerial commitment to e-procurement systems has been found to be necessary in coordinating technologies and human capital. However, best practices that can be applied to all levels of government have not been exhaustively identified. The need for customized approaches challenges the intellectual prowess of public procurement managers. Outsourcing for technological expertise in the form of systems design and customization represents the most significant cost that public procurement managers will face regarding e-procurement systems, other than certain hardware and software considerations. Therefore, public procurement managers will increasingly need to behold technological know-how to substantiate e-government initiatives taking place across the country at all levels of government. However, since the outsourcing of technological expertise in the form of systems design and customization are typically the most expensive costs of e-procurement systems, there is a need for the formulation of models and frameworks that public procurement managers can refer to in addressing the uniqueness of each respective public administrative system in the U.S. Additionally, the relationship among public sector participants has been improved by e-procurement but needs to be further researched.

Another research area to be addressed is related to public policy considerations. The swift advancement of technology creates a need for better understanding regarding the rights of purchasers and suppliers when dealing in a highly communicative environment. While transparency is of the essence, security and privacy issues continue to pervade e-procurement systems. The rise of NGOs has created a third sector that serves to add balance to the traditional roles of the private and public sector. However, the specific involvement of NGOs in public sector transactions is understudied in the U.S. and is even less understood. Both quantitative and qualitative research studies are warranted to further develop the role and impact of NGOs on the market place. E-procurement,

with its ability to centralize brokerage services to participants spanning immense geographic area, is a tool that may be utilized to provide interconnectivity to participants across sectors and levels of government. Further research is needed to establish methods and techniques of optimizing e-procurement connectivity between administration, government agencies, businesses, and the public.

CONCLUSION

Technology advancement and e-procurement in the U.S. are in the early stages of development. However, e-procurement has been established through application of economic rationale as a public procurement system that may assist public administration's transformation efforts to a system of e-governance. The synthesis of public sector participants including vendors, suppliers, NGO's, and the public is critical in achieving effective e-procurement. Interaction between human participants and technological components is central to the ability to design, customize, and maintain e-procurement systems. In the face of financial crisis and budgetary pressures, management practices are being relied upon to alleviate technological constraints. The reflexive nature of the underlying public sector environment indicates that relationships between businesses and government are becoming increasingly important. E-procurement, through the implementation of information, communication, and component technologies, has the potential to streamline public procurement practices and devolve managerial responsibilities in a cost-effective manner.

Technological advancements applicable to e-procurement in the U.S. have led to increases in transparency and accessibility to the participants of the market place. Administrations that have invested significantly in e-procurement have in some cases experienced phenomenal cost-savings, function improvements, and numerous other benefits.

However, adoption of e-procurement is largely overstated and the full potential of e-procurement systems is seldom achieved. Nonetheless, the recent numerous technological advancements related to e-procurement, especially in the areas of e-purchasing and information technology, have proven to positively contribute to administration's ability to serve the public sector and effectively relate to businesses. The willingness and intellectual capacity of the respective administration will largely determine the success of e-procurement systems at all levels of government.

REFERENCES

Achterstraat, P. (2011). *Compliance review report - Procurement reform of e-procurement and e-tendering.* Retrieved from http://www.audit.nsw. gov.au/ArticleDocuments/190/03_Vol_1_2011_ Compliance_Review.pdf.aspx?Embed=Y

Asian Development Bank. (2010). *Technical assistance report, Republic of Indonesia: Streangthing national public procurement process.* Manila, Phillipines: Asian Development Bank.

Attorney-General's Department. (2005). *Case studies on e-procurement implementations Italy, New South Wales, New Zealand, Scotland, Western Australia.* Canberra, Australia: Australian Government. Retrieved from http://www.finance.gov. au/publications/e-procurement-research-reports/ docs/Case_Studies_on_E-procurement_Implementations.pdf

Auriol, E. (2006). Corruption in procurement and public purchase. *International Journal of Industrial Organization, 24,* 867–885. doi:10.1016/j. ijindorg.2005.11.001

Bardhan, P. (1997). Corruption and development: A review of issues. *Journal of Economic Literature, 35*(3), 1320–1346.

Barr, S. (2008, January 24). OMB, GAO to go digital on key reports. *The Washington Post.*

Basheka, B. C. (2009). Public procurement corruption and its implications on effective service delivery in Uganda: An empirical study. *International Journal of Procurement Management, 2*(4), 415–440. doi:10.1504/IJPM.2009.026072

Batchelor, C. (1999, June 17). Logistics aspires to worldly wisdom. *The Financial Times,* p. 17.

Birks, C., Bond, S., & Radford, M. (2001). *Guide to e-procurement in the public sector: Cutting through the hype.* London, UK: Office of Government Commerce.

Bozeman, B., & Dietz, J. S. (2001). Research policy trends in the United States: Civilian technology programs, defense technology, and the development of the national laboratories. In Laredo, P., & Mustar, P. (Eds.), *Research and Innovation Policies in the New Global Economy: An International Comparative Analysis* (pp. 47–78). Northampton, MA: Edward Elgar Publishing, Inc.

Carter, R. Y., & Grimm, R. (2001). Journal of public procurement under the FAU-NIGP partnership. *Journal of Public Procurement, 1*(1), 3–8.

Chang, K. S. (2011). *Enhancing transparency through e-procurement.* The Republic of Korea. Retrieved from www.oecd.org/ dataoecd/47/30/49311011.pdf

Chen, H., Chau, M., & Zeng, D. (2002). CI spider: A tool for competitive intelligence on the web. *Decision Support Systems, 34,* 1–17. doi:10.1016/ S0167-9236(02)00002-7

Cooper, P. (2003). *Governing by contract: Challenges and opportunities for public managers.* Washington, DC: CQ Press.

Corini, J. (2000, March). Integrating e-procurement and strategic souring. *Supply Chain Management Review,* 3-7.

Croom, S., & Brandon-Jones, A. (2007). Impact of e-procurement: Experiences from implementation in the UK public sector. *Journal of Purchasing and Supply Management, 13*(4), 294–303. doi:10.1016/j.pursup.2007.09.015

Dunleavy, P., Margetts, H., Bastow, S., & Tinkler, J. (2006). *Digital era governance: IT corporations, the state, and e-government.* Oxford, UK: Oxford University Press.

Falvey, R., Greenaway, D., & Yu, Z. (2007). Market size and the survival of foreign-owned firms. *The Economic Record, 83,* 23–24. doi:10.1111/j.1475-4932.2007.00407.x

Fisman, R., & Gatti, R. (2002). Decentralization and corruption: Evidence across countries. *Journal of Public Economics, 83*(3), 325–345. doi:10.1016/S0047-2727(00)00158-4

Garvey, G. (1993). *Facing the bureaucracy: Living and dying in a public agency.* San Francisco, CA: Jossey-Bass Publishers.

Grace Commission. (1983). *The president's private sector survey on cost control. A Report to the President.* Washington, DC: Government Printing Office.

Hanna, N. K. (2010). *Transforming government and building the information society: Challenges and opportunities for the developing world.* New York, NY: Springer Verlag.

Hardy, C., & Williams, S. (2008). E-government policy and practice: A theoretical and empirical exploration of public e-procurement. *Government Information Quarterly, 25,* 155–180. doi:10.1016/j.giq.2007.02.003

Heilbrunn, J. R. (2004). *Anti-corruption commissions panacea or real medicine to fight corruption?* Washington, DC: The World Bank.

Henriksen, H., & Mahnke, V. (2005). E-procurement adoption in the Danish public sector: The influence of economic and political rationality. *Scandinavian Journal of Information Systems, 17*(2), 85–106.

Information Technology Management Reform Act. (1996, January 3). *104th congress, 2nd session.* S. 1124. Washington, DC: US Congress.

International Digital Communications. (1993). *Facilities management: The nature of the opportunity.* London, UK: IDC Publishers.

International Monetary Fund. (2010). *Maldives: Public financial management.* Washington, DC: IMF.

Johnson, M. (2002). *GSA awards task to improve information security in federal agencies.* GSA #9936. Retrieved from http://www.gsa.gov/portal/content/100287

Kerwin, C., & Furlong, S. (2011). *Rulemaking: How government agencies write law and make policy* (4th ed.). Washington, DC: CQ Press.

Kettle, D. (2002). *The transformation of governance.* Baltimore, MD: Johns Hopkins University Press.

Kettle, D. (2005). *The global public management revolution* (2nd ed.). Washington, DC: Brookings Institute Press.

Khanapuri, V. B., Nayak, S., Soni, P., Sharma, S., & Soni, M. (2011). *Framework to overcome challenges of implementation of e-procurement in Indian context.* Paper presented to International Conference on Technology and Business Management. Dubai, UAE.

Kurunmaki, L. (1999a). Making an accounting entity: The case of the hospital in Finnish healthcare reforms. *European Accounting Review, 8*(2), 219–237. doi:10.1080/096381899336005

Kurunmaki, L. (1999b). Professional vs. financial capital in the field of health care: Struggles for the redistribution of power and control. *Accounting, Organizations and Society, 24*(2), 95–125. doi:10.1016/S0361-3682(98)00030-0

Lee, M. (2010). An exploratory study on the mature level evaluation of e-procurement systems. *Journal of Public Procurement, 10*(3), 405–427.

Lee, S., Xin, T., & Trimi, S. (2005). Current practices of leading e-government countries. *Communications of the ACM, 48*(10), 99–104. doi:10.1145/1089107.1089112

MacManus, S. A. (2002). Understanding the incremental nature of e-procurement implementation at the state and local levels. *Journal of Public Procurement, 2*(1), 5–28.

Magrini, P. (2006). *Transparency in e-procurement: The Italian perspective.* Paper presented at 1st HIGH Level Seminar on E-Procurement. Naples, Italy. Retrieved from http://www.oecd.org/dataoecd/57/31/36238443.pdf

Mahmood, S. A. I. (2010). Public procurement and corruption in Bangladesh confronting the challenges and opportunities. *Journal of Public Administration and Policy Research, 2*(6), 103–111.

Malone, T., Yate, J., & Benjamin, R. (1987). Electronic markets and electronic hierarchies. *Communications of the ACM, 30*(6), 484–497. doi:10.1145/214762.214766

McHenry, W., & Pryamonosov, D. (2010). Emerging electronic procurement in Russia's regional governments. *Journal of Public Procurement, 10*(2), 211–246.

Moon, B. J. (2004). Consumer adoption of the internet as an information search and product purchase channel: Some research hypotheses. *International Journal of Internet Marketing and Advertising, 1*(1), 104–118. doi:10.1504/IJIMA.2004.003692

Mota, F., & Filho, J. (2011). Public e-procurement and the duality of technology: A comparative study in the context of Brazil and the state of Paraiba. *Journal of Information Systems and Technology Management, 8*(2), 315–330. doi:10.4301/S1807-17752011000200003

Mowery, D. C. (2001). The United States national innovation system after the cold war. In Laredo, P., & Mustar, P. (Eds.), *Research and Innovation Policies in the New Global Economy: An International Comparative Analysis* (pp. 15–46). Northampton, MA: Edward Elgar Publishing, Inc.

Nairn. (2000, November 1). Ripples from a quiet revolution bring net gains for manufacturing sector. *The Financial Times IT Survey*, p. 1.

National Performance Review. (1993). *From red tape to results: Creating a government that works better and costs less.* Washington, DC: United States Government Printing Office.

Ndou, V. (2004). E-government for developing countries: Opportunities and challenges. *The Electronic Journal of Information Systems in Developing Countries, 18*(1), 1–24.

Neef, D. (2001). *E-procurement: from strategy to implementation.* Upper Saddle River, NJ: Prentice Hall.

Neupane, A., Soar, J., & Yong, J. (2012). *Role of public e-procurement technology to reduce corruption in government procurement.* Paper presented at the 5th International Public Procurement Conference. Seattle, WA.

Office of Government Commerce. (2002). *A guide to e-procurement for the public sector.* London, UK: Office of Government Commerce. Retrieved from http://www.ogc.gov.uk

Organization for Economic Co-Operation and Development. (2004). *Information technology outlook.* Paris, France: Organization for Economic Co-Operation and Development.

Organization for economic co-operation and development. (2011). *Government at a glance 2011 country note: Finland.* Retrieved from http://www.oecd.org/dataoecd/60/25/47876433.pdf

Panda, P., Sahu, G., & Gupta, P. (2010). *Promoting transparency and efficiency in public procurement: E-procurement initiatives by government of India.* Paper presented at the 7th International Conference on E-procurement (ICEG). Banglore, India.

Pathak, R. D., Naz, R., Rahman, M. H., Smith, R. F. I., & Agarwal, K. N. (2009). E-governance to cut corruption in public service delivery: A case study of Fiji. *International Journal of Public Administration, 32*(5), 415–437. doi:10.1080/01900690902799482

Patton, K., & McKenna, T. (2005). Scanning for competitive intelligence. *Competitive Intelligence, 8*(2), 24–29.

Peachment, A. (1992). *The executive state: WA Inc and the constitution.* Perth, Australia: Constitutional Press.

Peters, B. G. (1996). *The future of governing: Four emerging models.* Lawrence, KS: University of Kansas Press.

Pooler, V., Pooler, D., & Farney, S. (2004). *Global purchasing and supply management: Fulfill the vision* (2nd ed.). Boston, MA: Kluwer Academic Publishers.

Quah, J. S. (1999). *Combating corruption in Mongolia: Problems and prospects.* Singapore, Singapore: National University of Singapore.

Quinn, J. (1992). *Intelligent enterprise.* New York, NY: Free Press.

Rose, N. (1999). *Powers of freedom: Reframing political thought.* Cambridge, UK: Cambridge University Press. doi:10.1017/CBO9780511488856

Sauter, V. (2005). Competitive intelligence systems: Qualitative DDS for strategic decision-making. *Business Information Review, 23*(1), 35–42.

Schapper, P. R., & Veiga Malta, J. (2004). Como hacer para que el estado compre mejor. *Gobierno Digital, 3,* 16–29.

Schapper, P. R., Veiga Malta, J., & Gilbert, D. (2006). An analytical framework for the management and reform of public procurement. *Journal of Public Procurement, 6*(1), 1–26.

Simon, H. (1973). Applying information technology to organizational design. *Public Administration Review, 33,* 268–278. doi:10.2307/974804

Simon. (1965). *The shape of automation for men and management.* New York, NY: Harper & Row.

Sun, S., Zhao, J., & Wang, H. (2012). An agent based approach for exception handling in e-procurement management. *Expert Systems with Applications, 39*(1), 1174–1182. doi:10.1016/j.eswa.2011.07.121

Talero, E. (2001). *Electronic government procurement, concepts and country experiences.* Washington, DC: The World Bank.

Thai, K. V. (2001). Public procurement re-examined. *Journal of Public Procurement, 1*(1), 9–50.

United Nations. (2010). *E-government survey 2010: Leveraging e-government at a time of financial and economic crisis.* New York, NY: United Nations.

United States Government Accountability Office. (2005). Competitive sourcing: Greater emphasis needed on increasing efficiency and improving performance. *Journal of Public Procurement, 5*(3), 401–441.

Vaidya, K., Sajeev, A. S., & Callender, G. (2006). Critical factors that influence e-procurement implementation success in the public sector. *Journal of Public Procurement, 6*(1), 70–99.

Varney, M. (2011). E-procurement- Current law and future challenges. *ERA-Forum, 12*(2), 185-204.

Vernon, M. (1999, March 24). Livelier image for a low-profile task. *The Financial Times*, p. 16.

Xu, M. (2007). *Managing strategic intelligence: Techniques and technologies.* Hershey, PA: IGI Global. doi:10.4018/978-1-59904-243-5

Zhang, H., & Yang, J. (2011). *Research on application of e-tender in China.* Paper presented to International Conference on Internet Technology and Applications (iTAP). New York, NY.

ADDITIONAL READING

Boyd, B., & Fulk, J. (1996). Executive scanning and perceived uncertainty: A multidimensional model. *Journal of Management, 22*(1), 1–21. doi:10.1177/014920639602200101

Buchanan, J. (1968). *The demand and supply of public goods.* Chicago, IL: Rand McNally.

Caiden, N., & Wildavsky, A. (1980). *Planning and budgeting in poor countries.* New Brunswick, NJ: Transaction Publishers.

Carter, N., Klein, R., & Day, P. (1995). *How organizations measure success.* London, UK: Routledge.

Chan, H., Lee, R., Dillon, T., & Chang, E. (2001). *E-commerce: Fundamentals and applications.* New York, NY: John Wiley & Sons.

Croom, S., & Brandon-Jones, A. (2009). Key issues in e-procurement: Procurement implementation and operation in the public sector. In Thai, K. (Ed.), *International Handbook of Public Procurement.* Boca Raton, FL: Taylor & Francis Group.

Donahue, J. (1991). *The privatization decision: Public ends, private means.* New York, NY: Basic Books.

Dooley, K., & Purchase, S. (2009). Factors influencing e-procurement usage. In Thai, K. (Ed.), *International Handbook of Public Procurement.* Boca Raton, FL: Taylor & Francis Group.

Gatsi, J., & Acquah, I. (2011). *Introduction to public procurement management in Ghana.* Saarbrucken, Germany: Lambert Academic Publishing.

Guba, E., & Lincoln, Y. (1981). *Effective evaluation.* San Francisco, CA: Jossey-Bass.

Hall, P. (2010). Historical institutionalism in rationalist and sociological perspective. In Mahoney, J., & Thelen, K. (Eds.), *Explaining Institutional Change: Ambiguity, Agency, and Power.* Cambridge, UK: Cambridge University Press. doi:10.1017/CBO9780511806414.009

Heady, F. (2001). *Public administration: A comparative perspective* (6th ed.). Boca Raton, FL: Taylor & Francis Group.

Heald, D., & Georgiou, G. (2000). Consolidation principles and practices for the UK government sector. *Accounting and Business Research, 30*(2).

Henley, D., Liekerman, A., Perrin, J., Evans, M., Lapsey, I., & Witheoak, J. (1983). *Public accounting and financial control.* London, UK: Chapman and Hall.

Hood, C. (1991). A public management for all seasons? *Public Administration, 69*(1). doi:10.1111/j.1467-9299.1991.tb00779.x

Jadoun, G. (1998). Public procurement training in Central and Eastern Europe. *Public Management Forum, 4*(2).

Kelman, S. (1990). *Procurement and public management: The fear of discretion and the quality of government performance.* Lanham, MD: University Press of America.

Mahoney, J., & Thelen, K. (2010). A theory of gradual institutional change. In Mahoney, J., & Thelen, K. (Eds.), *Explaining Institutional Change: Ambiguity, Agency, and Power.* Cambridge, UK: Cambridge University Press.

Nitse, P., Parker, K., & Dishman, P. (2003). Multiclass interest profile: Applications in the intelligence process. *Marketing Intelligence & Planning, 21*(5), 263–271. doi:10.1108/02634500310490210

North, D. (1990). *Institutions, institutional change, and economic performance.* Cambridge, UK: Cambridge University Press. doi:10.1017/CBO9780511808678

Prud'homme, R. (1995, August). On the dangers of decentralization. *World Bank Research Observer.* Washington, DC: World Bank.

Roldan, J., & Leal, A. (2003). Executive information systems in Spain: A study of current practices and comparative analysis. In Forgionne, G., Gupta, J., & Mora, M. (Eds.), *Decision Making Support Systems: Achievements and Challenges for the New Decade* (pp. 287–304). Hershey, PA: IGI Global. doi:10.4018/978-1-59140-045-5.ch018

Sang, H. (1988). *Project evaluation: Techniques and practices for developing countries.* New York, NY: Wilson Press.

Sherman, S. (1999). *Government procurement management.* Germantown, MD: Wordcrafters Publications.

Skocpol, T. (1994). *Social revolutions in the modern world.* Cambridge, UK: Cambridge University Press. doi:10.1017/CBO9781139173834

Stillman, R. (1999). *Preface to public administration: A search for themes and direction* (2nd ed.). Burke, VA: Chatelaine Press.

Thelen, K. (2004). *How institutions evolve: The political economy of skills in Germany, Britain, the United States, and Japan.* Cambridge, UK: Cambridge University Press. doi:10.1017/CBO9780511790997

Vaidya, K., Callender, G., & Sajeev, A. (2009). Facilitators of public e-procurement: Lessons learned from the U.K., U.S., and Australian initiatives. In Thai, K. (Ed.), *International Handbook of Public Procurement.* Boca Raton, FL: Taylor & Francis Group.

Waldo, D. (1980). *The enterprise of public administration.* Novato, CA: Chandler & Sharp Publishers.

Weidenbaum, M. (1969). *The modern public sector: New ways of doing the government's business.* New York, NY: Basic Books, Inc.

KEY TERMS AND DEFINITIONS

Economic Rationality: The exercise of reason as it relates to cost-savings and other financial metrics associated with efficiency of operations and systems.

E-Government: The political direction and control exercised over the members of business, state, and society using electronic interfaces and components to direct public affairs.

Integration: The act of bringing into harmony the behaviors of participants and outcomes of various functions related to the shared goals of organizations.

Reflexive: A characteristic of e-procurement and management systems in which the circular relationships regarding technology and human participants creates an environment where the potential for advancement is continual.

Synthesis: The seamless combination of diverse elements into a single or unified entity that is capable of operational excellence.

Transaction Costs: Fees, penalties, debits, or other disadvantages, which are associated with the exchange of goods and services.

Transparency: A level of visibility that is apparent to all participants so that core issues or concerns may be reasonably addressed without excessive investigation.

Chapter 6
The Rationale behind Implementation of New Electronic Tools for Electronic Public Procurement

Nataša Pomazalová
University of Defense, Czech Republic

Stanislav Rejman
AURA, s.r.o., Czech Republic

ABSTRACT

This chapter focuses on the effective implementation of new electronic tools for Public e-Procurement in public sector organizations. While an analysis of the characteristics of transformation processes necessary for the development of e-Government and the choice between Public e-Procurement tools is theoretically already well developed, there are still a number of ambiguities in the approaches of rationalization implementation of these. A deeper understanding of the decision-making phenomenon in general is provided. Flexibly adjusting the e-Government strategy on dynamics of the development of Public e-Procurement tool ex ante or leading in an effort to change the organizational structures, information flows, and constraints in which public sector organizations operate in the area of Public e-Procurement. Public e-Procurement tools are selected for the analysis, because interesting progress is expected here. Results from the nature of the dynamic transformation processes and decision-making show the need to support changes in the environment arising from the development of e-Government.

DOI: 10.4018/978-1-4666-2665-2.ch006

INTRODUCTION

The emerging importance of electronic public procurement in the public sector points to the advantages of the Internet, to an increase in efficiency, and is currently one of the crucial and debatable topics. The progressive development of new technologies and technological innovation opens up the new possibilities of electronic tools. However, it requires the transformation of the public sector, including changes in governance and management. Transformational changes in the public sector have already ceased to be understood and are still often perceived as conservative, but there is a shift towards a view of the public sector as authoritative, passive, and governmental. E-Government performance is left to the more proactive approach, where the public sector organizations could change their organizational structures and interest in the organizational and institutional constraints within which they operate. This is necessary in order to create the conditions for implementation of e-Government. The current acceleration of the e-Government in order to interconnect the public sector, citizens, and companies increases the importance of linking subjects across economic and social structures or processes. E-Government is an instrument for transforming the public sector as well as public procurement. E-Government supports the public e-procurement activities based on the law, flexibility, coordination, transparency, values, and needs of the public sector organizations, as well as private companies (Murray, 2009; Janssen & van Veenstra, 2005; Layne & Lee, 2001).

Being users of new knowledge, new methods and procedures leading to development of existing and innovative activities, the public sector organizations must make use of new technologies, which is also the case of the e-Government (Grönlund & Horan, 2004; Andersen & Henriksen, 2006). If e-Government is not implemented, then it is more difficult to gain the requisite spread over the information because any view of public sector organizational operations needs to be used with relation to many different data, information and knowledge and opportunities given by new information and communication technologies. Kolsaker (2006) stated developing e-Government to the information age and knowledge society. Lots of activities, including the public procurement, are performed in virtual environment of electronic business. The public sector cannot afford to fall behind essentially self-profiling economic and social trends mainly focusing on effective allocation of all social resources. Eyob (2004) discussed the complexity of investments in the public sector and highlighted evaluation of investments as a barrier of e-Government and transformational government development.

The theoretical portion of this chapter was intended to offer theoretical measures in relation to the empirical phenomenon in terms of contemporary attitudes towards e-Government. The intent was to choose some electronic public procurement tools that could result in loss prevention and that would further develop the electronic public procurement.

TRANSFORMATION PROCESSES AND E-GOVERNMENT IMPLEMENTATION

Transformation processes that are ongoing within the society are also reflected by the public administration. The public administration restructures and downsizes the number of personnel and equipment in the context of transformational processes (Bonham, Seifert, & Thorson, 2001; West, 2001, 2004; Scholl, 2005, 2006; Torres, Pina, & Royo, 2005). This restructuring and the efforts to reduce costs created space for efficient introduction of electronic tools into the sphere of public administration ably supported by legislation (Gil-Garcia & Martinez-Moyano,

2007). The principal reasons for introduction of e-Government could be (Danziger & Andersen, 2002; Gottschalk, 2009):

- **Political Reasons:** More effective cooperation of the public and private sectors.
- **Reasons within the Public Administration Itself:** After implementation of the electronic administration it will be possible, based on the increased labor productivity, to reduce numbers of public sector employees in a socially sensitive way.
- **Social Reasons:** Potential exploitation of knowledge and experience of experts working within the private sector.
- **Economic Reasons:** Envisaged long-term cost savings, quality improvements in any given area, better services and more flexibility when providing them, stimulation of electronic tools development by the private sector.

The transformational government concept has emerged from the fields of process-related challenges (Weerakkody & Dhillon, 2008; Dhillon, Weerakkody, & Dwivedy, 2008; Klievink & Janssen, 2009; Weerakkody, Janssen, & Dwivedi, 2011) as a response to the need for better understanding of closely related processes in governmental organizations and private companies. Moreover, transforming public sector organization is shaped through culture (Siau & Iong, 2005; Dhillon, Weerakkody, & Dwivedy, 2008; Weerakkody, Janssen, & Dwivedi, 2011). Culture shall be seen in managerial and social dimensions of radical change. Homburg (2009) and Weerakkody, Janssen, and Dwivedi (2011) emphasised the role of culture conditions, analysis of organizational structures and processes and importance of public authorities needed for transformational government. In analogy, they support this approach based on Business Process Reengineering (Hammer & Champy, 1993; Weerakkody & Dhillon, 2008; Weerakkody, Janssen, & Dwivedi, 2011), having

a direct influence upon challenges of core and support processes. Therefore, they refer to the manifestation of synchronization of processes, relatively homogenous implementation technologies, integration of information systems and decision-making. The decision-making process related to the implementation of e-Government and electronic public procurement must be system-based. To support a systematic incorporation of e-Government and electronic public procurement decision-making processes into the public administration, there must be basic tools enabling us to effect intensity, type, purpose and direction of financial and material flows within the public administration. Decision-making in the public sector is based more on political reasons than economics (Bannister, 2001; Heeks & Bailur, 2007; Heintze & Bretschneider, 2000).

According to Siau and Iong (2005) and de Brí (2009), the key issue for social, organizational, and technological challenges of public organizations is jumping from one stage to the next. These stages are:

- Web presence and e-enabling customer-facing services.
- Interaction.
- Transaction based on technologies to automate processes.
- Transformation as cultural, transformational change in public sector organizations.
- E-Democracy as political.

A new arena of possibilities, transformation processes, and e-Democracy are crucial for reorganization, improvement, undertaking, and delivery of governmental services in electronic form. Building on fundamental change of public administration processes, e-Government is implemented for achieving responsible interaction with governmental organizations, citizens or among companies within, on a Web portal consisting of personalized entrance and based on relevant public databases (Carter & Bélanger, 2005; Ho,

2002; Lee, 2010; Moon, 2002). However, current success rates of knowledge and profound experiences are emphasized for transformational government (t-Government) for digitalization of services (Irani, Love, & Montazemi, 2007; Janssen & Shu, 2008). As discussed by Weerakkody and Dhillon (2008) and Goldfinch, Gauld, and Herbison (2009), in many respects this is understandable, t-Government gained from a single point of contact and focuses on the uses of the modern work processes in making public sector organizations aware that many of their decisions have been grounded in control through rules finding out about. From the public sector standpoint, the process of profiling for e-Government could be limited. Van Veenstra, Klievink, and Janssen (2011) introduced impediments blocking governments from reaching transformational government and engaged a conceptual overview of selected and fundamental twenty-three impediments. Those findings are subsequently summarized and accomplished by additional most discussed and implemented typology as governance, organizational and managerial approach and technological.

LEGAL FRAMEWORK OF PUBLIC CONTRACT DIGITIZATION AND CURRENT EUROPEAN TRENDS IN ELECTRONIC PUBLIC PROCUREMENT

Legislation covering the electronic award of public contracts is comprised in the European Commission awarding directives. All provisions of the awarding directives related to the digitization of public contract award procedure have been taken over by the national legislation in the form of the Public Contracts Act. Legally, the electronic award of public contracts is equally legitimate as the "conventional" procedure based on paper documents.

European Union Legislation

Legislation covering the electronic award of public contracts is based on Commission Directive 2005/51/EC, Directive 2004/18/EC of the European Parliament and of the Council on the Coordination of Procedures for the Award of Public Works Contracts, Public Supply Contracts and Public Service Contracts, and Directive 2004/17/EC Coordinating the Procurement Procedures of Entities Operating in the Water, Energy, Transport, and Postal Services Sectors. These Directives form a complex framework for the electronic awarding of contracts in an open, transparent, and undiscriminating way, they define rules of electronic bidding, and terms and conditions of modern procurement methods based on electronic communication devices (Commission Implementing Regulation, 2011).

Coordination of procedures for the award of certain works contracts, supply contracts, and service contracts by contracting authorities or entities in the fields of defense and security is dealt with by the Directive 2009/81/EC of the European Parliament and of the Council of 13 July 2009. It is applicable to public contracts on:

- The supply of military equipment, including any parts, components, and/or subassemblies thereof.
- The supply of sensitive equipment, including any parts, components, and/or subassemblies thereof.
- Works, supplies and services directly related to the equipment referred to in points (a) and (b) for any and all elements of its life cycle.
- Works and services for specifically military purposes or sensitive works and sensitive services.

To implement a new legal framework of electronic public procurement, the European

Commission issued communication from the Commission to the Council, the European Parliament, the Economic and Social Committee and the Committee of the Regions No. SEC (2004) 1639 "Action Plan for the Implementation of the Legal Framework for Electronic Public Procurement" which implies a requirement to draw up national plans for the introduction of electronic public procurement by member states.

Current trends in European e-Government show increased interest in development of the electronic public procurement platform of the public administration at all management levels (Arlbjørn & Freytag, 2012). At the strategic level, the electronic public procurement issue is developing in the context of decision-making process focusing on access to the electronic public procurement and defining organizational strategy internally and externally. In addition, the lower management level is subject to vast theoretical and practical interest when searching for answers related to the electronic public procurement development and personnel capabilities advancement. The cause of this theoretical and practical interest is a mix of economic, social, and other reasons related, inter alia, to the activation of dormant potential of the organization.

In the European Union (EU) Action Plan, the European Commission is eager to modernize European public procurement markets, to make them more open, and to consolidate competitive environment. To this purpose, it proposes measures concentrated in the following areas:

- The functional internal EU market in electronic public procurement.
- Better efficiency in electronic public procurement and better public administration.
- International framework of electronic public procurement.

The European Commission believes that the substantial employment of electronic public procurement shall bring about following advantages:

- Better access to public contracts and increased transparency. The electronic public procurement improves access of potential suppliers to public contracts. The search for opportunities in the Internet is much quicker and cheaper than checking of paper documents. The electronic public procurement systems may be adjusted just to notify the suppliers of specific opportunities and to provide them with instant access to the project documentation. Also, the transparency is increased since the public procurement procedures are properly documented. This enables better monitoring of public contracts.

- Administrative cost reduction in relation to individual activities performed during the whole life cycle of the public contract. The electronic public procurement offers also opportunities to streamline the whole award process of public contracts.

- Potential to integrate public procurement markets within the EU. The electronic public procurement has the potential to mitigate obstacles caused by long distances and differences among national public procurement markets. It extends the pool of possible suppliers and it makes the markets grow. Despite not being able to change the role of distances or accessibility when performing the business itself and, thus, executing the public contract, it is a way to deal with the cost of participation in the public procurement process.

On 18 October 2010, the European Commission issued a strategic document, "Green Paper on Expanding the Use of e-Procurement in the EU" (European Commission, 2010b, 2010c). This document thoroughly examines the existing EU framework in relation to public contracts and it is offering a whole range of methods on how to face problems impeding successful transition to the electronic public procurement.

To be specific, some of these problems are passivity and concerns of contracting entities and suppliers, absence of standards for electronic public procurement processes, or non-existence of instruments enabling mutual recognition of domestic electronic solutions (Angelopoulos, Kitsios, Kofakis, & Papadopoulos, 2010; Chen & Dhillon, 2003). In addition to other things, the Green Paper defines following priorities for activities at the EU level:

- Positive and negative motivation of contracting entities and suppliers focusing on the timely introduction of electronic public procurement.
- Easier cross-border participation in the electronic public procurement.
- Support to standardization of crucial e-Procurement processes and supporting systems.
- Promotion of and support to dissemination of successful the Pan-European Public e-Procurement On-Line Project (PEPPOL) solutions at the market (Pan-European Public e-Procurement On-Line Project, 2011).
- International development and cooperation.

COMMON PATTERNS OF E-PUBLIC PROCUREMENT

Pan-European Public E-Procurement On-Line

European Commission initiative targeting the communication barriers in the e-Procurement is represented by the PEPPOL. The project shall increase interoperability in the e-Procurement within Europe and it has been also joined by the European administrators and/or providers of electronic tools (Pan-European Public e-Procurement On-Line Project, 2011). The project has been divided into eight areas – Working Parties (WP):

WP1: E-Signature
WP2: Virtual Company Dossier
WP3: E-Catalog
WP4: E-Ordering
WP5: E-Invoicing
WP6: Project management
WP7: Dissemination, awareness and consensus building
WP8: Solutions architecture, design and validation

Of all the above parties, we are interested mainly in WP3, the e-Catalog. Its objective is to produce solutions that will enable the suppliers to enter product–related data into electronic catalogs in the European e-Marketplaces (testing is going on solely at the markets run by association members). In terms of the performed standardization, the following outputs are of interest:

- The standard interface between individual European e-Marketplaces is European Committee for Standardization Business Interoperability Interfaces on public procurement in Europe' (CENBII) Phase 2 (WS/BII 2) (CEN, 2011).
- To test the established interface within a pilot operation, the following commodities have been selected.
- ICT – computers and printers (no reservations).
- Office and school furniture (no reservations).
- Medical material, devices, and medicaments (with reservations especially because of national standards and certificates).

The selection of the above categories has been done mainly on the basis of following criteria:

- Extension and quality of the applied classification determined by parameterization of commodity properties necessary for their characterization.
- Existence of registers describing parameters of purchased commodity.
- Cross-border potential.
- Traded volume at individual European e-Marketplaces.
- Existence of complex national laws pertaining to the selected commodity.

Effective Electronic Cross-Border Public Services to Public Administrations, Businesses, and Citizens

Interoperable Delivery of European e-Government Services to public Administrations, Businesses, and Citizens (IDABC) was a European Commission program aiming at widespread use of information and communication technologies to support cross-border delivery of public services to citizens and businesses in Europe to improve efficiency and cooperation between European public administration systems. The program outputs are especially:

- A feasibility study.
- Requirement analysis in terms of public procurement e-Invoicing.
- Static and dynamic simulators of the award procedure course (European Commission, 2009).

The IDABC Program is followed by the Interoperability Solutions for European Public Administrations Program (ISA) in 2010 – 2015. The ISA Program operates within a larger framework of EU-level policies and strategies on e-Government. It provides the European public administrations with a comprehensive approach to the establishment of electronic services that can easily co-operate across borders (European Commission, 2010 a).

European Committee for Standardization

European Committee for Standardization (CEN) is responsible for production and operation of EU standards for all economic areas except for electrical engineering and telecommunication. These standards are always produced in coordination with international ISO standards (CEN) (European Committee for Standardization, 2011).

The Business Interoperability Interfaces for Public Procurement in Europe Project has been run by the CEN since 2005 in connection with the EU Action Plan (European Commission, 2011a, 2011b). The objective of the project is an e-Marketplace standard used in public procurement.

The 1st phase of the project was concluded at the beginning of 2010. Besides the e-Marketplace standard, a data model has been defined characterizing also the part related to the description of purchased goods or services. To specify the purchased item, the United Nations Standard Products and Services Code (UNSPSC) Classification is recommended here. United Nations Standard Products and Services Code, classification system for goods and services created in 1998 and sponsored by the United Nations. The UNSPSC has 5 hierarchy levels and the classification code is formed by 8 digits. This classification system does not contain property definitions of individual classes (commodities) (United Nations, 2001).

Nonetheless, the author of the output also mentions the obligation to apply the Common Procurement Vocabulary (CPV) when performing public procurement in the "EU mode." CPV is a classification system for public contracts aiming at standardization of commodity names applied by contracting public authorities and contracting entities to describe public procurement subject matter. The CPV Classification is administered by the European Commission and it is published at the SIMAP Web portal (European Commission, 2008b; SIMAP, 2010, 2011).

However, it is necessary to highlight that the CPV and UNSPSC are classification systems that do not possess any other tools suitable for description of goods and services. The EU is aiming at:

- Functional internal EU market for electronic public procurement.
- Higher efficiency of public procurement and better functioning of public administration.
- International framework in electronic public procurement.
- Reduction of administrative costs of individual activities performed within the life cycle of a public contract.
- Better access to public contracts.
- Increased transparency of public procurement processes resulting in less opportunities for corruption.
- Standardization of procedures, regulations, and technical requirements for electronic tools of electronic public procurement.

This initiative also affects the electronic catalogs. These are today the foundation of the EU electronic marketplaces, but they are mostly built on individual needs and capabilities of either manufacturer or technological environment of business groupings and the electronic marketplace itself. The unifying property across all these solutions is the most extensive possible use of the eXtended Markup Language as a universal descriptive and depictive language. The catalogs enable search for, filtering and comparing of purchased commodities. Commodities, or goods and services, are described by standardized fields in the catalog and these are divided into attributes common for all types of commodities (commercial information) and attributes specific for individual types of commodities (technical specifications).

When publicly procuring within the EU, there is a duty to use the CPV. Besides the CPV, the EU documents mention also the UNSPSC Classification.

Standardization, Codification, and Classification in E-Government

Standardization is one of the concepts directly linked to the data quality. The aim of standardization (sometimes the word "normalization" is used as a synonym) is to define standards, meaning a common, uniform, and documented set of information so that it is possible to harmonize activities performed within any given area, based on that set. The result of such a standardized activity is a product (article, goods, service, data in Information System [IS], etc.) with predefined parameters. Normally, standardization is domain of specialized national or international organizations. Typical examples of standardization are the ISO Standards. Frequently, syndicates of manufacturers create their own standards and norms, just like public administration authorities.

Codification usually represents a system of uniformly arranged list of items (typically a catalog of goods, books, etc.). Sometimes the word codification is replaced by cataloging. The codification process is composed of two parts: classification and identification.

Classification is certain sorting out or assessment of an item in terms of its nature. In fact, it is a process of placing the item into a certain category. These categories (classes) associating items of similar kind are being assembled into tree structure lists known as Classification Systems. The purpose of each Classification System is to simplify the search for required items in the catalog and to support analyses of other operational or transactional data linked to the items in the catalog.

The practical codification usually employs internationally acknowledged classification systems UNSPSC, CPV, Statistical Classification of

Products by Activity (CPA) (European Commission, 2008a) or systems that proved useful within a specialized group of users or at a territory (like the NATO Codification System or German system eCl@ss) (NATO, 2003; eCl@ss, 2011).

E-Government and Open Technical Dictionaries

In case of public procurement, the e-Government is struggling to streamline the process of planning, preparation, and execution of electronic award procedures for purchase of goods and services. To digitize public procurement, it is desirable to make use of an open technical dictionary (Smith, 2009; Benson, 2010).

The Open Technical Dictionary (OTD) generated based on the ISO 22745 Standard is basically a data terminology dictionary containing concepts necessary to describe items registered and processed by the information systems.

The basic object in OTD defining each dictionary term is a so-called concept. The concept is granted a unique identifier that can be used to describe individuals, organizations, locations, goods, and services in codes.

The basic dictionary concept records are linked to concept names (terminology), detailed definitions of these concepts and graphical objects by the means of link relations. Terminology and definitions are provided with the language attribute so that the whole OTD can be appended with translations into any national language. Because of the fact that the exchange of OTD formatted data employs numeric concept identifiers for transfer, the OTD system is independent in terms of language.

Codification Using Open Technical Dictionaries

Technically speaking, the OTD supported codification does not differ from other codification systems using descriptive identification of codified items. Catalog items are described in pairs of property—value of the property. Individual properties (typical parameters of the item) are assembled in so-called Identification Guides (IGs) that represent some sort of template helping the user fill in required values of individual properties. Besides the property definition, the IG contains also rules applying to filling in of individual values, restrictive conditions for numeric values, lists of permitted units of measure, etc. This means that the practical application of OTD in codification is crucially affected by the accessibility to high-quality IGs.

The essential advantage of OTD supported codification is its total universality in terms of the type of codified (described) item. This shows that OTD can be potentially employed in all areas and activities supported by information systems.

The OTD can be used to codify individuals, organizations, locations, materials, goods, services, contracts, license rights, etc. This "subject matter" universality is complemented by language and, most importantly, communication universalities.

Another important advantage of data processed under OTD support is their portability between different information systems meaning between various software applications. Especially data of codified items—Master Data Items (MD Items), IG definitions, and requests for MD Items delivery (so called queries)—can be transferred. All 3 types of records standardized with OTD support are stored in text files in the eXtended Markup Language (XML) format. Portability of user data is becoming more and more important since requirements for cooperation among different Information Systems (ISs) are increasing and they are supported by the transfer of operational infrastructure of these ISs into the so-called cloud.

The cloud solution offers technical implementation of Software as a Service (SaaS) type service. When implementing the IS this way, the user works with a SW application via a Web browser and a computer connected to the Internet. Any other hardware and software infrastructure (hardware servers, their system SW, database SW) including the software application itself are located with the provider. The essential advantage of this cloud solution is how easy it can be put into operation by the user; minimum IS operational cost, easy performance scalability, and license model flexibility. The basic disadvantage of the cloud is its excessive novelty compared to the existing way of operating company applications in terms of infrastructure ownership, application, and user data. The situation when the whole IS and user data in particular are not stored and processed within a local (company) local area network and, moreover, they are administered by "other" service provider, is still an obstacle for the majority of Czech companies to decide in favor of such IS solution. In this area, it can expect positive influence of OTD compatible data formats, because the user of codification IS complying with OTD standards has his/her own data (master data to be more precise) at his/her immediate disposal in an easily readable standardized XML format and he/she does not have to be a bit concerned who is their owner.

Open Technical Dictionaries and ISO Standards

An important component in preparing the OTD system for its widespread application in the practical life was formulation of norms standardizing this system at the international level. These standards are ISO 22745 and ISO 8000. In both cases, the authors divided the standards in many parts in accordance with individual topics so that these are in fact, quite vast sets of standards.

The ISO 22745 Standard Set defines data model of open technical dictionaries and it specifies data structures (patterns) for XML files used to exchange data among OTD users. The ISO 8000 Standard Set is a methodical extension to the previous standard and it describes processes, rules, and methods for acquisition, maintenance, and exchange of high-quality data.

Electronic Commerce Code Management Association Open Technical Dictionary

After initial trials, taking place mainly within syndicate associations, to standardize description of catalog items universally applicable to any type of item (including non-material items such as services), the Electronic Commerce Code Management Association (ECCMA) has been established in 1999. This international association located in Pennsylvania, USA, wished to create a new codification system that would be acknowledged internationally, that would be universal in terms of codified items, and that would support measurable data quality. In the area of international standardization, this objective was met in 2010 by official publication of the ISO 22745 Standard specifying so-called open technical dictionaries and the ISO 8000 Standard defining procedures of master data processing and their quality. Alongside with the work on the above standards, the ECCMA was engaged in production of a technical dictionary structure and contents of which are in line with the above standards (Arnett, 2011; Radack, 2009).

ECCMA Open Technical Dictionary, sometimes also electronic Open Technical Dictionary (eOTD), data technical dictionary formed in compliance with the ISO 22745 Standards and enabling codification of items of any type. This dictionary has been published at ECCMA websites under the designation of eOTD. Individual properties defined in eOTD form sets of properties typical for item classes. These sets of typical properties, so-called Identification Guides, are the basis for description of items of any class. By using standardized data patterns, the IGs may be encoded (these are XML-Extensible Markup Language type text files) into such a form that is independent from the application software and that is easily portable between different information systems.

Customer-supplier communication is based on standardized queries and responses in the form of XML file imports and exports. Customer sends a query (eOTD-q-xml) for data provision plus a reference to an IG (eOTD-i-xml) which shall be the basis for product description. Supplier describes the product in compliance with the IG and sends the response (eOTD-r-xml) to the customer. The advantages of eOTD introduction are:

- Less labor intensity when searching for the items.
- Streamlined stock of standard items.
- Efficient stock share within the organization.
- Easy detection of replacement for missing or no longer supplied items.
- Codification of items is possible directly at the data source.

The eOTD does not contain any classification system; it is independent of classification systems. The eOTD can be attached to any classification system and, therefore, it can describe any goods and service by applying properties. The eOTD can be used for all commodity groups (segments) of the market.

E-GOVERNMENT, PUBLIC E-PROCUREMENT TOOLS, AND EFFICIENCY

Griffin and Halpin (2005) identified subsequent aspects evaluation of e-Government. The assumptions are related namely to perform:

- E-Government stages of growth.
- Electronic service delivery via the Internet.
- Involvement of stakeholders.
- Costs and benefits of e-Government.

In case of public administration, the efficiency assessment principles common in the market environment of the private sector cannot be fully applied (Schwester, 2009). The basic role is played here by political decisions in form of legislative measures like Acts.

In the public sector, the general tendency is inefficiency. To assess the efficiency of the public sector, there is a social result (benefit) which does not need to be quantifiable. The inputs can be quantified without substantial problems, but quantification of output, however, is more difficult. When representing efficiency of inputs and outputs in economic categories, we are talking about the so-called economic efficiency of the system, which assesses transformation of cost into result—benefit. In the following text, the general term "system" is replaced by the term "public administration entity." When assessing economic efficiency, it is necessary to clearly specify the assessed object—public administration entity.

At the general level, the resulting benefit can be expressed by Equation 1:

$$U = \sum_i U_i\left(+\right) - \sum_j U_j\left(-\right) - \sum_k Z_{Ek} \qquad (1)$$

knowing that:

- $U_i(+)$ is i^{th} component positive (desired) benefit (effect).
- $U_j(-)$ is j^{th} component negative (undesired) benefit (non-effect).
- Z_{Ek} is k^{th} component loss (parasitic) of the benefit.

The relation for total cost can be also expressed in an additive Equation 2:

$$C = \sum_i C_{ui} + \sum_j C_{zj} + \sum_k Z_{zk} \qquad (2)$$

knowing that

- C_{ui} is i^{th} component cost (resource) spent purposefully, increasing some $U_i(+)$.

- C_{zj} is j^{th} component cost (resource) spent un-purposefully, not increasing any $U_i(+)$.
- Z_{zk} is k^{th} component loss (useless, parasitic) of resources that will not enter the processes of benefit creation, but that is expended.

The problem of public administration economy is expressing the cost. To be able to express the cost, it is necessary that the organizations of this domain use accounting systems allowing differentiation of cost based not just on their type but also purpose and location of consumption.

When assessing efficiency of investment activities within the public sector, the time factor will be of essence for assessing the benefit. It is typical for technological units that operate in different modes. Therefore, it is necessary to employ time relations when expressing benefit and cost.

In case of e-Government and its tool, electronic public procurement, we are talking about purchase of required goods and services by a public administration authority representing a contracting entity. The following deliberations and subsequent proposals will reduce the time dimension of efficiency assessment to two statuses:

- Initial status at time t_0, when the public administration authority is functioning without a fully implemented e-Government. The initial status is described by the benefit of U_0 and the cost of C_0.
- Status at time t_1 after introduction of the e-Government. The public sector organisation making use of a fully implemented e-Government is achieving benefit of U_1 with total cost of C_1.

To assess economic efficiency, it is possible to employ indicator showing change of economic efficiency of a public administration organisation after implementation of the e-Government:

$$\Delta E = E_1 - E_0 \tag{3}$$

If $\Delta E > 0$, one can note that the implementation of the e-Government met the anticipated benefit. The economic efficiency is normally a quantity with a specific dimension because the benefit often cannot be expressed in monetary units. The selected solution of economic efficiency assessment of the e-Government is a procedure that is included into the framework of cost-benefit analysis methods.

Problems related to the benefit specification can be partially bypassed by introduction of a standard clearly defining specific e-Government outputs U_s. The issue of maximisation of economic efficiency meaning search for maximum of Equation 4:

$$E = \frac{U}{C} \tag{4}$$

is then reduced to the issue of minimisation of cost necessary to achieve the defined e-Government standard U_s.

Case Examples

Without changes of the current status when the contracting authority defines the subject matter of public contract only verbally not using any uniform standardized system of goods and services description, it is difficult to perform any efficient measures to further streamline processes of public procurement via digitization of public procurement.

Italy

According to Ancarani and Capaldoln (2005), in Italy, the Company CONSIP S.p.A. is a dedicated public limited company, completely owned by the Ministry of Treasury; this is accountable for the public sector purchase of goods and services through an e-procurement business model. CONSIP S.p.A. is owned 100% by the Ministry of Economic Development and Finance, formed the Public Administration Marketplace (MEPA) in 2003 (European Commission Directorarte, 2011). This electronic marketplace is used to award low-value contracts and "below threshold" public contracts. Since 2007, the central administration authorities must make use of MEPA for any public contract (Consip, Bertini, & Vidoni, 2009; Russo, 2009). MEPA is a Web application that is composed of three basic modules:

- **Catalog:** An electronic catalog enabling search for, filtering, comparison of products.
- **Orders:** This module enables selection of goods or service, generation of orders, and their electronic dispatch to the supplier.
- **Request for Quotation:** Module-enabling selection of relevant suppliers that will be addressed to make bids, assessment, and selection of the most convenient bid.

The whole purchase process is digitized except for eInvoicing and ePayment. The MEPA offers the contracting authorities two basic ways of purchase: direct order or request for quotation (a parallel to electronic auction). The latter method gives the contracting authority a chance to negotiate better terms in relation to price and quality of goods and services.

The electronic catalog is a basic component of MEPA. It is composed of catalogs of individual suppliers that showed interest in doing business via MEPA and that complied with basic qualification prerequisites. These suppliers fill in the catalog template and after being examined by CONSIP staff the catalogs are made accessible to contracting authorities in MEPA (Ministry of Economy and Finance, 2009).

Goods and services are described in the catalog in standardized fields that are divided into:

- Attributes common to all types of goods and services – commercial information such as name of supplier, short description, CPV, price, place, and time of delivery; and
- Attributes specific to individual types of goods and services – technical specifications such as weight, length, power consumption, etc.

Germany

In 2002, Germany started the Federal e-Government shop – Kaufhaus des Bundes Platform that enables the contracting authorities from individual federated states to do public procurement fully electronically. Since 2005, Kaufhaus des Bundes is used by the public administration authorities for procurement and its employment is being gradually extended also to local government entities. The operator of the Federal e-Government shop is Procurement Office of the Federal Ministry of the Interior (Federal e-Government Shop, 2009; Federal Institute for Risk Assessment, 2011; Procurement Office of the Federal Ministry of the Interior, 2011).

The Federal e-Government shop is a Web application enabling fully electronic procurement. Orders may be sent both in paper form and electronically using electronic signature. The basis of the marketplace is electronic catalogs of suppliers that are updated on a regular basis. In majority of cases, the suppliers are winners of electronic award procedure for framework contract for delivery of a specific commodity. The subject matter of the framework contract (i.e. the selected commodity) is defined using the CPV code. The electronic catalog, however, must be generated in compliance with the eCl@ss classification system (Schömann, 2008; Egeler & Funk, 2009).

eCl@ss is a branch standard for classification and description of products (goods and services) used to exchange information between customers and their suppliers. This standard is run by a non-profit organization eCl@ss e.V. charter members of which are representatives of large German concerns (BASF, Deutsche Bahn, Siemens, RWE and others).

The Czech Republic

Introduction of modern information and communication technologies into the public procurement process is one of the strategic objectives and measures taken by the Czech government. The key document for digitization of public procurement is the National Plan for the Introduction of Electronic Public Procurement over the Period 2006–2010 (hereinafter referred to as the "National Plan") (Czech Republic, 2006).

The National Plan has been followed by the Strategy of Digitization of Public Procurement from 2011 to 2015 (Czech Republic, 2010). The analysis of public procurement digitization status performed by the Czech Ministry for Regional Development on the sample of 1,334 public procurement contracting authorities in 2009 shows that 18% of contracting entities are currently making use of the electronic support. 32% of contracting entities are planning to introduce some kind of electronic support to award procedures in short-term or mid-term time horizon. The majority of contracting entities from the above 18% are employing electronic tools solely for implementation of component operations of the award procedure. Only 3% of them are performing full electronic award procedures. One half of all the contracting entities do not employ any electronic tools and they do not plan to employ them (Czech Republic, 2010).

In case the award procedures are electronically supported than the system in place, the uniform Public Procurement Information System and electronic marketplaces are used for "below threshold" contracts.

Looking at the digitization of the public contracts, the Czech Ministry of the Interior (MoI) represents a certain exception. To support centralized procurement within the MoI department, a Centralized Procurement Section (CPS) has been established in 2008 proposing to the Minister which assets and services shall be purchased in the year $n+1$ and it also proposes who will be the central contracting authority in award procedures.

The proposal of assets and services procured by the MoI department in the centralized manner is based on the analysis of MoI IS outputs and suggestions of individual contracting entities. After assets have been approved and after the CPS has nominated the authority, the assets specifications are being worked out in cooperation with standardization teams (representatives of designated units) so that it functionally complies as much as possible with the needs of the whole MoI department.

The CPS works out a draft of awarding documentation based on the requirement collection, which is submitted to the contracting authorities for comments. After considering all received comments, the documentation is handed over to the MoI legal department for implementation of the awarding procedure.

The central contracting authority carries out the awarding procedure and it concludes framework contracts solely on account of the public contracting entities. Before the awarding procedure is started, the central authority makes an agreement with MoI units defining rights and obligations in line with the Public Contracts Act (PCA). Once, the awarding procedure has been concluded, the authority hands over a framework contract to all involved suppliers and contracting entities. The involved contracting entities must perform their purchases based on the framework contract (execute award procedures – mini-tenders) in compliance with the PCA meaning that they have to request all framework suppliers for bids, evaluate received bids in line with the published criteria (typically the lowest bid price) and conclude a purchase contract.

The public contracting entity may organize mini-tenders as required during the whole period of framework contract duration. If an involved contracting entity has its reasons for purchase of assets with the same intended use like the standard assets defined in the framework contract; however, with different technical parameters (non-standard assets), it shall send requirement for non-standard assets approval to its senior authority with relevant substantiation and anticipated price. If the contracting entity proves to the CPS (by presenting the request, bids and contract draft) that the requested type of assets under the anticipated financial threshold of CZK 2 million VAT excluded, can be purchased under the same terms and conditions like in the framework contract from other than framework supplier, the senior authority approves so-called external purchase.

The whole process of mini-tender awarding from its announcement to contract conclusion including data pertaining to the actual delivery is being entered by the contracting entities into the MoI Internal Monitoring Information System in real time.

Even if the Czech MoI has its own specifications (so-called blank catalog) for a whole range of commodities purchased centrally, technical requirements are in free text (written description).

Another example of public procurement digitization is the use of the "SEPO" Web Application by the Czech Ministry of Defense (MoD). SEPO is the electronic tool of the defense department to purchase assets, services and construction works implemented in the form of low-cost public contracts in line with the PCA (i.e., below CZK 2 million VAT excluded for goods and services and below CZK 6 million VAT excluded for construction works). The main objective of SEPO is increased transparency and maximum possible reduction of corruption and thus increased cost-efficiency and effectiveness when acquiring as-

sets, purchasing services and construction works. Like the centralized purchases within the MoI, the SEPO also uses supplier catalogs to describe subject matter of the public procurement, however the description of purchased commodities itself is in free text.

National Infrastructure for Electronic Public Procurement

The draft model of the National Infrastructure for Electronic Public Procurement (NIPEZ) is one of the measures taken by the National Plan for the Introduction of Electronic Public Procurement over the Period 2006-2010 (Czech Republic, 2006). The NIPEZ Draft Model was adopted by the Government Resolution No. 574 of 4 May 2009 requiring the Government members and heads of other central bodies of public administration to guarantee execution of updated and new measures and tasks mentioned in the 2008 Report on Execution of the National Plan for the Introduction of Electronic Public Procurement over the Period 2006 – 2010 (Czech Republic, 2009). Main objectives of the NIPEZ Project are:

- Financial savings, both for contracting entities and suppliers, by reduction of purchased commodities cost and transaction cost related to the public procurement processes.
- Increased efficiency in public procurement and improvement in its administration process.
- Better access to public contracts and higher level of their transparency.
- Support to standardization of key processes of electronic public procurement.
- More data for statistic evaluation of the public procurement market by commodity aspect (using standardization to describe commodities through their properties) and improved conditions for monitoring of the Czech public procurement market.

NIPEZ is a modular set of information systems supporting processes of public procurement digitization. NIPEZ contains modules monitoring legal aspects—system of publication, e-Marketplace module, National Electronic Tool for Public Procurement (NEN), and interfaces with other internal and external information systems.

A part of NIPEZ is also software module called "NIPEZ Codebook" author of which is the Company AURA, s.r.o. The basis for the "NIPEZ Codebook" is the eOTD Dictionary enabling standardized description of products and services. ECCMA Open Technical Dictionary is a dictionary enabling standardized description of commodities using their properties in the "property – value pairs" system. Each commodity has its list of properties and the user fills in values based on specific parameters of the product. Definition of commodity description (IG) and data of the described item itself can be stored in XML files. eOTD content, XML file structures and eOTD maintenance and use are defined by the international standards ISO 22745 and ISO 8000. The eOTD is currently the most sophisticated system for parameterized description of goods and services. Its principles have been tested over the years in operation since it is technically based on the NATO Codification System (NCS). NCS is a system for codification of items that are purchased and used by defense departments. The NCS is used by more than 60 nations for standardized description of material items enabling easy data exchange among nations and supporting communication between the public sphere and its suppliers when carrying out procurement processes. Moreover, it is independent of existing classification systems because it is neutral in classification sense. Commodity property sets, so-called Identification Guides (IG) can be linked to any classification system including CPV or UNSPSC. Its undisputable advantage is that it uses universal descriptive and depictive language (XML) for manufacturer/supplier and customer communication. Descriptions of specific products and services like IGs are therefore easily transferable among different information systems. The basic classification of commodities uses the CPV, which is mandatory for contracting entities and contractors within the EU. Additional key data sources of the "NIPEZ Codebook" are, besides the CPV and eOTD, also NCS codebooks, the eCl@ss classification system and national branch codebooks (e.g., Drug Register, etc.).

The "NIPEZ Codebook" has two basic parts:

- A list of commodities.
- Property sets describing individual commodities.

The basis for the list of commodities is the CPV Codebook assembled in hierarchical tree structure enabling the users to easily find required commodity. The property set is formed by a group of parameters defining the commodity and enabling its description so that it cannot be interchanged for a different type of commodity. Based on their type, individual properties are complemented by rules and lists of approved values or units of measurement, which will allow the contracting entities for standardized commodity description when using relevant tools and the suppliers will apply the same system to prepare their products for offer. Each commodity at the lowest (end) level of the tree structure had to receive individual set of properties. Sets of service properties must have been generated because none of the used classification systems contains them in required quality. Each end commodity has its set of properties in the "NIPEZ Codebook."

Defense Research Project "EXCHANGE"

This project is implemented by the Czech Company AURA, s.r.o. for the Czech MoD and with its financial support in the period of 2010-2012. The project is a part of the research program No. 907980 Development of Achieved Operational Capabilities of the Armed Forces of the Czech

Republic and its full title is "Applied Research of Integrated Logistical Support System Technology Based on Automated Data Exchange between Defense Industry and MoD Department" (Rejman, 2010). The EXCHANGE Project has the following objectives:

- Applied research of modern methods of assets and services codification in compliance with eOTD focusing on classification and identification of services exploited by the defense department with the aim to streamline their planning, acquisition and evaluation.
- A draft of codification process methodology in compliance with eOTD and the ISO 22745 and ISO 8000 Standards which can be employed when improving assets and services acquisition support system within the defense department and when increasing compatibility with modern international standards.
- Analysis and use of the verification software application for evaluation of new codification methods based on the eOTD System.

The project makes full use of modern information technologies alongside with the methodical basis provided by the eOTD System and the ISO 22745 and ISO 8000 Standards. The resulting solutions have the following advantages:

- Support of effective communication between the defense department and industry in codification issues, Supplier Sourced Codification.
- Support of services codification in compliance with eOTD, drafts of services codification methodology as required by the defense department.
- A simplified and more efficient acquisition system and competitive tendering when purchasing assets and services.

So far, the following results have been achieved within the EXCHANGE Project:

- Status analysis of codification systems in the Czech Republic and abroad.
- Elaboration of a user requirements catalog for software application verification.
- A draft of the eOTD information system in support of acquisition processes within the MoD department.
- A draft of services codification methodology in support of specific needs of the MoD department.

One of the key results of the EXCHANGE Project is the methodology designed for codification of services using so-called descriptive identification in compliance with eOTD and the ISO 22745 Standard (Padalík, 2009). This type of codification based on standardized property description of the codified article has not been solved satisfactorily in the area of services. Internationally used classification systems either do not contain description of services using their properties or quality of such description is insufficient meaning that it is basically normal unstructured and hence non-standardized written description.

Project designers focused on the issues of the most complex and difficult portion of services codification which is preparation and creation of IGs that are actually templates for description of services. Comparative analysis and practical use within the defense department showed that it is neither suitable nor required to describe the processes ongoing during the execution of requested services. Instead, it is rather necessary to focus on the object affected by the activity and on the results and benefits which any given service provides the customer with. A specific IG, let's say, for "chimney sweeping" will not define the job technology, but it will stipulate types of chimneys based on heating output and fuels, service accessibility and list of possible additional activities (chimney examination, camera inspections, etc.).

A component result of the EXCHANGE Project is a complex draft of services codification methodology designed for specific needs of the defense department. Its part is also a methodological procedure when developing IGs for services. This can be seen in Figure 1.

Results of the EXCHANGE Project will be applied by the Czech defense department within the ongoing reform process of the acquisition system and streamlining of public procurement processes. It is also supposed that the existing ISs operated by the defense department and new electronic tools supported by eOTD will become parts of the NIPEZ System.

Even if the Czech Republic legally equalized the electronic public procurement with the "old-fashioned" way based on paper documents, only 3% of public contracting entities have fully electronic award procedure systems in place. There is no electronic support for specification of public procurement subject matter. Contracting entities are using verbal description to do this. Some ministries like MoI and MoD are trying to describe the subject matter of a public procurement by using parameters of so-called "blank catalogs" and technical specifications. Nonetheless, even "blank catalogs" and public procurement specifications define their subject matter in non-standardized verbal description.

Options for Process Rationalizations when Introducing New Electronic Tools for Public Procurement

When introducing new electronic tools to award public contracts in conjunction with the e-Government changes, it is necessary to prove the benefits of a new electronic tool (Blackstone, Boganno, & Hakim, 2005; Bertot, Jaeger, & Grimes, 2010; Rose & Grant, 2010). Starting point of potential rationalization is approach based on advantages of mathematical modeling of decision-making processes and on modern approaches towards

Figure 1. Methodological procedure when developing IGs for services

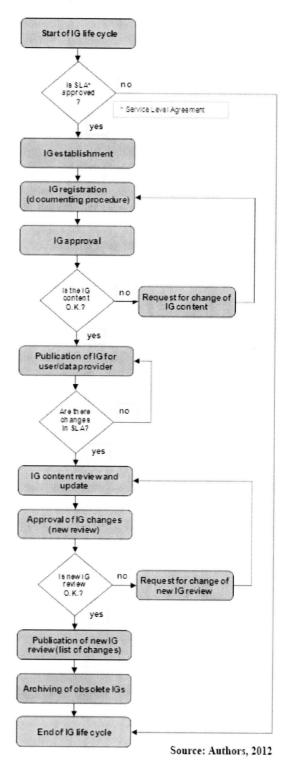

Source: Authors, 2012

electronic purchase of assets and services in compliance with the EU electronic public procurement principles, as it is stated in the case examples. There are different options of how to introduce electronic tools, but a public administration entity needs to know which of the tools is relevant for e-Government and when performing selection of a tool it is suitable to make use of exact approaches such as mathematical decision-making models. Basically, this is a broader implementation of e-Government, or electronic public procurement to be more specific.

The essence of the rationalization e-Government and Electronic Public Procurement is implementation of a pre-deliberation procedure aiming at:

- Evaluation of the current status in procurement of assets and services for public administration by an expert group of a public administration entity.
- Formulation of component evaluation criteria of the new electronic tool for electronic public procurement and stipulation of their importance levels.

Stipulation of Evaluation Criteria of New Electronic Tools

Basic evaluation criterion for implementation of new electronic tools into the public procurement is their cost-efficiency. The public administration entity shall judge component evaluation criteria and assign them importance levels expressed in percentage values.

To express a specific cost-efficiency Equation 1 can be used enabling definition of cost-efficiency (benefit) as a function of all component evaluation criteria. The defined benefit is very useful for the theory of multi-criteria decision making as the starting point for construction of a mathematical model supporting decision making in a public administration entity. A part of rationalization measures is stipulation of profitability of a new tool that

will be measured by a component criterion in the form cost savings in public administration entity. The importance levels of component evaluation criteria shall be stipulated by the mathematical model of multi-criteria evaluation to be described in the text to come.

To stipulate the cost-saving criterion (f_{i1}) as a component evaluation criterion, the following assumptions shall be observed (Pomazalová, 2010):

- Benefit is introduced for the purpose of economical evaluation.
- Benefit of an electronic tool is defined by a standard which enables the public administration entity to require compliance with this standard. A standard represents minimum values of component evaluation criteria required by the public administration entity.

All potential variants of the electronic tool must achieve just the standardized level. Offer in the variant A, offering the lowest cost C_A, however with "below-standard" benefit U_A, is excluded from the following procedures of offer evaluation. The best variant is the lowest-cost offer.

Component evaluation criterion of cost saving in i^{th} offer can be expressed by Equation 5:

$$f_{i1} - C - P_i \tag{5}$$

knowing that

- C represents *operating cost.*
- P_i is the price of the ith variant of the electronic tool.

In this context, it is necessary to note, that the C factor is specified if the public administration has completely functional system of internal accounting that can generate real operating cost. Important is also time comparability of C and P factors.

Definition of Importance Levels of Component Evaluation Criteria

The public administration entity shall define importance levels of component evaluation criteria. The total of percentage values of all component evaluation criteria can theoretically exceed the value of 100% and the stipulated importance levels of individual component criteria can be the same. The essence of this method is based on the assumption that the total of all component evaluation criteria will always state 100%. This assumption enables stipulation of importance levels of component evaluation criteria:

- Theoretical principles of multi-criteria decision making shall be respected.
- Computing algorithm stipulating the importance levels of component evaluation criteria shall be a part of endogenic functions in mathematical model to support decision making process in a public administration entity.

To be able to choose the most convenient variant of an e-Tool, we can use a classification method based on the fact that each member of the expert team of the public administration entity evaluates component evaluation criteria by assigning a certain amount of points to them based on a suitably selected classification scale. The advantage of such classification method is the possibility of more objective formulation of relations among importance levels of individual criteria. A considerable advantage is also the option to apply this method to cases where the offer is evaluated based on larger amount of component evaluation criteria.

Usually, a scale range of <0; 5> or <0; 10> is chosen. The higher classification is assigned to that criterion which is more important in the expert's view. The same classification can apply to more criteria. The importance of jth criterion as seen by the qth expert can be expressed by the following Equation 6 (Pomazalová, 2010):

$$\nu_{qj} = \frac{z_{qj}}{\sum\limits_{j=1}^{k} z_{qj}} \tag{6}$$

knowing that z_{qj} is number of classification scale assigned by the qth expert to j^{th} criterion.

The resulting ν_j importance level of the jth criterion defined based on the classification evaluation of all experts is hence expressed in Equation 7 (Pomazalová, 2010):

$$\nu_j = \frac{\sum\limits_{q=1}^{r} \nu_{qj}}{r} \tag{7}$$

knowing that r is number of experts.

The above method of how to define importance levels of component evaluation criteria, like other methods of this kind, that differ based on preference views of expert team members, are incorporated into the computing algorithms in the following text describing the concept of mathematical model supporting the decision making process during award procedure. The suggested concept of mathematical model supporting decision-making processes within a public administration entity takes into account that the set of endogenic relations will be amended by other different methods of criteria importance stipulation and the public administration entity will have the choice of a suitable method based on a specific situation.

Concept of Mathematical Model in Support of Decision-Making Process within Public Administration

Evaluation of e-Tool variants when choosing the most suitable variant is related to the evaluation of those properties that are reflecting the objectives defined by the public administration within the e-Government implementation. These aspects are specified in the set of component evaluation criteria.

Criteria may be expressed quantitatively—cost, loss, or qualitatively—quality, properties, etc. In their essence, these criteria are incomparable factors nature of which is generally "component profit" or "component loss." The final decision making process requires that individual criteria *quantify* related profits or loss. When respecting the basic evaluation criterion, it is necessary to aggregate component benefits and component loss in the form of a single factor. Such a factor is the cost efficiency.

The above assumptions of variant evaluation enable the issue of selecting the most convenient e-Tool variant to be transformed into the search for such a variant that maximizes benefit when applying the theory of multi-criteria decision making to the process of selecting the most convenient variant out of incomparable variants of decision-making. The basis of this rationalization measure is to outline this mathematical model applicable:

- a= *automatic method of variant evaluation.*
- b= *instrument for calculating importance levels of component criteria* based on individual views of expert team members when preparing the award procedure.

Selection of the most convenient e-Tool variant can be regarded as a task of multi-criteria evaluation of decision-making variants with the option of scalarization of the optimizing criterion. If we take into account the above formulated assumptions of properties of the component criteria set

evaluating the variants, the most suitable mathematical description of decision making processes within the selection will be any model based on the assumption saying that the complex criterion to evaluate suitability of the variants is the benefit function. Generally, these models are described by the benefit function $w(a)$ for the ith variant of decision in Equation 8 (Pomazalová, 2010):

$$w\left(a_i\right) = w\left\{w_1\left[f_1\left(a_i\right)\right], w_2\left[f_2\left(a_i\right)\right], ..., w_k\left[f_k\left(a_i\right)\right]\right\}$$

(8)

knowing that

- $w_j\, f_j(a_i)$ = component benefit function of the a_i decision variant in compliance with the f_j component evaluation criterion.
- k = amount of component evaluation criteria of decision variants.

Mathematical expression of benefit is shown in Equation 9:

$$w\left(a_i\right) = \sum_{j=1}^{k} v_j\, b_{ij}$$

(9)

knowing that

- v_j = importance level of the jth component evaluation criterion of the decision variant.
- b_{ij} = benefit level ratio of the ith decision variant based on the jth criterion.

The optimum decision variant is such variant in which the benefit Equation 2 reaches its maximum. When applying this mathematical model to evaluation procedures of variants, the following assignment is applicable:

- Benefit function of the ith decision variant.
- Cost efficiency of the ith offer.

- The jth component evaluation criterion of decision variant.
- The jth component criterion for offer evaluation.
- Under the same logic derived v_j importance levels and b_{ij} ratios.

The variants can be assembled based on decreasing values of economic efficiency. Importance levels of individual criteria for this type of multi-criteria variant evaluation models must comply with Equation 10 (Pomazalová, 2010):

$$\sum_{j=1}^{k} v_j = 1 \qquad (10)$$

When stipulating importance levels of component criteria, the multi-criteria decision-making theory is working on the assumption that the basic input for the v_j calculation are expert views expressed in the form of the z_{qj} points score that will be assigned by the qth expert from a predefined *assessing scale* as evaluation of importance level of the jth component criterion based on the principle the higher importance level the higher z_{qj} points score.

Structure of the Mathematical Model in Support of Decision-Making within Public Administration

The basis of this mathematical model is the algorithm calculating benefit function as of (2) which is thus representing its basic endogenic relation. Exogenic parameters of the mathematical model will be the z_{qj} values entered by individual experts expressing thus their individual assessment of importance level of the jth component evaluation criterion.

Another endogenic relation of the mathematical model is the algorithm recalculating the z_{qj} values for the v_j importance levels of the jth component evaluation criterion. There are also other

ways to stipulate importance levels; therefore, it is desirable to add, in a form of a selection menu to the endogenic relations, also algorithms of importance level calculation based on other methods. The contracting entity will have the option to choose the method on its own discretion.

A similar approach applies to the algorithm stipulating benefit level ratio. In the benefit function model as of (2), the benefit level ratio is described by Equation 11 (Pomazalová, 2010):

$$b_{ij} = \Phi\left\{f_j\left(a_i\right)\right\} \qquad (11)$$

expresses the fact that a certain a_i decision variant reached certain b_{ij} value in compliance with the f_j component evaluation criterion, bringing benefit to the public administration. Generally, the form of this function is dependent on the method applied in modelling of public administration preferences. Besides the quantitative criteria, one must take into account also qualitative—nominal criteria affecting such evaluations of individual variants like quality, etc. The main problem in using the multi-criteria decision making is to find a way allowing us to assign a common denominator to incomparable factors of component evaluation criteria using different types of evaluation scales.

Equation 5 can be subsequently interpreted as a procedure assigning relevant value of the b_{ij} evaluation scale, being interpreted as the benefit level ratio, to a specific value of jth component criterion acquired by the ith variant of the f_{ij} decision. The benefit level ratio is a simplified expression of the $w_j[f_j(a_i)]$ component benefit function from Equation 1 and used in Equation 2 representing the core of the mathematical model. Based on the assignment rules from Equation 5, individual methods of benefit ratio stipulation are differentiated.

For the purposes of practical applications of the proposed mathematical model, the point system is regarded as sufficiently objective and, at the same time, relatively simple.

The other group of endogenic functional relations in mathematical model is a set of methods performing assignment in compliance with Equation 5. The public administration entity can choose even the method of benefit ratio stipulation at its own discretion.

Solutions and Recommendations

The goal of the chapter is to contribute to a deeper understanding of the essential assumptions and implications of the emergence and existence of transformation of public sector organizations in shaping e-Government an e-Public procurement. Within the framework of this issue is focused in particular on:

- Finding an appropriate general theory-methodological approach to the solution, with regard to significant contemporary authors dealing with the issue of Public e-Procurement.
- Creating a set of research questions, their transformation into conceptual models and their operationalization.
- The design process of obtaining primary data, testing this approach and its evaluation and implementation.

Generation of a SW tool simultaneously enables:

- Creation and maintenance of IGs for individual commodities.
- Search for information about purchased commodities and their suppliers.
- Processing of catalog of purchased items including the blank catalog.
- Creation and maintenance of Master Data directly by external data sources (suppliers of commodities).
- Creation and maintenance of item data records must be in compliance with the ISO

22745 and ISO 8000 Standards when respecting specific requirements of the users.
- Electronic communication between the Master Data source and data user using data formats in compliance with the ISO 22745 Standard.
- Data update.
- Creation and specification of subject matters of public procurement using standardized commodity description in line with the relevant IGs.

FUTURE RESEARCH DIRECTIONS

Electronic platform for the e-Government has become a huge impulse for development of theoretical and practical Public e-Procurement and digitization of purchase processes.

Advantages of electronic public procurement in award procedures for purchase of goods and services are first and foremost:

- Online use of online means of mathematical decision making support; e.g. in the area of mathematical support of decision making processes this applies to importance level stipulation of component evaluation criteria all the way through to the selection of the most convenient offer.
- Use of mathematical modeling methods enabling not just accelerated but also more objective decision making especially when selecting the most convenient offer.
- Use of modern information and communication technologies especially in the area of parameter negotiating in relation to the outsourcing projects that are close to the market level.
- Significant reduction of potentially negative effects of subjective factors in such award procedures when bids of suppliers are being evaluated.

- Savings in transaction cost because of decreased administrative labor intensity of public procurement and Public e-Procurement.
- Increased price transparency of public contracts (it will be possible to monitor development of price levels within individual commodity categories).
- When using a standardized description of purchased commodities, it will be possible to mutually compare results of public procurement, to acquire data for statistical evaluation of public contract market including the commodity aspect and to perform more efficient audits and monitoring of the public procurement market.

Modern communication and information technologies offer new options not just in terms of service procurement but also in terms of rationalization of procedures that form a part of Public e-Procurement. Mathematical methods and mathematical modeling of decision-making processes in particular should be worked up for systematic use.

CONCLUSION

Public sector organizations should systematically organize key e-Government implementation and Public e-Procurement decisions together, based on legal framework and goals of transformation processes. The rational selection of a new electronic tool for Public e-Procurement is crucial for support of effective and transparent e-Government in regard of sense of transformation. Next common feature, that adds to the increased transparency and reduced corruption environment and thus supported efficiency and effectiveness when acquiring goods and services. e-Government and related e-Procurement platform established conditions for enabled government innovation and developmental potential.

Another important factor influencing the e-governance transformation is a complexity of tasks, possibility of decomposition of tasks between the agencies and coordination across the information and knowledge boundaries. The feasibility of information flows is a bottleneck as well as the development of the corresponding information system among the public sector organizations.

Standardizations, dictionaries, indicate the existence of common patterns of Public e-Procurement that describe the heterogeneous set of e-procurement tools. Because the possibilities of data use, preparing planning and install process of public sector organization cannot rely even on the specifics, create new Public e-Procurement device. One of these is creation of catalogs for increasing of efficiency of these processes. In this regard, progress in standardization of description of goods and services, development in creation of public procurement documentation is needed for information exchange based on international standards. Control is implemented by a mechanism based on and mathematical model, designed to fill the empty space in the implementation of new Public e-Procurement tools, to support governmental services and agencies solve transformational conflicts. Create a comprehensive picture of e-Government issue and Public e-Procurement phenomenon represents an enormous challenge introduced by transformational processes.

REFERENCES

Ancarani, A., & Capaldo, G. (2005). Supporting decision-making process in facilities management services procurement: A methodological approach. *Journal of Purchasing and Supply Management, 11*, 232–241. doi:10.1016/j.pursup.2005.12.004

Andersen, K. V., & Henriksen, H. Z. (2006). e-Government maturity models: Extension of the Layne and Lee model. *Government Information Quarterly, 23*, 236–248. doi:10.1016/j.giq.2005.11.008

Angelopoulos, S., Kitsios, F., Kofakis, P., & Papadopoulos, T. (2010). Emerging barriers in e-government implementation. In Wimmer, M. A. (Ed.), *International Federation for Information Processing: e-Government Conference* (pp. 216–225). Lausanne, France: IEEE.

Arlbjørn, J. S., & Freytag, P. V. (2012). Public procurement vs. private purchasing: Is there any foundation for comparing and learning across the sectors? *International Journal of Public Sector Management, 25*(3), 203–220. doi:10.1108/09513551211226539

Arnett, S. (2011). *The NATO codification system as the foundation for eOTD and ISO standards 22745 and 8000*. Retrieved November 14, 2011, from http://www.eccma.org/2011ECCMAconf/docs/Steven%20Arnett.pdf

Bannister, F. (2001). Dismantling the silos: extracting new value from IT investments in public administration. *Information Systems Journal, 11*(1), 65–84. doi:10.1046/j.1365-2575.2001.00094.x

Benson, P. (2010). Managing a data cleansing (cleaning) or cataloging project. *ECCMA*. Retrieved October 15, 2011, from http://www.eccma.org/resources/White_Papers.php#

Bertot, J. C., Jaeger, P. T., & Grimes, J. M. (2010). Using ICTs to create a culture of transparency: e-Government and social media as openness and anti-corruption tools for societies. *Government Information Quarterly, 27*, 264–271.

Blackstone, E., Boganno, M., & Hakim, S. (2005). *Innovations in e-government: The thoughts of governors and mayors*. Lanham, MD: Rowman & Littlefield.

Bonham, G., Seifert, J., & Thorson, S. (2001). *The transformational potential of e-government: The role of political leadership*. Paper presented at the 4th Pan European International Relations Conference. Kent, UK.

Carter, L., & Bélanger, F. (2005). The utilization of e-government services: Citizen trust, innovation and acceptance factors. *Information Systems Journal, 15*(1), 5–25. doi:10.1111/j.1365-2575.2005.00183.x

CEN. (2011). *CEN workshop on 'business interoperability interfaces on public procurement in Europe' phase 2 (WS/BII 2)*. Retrieved October 27, 2011, from http://www.cenbii.eu/about/

Chen, S. C., & Dhillon, G. S. (2003). Interpreting dimensions of consumer trust in ecommerce. *Information Technology Management, 4*, 303–313. doi:10.1023/A:1022962631249

Commission Implementing Regulation. (2011). No 842/2011 of 19 August 2011 establishing standard forms for the publication of notices in the field of public procurement and repealing regulation (EC) no 1564/2005. *Official Journal of the European Union, 222*(1). Retrieved August 30, 2011 from http://eur-lex.europa.eu/LexUriServ/LexUriServ.do?uri=OJ:L:2011:222:0001:0187:EN:PDF

Consip, Q., Bertini, L., & Vidoni, A. (2009). *The electronic marketplace of the public administration – MEPA, scenario, operation and trends.* Retrieved March 9, 2011, from http://www.eng.consip.it/on-line/en/Home/ActivityandResults/ProgramfortheRationalizationofPublicPurchases/ElectronicMarketplace/articolo613.html

Czech Republic. (2006). *National plan for the introduction of electronic public procurement over the period 2006–2010.* Retrieved August 15, 2011, from http://kormoran.vlada.cz/usneseni/usneseni_webtest.nsf/web/cs?Open&2006&05-10

Czech Republic. (2009). *National infrastructure for electronic public procurement (NIPEZ).* Retrieved August 21, 2011, from http://www.portal-vz.cz/NIPEZ

Czech Republic. (2010). Strategy of digitization of public procurement from 2011 to 2015. *Journal of Government for the Regional and Municipal Authorities, 9*(1), 4–22.

Danziger, J. N., & Andersen, K. V. (2002). The impacts of information technology on public administration: An analysis of empirical research from the "golden age" of transformation. *International Journal of Public Administration, 25,* 591–627. doi:10.1081/PAD-120003292

de Brí, F. (2009). An e-government stages of growth model based on research within the Irish revenue offices. *Electronic. Journal of E-Government, 7*(4), 219–228.

Dhillon, G. S., Weerakkody, V., & Dwivedi, Y. K. (2008). Realising transformational stage e-government: A UK local authority perspective. *Electronic Government. International Journal (Toronto, Ont.), 5*(2), 162–180.

eCl@ss. (2011). *Overview.* Retrieved August 30, 2011 from http://www.eclass.de/eclasscontent/standard/overview.html.en

Egeler, R., & Funk, J. (2009). Das kaufhaus des bundes – Ressortübergreifender einkauf der bundesverwaltung. The department store, the federal government - the federal government-wide purchasing. In Eßig, M., & Witt, M. (Eds.), *Öffentliche Logistik: Supply Chain Management für den öffentlichen Sektor Public Logistics: Supply Chain Management for the Public Sector.* (pp. 419–448). Berlin, Germany: Springer.

Eurlex. (2011a). Commission directive 2005/51/EC of 7 September 2005 amending annex XX to directive 2004/17/EC and annex VIII to directive 2004/18/EC of the European parliament and the council on public procurement. Retrieved October 27, 2011, from http://eur-lex.europa.eu/LexUriServ/LexUriServ.do?uri=OJ:L:2005:257:0127:0128:EN:PDF

Eurlex. (2011b). Communication from the commission to the council, the European parliament, the European economic and social committee and the committee of the regions – Action plan for the implementation of the legal framework for electronic public procurement {SEC(2004)1639}. Retrieved August 21, 2011, from http://eurlex.europa.eu/LexUriServ/LexUriServ.do?uri=CELEX:52004DC0841:EN:HTML

Eurlex. (2011c). *Directive 2004/17/EC of the European parliament and of the council coordinating the procurement procedures of entities operating in the water, energy, transport and postal services sectors.* Retrieved July 10, 2011, from http://eurlex.europa.eu/LexUriServ/LexUriServ.do?uri=OJ:L:2011:343:0077:0085:EN:PDF

Eurlex. (2011d). *Directive 2004/18/EC of the European parliament and of the council of 31 March 2004 on the coordination of procedures for the award of public works contracts, public supply contracts and public service contracts.* Retrieved October 27, 2011, from http://eurlex.europa.eu/LexUriServ/LexUriServ.do?uri=OJ:L:2004:134:0114:0240:EN:PDF

Eurlex. (2011e). *Directive 2009/81/EC of the European parliament and of the council of 13 July 2009 on the coordination of procedures for the award of certain works contracts, supply contracts and service contracts by contracting authorities or entities in the fields of defence and security, and amending directives 2004/17/EC and 2004/18/EC.* Retrieved October 17, 2011, from http://eurlex.europa.eu/LexUriServ/LexUriServ.do?uri=OJ:L :2009:216:0076:0136:EN:PDF

European Commission. (2008a). *Glossary: Statistical classification of products by activity (CPA).* Retrieved August 30, 2011 from http:// epp.eurostat.ec.europa.eu/statistics_explained/ index.php/Glossary:CPA

European Commission. (2008b). Commission regulation (EC) no 213/2008 is in use since 17/09/2008. *Official Journal of the European Union.* Retrieved May 10, 2011, from http://eur-lex.europa.eu/LexUriServ/LexUriServ.do?uri=O J:L:2008:074:0001:0375:EN:PDF

European Commission. (2009). *IDABC: The programme.* Retrieved from http://ec.europa.eu/ idabc/en/chapter/3.html

European Commission. (2010a). *Interoperability solutions for European public administrations: A commission-driven EU programme (2010-2015).* Retrieved August 21, 2011, from http://ec.europa. eu/isa/documents/isa_isapresentation_en.pdf

European Commission. (2010b). *Green paper on expanding the use of e-procurement in the EU SEC(2010) 1214.* Retrieved August 21, 2011, from http://eur-lex.europa.eu/LexUriServ/LexUriServ. do?uri=COM:2010:0571:FIN:EN:PDF

European Commission. (2010 c). *Commission staff working document evaluation of the 2004 action plan for electronic public procurement: Accompanying document to the green paper on expanding the use of e-procurement in the EU.* Retrieved August 30, 2011 from http://www.umic.pt/ images/stories/publicacoes4/Liv%20Verde%20 Cont%20Publ%20Aval%202004%20Plan%20 Cont%20Publi%20Electronico%20EN_2.pdf

European Commission. (2011 a). *2010-2013 action plan for European standardisation.* Retrieved August 30, 2011, from http://ec.europa. eu/enterprise/policies/european-standards/files/ standards_policy/action_plan/doc/standardisa- tion_action_plan_en.pdf

European Commission. (2011b). *European standards: Policy implementation action plan for European standardisation.* Retrieved August 30, 2011 from,http://ec.europa.eu/enterprise/poli- cies/european-standards/standardisation-policy/ implementation-action-plan/index_en.htm

European Commission Directorarte. (2011). *CONSIP SPA: General info.* Retrieved, October 23, 2011, from http://www.managenergy.net/ actors/1597

European Committee for Standardization. (2011). *Annual report.* Retrieved December 17, 2011, from http://www.cen.eu/cen/AboutUs/AR/Pages/ default.aspx

Eyob, E. (2004). E-government: Breaking the frontiers of inefficiencies in the public sector. *Electronic Government. International Journal (Toronto, Ont.), 1*(1), 107–114.

Federal eGovernment Shop. (2009). *eGovern- ment/eProcurement in Germany - Annual report of the European commission.* Retrieved, October 23, 2011, from http://www.kdb.bund.de/nn_1306306/ SharedDocs/Aktuelles/02__kdb__subsite/2009/ eGovernment.html

Federal Institute for Risk Assessment. (2011). *Procurement.* Retrieved, October 23, 2011, from http://www.bfr.bund.de/en/procurement-9810.html

Gil-Garcia, J. R., & Martinez-Moyano, I. J. (2007). Understanding the evolution of e-government: The influence of systems of rules on public sector dynamics. *Government Information Quarterly, 24,* 266–290. doi:10.1016/j.giq.2006.04.005

Goldfinch, S. F., Gauld, R., & Herbison, P. (2009). The participation divide? E-government, political participation, and trust in government in Australia and New Zealand. *Australian Journal of Public Administration, 68*(3), 333–350. doi:10.1111/j.1467-8500.2009.00643.x

Gottschalk, P. (2009). Maturity levels for interoperability in digital government. *Government Information Quarterly, 26,* 75–81. doi:10.1016/j.giq.2008.03.003

Griffin, D., & Halpin, E. (2005). An exploratory evaluation of UK local e-government from an accountability perspective. *Electronic. Journal of E-Government, 3*(1), 13–28.

Grönlund, Å., & Horan, T. A. (2004). Introducing e-gov: History, definitions and issues. *Communications of the Association for Information Systems, 15,* 713–729.

Hammer, M., & Champy, J. (1993). *Reengineering the corporation: A manifesto for business revolution.* New York, NY: Harper Business. doi:10.1016/S0007-6813(05)80064-3

Heeks, R., & Bailur, S. (2007). Analyzing e-government research: Perspectives, philosophies, theories, methods, and practice. *Government Information Quarterly, 24,* 243–265. doi:10.1016/j.giq.2006.06.005

Heintze, T., & Bretschneider, S. (2000). Information technology and restructuring in public organizations: Does adoption of information technology affect organizational structures, communications, and decision making? *Journal of Public Administration: Research and Theory, 10*(4), 801–829. doi:10.1093/oxfordjournals.jpart.a024292

Ho, A. (2002). Reinventing local governments and the e-government initiative. *Public Administration Review, 62*(4), 434–444. doi:10.1111/0033-3352.00197

Homburg, V. (2009). The social shaping of transformational government. In Weerakkody, V., Janssen, M., & Dwivedi, Y. K. (Eds.), *Handbook of Research on ICT-Enabled Transformational Government: A Global Perspective* (pp. 1–14). Hershey, PA: IGI Global. doi:10.4018/978-1-60566-390-6.ch001

Irani, Z., Love, P. E. D., & Montazemi, A. (2007). E-government: Past, present and future. *European Journal of Information Systems, 16,* 103–105. doi:10.1057/palgrave.ejis.3000678

ISO. (2009a). *ISO/TS 22745-30:2009: Industrial automation systems and integration – Open technical dictionaries and their application to master data, part 30: Identification guide representation.* Geneva, Switzerland: International Organization for Standardization.

ISO. (2009b). *ISO 8000-110:2009: Data quality, part 110: Master data: Exchange of characteristic data: Syntax, semantic encoding, and conformance to data specification.* Geneva, Switzerland: International Organization for Standardization.

ISO. (2010a). *ISO 22745-11:2010: Industrial automation systems and integration – Open technical dictionaries and their application to master data, part 11: Guidelines for the formulation of terminology.* Geneva, Switzerland: International Organization for Standardization.

ISO. (2010b). *ISO 22745-20:2010: Industrial automation systems and integration – Open technical dictionaries and their application to master data, part 20: Procedures for the maintenance of an open technical dictionary.* Geneva, Switzerland: International Organization for Standardization.

Janssen, M., & Shu, W. (2008). Transformational government: Basics and key issues: A workshop. *Proceedings of ICEGOV, Cairo Egypt., 2008*, 117–122. doi:10.1145/1509096.1509120

Janssen, M., & van Veenstra, A. F. (2005). Stages of growth in e-government: An architectural approach. *The Electronic. Journal of E-Government, 3*(4), 193–200.

Klievink, B., & Janssen, M. (2009). Realizing joined-up government - Dynamic capabilities and stage models for transformation. *Government Information Quarterly, 26*(2), 275–284. doi:10.1016/j.giq.2008.12.007

Kolsaker, A. (2006). Reconceptualising e-government as a tool of governance: The UK case. *Electronic Government, 3*(4), 347–355. doi:10.1504/EG.2006.010798

Layne, K., & Lee, J. (2001). Developing fully functional e-government: A four stage model. *Government Information Quarterly, 18*(2), 122–136. doi:10.1016/S0740-624X(01)00066-1

Lee, J. (2010). 10 year retrospect on stage models of e-government: A qualitative metasynthesis. *Government Information Quarterly, 27*, 220–230. doi:10.1016/j.giq.2009.12.009

Ministry of Economy and Finance. (2009). *The program for the rationalization of public authority purchases.* Retrieved October 23, 2011, from https://www.acquistinretepa.it/opencms/opencms/menu_livello_I/header/Inglese/PROGRAM

Moon, M. J. (2002). The evolution of e-government among municipalities: Rhetoric or reality? *Public Administration Review, 62*(4), 424–433. doi:10.1111/0033-3352.00196

Murray, J. G. (2009). Improving the validity of public procurement research. *International Journal of Public Sector Management, 22*(2), 91–103. doi:10.1108/09513550910934501

NATO. (2003). *Guide to the NATO codification system.* Retrieved April 22, 2011, from http://www.nato.int/structur/ac/135/ncs_guide/e_guide.htm

Padalík, M. (2009). *Software solution for codification based on NCS, eOTD and ISO 8000.* Retrieved November 26, 2009, from http://www.eccma.org/2009ECCMAconf/presentations/AURA.pdf

Pan-European Public e-Procurement On-Line Project. (2011). *About PEPPOL.* Retrieved May 26, 2011, from http://www.peppol.eu/about_peppol

Pomazalová, N. (2010). Possibilities of use the dynamic purchase system in the public procurement. In *The 16th International Conference The Knowledge-Based Organization*, (pp. 86-91). Sibiu, Romania: "Nicolae Bălcescu" Land Forces Academy Publishing House.

Procurement Office of the Federal Ministry of the Interior. (2011). *Electronic shopping: Procurement for the digital era.* Retrieved October 12, 2011, from http://www.bescha.bund.de/cln_100/nn_663232/sid_8010A7C909DE62EDA1D0003E313F439E/nsc_true/DE/OeffEinkauf/node.html?__nnn=true

Radack, G. (2009). *From the eOTD to international standards for open technical dictionaries (ISO 22745) and master data quality (ISO 8000-100).* Retrieved November 17, 2009, from http://www.eccma.org/2009ECCMAconf/presentations/GeraldRadack.pdf

Rejman, S. (2010). *Research program No. 907980: Applied research of integrated logistical support system technology based on automated data exchange between defense industry and MoD department*. AURA, s.r.o., Brno.

Rose, W. R., & Grant, G. G. (2010). Critical issues pertaining to the planning and implementation of e-government initiatives. *Government Information Quarterly, 27*, 26–33. doi:10.1016/j.giq.2009.06.002

Russo, A. (2009). *Italian public administration emarketplace*. Retrieved, October 23, 2011, from http://www.epractice.eu/en/cases/mepa1

Scholl, H. J. (2005). Organizational transformation through e-government: Myth or reality? *Lecture Notes in Computer Science, 3591*, 1–11. doi:10.1007/11545156_1

Scholl, H. J. (2006). Electronic government: Information management capacity, organizational capabilities, and the sourcing mix. *Government Information Quarterly, 23*(1), 73–96. doi:10.1016/j.giq.2005.11.002

Schömann, M. (2008). *Public electronic procurement in Germany*. Retrieved May 21, 2011, from http://www.ogasun.ejgv.euskadi.net/r51-3752/es/contenidos/informacion/20_seminario_internacional/es_3seminar/adjuntos/Manfred_Schomann.pdf

Schwester, R. W. (2009). Examining the barriers to e-government adoption: Electronic. *Journal of E-Government, 7*(1), 113–122.

Siau, K., & long, Y. (2005). Synthesizing e-government stage models-a meta-synthesis based on meta-ethnography approach. *Industrial Management & Data Systems, 105*, 443–458. doi:10.1108/02635570510592352

SIMAP. (2010). *CPV*. Retrieved September 2, 2011 from http://simap.europa.eu/codes-and-nomenclatures/codes-cpv/codes-cpv_en.htm

SIMAP. (2011). *Information system for European public procurement*. Retrieved September 2, 2011 from http://simap.europa.eu/index_en.htm

Smith, I. (2009). *Smart step codification phase III*. Retrieved December 12, 2010, from http://www.eccma.org/2009ECCMAconf/presentations/eOTDprocess.pdf

Torres, L., Pina, N., & Royo, S. (2005). e-government and the transformation of public administrations in EU countries. *Online Information Review, 29*(5), 531–553. doi:10.1108/14684520510628918

United Nations. (2001). *Using the UNSPSC: Why coding and classifying products is critical to success in electronic commerce*. United Nations Standard Products and Services Code White Paper. Retrieved September 2, 2011, from http://www.unspsc.org/documentation.asp

Van Veenstra, A. F., Klievink, B., & Janssen, M. (2011). Barriers and impediments to transformational government: Insights from literature and practice. *Electronic Government. International Journal (Toronto, Ont.), 8*(2/3), 226–241.

Weerakkody, V., & Dhillon, G. (2008). Moving from e-government to t-government: A study of process reengineering challenges in a UK local authority context. *International Journal of Electronic Government Research, 4*(4), 1–16. doi:10.4018/jegr.2008100101

Weerakkody, V., Janssen, M., & Dwivedi, Y. (2011). Transformational change and business process re-engineering (BPR): Lessons from the British and Dutch public sector. *Government Information Quarterly, 28*(3), 320–328. doi:10.1016/j.giq.2010.07.010

West, D. (2001). *e-Government and the transformation of public sector delivery*. Paper presented at the Annual Meeting of the American Political Science Association. San Francisco, CA.

West, D. (2004). e-Government and the transformation of service delivery and citizen attitudes. *Public Administration Review, 64*(1), 15–27. doi:10.1111/j.1540-6210.2004.00343.x

ADDITIONAL READING

Ancarani, A., & Capaldo, G. (2005). Supporting decision-making process in facilities management services procurement: A methodological approach. *Journal of Purchasing and Supply Management, 11*, 232–241. doi:10.1016/j.pursup.2005.12.004

Andersen, I. E., & Jaeger, B. (1999). Scenario workshops and consensus conferences towards more democratic decision-making. *Science & Public Policy, 26*(5), 331–341. doi:10.3152/147154399781782301

Andersen, K. (2002). Public sector process rebuilding using information systems. *Proceedings of Electronic Government: First International Conference, EGOV*. Berlin, Germany: Springer. *2002*, 37–44.

Andersen, K. V., Henriksen, H. Z., & Rasmussen, E. B. (2007). Re-organizing government using IT: The Danish model. In Nixon, P. G., & Koutrakou, V. N. (Eds.), *e-Government in Europe: Re-Booting the State* (pp. 103–118). London, UK: Routledge.

Angelopoulos, S., Kitsios, F., & Papadopoulos, T. (2010). New service development in e-government: Identifying critical success factors – Transforming government. *People. Process and Policy, 4*(1), 95–118.

Bannister, F. (2007). The curse of the benchmark: An assessment of the validity and value of e-government comparisons. *International Review of Administrative Sciences, 73*(2), 171–188. doi:10.1177/0020852307077959

Barzelay, M. (2001). *The new public management: Improving research and policy dialogue*. Berkeley, CA: University of California Press.

Baum, C., & Maio, A. D. (2000). *Gartner's four phases of e-government*. New York, NY: Gartner Group.

Blind, P. (2007). Building trust in government in the twenty-first century: Review of literature and emerging issues. In *Proceedings of UNPAN, 7thGlobal Forum on Reinventing Government, Building Trust in Government*. Vienna, Austria. Retrieved, October 23, 2011, from http://unpan1.un.org/intradoc/groups/public/documents/un/unpan025062.pdf

Cordella, A., & Iannacci, F. (2010). Information systems in the public sector: The e-government enactment framework. *The Journal of Strategic Information Systems, 19*, 52–66. doi:10.1016/j.jsis.2010.01.001

Coursey, D., & Norris, D. F. (2008). Models of e-government: Are they correct? An empirical assessment. *Public Administration Review, 68*(3), 523–536. doi:10.1111/j.1540-6210.2008.00888.x

Devadoss, P., Pan, S., & Huang, J. (2002). Structural analysis of e-government initiatives: A case study of SCO. *Decision Support Systems, 34*, 253–269. doi:10.1016/S0167-9236(02)00120-3

Ebrahim, Z., & Irani, Z. (2005). e-Government adoption: Architecture and barriers. *Business Process Management Journal, 11*(5), 589–612. doi:10.1108/14637150510619902

Gauld, R., Gray, A., & McComb, S. (2009). How responsive is e-government? Evidence from Australia and New Zealand. *Government Information Quarterly, 26*(1), 69–74. doi:10.1016/j.giq.2008.02.002

Government, H. M. (2006). *Transformational government enabled by technology annual report 2006*. Retrieved September 7, 2011, from http://webarchive.nationalarchives.gov.uk/20100304104621/http://www.cabinetoffice.gov.uk/media/140539/trans_gov2006.pdf

Government, H. M. (2007a). *Transformational government – Our progress in 2007 delivering better, more efficient services for everyone: Summary.* Retrieved October 23, 2011, from http://webarchive.nationalarchives.gov.uk/20100304104621/http://www.cabinetoffice.gov.uk/media/140574/tg_annual_report07sum.pdf

Government, H. M. (2007b). *Transformational government: Enabled by technology: Annual report 2006.* Retrieved October 20, 2011, from http://www.cio.gov.uk/documents/annual_report2006/trans_gov2006.pdf

Government, H. M. (2008). *Transformational government – Our progress in 2008 delivering better, more efficient services for everyone.* Retrieved August 15, 2011, from http://webarchive.nationalarchives.gov.uk/20100304104621/http://www.cabinetoffice.gov.uk/media/207649/tg08_part1.pdf

Government, H. M. (2010). *Government ICT strategy: Smarter, cheaper, greener.* Retrieved October 1, 2011, from http://webarchive.nationalarchives.gov.uk/20100304104621/http://www.cabinetoffice.gov.uk/media/317444/ict_strategy4.pdf#page=50

Helbig, N., Ramón Gil-García, J., & Ferro, E. (2009). Understanding the complexity of electronic government: Implications from the digital divide literature. *Government Information Quarterly, 26*(1), 89–97. doi:10.1016/j.giq.2008.05.004

Jaeger, P. T., & Bertot, J. C. (2010). Transparency and technological change: Ensuring equal and sustained public access to government information. *Government Information Quarterly, 27*(4), 371–376. doi:10.1016/j.giq.2010.05.003

Joss, S. (1999). Public participation in science and technology policy- and decision-making—Ephemeral phenomenon or lasting change. *Science & Public Policy, 26*(5), 290–293. doi:10.3152/147154399781782338

Lee, J., & Kim, J. (2007). Grounded theory analysis of e-government initiatives: Exploring perceptions of government authorities. *Government Information Quarterly, 24*, 135–147. doi:10.1016/j.giq.2006.05.001

OECD. (2003). *The e-government imperative: Main findings.* Paris, France: OECD.

OECD. (2009). *Rethinking e-government services: User-centered approaches.* Paris, France: OECD.

Reddick, C. G. (2004). A two-stage model of e-government growth: Theories and empirical evidence for US cities. *Government Information Quarterly, 21*(1), 51–64. doi:10.1016/j.giq.2003.11.004

Rosacker, K. M., & Olson, D. L. (2008). Public sector information system critical success factors. *Transforming Government: People. Process and Policy, 2*(1), 60–70.

Schiele, J. (2009). Contributions of public purchasing departments to competitive acquisition processes for consulting services. *Journal of Public Procurement, 9*(2).

Subramaniam, C., & Shaw, M. J. (2004). The effects of process characteristics on the value of B2B e-procurement. *Information Technology Management, 5*, 161–181. doi:10.1023/B:ITEM.0000008080.17926.2b

Tan, C., & Pan, S. (2003). Managing e-transformation in the public sector: An e-government study of the inland revenue authority of Singapore (IRAS). *European Journal of Information Systems, 12,* 269–281. doi:10.1057/palgrave.ejis.3000479

Wimmer, M. A., & Codagnone, C. (2007). Framework and metodology. In C. Codagnone & M. A. Wimmer (Eds.), *Roadmapping eGovernment Research: Visions and Measures towards Innovative Governments in 2020,* (pp. 11-34). Clusone, Italy: MY Print snc di Guerinoni Marco & C.

KEY TERMS AND DEFINITIONS

Award Procedure: Award procedure is a formal process used to select suppliers for a public contract. The award procedure can be started only by the means stipulated by legislation.

Electronic Catalog: Electronic catalog is a set of information containing prices of individual items of public contract subject matter, description of such items, plus other related data. Electronic catalog must comply with all requirements specified for electronic tools used for electronic communication in the Public Contracts Act.

Electronic Marketplace: A Web application enabling electronic public procurement using defined award procedures. An e-Marketplace is a completely electronic system and both contracting entity and supplier perform their activities electronically.

Electronic Public Procurement: Electronic public procurement is a process of public contract award when some or all transactions of the award procedure are implemented via electronic tools in connection with electronic means.

Electronic Tool: A technical device (i.e. hardware) or program (i.e. software). These are also individual applications used by contracting entities within the procurement process (e.g. electronic transfer of information for publication, for submitting and evaluation of bids or for electronic contracting). These applications can exist independently or they can be integrated into a complex solution for electronic public procurement (e.g. in the form of electronic marketplace).

Open Technical Dictionary (OTD): A dictionary of concepts where individual concepts with names, definitions and images have their identifiers using codes to describe individuals, organizations, locations, goods, and services.

Public Contract: A contract executed based on an agreement between a contracting entity and one or more suppliers' subject matter of which is delivery of goods, services or construction works against payment. Based on their subject matter, public contracts are divided into public contracts for supplies, services and works, based on anticipated cost they can be divided into "above threshold" public contracts, "below threshold" public contracts and low-value public contracts.

Chapter 7
Electronic Procurement in the Construction Industry

Robert Eadie
University of Ulster, UK

Srinath Perera
Northumbria University, UK

George Heaney
University of Ulster, UK

ABSTRACT

The benefits of e-business have been widely promoted but the Architecture, Engineering, and Construction (AEC) sector has lagged behind other sectors in the adoption of e-procurement. The prospective benefits for the AEC sector are suggested by the proven advantages of general e-procurement where adoption has been faster and deeper. However, several studies indicated that barely 20% of documentation is tendered electronically, suggesting there are barriers to e-procurement. In order to promote adoption of e-procurement in the AEC sector, it is important to establish the status of the industry and identify the drivers as well as barriers to e-procurement. This chapter provides a detailed discussion of the state of the industry and its drivers and barriers while ranking these according to its importance. It acts as a reference guide to allow those implementing e-procurement in construction to make informed decisions as to where to focus their efforts to achieve successful realisation incorporating the benefits and avoiding the pitfalls in the process. The chapter also provides some insight into the current state, trends, and future directions of e-procurement in the construction industry.

DOI: 10.4018/978-1-4666-2665-2.ch007

INTRODUCTION

E-business is defined as the application of Information Communication Technologies (ICT) to business activities and processes. The applications of e-business are too numerous to mention and are dealt with in other chapters of this book. However, one of the business processes that can gain significant benefit from the adoption of ICT is procurement. The construction industry is one such sector with a significant procurement component and in most countries contributes between 8-10% of the Gross Domestic Product (GDP). Therefore it can benefit from the substantial efficiency saving that e-procurement is purported to bring.

National Procurement Strategy for Local Government (2003) defined procurement as

the process of acquiring goods, works, and services, covering both acquisitions from third parties and from in-house providers. The process spans the whole life cycle from identification of needs, through to the end of a services contract or the end of the useful life of an asset. It involves options appraisal and the critical 'make or buy' decision.

The increased use of the Internet offers greater opportunity for e-Procurement, which can offer viable electronic alternatives to traditional paper-based processes. Rowlinson and McDermott (1999) define procurement for construction as "the acquisition of project resources for the realization of a constructed facility." The procurement process not only incorporates the buying of goods and services but is also a strategic actor within the construction process. The UK public sector has created a plethora of initiatives to explore methods of improving the strategy and processes of procurement over the last 12 years starting with the Modernising Government White Paper (1999) (Cabinet Office, 1999). This will be further developed and discussed later in the chapter indicating their impact on the construction industry.

General procurement actions can be clustered and defined in three different ways: indirect procurement, direct procurement and sourcing (Minahan & Degan, 2001). Indirect procurement comprises selecting, buying and management of supplies for daily operation of an organisation. In the construction industry, examples of indirect procurement are the office supplies, facilities management aspects of schemes and construction related computer software packages. Direct procurement is occasionally called supply chain management and involves purchasing goods and organising activities to manufacture a completed product or products. Construction industry examples include the purchase of materials, plant and labour services. According to Kim and Shunk (2003), sourcing pertains equally to indirect and direct procurement and is in the form of a four phase models (information, negotiation, settlement, and after-sales). In construction, project sourcing normally takes place on behalf of a client through the tender process. Tendering involves the first three stages of this model. Contractors' sources vary through a variety of means such as on-line catalogues and mini tenders.

One of the issues relating to procurement that has been identified as improving the process is electronic procurement. All of the above types of procurement in construction can be carried out electronically. E-Procurement is defined as "the use of electronic technologies to streamline and enable procurement activities" (Hawking, et al., 2004, p. 5). Rankin (2006) provides a fuller definition of e-procurement as the business-to-business purchase and sale of products and services by electronic means (today primarily using the Internet). E-Procurement improves numerous facets of the procurement process and therefore has great potential to improve public sector procurement.

One of promoted benefits of e-business generally is that it has been seen to promote sustainable use of energy (European Commission, 2010a). E-procurement (an application within e-business) has also been upheld as a way of producing cost savings through even partial adoption within the construction sector (European Commission, 2007).

Tendering is one of the main sub processes within construction procurement that provides the mode to procure the built asset concerned. IDEA (2008) defines completing the tendering process electronically (e-procurement) as "an electronic tendering solution that facilitates the complete tendering process from the advertising of the requirement through to the placing of the contract." Electronic procurement/tendering is not a strategy in itself but the use of electronic means to carry out the procurement/tendering process (Minahan & Degan, 2001). Hackett *et al.* (2007) further submit that the type of tendering procedure selected will depend greatly on the preferred procurement route. The National Joint Consultative Committee (NJCC, 1996) identifies the forms of competitive tendering as open tendering and selective tendering. Selective tendering can be a single stage or two stage process. It also incorporates serial tendering.

The Royal Institution of Chartered Surveyors (RICS, 2007) suggests that traditional tender documentation and procedures are more suited to manual and paper format based procurement. The documents included range from the drawings to Bills of Quantities. The introduction of e-tendering has revolutionised the laborious manual tendering process, as it is secure and cost effective resulting in reduced paper based procedures. However, a number of studies have shown that the uptake of e-procurement within construction has not been as expected (Eadie, et al., 2007, 2010a, 2010b; Martin, 2003, 2009). Although the uptake and subsequent benefits of e-procurement are well documented in other sectors, the reasons for slow uptake in construction procurement investigated in this chapter.

The courts have been helpful in clarifying some of the differences between general procurement and that in the construction sector. Eastern v.

EME Developments (1991) 55 BLR 114 defined the differences between construction contracts and general goods and services contracts. The decision stated:

the most important background fact which I should keep in mind is that building construction is not like the manufacture of goods in a factory. The size of the project, site conditions, and the use of many materials and the employment of various kinds of operatives make it virtually impossible to achieve the same degree of perfection that a manufacturer can. It must be a rare new building in which every screw and every brush of paint is absolutely correct.

This statement from the court indicates that construction is associated with the creation of a unique product, constructed at different geographical locations, with unknown individual features in accordance with a set of drawings and specifications. Conversely, manufacturing mass produces an item at minimum unit cost and maximum output, at a single location (normally a factory) also to drawings and specifications but without or limited variability of the unknown factors. Eadie *et al.* (2010a, 2010b) stated that the differences impacted on the ranking, and hence significance, of e-procurement drivers and barriers within the construction industry. There were some drivers and barriers to general e-procurement, which did not apply to construction. Unlike manufacturing, the construction industry is deeply fragmented with possible variations in the effect of each driver and barrier to construction procurement. This fragmentation within the industry exhibited itself across the public and private sectors and also across the fragmented disciplines within construction. This will be further examined in more detail later in this chapter.

The European Commission (2007) identified that the major driving force in the implementation of e-procurement in construction is driven by its introduction in large European construction enterprises. However, this Europe wide assessment gives little insight into the UK construction industry where 97.9% of construction businesses employ less than 49 employees (BIS, 2010). While the figure compares with the most of other European countries, the Europe wide impact on the construction industry is not much clear. E-Business Watch (European Commission, 2007) reports the second lowest level of adoption of e-business for the construction industry in a cross comparison of 10 major industries across Europe. In the UK, it is clear that it is the public sector that is driving the implementation of e-procurement in construction industry. The later sections of this chapter will further explore the use of e-procurement in the public sector while examining in detail the drivers and barriers for construction e-procurement.

This chapter investigates the state of adoption of e-procurement in the UK construction industry. It first traces the development of public sector e-procurement policy from the "Modernising Government White Paper" to the 2011 European Union initiatives to increase e-procurement. In the next section, it explores the use of electronic auctions for procurement in construction. It shows that the use of electronic auctions from a project perspective is against the ethos presented in many government reports on the construction industry. It then analyses the current implementation of e-procurement in the construction industry using statistics published in 2010 to determine e-procurement use among in the various construction disciplines both in private and public sectors. The final section discusses the drivers and barriers to e-procurement in construction and provides a ranked and classified list of the Drivers and Barriers for e-procurement in construction. The chapter concludes summarising the adoption of e-procurement in the construction industry providing insights in to further directions in promoting e-procurement in the construction industry.

DEVELOPMENT OF POLICY INITIATIVES PROMOTING E-PROCUREMENT

"Best Value" was the central core of the Modernising Government White Paper (Cabinet Office, 1999) which was published on 30th March 1999. This White Paper aspired to having public services available 24 hours a day; seven days a week provided there was a demand. The Cabinet Office (2000) measured progress against an original target of 100% of dealings with government to be delivered electronically by 2008. This target was subsequently amended to 100% of services to be electronically available by 2005. Dacorum Borough Council (2006) identifies procurement as a process under scrutiny in this report. The report incorporated a series of measurement indicators; among those was Best Value Indicator 157 (BVI157), which related to e-procurement (Dacorum Borough Council, 2006).

Best Value Indicator 157

DETR (2000) states, that the targets for BVI157 were 25% of services to be capable of electronic delivery by 2002 and 100% by 2005. BVI157 also identifies service delivery outcomes relating to procurement. However, The Hewson Group (2003) interestingly pointed out that BVI157 only asked for services to be e-enabled allowing councils to report that they had met the target. When the Hewson Group (2003) investigated, they found that with councils reporting 100% only 40% on average are successfully 'e-delivered' and the quality of the customer experience varies to a large extent with many customers finding it impossible or impractical to complete their transactions online. This indicates that there were difficulties with its implementation in a public procurement setting. While BV157 was general in application, it also applied to construction. However, the Glover Report (2008) indicated that electronic procurement for construction was still not 100% by 2008 and set a further date of 2012 for 100% implementation.

Developments in E-Business

In line with the Modernising Government (1999) document, OGC (2003) reported that, in order to improve the performance of central government departments as construction clients, larger government procurements should take advantage of available e-commerce solutions. This resulted in a proliferation of initiatives from 1999 onwards in the public sector promoting the use of the Internet

for procurement. These provided the infrastructure for the implementation for e-procurement adoption in construction. The Department for Education and Skills (DfES) produced a UK government Web portal promoting on-line business named "UKonline" in 2001. The Government Secure Intranet became a reality in 1998 (Caffrey, et al., 1999) and was revamped in 2004 (Public Technology, 2004). The public sector Initiatives that laid the foundations for e-procurement are presented in Figure 1.

The UKonline (2003) initiative to promote e-government and general use of the Internet was launched in 1999 and concluded in 2003. UKon-

Figure 1. UK initiatives with an impact on e-procurement

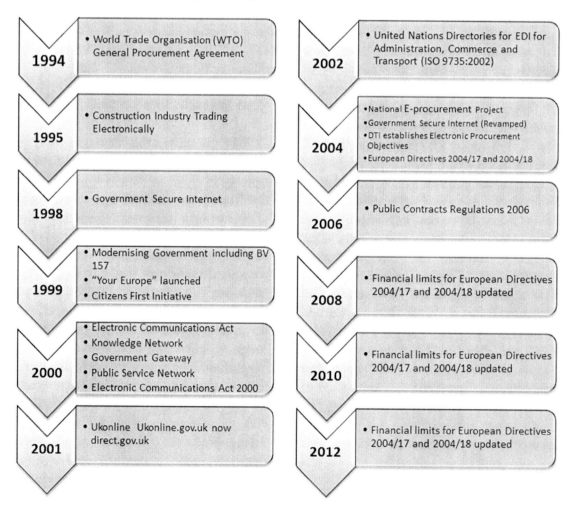

line (2003) in its final annual report shows that at the end of 2003, 56% of homes in the United Kingdom had Internet access. This indicated a significant success for the initiative as the increase was from a meagre 10% in 1999. UKonline centres were set up as part of this initiative to enable those without a private Internet connection access to government documentation including procurement documentation (UKonline, 2009). NTL (2004) reported on the European Communities website although 98% of local government organisations were set to meet the 2005 deadline for being fully electronic that only 8% of the sample population was aware of the e-government initiative. These clearly indicate there is lack of penetration of use to the population than expected.

Harindranath *et al.* (2008) report that the Regional Development Agency identified that 63% of SMEs were connected to the Internet, 46% had a website and 36% traded on-line. However, Pritchard (2006) states that 30% did not use computers in any way. This indicates there is low penetration of use with respect SME and business organisations as well.

HM Government (2009) shows the Government Gateway was launched in 2001 in order to fulfill the electronic requirements of the "Modernising Government" document relating to e-business and has since processed more than £66 million worth of transactions. Government Gateway (2009) allowed organisations to carry out many payment functions electronically, such as registering to pay taxes (VAT, tax returns) or check the ownership of land electronically through the land registry. The Cabinet Office (1999) states procurement by the departments was one of the services mentioned in the "Modernising Government" document as having to go electronic but has not yet been included on its website. Caffrey *et al.* (1999) shows that internally, the government provided the central civil service with the Government Secure Intranet. This has a specific construction application in that it allows the sharing and passing of commercial information such as priced bills of quantities between central government departments. The various government initiatives to promote and advance e-government have had a great influence in promoting e-procurement and providing the necessary infrastructure in the public sector. However, the spread and level of penetration of use of e-procurement in the construction sector is still limited. This was further established in a recent study published by Construct IT (2011) which stated there is very low usage of e-procurement related activities within the UK construction organisations.

Construction Industry Trading Electronically (CITE)

Another initiative to increase the uptake of e-procurement in construction resulted in a group being set up to provide a data exchange standard for electronic procurement documentation. Construction Industry Trading Electronically (CITE, 2009) is described on its website as "a collaborative electronic information exchange initiative for the UK construction industry." CITE was commissioned in April 1995. RICS (2005b) indicates that its aim was to give the construction industry a standard system of data interchange for tenders. CITE (2009) identified its original membership as having included some of the major contractors in the UK Construction Industry such as the Alfred McAlpine™ and Taylor Woodrow™.

CITE commenced with 180 member firms and has continued to grow. The aim was to get the industry to move forward as a unit using the same formats and systems and is currently working on a new XML tendering standard. CITE (2001) records that data exchange formats are made available. This allows CITE users to exchange data from multiple systems while providing and maintaining an industry wide common data exchange format. This format is based on the XML standards developed by the World Wide Web Consortium.

However, Martin (2003) who conducted a major survey of the UK Construction industry on electronic contract usage indicates it is little used. It states only 10% of the electronic documentation were sent out in CITE format.

CITE (2009) formats can be used to produce Bills of Quantities, valuations, project information, which is especially important in NEC-based contracts, enquires, quotations, orders, and invoices. The formats and the extensions used are detailed in Table 1.

RICS (2005b) refers to the CITE BOQ Reader. This takes CITE EBQ files and imports them into Microsoft Excel. E-Quantities (2009) show the EBQ Page layout is similar to a printed BOQ and there are 10 columns spaced across the page.

The CITE standard is *ASCII for both un-priced and priced Bills of Quantities (BOQ's), with associated documents.* This makes it compatible with the formats used by most estimating and bill preparation software packages. One of the benefits that CITE have accrued from moving to the XML schemas is that XML integrates better with fully Web based systems than the traditional EDI format (Li & Du, 2005). However, it was ahead of its time and suffered from construction industry fears over its legal status.

Electronic Communications Act 2000

One of the major advances in e-procurement history was the publication of the Electronic Communications Act. This allowed electronic contracts in every sector including construction to be recognised. The Electronic Communications Act is split into three main parts and a supplemental section (HM Government, 2012). The sections are cryptography service providers, facilitation of electronic commerce, and data storage. These are followed by the miscellaneous and supplemental section. Within the Act, the second part relates to electronic signatures. Although it takes a minimalist approach, it gives the principles of how electronic signatures are recognised by the law

Table 1. CITE format extensions

File Type	Extension	Exceptions
Control	.EBC	
Notes	.TXT	
BOQ	.EBQ	
Prelims	.PRL	Agreed proprietary format (e.g. .DOC, .PDF, .RTF, .LWP etc) or where they have priceable items they will be in an .EBQ file

(Brazell, 2004). There are outstanding changes to this act to bring it into line with Scottish legislation but do not affect the way that the act works with electronic signatures (HM Government, 2012).

DTI (2006) has established that Section 7(1) of the Electronic Communications Act of 2000 has elucidated that electronic signatures are admissible in evidence with respect to the authenticity or integrity of a communication or piece of data. Electronic signatures can come in many forms (DTI, 2009):

- Typewritten.
- Scanned in signature format.
- An electronic representation of a hand written signature.
- A unique sequence of characters.
- A digital representation of characteristics, e.g. fingerprint, retina.
- A signature created by cryptographic means.

However, the courts will recognise an electronic signature provided three sections are present and verifiable. The act states these as (1) the signature itself, (2) the means of producing, communicating, or verifying the signature, and (3) the procedure applied to the signature (HM Government, 2012).

Julià-Barceló and Vinje (1998) highlighted the resulting problems for many public sector departments as verification necessitates third party involvement. They show many Public Sector departments are reluctant to allow a third party to have access to sensitive data as this produces a security loophole. In order to overcome this difficulty the Government sponsored BIP systems to provide a vault for the transmission of electronic documentation for construction tendering and to verify whom the documents have come from and that they are unchanged through the tender process (BIPSolutions, 2004).

EUROPEAN AND WORLDWIDE INITIATIVES THAT PROMOTE E-PROCUREMENT AND THEIR IMPACT ON UK PROCUREMENT

A European wide initiative 'Your Europe' was launched in 1999 (European Commission, 2012) at the same time as the Northern Ireland's Citizens First initiative (DETNI, 2004). Both these were classic public sector approaches in bringing e-government in to reality. The 'Your Europe' Web-portal gives a record of all e-Europe initiatives including those on e-procurement across the European Union.

The European Union has been assessing the role of procurement in the public sector. Thoren (2004, p. 102) states "One of the proposed actions in the action plan for the information society of the European Union, eEurope 2005, is that, by the end of 2004, member states should have ensured that basic public services are interactive, where relevant, and accessible for all." The move to electronic contracts was enshrined in European legislation with the European Directives 2004/17 and 2004/18, which has a direct impact on construction industry. The move to electronic solutions for public sector activities including procurement is not exclusive to Europe. Thoren (2004) shows that the European agenda in regard to using electronic activity is being matched in countries such as Canada, Australia, and Singapore.

European Directives 2004/17 and 2004/18

European Law follows the stipulations in the World Trade Organisation (WTO) General Procurement Agreement (1994) Annex 4 Articles VII through XVI (WTO, 1994). The Hierarchy of legislation in the UK is shown in Figure 2.

However, as the WTO agreement was made prior to e-procurement becoming widely used it does not have any special provisions for it. In Europe, all procurement is subject to the Treaty on the Functioning of the European Union (TFEU). Europe has set within the European Directives 2004/17 (Eurlex, 2004a) and 2004/18 (Eurlex, 2004b) financial thresholds where additional rules regarding procurements above these limits were incorporated into European law on 31st March 2004. For the first time, European Directive 2004/17 (Eurlex, 2004a) Clause 20 acknowledged the use of electronic tendering and transmission of documents. This allowed it to be incorporated into the legislation of various national Governments.

It also confirmed that some electronic procurement systems could meet the principles of the European Union: equal treatment, non-discrimination, mutual recognition, proportionality, and transparency and could therefore be used for large European Union Tenders. Further enshrined in this clause for the first time was legislation allowing the use of dynamic purchasing systems such as electronic auctions. While these European Directives are not specifically for construction the rules within them must be applied to construction.

Public Contracts Regulations 2006

The European Directives 2004/17 (Eurlex, 2004a) and 2004/18 (Eurlex, 2004b) are incorporated into UK law through the Public Contracts Regulations 2006 (TSO, 2006). The current financial limits applied from 1 January 2012. From 2004 onwards the Finanancial Thresholds are reviewed by the

European Community every two years. The latest of these is European Commission Regulation (EU) No 1251/2011 resulting in the financial Thresholds defined in Table 2. The European Commission (2011/C 353/01) (2011) further show that the Sterling Equivalents were published by the European Union. These are also summarised in Table 2. The Public Contracts Regulations (TSO, 2006) defines those to whom Table 2 Schedule 1 applies as being UK Central Government Bodies.

Contracts meeting these thresholds have to be advertised in the Supplement to the Official Journal of the European Union (OJEU). All contracts above the thresholds in Table 2 must follow one of five procurement procedures. These cover the various procurement routes described earlier. They are:

1. The Open Procedure
2. The Restricted Procedure
3. The Negotiated Procedure
4. The Competitive Dialogue Procedure
5. A Dynamic Purchasing System

The first four are used for Construction Projects and the final one for Goods and Services Procure-

Figure 2. The hierarchy of procurement legislation

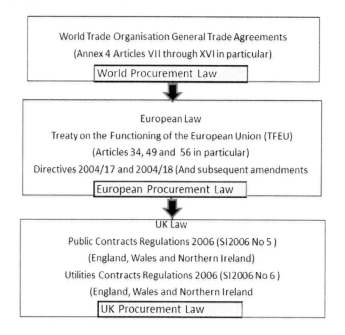

Table 2. Current European financial limits

Financial Threshold for:	Supplies	Services	Works
Entities listed in Schedule 1	£113,057 (€130,000)	£113,057 (€130,000)	£4,348,350 (€5,000,000)
Other public sector contracting authorities	£173,934 (€200,000)	£173,934 (€200,000)	£4,348,350 (€5,000,000)
Indicative Notices	£652,253 (€750,000)	£652,253 (€750,000)	£4,348,350 (€5,000,000)
Small Lots	£69,574 (€80,000)	£69,574 (€80,000)	£869,670 (€1,000,000)

ment. The amendment to the Public Contracts Regulations (TSO, 2009) adds the following two options for contracts already in place and removes the Dynamic Purchasing System:

- An existing supplier, for example, a strategic partnering arrangement with a particular supplier.
- An existing contract, for example a catalogue, an existing departmental contract or one let by another department.

TSO (2006) in Clauses 18, 19, 20, and 21 demonstrate that the first four procurement procedures can have their time limits reduced should e-procurement be adopted. These are summarised in Table 3. Reductions in time between 23% and 16% can be achieved through electronic documentation. The conclusion can be drawn that each of the procurement procedures above is therefore suitable for e-procurement adoption.

DFP (2009) identify limits and methods of procurement for contracts below the European financial threshold. These were first set on 17 February 2004 and revised in April 2006. A further revision took place on 1st January 2009 (DFP, 2009). The current limits and methods for public sector procurement below the European Financial Threshold are reproduced in Table 4.

United Nations Directories for EDI for Administration, Commerce, and Transport (ISO 9735:2002)

UNECE (2008) first released a standard for Electronic Data Interchange (EDI) in 1988. This document was agreed as an international standard for Data Interchange (ISO 9735). ISO 9735(2002) is now an International standard issued by ISO, which reproduces the UN/EDIFACT Syntax Rules. These rules have been agreed by the United Nations Economic Commission for

Table 3. Time reductions due to e-procurement

Open	Restricted	Negotiated	Competitive Dialogue
52 Days or 36 Days with Prior Information Notice (PIN)	First Stage 37 Days Second Stage 40 Days or 36 Days with PIN	First Stage 37 Days Second Stage time not specified	First Stage 37 Days Second Stage time not specified
Reduce the 52 Days to 45 Days for electronic contract notice or 29 Days with PIN	Reduce First Stage to 30 Days for electronic contract notice	Reduce First Stage to 30 Days for electronic contract notice	Reduce First Stage to 30 Days for electronic contract notice
Further reduce to 40 Days for electronic tendering	Reduce Second Stage to 35 Days for electronic tendering	Second Stage time not specified	Second Stage time not specified
Overall time reduction from 52 days to 40 days = 23%	Overall time reduction from 37+40 = 77 days to 30+35 = 65 days = 16%	Overall time reduction First stage only from 37 days to 30 days = 19%	Overall time reduction First stage only from 37 days to 30 days = 19%

Table 4. Financial limits and methods for public contracts below the European limits

Value	Procedure
Up to £1,500	2/3 oral quotations (Fax or Email confirmation should be obtained)
>£1,500 <£10,000	4 Selected Tenders
>£10,000 <£30,000	5 Selected Tenders
>£30,000 < EU Thresholds	Publically advertised tender competition

Adapted from DFP, 2010. Contracts below the European Thresholds do not have any specified reductions in time.

Europe (UN/ECE) as syntax rules for Electronic Data Interchange for Administration, Commerce and Transport (EDIFACT) and are part of the United Nations Trade Data Interchange Directory (UNTDID). GXS (2005) show that this standard controls the way any data interchange (data and money) is controlled worldwide.

The International Alliance for Interoperability (IAI)

BuildingSmart (2009b) is a merger of the International Alliance for Interoperability and the originally UK based CITE organisation discussed earlier. The IAI has a standard way of writing procedures for sharing information called Industry Foundation Classes (IFC). Each specification is called a class and these provide a set of agreed rules for a common language for constructing a format. The model produced (called a Building Information Model – BIM) can be shared and allows each operative the ability to define their own view of the objects contained within the model (BuildingSmart, 2009c). The documents can be viewed through a browser in HTML format.

BuildingSmart (2009d) aims produce a format, which will provide full interoperability for all building suppliers systems. It is especially important as it specialises in linking up construction specialists and allowing the transfer of AutoCAD drawings. This is represented diagrammatically in Figure 3.

AEC (Architecture, Engineering, and Construction) software is closely linked to this format of data exchange (AEC Software, 2012). An example of this being FastTrack Project management software which utilises the XML data interchange format.

Figure 3. Shared IAI interoperability model

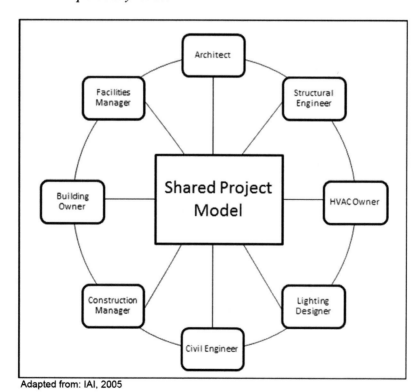

Adapted from: IAI, 2005

THE USE OF ELECTRONIC AUCTIONS FOR CONSTRUCTION PROCUREMENT

Arrowsmith (2001) defines reverse auctions as "a tendering procedure in which tenderers are provided with information on the other tenders, and are permitted to amend their own tenders on an on-going basis to beat those other tenders." Auctions are most commonly used as a means of driving down costs. According to Raghavan and Prabhu (2004) bidding continues until a pre-established bidding period ends or until no seller is willing to bid any lower, whichever comes first.

Teich *et al.* (2004, p. 2) states "The roots of electronic auction and negotiation mechanisms are in the auction and negotiation theory. Economists have investigated isolated, single good auctions. The ascending price English auction, the descending price Dutch auction and the Vickrey second-price sealed bid auction have been the most commonly studied auction mechanisms."

Arrowsmith (2001) and Teich *et al.* (2004) identify four different types of electronic auction.

1. **(Forward) Dutch:** Price descends until lowest price is reached.
2. **(Forward) English**: Price ascends until highest price is given.
3. **Reverse Dutch**: Prices rise until the first suppliers offer to supply at that price; least common of the four methods.
4. **Reverse English:** (Or, just "Reverse").

The price-only ethos of auctions seems at odds with the aspirations of the Latham and Egan reports into the UK Construction Industry. Smeltzer *et al.* (2003) comment that the use of auctions as a means of procurement results in a lack of loyalty as a buyer is only chasing a low price. Arminas (2002) points out no long-term relationship are therefore built up and the partnering ethos prescribed by Latham and Egan as a means of improving the Construction Industry

fails. Due to a short-term relationship being put into place by the auction, the initiative to invest in the quality of work provided, the incentive to train staff, revise work procedures, and make capital expenditure is lost. The NHS Purchasing eAuctions Pilot report (2004) identifies that only one of the 100 firms contacted refused to take part. This indicates that though there are apperent drawbacks there is market induced acceptance of the e-auction process. However, Smeltzer *et al.* (2003) points out how a long-term relationship is broken down by the use of an auction. This was due to the lowest sealed bid no longer being acceptable to the client and the client was seen to be saying that this did not meet expectations and they would "shop around" further. Smeltzer *et al.* (2003) exemplifies the drawbacks of e-auctions that in one instance of copper wiring, the supplier was so upset that it refused to bid with a customer with whom it had conducted business transactions with for over 7 years.

A quote from the European Construction Institute magazine ECI news (2003, p. 5) is pertinent in this regard "Reverse on-line auctions of subcontracts may drive down prices in the short-term, but they will do nothing to improve long-term industry performance and they are totally alien to an open book approach to alliancing and supply chain integration."

Don Ward is quoted in *Contract Journal* (Pearman, 2002, p. 3) as saying that he did not see how online auction tools could be used to assess the quality of the package offered. He considered electronic auctions as no more than a more efficient means of communication. He gives a view from a contractor's perspective, stating:

However, one contractor involved in a recent Dutch auction said: The only winner, apart from the auctioneer, is the cynical client who wants to screw the contractor.

The article also indicates that contractors question the validity of the cost saving produced through implementation of auctions. It suggests that most develop a strategy where they place their initial sealed price bid higher than if there had not been an auction. Yet, UK retail giant TESCO™ use Dutch Auctions for some of their construction work packages. They have reported savings of up to 3 percent through its controversial practice of reverse auction bidding (Contract Journal, 2003).

Initial price is the starting bid in the auction, therefore, although the studies show that auctions produce price savings it is only a price reduction on an inflated bid price. This may not be a saving at all should the tender have been let solely on sealed bids without the knowledge of a second stage (Pearman, 2002). The NHS Purchasing eAuctions Pilot report (2004) indicated savings of around 6% over normal tendering costs across the range of products piloted. However, they assume that the normal tendering costs are those after the first stage and not the figures after claims and therefore the figures should be treated with caution.

The use of electronic auctions best suits for standardised products and services where price alone is the governing criteria. In construction, price alone is rarely the key award criterion as both products and services vary. Another drawback in e-auctions is that its transparency results in commercially sensitive information given out over a website is visible to all competing bidders and that this meant the competition could see exactly what price others were supplying the goods and services.

Smeltzer *et al.* (2003) suggest that there is a possibility that those taking up the "challenge" of an auction may get caught in what they term as the "race." Bidders might get emotionally involved and end up submitting prices that are unreasonable. It has also been recorded that some bidders actually submitted prices below cost price in order to win or for quantities that they could not possibly deliver. In these situations, the bidders then tried to release themselves from what was a binding contract resulting in the whole acquisition process being slowed down and in some cases

the acrimony created resulted in the bidder being blacklisted (Smeltzer, et al., 2003). Pearman (2005) suggested that the Government may in the future examine the use of electronic auctions for construction activity in line with activity by large retailers such as TESCO™ for building projects. Katok *et al.* (2004) showed that electronic auctions are not suitable for all applications but can be used successfully for well-established commodity like items. They used examples such as plastic resin and personal computers as examples. They said however, that they are not suitable where there is a measure of uncertainty as in new products. In conclusion, therefore, auctions for construction products should only be used for certain goods and services where a long-term relationship with the supplier is not important and the items are clearly specified.

Raghavan and Prabhu (2004) propose a software framework for electronic auctions, negotiations, and settlements. This needs to be further developed to encompass the tendering process applicable to construction procurement. The User interface manager interfaces with a database management agent and the information submitted is stored in a database. The operation is carried out over the Internet. Raghavan and Prabhu (2004) model only deals with the e-auction process and not the logistics of e-tendering but could equally be adapted to do so.

ANALYSIS OF E-PROCUREMENT IMPLEMENTATION IN CONSTRUCTION

This section of the chapter deals with the implementation of e-procurement in construction. It shows that while e-procurement uptake has not been as expected within construction that the public sector and the initiatives described in the last part of the chapter are driving implementation within the sector. It further describes the implementation rates across the disciplines within construction showing that the public sector clients have the largest implementation rate.

The RICS carried out a major survey of the UK Construction Industry on the use of electronic contracts (Martin, 2003). The results showed that only 29% of the Bills of Quantities (BOQ)/Schedules of Rates and Prices (SORP) produced were sent to the contractor in electronic form. This equates to only 2.9% of the UK Construction Industry utilising the CITE format to convey contract documents. This low level of industry use has continued over many years. A similar study also conducted by Martin (2009, Table 2) shows that 15% of the Quantity Surveying Organisations said that they carried out e-procurement in construction five years on from his initial study. However, these studies were not related to public sector procurement specifically.

One of the first studies related to e-procurement in the public sector (Wamuziri & Seywright, 2005) reported an anticipated increase. Responses to their survey indicated 41% of local authorities in England included e-procurement as part of their overall procurement strategy. A further 45% of their sample was proceeding with the development of full e-procurement systems. This section of the sample indicated that in procurement of construction capital projects, different e-procurement systems were being trialed. One would expect that on completion of the trials, the benefits achieved through e-procurement will result in e-procurement for construction steadily increasing. In 2005, only a single local authority in England had a full working e-procurement system where tender documents could be downloaded and returned electronically (Wamuziri & Seywright, 2005). However, even this authority had not made its use compulsory.

Eadie *et al.* (2011) followed this with a study of public sector contractors and another subsequent study which examined the public sector clients. The first study focused on construction contractors who had worked partly for the public

sector. Roads Service Northern Ireland adopted an e-procurement system in late 2001. By creating a sample based on contractors who had recorded interest or tendered for their work (70 contractors out of a total of 114 civil engineering contractors registered with the Construction Industry Training Board [CITB] in Northern Ireland) it ensured that the sample would be familiar with e-procurement in construction. It also ensued that the sample was homogeneous, as all members would have shared convictions and beliefs, thus reducing ambiguity.

The study relating to public sector contractors (Figure 4) demonstrates that 47% of contractors within the sample received only 1-10% of their BOQ/SORP in electronic form. Of the remaining 53% of the sample, 26% received between 11% and 30% of documentation in electronic form. The 6% who had 91-100% of documentation in electronic form worked solely for Roads Service and hence used their e-procurement system. This again indicates that e-procurement adoption has lower levels of adoption within the construction industry.

Eadie *et al.* (2011) having chosen company sizes similar to those in Batenburg; (2007), compared their findings in construction with those in the General Goods and Services industries. The organisation sizes analysed in Eadie *et al.* (2011) were 11-20, 21-50, 51-100, and over 100. This determined that contractor size was not a factor in receiving electronic contract documentation. This would be expected, as the tender documentation is more likely to be produced from the clients design team in a traditional contract. The median percentage of contract documentation received electronically was around 25% for all sizes of contractor.

Batenburg (2007) indicates within the Goods and Services industries typically 50% of the small firms complete more than 5% of their purchases online. He further identifies that this percentage is slightly lower among the larger firms. Batenburg (2007) states that this indicates

Figure 4. Percentage of BOQ received in electronic form by contractors in Northern Ireland

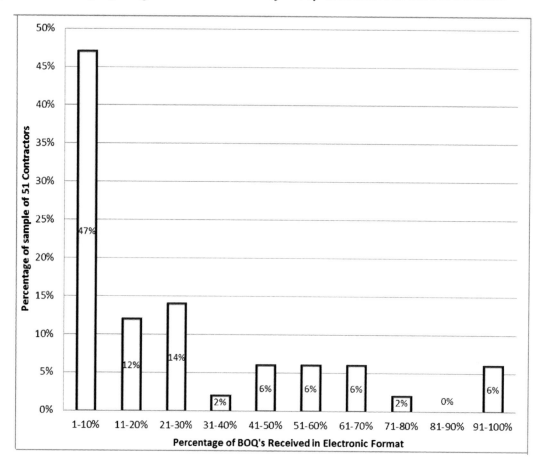

that size does determine the probabilities of e-procurement adoption but not the share of e-procurement in the total purchase process.

Eadie *et al.* (2011) indicate the opposite is true in relation to construction contractors. However, this is because use of e-procurement is primarily determined by the client/consultant due to the fragmentation of design and construction within the construction industry. The percentage by size remained around 25% for all sizes of contractors in relation to e-procurement adoption (Figure 5).

This was followed by a main survey, which was used to determine the extent of e-procurement implementation across England, Scotland, Wales and Northern Ireland. A variety of disciplines was surveyed to allow comparison between the public and private sectors. The sample contained quantity surveyors, public sector clients, architects, private sector clients, and consulting engineers.

Eadie *et al.* (2011) study surveyed a total of 775 construction organisations in 2008. This included 42 responses from the Public Sector and the remaining 732 from the private sector. The private sector distribution included 483 Surveyors, 172 Architects, 35 Private sector clients and 43 Consulting Engineers. The study thus provided statistics for use of e-procurement within the United Kingdom across the disciplines and sectors. Eadie *et al.* (2011) allowed comparison of the various disciplines within construction in the UK for the first time. Table 5 summarises the results. It indicates that the public sector clients were well ahead of the private sector in terms

Figure 5. Median percentage of electronic contract documentation by contractor size

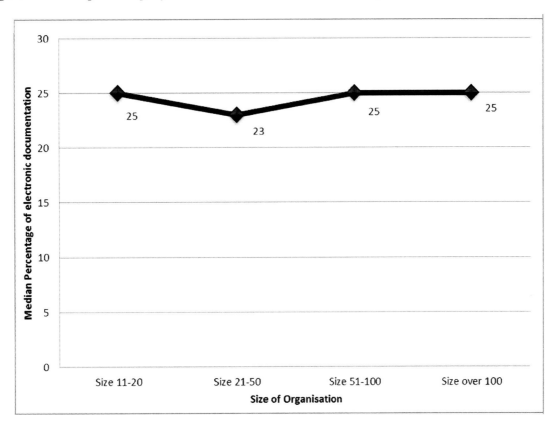

Table 5. Sample valid response breakdown by discipline

Discipline	Total Number of Organisations	Number Using E-Procurement/ Percentage	Number Not Using E-Procurement	Number Not Contactable, No Longer Trading or Unavailable for Comment	% Valid Response
Quantity Surveyors	483	83 / 25%	247	153	68%
Public Sector Clients	42	29 / 47%	10	3	93%
Architects	172	12 / 19%	156	4	98%
Private Sector Clients	35 in sample	0 / 0	35	Not applicable	
Engineers	43	4 / 15%	25	14	67%
	775	128 / 27%	473	174	77%

of adopting e-procurement within the industry with 47% having adopted it in some manner. This is substantially above the other disciplines and indicates that the public sector is driving e-procurement implementation within the industry.

There is a 22% gap between the public sector clients and the private sector Quantity Surveyors in the use of e-procurement (Note: quantity surveyors are the specialists professionals primarily entrusted the role of procurement in the UK construction industry). This may indicate that the various public sector initiatives to speed up the adoption of e-procurement in the public sector have paid off to some extent. This somewhat agrees with the findings of Wamuziri and Seywright, (2005) reported before with respect to the use of e-procurement in local authorities.

DRIVERS AND BARRIERS TO E-PROCUREMENT IN CONSTRUCTION

E-procurement is the acquisition of goods and services without the use of paper processes (Przymus, 2003). The factors which influence the implementation of e-procurement are divided into two sections within this chapter. These factors determine the likelihood of adoption of e-procurement. These are drivers promoting e-procurement and barriers causing challenges to its adoption within an organisation. Eadie *et al.* (2007) were also the first to investigate whether the construction procurement drivers and barriers were similar to those in other industries. They initially reviewed e-procurement in construction from a worldwide, European, and UK perspective. Eadie *et al.* (2007) compared e-procurement in construction initially with detailed studies on e-procurement in the goods and services sectors published in the United States and Australia. Westcott and Mayer (2002) rank the e-procurement uptake in these countries as first

and fourth in the world with Japan and Sweden occupying second and third place. The UK and Ireland are positioned fifth and sixth, respectively.

DRIVERS FOR E-PROCUREMENT

A detailed literature review on drivers and barriers for e-procurement provides the basis for the discussion provided in this section. These drivers and barriers were further processed and analysed for its applicability to the construction industry in Eadie *et al.* (2007, 2010a, 2010b). The following subsections provide a detailed discussion on how these affect construction e-procurement. A full list of classified and ranked drivers from Eadie *et al.* (2010a, 2010b) is provided later in the chapter.

Summary of E-Procurement Drivers Identified from Literature

Eadie *et al.* (2010a) revealed a collated set of 21 drivers for general e-procurement. These are summarised in Table 6.

Those drivers identified from the literature in Table 6 represent general e-procurement drivers and barriers and had not been verified as specific to construction. Eadie *et al.* (2010a) carried out a rigorous Delphi process to identify and rank the importance of each Driver and Barrier from a construction perspective. This allowed a number of drivers to be filtered out as lacking significance in construction. It also identified several new drivers that were shown to exist in the construction industry, which had not been identified in published literature from other industries. Further clarification resulted in some of the drivers in Table 6 being combined resulting in a final list of drivers and barriers specific to construction. Those deemed most important to construction are discussed below with their ranking for construction.

Table 6. Drivers to e-procurement identified from literature

No.	Drivers from Literature	Referenced In:
1	Process cost savings - (Tender/Purchase process)	Knudsen (2003), Minahan and Degan (2001), Martin (2009)
2	Service/Material/Product cost savings	Minahan and Degan (2001), Martin (2009) – Reduced Waste
3	Transaction administration cost savings	Davila et al. (2003) and Panayiotou et al. (2003)
4	Reduced administration costs	Egbu et al. (2003), Hawking et al. (2004), Raghavan and Prabhu (2004)
5	Increasing profit margins	McIntosh and Sloan (2001), Wong and Sloan(2003), Ribeiro (2001)
6	Strategic cost savings	Knudsen (2003)
7	Enhanced inventory management	Hawking et al. (2004), Martin (2009)
8	Decrease in costs through reduced staffing levels	Kong et al. (2001), Davila et al. (2003), Egbu et al. (2003)
9	Shortened overall procurement cycle times	Minahan and Degan (2001)
10	Shortened Communication Cycle Times	Knudsen (2003)
11	Reduction in time through greater transparency (Less objections)	Panayiotou et al. (2003)
12	Reduction in evaluation time	Panayiotou et al. (2003), Martin (2009)
13	Reduction in time through improved internal workflow	Panayiotou et al. (2003)
14	Reduction in purchasing order fulfillment time - Contract Completion	Davila et al. (2003)
15	Reduction in time through increased visibility	Kalakota et al. (2001)
16	Increased quality through increased competition	Kalakota et al. (2001)
17	Increased quality through benchmarking (Market Intelligence)	Hawking et al. (2004)
18	Increased quality through increased visibility in the supply chain	Minahan and Degan (2001) and Hawking et al. (2004)
19	Increased quality through increased efficiency	McIntosh and Sloan (2001), Ribeiro (2001), Martin (2009)
20	Increased quality through improved communication	Hawking et al. (2004)
21	Gaining competitive advantage	Wong and Sloan (2003)

Price Reduction in Tendering

Gebauer *et al.* (1988) in the US suggested that the two most important measures of the success of a procurement process are cost and time. This was followed by a study that suggested reduction in costs through the adoption of electronic processes was the most important factor for 75% of its respondents (National Institute of Governmental Purchasing, 2001). Hawking *et al.* (2004) confirm this with a result indicating it as most important for between 75 and 80% of their sample in Australia. The importance of Cost reduction

was also reported in the UK (Erridge, et al., 2001) and in China (Kong, et al., 2001). Rankin (2006) shows that this driver is also applicable to e-procurement in the construction industry in Canada and Knudsen (2003) indicates price reductions through efficiency. Sone (2011) indicates that e-procurement reduces time by days, speeds payment through visibility of accounts receivable, and generally reduces costs. Martin (2009) also considered this to be a major driver in cost savings through reduced waste.

In Construction, "Process, transaction, and administration cost savings" was the driver ranked highest by both the public and private sectors. This meant that overall it was the highest ranked in the 'Construction Industry Ranking.' This agrees with the findings of McIntosh and Sloan (2001) and Ribeiro (2001) in their assessment of the goods and services industries. More recently, Chen *et al.* (2011) identified that 76% of their sample considered that efficiency of business processes was the main driver for implementing e-business in construction. Any proposed e-procurement software that is implemented within the construction industry should therefore place maximum emphasis on the reduction of costs. "Price reduction in tendering" was ranked first for the goods and services industry in Australia by Hawking *et al.* (2004). In the US a similar result was achieved by Davila *et al.* (2003) whose study ranked "Purchasing transaction costs" in first position. Therefore, its importance is across all industries.

In 2003, the Office of Government Commerce (OGC) recognised this driver and realised that reduced costs could be achieved as a consequence of adopting e-procurement within the public sector (BravoSolution, 2008). This led to the OGC advertising a framework contract for the provision of e-procurement systems in the Official Journal of the European Union (OJEU) (BravoSolution, 2008). BravoSolution™ secured this contract in December 2003. BravoSolution™ has achieved results in trimming costs worldwide with its e-procurement solution; an example of this is Delta Airlines where savings of $300 million have been achieved (BravoSolution, 2012). In the construction industry, the implementation of BravoSolution's e-procurement system within both the public sector, through the OGC, and the private sector, through the Royal Institution of Chartered Surveyors (RICS), resulted in cost savings. However Eadie *et al.* (2012) report that the uptake in the construction private sector has been low and much more could be saved should further adoption be achieved. Martin (2009), reporting for the RICS (mostly for private sector quantity surveying organisations), discusses the

BravoSolution™ system and identifies the cost savings realised as a significant driver. Other systems exist and all purport to produce cost savings. It is evident from the literature above that both the public and private sectors of the construction industry could benefit from the cost savings achieved.

Convenience of Archiving Completed Work

In construction, public sector clients rank "Convenience of archiving completed work" in joint first place along with the "Process, transaction, and administration cost savings." Betts *et al.* (2006) highlighted this as a necessity to fulfill the legal requirements of e-tendering. Islington Council (2008) determined that when it decided to store all documents electronically including all contract documents that digital archiving will enable the removal of 250,000 pages, or 12 square metres of archive space, thereby saving £2,400 annually. The length of time specified in disposal schedules for local government contracts is six years after they become non-current and twelve years if they are contracts under seal as stipulated by the National Archives (2012) Clause 3.2. Local Councils follow this guidance, for example Blaby District Council (2004, p. 23) and the length of time and size of contract documentation means that substantial savings can be accrued through procurement being electronic due to the size of the storage medium. In Scotland for building and engineering work contract documents may be retained indefinitely by some government departments such as the Scottish Office (Gray, 2006). Those responding to Eadie *et al.* (2010b) therefore correctly identified the ability to archive electronically in the construction industry as one of the most important drivers for e-procurement within the public sector. This driver was also ranked joint second by the private sector organisations indicating that it is important for both sectors of the construction industry.

Increased Quality through Increased Accuracy

"Increased quality through increased accuracy (Elimination of errors through computer use)" was ranked third in the overall construction industry. However, this is much less highly ranked by the public sector where it is ranked it sixth in importance. Williams and Lynnes (2002) and Minahan & Degan (2001) all suggest improved contract compliance results from elimination of error-prone manual data entry during e-procurement. In the public sector, it is essential that it is confirmed that the construction project meets its objectives. These checks are carried out through the various stages of the Gateway process. Robust cost and content checks are adopted for construction contracts, which according to OGC (2009, 2006) have already created high quality contract documents. These checks are not present in the private sector meaning that more reliance is placed on the e-procurement system to highlight difficulties. Despite this Scalde *et al.* (2006) show that many public sector organisations from sectors such as healthcare and housing have moved to electronic procurement systems to boost the accuracy of procurement documentation. The private sector acknowledges the benefit of increased accuracy where market forces and high competition hone the need for precision and accuracy (Cartlidge, 2006).

Increased Quality through Increased Efficiency

Implementing e-procurement means that rates and associated information from construction tender documentation does not have to be copied or re-typed two or three times. This ensures that there are quality and time savings during the assessment and contract management process. The quality and efficiency enhancements e-procurement brings are also underlined by Tindsley and Stephenson (2008). The private sector organisations that rely on efficiency to survive during economically difficult times in the construction industry recognise the effect that efficiency gains can have on the performance of an organisation resulting in a higher rank than the respondents from public sector construction organisations—fourth and seventh place, respectively. McIntosh and Sloan (2001), Ribeiro (2001), and Martin (2009) all classify this as a driver but do not rank it. Therefore, comparison with other industries is limited.

Reduction in Time

Eighty-five percent of those in the Goods and Services industries suggested time savings could be achieved through E-Procurement adoption (National Institute of Governmental Purchasing, 2001). Further drivers related to sourcing materials for products such as emphasis on time to market, product quality-based competition, customer uncertainty and the need to improve bottom line costs were identified by Kalakota *et al.* (2001). Knudsen (2003) further comments on the speed and efficiency of e-procurement and calls it a "lean channel for communication." Minahan and Degan (2001) conclude that e-procurement results in shortened overall procurement cycle times.

McIntosh and Sloan (2001) in the US and Ribeiro (2001) in the UK both indicate that significant streamlining of the material procurement processes bringing speed, flexibility, efficiency, and increased profit margins to organisations could be achieved by the implementation of e-procurement. In construction, Rankin (2006) determines a reduction in overall procurement cycle time. With specific reference to the public sector, Panayiotou *et al.* (2003) state that "E-Procurement solutions make corporate purchasing activities more efficient and cost effective." They further suggest that e-procurement leads to a reduction in time through greater transparency (Less objections).

The speed of evaluation of bids is also a benefit raised by both Panayiotou *et al.* (2003) and Martin (2009). Davila *et al.* (2003) further highlights a reduction in purchasing order fulfillment time through early contract completion. The procurement communication time reduction was ranked in fourth position overall in the construction industry with the procurement cycle time ranked sixth. As most public sector construction contracts are above the European thresholds discussed earlier, the reduction in time through e-procurement becomes more important (ranked in third position for construction in the public sector) than private sector contracts where the European directives do not generally apply (resulting in a reduced ranking of ninth).

Lower Administration Costs

Rankin (2006) states that a decrease in paperwork and therefore lower administration costs were ranked as the second highest driver for e-procurement in construction in Canada. Hawking *et al.* (2004) investigates it as a driver for e-procurement. Another way of ascertaining if administration costs are lower is via the scrutiny of rents (profits that do not induce competition). Knudsen (2003) identified that Ricardian rents (efficiency savings) could be amplified by implementing e-procurement initiatives. Yet his work did not rank these efficiency savings alongside the other identified drivers for e-procurement. Lower transaction administration costs are highlighted by Davila *et al.* (2003) and Panayiotou *et al.* (2003). Egbu *et al.* (2003) show how the electronic management of the process can lower the administration costs. Raghavan and Prabhu (2004) show that this is applicable not only to the construction tender process but also to electronic auctions. During the Delphi process Eadie *et al.* (2010a) experts combined this with the process and transaction costs as a single driver which was determined to be the most important driver for e-procurement in construction.

Reduction in Procurement Staff

Egbu *et al.* (2003) provided an example of an 80% reduction in staff at a steel supplier through use of an e-procurement system on a multi-million pound project. Reduction in staff is one way in which competitive advantage through reduced costs can be achieved. Kong *et al.* (2001) and Davila *et al.* (2003) further support the argument that e-procurement means less staff. However, this is a simplistic viewpoint as other work by procurement staff takes the place of the less efficient paper based procedures resulting in increased quality. Staff reduction and turnover can be removed or incorporated into efficiency savings (Eadie, et al., 2010a).

Gaining Competitive Advantage

Remaining profitable depends on an organisation gaining competitive advantage over its competitors. Buchta *et al.* (2010) suggest that centralising functions such as payroll, procurement, and logistics in a single country may be one way of accomplishing this. In the public sector, centralized procurement has been used as a means of reducing public spending (Albano & Sparro, 2010). Electronic systems of procurement are ideal in this situation, as they are not bound by geographical or time limits. This is further emphasised by Kalakota (2001) who states that e-procurement "allows procurement activities 24 hours a day, 7 days a week, and 365 days a year." The gain in competitiveness is proved by Wong and Sloan (2003) in showing that gaining competitive advantage, reducing procurement costs, and increased profitability are perceived as three of the most important drivers for e-procurement. Rankin (2006) states that e-procurement in the construction sector results in increased productivity and greater market access. A number of studies also show that it is a means of gaining competitive advantage through increasing profit margins (McIntosh & Sloan, 2001; Wong

& Sloan, 2003; Ribeiro, 2001). According to McIntosh and Sloan (2001), Ribeiro (2001), and Martin (2009) not only do these bring financial gains but also improve the quality of the product through a more efficient process. Eadie *et al.* (2010a, 2010b) investigated these in relation to construction. Within Construction, the private and public sectors ranked this driver very differently. The private sector ranked these driver nine positions higher than the public sector, which ranked it in twentieth position. This shows that in a public sector scenario where generally competitive forces do not act in a similar way to the private sector, this driver is not deemed very important.

Improving Communication

Hawking *et al.* (2004) examined three separate communication drivers: "Improving visibility in supply chain management," "Improving visibility in customer demand," and "Increased compliance." With respect to improving communications, Rankin (2006) further identifies data transaction accuracy as a driver. Hawking *et al.* (2004) further suggest that improved communication also improves the quality of the end product.

Moreover, time reduction is considered as vital in construction with "Shortened Internal and External Communication Cycle times" being ranked highly. "Shortened Internal and External Communication Cycle times" rank as the fourth highest driver overall in Eadie *et al.* (2010b). In construction, the private sector ranks it sixth and the public sector ranks it fifth. This supports the view that e-procurement improves coordination and collaboration, therefore resulting in cost savings and reduced procurement cycle times (Gunasekaran, et al., 2009). Davila *et al.* (2003) ranked "Purchasing Cycle time" as third for the goods and services industry in USA.

Improved communication was deemed more important in construction contracts in the public sector as often large schemes are carried out with the application of European contract timescales over the financial thresholds mentioned earlier. As discussed earlier in the chapter the timescales can be reduced by implementing e-procurement as per the Public Contracts Regulations 2006 (TSO, 2006). The percentage reduction in time through e-procurement use can be significant. Williams (2007, p. 48) confirms that the first phase of the procurement can be reduced by 7 days. Table 2 earlier in the chapter shows how used e-procurement can reduce the overall time by up to 23%. It is seen as a little less significant to private organisations where the European Union constraints often do not apply to their procurement.

Improved Market Intelligence and Enhanced Decision-Making

Hawking *et al.* (2004) separated market intelligence from the decisions made on the information. As the decisions are only as good as the intelligence behind them, Eadie *et al.* (2007) considered these as a combined single entity for construction. Kalakota *et al.* (2001) indicate that the increase in competition leads to increased quality in the bid. The decision making process is vital to a correct bid and many organisations benchmark themselves against their competition. Hawking *et al.* (2004) indicates that this benchmarking process is easier through e-procurement and therefore results in greater market intelligence, which increases the quality of the bid. They along with Minahan and Degan (2001) suggest that e-procurement also increases quality through increasing the visibility of the supply chain. These are both investigated in the Eadie *et al.* (2010a, 2010b) studies and ranked for construction industry. The benchmarking process through e-procurement is ranked substantially more importantly by organisations in the public sector (ninth) as opposed to (seventeenth in) the private sector.

THE BARRIERS TO E-PROCUREMENT

Wong and Sloan (2004) state that less than half (48%) of the respondents to their study suggested that they were able to conduct e-commerce effectively. This indicates that there are still barriers to the implementation of e-procurement that need to be overcome.

Summary of E-Procurement Barriers Identified from Literature

Eadie *et al.* (2010a) revealed a collated set of 31 barriers for general e-procurement. These are summarised in Table 7. These were then investigated in a similar way to the drivers in a construction context.

Those barriers identified from the literature in Table 7 represent general e-procurement barriers and similar to the drivers had not been verified as specific to construction. Eadie *et al.* (2010a) also carried out a rigorous Delphi process to identify and rank the importance of each Barrier from a construction perspective. Clarification as a result of the Delphi process resulted in a final list of barriers specific to construction. These are discussed below.

Unsure of Legal Position of E-Procurement

Wong and Sloan (2004) identify ICT as improving communication in construction. However, only 26% of respondents considered that ICT was acceptable as admissible written proof should it be required as evidence in a court of law. This dropped further to 17% when asked if it was acceptable as a written notice. These questions relating to the legal validity of electronic information exchange must be considered a barrier to the implementation of an e-procurement system.

Prior to the Electronic Communications Act (2000), it was considered one of the main barriers to e-procurement in the European Union (Julia-Barcelo, 1999). The legal problems described by Julia-Barcelo were: lack of specific legal regulation, different national approaches, and validity, enforceability, and/or evidentiary problems. In America, similar sentiments were expressed by Pena-Mona and Choudary (2001). In a little way, the Electronic Communications Act (2000) went towards seeking a solution. However, the lack of legal challenges and therefore case law has been identified as a barrier by Hawking *et al.* (2004), Julia-Barcelo (1999), and Martin (2009).

Gebauer *et al.* (1988) highlight a number of legal issues such as security in the process. Can data be transmitted to the wrong person? Along with Julia-Barcelo (1999), they further suggest unauthorised viewing can compromise confidentiality. The possibility of documents being tampered with was also raised (Gebauer, et al., 1988; Pena-Mona & Choudary, 2001). This is still a concern for many but technological advances and the development of vault systems have minimised its impact. Legal issues relating to the validity of the signature will be covered under the security barrier.

Data transmission reassembly where incorrect reassembly of data transmitted in packets occurs and incomplete documentation being provided through technological glitches are also highlighted as problems by Jennings (2001).

In investigating data transmission and reassembly and partial data display, Eadie *et al.* (2010b) indicate these security and legal issues ranked highly in tenth position overall for construction overall. This concurs with the findings of the European Commission (2010b) where the complexity of e-procurement was perceived as the main challenge to take-up for technical and legal reasons. However, drilling down into their data and segregating the legal aspect results in "legal uncertainties for general e-procurement" in the fourth most important position.

Table 7. Barriers to construction e-procurement identified from literature

No.	Barriers from Literature	Referenced In:
1	Upper management support/Lack of leadership	Davila et al. (2003), Hawking et al. (2004)
2	Other competing initiatives	Kheng et al. (2002)
3	Resistance to change	Davila et al. (2003), Martin (2009)- Natural Inertia
4	Lack of a widely accepted solution	Davila et al. (2003), Martin (2009)
5	Magnitude of change	Kheng et al. (2002)
6	Lack of a national IT policy relating to e-procurement issues	Carayannis et al. (2005)
7	Lack of flexibility	Carayannis et al. (2005)
8	Bureaucratic dysfunctionalities	Carayannis et al. (2005)
9	Complicated procedures and extended relationships	Carayannis et al. (2005) show how excessive state intervention is a barrier to e-procurement.
10	Lack of technical expertise	Davila et al. (2003), Martin (2009)
11	Staff turnover	Kransdorff (1998)
12	Slowdown in the uptake of Internet services since the dotcom bubble burst	Christensen et al. (2002)
13	Company access to the Internet	Smith (2006) - BBC Webpage
14	Religious objections to the Internet	McMullan(2005) Correspondence to CPD
15	Insufficient assessment of systems prior to installation	Forrest (1999)
16	Security in the process - Data transmission to the wrong person	Gebauer et al. (1988), Kheng et al. (2002) -59% of Singapore sample cite security as the main barrier
17	Confidentiality of information - unauthorised viewing	Gebauer et al. (1988), Julia-Barcelo (1999)
18	Prevention of tampering with documents - changes to documents	Gebauer et al. (1988), Pena-Mona and Choudary (2001)
19	Data transmission reassembly - incorrect reassembly of data transmitted in packets	Jennings (2001)
20	Partial data display - incomplete documents provided	Jennings (2001)
21	Lack of pertinent case law	Hawking et al. (2004), Julia-Barcelo (1999), Martin (2009)
22	Different national approaches to e-procurement	Carayannis et al. (2005)
23	Proof of intent - electronic signatures	Julia-Barcelo (1999), Rawlings (1998), Dumortier et al. (1999), Wright (1999)
24	Clarity of sender and tenderer information	Wright(1999), Dumortier et al. (1999)
25	Enforceability of electronic contracts	Jennings (2001), CITE website (2004)
26	Information technology investment costs	Irani and Love (2002), Wong and Sloan (2004), Martin (2009)
27	Cost of assessment of systems to find correct system to fulfill tasks	Forrest (1999),Wong and Sloan (2004)
28	Internal compatibility	Davila et al. (2003), Boeing (1996)
29	External compatibility	Davila et al. (2003), Boeing (1996)
30	Investment in compatible systems	Davila et al. (2003)
31	Reluctance to 'buy-into' one off systems	Irani and Love (2002)

Company Culture and Upper Management Support

Carayannis *et al.* (2005) investigated traditional public procurement and found that complicated procedures and found the barriers to be: extended relationships, excessive state intervention, bureaucratic dysfunctionalities, absence of a clear national IT policy, large volume of paper, lack of flexible centralised control, lack of information quality and resistance to change. Eadie *et al.* (2010a) study in construction considered these as separate barriers. The European Commission (2011b) further highlighted the lack of standards, no means of facilitating mutual recognition of national electronic solutions, onerous technical requirements and managing a multi-speed transition to e-procurement as its most significant challenges. Apart from the reduction in paper in public procurement each of the identified barriers therefore remains. "Resistance to change" is the largest barrier to the introduction of construction e-procurement within the public sector (Eadie, et al., 2010b). Martin (2009) suggested that organisations had a natural inertia, which resulted in a lack of desiring to incorporate innovations within the construction industry. In the US resistance to change, lack of a widely accepted solution and lack of leadership, which are cultural issues, are also identified as barriers by Davila *et al.* (2003) (US) and Hawking *et al.* (2004) (Australia) thus showing that these barriers are global.

The difference in construction ranking between the public sector and the private sector in relation to "Resistance to change" is conspicuous in this regard. It was ranked first by the public sector while the private sector ranked it in sixth place (Eadie, et al., 2010b). Van den Belt *et al.* (2010) states that as organisations grow they become more complex with the result that single individuals make fewer decisions. This is especially the case in the public sector, which has a large number of staff. This results in different managerial styles and a reliance on procedures resulting in greater resistance to change. While size of organisation is a factor in resistance to change, cultural differences between the public and private sectors also play a part. Many studies indicate that the public sector is more restrained in its attempts to change and slow to adapt to changing working practices (Brookfield, 2000). Value for money policies have been adopted as they spend public money and desire that the taxpayer is best served in every policy and system implemented. To do this systemic practice, procedures and other precautions need to be in place before rollout across the public sector. In the private sector, change happens due to proven efficiencies being implemented. The much smaller chain of command results in decisions being taken more quickly, often with the background of intense economic pressure to increase efficiency by reducing costs and seeking competitive advantage to enhance their market share in the industry (Silverman, 1992).

One of the ways in which this barrier could be overcome is by showcasing the benefits already discussed earlier in this chapter. Once the benefits are fully evidenced, possibly through pilots of various systems, therefore trialing systems in the setting they will be used it will break down barriers such as this. Those who are actually using the system will see for themselves the positive aspects e-procurement brings and be more willing to adopt it. This could be combined with the formation of standard practice and procedures for the use of e-procurement. This will allay public sector concerns thus minimising or eradicating the effects of this barrier.

With these barriers, the accompanying slowdown in adoption results in a lack of benefit realisation. Cultural change within the public sector is required prior to and during the implementation of an e-procurement system. This includes the use of champions allocated to the task with full senior management support. Especially since the downturn in the economy, with the additional pressures on companies, other competing initiatives have taken priority in order that the organisation survives. Kheng *et al.* (2002) showed in Singapore other competing initiatives were the largest barrier to adoption. Sixty percent (60%) of the respondents to that study considered that other difficulties were of more importance than e-procurement. This further emphasises the need for cultural change via senior management support if successful e-procurement adoption is to be achieved. Christensen *et al.* (2002) indicate that there has been a slowdown in the uptake of Internet services since the dotcom bubble burst. This has led to a culture of caution in many organisations. Some have been identified as lacking access to even basic services such as the Internet even though it impacts on their profitability (Smith, 2006). Cultural problems also exist among an exclusive Brethren Group known as the Taylorites who oppose access to the Internet on religious grounds (McMullan, 2005). The European Commission (2011b) indicate that 60% of the respondents count the culture barrier of "overcoming inertia and fear" as one of the five most important challenges to e-procurement adoption. Eadie *et al.* (2010b) show that it is the most important barrier within the public sector of the construction industry.

Lack of IT Infrastructure, Costly IT Systems, and Lack of Technical Expertise

The first barrier in this regard is that an organisation may not have the necessary technological infrastructure to carry out e-procurement (Wong & Sloan, 2004). The price of some of the e-procurement systems on the market has resulted in some organisations not being able to afford it (Hawking, et al., 2004) and the last problem relates to the skills set of their existing workforce which may mean that they cannot operate IT (Hawking, et al., 2004; Davila, et al., 2003). Rankin (2006) shows that all three of these should be considered as barriers in the construction industry. Irani and Love (2002), Wong and Sloan (2004), and Martin

(2009) all identify the software costs as a barrier to full implementation of e-procurement systems. Forrest (1999) and Wong and Sloan (2004) even consider the research costs in the assessment of systems to find correct system to fulfil tasks as prohibitive. Eadie *et al.* (2011b) show that the lack of technical expertise ranks in thirteenth position for construction with the cost of systems well down the ranking in twenty-fifth place.

Reluctance to "Buy-Into" One Off Systems

Linked to the preceding barrier, Eadie *et al.* (2010b) rank "Reluctance to 'Buy-into' one off systems" in fourth position for construction but this barrier has the greatest difference in rank between the private and public sectors. Private Sector organisations rank its importance in second place whereas the public sector organisations place it in twenty-third place. Costs have already been highlighted as the most important driver for e-procurement. According to Kivijärvi *et al.* (2011) for any electronic system, costs can be separated into two categories: business costs (adaptation and administrative costs) and IT costs (continuous and one-off costs). If organisations are forced to implement new systems for each project it dramatically increases all these costs and could leave the organisation a number of systems to support. While the public sector has enough staff and money available to support multiple systems the private sector businesses are more profit oriented and multiplying systems for different schemes results in increased costs and decreased profitability. The private sector contract size is generally smaller with smaller profit margins and they will be therefore more reticent to implement a volatile and frequently changing system or multiple systems for contracts. Many larger schemes in recent years have had their own extranets. As the public sector is involved with many of these and varied systems it is viewed as less of a barrier.

Although Irani and Love (2002) identified this as a barrier in the goods and services industry it was not ranked. Therefore, a comparison with other industries is not possible at this time.

Lack of E-Procurement Knowledge/ Skilled Personnel and No Business Relationship with Suppliers Capable of E-Procurement

The issue of skilled personnel is primarily related to an older generation that has not kept up to the advances in ICT related issues. This proves a difficulty in procurement as many of those responsible for submitting tenders for construction work are experienced personnel who have the experience required to accurately price work. This means that some are used to and rely on traditional forms and means of procurement. Kransdorff (1998) also identify a problem due to staff turnover. When staffs are highly trained and efficient in submitting electronic tender documentation and move on to other organisations, it leaves a gap within the original organization, which is difficult to fill. A problem also occurs when clients choose to move to e-procurement as Hawking *et al.* (2004) identified the lack of business relationships with suppliers as a barrier. An e-procurement enabled supply chain is becoming more common as the technology advances but is another barrier to its implementation. Rankin (2006) shows that in the Canadian construction industry this barrier is ranked as second highest. Davila *et al.* (2003) and Martin (2009) suggest that a lack of a widely accepted solution produces a lack of knowledge and skills in the area. Carayannis *et al.* (2005) suggest that there is a need for a single widely accepted government solution. The Bravosolution™ software adopted through a Framework agreement for Government e-procurement in the UK has produced a solution for public sector procurement but the private sector implementation remains fragmented.

Security of Transactions

The most important barrier to e-procurement from an overall construction industry perspective is the "Prevention of tampering with documents— changes to documents" (Eadie, et al., 2010b). This barrier was investigated in Eadie *et al.* (2007) under the title of '*Security of Transactions.*' This barrier was broken down into its constituent parts in Eadie *et al.* (2010a, 2010b) to permit separate assessment in the construction industry. Paulo *et al.* (2010) indicate that across industries security of data is one of the main barriers to e-procurement adoption through their survey of 721 organisations in Portugal. Davila *et al.* (2003) agree, indicating that security and control mechanisms are important as they investigate "Lack of faith in transaction and data integrity." The smaller level of cost for items in the goods and services industries where they are procuring large numbers of similar items meant that it was ranked ninth. The much larger costs and the unique product in the construction industry mean that concern over level of security due to the magnitude of transaction is much greater. The findings in Hawking *et al.* (2004) in the Australian goods and services industry show that "Security of transactions" is also ranked ninth. This shows a lack of correspondence between the findings in each industry and indicates that security is much more important as the overall cost of the project rises.

Electronic signatures have become a problem for adoption of e-procurement. The difficulty of gravity in UK law has led to questions over enforcement of electronic contracts. A Europe wide consultation closed on Electronic Signatures closed on 15th April 2011. This will endeavour to clarify a common approach to the issue across all member states and will result in the European legislative framework on e-signatures being re-formed. This follows the required progress stated in action point 8 of the Digital Agenda for Europe. It should also address another issue highlighted by

Julia-Barcelo (1999), Rawlings (1998), Dumortier *et al.* (1999), and Wright (1999), which is the issue of proof of intent via electronic signatures as they only identify the person but do not address the issue of gravity. According to Wright (1999), and Dumortier *et al.* (1999) issues resulting from passwords being passed on, cloud the issue of sender identification for submission of tender information. Jennings (2001) suggests that this could call into question the enforceability of electronic contracts. The proposed amendments should allow the legal issue to be clarified not only in member countries but across the various borders in Europe.

Ranked in joint fourth position overall for construction is the barrier "Proof of intent—electronic signatures." It was ranked third by the private sector organisations and fourth by the public sector organisations.

Legislation has been passed by governments to give Electronic Signatures status (HM Government, 2012). However, the matters raised by Wright (1999) still express the variance between Public Key Infrastructure signatures (PKI) and those handwritten. Wright (1999) points out:

The PKI proponents are therefore wrong to equate PKI signatures with handwritten legal signatures. The purpose of a PKI signature is not to ensure that the signer was warned of the gravity of the document being signed or that the signer had a fair opportunity to review the words of the document. The sole purpose of a PKI signature (as it is classically understood) is to identify a person.

Identification and intent are different in law as the following quote also from Wright (1999) shows:

If a signature technology fails to express the signer's intent, in a way that fairly apprises the signer that the signature is being attached and what the signature means, then the signature cannot be valid. Handwritten signatures do so

express a signer's intent because they are physical events that derive their meaning from culture, tradition, and emotions. However, a signature based on nothing more than a mathematical key (which the signer cannot see) and a certificate is not fair to the typical signer because it involves no ceremony.

Recent literature indicates that professionals are still searching for a way to express proof of intent. Lenz (2012) acknowledges the problem of 'proof of intent and suggests biometric signatures may be the way forward. However, the infrastructure behind these is not yet in place and may be expensive. The difficulty with such solutions is that there has not been defining case law to support or reject the standing of such signatures. Leng (2011) describes and compares a single case in Singapore and the UK. He concludes that the decisions of the Singaporean (Joseph Mathew and Another v Singh Chiranjeev and Another) and English authorities (Nilesh Mehta v J Pereira Fernandes SA) are divided as to whether e-mail headers can satisfy the Statute of Fraud's signature requirement. However he concludes that both "agree that a typed signature in whatever form at the bottom of an e-mail message will satisfy the Statute." He further indicates that the UNCITRAL Working Group on the Model Law on Electronic Signatures discussed earlier differentiated between the legal idea of a 'signature' and the technical idea of an 'electronic signature.' They came to the conclusion that an electronic signature is "a term of art that does not necessarily cover legally significant signatures" (Leng, 2011). The Working Group further provided a distinction between "the use of the same technical tool for the production of a legally meaningful signature and for other authentication or identification functions." Only after the working group has reported and its recommendations fully tested for validity, in relation to construction contracts under United Kingdom (UK) and European law as a way of producing valid proof of intent, will this barrier be fully overcome. This barrier needs to be overcome at a world level as even within the EU the status of electronic signatures differs. UK law is different from German and other European law, which is proving a difficult obstacle to overcome (Wang, 2007). This barrier was ranked eighth in Hawking *et al.* (2004) for Australia under "Legal Issues." It was not separated under the "Proof of Intent" heading and therefore cannot be directly compared but its inclusion in that study shows that the issues around the "legality" of contract documentation is not restricted to the construction industry. European Commission (2011b) show that 80% of their respondents considered that the legislative changes are necessary to increase e-procurement uptake.

Historically security and legal issues have been identified by Gebauer *et al.* (1988) and Pena-Mona and Choudary (2001) who further underscore the security associated complications with e-procurement. Min and Galle (1999) show the "severity of security" is of fundamental importance as a barrier to Internet-based cyber-purchasing. Jennings (2001) states "The World Wide Web leaks like a sieve. Data transmitted on it can be garbled, can reassemble wrongly at the other end, or can display only partially because of incompatible software." Cybercrime and hacking is increasing. Banks acknowledge this and are constantly updating their systems to mitigate threats. Rankin (2006) shows that in construction this is one of the technical issues with e-procurement still to be surmounted.

Reilly (1999) shows Secure Electronic Transactions (SET) developed by VISA and MasterCard from 1996 onwards may apply to e-procurement. While this is being developed others such as Kim *et al.* (2009) propose security systems that guarantee non-repudiation, confidentiality, and integrity. All of these are concerns identified in 2011 by the European Commission (2011b). The Kim *et al.* (2009) system requests certification through a One-Time Password (OTP) by generating and holding the developed password asynchronously

among transaction parties along with certificate. Hawser (2008) states that despite high security levels, levels of fraud are increasing at banking institutions. Tran *et al.* (2011) highlights issues relating to financial fraud as a barrier to e-procurement in construction. As progress in electronic security systems increases the confidence of the industry will also increase resulting in greater uptake of e-procurement.

Huber *et al.* (2004) raised concerns over the security and confidentiality of the data which e-procurement required to be exchanged through electronic means. Eadie *et al.* (2010b) ranked Confidentiality of Information—unauthorised viewing in second place overall for e-procurement in construction. This shows that the top two barriers in construction relate to security issues. This concurs with Leith (2003) who identified the security risks resulting from unauthorized infiltration of transaction software and the failure to guard contract associated data during transmission or storage as one of the major barriers to general e-procurement. Angeles (2007) summarised literature on the security aspects and highlights the barrier under issues with immaturity of e-procurement software. Pena-Mora and Choudary (2001) also articulate concerns over tampering with contract documentation. This is an area that e-procurement systems need to more fully address in order to give confidence to those who use them. Confidentiality can only be preserved within a fully Internet based system if security systems and encryption are in place. Brandon-Jones and Carey (2010) linked confidentiality of procurement with professionalism and raked it seventh for general procurement. The link with professionalism shows that if the system cannot provide the security to prevent tampering with documents it will be abused with long-term relationships, reputation and trust damaged as a result. Eadie *et al.* (2010b) determined that in construction the public sector ranked this barrier in third place. This is despite most public sector organisations having internal security professionals specifically trained and employed to secure the IT infrastructure. A number of very embarrassing breaches of security in public sector data management activities have resulted in suggestions that employees could be fined (Hampson, 2012). While the suggestions have been contested, it has further highlighted the security concerns related to e-procurement. Ensuring confidentiality of information is of utmost importance in order to overcome this barrier and have successful implementation within the construction industry (Jones, 2009). Eadie *et al.* (2010b) show that in the private sector the impact is considered less with the barrier only being ranked in sixth place. This could be due to smaller contract sizes and a smaller risk of legal challenges. Supporting this view is that where the cost associated with the works diminishes such as in the goods and services industries Davila *et al.* (2003) highlight in their investigation of "Proprietary and confidential purchasing data will end up in competitors hands" that it falls to twelfth position in the rankings.

Interoperability Concerns

If all computers were standard with a standard set of programmes this would not be a difficulty. However, multiple programmes provide similar services. Organisations have implemented the programme that suits them best. This had led to the provision of electronic information causing interoperability concerns. Software companies have existed through making their product unique causing problems relating to exchange of data between systems. Boeing (1996) recognised this as a barrier and stipulated that all procurement should be using specific products. In order to overcome this difficulty CITE (Construction Industry Trading Electronically) was initiated. However, Martin (2003) proves that less than 30% of the construction industry has used CITE prescribed formats. Rankin (2006) concludes that compatibility, interfacing with other systems and

stability, are technical issues, which act as barriers to e-procurement implementation.

Angeles and Nath (2007) show, that this barrier is related to the immaturity of many e-procurement software packages. They draw a distinction between enterprise resources planning (ERP) software, which has been developed to a greater extent than many e-procurement packages. Some e-procurement packages relating to construction do not have features like invoicing, payment, reconciliation built in. This means that data must be transferred between systems resulting in interoperability issues. Eadie *et al.* (2010b) ranks this barrier in joint 13th position for construction organisations with the private sector considering it slightly more important than the public sector.

No Business Benefit Realized

Egbu *et al.* (2004) investigated the cost/benefit concern—where the expenses outweigh the benefits of moving to electronic procurement. This could result from insufficient assessment of systems prior to implementation resulting in large overruns in costs (Forrest, 1999). In general, e-procurement the European Commission (2011b) cites lack of justification/business case in fifth position in the additional barriers identified. In construction, Eadie *et al.* (2010b) show that this is much more important to the private sector (ranked 3rd) than the public sector (ranked 17th).

CLASSIFIED AND RANKED LIST OF DRIVERS AND BARRIERS TO E-PROCUREMENT IN CONSTRUCTION

This section provides a ranked list of drivers and barriers for e-procurement in the construction industry. These confirmed and verified drivers and barriers are classified into 6 different categories: General, Cost, Time, Quality, Cultural,

Infrastructure, Security, Legal, and Compatibility for further analysis (Table 8 and Table 9).

It is vitally important in the introduction of an e-procurement system to understand the importance of each of these drivers and barriers. This allows the developers to focus and prioritise their effort on aspects that are vital for the e-procurement system designed. Eadie *et al.* (2010a, 2010b) carried out three separate analyses on the rankings of construction drivers and barriers. Accordingly, all drivers and barriers were ranked to produce a list that is applicable to both private and public sectors of the construction industry. Tables 8 and 9 present these rankings in the order of importance.

This identifies that the two most significant drivers for e-procurement in Construction as "Pro-

cess, transaction and administration cost savings" and "Convenience of archiving completed work." This applies for both the public and private sectors.

In a similar manner, Table 9 identifies the e-procurement barrier rankings for the Private and Public Sectors across the UK.

Table 9 indicates that the barriers in the private and public sectors differ. However, in overall terms, the two most important barriers for e-procurement in construction are "Prevention of tampering with documents—changes to documents," followed by "Confidentiality of information—unauthorised viewing."

Table 8. Ranked drivers for e-procurement

Drivers in Rank Order	Banding	Private Sector Rank	Public Sector Rank	Construction Industry Rank
Process, transaction and administration cost savings	Cost	1	1	1
Convenience of archiving completed work	General	2	1	2
Increased quality through increased accuracy (Elimination of errors through Computer use)	Quality	2	6	3
Shortened internal and external communication cycle times	Time	6	5	4
Increased quality through increased efficiency	Quality	4	7	5
Shortened overall procurement cycle times	Time	9	3	6
Increased quality through Improved communication	Quality	5	10	7
Strategic cost savings	Cost	13	3	8
Service/Material/Product cost savings	Cost	8	10	9
Reduction in evaluation time	Time	10	7	10
Develops the technical Skills, knowledge and expertise of procurement staff	General	14	16	11
Increasing profit margins	Cost	7	19	12
Increased quality through benchmarking (Market Intelligence)	Quality	17	9	12
Reduction in purchasing order fulfillment time - Contract Completion	Time	11	13	14
Enhanced inventory management	General	17	14	15
Reduction in time through greater transparency (Less objections)	Time	16	12	16
Reduction in time through increased visibility	Time	14	18	17
Increased quality through increased visibility in the supply chain	Quality	19	17	18
Increased quality through increased competition	Time	20	14	19
Gaining competitive advantage	General	11	20	20

Table 9. Ranked barriers for e-procurement

Barriers in Rank Order	Banding	Private Sector Rank	Public Sector Rank	Construction Industry Rank
Prevention of tampering with documents - changes to documents	Security	1	2	1
Confidentiality of information - unauthorised viewing	Security	6	3	2
Resistance to change	Cultural	6	1	3
Reluctance to "buy-into" one off systems	Compatibility	2	23	4
Proof of intent - electronic signatures	Legal	3	4	4
Lack of a widely accepted e-procurement software solution	Cultural	6	4	6
Security in the process - data transmission to the wrong person	Security	10	4	6
Insufficient assessment of systems prior to installation	Infrastructure	3	17	8
Lack of a national IT policy relating to E-Procurement Issues	Cultural	6	10	9
Data transmission reassembly - incorrect reassembly of data transmitted in packets	Security	14	17	10
Partial data display - incomplete documents provided	Security	15	13	10
Bureaucratic dysfunctionalities	Cultural	18	7	12
Lack of technical expertise	Cultural	15	10	13
Internal and external interoperability of e-procurement software	Compatibility	11	13	13
Investment in compatible systems	Compatibility	11	19	15
Lack of flexibility	Cultural	17	13	16
Lack of publicity/awareness of best practice solutions	Cultural	13	10	17
Enforceability of electronic contracts	Legal	3	22	18
Upper management support/lack of leadership	Cultural	21	9	19
Magnitude of change	Cultural	18	13	20
Other competing initiatives	Cultural	23	7	21
Complicated procedures and extended relationships	Cultural	26	19	21
Clarity of sender and tenderer Information	Legal	23	19	21
Lack of a forum to exchange ideas	General	25	26	24
Information technology investment costs	Assessment Costs	18	29	25
Lack of pertinent case law	Legal	22	25	25
Perception of no business benefit realised	General	26	26	27
Different national approaches to e-procurement	Legal	26	26	28
Staff turnover	Cultural	30	23	29
Company access to the Internet	Infrastructure	30	30	30

TRENDS AND FUTURE DIRECTIONS IN E-PROCUREMENT

The construction industry is unique with respect to e-procurement. The size, scale, and complexity of the industry and its fragmented modes of operation make the industry unique. The public sector influenced by legislative and regulatory requirements, leads in the implementation of e-procurement. The UK government has identified e-business as a priority growth area and actively encourages adoption by micro and Small and

Medium Enterprises (SME). The private sector is primarily fragmented into large and micro and SME enterprises. Since, 99% of the construction industry in characterised by micro and SME organisations the use of e-procurement in the private sector is limited. However, there is significant potential for growth in the private sector. There is significant pressure developing from the rapid advancement of large-scale construction companies and the rate of development of technology. Cloud computing is in price advancing and reducing. As such, there will be significant growth in the private sector in e-procurement in the next decade. The public sector will achieve its target of 100% e-procurement albeit late in its achievement. Current research into BIM indicates the possibility of BIM enabled e-procurement becoming mainstream within the next decade. This will further drive down procurement costs but the cost effectiveness of BIM remains a concern.

There are developments that need to take place prior to an e-procurement system achieving its full potential in government organisations. The UNCITRAL Working Group on the Model Law on Electronic Signatures needs to address some of the security, proof of intent, validity and confidentiality related issues identified as barriers for e-procurement in this chapter. Standard and associated processes for e-procurement which addresses the barriers in this chapter should be produced. Government legislation has worked to some extent in introducing e-procurement to many public sector departments across the UK. However, to meet the target of 100% adoption stricter adherence to the targets set must be applied. Training for those involved in procurement is important to widen the pool of staff that is capable of carrying out e-procurement activity.

CONCLUSION

This chapter discussed the implementation of e-procurement within the construction industry. It found that while there are benefits in adopting e-procurement its low uptake within the construction sector means that there are barriers to be overcome. E-procurement is extensively used in general goods and services procurement but its adoption in the AEC sector is low. This chapter reviewed facets of e-procurement with a view of understanding the current state of development in the UK construction industry.

It found that there had been a substantial number of Government led initiatives to improve the uptake of e-procurement in the UK, commencing with the Modernising Government White Paper (Cabinet Office, 1999) and its associated Best Value Indicator (BV157). These developments in e-business and associated infrastructure resulted in Government departments driving adoption of e-procurement across the UK. The Glover Report (2008) indicated that e-procurement for construction was still not 100% by 2008 and set a further date of 2012 for 100% implementation. The private sector adoption still lags behind indicating that there could be substantial benefits still to be achieved.

The European Union also provided incentives for e-procurement adoption. The European Directives 2004/17 and 2004/18 acknowledged the use of electronic tendering and transmission of documents. The Public Contracts Regulations 2006 which brought these into UK law provided substantial time advantages should e-procurement be adopted. These apply to Construction Works, in addition to Goods and Services procurement.

The CITE initiative provided a standard format for transmitting electronic documents. BuildingSmart (2009b) is a merger of the International Alliance for Interoperability and CITE and its standard is still current for construction procurement. The Electronic Communications Act was the first legal attempt to address the thorny issue of electronic signatures. However, there are still a number of weaknesses in this legislation. Internationally, the results of the UNCITRAL Working Group on the Model Law on Electronic Signatures, and how findings on 'proof of intent,' 'gravity' and 'identification' are incorporated into UK law will be vital to improvement in e-procurement adoption.

The use of electronic auctions in construction in light of Latham and Egan principles proved controversial yet was adopted by some building clients. On this controversial topic, the chapter suggested that within construction auctions can be adopted successfully for materials procurement where the specification is precise. It is less successful for project procurement where unknowns could lead to an increase in claims due to the initial price being forced down.

This chapter further discussed the overall ranking of drivers and barriers to e-procurement in construction from a public procurement standpoint and contrasted these with the overall ranking and that of the private sector. The two most important drivers for UK construction organisations (both public and private) are "Process, Transaction and Administration Cost Savings" and "Convenience of archiving completed work." It was revealed that the cost savings from adoption of e-procurement has been widely documented. It is the most positive aspect of adopting e-procurement in construction. The squeeze in the global economy and the ensuing recession makes it important for the construction industry to adopt efficiency gaining process improvements such as e-procurement. The storage of bulky tender and procurement related documents is completely eliminated with the use of e-procurement while reducing electronic storage costs. Advancement of cloud technologies brings the benefits accruing from e-procurement to another level.

The discussion further revealed that resistance to change was the single most important barrier

causing difficulty in implementing e-procurement in the public sector. Overall, the two most important barriers for UK construction organisations (both public and private) are "Prevention of Tampering with Documents— changes to documents," followed by "Confidentiality of Information— unauthorised viewing." These were ranked second and third by the public sector. Improving awareness of benefits of e-procurement in construction is the main means of overcoming the "resistance to change" barrier. This could be combined with the formation of standard practice and procedures for use with e-procurement to alleviate public sector concerns. The outcomes of the UNCITRAL Working Group on the Model Law on Electronic Signatures is seen as vital to the progression of e-procurement in that it will address some of the industry wide vital issues relating to security. Developments in network security should also boost e-procurement adoption.

"Gaining Competitive Advantage" was given the lowest rank of all the drivers for e-procurement. This indicates that it has little relevance to the public sector and its relevance to the private sector is decreasing all the time as more organisations adopt e-procurement. On the barrier side, the lowest ranked barrier was company access to the Internet. This indicates that the majority of organisations are now on-line.

This chapter provides a useful insight into e-procurement in the construction industry with a detailed review of the state of the art developments in adoption of e-procurement in both public and private sectors of the UK constriction industry. It provides a detailed account of all drivers and barriers for construction e-procurement with a worldwide review of the state of application. E-procurement in construction is set accelerate in its adoption and use both in public and private sectors pushed primarily by the squeeze in the economy and advancement of technology with falling ICT price levels.

REFERENCES

Albano, G., & Sparro, M. (2010). Flexible strategies for centralized public procurement. *Review of Economics and Institutions, 1*(2), 1–32. doi:10.5202/rei.v1i2.17

Angeles, R., & Nath, R. (2007). Business-to-business e-procurement: success factors and challenges to implementation. *Supply Chain Management: An International Journal, 12*(2), 104–115. doi:10.1108/13598540710737299

Arminas, D. (2002). Are relationships going, going, gone? *Supply Management.* Retrieved January 28, 2012, from http://www.supplymanagement. com/news/2002/are-relationships-going-going-gone/?show=recent

Arrowsmith, S. (2001). E-commerse policy and the EC procurement rules: The chasm between rhetoric and reality. In *Kluwer Law International* (pp. 1447–1477). Dordrecht, The Netherlands: Kluwer.

Batenburg, R. (2007). E-procurement adoption by European firms: A quantitative analysis. *Journal of Purchasing and Supply Management, 13*(3), 182–192. doi:10.1016/j.pursup.2007.09.014

Betts, M., Black, P., Christensen, S., Dawson, E., Du, R., & Duncan, W. ... Gonzalez Nieto, J. (2006). Towards secure and legal e-tendering. *Journal of Information Technology in Construction, 11,* 89-102. Retrieved January 28, 2012, from http://itcon.org/cgi-bin/works/Show?2006_7

BIPSolutions. (2004). *Vault secure e-tendering document exchange service.* Retrieved January 28, 2012, from http://www.sopo.org/rtfs/vaultfaq.htm

BIS. (2010). *Small and medium-sized enterprise (SME) statistics for the UK and regions 2009 (SME statistics).* Retrieved January 28, 2012, from http://webarchive.nationalarchives.gov.uk/+/http://stats.bis.gov.uk/ed/sme/

Blaby District Council. (2004). *Document retention and destruction procedures and guidelines.* Retrieved January 28, 2012, from http://idocs. blaby.gov.uk/external/council-democracy/dp-foi/foi-council-retention-schedule.pdf

Boeing. (1996). *Supplier network technical data interchange (SNET-TDI).* Retrieved January 28, 2012, from http://www.boeing.com/companyoffices/doingbiz/tdi/faq.html

Bravosolution. (2008). *Government makes key cost and effective savings with innovative technology.* Retrieved January 28, 2012, from https://www.bravosolution.com/cms/news-events/press-center/08-july-2008-1/

Bravosolution. (2012). *Analyst industry reports.* Retrieved January 28, 2012, from https://www.bravosolution.com/cms/uk/resource-center/analyst-industry-reports/copy3_of_Knowledge%20Economy

Brazell, L. (2004). *Electronic signatures law and regulation: Law and regulation.* London, UK: Sweet & Maxwell.

Buchta, D., Eul, M., & Schulte-Croonenberg, H. (2010). *Strategic IT management, increase value, control performance, reduce costs.* Wiesbaden, Germany: Gabler.

Building Smart. (2009a). *CITE bills of quantities standard - Version 4.2.* Retrieved January 28, 2012, from http://146.87.15.57:9080/buildingSmart/CITE/standards/ascii-flat-file-members-only/cite-bills-of-quantities-standard

Building Smart. (2009b). *What is BuildingSmart?* Retrieved January 28, 2012, from http://www.buildingsmart.org.uk/buildingSMART/what-is-the-iai

Building Smart. (2009c). *BuildingSmart international.* Retrieved January 28, 2012, from http://www.buildingsmartalliance.org/

Building Smart. (2009d). *Frequently asked questions.* Retrieved January 28, 2012, from http://buildingsmart-tech.org/implementation/faq

Cabinet Office. (1999). *Modernising government.* Retrieved January 28, 2012, from http://www.archive.official-documents.co.uk/document/cm43/4310/4310-00.htm

Cabinet Office. (2000). *Progress report against the executive summary of the modernising government white paper 1999.* Retrieved January 28, 2012, from http://archive.cabinetoffice.gov.uk/moderngov/whtpaper/summary_progress.htm#4d

Caffrey, L., Rogers, W., & Okot-Uma, O. (1999). *Government secure intranets.* London, UK: Commonwealth Secretariat.

Carayannis, E., & Popescu, D. (2005). Profiling a methodology for economic growth and convergence: Learning from the EU e-procurement experience for central and eastern European countries. *Technovation, 25,* 1–14. doi:10.1016/S0166-4972(03)00071-3

Cartlidge, D. (2006). *New aspects of quantity surveying practice.* Oxford, UK: Elsevier Butterworth-Heinemann.

Chaffey, D. (Ed.). (2004). *E-business and e-commerce management.* Upper Saddle River, NJ: Prentice Hall.

Chen, S., Ruikar, K., Carrillo, P., Khosrowshahi, F., & Underwood, J. (2011). *Construct IT for business, e-business in the construction industry.* Loughborough, UK: Loughborough University.

Christensen, J., Schmidt, M., & Larsen, M. (2002). *The industrial dynamics of internet services.* Paper presented at the DRUID Summer Conference. Retrieved January 28, 2012, from http://www.druid.dk/conferences/summer2002/Papers/Christensen.pdf

CITE. (2009). *What is CITE? BuildingSmart website.* Retrieved January 28, 2012, from http://www.buildingsmart.org.uk/about/cite/cite/?searchterm=CITE

Contract Journal. (2003). *Contractors urged to shun Tesco's Dutch auctions.* Retrieved January 28, 2012, from http://business.highbeam.com/410604/article-1G1-110665058/contractors-urged-shun-tesco-dutch-auctions

Dacorum Borough Council. (2006). *IEG5 report.* Retrieved January 28, 2012, from www.bipsolutions.com/docstore/doc/12757.doc

Davila, A., Gupta, M., & Palmer, R. (2003). Moving procurement systems to the internet: The adoption and use of e-procurement technology models. *European Management Journal, 21*(1), 11–23. doi:10.1016/S0263-2373(02)00155-X

DETNI. (2004). *NICS strategic initiatives appendix B.* Retrieved January 28, 2012, from http://www.detini.gov.uk/nics_strategic_drivers.pdf

DETR. (2000). *Best value and audit commission performance indicators for 2001/2002: The gold book.* Retrieved January 28, 2012, from http://www.communities.gov.uk/archived/publications/localgovernment/bestvalueperformance

DFP. (2009). *Central procurement directorate procurement guidance note 03/10 procurement control limits.* Retrieved January 28, 2012, from http://www.dfpni.gov.uk/index/procurement-2/cpd/cpd-policy-and-legislation/content_-_cpd_-_policy_-_procurement_guidance_notes/content_-_cpd_procurement_guidance_notes_pgn_03_-_10/pgn-03-10-26012011.pdf

DTI. (2006). *Electronic signatures factsheet.* Retrieved January 28, 2012, from http://webarchive.nationalarchives.gov.uk/+/http://www.berr.gov.uk/files/file34339.pdf

DTI. (2009). *Electronic signatures and associated legislation.* Retrieved January 28, 2012, from http://webarchive.nationalarchives.gov.uk/+/ http://www.berr.gov.uk/files/file49952.pdf

Dumortier, J., & Van Eecke, P. (1999). The European draft directive on a common framework for electronic signatures. *Computer Law & Security Report, 15*(2), 106–112. doi:10.1016/ S0267-3649(99)80022-3

E-Quantities. (2009). *What is CITE?* Retrieved January 28, 2012, from http://www.e-quantities. com/bqfilter/cite.htm

Eadie, R., Millar, P., Perera, S., Heaney, G., & Barton, G. (2012). E–readiness of construction contract forms and e–tendering software. *International Journal of Procurement Management, 5*(1), 1-26. Retrieved January 28, 2012, from http://inderscience.metapress.com/ content/9580t2p387mu1228/

Eadie, R., Perera, S., & Heaney, G. (2010a). Identification of e-procurement drivers and barriers for UK construction organisations and ranking of these from the perspective of quantity surveyors. *Journal of Information Technology in Construction, 15*, 23-43. Retrieved January 28, 2012, from http://www.itcon.org/cgi-bin/works/ Show?2010_2

Eadie, R., Perera, S., & Heaney, G. (2010b). A cross discipline comparison of rankings of e-procurement drivers and barriers for UK construction organisations. *Journal of Information Technology in Construction, 15*, 217-233. Retrieved January 28, 2012, from http://www.itcon.org/cgi-bin/ works/Show?2010_17

Eadie, R., Perera, S., & Heaney, G. (2011). Analysis of the use of e-procurement in the public and private sectors of the UK construction industry. *Journal of Information Technology in Construction, 16*, 669 – 686. Retrieved January 28, 2012, from http://www.itcon.org/cgi-bin/ works/Show?2011_39

Eadie, R., Perera, S., Heaney, G., & Carlisle, J. (2007). Drivers and barriers to public sector e-procurement within Northern Ireland's construction industry. *Journal of Information Technology in Construction, 12*, 103-120. Retrieved January 28, 2012, from http://www.itcon.org/cgi-bin/ works/Show?2007_6

Egbu, C., Vines, M., & Tookey, J. (2004). The role of knowledge management in e-procurement initiatives for construction organisations. In *Proceedings of the ARCOM Twentieth Annual Conference 2004,* (Vol. 1, pp. 661-671). Reading, UK: Arcom.

Erridge, A., Fee, R., & McIlroy, J. (2001). *Best practice procurement: Public and private sector perspectives.* Burlington, VT: Gover Publishing Company.

Eurlex. (2004a). *European Union directive 2004/17 coordinating the procurement procedures of entities operating in the water, energy, transport and postal services sectors.* Retrieved January 28, 2012, from http://eur-lex. europa.eu/LexUriServ/LexUriServ.do?uri=- CELEX:32004L0017:en:HTML

Eurlex. (2004b). *European Union directive 2004/18 on the coordination of procedures for the award of public works contracts, public supply contracts and public service contracts.* Retrieved January 28, 2012, from http://eur-lex. europa.eu/LexUriServ/LexUriServ.do?uri=- CELEX:32004L0018:En:HTML European Commission. (2012). *Your Europe website.* Retrieved January 28, 2012, from http://ec.europa. eu/youreurope/

European Commission. (2007). *The European e-business report, a portrait of e-business in 10 sectors of the EU economy: 5th synthesis report of the e-business W@tch*. Retrieved January 28, 2012, from http://ec.europa.eu/enterprise/archives/e-business-watch/key_reports/documents/EBR06.pdf

European Commission. (2010). *ICT and e-business for an innovative and sustainable economy: 7th synthesis report of the sectoral e-business watch*. Retrieved January 28, 2012, from http://www.ebusiness-watch.org/key_reports/documents/EBR09-10.pdf

European Commission. (2011a). *Communication from the commission — Corresponding values of the thresholds of directives 2004/17/EC, 2004/18/EC and 2009/81/EC of the European parliament and of the council 2011/C 353/01 (2011)*. Retrieved January 28, 2012, from http://eur-lex.europa.eu/LexUriServ/LexUriServ.do?uri=OJ:C:2011:353:FULL:EN:PDF

European Commission. (2011b). *Public consultation (green paper) on expanding the use of e-procurement in the EU*. Retrieved January 28, 2012, from http://ec.europa.eu/internal_market/consultations/docs/2010/e-procurement/synthesis_en.pdf

Forrest, A. (1999). *Fifty ways towards a learning organisation*. Sterling, VA: Stylus Publishing Inc.

Forrester. (2003). ISM/Forrester report on ebusiness. *Institute for Supply Management (ISM)*. Retrieved January 28, 2012, from http://www.forrester.com/rb/Research/ismforrester_report_on_ebusiness_q1_2003/q/id/16792/t/2

Gebauer, J., Beam, C., & Segev, A. (1998). Impact of the internet on purchasing practices. *Acquisitions Review Quarterly, 5*(2), 167–184.

Glover, A. (2008). *Accelerating the SME economic engine: Through transparent, simple and strategic procurement*. London, UK: HM Treasury.

Government, H. M. (2009). *What is the government gateway?* Retrieved January 28, 2012, from http://www.direct.gov.uk/en/Diol1/DoItOnline/Doitonlinemotoring/DG_10035603

Government, H. M. (2012). *Electronic communications act 2000*. Retrieved January 28, 2012, from http://www.legislation.gov.uk/ukpga/2000/7/part/II/data.pdf

Government Gateway. (2009). *Government gateway*. Retrieved January 28, 2012, from http://www.gateway.gov.uk/

Gray, P. (2006). *The management, retention and disposal of administrative records*. Retrieved January 28, 2012, from http://www.sehd.scot.nhs.uk/mels/HDL2006_28.pdf

Gunasekarana, A., McGaughey, R., Ngaic, E., & Rai, B. (2009). Impact of e-procurement: Experiences from implementation in the UK public sector. *Journal of Purchasing and Supply Management, 13*, 294–303.

GXS. (2005). *EDIFACT standards overview tutorial*. Retrieved January 28, 2012, from http://edi.gxs.com/wp-content/themes/EDI/media/Tutor_EDIFACT_GXS.pdf

Hackett, M., Robinson, I., & Stratham, G. (2007). *The aqua group guide to procurement, tendering and contract administration*. Oxford, UK: Blackwell Publishing.

Hampson, T. (2012). Fining public sector staff for data breaches 'will not work'. *UKauthorITy*. Retrieved January 28, 2012, from http://www.ukauthority.com/NewsArticle/tabid/64/Default.aspx?id=3499

Harindranath, G., Dyerson, R., & Barnes, D. (2008). ICT adoption and use in UK SMEs: A failure of initiatives? *Electronic Journal Information Systems Evaluation, 11*(2), 91–96. Retrieved January 28, 2012, from http://www.ejise.com

Hawking, P., Stein, A., Wyld, D., & Forster, S. (2004). E-procurement: Is the ugly duckling actually a swan down under? *Asia Pacific Journal of Marketing and Logistics, 16*(1), 1–26. doi:10.1108/13555850410765140

Hawser, A. (2008). *Who should be liable for on-line fraud? Fighting fraud.* Retrieved January 28, 2012, from http://fightingfraud.blogspot.com/2008/10/who-should-be-liable-for-online-fraud.html

Hewson Group. (2003). *e-Government: Can it meet public expectations through a successful CRM programme?* Retrieved January 28, 2012, from http://crmguru.custhelp.com/ci/fattach/get/314/

Huber, B., Sweeney, E., & Smyth, A. (2004). Purchasing consortia and electronic markets – A procurement direction in integrated supply chain management. *Electronic Markets, 14*(4), 284–294. doi:10.1080/10196780412331311739

IAI. (2005). *IAI website.* Retrieved January 28, 2012, from http://eetd.lbl.gov/eetd-software-iai.html

IDEA. (2004). *The benefits of e-procurement.* Retrieved January 28, 2012, from http://www.idea.gov.uk/idk/aio/70780

IDEA. (2008). *e-Tendering.* Retrieved January 28, 2012, from http://www.idea.gov.uk/idk/core/page.do?pageId=82667

Irani, Z., & Love, P. (2002). Developing a frame of reference for ex-ante IT/IS investment evaluation. *European Journal of Information Systems, 11*(1), 74–82. doi:10.1057/palgrave/ejis/3000411

Islington Council. (2008). *Paper-free working improves service delivery for Islington council.* Retrieved January 28, 2012, from http://www.publictechnology.net/content/18250

Jennings, D. (2001, September 6). Secure trading. *Supply Management*, 52-53.

Julia-Barcelo, R. (1999). Electronic contracts: A new legal framework for electronic contracts: The EU electronic commerce proposal. *Computer Law & Security Report, 15*(3), 147–158. doi:10.1016/S0267-3649(99)80032-6

Julià-Barceló, R., & Vinje, T. (1998). Towards a European framework for digital signatures and encryption: The European commission takes a step forward for confidential and secure electronic communications. *Computer Law & Security Report, 14*(2), 79–86.

Kalakota, R., Tapscott, D., & Robinson, M. (2001). *E-business 2.0: Roadmap for success* (2nd ed.). Reading, MA: Addison-Wesley Publishing Company.

Katok, E., & Roth, A. (2004). Adoption of electronic commerce tools in business procurement: Enhanced buying center structure and processes. *Management Science, 50*(8), 1044–1063. doi:10.1287/mnsc.1040.0254

Kheng, C., & Al-hawamdeh, S. (2002). The adoption of electronic procurement in Singapore. *Electronic Commerce Research, 2*(1-2), 61–73. doi:10.1023/A:1013388018056

Kim, J., & Shunk, D. (2003). Matching indirect procurement process with different B2B e-procurement systems. *Computers in Industry, 53*(2), 153–164. doi:10.1016/j.compind.2003.07.002

Kivijarvi, H., Hallikainen, P., & Penttinen, E. (2011). Supporting the supplier scheduling decisions in the e-invoicing implementation projects - An application of the ANP method. In *Proceedings of 44th Hawaii International Conference on System Sciences (HICSS)*, (pp. 1-12). Kauai, HI: IEEE.

Knudsen, D. (2003). Aligning corporate strategy, procurement strategy and e-procurement tools. *International Journal of Physical Distribution & Logistics Management, 33*(8), 720–734. doi:10.1108/09600030310502894

Kong, C., Li, H., & Love, P. (2001). An e-commerce system for construction material procurement. *Construction Innovation, 1*(1), 43–54.

Kransdorff, A. (1998). *Corporate amnesia keeping the know-how in the company*. Oxford, UK: Butterworth-Heinemann.

Latham, M. (1994). *Constructing the team. Joint Government of Industry Review of Procurement and Contractual Arrangements in the UK*. London, UK: Construction Industry.

Lenz, J. (2012). Taking dynamic signatures seriously. *Biometric Technology Today, 2011*(11–12), 9–11.

Li, E., & Du, T. (2005). *Advances in electronic business*. Hershey, PA: IGI Global.

Martin, J. (2003). *E-procurement and extranets in the UK construction industry*. Paper presented at FIG Working Week. Paris, France. Retrieved January 28, 2012, from www.fig.net/pub/fig_2003/TS_6/TS6_4_Martin.pdf

Martin, J. (2009). *2009 BCIS etendering survey report*. Retrieved January 28, 2012, from http://www.bcis.co.uk/downloads/2009_BCIS_eTendering_Survey_Report_pdf__2_.pdf

McIntosh, G., & Sloan, B. (2001). The potential impact of electronic procurement and global sourcing within the UK construction industry. In A. Akintoye (Ed.), *Proceedings of Arcom 17th Annual Conference 2001*, (pp. 231-239). Manchester, UK: University of Salford.

McMullan, C. (2005). *Letter to CPD: Central procurement directorate*. Belfast, Ireland: Clare House.

Min, H., & Galle, W. (1999). Electronic commerce usage in business-to business purchasing. *International Journal of Operations & Production Management, 19*(9), 909–921. doi:10.1108/01443579910280232

Minahan, T., & Degan, G. (2001). *Best practices in e-procuremen*. Boston, MA: Aberdeen Group. Retrieved January 28, 2012, from http://www.inkoopportal.com/inkoopportal/download/common/e-procurement_1_.pdf

National Archives. (2012). *Records management: Retention scheduling 5: Contractual records*. Retrieved January 28, 2012, from http://www.nationalarchives.gov.uk/documents/information-management/sched_contractual.pdf

National Procurement Strategy for Local Government. (2003). *National procurement strategy for local government in England 2003-2006*. Retrieved January 28, 2012, from http://www.communities.gov.uk/publications/localgovernment/nationalprocurementstrategy

News, E. C. I. (2003). *ECI newsletter – Achieving continuous improvement and value*. Retrieved January 28, 2012, from http://www.researchandmarkets.com/reports/1530394/long_term_partnering_achieving_continuous

NIFHA. (2007). *NIFHA database*. Retrieved January 28, 2012, from http://www.nifha.org/housing-association-database/

NJCC. (1996). *Code of practice for two stage selective tendering.* London, UK: NJCC.

OGC. (2003). *Building on success.* Retrieved January 28, 2012, from http://www.ccinw.com/images/publications/OGC%20Acheiving%-20Excellence%20in%20Construction.pdf

OGC. (2005). *e-Procurement in action – A guide to e-procurement for the public sector.* Retrieved January 28, 2012, from http//www.umic.pt/images/stories/publicacoes/embedded_object[1].pdf

OIG. (1997). *Audit of the office of program and integrity reviews special studies.* Retrieved January 28, 2012, from http://oig.ssa.gov/audit-office-program-and-integrity-reviews-special-studies

Panayiotou, N., Sotiris, G., & Tatsiopoulos, I. (2003). An e-procurement system for governmental purchasing. *International Journal of Production Economics, 90*(1), 79–102. doi:10.1016/S0925-5273(03)00103-8

Paulo, A., Bráulio, A., Tiago, O., Varajão, Q., & Eduardo, J. (2010). Electronic procurement: Dealing with supplier adoption. In Cruz-Cunha, M., Putnik, G., & Trigo, A. (Eds.), *ENTERprise Information Systems, Communications in Computer and Information Science* (*Vol. 109*, pp. 168–179). Berlin, Germany: Springer.

Pearman, R. (2002). E-bidding: Who can you trust? *Contract Journal.* Retrieved January 28, 2012, from http://business.highbeam.com/410604/article-1G1-85005041/ebidding-can-you-trust

Pena-Mora, F., & Choudary, K. (2001). Web-centric framework for secure and legally binding electronic transactions in large-scale A/E/C projects. *Journal of Computing in Civil Engineering, 15*(4), 248–259. doi:10.1061/(ASCE)0887-3801(2001)15:4(248)

Pritchard, S. (2006). How can so many businesses cope without computers? *Financial Times.* Retrieved January 28, 2012, from http://www.ft.com/cms/s/1/cc145e2e-47f5-11db-a42e-0000779e2340.html

Przymus, K. (2003). *E-procurement for a municipal government.* Retrieved January 28, 2012, from http://www.toronto.ca/inquiry/inquiry_site/cd/gg/add_pdf/77/Procurement/Electronic_Documents/Miscellaneous/Municipal_EProcurement_Study.pdf

PublicTechnology. (2004). *Next-generation Energis-supplied government secure intranet goes live.* Retrieved January 28, 2012, from http://www.publictechnology.net/content/568

NHS Purchasing and Supply Agency. (2004). *NHS PASA eAuctions pilot report.* London, UK: National Health Service.

Raghavan, N., & Prabhu, M. (2004). Object-oriented design of a distributed agent-based framework for e-procurement. *Production Planning and Control, 15*(7), 731–741. doi:10.1080/09537280412331298229

Rankin, J., Chen, Y., & Christian, A. (2006). E-procurement in the Atlantic Canadian AEC industry. *Journal of Information Technology in Construction, 11*, 75-87. Retrieved January 28, 2012, from http://www.itcon.org/cgi-bin/works/Show?2006_6

Rawlings, J. (1998). Electronic commerce on the internet – Part 1. *Network Security, 7*, 11–14. doi:10.1016/S1353-4858(98)80010-X

Records Management Society of Great Britain, Local Government Group. (2003). *General disposal guidelines for local authorities.* Retrieved January 28, 2012, from http://www.esd.org.uk/foi/records management retention guidlines for LG.pdf

Reilly, D. (1999). *Secure electronic transactions: An overview*. Retrieved January 28, 2012, from http://www.davidreilly.com/topics/electronic_commerce/essays/secure_electronic_transactions.html

Ribeiro, F., & Henriques, P. (2001). How knowledge can improve e business in construction. In *Proceedings of 2nd International Postgraduate Research Conference in the Built and Human Environment*. Oxford, UK: Blackwell Publishing.

RICS. (2005b). *E-tendering: RICS guidance note*. Retrieved January 28, 2012, from https://www.ricsetendering.com/web/RICS%20Guidance%20Note%20-%20e-Tendering.pdf

RICS. (2007). *RICS e-tendering means paper free procurement*. Retrieved January 28, 2012, from http://www.bcis.co.uk/site/scripts/news_article.aspx?newsID=73

Rowlinson, S., & McDermott, P. (1999). *Procurement systems*. New York, NY: E & FN Spon.

Smeltzer, L., & Carr, A. (2003). Electronic reverse auctions promises, risks and conditions for success. *Industrial Marketing Management, 32*(6), 481–488. doi:10.1016/S0019-8501(02)00257-2

Smith, J. (2006). *Blogs making their impact felt. BBC Website*. Retrieved January 28, 2012, from http://news.bbc.co.uk/2/hi/technology/4976276.stm

Software, A. E. C. (2012). *Fasttrack schedule 10*. Retrieved January 28, 2012, from https://www.aecsoftware.com/

Sone, J. (2011). *E-governance in central Texas: Patterns of e-gov adoption in smaller cities*. Retrieved January 28, 2012, from http://ecommons.txstate.edu/arp/381

Spalde, C., Sullivan, F., de Lusignan, S., & Madeley, J. (2006). e-Prescribing, efficiency, quality: Lessons from the computerization of UK family practice. *Journal of the American Medical Informatics Association, 13*(5), 470–475. doi:10.1197/jamia.M2041

Teich, J., Wallenius, H., Wallenius, J., & Koppius, O. (2004). Emerging multiple issue e-auctions. *European Journal of Operational Research, 159*(1), 1–16. doi:10.1016/j.ejor.2003.05.001

Thoren, C. (2004). The procurement of usable and accessible software. *Information Access in the Information Society, 3*(1), 102–106.

Tindsley, G., & Stephenson, P. (2008). E-tendering process within construction: A UK perspective. *Tsinghua Science and Technology, 13*(1), 273–278. doi:10.1016/S1007-0214(08)70161-5

Tran, Q., Huang, D., Liu, B., & Ekram, H. (2011). A construction enterprise's readiness level in implementing e-procurement: A system engineering assessment model. *Systems Engineering Procedia, 2*, 131-141. Retrieved January 28, 2012, from http://www.sciencedirect.com/science/article/pii/S2211381911001056

TSO. (2006). *Public contracts regulations 2006*. Retrieved January 28, 2012, from http://www.opsi.gov.uk/si/si2006/uksi_20060005_en.pdf

TSO. (2009). *Public contracts (amendment) regulations 2009*. Retrieved January 28, 2012, from http://www.legislation.gov.uk/uksi/2009/2992/contents/made

UKonline. (2003). *UK online annual report 2003*. Retrieved January 28, 2012, from http://collection.europarchive.org/tna/20040722012352/http://e-government.cabinetoffice.gov.uk/MediaCentre/NewOnSiteArticle/fs/en?CONTENT_ID=4006060&chk=rIWVHj

UNECE. (2008). *UNEDIFACT draft directory.* Retrieved January 28, 2012, from http://www.unece.org/trade/untdid/welcome.htm

Wamuziri, S., & Seywright, A. (2005). Procurement of construction projects in local government. *Municipal Engineer, 158*(2), 145. doi:10.1680/muen.2005.158.2.145

Wang, M. (2007). Do the regulations on electronic signatures facilitate international electronic commerce? A critical review. *Computer Law & Security Report, 23*(1), 32–41. doi:10.1016/j.clsr.2006.09.006

Wang, Y., Chang, C., & Heng, M. (2004). The levels of information technology adoption, business network, and strategic position model for evaluating supply chain integration. *Journal of Electronic Commerce Research, 5*(2), 85–98.

Westcott, T., & Mayer, P. (2002). Electronic tendering: is it delivering? A UK and European perspective. In *Proceedings of RICS Foundation Construction and Building Research Conference – COBRA 2002.* Nottingham, UK: Nottingham Trent University.

Williams, C., & Lynnes, R. (2002). e-Business without the commerce. In *Proceedings of the Water Environment Federation,* (pp. 298-303). WEF/AWWA.

Williams, R. (2007). Briefing: The public contracts regulations 2006. In *Proceedings of the Institution of Civil Engineers Management Procurement and Law,* (pp. 45-49). Retrieved January 28, 2012, from http://www.icevirtuallibrary.com/content/article/10.1680/mpal.2007.160.2.45

Wong, C., & Sloan, B. (2004). Use of ICT for e-procurement in the UK construction industry: A survey of SMES readiness. In F. Khosrowshami (Ed.), *Proceedings of ARCOM Twentieth Annual Conference 2004,* (Vol. 1, pp. 620-628). Reading, UK: Arcom.

Wright, B. (1999). Electronic signatures: Making electronic signatures a reality. *Computer Law & Security Report, 15*(6), 401–402. doi:10.1016/S0267-3649(99)80090-9

WTO. (1994). *The Uruguay round final act annex 4 in legal texts: The WTO agreements.* Retrieved January 28, 2012, from http://www.wto.org/english/docs_e/legal_e/final_e.htm

ADDITIONAL READING

Dillon, T., Wu, C., & Chang, E. (2010). Cloud computing: Issues and challenges. In *Proceedings of 24th IEEE International Conference on Advanced Information and Applications,* (pp. 27-33). IEEE Press. Retrieved January 28, 2012, from http://www.techpdf.in/files/cloud/Cloud%20Computing%20Issues%20and%20Challenges.pdf

Eadie, R., Millar, P., Perera, S., Heaney, G., & Barton, G. (2012). E-readiness of construction contract forms and e-tendering software. *International Journal of Procurement Management, 5*(1), 1–26. doi:10.1504/IJPM.2012.044151

Eadie, R., Perera, S., & Heaney, G. (2011). Key process area mapping in the production of an e-capability maturity model for UK construction organisations. *Journal of Financial Management of Property and Construction, 16*(3), 197–210. doi:10.1108/13664381111179198

Guillermo, A., & Stewart, P. (2005). Barriers to e-business adoption in construction: International literature review. In *Proceedings of QUT Research Week 2005.* Retrieved January 28, 2012, from http://eprints.qut.edu.au/27334/

Laudon, K., & Laudon, J. (2002). *Management information systems: Managing the digital firm.* Upper Saddle River, NJ: Prentice-Hall Inc.

Li, F. (2007). *What is e-business? How the internet transforms organizations.* Oxford, UK: Blackwell Publishing Ltd.

Lockley, S., Watson, R., & Shaaban, S. (2002). Managing e-commerce in construction - Revolution or e-business as usual? *Engineering, Construction, and Architectural Management, 9*(3), 232–240.

Mell, P., & Grance, T. (1999). *Draft NIST working definition of cloud computing.* Retrieved January 28, 2012, from http://www.scribd.com/doc/19002506/Draft-NIST-Working-Definition-of-Cloud-Computing-v15

Prananto, A., Mckay, J., & Marshall, P. (2001). Frameworks to support e-business growth strategy. In *Proceedings of the 9th European Conference on Information Systems,* (pp. 1255-1263). Bled, Slovenia. Retrieved January 28, 2012, from http://is2.lse.ac.uk/asp/aspecis/20010091.pdf

Sultan, N. (2010). Cloud computing for education: A new dawn? *International Journal of Information Management, 30,* 109–116. doi:10.1016/j.ijinfomgt.2009.09.004

KEY TERMS AND DEFINITIONS

Barriers for E-Procurement: Those issues which inhibit or challenge its adoption.

Bill of Quantities (BOQ): An itemization of all work that is required to complete a construction project. It forms the basis of a tender for procurement of a construction project.

Construction Industry Trading Electronically (CITE): A collaborative electronic information exchange initiative for the UK construction industry.

Construction Procurement: The method of procuring projects, materials, plant, labour, or services for construction projects and related activities.

Drivers for E-Procurement: Those issues which promote the likelihood of its adoption.

E-Business: The use of electronic technologies to support of all the activities of a business. It is innovation lead by information communication technologies.

E-Procurement: Electronic procurement or the use electronic technology in procurement activity to create a leaner and more efficient procurement.

European Procurement: Procurement that must follow regulations in the European Directives that control procurement in the public sector across Europe's member states.

E-Tendering: The use of electronic means to carry out the tendering process.

General Procurement: The method of purchasing goods, works or services. This includes the whole life cycle of purchasing from third parties or in-house providers. It further involves the strategic elements of purchasing from identification of needs, through to disposal/demolition of an asset.

Interoperability: The ability of different software packages/systems to communicate with each other through common or standard data structures.

Quantity Surveyor: A professional within the construction industry that deals specifically with all aspect of construction costs. The profession of quantity surveying originated in the UK and is widely practiced in the British Commonwealth, the Middle East, and Asia. The Quantity Surveyor in Europe is often known as a Construction Economist.

Tendering: One of the main sub processes within construction procurement that provides the mode to procure the built asset concerned. It can be open tendering (anyone can tender) or selective tendering (only certain organisations which meet set criteria can tender) in a single or two-staged process.

Chapter 8

European Union Public Procurement Remedies Regimes:
The Nordic Experience

Kai Krüger
Emeritus University of Bergen, Norway

ABSTRACT

The chapter explores the Nordic statutory EU-based remedy regimes. Due to the European Economic Area (EEA) agreement, the EU commitments do not vary between EU member states, Denmark, Finland, and Sweden and (non-members) Norway and Iceland. The legislation on procurement remedies is assumed to be EU/EEA compliant. There are however material differences in the set up for handling disputes and complaints—also subsequent to the 2010-2012 Nordic adaptation of EU Directive 2007/66/EC on enhanced procurement remedies. The pending issue is whether the EU "sufficiently serious breach" principle on treaty infringements applies on liability for procurement flaws. Loss of contract damage has been awarded in all Nordic countries, whereas cases on negative interest (costs in preparing futile tender bids) seem more favorable to plaintiffs. Per mid-2012, there are no Nordic rulings on the effect of the recent somewhat ambiguous EU Court of Justice Strabag and Spijkers 2010 rulings.

INTRODUCTION

The Swedish and Finnish dual court pillar systems distinguish between public administrative courts authorized to issue injunctions, impose penalties, and declare contracts ineffective as opposed to civil courts, which handle claims for damages and regular contract disputes between contract-ing authorities and private suppliers. The Danish public procurement remedies are placed with the semi-judicial fully authorized Danish Complaint Board as an optional alternative to court litigation. Adversely, competences on injunctions, penalties, ineffective contracts, and damages are in Norway handled by general civil courts, whereas the KOFA Complaint Board is only resorted to

DOI: 10.4018/978-1-4666-2665-2.ch008

for advisory non-binding opinions. Questions on damage formal-procurement have been raised in all Nordic Supreme Courts, leaving a somewhat scattered picture both on the basis for liability.

Global Setting: UNCITRAL, WTO/GPA, EU, and IBRD

Award of public contracts has moved from domestic law into rapidly growing overarching transborder or regional comprehensive legal regimes. These vary in their structure and contents.

1. The UNCITRAL 2011 Model Law on Public Procurement is a suggested template for state legislation, whereas World Trade Organisation – Government Procurement Agreement (WTO GPA) agreement on government procurement (1996) is a multilaterally binding regime on EU and 13 member states.[1] The aim of the GPA is to ensure free trade transparency in relation to laws, regulations, and procurement practice, provide for well-functioning markets and better use of resources, by enabling international competition on deliveries to states and local authorities, and reduce corruption and other dubious business practices. Surveillance and dispute handling is dealt with within the general WTO umbrella. WTO Dispute Settlement Body – open to WTO/GPA Member States.[2]

2. The World Bank (IBRD) involvement in financial projects assumes receivers' acceptance of a set of guidelines (2011) on procurement under IBRD Loans and IDA Credits. Surveillance on compliance has as the primary remedy a withdrawal of financial resources from the recipient.

3. The EU regime on public procurement law is effective in all 27 (28) Member States (including Denmark, Finland, and Sweden) and the relevant directives on procedures and remedies extends also to the legislation in non-member states Iceland, Norway and Liechtenstein under the EEA (European Economic Area) Agreement.[3]

The primary purpose of EU/EEA procurement law is to facilitate and enhance inner market regulated transparent non-discriminatory mobility for public supplies and services, but its anti-corruptive side effect is acknowledged as well.[4] The EU procurement regime has developed since the first procedural directives in the 1970s up until the comprehensive Directive 2004/18/EC (public "classical")[5] (plus Dir. 2004/17(utilities)[6] and Dir. 2009/81 (defense) as noted Kotsonis (2010).[7] A procurement law reform is scheduled 2012 by Commission Draft directives COM (2011) 896 and COM (2011) 895 (see Kotsonis, 2010). The Lisbon Teaty transition from EC/EU into the 2008 Treaty on the Functioning of the European Union (TFEU) changed the numbering of certain provisions relevant on procurement law, renamed the EU Court of Justice (EUCJ), and EU General Court (EUGC), but brought otherwise no amendments in substance with specific bearing on public contracting or—in the context of this chapter—remedies for infringements.

Many EU/EA states such as the Nordic states have chosen to regulate sub-threshold contracts [8] and B-services[9] basically falling outside the scope of EU law, adopting remedies similar to the EU/EEA relevant provisions.

4. Domestic national regimes may apply in addition or—when appropriate—instead of supranational regimes. One such is the comprehensive US federal (1996) FAR (Federal Acquisition Regulation) regime on US federal acquisition with complementary GAO (Government Acquisition Office) surveillance apparatus for the monitoring and ruling out of un-authorized contracts (Robinson in Thai, 2009).

Procurement law such as the UNCITRAL (2011) regime may deal only with procedures. Normally, however, legislation on public contracting distinguishes between procedural rules as opposed to mandatory remedies when the rules are infringed—by general courts, specialized courts, market tribunals competition authorities, or expert staffed Complaint Boards. These vary greatly in the EU system. A survey of the various Nordic institutions follows *infra*.

The topic of this chapter is not procedural procurement law, but rather the various instrumental devices, which have as their objective to dissuade sloppy, corruptive, fraudulent, improper, or otherwise non-compliant administration of public contracting. The focus is primarily on Norwegian law, but with comparative side views to status in Danish, Finnish, and Swedish law. Such rules and updates are derived partly from EU black letter directives, partly from a great number of EUCJ rulings the last decades, some now embodied in the Dir. 07/66. The focus *infra* is on Nordic EU/EEA responses to EU commitments.

A characteristic feature since 1989 has been the EU legislation on enforcement of procurement law. Two remedy' directives address public (Dir. 89/665/EC) and utilities procurement (Water/Energy/Post/Transport) (Dir. 92/13/EC). A recent Dir. 2009/81on Defence procurement includes provisions on damages in article 56 (1) b. The public and utilities' remedy directives are still in force, but were amended through Dir. 07/66 on enhanced sanctions and, in particular, standstill requirements and a rule on mandatory "ineffective contract" for grave procurement flaws.

EU/EEA Level Remedies Dimension: Surveillance and EUCJ Precedence–Interplay with Domestic Regimes

The EU approach to procurement surveillance and enforcement is to combine EU institutional monitoring (Commission) with a latitude for domestic legislator, provided that preset remedies' directive based minimums are observed to ensure effective sanctions and remedies reasonable equivalent to similar domestic practice. Basically, the EU approach has been to require a horizontal remedy regime in which procedural or economic claims are available to unsuccessful runner-up candidates as well as to any person/undertaking affected through rejection of tender bid, non-observance of mandatory publication of invitation to submit offers—or misleading contract documentation. In this, the procurement remedies differ from enforcing competition law, where national and EU Commission are authorised to investigate infringements, prohibit certain actions, and issue penalties.[10]

The regime for public/utilities procurement is complex (Arrowsmith, 1993; Fargieve & Lichére, 2011). Institutional surveillance on legislation and current national practices is provided for through EU Commission (EU) and EFTA Surveillance Authority (ESA)—in cooperation with domestic surveillance.[11] Failing to reach settlements in dialogue with domestic governmental authorities' alleged violations[12] may be instigated by court action either in EUCJ or in the EFTA Court. There are a great number of such cases in the EU court system, but per date none in the EFTA court. Alternatively, procurement issues such as on proper remedies may be raised in preliminary rulings in either of these courts, responding to questions submitted by courts in domestic litigation.

EU/EEA procurement law has to a great degree been developed in these rulings—and the number of submittals has grown dramatically the last decades, both on procedural matters and on domestic handling of remedies provided for either indirectly in the Treaty (Treumer, 2007)[13]—or more expressly in the remedy directives.

The EEA match to the Treaty preliminary EUCJ/EUGC rulings is the EEA and ODA Agreement[14] optional submittal to the EFTA Court for advisory opinions.[15] The EEA (Norwegian/Icelandic/Liechtenstein) dimension on law in substance is identical to the EU. The EFTA Surveillance Authority (ESA) investigates procurement infringement cases in private complaints or *ex officio,* but mainly to correct or to call attention to errors made and with the objective to improve the future practice (Delsaux, 2004).[16] Private operators and their interest in compensation for faulty procurement would normally only benefit indirectly from such proceedings.

The European Court of Justice (EUCJ) has dealt with procurement remedies in a great number of cases. Most of these are about efficiency and transparency requirements[17] and the focus is on inaccurate or insufficient statutory national implementation of the remedies' requirements—either in cases on Treaty violations—or in preliminary rulings where MS' legislation is challenged. Few cases—preceding the 2010 *Strabag* and *Spijkers*[18] rulings (to be discussed *infra* 6.)—deal with the proper interpretation of the remedies' provisions on damages for procurement infringements.[19] Whereas few cases have dealt with the proper interpretation of the provisions on damages for procurement infringements by Member States, several cases on damages have been litigated in the EU General Court (EUGC)[20] as first instance claims under TFEU articles 256 and 268 for EU institutions' own contract awards (Fredriksen & Haukeland, 2010).[21] Most such cases have been dismissed and are therefore of less interest in the context of this chapter. The EUGC claim for damages T-160/03 *AFCon Management Consultants and others v. Commission* (2005-03-17) came out successful for the plaintiff, but only for costs plus interests (Braun, 2005)[22] incurred in challenging the tendering procedure.[23] Claims for loss of profit, 'loss of profile' and 'harm to reputation' were rejected in that case.

The directives on public and utilities remedies were not included in the 2004 EU law reform package. The later 2007 law reform on remedies in public and utilities procurement (Dir. 2007/66/EC[24]) introduced a standstill period, penalties and sanctions on certain grave procurement violations - and in particular "direct purchasing" - without

a public call for competition (Tender Electronic Daily – TED).

However, the 2007 regime did not change the law on damages (Dir. 89/665/EC article 2-1[c]), but might possibly extend the litigation arena for damages in the situation where a contracting authority through terminating the contract potentially incurs liability towards a presumed innocent selected contractor.

The current 2011 Draft Directive on public procurement[25] launched in December 2010—now on the agenda for a forthcoming in-depth law reform—does not include let alone envisage amendments in procurement remedies at all.[26]

Nordic Procurement in the EU/EEA Setting

Nordic[27] law may in certain respects be classified as a separate legal family, distinct from common law and civil law codifications such as Germany, France and the Mediterranean countries. Historically the Nordic countries have cooperated on major legislative projects in private law. Obvious reasons for this lie in historical facts, geographical closeness, and communicative restrictions due to languages not shared in other European countries. The Scandinavians in Denmark, Norway, and Sweden understand each other, although this is not true when it comes to Iceland and Finland.

EU/EEA procurement legal commitments have been complied with in all Nordic countries. In that context, it is still surprising that the design, format, and layout of procurement legislation both on procedures and on remedies differ. The EEA separate status for Iceland and Norway is not the explanation since the EEA agreement levels out the distinctions between EU and EEA procurement law. There are however inter-Nordic differences both in substance and on procedural matters as will be explained *infra*.

A first question is whether the incorporation of (identical) EU/EEA procurement law in the Nordic countries as stated in TFEU or EEA is compliant with the overarching commitments—either on procurement regimes as such or specifically on the remedies' regimes.

The short answer is that Nordic procurement law has not per date been often challenged or tested in the EUCJ or EFTA Court setting.[28] There are a few incidents in the EU context (Denmark, Sweden, Finland).

An old C-243 (J 1993-06-22) *Storebælt* is a Treaty violation case preceding the directives' regime, in which Denmark was found to have violated the ban-on-negotiations assumption in tender procedures. A later Finnish C-195/04 (J 2007-04-26) case was dismissed by the Court. This is history since later domestic law reforms and case law development has amended earlier flaws.

A spectacular Finnish case C-513/99 (J 2002-09-17) *Concordia* is a preliminary EUCJ ruling on environmental award criteria, later to inspire the present Dir. 2004/18 article 53. There is also a Danish preliminary ruling C-275/98 (J 1999-11-18) answering some questions raised by the Danish Complaints Board "Klagenævn."

EUCJ has no jurisdiction under the EEA Agreement (Norway-Iceland). Procurement disputes would fall under the EFTA Court either as cases on infringements (ESA vs. EFTA state) or as preliminary opinions requested by Norwegian or Icelandic national courts). However, per date no Norwegian procurement legal issues have been submitted before the EFTA Court since the EEA came into force in 1994.[29] Non-Member State Iceland has experienced one single case before the EFTA Court—the *Fagthun* case (1999) ruling out *in casu* irregular ban-on-negotiations.[30]

The latest Dir. 2007/66/EC extends the previous Dir. 89/665 procurement remedies to comprise: (1) a mandatory standstill period between award decision and contract conclusion plus; (2) a rule on ineffective contracts on grave procurement flaws (amending Dir. 89/665 article 2d). The law reform (relevant also to EEA Norway and Iceland) has been effectuated in Denmark,[31] Finland,[32] and

Sweden,[33] and passed Norwegian parliamentary preparation 27 March 2012.[34]

In lack of EUCJ/EFTA Court rulings[35] specifically addressing Nordic procurement statutes/regulations domestic Supreme Court rulings prevail in these matters, but as will be shown: The Nordic EU and EEA courts at all levels pay attention to a vast number of EUCJ procurement rulings related to non-Nordic EU jurisdictions.[36]

Whether Nordic national law on procurement remedies is EU/EEA compliant is therefore not primarily about the provisions as such, but on the borderline exercise undertaking by the national courts to apply the relatively widely phrased provisions on faulty procurement (transparency, insufficient reasons for (award) decisions, accountability, proportionality, and others) when challenged by affected claimant/plaintiff such as a runner-up bidder or non-tendering market operators challenging an alleged foul award or a purchase not published with the mandatory market call for competition.

VARIOUS NORDIC PROCUREMENT REMEDIES INSTITUTIONS: A SURVEY AND AN ASSESSMENT

Norwegian Public Procurement Law

Norwegian public procurement law[37] consists of a short 1999-07-16 No 69 framework statute ("*Lov om offentlige anskaffelser*") authorising a comprehensive set of ministerial regulations both on EU/EEU level[38] and on (non-EEA) sub-threshold contracts.[39] The basic structure was maintained in the 2006 implementation of the two 2004 public procurement directives and will apply also after the Dir. 2007/66/EC law reform by spring/summer 2012. Remedies are dealt with in the 1999 act and in a separate ministerial regulation on bid protests (complaints) as of 2002.[40] Ministerial adaptation to Dir. 07/66, i.e. amendments in

2006 procurement and 2002 complaints procedure regulations is presently effectuated in a spring 2012 parliamentary law reform.[41]

The domestic Competition Surveillance Authority ("*Konkurransetilsynet*") is the administrative host of the KOFA Complaint Board secretariat, but exercises no authority on procurement violations. That means that there is no civil public authority (except ESA) to investigate procurement law flaws such as direct purchases, corruptive contracting or the like. Criminal proceedings fall under general state attorney authorities, assisted by "*Økokrim*" (The Norwegian National Authority for Investigation and Prosecution of Economic and Environmental Crime)—and above all strongly supported by critical media focus on dubious public contracting such as "bid rigging," corruptive fraud, abuse of political power, nepotism and bribery in the handling of contract awards.[42]

The optional Norwegian Procurement Complaint Board ("*Klagenemnd* for *Offentlige Anskaffelser*") (KOFA) established under the 1999 Act on procurement § 7a (effective as from 2003), is a responsive expert panel,[43] authorised by statutory regulations to respond on complaints submitted by interested parties (other than the contracting authority). The procedure is based on contradictory exchange of pleas from the parties and may take anywhere between 6 and 12 months. In KOFA cases the board may only opine on whether a submitted bid protest is legally substantiated or not. An interim injunction to freeze or reverse contract awards is not a KOFA matter. Such as well as full trial of damages and—prior to contract—reversal/corrections in a current award procedure are exclusively a matter for the civil courts at first instance.

Even if the KOFA is in lack of legal "muscles" and even if the time span for a submitted complaint is considerable, the KOFA opinions enjoy recognition in the Norwegian procurement environment, thereby probably eliminating costly litigation.[44]

KOFA deals with complaints filed by any party or person having an interest in viewing the procedure or decisions of a contracting authority.[45] Since 2007, the Board has in addition been authorised to impose penalties up until 15% of contract value ("*overtredelsesgebyr*") for serious direct purchases—and has done so in 25 cases by the end of 2011. The Board is otherwise authorised to issue advisory opinions on alleged violations, which, if justified, may be solved voluntarily by correcting, terminating or reversing the award procedure. Alternatively, or where contracting authority challenges the KOFA opinion, the complainant may submit the award to court litigation.[46] The Board may not award—but can opine on—damages when so requested by complainant, but will normally not do so since the complaint procedure is based on written documents and somewhat summary with limited access to evidence required when the liability issue is to be clarified. Furthermore, KOFA does not have the authority to order a standstill in the award procedure. The majority of complaint outputs are therefore responses subsequent to conclusion of the contested contract and therefore only useful for å subsequent court suit. It is for the complainant—independently of the KOFA procedure—to submit a request for judicial interim injunction ("*midlertidig forføyning*") under Civil Procedure Act ("*Tvisteloven*") 2005-06-17 No 90 Chap 34.

For apparent reasons, the out-of-court KOFA Board is not considered a "review body" under any of the Dir. 89/665, 92/13 or 2007/66 Remedies' Directives.[47]

Under the Norwegian dual track system, a private party may initiate court proceedings for damages directly subsequent to the KOFA favourable advisory opinion, but may of course also choose to initiate court proceedings without having had the case reviewed by KOFA at first. KOFA opinions tried in subsequent court litigation show that relatively few opinions are challenged, that the majority court rulings sustain the KOFA opinion although there are cases where the courts have reversed the opinion.[48]

Under the 2012 Norwegian law reform, KOFA will remain only advisory without extended authorities to impose penalties or award damages.

Danish Public Procurement Law

Danish (EU MS) EU procurement ("*udbud*") law on procedures is the black letter procurement directives as such[49] with some supplementary regulations outside the scope of the directives themselves (sub-threshold and B-services).[50] Remedies are addressed in the 2010-05-12 No. 492 Act on remedies ("*håndhævelse*").

The optional (and most often preferred) Complaints Board "*Klagenævnet for udbud*"[51] handles (since 1992) out-of-court bid protests. The board (staffed with 9 judges and 19 procurement law experts) is an optional alternative to court law suits. The procedure is based on contradiction either written on based on oral hearings. It may rule on EU Dir. 89/665 and 07/66 remedies such as stand still injunctions, reversal of procedure, declaration of ineffective contract, penalties and even award damages (subject to optional court review). Steen Treumer argues that complaint cases on damages are more inclined to award damages based on strict liability for violations than the Danish courts (Treumer, 2006c).[52] The annual output of the Board is (2011) approximately 100 rulings.

The Danish Competition and Consumer Authority ("*Konkurrence- og Forbrugerstyrelsen*") may also respond by opinions in procurement disputes—and if not followed by the contracting authority may even submit complaints before the Complaints Board.

The Danish Complaint Board enjoys authority in the Danish procurement environment and its rulings are not often challenged by court proceedings. EUCJ has recognised the Danish board as

a review body authorised to submit preliminary questions to the court.[53]

In Denmark, the new competences on "ineffective contracts" fall under the Complaint Board ("*Klagenævn for udbud*").[54]

Criminal procurement proceedings fall under Director of Public Prosecutions *("Statsadvokaten for Særlig Økonomisk Kriminalitet")*, which acts upon notification by the Complaints Board.

Finnish Public Procurement Law

The Finnish legislation on procurement[55] consists of two comprehensive statutes on public and utilities procurement—with provisions on remedies in the statute on public procurement 30.3.2007/348 (with later amendments 30. April 2010 No 321) Part IV Chaps 10-11 (73-1074 §§) (on utilities 30.3.2007/349), in which there is a reference to the public sector provision on damages (61 § "Rättsmedel")—Ministerial regulations 24.5.2007/614. Remedies are dealt with in Chap 11 ("Ändringssökande och påföljder").

The Finnish special two pillar administrative court Market Court ("Marknadsdomstolen") rules on submitted procurement complaints (85 §).[56] The procedure is either written or oral. Rulings may be appealed to Finnish Supreme Court. The Dir. 07/66 amendments are effective as from 1 June 2010.

Swedish Public Procurement Law

Swedish (EU MS) EU procurement ("*upphandling*") law is a comprehensive act SFS 2007:1091 (amended on the occasion on EU Dir. 07/66 SFS 2010:571).[57]

The Swedish remedial two-pillar regime authorises the public administrative pillar courts ("*Allmän förvaltningsdomstol*") to rule on violations whereas the civil courts will deal with liabilities (Bjørklund & Madell, 2008).

Amended provisions on remedies for faulty procurement are since 2010 inserted SFS 2007:1091 Chap 16[58], updated on the occasion of Dir. 2007/66 by SFS 2010:571 (in force 2010-07-15).[59] The public pillar court employ the Dir. 89/665 article 2 remedies on injunctions, reversal of the procedure—or amendments.

The Swedish Competition Authority (*"Konkurrensverket"*) is authorised to investigate procurement infringements, acting *ex officio* or on external notification. The authority has however no remedial authorities except instigating a case before the public administrative court.

SELECT 2010/2012 LAW REFORM ISSUES

Standstill and Injunctions: C-81/98 "Alcatel" – (Dir. 06/77 Amended) Dir. 89/665/EC

EU Setting

A provision on mandatory "interlocutory procedures" prior to contract conclusion is set in Dir. 89/665 article 2 No 1 (a)-(c). That directive is however silent on standstill period from award decision until contract conclusion. The *Alcatel* pause originated in the EUCJ C-81/98 (J 1999-10-28) ruling, subsequently expressly addressed in the Dir. 07/66 amended provisions articles 2 (3), 2a (2), sanctioned by the "ineffective contracts" rule in article 2d (*infra*). Article 2a (2) is the statutory response to the *Alcatel* ruling whereas article 2 (3) requires an additional standstill suspension of contract conclusion during a pending application for interim measure or for review.

Norway

The ministerial Regulation FOR 2006-04-07 No 402 provision § 22-3 states a reasonable time standstill period (*"rimelig tid"*) between award

decision and contract signature replaced with a 10/15 days calendar suspension period,[60] allowing time for complainant/plaintiff to initiate court standstill injunction.

An optional court injunction for further suspension following the statutory standstill period is dealt with in the general Civil Procedure Act 17 June 2005-06-17 No 90 Chap 34. Award of interim injunction has per date only been effective as from the final court decree which means that the contracting authority has had the option to award *and conclude* the contract while the injunction submittal is still pending.[61] In the amended provision Procurement Act 1999 § 9 the suspension/standstill rule may by ministerial regulation apply already from the submittal of the injunction application, allowing the complainant/plaintiff to act effectively before the standstill period elapses. The duration of the injunction impeding contract conclusion is a matter for the judge to decide on.

Denmark, Sweden, Finland

The Danish response to Dir. 07/66 article 2 1. (a) is the amended Act 2010-05-12 No 492 § 12 authorizing the Complaint Board to decide on suspension (*"opsættende virkning"*). A complaint submitted in the "Alcatel" period impedes contract conclusion temporarily until the Board—on strong indications (*"særlige grunde"*)—has decided on further suspension until the complaint has been concluded by a decision.

The Swedish injunction (*"avtalsspärr"*) under public administrative court (*"allmän förvaltningsdomstol"*) is dealt with in the (2010) amended SFS 2007:1091 Chap 16 1-3 §§ and 8-10 §§. During the period for review of the procurement, the contracting authority may not conclude contract (*"förlängd avtalsspärr"*), subject to exception decree by the court (Act SFS 2011:1030).

The Finnish Market Court (*"Marknadsdomstolen"*) is similarly authorized to issue injunctions (91-93 §§).

"Ineffective Contract": Dir. 07/66 Article 2d

EU Setting

Codifying the C-81/98 *Alcatel* ruling on stand-still period between award decision and contract signing, the Dir. 07/66 law reform has gone on to penetrate the earlier Dir. 89/665 article 2 No 6 barrier for contractual closure effects. It is now stated that certain grave procurement infringements under EU/EEA law makes a contract mandatorily ineffective—Dir. 07766 article 2d now refer to the cases of "direct purchase," violation of extended standstill periods—articles 2d (1) (a) referring to articles 1 (5), 2 (3), 2a (2) - with certain qualifications set in article 2d (1) b as to infringing the complainant's legal options to challenge the procedure.

The main rule still applies otherwise: With exception of the express provisions in article 2d procurement flaws and errors are without contractual effects once the contract has been concluded. Even if contract is manifestly infected by faulty procurement, national law will prevail both on validity and interpretation of the contract, as stated in Dir. 89/665 article 2 (7).[62]

Norway

Forthcoming amended 1999 Act § 17 will state authority for general civil courts at first instance—when engaged by plaintiff—to declare "ineffective" contract according to Dir. 07/66—proactively *ex nunc* or—if restitution in substance is essentially possible—retroactively *ex tunc*. Provisions on alternative shortening of contract duration are inserted in § 14 and on alternative penalties.

Denmark, Sweden, Finland

The Danish Complaint Board (*"Klagenævnet"*) is under Act 492 12 May 2010 §§ 17-18 authorized to declare the contract ineffective (*"uden virkning"*)

proactively (*ex nunc*), but may also—provided strong policy considerations so indicate (*"særlige forhold"*)—impose a retroactive (*ex tunc*) disapproval if restitution can take place.

The Swedish ineffective contract rule is stated in SFS: 571 Chap 16 13 §, authorizing public pillar court to declare the unlawful contract invalid (*"ogiltig"*), i.e. assuming *ex tunc* restitution without any exception.

Finnish ineffective contract rule provided for in provided for in Act 30.3.2007/348 (amended 30.4.2010/321 in force 1.6.2010) 96 § Market Court (*"Marknadsdomstolen"*) authority—invalid *ex tunc* as in the Swedish act.

Dissuasive Penalties

EU Setting

Dir. 89/665 does not contain provisions on penalties as does the utilities Dir. 92/13 (article 2 (1) c). In the Dir. 07/66 amendments, however, effective, proportionate, and dissuasive penalties are set to interact with ineffective contract rule—provisions on this are found in articles 2d (3) and 2e (1) and (2).

Norway

A 2006 amendment to the 1999 statute introduced a KOFA deterrent penalty (*"overtredelsesgebyr"*) for grave un-authorised direct purchases both EU and sub-threshold public contracts (effective as from 2007). Such penalty requires grave error (deliberate or gross negligence), strong appropriate indications—with limitation to 15% of contract value. The pending law reform spring 2012 on Dir. 2007/66 substitutes the KOFA dissuasive penalty with authorization for general civil courts to integrate penalties with the "ineffective contract" remedy stated in Dir. 200766 article 2d—draft § 14.

Denmark, Finland, Sweden

Provisions on combination of ineffective contract and penalties are inserted in the Danish Act 492 12. May 2010, §§ 19, the Finnish (amended) Act 24. May 2007 98 § and the Swedish (amended 2010) SFS 2007:1091 Chap 17.

Compensation Procurement Damage (Positive and Negative Interest): EUCJ Rulings and Domestic Case law

EU Setting[63]

The question of damages for procurement violations is somewhat vaguely provided for in the three EU remedies' directives on public, utilities, and defence contracting. The Public Procurement Remedies' Dir. 89/665 article 2 No 1 (c) simply state that the remedy of damages under national procurement legislation shall be available to harmed interests such as defined in the provision on "legal standing" (Dir. 89/665 article 1 (3) "any person having or having had an interest in obtaining…a contract…").[64] The remedy provisions on damages were not reviewed in the 2007 law reform (and are not addressed in the 2010 draft law reform).

Few cases have dealt with the proper interpretation of the remedies' provisions on damages for procurement infringements.[65]

Two recent EUCJ 2010 rulings attempt to refine the arguments on the damage issues.

The *C-314/09 Strabag* (2010-09-30)[66] preliminary ruling strikes down an Austrian 1998 piece of legislation stating that the right to damages for an infringement of public contract law (*in casu* a non-compliant tender bid for asphalt supplies) is conditional on *culpa* modified with a presumption that the contracting authority is at fault so that the authority will have to rebut the onus that it is not accountable for the alleged infringement.

EUCJ—reminding of the Dir. 89/665 Recitals—reiterates in (31) the Member States' duty to take measures necessary to ensure the existence of effective and rapid review of procurement decisions—in (32) specified on powers to award damages to persons harmed by an infringement.

Whereas the directive only lays down a "minimum" level of conditions for review procedures, the ruling goes on to acknowledge Member States' competences to legislate in domestic law on:

(33) … the measures necessary to ensure that the review procedures effectively award damages to persons harmed by an infringement of the law on public contracts (see, by analogy, GAT, paragraph 46).

Furthermore,

(34) […] the implementation…in principle… comes under the procedural autonomy of the Member States limited by the principle of equivalence and effectiveness…

However, it must be noted that

[---] it is necessary to examine whether that provision, interpreted in the light of the general context and aim of the judicial remedy of damages, precludes a national provision such as that at issue in the main proceedings from making the award of damages conditional in the circumstances set out in paragraph 30 of this judgment, on a finding that the contracting authority's infringement of the law on public contracts is culpable.

The remedy of damages under article 2 (1) (c) thus opens for national implementation:

(35) [---] in no way indicates that the infringement in the public procurement legislation liable to give rise to a right of damages in favour of the person harmed should have specific features such as be-

ing connected to fault –proved or presumed on the part of the contracting authority, or not being covered by any ground for exemption of liability.

And, to comply with the principle of effectiveness:

(39) [----] is no more dependent than the other legal remedies provided for in article 2 (1) of Directive 89/665 on a finding that the contracting authority is at fault.

These passages have been read to eliminate literally not only black letter statutory culpable requisites for liability (even as in the Austrian act supplied with a burden of proof disfavouring the contracting authority to the benefit of the complainant),[67] but also the *Factortame III*[68] inspired "sufficiently serious breach" formula.

With some uncertainty lingering in the procurement world, the Court recapitulated the damage issue few months later.

The damage issue still pending, the 2010 *Strabag* ruling is not stating that *any* public procurement violation causing losses to relevant harmed interests should be compensated according to Dir. 89/665 art 2 1(c) on a strict liability basis. But it is worth observing that he *Factortame III* "sufficiently serious breach" test advocated by many in relation to article 2 (2) (c) is not referred to at all in the ruling. On the contrary,

(35) ---the wording of ...Article 2 (1)....and the sixth recital in the preamble to Directive 89/556 in no way indicates that the infringement of the public procurement legislation liable to give rise to a right to damages in favour of the person harmed should have specific features, such as being connected to fault—proved or assumed—on the part of the contracting authority, or not being covered by any ground for exemption from liability (emphasis added).

The *Strabag* ruling therefore could be said not only to reiterate C-275/03 *Commission v Portugal* (2004-10-10) extended into ruling out not only statutory excessively burdensome procedural impediments on the claimant litigating for damages[69]—but also to strike down other restrictions on liability of "specific features" such as the "sufficient serious breach" formula.

Arguably one might envisage two scenarios, one where the public contracting authority such as a regional municipality applying a *compliant* national implementation of the EU *acquis* incurs liability for mal-procurement—a point blank Dir. 89/665 article 2 (1) (c) arena, whereas alternatively the government legislative body might have been found liable in damages for non-compliant legislation on liability[70]—but protected under the *Factortame III* qualified level for liability, such as making damage cover dependent on culpa or any other "special features."

In dealing with domestic legislation the *Strabag* case the setting is of limited interest to the Nordic legislature since there have so far been no attempts in reported litigation or complaint board cases to challenge the various Nordic provisions expressly on procurement damage for being in their wording or preparatory documents non-compliant with EU/EEA law.[71]

The subsequent December 2010 ruling C-568/08 *Spijkers* (2010-12-09) on substantial irregular changes in the contract documentation after time limit for submittal of tender bids for bridge construction works project in Holland) appears to restore the *Factortame III* threefold formula on liability (conferred rights, sufficiently serious breach, causal link). Somewhat confusing, the Dir. 89/665 article 2 (1) (c) on contracting authority's liability is in (87) and (92) now displayed as a rule on *State* liability, whereas the directive states *contracting authority's* liability (McGowan, 2011).

Accepting (88) that EU case law at present (and even after Dir. 07/66) has not set out more detailed criteria for mal-procurement damage, it is:

(90) ...for the legal order of each Member State to determine the criteria on the basis of which damage arising from an infringement of EU law on the award of public contracts must be determined and estimated...provided the principles of equivalence and effectiveness are complied with...

In that context, the subsequent reasoning in (92) is a two-fold exercise. The *Factortame III* "sufficiently serious breach" fragment is not rigidly set under EU procurement law (as many have suggested), but short of such:

(92) ...it is for the internal legal order of each Member State, once those conditions have been complied with, to determine the criteria on the basis of which the damage arising from an infringement of EU law on the award of public contracts, must be determined and estimated, provided the principles of equivalence and effectiveness are complied with (emphasis added)

Spijkers develops *Strabag* in so far as the ruling—reiterating *Factortame* III "sufficiently serious breach"—also seems to leave appreciable latitude for national autonomous handling of principles on equivalence and effectiveness in setting the threshold for relevant breaches. Even if "fault" is ruled out as a statutory condition for damages, subjective elements on part of the contracting authority might arguable still form part of the test for which breach—cumulative breaches—are sufficient in a given case for damages.

Neither of the two cases seems to appreciate a distinction between a contracting authority's liabilities for faulty procurement as opposed to a Member State's liability for non-compliant EU legislation on damages. The Dir. 89/665 article 2.1 (c) only states that the person harmed shall be compensated for damages without distinguishing

legislator's derogation and contracting authority's faulty procurement. So *query*, does EUCJ impliedly assume the same basis for liability in the two scenarios whereas EU/EEA case law so far only is about derogatory non-compliant MS legislation? Might the policy objectives to ensure deterrent remedies for mal-procurement allow for more severe sanctions than if the case is for statutory infringement of the procurement *acquis*? Admittedly, however, the Directive 89/665 article 2 (1) (c) makes no literal distinction between the two scenarios and the *Spijkers* references on state liability are expressly related to the national remedy statutory provision.

Whereas the EU case law on procurement damages have dealt with MS' inaccurate or questionable statutory implementation of the remedy directives (or EU institutions procurement), as already explained none of the Nordic provisions on procurement damage have as yet been challenged in EUCJ or in the EFTA-court (Norway – Iceland) litigation.[72]

The "ineffective" rule in Dir. 07/66 article 2d[73] raises a new problem, namely whether the affected supplier left without a contract (*ex tunc* or *ex nunc*) should be barred from claiming damages from his public counter party under Dir. 89/665 article 2d. The Danish and Swedish preparatory documents assume that the supplier (save contributory negligence) may claim for damages[74] whereas the Norwegian committee preparing the amendment expressed doubts as to whether the "ineffective" rule would be undermined, at least if the supplier were allowed to claim for loss of contract.[75] The ministerial and parliamentary response is that the question on liabilities should be left to development in case law.[76]

Norway

Damages in a court case of faulty procurement—initially raised or raised subsequent to a KOFA complaints Board statement—is addressed in the 1999 Act § 10, only stating in a single sentence that the contracting authority violating the statute—or regulations issued under the statute—incurs liability for the loss inflicted on the harmed party.[77] Supreme Ct has applied the *Factortame III,* "sufficiently serious breach" formula on loss of contract litigation—Rt. 2001.1062 *Nucleus.*[78]. On negative interest, the ruling Rt. 2008.982 *"Catch-Ventelo"* awards cover for plaintiffs financial efforts to abort an erroneous procedure, whereas Rt. 1997.574 *Firesafe* dismisses a negative interest claim for lack of causation.[79] Rt. 3007.983 *RenoVest* is also a case on lack of causation: if the actual award could not sustain the alternative would have been an in-house performance. There are no subsequent express rulings on negative interest.

Denmark

The Danish Complaints Board is since 2003 authorized to award as binding awards damages in infringement cases—optional to civil court litigation[80]—and has done so in a number of cases, some of which have been reviewed by the courts.[81] The law reform 12 May 2010 No 482 (*"Lov om håndhævelse af udbudsreglerne"*) reiterates the rule on damages in statutory § 14.

There are in addition a handful of Danish Supreme rulings on damages—both on positive interest and on negative interest. Earlier cases on procurement published with an obligation to award to lowest bidder (*"bunden licitation"*) is UfR 1997.1308 *Horsens Byhus* (sub-EU threshold)[82], later rulings on positive interest are UfR 2000.1561 *Fårup Sommerland* (award), UfR.2007.2106 *"Arriva"* (utilities – award), UfR 2011.1955 *Amager Strandpark.* Cases on negative interests are UfR 2002.1180 H *KKS* (dismissed), UfR 2004.1294 H *Skjortegrossisten* (dismissed) and UfR 2005.1799 H *Ørestad Metro* (dismissed).

Finland

The Finnish rule on procurement damage liability is a provision in Act 30. March 2007 No. 348 (amended 30 April 2010 No 321) 107 §, partly similar to the Swedish rules. Whereas Market Court (*"Marknadsdomstolen"*) is authorized to impose penalties and declare contracts invalid, it follows from 107 § that litigation for damages is a matter for ordinary general civil courts.

Sweden

The Swedish regime on damages is a single track civil court regime, running parallel to the public pillar courts competences to award suspension and injunctions, award penalties and declare contracts invalid (*"ogiltig"*).

Damage to runner-up candidates or potential bidders is dealt with in Swedish statute SFS 2007:1091 amended on the occasion of EU Dir. 07/66 in SFS 2010: 571. The provision on damage is inserted in Chap as 20-21 §§. Several previous cases on (positive interest) damage for procurement damage have been litigated in Supreme Court such as case—NJA 1998.873 *Arkitekttjänst* (award)[83], NJA 2000.712 *Tvättsvamparna* (dismissed), and NJA 2007.349 *Ishavet—Virgo* (award). It is believed that existing Supreme Court case law is sustained under the 2010 regime.

Corruption and Fraud Remedies: UN 2003 and Council of Europe 1999 Regimes - A Norwegian Puzzle

Corruption and fraudulent behavior is only indirectly addressed in EU procurement law. Corruptive award of contracts not opened for a mandatory call for competition would under Dir. 07/66 normally be a unauthorized "direct purchase" subject to "ineffective contract" declaration and/ or penalties. In addition the EU regime include provisions on mandatory exclusion of contract candidates or tenderisers who has been convicted for *inter alia* corruption or fraud (Dir. 2004/18 article 45 [1][b][c]). Furthermore, contracting authorities may exclude candidates found guilty of grave professional misconduct (article 45 [2] [d]). Such cases are rare in the Nordic histology. One Norwegian 2009 incident (subject to parliamentary hearing) dealt with the issue of time span for optional exclusion and on the handling of a dispute where the candidate objected to the contracting authority's interpretation of the provision allegedly violated fraudulently by the candidate.

Combating corruption has also entered the UN agenda by Convention against corruption 2003 (with provisions on corruptive procurement in article 9). Further initiatives have been taken by Council of Europe (civil and criminal law on corruption 1999).[84]

Plain bribery, fraud, and similarly corruptive actions to achieve irregular public contracts will normally imply one or more insiders' complicity or collusion and therefore constitute violations of procurement rules such as unlawful direct purchasing, improper contract administration and others. Corruptive contracts might therefore most often be considered *ineffective* under the Dir. 2007/66 regime article 2d. Furthermore, the remedies' rules under Dir. 89/665 and Dir. 92/13 would enable honest competitors to claim for *damages* from the contracting authority, applying (classical) Dir. 89/665 article 2 (1) (c) or (utilities) Dir. 92/13 article 2 (1) (d).

Implementation of the 1999 Council of Europe Civil Law on Corruption articles 3-7[85] took place in Norway 2008 by inserting a provision in the 1969-06-13 No 26 Act on Civil Liability Sect 1-6,[86] stating liability for the person guilty of corruption as defined in amended 1902-05-22 No 10 Criminal Code Sections 276a-276c as well as semi-subjective vicarious liability for the guilty person's principal/employer. Liability may not incur if the principal/employer ("*arbeidsgiver*") can prove that all reasonable precautions have

been undertaken to avoid corruption *and* furthermore—alternatively—that liability should not be imposed in view of an overall assessment of the merits of the case. That provision may very well overlap a typical fraudulent direct purchase under procurement Dir. 07/66.

The 1969 statutory provisions on contributory negligence (§ 5-1) were not considered by the 2008 amendment. Nor was the Norwegian procurement liability provision in § 10. It could therefore be argued that the public authority itself might be barred from claiming damages if a corruptive award of contract did take place vicariously by a disloyal staff member operating without any interference or knowledge on part of his superiors.

The corruption provision might overlap the otherwise applicable provisions on liability for faulty procurement when the activities addressed involve award of public contracts. The 2008 insertion does not exclude or limit further going liability in procurement law. However, the corruption rule might itself go beyond procurement remedies and open up for claims by innocent competitors raised against the not-so-innocent corruptive co-supplier for loss of contract or negative costs.

The Norwegian implementation of the 1999 Council of Europe Civil Law on Corruption (articles 3-7) is badly coordinated with procurement statutory remedies and implications in relation to Dir. 89/665 and Dir. whereas 2007/66 article 2(1)(c) and the 1999 Act § 10 have apparently not been observed.

FUTURE RESEARCH DIRECTIONS

Future challenges in the procurement remedy setting would be to explore the actual effect of the various approaches chosen by the legislators in the Nordic countries, such as the Swedish/Finnish procedural separation between public administrative courts as opposed to civil court litigation on compensation for positive and negative costs. The separation is burdensome for the litigants and therefore obviously questionable under the EU Dir 89/665 article 1 requirement, which is to ensure effective and rapid measures for review of procurement procedures. In the Danish setting, one might need to examine pros and contras of the optional quasi-judicial Complaints Board authorized to impose penalties, ʹto award damages and to declare contracts ineffective. Similarly, the Norwegian purely responsive Complaints Board (KOFA) is the chosen "soft" alternative to court review, but there is as yet no comprehensive research on whether these purely advisory opinions on procurement compliance lead to acceptable out-of-court settling of disputes over contract awards, let alone documentation on the perceptible outcome of cases in various civil courts subsequent to the KOFA opinions.

The Dir. 2007/66/EU enhanced sanctions implemented 2010-2012 have not yet reached court litigation nor do complaints board reviews. It is expected that the impact of the law reform will be monitored closely both by academics, legislators and the law profession. Time will show.

CONCLUSION

The Nordic remedies' legislation on procurement remedies appears to be basically EU/EEA compliant[87] and very few of the statutory implementations of the EU procedural directives have per date been challenged or subject to preliminary reviews in the EU Court of Justice or the EFTA Court (Norway/Iceland)—excepting the Danish C-243/89 *Storebælt* case (1993) and the Finnish C-195/04 (J 2007-04-26) (case dismissed).

Only two Nordic procurement cases have been submitted for preliminary questions. Denmark, Finland and Sweden have duly implemented the Dir. 07/77 amendments per 2010, whereas Norway will have the statutory amendments in place and in force before or by the end of 2012.

The non-member EFTA/EEA states Iceland and Norway have separate arrangements for supra national surveillance of procurement law—the EFTA Surveillance Authority ESA (corresponding to EU Commission) and the EFTA Court (corresponding to the EU Court of Justice although only advisory and consequently limited jurisdiction). Several ESA incidents have occurred in procurement communication with Norway and Iceland, but per date only one procurement ruling by the EFTA Court—the Icelandic E-5/98 (1999-05-12) *Fagthun* case.

Questions on damage compensation (loss of contract, costs in challenging a contract award and negative interest costs in participating in a mal-administered award procedure) have been raised in all Nordic countries, leaving a somewhat scattered picture both on the basis for liability (pending issue whether the EU *Factortame III* "sufficiently serious breach" principle applies and on causation. Loss of contract damage has been awarded in Denmark, Finland, and Norway. It is somewhat doubtful whether there is a basis for distinguishing between loss of contract issues (positive contract interest) and negative interest. Per mid-2012 there are no Nordic rulings on the effect of the EUCJ *Strabag* and *Spijkers* rulings.

There are material differences in the set up for handling disputes and complaints. The Swedish and Finnish dual court pillar systems distinguish between public administrative courts authorized to issue injunctions, impose penalties, and declare contracts ineffective as opposed to civil courts which handle claims for damages and regular contract disputes between the public and private parties. The Danish system is also dual, but the core of EU-based remedies is placed with the Danish Complaint Board, although procurement damage claims may be handled both in the Complaint Board and in civil courts as an optional alternative or subsequent to a Complaint Board ruling (several Supreme Court rulings). The Norwegian system is as from 2012 a single-track review apparatus. Effective competences on injunctions, penalties, ineffective contracts, and damages are all handled by general civil courts, whereas the KOFA Complaint Board is only resorted to for advisory opinions. In spite of this (and lengthy time for dispute handling) the workload for the KOFA is considerable.

REFERENCES

Act 30. March 2007 No. 348. (2007) C-314/09 Strabag (2010-09-30) and C-568/08 Spijkers (2010) C-395/95 Geotronics SA v Commission (1997-04-22) E.C.R. I-2271 (1997)

Danish Act No 492 2010-05-12 in effect 2010-07-01, subsequent Complaints Board (2010)

Dir. 07/66/EU (2010)

Dir. 07/77/EU (2010)

Dir. 2004/18/EU (2010)

Dir. 2007/66/EU (2010) Draft COM (2011)

Dir. 89/665/EU (2010)

Dir. 92/13/EU (2010)

EFTA Court - the Icelandic E-5/98 (1999-05-12) Fagthun case (1999)

EU Court of Justice – the Finnish C-513/99 (J-2002-09-17) Concordia ruling and the Danish Unitron Skandinavia case C-275/98 (J 1999-11-18) (2002)

Finnish Act 2010-04-30 No 321 (in force 2010-06-01) amending Act 30.3.2007/348 (2010)

Kotsonis, T. (2011). A novelty is a commission draft directive on concession awards COM(2011)897, previously only dealt with in EUCJ rulings on *quasi*-procurement interpretation of EU treaty principles: Commenting on commission draft directives COM (2011) 896 and COM (2011) 895 (2010). *Public Procurement Law Report, 20*(5), 51.

Standstill and injunctions – C-81/98 "Alcatel" – (Dir. 06/77 amended) Dir. 89/665/EC (2010)

World Trade Organisation. (1996). *Government procurement agreement: Agreement on government procurement.* New York, NY: WTO.

WTO. (2011). *The WTO regime on government procurement: Challenge and reform.* Cambridge, UK: Cambridge University Press.

ADDITIONAL READING

Arrowsmith, S. (Ed.). (1993). *Remedies for enforcing the public procurement rules.* Peterborough, UK: Earlsgate Press.

Arrowsmith, S. (2008). *The law of public and utilities procurement* (2nd ed.). London, UK: Sweet and Maxwell.

Arrowsmith, S., & Anderson, R. D. (Eds.). (2011). *The WTO regime on government procurement: Challenge and reform.* Cambridge, UK: Cambridge University Press. doi:10.1017/CBO9780511977015

Bjørklund, D., & Madell, T. (2008). Skadestånd vid offentlig upphandling. *Svensk Juristtidning,* 579–602.

Braun, P. (2005). Commenting on T-160/03 AFCon management consultants and others v commission (2005-03-17). *Public Procurement Law Report, 14,* 98.

Dischendorfer, M. (2005). Commenting on commission v Germany C-126/03 (18.11.2004). In *14 PPLR NA80*.

Fairgrieve, D., & Lichère, F. (Eds.). (2011). *Public procurement law: Damages as an effective remedy*. London, UK: Hart.

Fredriksen, H. (2010). Objektivt ansvar for anbudsfeil?. *Lov og Rett, 600*.

Høg, T. (2012). *Erstatningsansvar I forbindelse med udbud*. Retrieved from http://www.udbudsportalen.dk

McGowan, D. (2011). Commenting on C-568/08 spijkers (2010-12-09). *Public Procurement Law Report, 20*, 64.

Olykke, G. S. (2010). *Abnormally low tenders, with an emphasis on public tenderers*. Copenhagen, Denmark: DOJF.

Poulsen, S. T., Jakobsen, P. S., & Kalsmose-Hjelmborg, S. E. (2011). *EU udbudsretten*.

Robinson, K. C. D. (2009). Federal government procurement. In Thai, K. V. (Ed.), *International Handbook of Public Procurement* (p. 291). London, UK: Auerbach Press.

Sanchez Graells, A. (2010). More competition-oriented public procurement to foster social welfare. In Thai, K. V. (Ed.), *Towards New Horizons in Public Procurement* (p. 81). Boca Raton, FL: Academic Press.

Sanchez Graells, A. (2011). *Public procurement and the EU competition rules*. Oxford, UK: Hart Publishing.

Snider Smith, J. J. (2008). Competition and transparency: What works for public procurement reform. *Public Contract Law Journal, 38*, 85.

Steinicke, M., & Groesmeyer, I. (2011). *EU's udbudsdirektiver*.

Taylor, S. (2011). The challenge of competitive neutrality in public procurement and competition policy: The UK health sector as case study. *CPI Journal, 7*.

Treumer, S. (2006c). Commenting on Danish complaint board cases. *Public Procurement Law Report, 4*, 159–170.

Treumer, S. (2007a). Towards an obligation to terminate contracts concluded in breach of the EC public procurement rules: The end of the status of concluded contracts as sacred cows. *Public Procurement Law Report, 16*(6), 371.

Treumer, S. (2007b). Commenting on commission v Germany C-126/03 (18.11.2004). *Public Procurement Law Report, 16*(6), 371.

KEY TERMS AND DEFINITIONS

Corruption: Improper attempts to bribe or otherwise induce a contract award such as direct purchasing without a public call for competition (UN Convention 2003 and others).

Damages: Public mandatory commitments to compensate for costs in preparing contract offer to public contracting authorities.

EU Procurement Remedies: EU law based surveillance of government/municipal contracting, including submittal of bid protests.

Ineffective Contracts: EU/EEA based commitments to invalidate contracts awarded through certain grave procurement flaws.

Injunctions: Procedural remedies for complainants to achieve court preliminary orders for additional suspension of award procedure.

Nordic Legal Family: History based features in Nordic legal tradition distinct from common law or civil (continental) law.

Public Contracts: Government or municipal contracts awarded to private suppliers/contractors (goods, service,s or construction works).

Standstill Period: Mandatory time limit suspension of contract conclusion to allow for bid protest on reversing or abortion of ongoing award procedure.

ENDNOTES

1   GPA is reflected in the EU directives' regime as from 1997 EEC Dir. 97/52 of 13. October 1997 amending Directives 92/50/EEC, 93/36/EEC and 93/37/EEC (Services, Works, Supplies), in Non-EU member Norway GPA inserted in the earlier 1992 Act on public procurement in 1996.

2   In November 2001, at the Doha Ministerial Conference, member governments agreed to negotiate to improve and clarify the Dispute Settlement Understanding. These negotiations take place in special sessions of the Dispute Settlement Body (DSB) (Arrowsmith, 2011).

3   Signed Oporto 1992-05-02 – no subsequent amendments. The agreement extends *inter alia* EU inner market regime and competition law to apply in EFTA states Iceland, Liechtenstein and Norway (EFTA-state Switzerland is not a member of the Agreement). Initial EEA members Austria, Finland, and Sweden acceded to the European Union on 1 January 1995.

4   More explicit in the Draft COM(2011) 896 article 22 ("illicit conduct"), cfr UN 2003 Convention Against Corruption article 9 addressing corruptive procurement expressly.

5   Directive 2004/18 of the European Parliament and of the Council of 31. March 2004 on the coordination of procedures for the award of public works contracts, public supply contracts and public service contracts.

6   Directive 2004/17/EC of the European Parliament and of the Council of 31. March 2004 coordinating the procurement procedures of entities operating in the water, energy, transport and postal services sectors.

7   Directive 2009/81 of the European Parliament and of the Council of 13 July 2009 on the coordination of procedures for the award of certain works contracts, supply contracts and service contracts by contracting authorities or entities in the field of defence and security, and amending Directives 2004/17/EC and 2004/18/EC.

8   Threshold figures set in Dir. 2004/18 Section 1 (articles 7-9).

9   Dir. 2004/18 article 20 reference to Annex II A (such as health and social services).

10   Draft Dir. COM(2011)896 introduces a Title V on "Governance" on Enforcement (articles 83-88) with *inter alia* "Oversight bodies" (article 84) monitoring public procurement activities.

11   In Denmark, Finland, and Sweden the EU Commission acts in cooperation with national Competition authorities. In Norway, the national Competition Surveillance Authority does not handle procurement disputes (but may investigate collusive tendering and on non-compliant state aid "abnormally low tenders" – Dir. 2004/18 article 55). The EFTA Surveillance Authority ESA communicates on procurement disputes with the relevant Government Ministry and if unresolved dispute the case may be brought before the EFTA Court (no such Nordic cases per date).

12   *Ex officio* or in response to complaint from affected parties.

13   Stating that EU supranational law requires transparency, accountability, equal treatment, and proportionality whether or not this can be derived from the wording or implications of the Treaty provisions or based on the

directives' texts. The most spectacular case is C-81/98 *Alcatel* (J 1999-10-28) (standstill period suspending contract conclusion), C-503/04 Commission v Germany (J 2007-07-18), Cf Commission v Germany C-126/03 (18.11.2004) with comments by S. *Treumer* op.cit. s. 373 and *M Dischendorfer* (2005) 14 PPLR NA80.

14 Agreement between the EFTA States on the Establishment of a Surveillance Authority and a Court of Justice 2 May 1992 (anticipated in the EEA Agreement 1992 article 108).

15 Only one procurement preliminary ruling in the EFTA Court - E-5/98 (1999-05-12) *Fagthun* (Iceland).

16 ESA cases are reported in Annual Reports. In 2004, ESA dealt with appr. 20 cases, all Norwegian cases. As to Commission's surveillance. Since the establishment of the Norwegian Complaint Board KOFA in 2003, the number of ESA procurement investigations has gone down (annual reports on <eftasurv.int>. There is only one EFTA Court procurement case, the Icelandic E-5/98 (1999-05-12) *Fagthun*. No EFTA court cases raised by ESA on procurement remedies as yet.

17 On non-acceptable national procedural conditions or time limits for such claims, C-470/99 *Universale Bau* (2002-12-12) and C-406/08 *Uniplex* (2010-01-28) or on questionable subjective liability conditions, C-275/03 *Commission v Portugal* (2004-10-10) on non-acceptable Portuguese legislation requiring fraud or fault as conditions for damages.

18 C-314/09 *Strabag* (2010-09-30) and C-568/08 *Spijkers* (2010-12-09), to be discussed *infra 4*.

19 C-395/95 *Geotronics SA v Commission* (1997-04-22) [1997] E.C.R. I-2271 on procedure, C-275/03 *Commission v Portugal* (2004-10-14) on non-compliant Portuguese

legislation requiring fraud or fault as conditions for damages, followed by a ruling on financial penalty for failing to amend legislation C-70/06 (2008-01-10).

20 Ex Court of First Instance CFI - TFEU article 256.

21 Cf. on the EU institutions' civil contract and tort liabilities such as in the area of award of contracts, TFEU article 340 (ex TEC article 288), with somewhat vague references not to EU law but to 'the law applicable to the contract in question' and (non-contractual) to 'the general principles common to the laws of the Member States.' Whether this rules out the 2010 *Strabag* drift towards strict liability (infra) could be questioned. Strong policy considerations indicate that EU institutions should not benefit from more lenient rules on liability than contracting authorities in EU/EEA Member States. EU competitive contract awards are also about inner market mobility.

22 Recitals (109) and (133) - EU Central Bank interest rate plus 2% p. a., in addition compound interest subsequent to judgment. Case comment by P. Braun (2005) 14 PPLR NA98, and P. Kalbe (2005) 14 PPLR NA121.

23 EU procurement law is basically restricted to regulate contracting authorities, so both contracting in disregard of the standstill period as well as direct contracting without a call for competition could evidently be said to harm the interests of the private party affected.

24 Directive 2007/66/EC of the European Parliament and of the Council of 11 December 2007 amending Council Directives 89/665/EEC and 92/13/EEC with regard to improving the effectiveness of review procedures concerning the award of public contracts.

25 On Utilities Procurement COM(2011)895 furthermore (a new) COM(2011)897 Draft Directive on the award of concession contracts).

26 Excepting draft article 84 on "Public Oversight."

27 "Nordic" includes Denmark, Finland, Iceland, Norway and Sweden. "Scandinavian" is often used as a synonym for Nordic although the Scandinavian peninsular/ language region could more accurately be said to include only Denmark, Norway, and Sweden *("Store Norske Leksikon")*.

28 ESA Annual Reports (<eftasurv.int>) display communication between the surveillance authority and EEA states on procurement matters. In Norway, the KOFA Complaints Board has taken over most of such cases. In the last years only very few procurement disputes have been handled by ESA (Brussels).

29 On ESA involvement in Norwegian procurement disputes, reference is made to (Norwegian commission report) (Norges Offentlige Utredning) NOU 2012::2 "Utenfor og innenfor" pp. 411-412 and on remedies in the EEA regime in general pp. 198 et seq with a list of EU/EEA-related court cases (Supreme Court and subordinate courts) Annex 7 (pp 903) (whereof 27 cases on public procurement).

30 E-5/98 (1999-05-12) *Fagthun*.

31 Danish Act No 492 2010-05-12 in effect 2010-07-01, subsequent Complaints Board ("Klagenævnet for Udbud") cases 2012-01-03 Danske Arkitektvirksomheder mod Thisted Gymnasium og Kurser, 2012-01-03 Danske Arkitektvirksomheder mod Skanderborg Gymnasium.

32 Finnish Act 2010-04-30 No 321 (in force 2010-06-01) amending Act 30.3.2007/348.

33 Swedish Act SFS 2010:571 (amending SFS 2007:1091 and 1092) in effect 2010-07-15.

34 Parliamentary Innst 185 L (2011-2012), (ministerial) Prop. 12 L (2011-2012), (committee Report) NOU 2010:2 "Håndhevelse av offentlige anskaffelser")—parliamentary decision 2012-03-27.

35 Communication based on E-Commission requests to Member States' governments on possible infringement is not observed here.

36 The total volume of EUCJ procurement rulings is massive, both Treaty infringement cases (Commission vs Member State) and preliminary rulings on questions submitted by national courts in current litigation. Add to this cases where private operators challenge contract awards by EU own institutions, reviewed at first instance in EU General Court (EUGC), cfr TFEU articles 256 and 340.

37 Accessed (in Norwegian) on official website <lovdata.no>.

38 Ministerial Regulation ("forskrift") 2006-04-07 No 402 Parts I and III.

39 2006-04-07 No 402 Parts I and II, extending national rules further than required under Dir. 2004/18 (sub-threshold and B-services). On abolishing the distinction between A and B services, se now Draft Directive COM(2011)896 Explanatory Memorandum at p. 8.

40 "Klageforskrift" 2002-11-15 No 1288 FAD.

41 Ministerial Prop L 12 (2011-2012) on statute amendments passed in Parliament 2012-03-27.

42 UN 2003 Convention against corruption inspired provisions on corruption in 1902-05-22 No 10 Criminal Code §§ 276a-276c. "Økokrim" is since 1989 the central Norwegian hub unit for investigation and prosecution of economic and environmental crime, and the main source of specialist skills for the police and the prosecuting authorities in their combat against crime of this kind. Økokrim is both a police specialist agency and a public prosecutors' office with national authority, cf *infra* 4. e.

[43] 10 Board Members: 4 judges, 4 procurement attorneys including the chairman, 1 university emeritus professor (KK). The Board has per end of 2011 dealt with appr 1500 cases since 2003.

[44] The fee for KOFA complaint submittal is per date modest compared to court fees and litigation costs – NOK 860 (= appr 100 euro). A ministerial proposal for raising the fee to 8000 NOK is pending.

[45] Regulation on procurement complaints ("Klageforskriften") 2002-11-15 No 1288 § 6.

[46] The contracting authority will normally only challenge a KOFA-response if the complainant instigates court review in a case for remedies (such as damages).

[47] Compare the Danish Complaints Board ("Klagenævnet for udbud"), which is recognized as a "review body" authorised to submit questions for preliminary rulings by EUCJ – C-275/98 (J 1999-11-19).

[48] Supreme Court rulings supporting KOFA opinions are Rt. 2007.983 "RenoVest", Rt. 2007.1489 "Byggholt", Rt. 2008.982 "Catch/Ventelo." Adverse outcome in Rt. 2008.1705 "Trafikk og Anlegg."

[49] Bekendtgørelse (decree) nr. 937 2004-09-16 (amended 2006-06-12). [<rettsinformation>].

[50] Act on sub-threshold procurement 2005-05-18 No 338 ("Tilbudsloven")(amended 2007-06-06 No 572), furthermore Act on procurement remedies No 2010-05-12 No. 492, replacing Act on Complaints Board ("Klagenævnet") 2000-05-31 No 415.

[51] <www.klfu.dk>.

[52] Commenting on the Complaint Board ruling 2005-03-01 *BN Produkter Danmark AS mod Odense Renovationsselskab.* In a number of later rulings, it appears as if the Complaint Board's practice is to consider claims for damages without assuming or addressing any qualified conditions for liability, such

as the 2009 on negative interest 2009-01-09 *C C Brun Entreprise v AS Storebælt,* 2009-01-12 *Jysk Erhvervsbeklædning ApS v Hjørring Kommune,* 2009-05-18, *Brøndum AS v Boligforeningen Ringgården,* 2009-07-24 *Lyreco Danmark AS v Varde Kommune.* On the Danish more reluctant court cases see below.

[53] C-275/98 (J 1999-11-18).

[54] 2010-05-12 No 492 Remedies ("Håndhævelse") Act § 18.

[55] Official website <finlex.fi/sv>.

[56] And on competition law infringements.

[57] Official website <notisum.se>.

[58] SFS 2007:1092 on utilities.

[59] The law reform initiated 2009-12-17 ("Lagrådsremiss"), followed by Reg. Prop. 2009/10:180 and Act SFS 2010:571 in force as from 2010-07-15, transposed EU Dir. 2007/66 (amending Dir. 89/665) with provisions on damage for faulty procurement - Chap 16 sects 20-21 (comments Prop. pp 225-226 in case of ineffective contracts).

[60] Prop 12 L (2011-2012) p 71 and p 72, followed early 2012 by parliamentary Innst. 185 L (2011-2012) on conclusive mutual contract signature.

[61] In the Rt. 2008-982 *"Catch Ventelo"* case, the plaintiff was therefore definitely barred from suspension even where the contract was concluded during court proceedings. The plaintiff did not earn invoked damages as from the contract conclusion.

[62] A Norwegian illustration: A blatant violation of the ban-on-negotiation rule (Commission Statements 1994 supplementing Dir. 2004/18 arguably valid also under the forthcoming law reform) forced the selected candidate in the tender procedure to waive an undisputedly valid reservation on price index escalation. Supreme court stated that the contract as amended was to apply—Rt. 2005.1481 *"SØRAL."* Dir. 89/665 article 2 (7) assumes that the contract as such

prevails, but does arguably not exclude award of damages for pre-contractual flaws infecting the contract such as un-authorised amendments or variations in tenderer's bid in an otherwise non-negotiable tender procedure—Commission's statements Official Journal of the European Communities No L 111/114 (1994).

[63] Articles on procurement damages in D Fairgrieve and F Lichère op cit.

[64] Cfr. Short provision in Defence Procurement Dir. 2009/81 article 56 (1)(b). A more sophisticated rule on negative interest cover for loss of chance is set out in the Utilities Remedies' Dir. 92/13 article 2 (1) (d) as elaborated in article 10 (7). That provision has not been effectively applied in any of the Nordic Supreme Court rulings. Instead, it has (2010) been inserted as *the* public procurement rule both in the Finnish Act 30. March 2007 Act (amended 2010) 107 § and in the Swedish (amended 2010) SFS 20 § second paragraph. The Danish Act 492 12. May 2010 § 14 2nd paragraph mirroring Dir. 91/13 article 2 (1) (d) states correctly that the "loss of chance" rule only applies as a liability remedy in utilities' procurement.

[65] C-395/95 *Geotronics SA v Commission* (1997-04-22) [1997] E.C.R. I-2271 on procedure, C-275/03 *Commission v Portugal* (2004-10-14) on non-compliant Portuguese legislation requiring fraud or fault as conditions for damages, followed by a ruling on financial penalty for failing to amend legislation C-70/06 (2008-01-10).

[66] Comment by *T Kotsonis* (23011) 20 PPLR NA59. In Norwegian literature, the case is discussed by H.H.Fredriksen *"Objektivt ansvar for anbudsfeil?"* LoR 2010 pp. 600-615, L Simonsen in (restatement) Gyldendal Rettsdata <rettsdata.no>.

[67] Reiterating C-275/03 *Commission v Portugal* (2004-10-10) extended to rule out also exces-

sively burdensome procedural impediments on the claimant litigating for damages.

[68] Joined cases C-46/93 and C-48/93 [1996] E.C.R I-1029 (55-56).*Brasserie du Pêcheur and Factortame III.*

[69] Such as unreasonable time limits and others. C-145/08 *Club Hotel Loutraki* (2010-05-06) rules out Greek statute which deprives an individual member of a temporary association to claim for damages suffered individually in a particular procedural setting, compare earlier cases C-327/00 (2003-02-23) *Santex* and C-315/01 (2003-06-19) *GAT.*

[70] Possibly extended to liability for erroneous domestic court rulings.

[71] Although the Norwegian 1999 law reform leaving out the utility loss of chance rule may have been questioned under Remedy Dir. 92/13 article 2 No 7.

[72] The only EFTA Court procurement case *Fagthun* E-5/98 (1999-05-12) is not about liabilities.

[73] In cases of unlawful direct purchasing or on concluding contract in disregards of statutory "standstill" obligations – Dir. 2007/66 article 2d with further references.

[74] Danish L110 (2010-01-27) p. 22, Swedish Reg. Prop. 2009/10:180 pp. 225-226.

[75] NOU 2010:2 pp. 174-176. The consequential effects of article 2d on subcontracts for construction works, consultant services or supplies is not provided for in the directive or in the Nordic 2010-2012 law reform documents. Implications on termination, cancellation etc must be solved under the relevant contract regime or otherwise default contract law principles depending on the contract category.

[76] NOU 2010:2 p 175, Prop. 12 L (2011-2012 p. 64, Innst 185 L (2011-2012) p. ++,) The 2010 EUCJ *Strabag* ruling is observed (prior to *Spijkers*), but with the remark that it should be up to the courts to assess its impact in subsequent cases.

[77] In contrast to the other Nordic countries, the Norwegian implementation was (replacing a short 1992 act with regulations) effectuated in a short 1999 framework 1999 act (§§ 1-12) with additional comprehensive ministerial regulations for public (2006-04-07 No 402) and utilties (2006-04-07 No 401) sectors. The act states the general principles such as the liability rule in § 10 whereas the regulations deal with all the details, some taken from the directives, others filling in lacunas in the EU regime or even reiterating pre-EEA government procurement law from regulations of 1899, 1927 and 1978 ("REFSA"). A ministerial EEA-adapted 2006 advisory Guideline ("FAD Veileder") explains certain aspects of the black letter provisions to help public authorities (COs) in their contracting activities.

[78] "Rt." = Norwegian Supreme Court (paper) Law Reports ("Norsk Retstidende") – quoted< year.page start>.

[79] There was indeed a sufficiently serious breach in openly disregarding a preset qualification on apprentices, but assuming that all candidates would have submitted their bids even hypothetically aware of such the chain of events precluded a relevant loss.

[80] Act 2010-05-12 No. 492 § 14 succeeding preceding provisions on Complaint Board's competences on damages Act 2000-05-31 No. 415 § 6 3rd paragraph. The utilities

"loss of chance" rule is expressly stated in second paragraph of the 2010 Act Sect 14. On Danish damage awards of public procurement cf. M Steinicke –L Groesmeyer *"EU's Udbudsdirektiver"* (2nd ed 2008) pp 132 et seq, S.T.Poulsen – P.S. Jakobsen – S.E. Kalsmose-Hjelmborg *"EU Udbudsretten"* (2nd ed) pp 560 et seq. T. Høg *"Erstatningsanscvar I forbindelse med udbud"* (displayed <udbudsportalen.dk>).

[81] The Danish Complaint Board has been recognised as a "review body" authorized to submit questions for preliminary rulings by ECJ - C-275/98 (J 1999-11-18).

[82] "UfR" = Ugeskrift for Retsvæsen (section A) Danish Supreme Court (paper) Law Report. – quoted< year.page start>.

[83] "NJA" = Nyt Juridiskt Arkiv (I) Swedish Supreme Court Law Report – quoted< year. page start>.

[84] Plus OECD Convention on Combating Bribery in Foreign Officials 1997.

[85] Dealing with Compensation for damage (article 3), Liability (article 4), State responsibility (article 5), and Contributory negligence (article 6).

[86] Dated 11, January 2008 in force 1 March 2008 - prepared in ministerial Ot prp nr 73 (2006-2007).

[87] Excepting certain discrepancies on utilities "loss of chance" provision in Dir. 92/13 article 2 No 7.

Chapter 9
Conditions Determining the Success of Public E-Procurement

Nirmala Dorasamy
Durban University of Technology, South Africa

ABSTRACT

The dynamic global environment has necessitated governments to adopt a systems approach of integrating suppliers, customers, and information linkages in an endeavor to create and sustain value for public services. The evolution of the concept "the customer is king" has placed the customer foremost in public management thinking. As a result, optimizing customer value in the public domain has become a focal point in managing procurement. The large quantity of public resources used for service delivery points to the importance of efficiency and effectiveness in expenditures as well as accountability. E-Procurement systems provide mechanisms for controlling, simplifying, and automating goods and services from different suppliers. While benefits like stricter control over spending authorization, easier transaction processing and elimination of redundant stock are achieved through automated procurement processes; the viability and success of e-procurement for the public sector is determined by various conditions. The conditions for successful implementation of an e-procurement system are explored as every government activity involves the spending of public monies on goods and services. Any failings in e-procurement practices can create possibilities for large-scale losses through incompetence, waste, and fraud, which directly impact the public.

DOI: 10.4018/978-1-4666-2665-2.ch009

INTRODUCTION

E-Procurement evolved from the need for better governance mechanisms to procure goods and services and engage with suppliers, resulting in an information system enabled innovation in business.

Businesses today are extending e-procurement beyond merely controlling the purchase of office supplies and goods. However, while there are benefits in the direct-goods environment, e-procurement is viable for goods of a generic nature that are purchased in large volumes on a regular basis. Strategic procurement of highly customized goods is generally not viable for e-procurement.

Generally, large corporations or a group of businesses that share common buying patterns may use e-procurement. In the public sector, governments must aim for the optimum supply of goods and services from suppliers in terms of cost, quality, timeliness, risk management, and ethical practices. This is necessary in view of government spending on goods and services, which is generally more than the Gross Domestic Product. Well-managed e-procurement systems can add stability to the country's macro economy, increase levels of service delivery through efficient allocation of resources, stimulate micro economic activity, and retain expenditures within the value and timing boundaries of the budget. The purchasing of goods and services in the public sector is central as it supports all functions of government to achieve its mission. As an important function of government, public procurement has to promote the basic principles of good governance: transparency, accountability, and responsibility. In attempting to preserve good governance principles, government procurement operates within an established milieu of regulations and policies that embrace public interest and non-discriminatory practices. The transparent management information provided by e-procurement facilitates the monitoring of compliance with the regulatory framework of the public sector and performance in terms of effectiveness and efficiency of the public governance agenda. Further, governments are expected to promote social, economic, and financial imperatives in the quest for good governance. Interest in e-procurement was underpinned by its potential to improve efficiencies and transparency in government procurement processes, since imperatives to improve services and curb public expenses are forceful. Public e-procurement has policy implications in advancing initiatives that drive such imperatives. This can further ignite conflicts with other policy areas because of competing priorities, changing political landscapes and different information systems. There could be able to a shift in focus from pure cost efficiency to more qualitative measures like green procurement. Further, opportunism costs associated with public procurement may emanate in an endeavor to broaden competition and maximize opportunities for value for money.

In view of the focus on value for money for goods and services in the public sector, the advantages offered by e-procurement are significant. As such, e-procurement is considered as revolutionary in that it has been in influential in enhancing the nature of the purchasing function within organizations. Despite the promotion of e-procurement being appropriate for all types of organizations and being an enabling initiative to make e-procurement cost and time effective, generally, the purchasing community has been slow in committing to e-procurement. This is especially so in poor and developing regions which have limited access to information technology to drive economic and social changes. Further, the divide may also exist between small and large organizations and between urban and rural communities within nations. However, Jae Moon (2005, p. 58) argues that large governments with financial capacity and service demand are more likely to adopt an innovation, since they are under pressure to find alternative ways of providing public services. Further, public sector purchasing volume represents a great potential for establishing national electronic marketplaces, while large standardized purchases by governments can increase procurement efficiency through e-procurement. However, effective and efficient ways to access information about suppliers and their goods and services, transact, pay, and gather information about the strategic public sector environment is dependent on a well-integrated and managed e-procurement system, which ultimately saves cost and time. Despite prerequisite conditions for the successful implementation of an e-procurement system, great strides have been made to integrate data across function boundaries within and between organizations. However, it is still imperative to examine improvement initiatives that focus on streamlining processes that ultimately contribute to the general effectiveness of the various tasks that are completed in e-procurement. This is vital since the public procurement function plays an integral role in the provision of services by public sector organizations and every endeavor should be pursued to ensure that taxpayer funds are spent in the most efficient and effective way.

BACKGROUND

E-procurement is generally viewed as a component of supply chain management. Supply chain management facilitates observation of every action, transaction, and activity that takes place from the sourcing of products or raw materials to the delivery of the final product to the customer. E-procurement, as a subset of supply chain management, contributes to the controlling, simplifying and automating of the purchase of goods and services from several suppliers. The main tasks of e-procurement include: support of basic transactions like requisitioning, ordering and payment, facilitating processes like supplier selection, value analysis and performance evaluation, enhancing advanced applications such as cross functional and cross-organizational co-operation and integration, and assisting in relationship management (Cronje,

van Biljon, Naude, Nel, & Poulter, 2011, p. 224). Efficient procurement practices play a key role in the global economy as they limit wasteful activities in the procurement process. Achieving such efficiency requires conditions relating not only to the process, but also to the legal framework, political environment, and market structure to be addressed. Figure 1 and Figure 2 highlight the differences between a paper-based process and an electronic process for procurement.

Traditional procurement is a paper-based process that is exemplified by fragmented purchasing, off-contract buying, and lack of control over expenditures. E-Procurement facilitates, integrates, and streamlines the supply chain process through electronic means. The e-procurement process reduces the number of activities involved in the paper-based process. This not only reduces cycle time but also costs; process, efficiency, flexibility, and strategic benefits from e-procurement are also visible.

E-Procurement shifts the focus away from routine purchasing tasks to issues such as negotiating broad purchasing contracts and establishing contacts with suppliers of goods and services. Procurement tasks include tactical (specifying, selecting, contracting) and operational (ordering, monitoring and servicing). According to Adendorff, Bothma, Fourie, and Walters (2004, p. 264), most often the focus is on the operational tasks, which ought to be automated, rather than on the tactical tasks. By focusing on tactical procurement and automating operational procurement, the costs associated with purchase orders can be controlled. Invariably, there is a shift from spending time managing repetitive documentary type activities to simplifying procurement processes through automation, thereby redirecting focus on meaningful activities. The effect is efficiency improvement from a time and cost savings perspective. Therefore, by focusing on process in the total value stream, inefficiencies can be eliminated.

Further, the transition from the traditional procurement to e-procurement requires the analysis

Figure 1. Paper-based procurement process

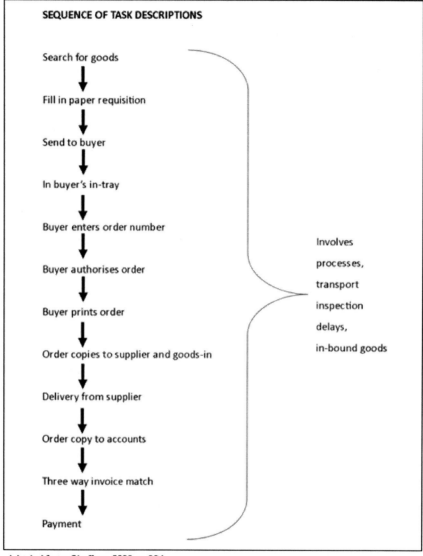

SEQUENCE OF TASK DESCRIPTIONS

Search for goods

Fill in paper requisition

Send to buyer

In buyer's in-tray

Buyer enters order number

Buyer authorises order

Buyer prints order

Order copies to supplier and goods-in

Delivery from supplier

Order copy to accounts

Three way invoice match

Payment

Involves processes, transport inspection delays, in-bound goods

Adapted from: Chaffrey, 2009, p. 384

and design of new processes in an attempt to reduce meaningless information circulation, definition of clear job descriptions and economical procurement within defined deadlines. The successful transition, from a government perspective, is subject to a number of inhibitors generally incurred by legislation, which attempt to guarantee the transparent management of public resources (Panayiotou, Gayialis, & Tatsiopoulos, 2004, p.

82). Two common models for e-procurement are in Figures 3 and 4.

In Figure 3, the buying organization creates a link between itself and suppliers in respect of information relating to ordering, type of goods and payment. In the single entity model, policies and guidelines for suppliers are specified. Through registration, suppliers can integrate their own systems with that of the buying organization.

Figure 2. E-procurement process

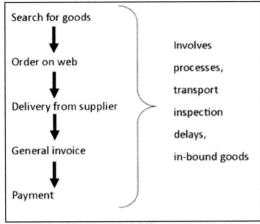

Adapted from Chaffrey, 2009, p. 385

Generally, registered suppliers bid for the supply of a required product. All processing is electronically executed.

In Figure 4, several buying organizations with similar buying needs interact with different suppliers. The e-procurement system is generally managed by a third party procurement hub (Bothma, 2000, p. 117). Various buyers and suppliers adapt their inventory electronic transfer, order processing and electronic payment systems to the e-procurement hub or e-marketplace.

The single entity and third party e-procurement models result in the following benefits (Bothma, 2000, p. 120):

- Reduction in the costs incurred during the purchasing process, which is often hidden.
- The consideration and integration of automated purchasing systems allows organizations to engage in self-service during the operational phase, thereby facilitating greater focus on strategic procurement.
- Costs and time incurred by suppliers is minimized.
- Fictitious or fraudulent purchases and administrative errors are better controlled.

Figure 3. Single entity e-procurement model

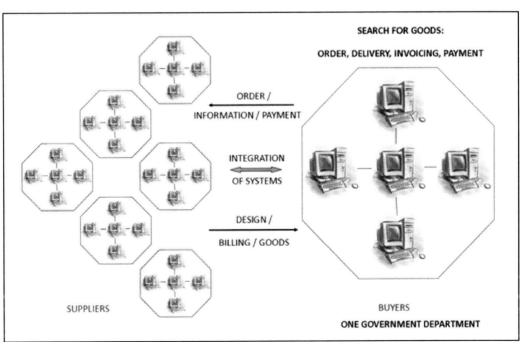

Adapted from: Bothma, 2000, p. 116;
in Hugo, Badenhorst-Weiss, & van Biljon, 2004, p. 262

Figure 4. Third party e-procurement model

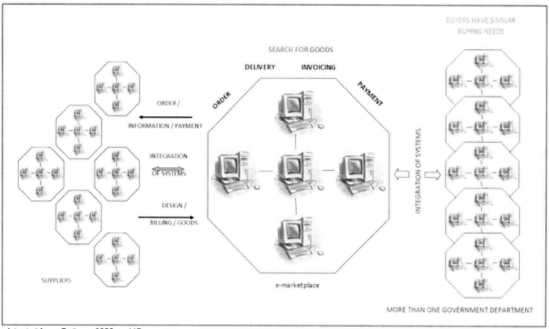

Adapted from: Bothma, 2000, p. 117;
in Hugo, Badenhorst-Weiss, & van Biljon, 2004, p. 263

- Automated purchased activities ensure consistency in the application of purchasing guidelines and procedures; thereby reducing discrepancies.
- By interacting only with registered suppliers, organizations can aggregate purchasing expenditure.
- Less time is spent on negotiating contracts, thereby saving costs and reducing the purchasing cycle time.
- Cost reduction through automation can reduce final prices.
- Cost tracking with different suppliers gives an indication of amounts paid to different suppliers.
- Efficient procurement systems produce high inventory turnover.
- Buyers benefit from established minimum service standards, improved distribution economics and better prices through aggregating purchasing power.

- Suppliers are exposed to low credit risks, coordinated terms of trade, low cost of order processing and immediate access to a large market.
- Enhanced budgeting control.

E-Procurement can be considered an "evolutionary shift" from poor planning, inconsistent quality of goods and services and general unpredictability in the relationships between buyers and sellers. The evolutionary shift results in the following manifestations (Neef, 2001, p. 38):

- Shift in management's focus toward horizontal processes that form part of a single, fully integrated process that empowers individual employees in a decentralized system, which focuses on total cost rather that silo-based incentives.
- Information technology has replaced human labor extensively through auto-

mated requisitioning, approval, receiving progress reports, payment, routing, and tracking.

- Development of the extended enterprise where integrated process and systems create a seamless electronically initiated and monitored exchange of information, goods, and services.

According to Baily, Farmer, Jessop, and Jones (1994, p. 165), the ultimate benefit of e-procurement is improved performance for each of the "five rights": right price, right source, right time, right quality, and right quantity.

However, despite the potential benefits of e-procurement, it may not be viable for all organizations to adopt e-procurement. Some of the potential factors that may influence the adoption of e-procurement include (Walker & Harland, 2007, p. 836):

- **Organizations:** Large organizations with adequate resources, information technology infrastructure and expertise in information systems are likely to adopt e-procurement. Further, high volume operations that require repetitive purchases is suitable for higher levels of electronic integration between buyers and suppliers.
- **Readiness:** Organizations that have comprehensively evaluated appropriate purchasing applications amidst the impact on organizational change and have identified internal barriers show a greater readiness to reap the benefits of e-procurement.
- **Supply:** Organizations that have dispersed supply chains may consider e-procurement as it facilitates co-ordination, establishment of information exchange infrastructures and has a supplier base that is capable of dealing with integrated systems.
- **Strategy:** Organizations that focus on improving performance and establishing a competitive edge, may adopt e-procure-

ment as part of their business strategy. The use of electronic media at a strategic level facilitates its alignment with organizational processes. Therefore, by being strategic in e-procurement adoption, organizations can integrate their e-procurement strategy with the wider organizational strategy.

- **Policy:** E-Procurement can support broader government policies that encourage transparency, efficiency, cost reduction, and value for money. E-Procurement can be used as an instrument to promote social issues relating to environmentally friendly products and services, while stimulating developmental objectives. In view of the increased global emphasis on corporate social responsibility, organizations may adopt e-procurement as an organizational strategy to reflect their commitment to environmental and social issues.

In addition, any e-procurement initiative has to be a genuine exercise in collaboration, based on the development and conformation of a strategy to fit the organization, while being stakeholder driven. Since government cannot be viewed as a single business, it is important to realize that as a multiple public services and goods provider, it has to align to its strategy and technology platform with the way the public sector operates in the global arena.

CONDITIONS FOR PUBLIC E-PROCUREMENT

Government e-procurement can have a profound effect on the economy, in view of the staggering amounts spent by government. Government purchasing not only accounts for a huge amount of taxpayer revenue, but also sustains a large number of suppliers throughout the world (Neef, 2001, p. 110). As highlighted by Riggins and Mitra (2007, p. 6; in Chaffey, 2009, p. 387), e-procurement for the public sector can increase the quality of management information (planning), accelerate development (development), gain greater efficiency through paperless transactions (inbound), avoid limiting manufacturing by poor availability of parts (production), and achieve efficient public response (outbound). A possible framework for evaluating the benefits of e-procurement is illustrated in Table 1.

Government purchasing systems have similar features with that of the private sector due to both sectors being driven to find sources of supply at a potential cheapest price and between acceptable levels of quality (Panayiotou, Gayialis, & Tatsio-poulos, 2004, p. 82). However, public procurement differs in the following aspects: the procurement

Table 1. Framework for evaluating e-procurement benefits

Dimension	Value Creation
Changes to total acquisition costs	• Reduction in cost per order • Requirements consolidated • Reduction in requisition order process costs • Increased access to suppliers • Increased internal compliance • Increased leverage over prices
Changes to governance structures	• Improved communication with suppliers • Increased knowledge sharing • Transparency in supply processes • Increased supplier compliance • Improved aggregation of demand
System specification	• Higher concern for integration with existing systems • Data management • Improved control over management information
Changes to total organizational characteristics	• Establishment of training units • Training for suppliers • Enhanced status of purchasing functions • Improved accessibility • Establishment of help support centre • Encouragement of users to comply • Increased internal service perceptions
Implementation management	• Management of roll out of goals and services • Management of roll out of suppliers • Determining return on investment

Adapted from: Croom & Brandon-Jones, 2007, p. 298.

system administrates money that belongs to all, procurement is subjected to prescribed procedures resulting from laws, administrative, and political decisions, transparency is imperative for purchasing procedures, all government departments are subjected to uniform public procurement plans. Therefore, when considering any e-procurement system, government has to ensure that it maximizes specific service objectives and considers the impact on processes across all public sector organizations. By adopting e-procurement, governments can provide a valuable incentive for suppliers to become Web-enabled, thereby stimulating growth in this area. While government may provide an important endorsement for a shift toward the accountability and efficiencies that derives from procuring online, the success of e-procurement is largely dependent on various determinants. The determinants which can share areas of commonality across both the macro and micro environments are shown in Table 2.

POLITICAL CONDITIONS FOR PUBLIC E-PROCUREMENT

E-Government initiatives seek to innovate communication with and participation by citizens through electronic means in areas like public service delivery and voting. In fulfilling their public function of purchasing goods and services, governments have adopted procurement innovation through e-procurement, which can be considered as an effective public procurement policy to successfully deliver on public sector imperatives. Governments which have adopted e-procurement have realized the opportunity for efficiency gains in the public sector and benefitting from lower prices due to centralized spending.

However, in adopting e-procurement government has to focus on issues like public policy implementation, especially in a complex inter- and intra-governmental organizational system. This is further exacerbated by bureaucratic processes,

Table 2. Determinants for public e-procurement

Dimension	Value Creation
Changes to total acquisition costs	• Reduction in cost per order • Requirements consolidated • Reduction in requisition order process costs • Increased access to suppliers • Increased internal compliance • Increased leverage over prices
Changes to governance structures	• Improved communication with suppliers • Increased knowledge sharing • Transparency in supply processes • Increased supplier compliance • Improved aggregation of demand
System specification	• Higher concern for integration with existing systems • Data management • Improved control over management information
Changes to total organizational characteristics	• Establishment of training units • Training for suppliers • Enhanced status of purchasing functions • Improved accessibility • Establishment of help support centre • Encouragement of users to comply • Increased internal service perceptions
Implementation management	• Management of roll out of goals and services • Management of roll out of suppliers • Determining return on investment

generally underpinned by legislation to guarantee the transparent administration of public resources. Further, government needs to address the impact of e-procurement on financial, legal, and human resource constraints. Panayiotou *et al.* (2004, p. 84) cite the case of e-procurement resulting in staff reduction, but there may be no justification to reduce staff due to legislative constraints. Further, changes in bureaucratic practices may be necessary because of the need for process—change in adopting e-procurement. Then, any changes in bureaucratic practices may result in conflicting goals with existing legislation. Therefore, it becomes necessary to not only consider the functional specifications of an e-procurement system, but also technological advancement and

changes required in the public sector legal framework. In this regard, Panayiotou *et al.* (2004, p. 95) suggests the adoption of e-procurement in an "incremental change" manner since public sector procurement has to work within regulations and policies established to achieve desirable economic and social goals. Aspects like inclusiveness and broad competition may be emphasized to promote the general welfare of all citizens.

MacManus (2002, p. 10) further argues that governments frequently embark on e-procurement from a purely technological stance. This often results in e-procurement initiatives commencing in a very haphazard way, since policy and organizational issues are addressed much later, yet these should be focused upon first. Public purchase policies are quite significant in directing procurement and adherence to policy directives like non-discriminatory clauses or qualitative measures like green procurement cannot be in conflict with e-procurement processes especially if such issues are given high priority in public processes. This is especially so as the "one size fits all" practice cannot be employed if public sector institutions vary in size and functional responsibilities. In addition, governments have been criticized for the following: lagging behind in revising processes and procedures, poor financial management, slow implementation of mandated policies, failure to engage in strategic planning, haphazard integration (MacManus, 2002, p. 14). Therefore, while governments consider the role that social and political factors play in public policy making, they also need to realize that a successful procurement system can only generate best quality economic value if it is driven by results.

Henriksen and Mahnke (2005, p. 96) raise political rationality as another issue to be considered within the political landscape. In a study conducted in Denmark, their findings showed that local political interests, rather than the pursuit of efficiency alone, dominated e-procurement adoption patterns. Herein, is an important consideration for government officials to be willing to sacrifice decentralized layers of public hierarchies toward a transparent central e-marketplace? If the focus is on maximizing power positions, budgets and voter support, instead of caring for the greater public interest, then the successful adoption of e-procurement can be jeopardized (Henriksen & Mahnke, 2005, p. 96). In addition, if there is a large measure of decentralization, then consideration has to be given as to whether economically independent public organizations are interested in supporting centralized procurement processes. Further, in decentralized government systems, administrators have gained a more influential position in establishing visions, goals, and strategies compared to the top-down approach where politicians issued directives. Therefore, government has to address challenges within the political landscape, which can impact an e-procurement adoption.

LEGISLATIVE AND REGULATORY FRAMEWORK

The procurement system must be guided by legislation and stipulated processes for public sector e-procurement. Comprehensive e-procurement management and control systems have to be based on adherence to any government's financial management system and other relevant policy guidelines. Important mechanisms like "check and balance" and "division of authority" principles must be implemented within the e-procurement system (Pauw, Woods, van der Linde, Fourie, & Visser, 2009, p. 347). The policy and regulatory approach must not only prescribe minimum systems requirements, but also articulate the solution to doing things correctly and ways of discouraging fraudulent activities. While there may be an adequate regulatory framework governing purchasing transactions, optimizing value for money from government's massive spending

responsibilities is also important. Some notable reforms in procurement practices include (Pauw, et al., 2009, p. 230):

- Shifting authority and responsibility to individual government departments and their accounting officers.
- Compulsory expenditure planning and budgetary control across all operations in each government department.
- Application of the principle of value for money for performance budgeting, whereby managers strive to achieve more than what the budget and costs specified.
- Decentralized procurement systems, which are less prescriptive, thereby according greater managerial responsibility.
- Minimizing risk through increased internal control within government departments.
- Monitoring mechanisms to identify unauthorized, wasteful, and irregular expenditure as determined by regulations.

In the case of bidding, the bidding evaluation and adjudication committees must evaluate bids in accordance with the specifications for procurement. In this regard, performance guarantees should be stipulated in the standard conditions of contract. This is an important risk management mechanism in protecting the public sector from poor supplier services. Varney (2011, p. 201) argues that while governments may offer clear frameworks under which e-procurement may proceed, it further requires coordinated action from the legal, political, organizational and technical fronts.

Government intervention maybe required to prevent hardware, software, and telecommunication businesses from exploiting domestic markets. However, government needs to exercise caution not to compromise compatible operating systems while limiting market power. A further challenge is that in some countries, there is inadequate investment in technology development and access maybe costly. These can have serious hindrances for the expansion of e-procurement (Fraser, et al., 2001, p. 18).

In the global arena, governments need to address issues around consumer protection, privacy, intellectual property laws, and taxation. These issues require cooperation between governments to ensure that national differences in legal requirements do not limit the potential benefits of e-procurement, but rather are consistent with the development of it.

SUPPLIER COMPATIBILITY

In any e-procurement system, supplier integration is integral. If the supplier's system is incompatible, then systems integration across the e-procurement landscape can be inhibited. In a study by Croom and Brandon-Jones (2007, p. 298), concern was raised by respondents on the lack of capability of their supplier base to fully engage in the integration of e-procurement. The use of a variety of forms of governance structures to facilitate buyer-suppler communications include: public Web, exchange venue, seller extranet, market place, and company hub (Croom, 2003, p. 540). Governance structures can have a significant influence on contract compliance, accountability, communication, and knowledge sharing (Croom & Brandon-Jones, 2007, p. 299). Further, if suppliers are involved early in the e-procurement adoption process, they can offer feedback on practices requiring improvement. Educating suppliers on e-procurement benefits can encourage them to conduct business electronically with the public sector, increase their e-readiness and provide an important platform to discuss issues relating to the public e-procurement initiative (Vaidya, Sajeev, & Callender, 2006, p. 83).

MANAGEMENT PERCEPTIONS

E-Procurement should consider strategy first and technology second. Strategy is about defining the best way to get the right products and services, at the right time and at the lowest cost, while e-procurement plays an important role in that strategy. Since e-procurement affects almost every function in any public sector organization, government needs to consider how it wants e-procurement to affect its relationship with suppliers. It is only when it is decided what types of procurement services government wants to buy, outsource or keep in house, can it think about technology platforms. Therefore, the magnitude of the adoption and implementation of e-procurement is largely influenced by the general disposition of government as a whole (Croom & Jones, 2007, p. 295).

Further, lack of clarity around the business context and failure to understand the strategic importance of e-procurement can result in a lack of support from key organizational leaders. Unless key organizational leaders are actively involved in providing input and support in the early planning phase of e-procurement, there is the likelihood of continuous debate over purpose and value and to over run in terms of time and budget (Neef, 2001, p. 143). Hence, without management satisfaction in the development, adoption and implementation, improvement in performance would be a challenge. Management needs to address the following (Cronje, et al., 2011, p. 226; Neef, 2001, p. 138):

- Based on total spending relating to manual processes, management can consider restructuring for self-service procurement.
- Clear understanding of the risks and benefits of e-procurement.
- Information sharing with suppliers by determining what information is to be shared and with which partners should it be shared.
- Develop a strong and honest communication plan regarding the approach, sched-

ules, and impact of e-procurement on the organizational structure.

- Establish why e-procurement is necessary, what it entails, and the expected return on investment.
- Develop a single, all-encompassing e-business strategy that incorporates coordinated and prioritized initiatives that are not in conflict.
- Develop an agreed upon change transition plan which includes a comprehensive communication and employee participation plan so that there is "buy in" throughout public sector departments.
- Avoid an attitude of wait-and-see when organizations have to select suppliers and e-marketplaces.
- Determining the authenticity of suppliers for transactions.
- Ensuring the transmission of information is not tampered with.
- Ensuring privacy of contractual details.
- Securing access to role players who have a legal right to use e-procurement systems.
- Establishing strategic perspectives relating to trust, commitment, and long-term relations between the organization and suppliers.

Ultimately, management support will be reflected in its commitment to improvement efforts by walking the walk and talking the talk by empowering employees to exercise the authority to make changes based on added value for public benefit. Further, an awareness of the need for change and an understanding of what needs to be changed are important considerations. Management should facilitate the requisite understanding so that employees can implement the changes. This requires setting the vision and goals, bringing about collective commitment for change in process and institutionalizing policies and strategies to implement the e-procurement initiative. This necessitates a change management programme

focusing on consultation, communication and participation in resolving issues, so that learning and effort by users is not marginalized.

PROPOSING A BUSINESS CASE

The e-procurement initiative has to be championed by a business case that highlights the benefits and risks. Only if users are willing to change the way they work, can a "buy-in" be ensured. Support from management can be largely influenced by highlighting the costs and benefits of the e-procurement initiative. The analysis should focus on the following (Neef, 2001, p. 145; Fraser, Fraser, & McDonald, 2001, p. 150):

- Identify transactions by cost and quality. Determine whether products or services can be classified by their strategic or tactical nature.
- Calculate labour costs for manual data processing.
- Analyse current procurement contracts in terms of types and levels of control within the organization.
- Analyse the nature of the tendering process.
- Calculate percentages from the purchased budget paid to suppliers.
- Analyse supplier performance.
- Examine payment options.
- Identify possible supplier resistance to e-procurement.
- Examine whether the costs of learning from mistakes with new technology can be offset in the short term, long term or not at all.
- Identify sections within the organization that will not operate effectively with e-procurement in the short term, long term or not at all.
- Examine whether the solutions relating to e-procurement will lead to sustainable benefits.

The aforementioned analysis will provide an objective return on investment picture, determining the feasibility of adopting e-procurement. The strategy adopted should determine the magnitude and time of an e-procurement system that leads to the best cost-benefit outcomes of e-procurement.

In proposing a business case, changes to process and work activities can be highlighted in an implications analysis. In addition, a transition plan which communicates the changes throughout the organization is vital. By communicating the structure and direction of an e-procurement system, there will be greater clarity and "buy-in" by all role-players.

Neef (2001, p. 148) argues for a business case that is founded on changes to strategy and process and not merely technology. The adoption of an enterprise wide e-procurement approach ensures that operational strategy is clearly aligned to change programs that reflect organizational benefits through an analysis of the e-procurement process. By engaging in this exercise, employees are made aware of the multiple financial costs and sign offs that hinder the procurement process and increases costs. A strong business case can highlight antiquated, over audited approaches to procurement, while helping to enlist employee buy-in. An e-procurement strategy that is procurement and technology driven can help in emphasizing the importance of e-procurement in the public sector, while highlighting the accompanying need for process and organizational change.

ORGANIZATIONAL CULTURE

Relationships in the public sector are part of its culture. Complex and dynamic formal and informal relationships influence the efficiency levels of any organization. Change through e-procurement can impact on these relationships because it introduces change in the organizational organogram, work process and at a social level. Different types

of cultural orientation may be required as shown below (Chaffey, 2009:589):

- **Survival:** The organization has to consider the external environment, which is influential in governing organizational strategy. It is driven by customer demand.
- **Productivity:** Interaction with the external environment is well structured and is driven by sales.
- **Human Relations:** Interpersonal relations are considered important. Focus on staff development and empowerment.
- **Stability:** The environment is ignored, with managers focusing on internal efficiency.

Within any cultural orientation approach, it is important to take cognizance of the nature of change. In the case of e-procurement management, it is important to consider the nature of change and how to control it impact. These changes potentially include changes in the values held by employees within the organization, embedded processes, and policies guiding decision-making and the nature of relationships within any system (Schiele & McCue, 2011, p. 216). Governments with an innovative managerial culture are more likely to adopt e-procurement since they are likely to be more receptive to new practices (Jae Moon, 2005, p. 59). Studies by Coggburn (2003; in Jae Moon, 2005, p. 59) found a close association between managing for results performance and innovative procurement practices in the public sector. Therefore, implementing e-procurement requires strong policy leadership and managerial willingness to innovate, both of which are challenges for many governments. It appears that the real challenges for government may not really be technical, but rather organizational and managerial. This is highlighted in a study by Liau, Cheng, Liao, and Chen (2003) in Croom and Brandon-Jones (2003, p. 374) on Taiwanese military procurement which identified cultural resistance to changes in established processes and practices as a major challenge.

Further, consideration has to be taken of bureaucratic processes in the public sector that can impede efforts for change. Therefore, any e-procurement initiative has to examine the possibility of remaining barriers preventing e-procurement from being implemented. However, this has to be preceded by the identification of gaps between existing practices and best practices associated with e-procurement (Schoenherr & Mabert, 2011, p. 835). Managing the impact of change can be undertaken collaboratively, consultatively, directly, or coercively. However, it is important to influence the following groups who can be influential in achieving overall organizational change (Chaffey, 2009, p. 589):

- Key stakeholders in the e-procurement process who can act as a source of support for the system.
- Experts who protect the norms and values of the system.
- Opinion leaders who have little formal power, but are regarded as "good idea" individuals.

ETHICAL STANDARDS

Public sector organizations are stewards of the public financial resources they spend and they operate in a more complex and regulated environment. Hence, they are more susceptible to scrutiny and criticism by the general public. Therefore, employees need to be aware of ethical standards in the execution of their e-procurement duties, so that they represent the best interest of the public sector.

A code of ethics for all officials and role players in the e-procurement system must be established. This is an imperative to promote trust, integrity, fairness, and transparency. The code of ethics for

procurement should be underpinned by the following (Adendorff, et al., 2004, p. 249):

- Reporting of irregular conduct in the procurement system.
- Equitable and fair treatment of registered and potential suppliers.
- Declaration of benefits promised, offered, or granted.
- Withdrawal from the procurement process if any role player has links with particular suppliers.
- Scrupulous use of state property.

The adoption of a code of ethical conduct ought to be binding on all relevant role players in the procurement process. The approach to ethics in procurement can be rule oriented (obeying rules and regulations governing public management), utilitarian (by promoting public interest, the principle of "the greatest good for the greatest number is observed), or virtue ethics (promoting honesty and integrity in the public sphere through the virtuous disposition of employees and the organization). Since employees in the public sector are expected to serve public interest with fairness and to manage public resources effectively and efficiently, public trust can be incurred through fair, equitable, and reliable services. In terms of e-procurement, processing systems should be driven by optimal service delivery, where value for money is sought. In so doing, employees involved in e-procurement should be aware of their ethical obligations to their employers (loyalty), suppliers (fair play), and colleagues (reputation).

Vaidya *et al.* (2006, p. 84) relate the need for buyers and suppliers to have confidence and trust in the underlying security infrastructure because of the sensitivity of government data. Jae Moon (2005, p. 58) posits that an organization with a high level of ethics is more receptive to changes and tends to value effectiveness and efficiency. He argues that legislative ethics and reformed procurement practices normally share a positive relationship.

VALUE ADDING

E-Procurement is dynamic, underpinned by changes in relationships, capabilities, and demand. Therefore, optimization strategies have to be designed and reviewed as changes take place. "Value stream" mapping focuses on value creation for buying organizations. A map of the value stream highlights ineffective and obsolete activities in the procurement system. Simple and adaptable processes to changing conditions can avoid wastages like wasting time, delays, and excessive lead times. Further, time management as a component of the value stream mapping increases responsiveness and faster reaction capabilities in managing demand changes, improved services from suppliers and the development of a learner procurement system (Adendorff, et al., 2004, p. 82). In addition, Pauw *et al.* (2009, p. 354) suggest the following aspects to enhance quality:

- Performance budgeting identifies predetermined outputs to be achieved, while monitoring costing and wastage.
- Regular reporting allows for closer monitoring and detection of deviations.
- Alignment and maintenance of accounting standards with international standards ensures the implementation of best practice.
- Internal control measures like segregation of duties, information systems, internal audits and risk plans strengthens quality.

Adendorff *et al.* (2004, p. 166) stress the integration of three components of quality management: supplier quality system, internal quality system of the buyer and the quality system of the customer. The integration is evident in a number of quality management approaches identified by Dobler and Starling (2003, p. 10; in Adendorff,

et al., 2004, p. 168): Six Sigma, Ectal quality management, continuous improvement, quality management system and just-in-time. All approaches have contributed to the success of quality management in e-procurement systems. The integration can also be aligned to "lean thinking" whereby the buyer and supplier work together to improve customer satisfaction levels. This requires looking at processes where value can be added through improvement from a customer's perspective (Schiele & McCue, 2011, p. 215). According to Schiele and McCue (2011, p. 216), "by understanding the value adding process from the customer's perspective, organizational procurement processes becomes customer oriented."

Further, value adding can be inhibited if integration within the e-procurement system does not take place. Croom and Brandon-Jones (2007, p. 296) argue that a major causal determinant of an effective and efficient system is integration of the buyers' information infrastructure with links to suppliers. Such integration facilitates timeous changes to changing prices, product and service specifications and account details from a supplier perspective. There, if the supplier base is not effectively managed and maintained, then the e-procurement system can be compromised by inaccurate and inconsistent information. Further, e-procurement systems are not independent systems. Data management in respect of financing systems, requisition, order and payment processes, data formatting, and communication systems to transmit data are indicative of the need for integrating information flows within the e-procurement system.

CAPACITY TO MANAGE PERFORMANCE MEASURES

Central to quality management approaches is performance evaluation of the e-procurement system, aimed at a value assessment of the critical dimensions of e-procurement. Evaluation provides valuable input about the degree of success with which e-procurement activities are carried out and can be used by management to measure the success of the initiative (Cronje, et al., 2011, p. 36). Procurement performance indicators can provide quantitative values for different procurement activities or focus on subjective measures like commodity knowledge, negotiating ability, and professionalism. Therefore, it is vital that before adoption and implementation, the capacity to manage pre-determined measures is explored.

Continuous measurements are vital for the successful implementation of the business case. Measurement spurs on behavior and is a driver to making change a success. Measurement capability ensures that management has tools for evaluating e-procurement progress and tracking benefits. Performance measures provide a yardstick for the practical evaluation of e-procurement performance. Cronje *et al.* (2011, p. 39) state that irrespective of the type of measure used to indicate performance, evaluation levels of measure must focus on the following three levels:

- Procurement management, which uses management elements as performance measures. Development of individual and organizational goals and objectives, personal training and communication can qualitatively assess performance at a managerial level.
- Determining the extent to which the procurement function has achieved the objectives of its function by evaluating pricing proficiency, supplier performance, materials flow and quality.
- Determining efficiency levels by evaluating cost savings, administrative performance, and workload.

Therefore, setting measures to indicate performance is decisive for the determination of performance of e-procurement systems. Further, predetermined measurements must be accurate

and reliable indicators of performance, highlighting that achieving target levels will result in meaningful improvements in procurement and for the organization as a whole. Neef (2001, p. 166) suggests that by attaching objective numbers, performance indicators can reveal the advantages and disadvantages of changing to e-procurement.

In addition, Croom and Brandon-Jones (2007, p. 296) highlight challenges relating to implementation management that can impact on performance. Measures like human deficiencies and faults need to be considered in the implementation process as challenges like corruption and inefficiency can identified as potential factors impacting on performance.

TECHNOLOGY

An analysis of the level of integration required between the e-procurement initiative and existing information technology systems will determine the extent to which existing processes will need to be changed or adapted (Vaidya, et al., 2006, p. 84).

The consolidation of information through technology can provide buyers and suppliers with revolutionary ways to transfer goods and services, capture previously inaccessible markets and increase productivity through automation. According to Cronje *et al.* (2011, p. 224), organizations need to consider the following relating to technology:

- Sufficient capital to buy and implement the technology required for e-procurement.
- Managing technical requirements for information and data interchange.
- Adequately trained employees to implement the system.
- Comprehensive regulatory framework for reliable e-procurement transactions.
- "Buy-in" from suppliers to participate in e-procurement.

- Low level of technical sophistication and variances in supplier needs to be recognized.
- Establishment of a standardized interchange format for e-procurement.
- Establishment of systems compatibility within the organization.

In the case of third party electronic trading hubs, cognizance has to be taken of the following if they are to provide comprehensive procurement services that basically undertake or guarantee the success of transactions between suppliers and buying organizations (Neef, 2001, p. 121):

- Integration of transaction information in buyers and sellers electronic systems.
- Monitoring transactions between buyer and seller by tracking order fulfillment, payment, and delivery services.
- Complex services may require automated inventory replenishment and logistics services.
- Supporting different systems for tax, export, language, and currency if global sales occur.

Issues relating to information systems development and adoption are vital for e-procurement implementation. Knowledge sharing systems enable greater communication and co-ordination in areas of innovation sourcing and supply management (Croom & Brandon-Jones, 2005, p. 376).

According to Baily, Farmer, Crocker, Jessop, and Jones (2008, pp. 394-400), e-procurement is dependent on the following three categories associated with technology for successful results:

- **E-Sourcing:** The sourcing team, when dealing with contractual processes should be able to gather and record relevant information regarding suppliers, assist in decision making relating to complex purchasing activities, automate steps in the purchasing cycle, assist in supplier collaboration, involve suppliers in planning for e-procurement and re-engineer the bidding process. Since e-sourcing may not be viable for all organizational requirements, it must be considered against the strategic importance of required goods and services and the influence of global markets.
- **E-Transactions:** Can be conducted in e-marketplaces, where organizations and suppliers interact to conduct business-to-business transactions. In addition, e-catalogues provide information relating to suppliers, and prices of their goods and services as well as electronic ordering systems which provide specific data to buying organizations such as quantities ordered, prices paid and delivery dates of transactions. While e-transactions provide improved communication between role-players, information interchange must be regularly monitored.
- **E-Payment:** Facilitates the conclusion of the purchasing order. Since e-payment entails the use of electronic tools like e-invoicing, standard payment procedures have to be re-engineered.

The above categories of e-procurement require not only technological support, but also competent staff to oversee each category, thereby contributing to an efficient e-procurement function.

EDUCATION AND TRAINING

The efficiency benefits of e-procurement cannot be achieved only through the implementation of a new system. It needs to be underpinned by continuous education and training of users of e-procurement. Government needs to identify the expertise required for e-procurement. Further, the availability of the following skills internally needs to be determined:

- Leading practice procurement strategies.
- Leading operational level e-procurement practices.
- Process mapping and design.
- Financial and payment support for integration with internal payment processing and for third-party financial services support.
- Data management and security.
- Performance measurement.
- Business processes redesign training.

Reengineering processes and managing change may require benchmarking from outside specialists, not specifically focusing only on technical support for technology, but also on e-procurement processes and organizational transformation. The benefits of the e-procurement system can only be appreciated if end-users understand operational functionalities (Vaidya, et al., 2006, p. 82).

Training users on the tools and techniques required for e-procurement is necessary before pursuing the implementation of any change. Such exposure will enlighten employees on the value stream associated with e-procurement. Education and training is effective in developing employees' ability to apply different tools and techniques to aid improvement efforts, since technology alone does not ensure the success of e-procurement. If users are technology unaware and are unwilling to change and accept new internal processes, then support can be compromised.

In addition, Croom and Brandon-Jones (2007, p. 298) highlight the importance of day-to-day support provision in e-procurement implementation. Comprehensive support for e-procurement system users can have a significant influence on the level of internal service provision compliance, reputation of the purchasing function facilitating procurement and the general amenability of the organization to support e-procurement. While the authors support the view that e-procurement implementation creates the potential to improve compliance, it cannot be assumed that compliance

is a given. Further, support given to e-procurement users can have a significant effect on maverick spending (Croom & Brandon-Jones, 2007, p. 301).

REGISTRATION OF SUPPLIERS

Without supplier participation, e-procurement cannot be successfully implemented. Government should not take supplier willingness to engage in e-procurement for granted, since suppliers generally do not see technology as a core competency and do not see the value of a complex, costly and time consuming electronic investment that does not reflect immediate visible returns. Therefore, there should be "buy in" of the business case not only from management, but also from suppliers who should be part of the e-procurement project and change management plan. Supplier involvement in e-procurement planning can highlight beneficial milestones to all role players. Further, to avoid risks associated with suppliers especially if large volumes of goods and services are required to support strategic and operational commitments, it is imperative that prospective suppliers are evaluated before registering on the e-procurement database. The evaluation process should consider the following (Fourie & Opperman, 2011, pp. 341-345):

- Identification and tax references.
- Business history.
- Any direct or indirect employment history with the state.
- Evidence of a reliable quality assurance and quality control procedure.
- Installation of an integrated IT system which can provide reliable information.
- Profiling of supplier's management philosophy, financial status, and production capacity.
- Compliance with 150 9000 quality standards.

Lists of registered suppliers must be updated regularly to include additional suppliers, new goods and services and to identify listed or prospective suppliers who have been prohibited from conducting business with the public sector. Regular review of registered suppliers is important for performance management of suppliers.

RISK IDENTIFICATION

Organizations operate in an ever-changing environment, thereby creating uncertainty, which can result in deviation of actual results from desired or expected results. Further, a security risk is another significant factor hindering organizations adopting e-procurement. In the absence of transactions between different systems being exchanged in secure ways, vulnerability to fraud may emerge. Potter (2000, p. 20) states that security fears relating to the following are a frequently cited concern relating to e-procurement: data corruption, fraud, hacking by unauthorized outsiders, staff misuse of information systems, malicious software and phishing. Any organization has to consider how the following risks can be managed (Cronje, et al., 2011, p. 97):

- Core business risks impact directly on the operating profit of an organization, as they are inherent in the main business of the organization.
- Incidental risks like escalating interest rates, liquidity risk and fluctuations in foreign exchange are generally financial risks, which arise from the continuation of the main business of the organization.
- Operational risks arising from the failure of technology, insufficient procurement processes, and incompetent human resources are generally internal shortcomings that expose an organization to losses.
- External downside risks like natural disasters, supplier risks, labor strikes, and

security are difficult to control proactively. Therefore, organizations need to anticipate these risks so that their adverse effects can be minimized.

Organizations can manage risks by considering the following options: risk avoidance, risk assumption, risk elimination, risk reduction; risk transfer. However, security risks relating to information can be addressed through the implementation of an information security management system based on the development of an in-house policy or the adoption of an international standard.

From the preceding discussion, it is clear that there can be conditions that emanate from the macro-environment but may have to be managed within the microenvironment. Imperatives like technology, risk identification, and registration of suppliers can be located in both environments. It is clear that support for change in the organizations procurement process has to be underpinned by management "buy-in," comprehensive understanding of the magnitude of change and a deviation from existing working practices. Central to this is effective education and training. Education and training will not only make individuals understand the concepts and technologies necessary to operate e-procurement systems, but also the value proposition behind e-procurement adoption (Ross, 2003, p. 269).

Solutions and Recommendations

Government expenditure is of such magnitude that it is a significant part of economic and social progress. Therefore, cognizance needs to be taken of the following factors when governments are developing e-procurement policies for implementation:

- Sensitivity to local socio-economic imbalances within the context of a global economy.

- Institutionalization of a code of ethics for all e-procurement users within government, underpinned by regular education and training supporting e-procurement implementation management.
- A coherent and comprehensively resourced e-procurement regulatory framework that addresses national policy imperatives.
- Developing human resources adequately to operate within an e-procurement environment.
- Developing in-country technological capacity, especially in developing economies to manage e-procurement.
- Constructive local and international participation in developing policies and systems to support e-procurement.
- Investigating public sector incentives that can drive e-procurement compatibility with suppliers.
- Researching an "enterprise-wide" initiative within government, given the overlapping and competing power interests.
- Provision of government technology support structures to assist businesses in providing trading portals and exchange services.
- Research into horizontal processes that integrate the supplier-buyer interface, rather than only sharing critical inventory information with suppliers.
- Investigating more effective means of real time measurement of service performance since service quality measurement is difficult and complex.

FUTURE RESEARCH DIRECTIONS

Future research in the area of determinants for public e-procurement success is wide. Focus areas worthy of further exploration include:

- Comparing influencing determinants in the private and public sectors for the choice of a procurement mode. While the determinants may be common to both sectors, their differing influential levels should be investigated.
- Quantitative and qualitative measures in the public sector should be identified for developing economies to ascertain factors that mitigate the implementation of e-procurement in such economics.
- While there is a plethora of research to support the adoption and implementation of e-procurement, existing literature is limited on reasons why adoption and implementation of e-procurement in different global environments has been slow.
- The extant literature on e-procurement does not provide empirical insights into social responsibility by private and public sector organizations with respect to their purchasing policies and practices. Such research will provide valuable findings on empowerment, growth, and development, especially in emerging economies.
- The nature of e-procurement and it's diffusion into the public sector needs to be more rigorously analyzed. The critical success factors for public e-procurement in different contexts are also not well studied.
- More vigorous studies are also need to identify which of the generally recognized deterrents to e-procurement are most applicable in the public sector.

CONCLUSION

Public sector e-procurement, which has a major impact on the macro-economy, can be used as a tool by governments to achieve economic goals. Further, an effective and efficient e-procurement system enables government to deliver quality public services. Being the largest buyer in any country, government has to ensure that public sector procurement subscribes to international best practice, while advocating good governance. While international best practice points to e-procurement, governments can only benefit from e-procurement if the imperatives underpinning successful implementation of e-procurement systems is identified. Conditions like management "buy in," technology, quality, risk management, establishment of e-sourcing, e-transactions, and e-payment systems and the regulatory framework are important considerations for an effective and efficient e-procurement system to operate. By being responsive to the conditions determining the success of e-procurement, governments can reap the benefits of value for money, cost reduction, enhanced service provision, and ultimately contribute to quality procurement systems and practices.

Ideally, a cost-effective e-procurement system should promote government's socio-economic imperatives within a fair, transparent, and equitable environment. The administrative capacity of government should not be over-burdened, while not exposing government to unnecessary risks. While value-for-money is of paramount importance, a collective partnership between public sector organizations and suppliers ensures that all role players within the e-procurement system perform effectively and efficiently.

The sheer magnitude of government spending provides an enticing market expansion opportunity for software vendors, private businesses and IT specialists. Once ignited, e-procurement can be a powerful incentive to all role-players in the global economy. However, it should be noted that the determinants for successful e-procurement are diverse and may necessitate costs to be initially incurred. Therefore, it may take time before governments may fully enjoy the strategic and operationally benefits of e-procurement initiatives.

REFERENCES

Adendorff, S. A., Bothma, C., Fourie, I., & Walters, J. (2004). E-commerce and SCM. In Hugo, W. M. J., Badenhorst-Weiss, J. A., & van Biljon, E. (Eds.), *Supply Chain Management*. Pretoria, South Africa: Van Schaik.

Baily, P., Farmer, D., Crocker, B., Jessop, D., & Jones, D. (2008). *Procurement principles and management*. Harlow, MA: Prentice Hall.

Baily, P., Farmer, D., Jessop, D., & Jones, D. (1994). *Purchasing principles and management*. London, UK: Gower Publishing.

Bothma, C. H. (2000). *E-commerce for South African managers*. Pretoria, South Africa: Interactive Reality.

Chaffey, D. (2009). *e-Business and e-commerce management*. Essex, UK: Prentice Hall.

Cronje, T., van Biljon, E., Naude, M., Nel, D., & Poulter. (2011). The task of purchasing and task management. In W. M. J. Hugo & J. A. Badenhorst-Weiss (Eds.), *Purchasing and Supply Management*. Pretoria, South Africa: Van Schaik.

Croom, S., & Brandon-Jones, A. (2007). Impact of e-procurement in the UK public sector. *Journal of Purchasing and Supply Management, 13*, 294–303. doi:10.1016/j.pursup.2007.09.015

Croom, S., & Johnston, R. (2003). E-service: Enhancing internal customer service through e-procurement. *International Journal of Service Industries Management, 14*(5), 539–555. doi:10.1108/09564230310500219

Croom, S. R., & Brandon-Jones, A. (2005). Key issues in e-procurement: Procurement implementation and operation in the public sector. *Journal of Public Procurement, 5*(3), 367–387.

Fourie, M. L., & Opperman, L. (2011). *Municipal finance and accounting*. Pretoria, South Africa: Van Schaik.

Fraser, J., Fraser, N., & McDonald, F. (2001). The impact of electronic ecommerce on purchasing in the supply chanin. In A. Erridge, R. Fee, & McIlroy (Eds.), *Best Practice Procurement: Public and Private Sector Perspectives*. Hampshire, UK: Gower Publishing.

Henriksen, H. Z., & Mahnke, V. (2005). e-Procurement adoption in the Danish public sector. *Scandinavian Journal of Economic Systems, 17*(2), 85–106.

Jae Moon, M. (2005). Procurement management in state governments: Diffusion of e-procurement practices and its determinants. *Journal of Public Procurement, 5*(1), 54–72.

MacManus, S. (2002). Understanding the incremental nature of e-procurement at the state and local levels. *Journal of Public procurement, 2*(1), 5-28.

Neef, D. (2001). *e-Procurement: From strategy to implementation*. Upper Saddle River, NJ: Prentice Hall.

OECD. (2005). *Paris declaration on aid effectiveness*. Paris, France: OECD.

Panayiotou, N. A., Gayialis, S. P., & Tatsiopoulos, I. P. (2004). An e-procurement system for government purchasing. *International Journal of Production Economics, 90*, 79–102. doi:10.1016/S0925-5273(03)00103-8

Pauw, J. C., Woods, G., van der Linde, G. J. A., Fourie, D., & Visser, C. B. (2009). *Managing public money: Systems from the south*. Johannesburg, South Africa: Heinemann.

Potter, C. (2000). *Trust.... not built at e-speed: Trust issues in B2B e-procurement. Price-Waterhouse Coopers Report*. London, UK: PriceWaterhouse Coopers.

Riggins, F., & Mitra, S. (2007). An e-evaluation framework for developing net-enabled business metrics through functionality interaction. *Journal of Organizational Computing and Electronic Commerce, 17*(2), 175–203. doi:10.1080/10919390701294129

Ross, D. F. (2003). *Introduction to e-supply chain management*. Boca Raton, FL: St. Lucie Press.

Schiele, J. J., & McCue, C. P. (2011). Lean thinking and its implications for public procurement: Moving forward with assessment and implementation. *Journal of Public Procurement, 11*(2), 206–239.

Schoenherr, T., & Mabert, V. A. (2011). A comparison of online and offline procurement in B2B markets: Results from a large scale survey. *International Journal of Production Research, 49*(3), 827–846. doi:10.1080/00207540903473359

Vaidya, K., Sajeev, A. S. M., & Callender, G. (2006). Critical factors that influence e-procurement implementation success in the public. *Journal of Public Procurement, 6*(113), 70–79.

Varney, M. (2011). *e-Procurement current law and future challenges*. Paper presented at the Annual Conference an European Public Procurment Law. Trier, Germany.

Walker, H., & Harland, C. (2007). e-Procurement in the United Nations: Influences, issues and impact. *International Journal of Operations & Production Management, 28*(9), 831–857. doi:10.1108/01443570810895276

ADDITIONAL READING

Aboelmaged, G. M. (2009). Predicting e-procurement adoption in a developing country: An empirical integration of technology acceptance model and theory of planned behavior. *Industrial Management & Data Systems, 110*(3), 392–414. doi:10.1108/02635571011030042

Badley, A., & Lewis, E. (2008). Debate: Why aren't we all lean? *Public Money & Management, 23*(1), 10–11.

Basheka, B. C. (2009). Procurement planning and local governance in Uganda: A factor analyses approach. *International Journal of Procurement Management, 2*(2), 191–209. doi:10.1504/IJPM.2009.023407

Camillus, J. C. (2008). Strategy as a wicked problem. *Harvard Business Review, 86*, 98–101.

Collin, K., & Muthusamy, S. (2007). Applying the Toyota production system to a healthcare organization: A case study on a rural community healthcare provider. *The Quality Management Journal, 14*(4), 41–52.

Croom, S. (2005). The impact of e-business on supply chain management. *International Journal of Operations & Procurement Management, 25*(1), 55–73. doi:10.1108/01443570510572240

Diniz, J. D. A. S., & Fabbe-Costes, N. (2007). Supply chain management and supply chain orientation: Key factors for sustainable development projects in developing countries? *International Journal of Logistics: Research and Applications, 10*(3), 235–250.

Feinstein, L., Lupton, R., Hammond, C., Mujtaba, T., Salter, E., & Sorhaindo, A. (2008). *The public value of social housing: A longitudinal analysis of the relationship between housing and life chances.* London, UK: Smith Institute.

Green, K., Morton, B., & New, S. (1996). Purchasing and environmental management: Interactions, policies and opportunities. *Business Strategy and the Environment, 5*(3), 188–197. doi:10.1002/(SICI)1099-0836(199609)5:3<188::AID-BSE60>3.0.CO;2-P

Holzer, M., Charbonneau, R., & Kim, Y. (2009). Mapping the terrain of public service quality improvement: Twenty-five years of trends and practices in the United States. *International Review of Administration Sciences, 75*(3), 403–418. doi:10.1177/0020852309341330

Kauffman, R. J., & Mohtadi, H. (2004). Proprietary and open systems adoption in e-procurement: A risk augmented transaction perspective. *Journal of Management Information Systems, 21*(1), 137–166.

Khalid, S., Ahmad, S., & Irshad, M. Z. (2011). e-Procurement in the organization performance: Business case of export based textile industry. *Interdisciplinary Journal of Contemporary Research in Business, 3*(1), 494–502.

Kirchgeorg, M., & Winn, M. I. (2006). Sustainability marketing for the poorest of the poor. *Business Strategy and the Environment, 15*(3), 171–184. doi:10.1002/bse.523

Kollberg, B., Dahlgaard, J. J., & Brehmer, P. (2007). Measuring lean initiatives in health care services: Issues and findings. *International Journal of Productivity and Performance Management, 56*(1), 7–24. doi:10.1108/17410400710717064

Lamothe, M., & Lamothe, S. (2009). Beyond the search for competition in social service contracting: Procurement, consolidation, and accountability. *American Review of Public Administration, 39*(2), 164–188. doi:10.1177/0275074008316557

Lamothe, S., Lamothe, M., & Feiock, R. C. (2008). Examining local government services delivery arrangements over time. *Urban Affairs Review, 44*(1), 27–56. doi:10.1177/1078087408315801

Linton, J. D., Klassen, R., & Jayaraman, V. (2007). Sustainable supply chains: An introduction. *Journal of Operations Management, 25*(6), 1075–1082. doi:10.1016/j.jom.2007.01.012

Loader, K. (2009). Is local authority procurement 'lean'? An exploration to determine if 'lean' can provide a useful explanation of practice. *Journal of Purchasing and Supply Management, 16*(1), 41–50. doi:10.1016/j.pursup.2009.10.001

Mason, C., Kirkbride, J., & Brde, D. J. (2007). From stakeholders to institutions: The changing face of social enterprise governance theory. *Management Decision, 45*(2), 284–301. doi:10.1108/00251740710727296

Matos, S., & Hall, J. (2007). Integrating sustainable development in the supply chain: The case of life cycle assessment in oil and gas and agricultural biotechnology. *Journal of Operations Management, 25*(6), 1083–1102. doi:10.1016/j.jom.2007.01.013

Meehan, J., & Bryde, D. (2011). Sustainable procurement practice. *Business Strategy and the Environment, 20*, 94–106. doi:10.1002/bse.678

Neves, P. (2009). Readiness of change: Contributions for employee's level of individual change and turnover intentions. *Journal of Change Management, 9*(2), 215–231. doi:10.1080/14697010902879178

Pettijohn, C., & Qiao, Y. (2000). Procuring technology: Issues faced by public sector organisation. *Journal of Public Budgeting Accounting and Financial Management, 12*(1), 441–461.

Preuss, I. (2007). Buying into our future: Sustainability initiatives in local government procurement. *Business Strategy and the Environment, 16*(5), 354–365. doi:10.1002/bse.578

Prince, P. M., & Harrison, N. J. (2009). Purchasing and personality: A review of the literature and a case for future research. *International Journal of Procurement Management, 2*(1), 62–78. doi:10.1504/IJPM.2009.021730

Puschmann, T., & Rainer, A. (2005). Successful use of e-procurement in supply chains. *Supply Chain Management, 10*(2), 122–133. doi:10.1108/13598540510589197

Rai, A., Tang, X., Brown, P., & Keil, M. (2006). Assimilation patterns in the use of electronic procurement innovations: A cluster analysis. *Information & Management, 43*(3), 336–349. doi:10.1016/j.im.2005.08.005

Rajkumar, T. (2001). E-procurement: business and technical issues. *Information Systems Management, 18*(4), 52–61. doi:10.1201/1078/43198.18.4.20010901/31465.6

Schiele, J. J., & McCue, C. P. (2006). Professional service acquisition in public sector procurement: A conceptual model of meaningful involvement. *International Journal of Operations & Production Management, 26*(3), 300–325. doi:10.1108/01443570610646210

Schoenherr, T., & Mabert, V. A. (2011). A comparison of online and offline procurement in B2B markets: Results from a large scale survey. *International Journal of Production Research, 49*(3), 827–846. doi:10.1080/00207540903473359

Shakir, M., Smith, G., & Gule, E. (2007). E-procurement: Reaching out to small and medium businesses. *MIS Quarterly Executive, 6*(4), 225–238.

Smart, A. (2009). Exploring the business case for e-procurement. *International Journal of Physical Distribution & Logistics Management, 40*(3), 181–201. doi:10.1108/09600031011035083

Stone, D. (2009). Rapid knowledge: Bridging research and policy at the overseas development institute. *Public Administration and Development, 29*(4), 303–315. doi:10.1002/pad.540

Tanner, C., Woelfle, R., Schubert, P., & Quade, M. (2008). Current trends and challenges in electronic procurement: An empirical study. *Electronic Markets, 18*(1), 6–18. doi:10.1080/10196780701797599

Tatsi, V., Mena, C., Van Wassenhove, L., & Whicker, L. (2006). E-procurement in the Greek food and drink industry: Drivers and impediments. *Journal of Purchasing and Supply Management, 12*, 63–74. doi:10.1016/j.pursup.2006.04.003

Ung, S. T., Bonsall, S., Wall, A., & Wang, J. (2007). The application of six-sigma concept to port security process quality control. *Quality and Reliability Engineering International, 23*(5), 631–639. doi:10.1002/qre.855

Van Dijk, R., & van Dick, R. (2009). Navigating organisational change: Change leaders, employee resistance and work-based identities. *Journal of Change Management, 9*(2), 143–163. doi:10.1080/14697010902879087

Yin, R. K. (2008). *Case study research: Design and methods*. Newbury Park, CA: Sage Publications.

KEY TERMS AND DEFINITIONS

E-Procurement: Electronic procurement where the whole process of order processing, receipt inspection and payment of suppliers is time efficient because of automated procurement process.

Ethics: Guidelines or rules of conduct by which an organization conducts its activities.

Maverick Purchasing: Ordering of items that are unnecessary or too expensive by originators who are empowered to buy their own items.

Phishing: Accessing personal information electronically through e-mails and sites, in hereby one party masquerades as someone else.

Procurement: Activities relating to the acquisition receipt and storage of purchased goods and services required by an organization.

Public Procurement: Government administrative activities focusing on the purchasing of goods and services from the private sector.

Chapter 10

Public Procurement in the Czech Republic:
Focused on Regional Development and E-Procurement

Jiří Novosák
Tomas Bata University in Zlín, Czech Republic

Oldřich Hájek
Tomas Bata University in Zlín, Czech Republic

Jiří Machů
Tomas Bata University in Zlín, Czech Republic

ABSTRACT

Relations between public procurement, regional development, and e-procurement are discussed in this chapter. First, main themes of the debate are reviewed. Subsequently, some relations between public procurement, regional development, and e-procurement are discussed. The Czech Republic is used as a case study in this regard. The authors' findings confirm the potential of public procurement to stimulate development of Czech regions. Spatially, public procurement may not be regarded as a suitable tool for reduction of regional disparities. However, there seems to be an important impact of public procurement on the development of local small and medium enterprises. In addition, the authors' findings point at some links between public procurement and the concepts of sustainable development and competitiveness. Nevertheless, the dominant position of price as evaluation criterion indicates that the linkages are rather weak. Finally, the increasing interest of the Czech Republic in e-procurement was documented.

DOI: 10.4018/978-1-4666-2665-2.ch010

INTRODUCTION

Historically, regional development was understood in an economic way. Increasing number of jobs and increasing average income were regarded as traditional indicators of regional development (e.g. Callois & Aubert, 2007). However, this narrow definition of regional development appeared not to be in accord with increasing quality of life. Consequently, a number of other aspects were added as ingredients of regional development. Social justice, environmental sustainability, civic society building, and cultural heritage protection are only some of them (Pike, Rodríguez-Pose, & Tomaney, 2007). Altogether, regional development is a quite intricate concept and there is not one, all encompassing definition of the term.

The abovementioned shifts in the understanding of regional development are closely connected with changes in theoretical approaches, which try to explain the essence of regional development. In this respect, there are an increasing number of aspects, which are regarded as highly relevant for regional development. Besides traditional factors such as population, transport infrastructure, or human capital, a number of other factors are becoming more and more accentuated in scholar literature on regional development. These factors include among others innovations, institutional quality, social capital and creativity, or quality of environment. On this basis, regional development is now an extremely complex phenomenon. In this situation, the public sector faces new challenges how to solve more and more demanding tasks. Svensson, Trommel, and Lantink (2008), for example, speak about a shift of public sector activities from a bureaucratic form of organization towards an organization with obvious market features (e.g. privatization, outsourcing, networking, and others). These features belong to the cornerstones of the politically influential New Public Management concept. Essig and Batran (2005) and Bogason and Toonen (1998) give the following typical characteristics of the concept:

- Concentration on key tasks and elimination of inefficient operations (outsourcing, privatization).
- Emphasis on efficiency and cooperation.
- Human capital development and ethical behavior.

The first and second abovementioned aspects are of great importance for our chapter. In this regard, a number of public sector operations were outsourced with the goal to increase their efficiency. More and more limited public budgets may be regarded as an important stimulus of this efficiency discussion. It is noteworthy that public procurement is a typical mechanism how public authorities buy goods, works, and services. Altogether, it is not surprising that research on public procurement has become highly relevant also for regional development. In this respect, public procurement may represent an important source of financing for regional development. The goal of this chapter is oriented just in this direction—to review the current state of research on public procurement and regional development and subsequently to discuss some relations in the case of the Czech Republic. Special attention is given to e-procurement. Just this form is often regarded as a promising way to increase efficiency of public procurement procedures.

BACKGROUND

Increasing competition of regions may be understood as a typical feature of globalization (see e.g. Nijkamp, Van der Burch, & Vindigni, 2002). In this environment, regions are forced to search various strategies how to reinforce their development potential. There are a number of political tools applied in this regard. Hood (2007), for example, distinguishes administrative, economic, institutional, and information tools of regional development. Economic tools traditionally include various forms of subsidies. Their allocation is expected to strengthen regional competitiveness on one side and economic, social, and territorial cohesion on the other (see e.g. Fratesi, 2008; Boldrin & Canova, 2001). However, recently, there is also a growing interest in research on public procurement as a policy tool (e.g. McCrudden, 2004). In this regard, Arrowsmith (2003) mentions various political areas of interest. Two types of policies are defined. Primary policies are focused on obtaining goods, works, and services on the best terms. Secondary, or horizontal, policies embed public procurement in broader economic, social, and environmental relations (Arrowsmith, 2003; Walker & Brammer, 2009). Thus, public procurement becomes highly relevant also for regional development (Peck & Cabras, 2008).

The importance of public procurement as a development tool is typically highlighted by the ratio of total volume of public procurement to GDP of particular territorial units. This ratio is estimated between 8% and 25% in the OECD countries and at 16% in the EU (e.g. Brammer & Walker, 2011; Preuss, 2009; Peck & Cabras, 2008; Cabras, 2011). Such an amount of money creates a huge potential to influence development paths of regions, e.g. on the basis of market expansion through government-led demand (Palmujoki, Parikka-Alhola, & Ekroos, 2010; Preuss, 2009). The value for money principle, closely related to the efficiency and effectiveness concepts, is a key rule in public procurement allocation (Raymond, 2008; Preuss, 2009). In many cases, the rule is understood on the lowest price basis. Thus, Peck and Cabras (2008), Cabras (2011), among others, mention just price as the decisive evaluation criterion of public procurement. However, the idea of the most economically advantageous tender extends this simple understanding also by other types of evaluation criteria such as quality, technical merit, functional characteristics, after-sales services, or environmental characteristics (compare with Palmujoki, Parikka-Alhola, & Ekroos, 2010; Lorentziadis, 2010). In this way, we get back to the abovementioned issue on public

procurement and secondary policies. Sustainable development belongs to the most prominent policies of this kind.

Traditionally, sustainable development is understood as the kind of development, which satisfies the needs of the present generation without compromising the ability of future generations to meet their needs. In addition, sustainable development creates a balance among economic, social, and ecological interests (see e.g. Winston & Eastaway, 2008; Moffatt, 1996). Such a balance represents also the cornerstone of sustainable procurement, although social and environmental aspects are usually stressed (e.g. Brammer & Walker, 2011). Scholar literature gives several features typical for sustainable procurement, including contracting with local businesses as a source of benefits for local economy, involvement of community benefits into tendering process, or focus on environment-friendly purchases and services as sources of environmental benefits (Preuss, 2009; Arrowsmith, 2003). Moreover, the position of ethnic minorities, contracts with social enterprises or voluntary sector, gender equality, and working conditions for employees are also typical characteristics of sustainable procurement (see e.g. McCrudden, 2004 for a review of linkages between public purchasing and social outcomes). Note that Carter and Jennings (2004) generalized the features of sustainable procurement into the so called Purchasing Social Responsibility concept. This concept consists of five dimensions—environment, diversity, safety, human rights, and philanthropy—reflecting especially social and environmental goals of sustainable development.

Sustainable procurement was a subject of research in several subthemes. Walker and Brammer (2009) dealt with the most important aspects of sustainable procurement, using the questionnaire survey among relevant stakeholders. Contracting with local small and medium enterprises (also Brammer & Walker, 2011, for international perspective), health threats and working conditions were chosen as the most important aspects. It is noteworthy that social dimension of sustainable procurement was ranked higher than environmental. This is surprising if considering, e.g. McCrudden's claim on earlier development of the green procurement concept (McCrudden, 2004). Preuss (2009) identified the most important barriers of progress in sustainable procurement practices. Higher costs and low priority of sustainable procurement were upheld in this regard (compare with the same finding in Walker & Brammer, 2009). Palmujoki, Parikka-Alhola, and Ekroos (2010) concerned with environmental evaluation criteria in public procurement contracts. Palmujoki, Parikka-Alhola, and Ekroos (2010) point at a rather wide application of these criteria, however, a more or less vague formulation is emphasised. Peck and Cabras (2008) considered characteristics of suppliers in their research on public procurement. Findings of the authors showed a rather strong position of local small and medium enterprises in accord with the basic features of sustainable procurement. In this regard, Cabras (2011) warns from the threads of an undue emphasis on efficiency of public procurement. The rationale of the threads rests on the efforts to cumulate small tenders into larger, and more efficient, ones. However, such an approach may disqualify many small and medium enterprises from their participation in public procurement tenders (compare also with Arrowsmith, 2003). It is noteworthy that Peck and Cabras (2008) regard long-term relations, lower risk and image building as the main motivations of suppliers to participate in public procurement. On the contrary, bureaucracy is mentioned as the main barrier.

Besides sustainable development, regional competitiveness may be understood as a prominent development concept of these days. A number of factors influence the ability of regions to succeed in fierce global competition. These factors include among others labour market, transport costs, innovative capacity, untraded inter-dependencies and many others (see e.g. Budd & Hirmis, 2004). Search for new ways how to strengthen regional

competitiveness increased also the interest in public procurement. In this respect, the linkages between public procurement and innovations are in the heart of political debate (see e.g. Aschoff & Sofka, 2009; Rolfstam, 2009; Edler & Georghiou, 2007). It is noteworthy that innovation is understood as a cornerstone of regional competitiveness (e.g. Asheim & Coenen, 2005; Tödtling & Trippl, 2005). What is the rationale of linkages between public procurement and innovations? Aschoff and Sofka (2009) explain the essence of these linkages by the differences between standard products and services on one side and new products and services on the other. Public procurement focused on the second type of products and services may be regarded as an innovation policy tool because governments create demand for innovative products and services (Edler & Georghiou, 2007; Arrowsmith, 2003). Thus, Aschoff and Sofka (2009) speak about positive impacts of public procurement on innovations. In addition, Aschoff and Sofka (2009) emphasise the importance of public procurement especially for innovative processes in small enterprises with limited resources because public procurement provides relatively large amount of money for innovative activities. Moreover, purchase of innovative products or services is at least partially ensured and risk is generally low.

Another theoretical question is related to spatial pattern of public procurement. Is public procurement more concentrated in lagging or non-lagging regions? Thus, may we understand public procurement as a tool supportive for the traditional goal of regional policy—to reduce spatial disparities? It is noteworthy that, unlike subsidies, spatially oriented evaluation criteria are not allowed in public procurement tendering. Thus, it is unlikely that lagging regions are relatively more important beneficiaries of public procurement than the largest metropolitan regions. Moreover, it seems to be substantiated that local and regional governments prefer allocation of public procurement locally. This assumption further reinforces the position of the largest metropolitan regions in public procurement allocation because of their more important position as contractor compared to peripheral regions. Cabras (2011) adds other pieces to the mosaic posing the questions on the ability of peripheral regions to secure some specialized goods and services locally and on the role of e-auctions in the choice of suppliers. On the other hand, Pinch and Patterson (2000) stress more balanced spatial distribution of public services, and public procurement consequently, compared to producer services. This assumption is in favor of spatially even distribution of public procurement.

The aforementioned questions are highly relevant for recognition of linkages between public procurement and regional development. However, research on this theme is rather scarce. Cabras (2011) explains this research gap by the lack of data on public procurement at regional and local level. Cabras (2011) belongs to few exceptions in this regard. His research on the spatial pattern of public procurement in the Cumbria region shed some light on the issue. Thus, a relevant share of public procurement contracted by local authorities was kept in the region. Furthermore, small and medium enterprises were overrepresented in the sample of local suppliers and simultaneously they were more often suppliers of relatively small public procurement. Finally, the link between local contractors and local suppliers is sector-specific. The leakage of public procurement from region is less typical for sectors like construction or social care and more typical for sectors like consultancy and transportation (compare with the same findings in Peck & Cabras, 2008). In the latter case, Cabras (2011) speaks about the "London effect" because of a high share of suppliers located in the capital of the United Kingdom. Moreover, the question on real spatial allocation along the supply chain is raised. Altogether, much more research is needed to reveal linkages in the nexus of public procurement and regional development.

The calls for increasing efficiency and effectiveness and the value-for-money principle were mentioned as highly relevant goals of public procurement procedures of these days. Consequently, a number of support tools have been developed to achieve these goals. E-procurement belongs to the most prominent of them. Cabras (2010) gives three main reasons why e-procurement is regarded as a promising tool in this regard. First, e-procurement may increase competition for public procurement because spatial barriers are reduced. Second, e-procurement may substantially reduce administration costs. Third, e-procurement may speed up the public procurement procedures. There are various forms of e-procurement tools including e-tendering, e-auctions, or transmission of invoices online. It is noteworthy that especially e-auctions may represent an interesting tool how to reduce not only transaction costs but also the final price of public procurement contracts. Altogether, it is not surprising that e-procurement has its firm position in scholar literature. Croom and Brandon-Jones (2007) give five research themes in this respect. These themes include changes in total costs, changes to organizational characteristics and governance structure, system specification, and implementation management. Moreover, Cabras (2010) extends this review by the links between e-procurement and regional development, formulating the question on negative impacts of e-procurement on the ability of local and regional suppliers to be successful in a more intensive competition with non-local and non-regional firms.

THE CASE OF THE CZECH REPUBLIC

The background of this chapter summarized the most important theoretical issues of public procurement and regional development research. The importance of e-procurement was stressed as well. Now, let us turn our attention to evaluation of these issues in the Czech Republic.

Transformation Processes, Public Sector, and E-Procurement

Transformation processes in the Czech Republic after 1989 are closely related to changing missions of public sector in the country. A number of reforms have been realized since then. Recently, the nature of these reforms is focused also on the issues of efficiency and effectiveness in accord with the New Public Management concept. The tools like CAF, benchmarking, balanced scorecard, and others tend to be more often implemented now. However, these tools are still underrepresented in public sector management in the Czech Republic.

Public sector modernization in the Czech Republic is also closely related to ICT technologies. This sphere was traditionally affected by the lack of funds. However, the EU accession of the Czech Republic in 2004 substantially improved the situation. It is noteworthy that a number of projects focused on ICT in public sector were supported by EU cohesion policy in the Czech Republic. For our theme, it is important that this development created necessary assumptions for a wider use of e-forms of public procurements. What is the situation on e-forms of public procurements in the Czech Republic now?

There is an increasing interest in e-procurement in the Czech Republic now. Law on e-procurement is based on two EU Directives—2004/18/EC of the European Parliament and the Council of 31 March 2004 on the coordination of procedures for the award of public works contracts, public supply contracts and public service contracts on one hand and 2004/17/EC of the European Parliament and of the Council of 31 March 2004 coordinating the procurement procedures of entities operating in the water, energy, transport and postal services on the other. These Directives provide a complex framework for e-procurement in EU countries. The Czech Republic transposed the Directives into national law in 2006. Thus, Czech law on e-procurement consists of Act No. 137/2006 Coll.

on Public Contracts and Act No. 139/2006 Coll. on Concession Contracts and Concession Procedure. In addition, National Plan for the Introduction of Electronic Public Procurement over the period 2006-2010 was approved by Czech government in 2006 (see MRD, 2006), followed by Strategic Document on Electronic Public Procurement over the period 2011-2015 approved in 2011 (see MRD, 2011). The main goal of these documents is to create a fundamental strategic framework for implementation of ICT technologies into public procurement procedures.

The actual strategic document on e-procurement in the Czech Republic summarizes the state-of-the art in the theme. First, a rather low share of contractors (18%) uses electronic forms of procurement procedures. Moreover, only partial tasks are usually realized through e-procurement. However, there is a rather huge potential in this regard because 32% of contractors declare their interest in e-procurement implementation in short-term or middle term time frame. The strategy mentions also the most important barriers in wider implementation of e-procurement procedures. These include especially insufficient IT support to complex forms of e-procurement procedures on one side and a rather blurred legislative background on the other (see MRD, 2011). It is noteworthy, that the task to create robust IT support of e-procurement procedures was already mentioned in the National Plan for the Introduction of Electronic Public Procurement over the period 2006-2010 (compare with MRD, 2006). Nevertheless, this task has not been fulfilled yet.

Implementation of electronic tools belongs to the most important directions how to improve efficiency and effectiveness of public sector in the Czech Republic. E-government and smart administration are the leitmotifs in this regard. E-procurement procedures are firmly positioned in these directions. Thus, what are the most important goals of the actual Strategic Document on Electronic Public Procurement over the period

2011-2015? The main goal of the Strategy declares that all contractors in the Czech Republic are expected to have the opportunity to use some IT support tool for complex public procurement procedures by 2015. Thus, all legislative, financial, and technological barriers should be removed. In addition, it is expected that 50 billion CZK will be saved through e-procurement. These main goals are subsequently extended in the form of measurements, which include among others (MRD, 2011):

- The NIPEZ project tries to solve the problem of insufficient IT support to complex e-procurement. The NIPEZ solution is proposed as a modular IT interface to support all areas of e-procurement procedures. Two modules form the cornerstone of the NIPEZ project. The e-marketplace module is focused on operational purchases such as health material while the national e-tool module on complex (strategic) purchases such as highway construction works and others.
- Several measurements are mentioned with respect to cost reduction. Thus, it is recommended to cumulate public procurement contracts, and to use e-auctions and e-evaluation more frequently in public procurement competitions. In addition, electronic forms are recommended also in subsequent procedures related to procurement contracts or financial issues.

Public Procurement, Regional Development, and E-Auctions

It was claimed in the background of the chapter that there is an important impact of public procurement on regional development. The Czech Republic is no exception in this regard. Table 1 shows basic statistics on public procurement contracts registered in the official information system of the Czech Ministry for Regional Development. The total volume of officially registered public procurement in the Czech Republic was about 8-9% of its GDP in the period 2006-2010. It is noteworthy that government estimates speak about much higher shares between 14-17% of GDP. Comparison of these two figures indicates that a large share of public procurement is not registered in the official information system. However, the both figures confirm the importance of public procurement for Czech economy.

In this section, we would like to extend the abovementioned findings by some additional information from our research on the public procurement contract level. For the purpose of the analysis, we compiled a database of 1,481 public procurement contracts realized during the months September and December in the year 2011. The total financial allocation for these contracts was 21.1 billion CZK. Several attributes of these contracts were added into the database. Subsequently, the database became the main source of information for our analysis. Overall, we dealt with five areas of interest.

Table 1. Public procurement contracts registered in the information system on public procurement: basic statistics

Year	2006	2007	2008	2009	2010
Total number	8.993	7.280	8.155	9.778	8.922
Total volume (CZK)	303.3 billion	218.6 billion	307.3 billion	299.3 billion	268.6 billion

Source: Ministry for Regional Development – Information System on Public Procurement

Public Procurement and Balanced Regional Development

In the background of the chapter, we formulated several spatial issues related to public procurement research. First, our interest is focused on the linkages between public procurement and balanced regional development. The main goal of this development concept is traditionally focused on various forms of support given to lagging regions. However, such an approach is not allowed in the public procurement evaluation process. Thus, what is the relationship between public procurement and balanced regional development in our sample of public procurement contracts?

To answer the abovementioned question we use two approaches how to understand lagging and non-lagging regions. The first approach is based on the so called "regions with a concentrated state support" as given in relevant Czech law. We regard just these regions at the county level as lagging regions because Czech regional policy declares some forms of preference to them. The second approach follows regional/urban hierarchy of the Czech Republic. Four categories of regions were defined in this respect. The first category includes Counties of four largest cities in the Czech Republic. The remaining counties are categorized according to two attributes—number of inhabitants and population density. counties in the fourth category, with the lowest number of inhabitants and population density, are perceived as lagging regions.

Our solution to the first research problem was based on location of suppliers' headquarters for each analyzed contract. The county level was decisive in this regard to categorize contracts either into lagging or non-lagging regions on one side and into a category of regional hierarchy on the other. Subsequently, absolute public procurement allocation for the two types of regions and the four categories of regional hierarchy was summed and recalculated per 1 inhabitant. Table 2 shows results. The main conclusion of our analysis points at higher relative figures of non-lagging regions. This finding is obvious according to the both definitions of lagging regions. It is noteworthy that also financially more demanding public procurement contracts are realized in non-lagging regions. Overall, there is no sign that public procurement contributes to balanced regional development in the Czech Republic. On the contrary, more developed regions seem to be favored in this regard.

Public Procurement and Local/Regional Development

Although the spatial dimension is not allowed as an evaluation criterion in public procurement tendering there are several factors, which favor local or regional suppliers. These factors include, among others, lower transaction costs because of general familiarity with the territory. Consequently, the second research problem is focused on the match between spatial location of suppliers and contractors of the analyzed public procurement contracts.

Table 2. Public procurement allocation: distribution between lagging and non-lagging regions and categories of regional hierarchy

Regions with a Concentrated State Support	Non-Lagging Regions		Lagging Regions	
Allocation per 1 inhabitant	2,577		795	
Regional Hierarchy Category	1	2	3	4
Allocation per 1 inhabitant	5,432	3,027	1,112	646

Source: Authors' elaboration based on Ministry for Regional Development – Information System on Public Procurement

Our solution to the second research problem is based on two spatial levels of Counties and Regions. Note that there are 14 Regions in the Czech Republic—the higher administrative units. The County level provides more detailed analysis at a lower spatial level with 77 spatial units. Our conclusions may be summarized as follows. There are 709 public procurement contracts in our sample where the same Region of both, contractor's and supplier's headquarters, was identified. Thus, almost 50% of contracts were realized in the same Regions as the location of contractors' headquarters. The share is even slightly higher (52%) for total financial allocation. The match between location of contractors' and suppliers' headquarters is weaker at the County level. However, the corresponding shares remain rather high with 37% of contracts realized and 42% of funds allocated in the same Counties.

Overall, spatial proximity seems to be a relevant aspect of public procurement allocation. In addition, there is a question on the importance of this aspect when considering differences between lagging and non-lagging regions. Table 3 shows some findings related to the question. A higher share of regionally located suppliers is characteristic for non-lagging regions. Thus, the impact of public procurement on the development of lagging regions seems to be further questioned if the location of suppliers is considered.

Thematic Focus of Public Procurement

The relationship between public procurement and competitiveness on one side and sustainable development on the other is widely discussed in scholar literature. We considered this relationship in two aspects of public procurement. The first aspect was related to the thematic focus of public procurement contracts while the second aspect to the content of weighted evaluation criteria. Results of our first evaluation showed the highest share (31%) of the theme "Infrastructure of public services and public space" on the total number of public procurement contracts. The themes "Other services and goods" (23%), "Environmental aspects of development" (15%), and "Transport infrastructure" (12%) were ranked second, third, and fourth in this regard. However, this ranking was different when the total volume of public procurement had been chosen for evaluation. Then, the theme "Infrastructure of public services and public space" (27%) was ranked first and the themes "Other services and goods" (27%) and "Environmental infrastructure" (17%) followed. Altogether, there seem to be some links between the themes related to sustainable development and competitiveness concepts. It is noteworthy, that the importance of social dimension of the sustainable development concept was rather negligible

Table 3. Public procurement allocation: match between location of contractors' and suppliers' headquarters (% of cases); breakdown by lagging and non-lagging regions and regional hierarchy

Regions with a Concentrated State Support	Non-Lagging Regions		Lagging Regions	
Supplier from the same county as contractor	38%		27%	
Supplier from a different county than contractor	62%		73%	
Regional Hierarchy Category	1	2	3	4
Supplier from the same county as contractor	45%	32%	21%	25%
Supplier from a different county than contractor	55%	68%	79%	75%

Source: own elaboration based on Ministry for Regional Development – Information System on Public Procurement

218

compared to environmental dimension. Table 4 extends our findings on the relationship between the thematic focus of public procurement on one side and the match between location of contractor and supplier headquarters on the other. In this regard, the theme "Infrastructure of public services and public space" was more typical for regionally located suppliers compared especially with large infrastructure public procurement contracts.

There were not complete data on evaluation criteria for all analyzed public procurement contracts. Thus, our analysis is based on the sample of 576 contracts. Price related evaluation criteria were by far the most important type of them. This type of evaluation criteria was in some form used in all contracts, with an average weight of 78%. It is noteworthy that the weight of 100% was the most frequent one (31% of all contracts). Other evaluation criteria were used in substantially less contracts with lower average weights (see Table 5). Thus, the price for value concept seems to be prevalent in the sample of the analyzed public procurement contracts with a rather marginal role of secondary policies.

Characteristics of Suppliers

Our fourth research problem is related to some characteristics of suppliers. The theoretical background of this chapter highlighted especially the importance of public procurement for small and medium enterprises. Thus, the first characteristic of our concern is focused on size of suppliers as given by the number of employees. Three categories of suppliers are defined in this regard. The first category contains the suppliers with less than 50 employees (small suppliers), the second category the suppliers with more than 49 but less than 250 employees (medium suppliers), and the third category the suppliers with more than 249 employees (large suppliers). In addition, the institutional background is followed as the second characteristic of suppliers in our sample. We distinguish three categories of

Table 4. Public procurement allocation: match between location of contractor and supplier headquarters (the first figure % of cases; the second figure% of financial allocation); breakdown by the selected thematic focus

Themes	Supplier From			
	Same County as Contractor		Different County from Contractor	
Environmental infrastructure	28%	22%	72%	78%
Infrastructure of public services and public space	45%	60%	55%	40%
R&D and innovation	43%	43%	57%	57%
Transport infrastructure	35%	32%	65%	68%

Source: Authors' elaboration based on Ministry for Regional Development – Information System on Public Procurement

Table 5. Evaluation criteria used in public procurement contracts: basic characteristics

Evaluation Criterion	Used In	Average Weight	Range of Weight
Price related	576 contracts	78%	20% – 100%
Quality of proposal	71 contracts	33%	5% – 80%
Technical merit	80 contracts	33%	2% – 80%
Quality of working team	6 contracts	15%	5% – 25%
Sanctions	123 contracts	15%	2% – 40%
Time-plan	140 contracts	18%	2% – 40%
After-sales services	189 contracts	16%	3% – 45%
Other criteria	23 contracts	18%	5% – 40%

Source: Authors' elaboration based on Ministry for Regional Development – Information System on Public Procurement

suppliers—public organizations, private subjects, and non-government organizations.

Our findings point at the highest share of small and medium suppliers in our sample if considered the number of contracts. Thus, the share of the small supplier category was 43.2%, the share of the medium supplier category was 35.9%, and the share of the large supplier category was

19.0%. However, the position of the large supplier category was substantially strengthened in the evaluation of total financial allocation. In this respect, the share of the large supplier category was more than 1.6 fold higher (31.9%). On the contrary, the share of the small supplier category was almost halved (24.8%).

In addition, we deal with the size of suppliers considering the match between location of contractor and supplier headquarters. Table 6 shows the main findings of our evaluation on two spatial levels—Counties and Regions. There is some tendency of location of small and medium suppliers in their home regions. The headquarters of large suppliers were more often located in different Counties and Regions than the headquarters of contractors. Thus, public procurement seems to be an important financial tool how to support regional development based on local small and medium enterprises. Question remains what the position of public and private sector was in our sample of suppliers. In this respect, the share of private enterprises was almost 98%.

Public Procurement and E-Auctions

Finally, our fifth research question is related to e-auctions. E-auctions are regarded as a promising tool how to increase efficiency and effectiveness of public procurement procedures. In addition, e-auctions may weaken the links established between local and regional contractors and suppliers. Thus, our analysis is focused on three aspects of e-auctions. First, we are interested in the question how often e-auctions were used in our sample of public procurement contracts. Second, the differences between anticipated and final prices of public procurement contracts realized on the basis of e-auctions are analyzed. Third, the regional match between contractors' and suppliers' location is of our concern. What are the findings?

Table 6. Public procurement allocation: match between location of contractor and supplier headquarters (% of cases); breakdown by size of suppliers

Size of Suppliers	Small	Medium	Large
Same county as contractor	41%	37%	28%
Different county than contractor	59%	63%	72%
Same region as contractor	53%	51%	33%
Different region than contractor	47%	49%	67%

Source: Authors' elaboration based on Ministry for Regional Development – Information System on Public Procurement

Solutions and Recommendations

First, it is necessary to uphold that e-auctions were used only in 53 public procurement contracts in our sample (4%). Thus, e-auctions do not seem to be a frequent tool in public procurement procedures in our sample. Second, the differences between anticipated and final prices of public procurement contracts were analyzed considering the role of e-auctions. In this regard, the real price of public procurement contract was lower than the anticipated one in almost 55% of the cases based on e-auctions. Nevertheless, e-auctions do not seem to be a differentiated feature of public procurement savings. Thus, the share of public procurement contracts with a lower final price is the same regardless realization based on e-auctions. Third, there are rather significant differences in the match between contractors' and suppliers' location when e-auctions are taken for a discrimination criterion. Thus, the share of the regional match of contractors and suppliers is lower if e-auctions are used.

FUTURE RESEARCH DIRECTIONS

The findings revealed from our preliminary research on public procurement and regional development in the Czech Republic showed opportunities how to use the existing sources of information for a detailed analysis of relations between public procurement and regional development with a special attention given to e-procurement. However, because of a rather limited number of analyzed public procurement contracts it is necessary to extend the contract coverage of our evaluation. This is the first direction of our further research.

Our preliminary research showed a close match between location of contractor and supplier headquarters. This is an important finding if considering that spatial aspects are not included in the evaluation process. However, it is rather intuitive that local and regional governments may try to allocate public procurement to local and regional suppliers. In this way, regional development may be supported. Based on this rationale, research on legal mechanisms how to use public procurement for regional development may be fruitful. This is the second direction of our further research.

The Information System of Public Procurement in the Czech Republic offers several other interesting research directions. These research directions may be summarized as follows.

The Czech Information System of Public Procurement provides necessary information for evaluation of the differences between anticipated and real prices of public procurement. Thus, the research question whether public procurement tenders reduce the real prices may be answered. Subsequently, the factors which explain the differences may be surveyed. The role of e-auctions may be considered in this regard.

There is a unique opportunity for the Czech Republic to draw financial means from EU structural funds in the programming period 2007-2013. The main goal of these structural operations is to reduce regional disparities and in this way to strengthen economic, social and territorial cohesion. The Czech Information System of Public Procurement allows us to distinguish between the public procurement supported from EU structural funds on one hand and not supported on the other. The differences between the two types of public procurement contracts may be followed subsequently.

The themes of further research on public procurement in the Czech Republic may provide fruitful benefits in understanding relations between public procurement, regional development, and e-procurement. We think that the importance of these relations is going to increase in near future. The Czech Republic belongs to the group of post-communist countries. Consequently, there are substantially less experience with many market mechanisms applied in public sector. Thus, cross-country research on the relations between public procurement and regional development may be useful to draw lessons for the Czech Republic.

CONCLUSION

There is an increasing research on public procurement as a tool of regional development now. Various themes are discussed in this regard. They include, among others, relations between public procurement on one side and sustainable development and regional competitiveness on the other. Moreover, public procurement are also connected with other themes of regional development, such as balanced regional development or endogenous regional development on the basis of local small and medium enterprises. It is noteworthy that these relations attract strong political attention now. This fact may be substantiated by a relatively high share of public procurement in GDP and by the emphasis, which is given on the efficiency and effectiveness concepts in the Czech Republic.

The goal of this chapter was focused on discussion of some relations between public procurement, regional development, and e-procurement in the Czech Republic. The most important findings of our preliminary research may be summarized as follows:

- The share of public procurement is officially estimated at 16% of GDP. Thus, there is an important position of public procurement as a source of funds for financing of regional development activities. In addition, there is an increasing interest in e-procurement procedures in the Czech Republic now.
- Public procurement seems to be not a suitable tool for reduction of regional disparities. Public procurement contracts are relatively more often allocated in non-lagging and core regions, not in peripheral regions. It is noteworthy that public procurement plays an important role in projects, which are supported from EU structural funds. On this basis, question on coherence of public procurement on one side and the main cohesion policy goal to reduce regional disparities arises.
- Public procurement seems to be an important source of funds for stimulation of endogenous development based on local and regional small and medium enterprises. Some themes (e.g. construction) are more regionally closed than others (e.g. transport or environmental infrastructure).
- Some linkages between public procurement on one hand and sustainable development and regional competitiveness on the other were identified. However, these linkages seem to be still rather weak.

On the basis of these findings, several directions of our further research are suggested.

ACKNOWLEDGMENT

The authors are thankful to the Internal Grant Agency of Tomas Bata University in Zlin for the grant No. IGA/50/FaME/2012/019, "Evaluation of Impacts of Public Financial Schemes on Development of Lagging Regions in the Czech Republic," which provided financial support for this survey.

REFERENCES

Arrowsmith, S. (2010). Horizontal policies in public procurement: A taxonomy. *Journal of Public Procurement, 10*(2), 149–186.

Aschoff, B., & Sofka, W. (2009). Innovation on demand – Can public procurement drive market success of innovations? *Research Policy, 38*(8), 1235–1247. doi:10.1016/j.respol.2009.06.011

Asheim, B. T., & Coenen, L. (2005). Knowledge bases and regional innovation systems: Comparing Nordic clusters. *Research Policy, 34*(8), 1173–1190. doi:10.1016/j.respol.2005.03.013

Bogason, P., & Toonen, T. A. J. (1998). Introduction: Networks in public administration. *Public Administration, 76*(2), 205–227. doi:10.1111/1467-9299.00098

Boldrin, M., & Canova, F. (2001). Inequality and convergence in Europe's regions: Reconsidering European regional policies. *Economic Policy, 16*(32), 207–253. doi:10.1111/1468-0327.00074

Brammer, S., & Walker, H. (2011). Sustainable procurement in the public sector: An international comparative study. *International Journal of Operations & Production Management, 31*(4), 452–476. doi:10.1108/01443571111119551

Budd, L., & Hirmis, A. K. (2004). Conceptual framework for regional competitiveness. *Regional Studies, 38*(9), 1015–1028. doi:10.1080/0034340042000292610

Cabras, I. (2010). Use of e-procurement in local authorities' purchasing and its effects on local economies: Evidence from Cumbria, UK. *European Planning Studies, 18*(7), 1133–1151. doi:10.1080/09654311003744209

Cabras, I. (2011). Mapping the spatial patterns of public procurement: A case study from a peripheral local authority in Northern England. *International Journal of Public Sector Management, 24*(3), 187–205. doi:10.1108/09513551111121338

Callois, J. M., & Aubert, F. (2007). Towards indicators of social capital for regional development issues: The case of French rural areas. *Regional Studies, 41*(6), 809–821. doi:10.1080/00343400601142720

Carter, C. R., & Jennings, M. M. (2004). The role of purchasing in the socially responsible management of the supply chain: A structural equation analysis. *Journal of Business Logistics, 23*(1), 145–186. doi:10.1002/j.2158-1592.2002.tb00020.x

Croom, S. R., & Brandon-Jones, A. (2007). Impact of e-procurement: Experiences from implementation in the UK public sector. *Journal of Purchasing and Supply Management, 13*(4), 294–303. doi:10.1016/j.pursup.2007.09.015

Edler, J., & Georghiou, L. (2007). Public procurement and innovation – Resurrecting the demand side. *Research Policy, 36*(7), 949–963. doi:10.1016/j.respol.2007.03.003

Essig, M., & Batran, A. (2005). Public-private partnership: Development of long-term relationships in public procurement in Germany. *Journal of Purchasing and Supply Management, 11*(5-6), 221–231. doi:10.1016/j.pursup.2006.01.001

Fratesi, U. (2008). Regional policy from a supra-regional perspective. *The Annals of Regional Science, 42*(3), 681–703. doi:10.1007/s00168-007-0167-x

Hood, C. (2007). Intellectual obsolescence and intellectual makeovers: Reflections on the tools of government after two decades. *Governance: An International Journal of Policy, Administration and Institutions, 20*(1), 127–144. doi:10.1111/j.1468-0491.2007.00347.x

Lorentziadis, P. L. (2010). Post-objective determination of weights of the evaluation factors in public procurement tenders. *European Journal of Operational Research, 200*(3), 261–267. doi:10.1016/j.ejor.2008.12.013

McCrudden, C. (2004). Using public procurement to achieve social outcomes. *Natural Resources Forum, 28*(4), 257–267. doi:10.1111/j.1477-8947.2004.00099.x

Moffatt, I. (1996). *Sustainable development: Principles, analysis and policies*. New York, NY: Parthenon.

MRD. (2006). *National plan for the introduction of electronic public procurement over the period 2006-2010*. Prague, Czech Republic: Ministry for Regional Development of the Czech Republic.

MRD. (2011). *Strategie elektronizace zadávání veřejných zakázek pro období let 2011 až 2015* [Strategic document on electronic public procurement over the period 2011-2015]. Prague, Czech Republic: Ministry for Regional Development of the Czech Republic.

Nijkamp, P., Van der Burch, M., & Vindigni, G. (2002). A comparative institutional evaluation of public-private partnerships in Dutch urban land-use and revitalisation projects. *Urban Studies (Edinburgh, Scotland), 39*(10), 1865–1880. doi:10.1080/0042098022000002993

Palmujoki, A., Parikka-Alhola, K., & Ekroos, A. (2010). Green public procurement: Analysis of the use of environmental criteria in contracts. *Review of European Community & International Environmental Law, 19*(2), 250–262. doi:10.1111/j.1467-9388.2010.00681.x

Peck, F., & Cabras, I. (2008). *Public procurement and regional development: The impact of local authority expenditure on local economies.* Paper presented to the Regional Studies Association International Conference Regions: The Dilemmas of Integration and Competition. Prague, Czech Republic.

Pike, A., Rodríguez-Pose, A., & Tomaney, J. (2007). What kind of local and regional development and for whom? *Regional Studies, 41*(9), 1253–1269. doi:10.1080/00343400701543355

Pinch, P. L., & Patterson, A. (2000). Public sector restructuring and regional development: The impact of compulsory competitive tendering in the UK. *Regional Studies, 34*(3), 265–275. doi:10.1080/00343400050015104

Preuss, L. (2009). Addressing sustainable development through public procurement: The case of local government. *Supply Chain Management: An International Journal, 14*(3), 213–223. doi:10.1108/13598540910954557

Raymond, J. (2008). Benchmarking in public procurement. *Benchmarking: An International Journal, 15*(6), 782–793. doi:10.1108/14635770810915940

Rolfstam, M. (2009). Public procurement as an innovation policy tool: The role of institutions. *Science & Public Policy, 36*(5), 349–360. doi:10.3152/030234209X442025

Singer, M., Konstantinidis, G., Roubik, E., & Beffermann, E. (2009). Does e-procurement save the state money? *Journal of Public Procurement, 9*(1), 58–78.

Svensson, J., Trommel, W., & Lantink, T. (2008). Reemployment services in the Netherlands: A comparative study of bureaucratic, market and network forms of organization. *Public Administration Review, 68*(3), 505–515. doi:10.1111/j.1540-6210.2008.00886.x

Tödtling, F., & Trippl, M. (2005). One size fits all? Towards a differentiated regional innovation policy approach. *Research Policy, 34*(8), 1203–1219.

Walker, H., & Brammer, S. (2009). Sustainable procurement in the United Kingdom public sector. *Supply Chain Management: An International Journal, 14*(2), 128–137. doi:10.1108/13598540910941993

Winston, N., & Eastaway, M. P. (2008). Sustainable housing in the urban context: International sustainable development indicator sets and housing. *Social Indicators Research, 87*(2), 211–221. doi:10.1007/s11205-007-9165-8

ADDITIONAL READING

Baily, P., Farmer, D., Crocker, B., Jessop, D., & Jones, D. (2008). *Procurement principles and management.* London, UK: Pitman Publishing.

Blažek, J., & Macešková, M. (2010). Regional analysis of public capital expenditure: to which regions is public capital expenditure channelled – To 'rich' or to 'poor' ones? *Regional Studies, 44*(6), 679–696. doi:10.1080/00343400903002713

Boldrin, M., & Canova, F. (2001). Inequality and convergence in Europe's regions: Reconsidering European regional policies. *Economic Policy, 16*(32), 207–253. doi:10.1111/1468-0327.00074

Brüllhart, M., & Trionfetti, F. (2001). Industrial specialisation and public procurement: Theory and empirical evidence. *Journal of Economic Integration, 16*(1), 106–127.

Caldwell, N., Walker, H., Harland, C., Knight, L., Zheng, J., & Wakeley, T. (2005). Promoting competitive markets: The role of public procurement. *Journal of Purchasing and Supply Management, 11*(5-6), 242–251. doi:10.1016/j.pursup.2005.12.002

Caranta, R., & Trybus, M. (2010). *The Law of green and social procurement in Europe*. Copenhagen, Denmark: Djoef Publishing.

Carter, C. R., & Jennings, M. (2004). The role of purchasing in corporate social responsibility: A structural equation analysis. *Journal of Business Logistics*, *25*(1), 145–186. doi:10.1002/j.2158-1592.2004.tb00173.x

Coggburn, J. D. (2004). Achieving managerial values through green procurement? *Public Performance & Management Review*, *28*(2), 236–258.

Croom, S. R., & Brandon-Jones, A. (2005). Key issues in e-procurement: Procurement implementation and operation in public sector. *Journal of Public Procurement*, *5*(3), 367–387.

Dooley, K. (2006). Factors influencing e-procurement usage. *Journal of Public Procurement*, *6*(1-2), 28–45.

Edquist, C., & Hommen, L. (2000). Public technology procurement and innovation theory. In Edquist, C., Hommen, L., & Tsipouri, L. (Eds.), *Public Technology, Procurement and Innovation* (pp. 5–70). Dordrecht, The Netherlands: Kluwer Academic Publishers. doi:10.1007/978-1-4615-4611-5_2

Erridge, A. (1994). Public procurement, competition and partnership. *European Journal of Purchasing & Supply Management*, *1*(3), 169–179. doi:10.1016/0969-7012(94)90006-X

Essig, M., & Batran, A. (2005). Public-private partnership – Development of long-term relationships in public procurement in Germany. *Journal of Purchasing and Supply Management*, *11*(5-6), 221–231. doi:10.1016/j.pursup.2006.01.001

Falagario, M., Sciancalepore, F., Constantino, N., & Pietroforte, R. (2012). Using a DEA-cross efficiency approach in public procurement tenders. *European Journal of Operational Research*, *218*(2), 523–529. doi:10.1016/j.ejor.2011.10.031

Geroski, P. A. (1990). Procurement policy as a tool of industrial policy. *International Review of Applied Economics*, *4*(2), 182–198. doi:10.1080/758523673

Howes, R., & Robinson, H. (2005). *Infrastructure for the built environment: global procurement strategies*. Amsterdam, The Netherlands: Elsevier.

Hudson, R. (2007). Regions and regional uneven development forever? Some reflective comments upon theory and practice. *Regional Studies*, *41*(9), 1149–1160. doi:10.1080/00343400701291617

Johnstone, N. (2003). *The environmental performance of public procurement: Issues of policy coherence*. Paris, France: Organization for Economic Cooperation and Development.

Lolos, S. E. G. (2009). The effect of EU structural funds on regional growth, assessing the evidence from Greece, 1990-2005. *Economic Change and Restructuring*, *42*(3), 211–228. doi:10.1007/s10644-009-9070-z

Martin, P. (1999). Public policies, regional inequalities, and growth. *Journal of Public Economics*, *73*(1), 85–105. doi:10.1016/S0047-2727(98)00110-8

McLean, I., & McMillan, A. (2005). The distribution of public expenditure across the UK regions. *Fiscal Studies*, *24*(1), 45–71. doi:10.1111/j.1475-5890.2003.tb00076.x

North, D., & Smallbone, D. (2000). Innovative activity in SMEs and rural economic development: Some evidence from England. *European Planning Studies*, *8*(1), 87–105. doi:10.1080/096543100110947

Palmberg, C. (2000). Industrial transformation through public technology procurement? The case of Nokia and Finnish telecommunications industry. In Edquist, C., Hommen, L., & Tsipouri, L. (Eds.), *Public Technology, Procurement and Innovation* (pp. 167–196). Dordrecht, The Netherlands: Kluwer Academic Publishers. doi:10.1007/978-1-4615-4611-5_8

Reiner, M. (1999). *Regional dimension in European public policy: Convergence or divergence?* New York, NY: Palgrave Macmillan.

Rothwell, R. (1984). Technology based small firms and regional innovation potential: The role of public procurement. *Journal of Public Policy*, *4*(4), 307–332. doi:10.1017/S0143814X00002774

Srivastava, S. K. (2007). Green supply-chain management: A state-of-the-art literature review. *International Journal of Management Reviews*, *9*(1), 53–80. doi:10.1111/j.1468-2370.2007.00202.x

Thomson, J., & Jackson, T. (2007). Sustainable procurement in practice: Lessons from local government. *Journal of Environmental Planning and Management*, *50*(3), 421–444. doi:10.1080/09640560701261695

Vaidya, K., Sajeev, A. S. M., & Callender, G. (2006). Critical factors that influence e-procurement implementation success in public sector. *Journal of Public Procurement*, *6*(1-2), 70–99.

Worthington, I., Ram, M., Boyal, H., & Shah, M. (2008). Researching the drivers of socially responsible purchasing: A cross-national study of supplier diversity initiatives. *Journal of Business Ethics*, *79*(3), 319–331. doi:10.1007/s10551-007-9400-x

Yülek, M. A., & Taylor, T. K. (2011). *Designing public procurement policy in developing countries: How to foster technology transfer and industrialization in the global economy*. Berlin, Germany: Springer.

KEY TERMS AND DEFINITIONS

Balanced Regional Development: Development of regions without harmful disparities.

Competitiveness of Regions: The ability of regions to compete with other regions.

Development Based on Small and Medium Enterprises: Usually endogenous form of development based on relatively small enterprises.

Green Procurement: Public procurement in accord with environmental requirements.

Public Procurement: Process by which governments purchase goods, works, and services.

Regional Competition: The ability of regions to compete with other regions in the current era of globalization.

Regional Development: Improving of values of various indicators related to quality of life.

Sustainable Development: The kind of development, which satisfies the needs of the present generation without compromising the ability of future generations to meet their needs.

Secondary Policies of Public Procurement: Policies which are indirectly influenced by public procurement (e.g. sustainable development, regional competitiveness).

Chapter 11
The Architecture of the EU Structural Instruments in Romania:
Public Administration Bodies Functioning, Econometric Modeling, and E-Solutions

Oana Gherghinescu
University of Craiova, Romania

Paul Rinderu
University of Craiova, Romania

Demetra Lupu-Visanescu
University of Craiova, Romania

ABSTRACT

The present chapter, after a short introduction presenting basic information about the European Union cohesion policy, presents the seven operational programmes that have been negotiated by Romania with the European Commission for the current programming period. The difficulties deriving from public procurement-acquisition procedures in Romania are identified; such difficulties are encountered during the implementation of European projects, thus questioning the effectiveness of the Electronic Public Procurement-Acquisition System. Although it was created with a view to securing the transparency of public funds distribution, it does not allow for tracking the concluded contracts compliance with procurement-acquisition terms. It is at this stage that the most serious problems related to public funds effective use arise. Emphasis is also placed on innovative tools used for submitting, evaluating, and monitoring projects, emphasizing the role of Management Authorities, as public bodies for managing this process. For each operational programme, an econometric model GARCH-like has been developed and applied for realizing this analysis at the level of NUTS2. Bucharest-Ilfov region has been chosen

DOI: 10.4018/978-1-4666-2665-2.ch011

as a case study. Conclusions emphasize the beneficial role of such models especially for assessing the current status of absorbing the structural funds as well as for formulating suggestions for improvement as regards the next programming period. The chapter also pays special attention to the potential use of innovative tools in the application and implementing process as drivers for increasing the efficiency and effectiveness of the process.

INTRODUCTION

During the 2007-2013 period, the European Regional Development Fund (ERDF), the European Social Fund (ESF), and the Cohesion Fund will contribute to achieving the three objectives of the Cohesion policy: Convergence (ERDF; ESF and Cohesion Fund), Regional Competitiveness and Employment (ERDF; ESF) and European Territorial Co-operation (ERDF). Regions with a GDP below 75% of the EU average are eligible under the Convergence objective while the other regions eligible under the Regional Competitiveness and Employment objective. Geographic eligibility of regions under the European Territorial Co-operation objective concerns either cross-border regions or those belonging to trans-national co-operation areas. The objectives, eligible regions, and allocations are as follows:

- The rationale of the Convergence objective is to promote growth-enhancing conditions and factors leading to real convergence for the least-developed Member States and regions. In an EU-27, this objective concerns—within 17 Member States—84 regions with a population of 154 million, whose per capita GDP is less than 75% of the Community average, and—on a "phasing-out" basis—another 16 regions with 16.4 million inhabitants with a GDP only slightly above the threshold, due to the statistical effect of the larger EU.

- Outside the Convergence regions, the Regional Competitiveness and Employment objective aims at strengthening regions' competitiveness and attrac-

tiveness, as well as employment, through a two-fold approach. First, development programmes will help regions to anticipate and promote economic change through innovation and the promotion of the knowledge society, entrepreneurship, the protection of the environment, and the improvement of their accessibility. Second, more and better jobs will be supported by adapting the workforce and by investing in human resources. In an EU-27, a total of 168 regions will be eligible, representing 314 million inhabitants.

- The European Territorial Co-operation objective will strengthen cross-border co-operation through joint local and regional initiatives, trans-national co-operation aiming at integrated territorial development, and interregional co-operation and exchange of experience. The population living in cross-border areas amounts to 181.7 million (37.5% of the total EU population), whereas all EU regions and citizens are covered by one of the existing 13 transnational co-operation areas. EUR 7.75 billion (2.5% of the total) available for this objective is split as follows: EUR 5.57 billion for cross-border, EUR 1.58 billion for transnational and EUR 392 million for inter-regional co-operation.

The Structural Funds are managed through a de-centralised system. This means that once the agreement on the financial allocation and the type of activities to be funded is signed between the European Commission and the Governments of the EU Member States, the national authorities have much freedom in the management of the Funds. In Romania the structural funds interventions are realised via seven Operational Programmes (OPs) as described here below. All these OPs are managed by Public Administration Bodies (Managing Authorities and Intermediate Bodies). The main objectives of this chapter will point to the following: (1) to present the architecture of the operational programmes, (2) to present the potential use of econometric models for analyzing the absorption of structural funds at NUTS2 regional level, (3) to present innovative tools in the process of programme implementation at NUTS2 regional level, (4) to depict conclusions on how the proposed models could be used/enhanced, (5) to depict conclusions on how the use of innovative tools can be up-scaled and extended.

The implementation of the projects financed from European financing is influenced directly by the ongoing way of the public acquisitions ran through the Electronic System of Public Acquisitions. Though at Romania's level the European directives which were transposed set the legal frame of development for the public acquisitions, the difficulty of the ongoing procedures for acquisitions is determined by the different interpretations of law. The problem is very complex and implies an ample analysis both in terms of theory and practice. Within the chapter, we intended to analyze only the most important aspects imposed by the right functionality of this market segment and also the disadvantages generated by plenty of legislation.

BACKGROUND

Operational Programmes Architecture

The Regional Operational Programme (ROP)

The Regional Operational Programme 2007-2013 (ROP) addresses all 8 Development Regions of Romania as settled by the Regional Development Law no. 151/1998, which was later amended by Law no. 315/2004, in line with the provisions of EC Regulation No. 1059/2003 with regard to the establishment of a common statistical classification of territorial units.

The legal basis is represented by Commission Regulation no. 1828/2006 setting out rules for the implementation of Council Regulation no. 1083/2006 and of Council and European Parliament Regulation no. 1080/2006, the Council Regulation no. 2988/95 on the protection of the European Communities' financial interests.

ROP is co-financed by the European Regional Development Fund (ERDF). The EU contribution will represent up to 85% of the total public expenditure. The total budget allocated to the ROP is approximately 4.4 billion euros for the financial exercise 2007-2013.

All Romanian NUTS II regions, including Bucharest-Ilfov, have a per capita Gross Domestic Product (GDP) of less than 75% of the Community average. Therefore, they are all eligible for EU Structural Fund support, under the "Convergence" objective, as specified in the Art. 5 of Council Regulation No. 1083/2006[1].

The ROP intervention is articulated into several steps which take into consideration the limited programming capacity available at the local level and the experience built in several years of EU-supported institution building in the field. Indicative financial allocations are made at the regional level based on local development level by privileging the less developed Regions through a financial allocation mechanism indirectly proportional to their GDP/capita level amended with the population density index, so that the less developed Regions could proportionally receive higher amounts of financial allocation within the framework of the agreed priority axes and in line with development strategies agreed at the regional level by the local authorities through their regional development boards.

The main features of ROP distinguishing it from the other Operational Programmes are:

- It has a clear local dimension in addressing socio-economic problems from the local point of view and capitalizes on local resources and opportunities.
- It privileges Regions relatively lagging behind and less developed areas by ensuring a minimum set of preconditions for growth but does not have redistributive purposes per se.
- ROP key areas of intervention are complementary to those of the other OPs and expected to operate in synergy with the former.
- It fosters a bottom-up approach to economic development.

ROP includes the following priority axes:

Priority Axis 1: Support to sustainable development of urban growth poles.
Priority Axis 2: Improvement of regional and local transport infrastructure.
Priority Axis 3: Improvement of social infrastructure.
Priority Axis 4: Strengthening the regional and local business environment.
Priority Axis 5: Sustainable development and promotion of tourism.
Priority Axis 6: Technical assistance.

The Sectoral Operational Programme "Increasing Economic Competitiveness" (SOP IEC)

The Sectoral Operational Programme "Increasing Economic Competitiveness," further referred to as SOP IEC, aims strengthening the strategic focus of the Economic and Social Cohesion policies and to make the correct and appropriate linkages to the European policies and the Lisbon Strategy for growth and job creation.

SOP IEC directly addresses the first priority of the National Development Plan (NDP) 2007-2013, i.e. "Increase of economic competitiveness and development of knowledge-based economy" and the second priority of the National Strategic Reference Framework (NSRF) 2007-2013, i.e. "Increasing the Long Term Competitiveness of the Romanian Economy," and contributes, to a certain extent, to the implementation of all NSRF priorities.

The starting point for SOP IEC is the analysis of the current situation of entrepreneurship and innovation, with special emphasis on the small and medium-sized enterprises sector (SMEs), on resources for research and development, on ICT sector on energy efficiency and environment protection issues in the energy and industry sectors.

The general objective of SOP IEC is the increase of Romanian companies' productivity, in compliance with the principle of sustainable development, and reducing the disparities compared to the average productivity of EU. The target is an average annual growth of GDP per employed person by about 5.5%. This will allow Romania to reach approx. 55% of the EU average productivity by 2015. In terms of figures, the EU contribution to SOP IEC budget for the 2007-2013 programming period is 2,554 million Euros.

All initiatives developed under SOP IEC will be related to the following priority axes:

Priority Axis 1: An innovative and eco-efficient productive system.

Priority Axis 2: Research, Technological Development and Innovation for competitiveness.

Priority Axis 3: ICT for private and public sectors.

Priority Axis 4: Increasing energy efficiency and security of supply, in the context of combating climate change.

Priority Axis 5: Technical Assistance.

The Sectoral Operational Programme "Human Resources Development" (SOP HRD)

The Sectoral Operational Programme "Human Resources Development" (SOP HRD) sets the priority axes and the key areas of intervention in Romania in the human resources field in order to implement the EU financial assistance through the European Social Fund.

Elaborated in the context of National Development Plan 2007-2013 and in line with the Priorities of the National Strategic Reference Framework, SOP HRD is an important instrument in supporting the economic development and structural changes. Moreover, the investments in human capital will complement and will confer sustainability to the increase of productivity on a long term.

A highly qualified labour force, with a high level of education, having the capacity to respond to the new technologies and to the changing needs of markets, is essential for a competitive and dynamic economy. Romania will promote active labour market policies to increase the adaptability and flexicurity of labour force. It is envisaged to be reached a higher level of participation on the labour market, as a base for a competitive knowledge based economy.

The ESF intervention in Romania shall support the achievement of the general objective and the specific objectives in the field of human resources development, making a real contribution to the implementation of European Employment Strategy and to the overall objective of growth and jobs.

The general objective of SOP HRD is the development of human capital and increasing competitiveness, by linking education and lifelong learning with the labour market and ensuring increased opportunities for future participation on a modern, flexible, and inclusive labour market for 1,650,000 people.

The EU allocation for SOP HRD is 3,476 million Euro, representing 85% of the total value of the Programme. The National public counterpart is estimated at 613 million Euros.

The SOP HRD is structured on seven priority axes:

Priority Axis 1: Education and training in support for growth and development of knowledge based society.

Priority Axis 2: Linking lifelong learning and labour market.

Priority Axis 3: Increasing adaptability of workers and enterprises.

Priority Axis 4: Modernizing the public employment service.

Priority Axis 5: Promoting active employment measures.

Priority Axis 6: Promoting social inclusion.

Priority Axis 7: Technical assistance.

The Sectoral Operational Programme Transport (SOPT)

Through increasing and improving the quality of investment in physical capital, the Sectoral Operational Programme Transport (SOPT) aims at speeding up the convergence process by improving conditions for growth and employment.

The Sectoral Operational Programme Transport complies with the Community Strategic Guidelines for Cohesion Policy and the Lisbon Strategy for Growth and Jobs and the overall European transport policy as defined in the document "European Transport Policy for 2010, Time to Decide" and "Keep Europe Moving" The total budget of the SOPT for the programming period

2007–2013 is about 5.7 billion EUR. Out of these, 4.57 billion represent the EU financial support.

For the 2007-2013 period, the overall Romanian transport strategy focuses on clear national priorities and the EU policies, such as development of the Trans-European Network Transport (TEN-T), especially TEN-T priority projects, mode balancing and improvement of traffic safety. This approach comes as a natural reaction to the political commitments as well as to the needs assessment done so far on the whole transport network prior to entering the programming period.

The following Priority Axes have been identified in the SOPT:

Priority Axis 1: Modernization and development of TEN-T priority axes aiming at sustainable transport system integrated with EU transport networks.

Priority Axis 2: Modernization and development of the national transport infrastructure outside the TEN-T priority axes aiming at sustainable national transport system.

Priority Axis 3: Modernization of transport sector aiming at higher degree of environmental protection, human health and passenger safety.

Priority Axis 4: Technical assistance.

The Sectoral Operational Programme Environment (SOP ENV)

The SOP ENV has been drawn up in correlation with the third Priority of Romania's NDP 2007-2013—"Protection and improvement of environment quality" and the priorities under NSRF—"Develop Basic Infrastructure to European Standards." The SOP ENV contains essential elements for the successful implementation of the NDP and NSRF referring to environmental protection development; its basic objective is to promote sustainable development of the country.

The SOP's total budget for the 2007-2013 programming period amounts to about Euro 5.6 billion. Out of this, about Euro 4.5 billion is envisaged as Community support, which represents about 23.5% of the financial envelope of the NSRF, and about Euro 1.1 billion comes from national contribution. The Community sources that will support SOP ENV implementation are Cohesion Fund and European Regional Development Fund.

The SOP ENV strategy for 2007-2013 focuses on investments and collective services, which are required to increase long term competitiveness, job creation and sustainable development. Basic infrastructures and services will need to be created, upgraded, and expanded in order to open up regional and local economies, set up an effective business support framework and exploit opportunities afforded by the European Market. Establishment of effective water and environmental infrastructure will create potential for new jobs (construction, services, SMEs, etc.) and in a way reduce the workforce migration giving possibilities for population to develop businesses or to attract other investors by using also local competitive advantages (cheaper resources, valuable natural areas, etc.). In order to put in practice this strategy, the following priority axes are identified:

Priority Axis 1: Extension and modernization of water and wastewater systems.

Priority Axis 2: Development of integrated waste management systems and rehabilitation of historically contaminated sites.

Priority Axis 3: Reduction of pollution and mitigation of climate change by restructuring and renovating urban heating systems towards energy efficiency targets in the identified local environmental hotspots.

Priority Axis 4: Implementation of adequate management systems for nature protection.

Priority Axis 5: Implementation of adequate infrastructure of natural risk prevention in most vulnerable areas.

Priority Axis 6: Technical assistance.

The Operational Programme "Administrative Capacity Development" (OP ACD)

The revised Lisbon Strategy calls for better legislation, policy design, and delivery in order to create the conditions for economic growth and job creation. Administrative capacity development can make a direct contribution to the achievement of these objectives. The OP ACD will be financed by the EU with EUR 208 million and the national co-financing is expected to be EUR 38 million.

Public institutions can contribute to socio-economic development programmes through the performance of the following functions:

- Improving decision making processes, including the quality of major investment.
- Choices (knowledge and human resources) and project selection (information, regulation, and feed-back mechanism).
- Ensuring a better implementation and enforcement of legislation.
- Improving the regulation mechanism especially through setting up a standardized model for quantifying the compliance costs imposed by issued regulation.
- Ensuring adequate framework for economic activities (human resources, data, legal aspects).
- Improving the public decision making processes.
- Ensuring quality and efficiency in public service delivery.
- Increasing the number of civil servants who hold professional qualification in HRM, finance, economics, and law.

The Government has identified the following main priority areas where interventions are most needed and are likely to have the highest value-added:

- Building effective decision making and accountability processes that enhance organizational effectiveness.
- Improving the quality and efficiency standards in the delivery of public services, primarily on a decentralized basis.

There are three priority sectors for support—health, education, and social assistance. This was based on the stage of their decentralization process—the three sectors being the most advanced—and their overall contribution to the socio-economic development, as indicated by their size in the public expenditure, the number of public servants employed in the sectors, the number of subordinated/decentralized institutions and the extent of the population that is reached.

Taking into consideration the above mentioned, the OP ACD will be implemented through the following Priority Axes:

Priority Axis 1: Structural and process improvements of the public policy management cycle.

Priority Axis 2: Improved quality and efficiency of the delivery of public services on a decentralised basis.

Priority Axis 3: Technical assistance.

The Operational Programme Technical Assistance (OP TA)

The OP TA was prepared by the Ministry of Economy and Finance in agreement with other Ministries acting as Managing Authorities for the other OPs, as well as other relevant institutions. The suggested objectives, Priority Axes and key areas of intervention are horizontal, and were split between OP TA and the remaining OPs on the basis of the principles of complementarity, subsidiarity, and logical coherence, with due concern for the guidelines underlying the Structural Instruments implementation system.

The technical assistance priority axes within the other OPs will provide specific assistance for project preparation, monitoring, evaluation, and control, as well as for communication activities ensuring appropriate publicity, only with regard to specificity of each OP. This specific assistance is to be complemented with horizontal assistance tools addressing the common needs of all structures and actors involved in the management and implementation of the Structural Instruments, with the development of an effective Single Management Information System able to provide transparent information on fund absorptions, with horizontal activities aiming at general public awareness on the role of the Community support and a general understanding of the interventions of Structural Instruments. These three general areas of intervention require the preparation and implementation of a horizontal operational programme for technical assistance.

It is expected that about 75% of the total technical assistance for structural policy tasks financed from the Structural and Cohesion Funds under the Convergence Objective will be allocated to TA priority axes within the OPs. The remaining balance of technical assistance funds will be spent on implementing interventions within OP TA.

The priority axes and interventions under OP TA will be entirely co-financed from the European Regional Development Fund. The OP's total budget envisaged for the period 2007-2013 is approximately 212.8 mil. Euro, out of which 170.24 mil. Euro is envisaged as Community support (80%) and around 42.56 mil. Euro (20%) will come from public sources. Hence, in accordance to the above mentioned, the following Priority Axes have been identified within OP TA:

Priority Axis 1: Support to the implementation of Structural Instruments and coordination of programmes.

Priority Axis 2: Further development and support for the functioning of the Single Management Information System.

Priority Axis 3: Dissemination of information and promotion of Structural Instruments.

Public Procurement

The creation of the European Union imposed the accomplishment of standards that can be applied in a unitary way in all member countries. We consider that the necessity to eliminate barriers in national public procurement systems represents a key-element of economic integration at European level. We rely for this assertion on the major volume of public procurement, which at the level of the European Union represents an important market counting more than 1,000 billion Euros a year or approximately 19% of GDP. Under the circumstances of the current economic crisis, this sector constitutes an essential element for growth. In this context, the harmonization of national legislations in the domain, as well as the process of facilitating the interconnection of national public procurement systems imposed the achievement of specific standards, which allow the access of all economic operators to the European market, by the participation to procedures initiated by contracting authorities from any member state. For this purpose, the European Parliament has issued Directives 2004/17/EC and 2004/18/EC, which establish the legal framework for carrying out public procurement. With the help of the working group ISSS WS BII ("Business Interoperability Interfaces on public procurement in Europe") CEN—the European Committee for Standardization—aimed to create a European standard for interoperability in e-procurement. The profiles describe rules and scenarios that are applied to electronic messages exchange within procurement procedures. Starting from the requirements formulated by participant countries, there have been identified several profiles afferent to the phases included in the process of carrying out public procurement, until the contract award and in the period following and supervising its execution. A first implementation of the new standard has been achieved within the pilot project PEPPOL (Pan-European Public Procurement Online), initiated by the European Commission, which aims to design a model of common virtual market for European public procurement, by the interconnection of current e-procurement systems at national or regional level. In order to join and adhere to the interoperability model, member states must adapt the e-procurement systems, the standards, and the national legislation. At the moment, only eleven countries participate in this pilot project (Austria, Denmark, Finland, France, Germany, Greece, Italy, Norway, Portugal, Sweden, and the United Kingdom of Great Britain). It is estimated that the replacement of classic methods for the accomplishment of public procurement with electronic methods at the level of the entire European Union would lead to annual savings between 50 and 75 billion Euros.

Romania's accession to the European Union imposed the alignment to the requirements of European standards in all domains and consequently, in the domain of public procurement. Thus, European legislation was transposed into national legislation. We consider that this was not efficiently achieved, since a new intricate and too elaborate legislation, abounding in exceptions, was generated. The Electronic Public Procurement System, created to comply with the requirements imposed by the European Union, does not yet contribute to the setting up of a competitive business environment, as it does not contribute to the increase of transparency in the way public money is spent, as we will demonstrate further on.

The main causes of syncope registered in performing procurement procedures find their origin in the ambiguity of legislation and especially in the different interpretation by different institutions which have control attributions in this sector. The fact that legislative interpretations given by

the National Authority for the Regulation and Monitoring of Public Procurement regarding the same issue are different from one year to another is also paradoxical.

Taking into account the fact that the execution of any public procurement, irrespective of the fact that this procedure can take place through and by means of the electronic system, starts from determining the estimated value, we consider it is important to briefly analyze this aspect. A major difficulty in the Romanian public procurement system is represented by the determination of the estimated value of contracts. The estimated value constitutes an essential piece of information for planning and carrying out procurement. Though the legislation in the field establishes a set of rules for estimating the value of public procurement contracts, these are summary and evasive, and they have thus led to different interpretations. If initially the estimated value was considered to be calculated at the level of each CPV code, there was subsequently proposed, as preventive measure, the reporting and relating of the estimated value of the public procurement contract not to a CPV code, but to a necessity, to which there can be attributed one or several CPV codes (of products/services/works). However, this "necessity" was not clearly defined, so we are asking ourselves: till where can the interpretation be extended and till where can the "necessity" be determined? It is a question to which the legislator does not have a concrete answer that can eliminate the ambiguity, ambiguity that can engender a breach of the principles of public procurement and can raise correctness issues in the carrying out of the whole process. Moreover, in the case of procurement procedures undergone for implementing projects financed from European funds, the point of view of the authority initially considered that "procurement procedures that have been completed correspond to the satisfying of some necessities of the contracting authority in its whole, irrespective of the financing source," and afterwards, the perspective changed so that "each project financed from European funds has specific implementation necessities, and the procurement procedures relate only to that specific project." In conclusion, we assert that we need to take further action and we need regulation measures that can allow the contracting authorities to determine the estimated value of public procurement contracts in a unitary way.

The Electronic Public Procurement System (SEAP) was conceived with the aim to become a virtual market for the acquisition of goods, services, and works that allow performing public procurement procedures in the conditions of a fair behavior on behalf of all participants, whether they represent contracting authorities, or they are bidders. From the moment of its launch until now, SEAP has suffered a series of changes that allowed a greater transparency of procurement procedures. Otherwise, it is foreseen in the regulations that all procedures of awarding, of open tendering, restrained tendering, procurement notice, negotiation with the publication of a preliminary contract notice, competitive dialogue and competition of solutions, be carried out through SEAP, except for negotiations without preliminary contract notices. The system allows the execution of these procedures entirely by electronic means or just finalizing off-line procedures with a final phase of electronic bidding. The use of electronic means for performing public procurement procedures is a key-element for achieving the aim of interoperability between procurement systems from different European Union states.

In Romania, the Electronic Public Procurement System (SEAP) allows performing the following operations:

- Transmission of awarding documentation and of explanatory notes to be validated by the National Authority for the Regulation and Monitoring of Public Procurement.
- Publication of contract notices.
- Carrying out the initial phase of electronic bidding.

- Performing the entire procurement procedure online.
- Publication of contract award notices.

Through SEAP, a digital catalogue for direct procurement of services and works is placed at the disposal of those interested by the contracting authorities.

The system's functionality, even though it has substantially improved lately, can generate errors, which determine the non-completion or the repetition of the entire procurement process. We consider that this fact can lead to loss of financing and can engender supplementary costs uselessly paid from public funds. On the one hand, there are cases where the wrong configuration of an electronic bidding as final phase of an off-line procedure has led to the annulment of the entire procedure, since the system did not allow coming back to the initial phase (before the launch of the final phase of electronic bidding). On the other hand, we can raise the issue of the legality of the financial offer within the electronic bidding. As it is well known, the modification of the financial offer imposes declaring it non-conforming. We are wondering ourselves if we are not at the border of legality by allowing economic operators to change their financial offer or proposal. Another debatable issue that draws critical comments regarding the initial phase of electronic bidding is linked to the fact that applying it can engender a breach of the principle of efficient use of public funds. Being informed by the procurement data sheet and by the contract notice, the economic operators create a strategy to tender a value as close as possible to the estimated value published in the Electronic Public Procurement System, sometimes tendering precisely at the level of this value. We encounter rare cases when these economic operators bid a right price before the phase of electronic bidding. We can say that they all count on the fact that during the phase of electronic bidding they will lower the price no matter how much in order to win the contract. However, there are often cases when during the final stage of electronic bidding only one admissible offer is qualified, and the economic operator is not anymore interested to lower the price initially tendered. We assert that in these cases the principle of efficient use of public funds is breached since there is no real competition between economic operators. This is justified by the fact the awarding of the contract is done at the estimated value determined by the contracting authority, which most of the times is situated at a high level. This should not be reproached to those who determine the estimated value, since they do not have access to discounts or other advantages offered by suppliers to different dealers.

A recent study coordinated by the Institute for Public Policies (IPP) and carried out with the help of the United States' Embassy in Bucharest, within the Program Democracy Grants, reveals the fact that each year, in Romania, there are performed over 80,000 procedures through the Electronic Public Procurement System. The same study mentions the fact that 62% of the contracts awarded through SEAP in 2009 and 2010 in Romania were concluded following an online procedure, but their value is relatively low, raising at the level of 2.8 billion Euros, that is approximately 14% of the total value of acquisitions. On the other hand, the rest of 38% of the number of procurement procedures executed through SEAP were not performed online, but their value was of over 16.9 billion Euros, that is approximately 86% of the total value. The same study draws the conclusion that, by relating only official numbers regarding the volume of acquisitions annually transacted through the Electronic Public Procurement System to the average of public procurement carried out at the level of member states of the European Union, only a percentage of 40% is performed through SEAP (only advertising or thoroughly), the rest being performed outside this platform.

If as regards the transparency in the performance of procurement procedures, we can appreciate that the Functionality of SEAP is as-

sured, the same thing does not apply in the stage of supervision of procurement contracts, stage during which some contracting authorities can change technical solutions or can increase without any justification, over the legal limits, the initially awarded value.

Analyzed on the whole, the process of public procurement in Romania is faced with deficiencies, for it is governed by a legislation which leaves space for interpretations and it is supervised by a series of institutions which have different points of view (the National Authority for the Regulation and Monitoring of Public Procurement, the Unit for Coordinating and Checking Public Procurement within the Ministry of Finances, the National Council for Solving Contestations, the Court of Auditors). We often encounter cases in which different institutions—acknowledged for the control of public procurement—adopt conflicting decisions. We can easily notice that we are witnessing a too wide distribution of responsibility.

From our point of view, in order to improve the Romanian public procurement system, the following measures must be taken: the elaboration of a less intricate legislation, but at the same time coherent and clear, without ambiguities; a considerable enhancement of the functionality of the Electronic Public Procurement System; the constitution of a single body competent in performing the control, since in this situation the responsibility is objectively identified.

Theoretical Models

A key point of interest in this phase of the implementation of operational programmes in Romania is to understand how absorption is ensured as a pre-requisite for the N+3/N+2 rule compliance in the short run but also as a pre-requisite for ensuring the expected impact in the medium and long run.

For performing the analysis, an Autoregressive Conditional Heteroskedasticity (ARCH) model has been developed (Bowerman, 2004; Stewart, 2005), based on the block diagram presented in

Figure 1. Such models are specifically designed to model and forecast conditional variances. The variance of the dependent variable is modeled as a function of past values of the dependent variable and independent, or exogenous variables. The significance of all variables used in Figure 1 are described in Table 1.

ARCH models were introduced by Engle (1982) and generalized as GARCH (Generalized ARCH) by Bollerslev (1986). These models are widely used in various branches of econometrics, especially in financial time series analysis. See Bollerslev, Chou, and Kroner (1992) and Bollerslev *et al.* (1994) for recent surveys. Another relevant characteristic for the scope of this chapter is that such models provide a stable behaviour in the case of systems characterized by a high degree of volatility or non-determination (in the sense that there are exogeneous variables with hard to be predicted evolution).

In a classical approach, a GARCH (1,1) model is characterized by the following set of equations:

$$y_t = x'_t \gamma + \varepsilon_t; \qquad (1)$$

$$\sigma_t^2 = \omega + \alpha \varepsilon_{t-1}^2 + \beta \sigma_{t-1}^2 \qquad (2)$$

where the mean equation given in Equation 1 is written as a function of exogenous variables with an error term. Since σ_t^2 is the one-period ahead forecast variance based on past information, it is called the conditional variance. The conditional variance equation specified in Equation 2 is a function of three terms:

1. ω : The mean.
2. ε_{t-1}^2 : News about volatility from the previous period, measured as the lag of the squared residual from the mean equation—the ARCH term.
3. σ_{t-1}^2 : Last period's forecast variance—the GARCH term.

Figure 1. The generic econometric model conceived/used for performing the analysis

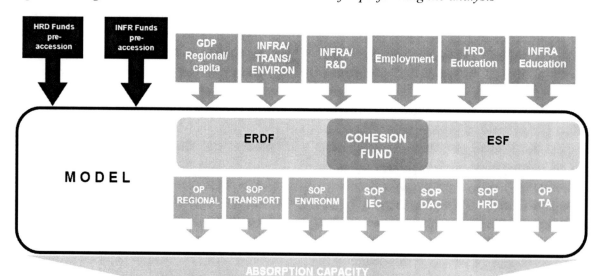

Table 1. Variables of the econometric model

Variable	Description
ABS_POAT_P	Time serie with payments for OP TA
ABS_POAT_V	Time serie with contracted amounts for OP TA
ABS_PODCA_P	Time serie with payments for OP ACD
ABS_PODCA_V	Time serie with contracted amounts for OP ACD
ABS_POR_P	Time serie with payments for ROP
ABS_POR_V	Time serie with contracted amounts for ROP
ABS_POSCCE_P	Time serie with payments for SOP IEC
ABS_POSCCE_V	Time serie with contracted amounts for SOP IEC
ABS_POSDRU_P	Time serie with payments for SOP HRD
ABS_POSDRU_V	Time serie with contracted amounts for SOP HRD
ABS_POSMEDIU_P	Time serie with payments for SOP ENV
ABS_POSMEDIU_V	Time serie with contracted amounts for SOP ENV
ABS_POSTRANS_P	Time serie with payments for SOP T
ABS_POSTRANS_V	Time serie with contracted amounts for SOP T
CD_PRE_BIF	Time serie number of persons RTD sector – BIF Region
DR_PRE_BIF	Time serie length of roads – BIF Region
DRDENS_PRE_BIF	Time serie density of roads – BIF Region
DRM_PRE_BIF	Time serie lengths of modernized roads – BIF Region
HRD_PRE_BIF	Time serie pre-accession funds HRD type – BIF Region
INFRA_PRE_BIF	Time serie pre-accession funds INFR type – BIF Region
IRU	Table HR indices (regional level - 15 variables)
PIB_REG	GDB/capita at the level of development regions
PO_AT_P_X	Payments performed at regional level OP TA
PO_AT_PROC_X	Percentage payments/contracted amounts OP TA at regional level
PO_AT_V_X	Contracted amounts OP TA at regional level
PO_DCA_P_X	Payments performed at regional level OP ACD
PO_DCA_PROC_X	Percentage payments/contracted amounts OP ACD at regional level
PO_DCA_V_X	Contracted amounts OP ACD at regional level
PO_PROC_X	Percentage payments/contracted amounts for OP
POP_REG	Number of inhabitants at the level of development regions
POR_P_X	Payments performed at regional level ROP
POR_PROC_X	Percentage payments/contracted amounts ROP at regional level
POR_V_X	Contracted amounts ROP at regional level
POS_CCE_P_X	Payments performed at regional level SOP IEC
POS_CCE_PROC_X	Percentage payments/contracted amounts SOP IEC at regional level
POS_CCE_V_X	Contracted amounts SOP IEC at regional level
POS_DRU_P_X	Payments performed at regional level SOP HRD

continued on following page

Table 1. Continued

Variable	Description
POS_DRU_PROC_X	Percentage payments/contracted amounts SOP HRD at regional level
POS_DRU_V_X	Contracted amounts SOP HRD at regional level
POS_MED_P_X	Payments performed at regional level SOP ENV
POS_MED_PROC_X	Percentage payments/contracted amounts SOP ENV at regional level
POS_MED_V_X:	Contracted amounts SOP ENV at regional level
POS_TR_P_X	Payments performed at regional level SOP T
POS_TR_PROC_X	Percentage payments/contracted amounts SOP T
POS_TR_V_X	Contracted amounts SOP T at regional level
RU	Table values HR (regional level - 15 variables)
SOMAJ_BIF	Time serie unemployment BIF Region

The (1,1) in GARCH(1,1) refers to the presence of a first-order GARCH term (the first term in parentheses) and a first-order ARCH term (the second term in parentheses). An ordinary ARCH model is a special case of a GARCH specification in which there are no lagged fore- cast variances in the conditional variance equation.

ARCH models in EViews are estimated by the method of maximum likelihood under the assumption that the errors are conditionally normally distributed. For example, for the GARCH(1,1) model, the contribution to the log likelihood from observation t is:

$$l_t = \frac{-\frac{1}{2}\log\left(2\pi\right) - \frac{1}{2}\log\sigma_t^2 - \frac{1}{2}\left(y_t - x_t'\right)^2}{\sigma_t^2} \qquad (3)$$

where:

$$\sigma_t^2 = \omega + \alpha\left(y_{t-1} - x_{t-1}'\gamma\right)^2 + \beta\sigma_{t-1}^2 \qquad (4)$$

There are two alternative representations of the variance equation that may aid in the interpretation of the model:

• If we recursively substitute for the lagged variance on the right-hand side of Equation 2, we can express the conditional variance as a weighted average of all of the lagged squared residuals:

$$\sigma_t^2 = \frac{\omega}{1-\beta} + \alpha\sum_{j=1}^{\infty}\beta^{j-1}\varepsilon_{t-j}^2 \qquad (5)$$

• We see that the GARCH (1,1) variance specification is analogous to the sample variance, but that it down-weights more distant lagged squared errors.
• The error in the squared returns is given by $v_t = \varepsilon_t^2 - \sigma_t^2$.

Substituting for the variances in the variance equation and rearranging terms we can write our model in terms of the errors:

$$\varepsilon_t^2 = \omega + \left(\alpha + \beta\right)\varepsilon_{t-1}^2 + v_t - \beta v_{t-1} \qquad (6)$$

- Thus, the squared errors follow a heteroskedastic ARMA(1,1) process. The autoregressive root which governs the persistence of volatility shocks is the sum of $\alpha + \beta$. In many applied settings, this root is very close to unity so that shocks die out rather slowly.

Equation 2 may be extended to allow for the inclusion of exogenous or predetermined regressors, z, in the variance equation:

$$\sigma_t^2 = \omega + \alpha \varepsilon_t^2 + \beta \sigma_{t-1}^2 + \pi z_t \qquad (7)$$

The x in Equation 2 represents exogenous or predetermined variables that are included in the mean equation. If we introduce the conditional variance into the mean equation, we get the ARCH-in-Mean (ARCH-M) model (Engle, et al., 1987):

$$y_t = x_t' \gamma + \sigma_t^2 + \varepsilon_t \qquad (8)$$

A variant of the ARCH-M specification uses the conditional standard deviation in place of the conditional variance. In this case, due to high dynamic of the variables flow, it was chosen a set of constant regression factors, hence preventing the increase of the hyper-reactivity of the model.

MAIN FOCUS OF THE CHAPTER

One of the main original aspects of the current chapter is represented by the fact that, despite the lack of historical data about the absorption of structural funds via the seven Operational Programmes, it is worth observing what was happening during the pre-accession period and to consider time series characterizing the absorption of pre-accession funds at the level of NUTS 2 development regions (Bagliano & Bertola, 2004;

Bradley & Zaleski, 2003; Bradley & Morgenroth, 2003; Capello, 2007; Gherghinescu, et al., 2010; Kejak & Vavra, 2005; Rinderu, et al., 2009). In this way it was possible to extrapolate the analysis over a larger interval (from 3 to 10 years) via a function which can induce discontinuities as most up to the first degree one, hence staying within the continuity assumptions when considering such approaches. This section will focus on building econometric models for analyzing the absorption of structural funds considering projects implemented within each Operational Program at the level of the weal thiest—NUTS2 region in Romania—Bucharest-Ilfov (BIF). The process of submitting and implementing projects, considering the specificities of the OPs will be also discussed (see Figures 2, 3, 4, 5, 6, 7, and 8; and corresponding Tables 2, 3, 4, 5, 6, 7, and 8).

Innovative Tools and their Potential Contribution to an Efficient, Effective Implementation of Operational Programmes in Romania

Pre-accession programmes implementation in Romania has been characterized to a very large extent by a "classical approach" to submitting projects and reporting their implementation. Although the quantity of paper to be used for implementing a project may not be the best indicator of the complexity of procedures and the administrative burden on beneficiaries, it still is a clue aspect.

The shift to the structural instruments has brought new approaches and instruments in the interface between beneficiaries and managing authorities.

A Web-based solution widely used in one of the operational programmes (Sectoral Operational Programme Human Resources Development) is Actionweb[2]. It is managed by the Managing Authority of SOP HRD and offers multi-level access for potential beneficiaries, beneficiaries, intermediate bodies and the managing authority

Figure 2. Correlogram of standardized residuals – ROP – BIF region

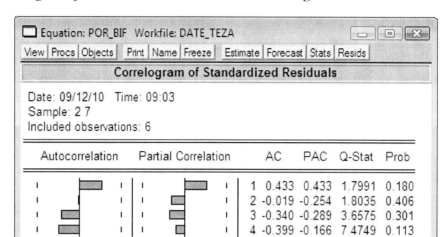

Table 2. Econometric model ROP – BIF region

Dependent Variable: Implicit Equation Estimated by GMM				
Method: ML - ARCH				
Date: 09/11/10		Time: 21:00		
Sample(adjusted): 2 7				
Included Observations: 6 after adjusting endpoints				
Convergence achieved after 1 iteration				
LOG(POR_P_X(8,1))-(C(1)*LOG(POR_V_X(8,1)*POP_REG(8,1) *PIB_REG(8,1))+C(2)*LOG(INFRA_PRE_BIF(-1)) +C(3) *LOG(DR_PRE_BIF(-1)*PIB_REG(8,1)*POP_REG(8,1) *DRM_PRE_BIF(-1)*DRDENS_PRE_BIF(-1)))				
	Coefficient	Std. Error	z-Statistic	Prob.
C(1)	0.398498	0.006857	58.11597	0.0000
C(2)	-2.87E-13	0.000106	-2.71E-09	1.0000
C(3)	0.000000	7.62E-05	0.000000	1.0000
C(4)	3.52E-27	0.000303	1.16E-23	1.0000
C(5)	0.150000	22.51351	0.006663	0.9947
C(6)	0.600000	7.211531	0.083200	0.9337
Akaike info criterion:	-55.43057		Sum squared resid:	3.25E-26
Schwarz criterion:	-55.63881		Log likelihood:	172.2917
Durbin-Watson stat:	0.465604			

Figure 3. Correlogram of standardized residuals – SOP IEC – BIF region

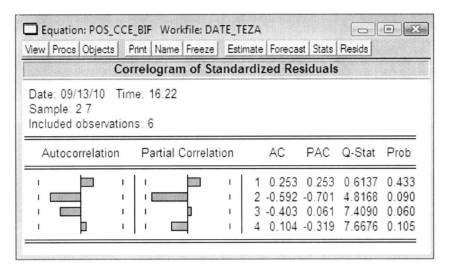

Table 3. Econometric model SOP IEC – BIF region

Dependent Variable: Implicit Equation Estimated by GMM				
Method: ML - ARCH				
Date: 09/11/10		Time: 21:35		
Sample(adjusted): 2 7				
Included Observations: 6 after adjusting endpoints				
Convergence achieved after 1 iteration				
LOG(POS_CCE_P_X(8,1))-(C(1)*LOG(POS_CCE_V_X(8,1) *POP_REG(8,1)*PIB_REG(8,1))+C(2)*LOG(INFRA_PRE_BIF(-1) *CD_PRE_BIF(-1)) +C(3)*LOG(HRD_PRE_BIF(-1)*PIB_REG(8,1) *POP_REG(8,1)*IRU(8,1)*IRU(8,9)))				
	Coefficient	**Std. Error**	**z-Statistic**	**Prob.**
C(1)	0.403396	0.000969	416.3396	0.0000
C(2)	-3.86E-13	4.30E-05	-8.97E-09	1.0000
C(3)	8.22E-13	2.67E-05	3.08E-08	1.0000
C(4)	4.05E-26	1.96E-05	2.06E-21	1.0000
C(5)	0.150000	15.65835	0.009580	0.9924
C(6)	0.600000	7.139587	0.084038	0.9330
Akaike info criterion:	-53.12744		Sum squared resid:	3.74E-25
Schwarz criterion:	-53.33568		Log likelihood:	165.3823
Durbin-Watson stat:	1.211053			

Figure 4. Correlogram of standardized residuals – SOP HRD – BIF region

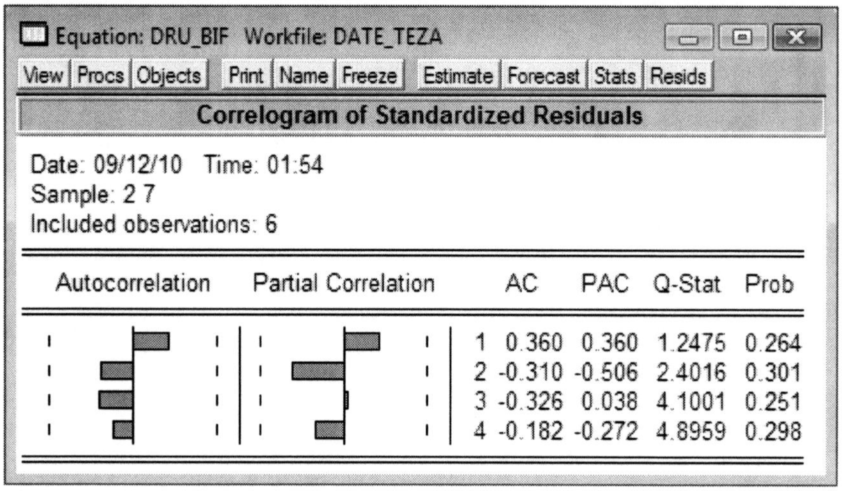

Table 4. Econometric model SOP HRD – BIF region

Dependent Variable: Implicit Equation Estimated by GMM				
Method: ML - ARCH				
Date: 09/11/10		Time: 20:43		
Sample(adjusted): 2 7				
Included Observations: 6 after adjusting endpoints				
Convergence achieved after 1 iteration				

LOG(POS_DRU_P_X(8,1))-(C(1)*LOG(POS_DRU_V_X(8,1)
    *POP_REG(8,1)*PIB_REG(8,1))+C(2)*LOG(HRD_PRE_BIF(-1)
    *POS_DRU_V_X(8,1)*IRU(8,1)*IRU(8,2)*IRU(8,3)*IRU(8,4)
    *IRU(8,5)*IRU(8,6)*IRU(8,9)*IRU(8,10)*IRU(8,11)*IRU(8,12))+C(3)
    *LOG(SOMAJ_BIF(-1)*POS_DRU_V_X(8,1)*IRU(8,1)*IRU(8,2)
    *IRU(8,3)*IRU(8,4)*IRU(8,5)*IRU(8,6)*IRU(8,9)*IRU(8,10)*IRU(8,11)
    *IRU(8,12)))				

	Coefficient	**Std. Error**	**z-Statistic**	**Prob.**
C(1)	0.405034	0.015304	26.46543	0.0000
C(2)	2.10E-12	4.58E-05	4.59E-08	1.0000
C(3)	1.84E-12	0.000208	8.82E-09	1.0000
C(4)	3.20E-25	0.000184	1.74E-21	1.0000
C(5)	0.150000	78.27955	0.001916	0.9985
C(6)	0.600000	66.70175	0.008995	0.9928
Akaike info criterion:	-51.13400		Sum squared resid:	2.95E-24
Schwarz criterion:	-51.34224		Log likelihood:	159.4020
Durbin-Watson stat:	0.770866			

Figure 5. Correlogram of standardized residuals – SOPT – BIF region

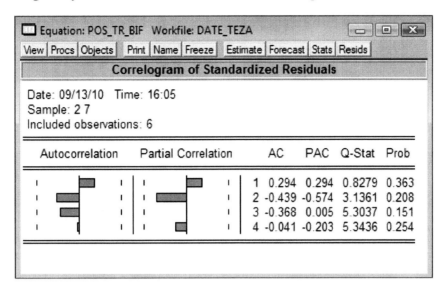

Table 5. Econometric model SOPT – BIF region

Dependent Variable: Implicit Equation Estimated by GMM				
Method: ML - ARCH				
Date: 09/13/10		Time: 16:04		
Sample(adjusted): 2 7				
Included Observations: 6 after adjusting endpoints				
Convergence achieved after 1 iteration				
LOG(POS_TR_P_X(8,1))-(C(1)*LOG(POS_TR_V_X(8,1)*POP_REG(8,1) *PIB_REG(8,1))+C(2)*LOG(INFRA_PRE_BIF(-1)*PIB_REG(8,1)) +C(3)*LOG(POS_TR_V_X(8,1)*DR_PRE_BIF(-1)*DRM_PRE_BIF(-1)*DRDENS_PRE_BIF(-1)))				
	Coefficient	**Std. Error**	**z-Statistic**	**Prob.**
C(1)	0.368585	0.005110	72.13626	0.0000
C(2)	-1.43E-11	0.000137	-1.04E-07	1.0000
C(3)	4.21E-11	7.06E-05	5.96E-07	1.0000
C(4)	2.09E-24	2.27E-05	9.18E-20	1.0000
C(5)	0.150000	9.197808	0.016308	0.9870
C(6)	0.600000	18.08575	0.033175	0.9735
Akaike info criterion:	-49.25466		Sum squared resid:	1.93E-23
Schwarz criterion:	-49.46290		Log likelihood:	153.7640
Durbin-Watson stat:	0.901415			

Figure 6. Correlogram of standardized residuals – SOP ENV – BIF region

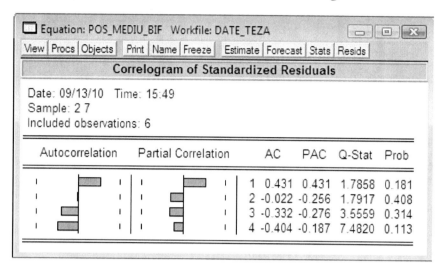

Table 6. Econometric model SOP ENV – BIF region

Dependent Variable: Implicit Equation Estimated by GMM				
Method: ML - ARCH				
Date: 09/11/10		Time: 21:08		
Sample(adjusted): 2 7				
Included Observations: 6 after adjusting endpoints				
Convergence achieved after 1 iteration				
LOG(POS_MED_P_X(8,1))-(C(1)*LOG(POS_MED_V_X(8,1) *POP_REG(8,1)*PIB_REG(8,1))+C(2)*LOG(INFRA_PRE_BIF(-1) *PIB_REG(8,1)) +C(3)*LOG(POS_MED_V_X(8,1)*DR_PRE_BIF(-1)))				
	Coefficient	Std. Error	z-Statistic	Prob.
C(1)	0.414167	0.017447	23.73888	0.0000
C(2)	5.74E-13	0.000910	6.30E-10	1.0000
C(3)	0.000000	0.000540	0.000000	1.0000
C(4)	1.41E-26	0.000736	1.92E-23	1.0000
C(5)	0.150000	53.01841	0.002829	0.9977
C(6)	0.600000	18.55306	0.032340	0.9742
Akaike info criterion:	-54.04070		Sum squared resid:	1.30E-25
Schwarz criterion:	-54.24894		Log likelihood:	168.1221
Durbin-Watson stat:	0.469848			

Figure 7. Correlogram of standardized residuals – SOP ACD – BIF region

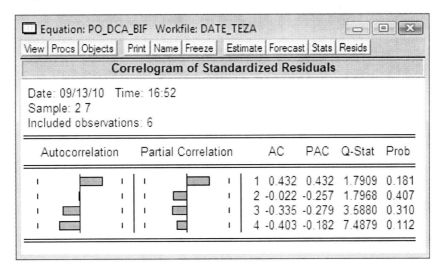

Table 7. Econometric model OP ACD – BIF region

Dependent Variable: Implicit Equation Estimated by GMM				
Method: ML - ARCH				
Date: 09/11/10		Time: 21:49		
Sample(adjusted): 2 7				
Included Observations: 6 after adjusting endpoints				
Convergence achieved after 1 iterations				
LOG(PO_DCA_P_X(8,1))-(C(1)*LOG(PO_DCA_V_X(8,1) *POP_REG(8,1))+C(2)*LOG(INFRA_PRE_BIF(-1)*PIB_REG(8,1)) +C(3)*LOG(HRD_PRE_BIF(-1)*POP_REG(8,1)*IRU(8,1) *IRU(8,9)))				
	Coefficient	**Std. Error**	**z-Statistic**	**Prob.**
C(1)	0.485913	0.005203	93.38796	0.0000
C(2)	-5.74E-13	0.000648	-8.85E-10	1.0000
C(3)	0.000000	0.000108	0.000000	1.0000
C(4)	1.42E-26	0.000738	1.92E-23	1.0000
C(5)	0.150000	34.98232	0.004288	0.9966
C(6)	0.600000	46.63301	0.012866	0.9897
Akaike info criterion:	-54.03705		Sum squared resid:	1.31E-25
Schwarz criterion:	-54.24529		Log likelihood:	168.1112
Durbin-Watson stat:	0.469535			

Figure 8. Correlogram of standardized residuals – OP TA – BIF region

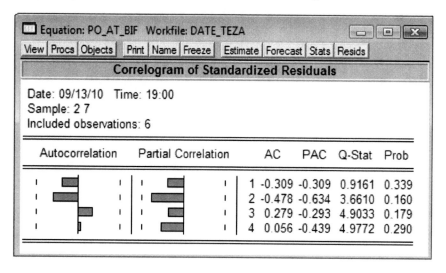

Table 8. Econometric model OP TA – BIF region

Dependent Variable: Implicit Equation Estimated by GMM				
Method: ML - ARCH				
Date: 09/13/10		Time: 19:00		
Sample(adjusted): 2 7				
Included Observations: 6 after adjusting endpoints				
Convergence achieved after 19 iterations				
LOG(PO_AT_P_X(8,1))-(C(1)*LOG(PO_AT_V_X(8,1)*CD_PRE_BIF(-1) *IRU(8,1)*IRU(8,9))+C(2)*LOG(INFRA_PRE_BIF(-1) *PIB_REG(8,1)) +C(3)*LOG(HRD_PRE_BIF(-1)*POP_REG(8,1)))				
	Coefficient	Std. Error	z-Statistic	Prob.
C(1)	0.469497	0.013111	35.81046	0.0000
C(2)	-0.037027	0.038307	-0.966589	0.3337
C(3)	0.053421	0.028471	1.876337	0.0606
C(4)	4.63E-05	0.000562	0.082389	0.9343
C(5)	-0.144660	1.611911	-0.089744	0.9285
C(6)	0.578882	6.330025	0.091450	0.9271
Akaike info criterion:	-4.677062		Sum squared resid:	0.000469
Schwarz criterion:	-4.885303		Log likelihood:	20.03119
Durbin-Watson stat:	2.514542			

itself. The main three phases in the life cycle of a POS DRU project supported by Actionweb are:

1. The project identification and submission.
2. The project assessment.
3. The project implementation.

Project Identification and Submission

Unlike the classical approach of project submission in hard copy, MA SOP HRD offers potential beneficiaries the opportunity of creating and submitting their project online.

By a very simple process of registration, every potential beneficiary can get the credentials for its account, which will host all the applications submitted, rejected, approved, and implemented for the respective entity.

After registration, the Web platform offers information on the guidelines of the open available calls. Once opened a project application, the beneficiary has access to the specific labels, which are not much different from the ones that are included in any project application form. Main sections refer to: the applicant, its partners, the project objectives, activities description and planning, results, indicators including the ones related to the target group, horizontal aspects and the budget. Limited quantity of text is allowed for every label; therefore, the beneficiary has to select the most relevant one when writing the application.

The online application form allows changes of the information until the moment when it is finally submitted and closed by the applicant. From this moment on, the beneficiary is not allowed to change its content.

The finalization of the online submission will generate a list of annexes to be sent in hard copy to the Managing Authority/Intermediate Bodies, whose number and dimension are really low.

Project Assessment

When filling in the application form, the potential beneficiary has to pay attention not to disclose its identity in most of the labels. If such a thing happens, the application will be rejected.

Independent evaluators have access to the labels of the application form which do not disclose the identity of the beneficiary and therefore the impartiality and independence are fully ensured.

Project Implementation

Successful applications are shown in the system as approved and the contracting process can start. This step is mainly based on the submission of hard copies. After the contract has been signed, the project is displayed in Actionweb as started and new labels are available, linked to the financial and technical implementation of the project.

- **Financial Implementation:** The list of expenses and supporting documents can be filled in online by the applicant.
  For the first reimbursement request, the online data is accompanied by supporting documents in hard copies for all the expenditure reported. Starting the second reimbursement request and depending on the risk class of the project, Actionweb generates a sample of documents that need to be submitted on hard paper.
- **Technical Implementation:** Actionweb offers a module for the evidence of the target group.
  The main advantages of Actionweb can be summarized as follows:
  - A practical way of ensuring access to information for potential beneficiaries, beneficiaries, evaluators and staff of the MA/IBs.
  - A practical way of following the status of a project in various phases of its life cycle.

○ A practical way of submitting a project, avoiding the handling of large piles of papers.

○ A practical way of evaluating a project.

○ An effective way of financial reporting.

Although such an approach may not be a key factor for increasing absorption, it is an important tool to reduce the bureaucratic burden for beneficiaries in the process of submitting and implementing projects. As a matter of fact, SOP HRD is one of the most addressed operational programmes in Romania.

Solutions and Recommendations

After running the models for each region, the following set of specific conclusions has been depicted:

- Due to the differences in magnitude order of several variables it was considered a logarithmic scale in order to facilitate the convergence process. A very peculiar task was to slightly modify the values of time-series in cases when the same value for two consecutive years appeared, hence to eliminate the overflow errors.

- All models converge, but present a quite high degree of volatility. This is explained both by the limited number of observations and by the impossibility of modeling some external factors (e.g. political changes in the legislation, etc.).

- All applied statistical tests (Akaike, Schwarz, Durbin-Watson) and the corresponding correlograms present normal values and shapes.

- It is very much sensitive to assess the quality of the absorption process at regional level.

- The model might be used for future analyses concerning the absorption of structural funds in Romania.

- The model could be refined by introducing supplementary variables and could be also serve as a powerful instrument in developing future strategies for absorbing the structural funds in Romania, to have better programming exercises in the future.

- Absorption depends to a large extent to the simplification of bureaucratic arrangements in the management of operational programmes. The chapter has shown an example of best practice in increasing the effectiveness of communication between MA and beneficiaries by the use of a Web platform.

- Online tools cannot, however, support big steps forward when it comes to absorption if they are not complemented by strong monitoring arrangements for incentivating projects to spend and report regularly; administrative measures to allow the MA and IB to process reimbursements faster; favoring projects which are resorting to simple implementation procedures and therefore can spend faster.

CONCLUSION

The general conclusions of this chapter refers to three main aspects: (1) The use of structural funds via the operational programmes at country/regional level represents the most important tool for sustainable development and socio-economic progress; (2) The proposed models for analyzing the absorption of these funds are highly original and might constitute a precise tool for further programming exercises and assessment of their efficiency and effectiveness; (3) the proposed models could be used for performing the same type of analysis for the other seven NUTS2 development regions in Romania and, further on, a global model at country level could be used; (4) new mechanisms to foster absorption have to be identified in relation to how the calls are designed; how the MA and IB deal with the process of issuing calls, project evaluation, contracting, monitoring, expenditure verification; how the beneficiaries can increase their commitment to project implementation, spending, and reporting; (5) among the many possible directions of simplification of procedures, the use of Web platforms in the implementation of an operational programme can be considered.

ACKNOWLEDGMENT

This work was supported by the strategic grant POSDRU/89/1.5/S/61968, Project ID61968 (2009), co-financed by the European Social Fund within the Sectoral Operational Programme Human Resources Development 2007 – 2013.

REFERENCES

Bagliano, F. C., & Bertola, G. (2004). *Models for dynamic macroeconomics*. Oxford, UK: Oxford University Press. doi:10.1093/0199266824.001.0001

Bollerslev, T., Chou, Y. R., & Kroner, F. K. (1992). Arch modeling in finance: A review of the theory and empirical evidence. *Journal of Econometrics, 52*, 5–59. doi:10.1016/0304-4076(92)90064-X

Bowerman, L. B., O'Connell, T. R., & Koehler, B. A. (2004). *Forecasting, time series, and regression: An applied approach*. Chula Vista, CA: South-Western College Publication.

Bradley, J., & Morgenroth, E. (2004). *A study of the macro-economic impact of the reform of EU cohesion policy*. Retrieved from http://ec.europa.eu/regional_policy/sources/docgener/studies/pdf/3cr/macro_impact.pdf

Bradley, J., & Zaleski, J. (2003). *Modeling EU accession and structural fund impacts using the new Polish HERMIN model - Report*. Retrieved from http://www.funduszestrukturalne.gov.pl/NR/rdonlyres/76D3C5FA-B01A-494C-AB9D-D31C3F624193/14808/REVISEDJBradleyJZaleski_HERMIN-PolandafterCopenhage.pdf

Capello, R. (2007). *Regional economics*. London, UK: Routledge.

Gherghinescu, O., Rinderu, P., & Iova, C. (2010). *Econometric modeling - Between relevance and simplicity*. Paper presented at 6th International Conference on Applied Business Research. Dubai, United Arab Emirates.

Kejak, M., & Vavra, D. (2005). *The impact of EU structural funds on the Czech macroeconomy: Some preliminary results from the HERMIN model, report*. Prague, Czech Republic: Czech National Bank.

Rinderu, P., Iova, C., Gherghinescu, O., & Neagoe-Bacanu, D. (2009). *Comparison between HRD pre-accession funds and European social fund absorption at regional level in Romania*. Paper presented at 5th International Conference on Applied Business Research. Malta, Malta.

Stewart, G. K. (2005). *Introduction to applied econometrics*. London, UK: Thomson Brooks.

ADDITIONAL READING

Andrews, D. W. K., & Christopher, M. J. (1992). An improved heteroskedasticity and autocorrelation consistent covariance matrix estimato. *Econometrica, 60*, 953–966. doi:10.2307/2951574

Armstrong, H., & Taylor, J. (2000). *Regional economics and policy*. Oxford, UK: Blackwell.

Dobrescu, E. (2006). *Macromodels of the Romanian market economy*. Bucuresti, Romania: Editura Economică.

European Council. (2005). *Financial perspective 2007-2013*. Brussels, Belgium: European Council.

Ezekiel, M., & Fox, K. A. (1961). *Methods of correlation and regression analysis*. New York, NY: John Wiley & Sons, Inc.

Fahrmeir, L., & Tutz, G. (1994). *Multivarinte statistical modeling based on generalized linear midels*. London, UK: Springer.

Feldkircher, M. (2006). *Regional convergence within the EU-25: A spatial econometric analysis*. Paper presented in OeNB Workshops - New Regional Economics in Central European Economies: The Future of CENTROPE, OeNB. Vienna, Austria.

Fota, C. (2007). *Integrarea României în Uniunea Europeană*. Bucharest, Romania: Editura Sitech.

Gherghinescu, O. (2007). *Fondul social European – Manual universitar*. Craiova, Romania: Editura Sitech.

Gherghinescu, O., Iova, C., & Rinderu, P. (2009). Financing human resources development at regional level: Comparison between HRD pre-accession funds and European social fund absorption. *Metalurgia International, 14*(13), 89–93.

Gherghinescu, O., & Neagoe-Băcanu, D. (2007). *Există un model pentru alocarea sectorială optimă a fondurilor structurale şi de coeziune?* Paper presented at Jean Monnet Seminar - European Open Gates. Craiova, Romania.

Gherghinescu, O., Rinderu, P., & Spulbar, C. (2009). *Analysis of structural and cohesion funds absorption in Romania*. Retrieved from http://ideas.repec.org/a/aio/fpvfcf/v1y2009i9p223-230.html

Gherghinescu, O., Rinderu, P., Spulbar, C., & Berceanu, D. (2009). *Structural and cohesion funds absorption in Romania*. Paper presented at 5th International Conference on Applied Business Research. Malta, Malta. Retrieved from http://www.icabr.com

Gujarati, N. D. (2003). *Basic econometrics* (International Edition). Bucharest, Romania.

Howells, J. (1999). Regional systems of innovation? In Archibugi, D., Howells, J., & Michie, J. (Eds.), *Innovation Policy in a Global Economy*. Cambridge, UK: Cambridge University Press. doi:10.1017/CBO9780511599088.007

IPP. (2012). *The current economic challenges – An opportunity for increasing transparency and accountability in spending public resources through the public procurement process coordinated by the institute for public policies (IPP)*. Retrieved from http://www.ipp.ro/pagini/transparen355a-eficacitatea-351i-.php

Lazar, S. (2010). *Public acquisitions – Principles – Procedures – Operations – Methodology*. Berlin, Germany: Wolterskluwer.

Paas, T., & Schlitte, F. (2008). Regional income inequality and convergence process in the EU-25: Scienze regionali. *Italian Journal of Regional Science, 7*(2), 29–49.

Paas, T., Vokb, A., Kuuskc, A., & Schlitted, F. (2006). *Modeling regional income convergence în EU-25*. Tartu, Estonia: University of Tartu.

Petrakos, G. (2000). The spatial impact of east-west integration in Europe. In Petrakos, G., Maier, G., & Gorzelak, G. (Eds.), *Integration and Transition in Europe*. London, UK: Routledge.

Rinderu, P. (2008). Econometric model for analyzing HRD funds absorption at regional level – North-East region. *Annals of the University of Craiova – Economic Series, 2*(36), 643-649.

Rinderu, P., Gherghinescu, O., & Iova, C. (2009). *An econometric model for analysing the structural funds absorbtion at regional level.* Paper presented at 6th Conference on Management of Technological Changes. Retrieved from http://www.cetex.tuiasi.ro/mtc2009

Rinderu, P., & Iova, C. (2006). Reforma politicii de coeziune a Uniunii Europene pentru intervalul 2007-2013. *Jurnalul Economic, 9*(22), 113–118.

Rodrigues-Pose, A., & Fratesi, U. (2004). Between development and social policies: The impact of European structural funds in objective 1 region. *Regional Studies, 38*(1).

Serban, D. D. (2011). *Public acquisitions: The jurisprudence of the European court of justice.* Bucharest, Romania: Hamangiu.

Storti, G. (2006). Minimum distance estimation of GARCH (1, 1) models. *Computational Statistics & Data Analysis, 51*(3), 1803–1821. doi:10.1016/j.csda.2005.11.020

(2007). Transparency of academic qualifications and competences as a gateway for labour mobility in Europe. InRinderu, P. (Ed.), *Proceedings LdaV/Ref/C/84252.* Bucharest, Romania: LdaV.

KEY TERMS AND DEFINITIONS

ARCH Models: Econometric models that models are specifically designed to model and forecast conditional variances.

European Regional Development Fund (ERDF): One of the Structural Funds, mainly financing "hard," infrastructure projects.

European Social Fund (ESF): One of the Structural Funds, mainly financing "soft," Human Resources Development related projects.

Nomenclature of Territorial Units for Statistics II (NUTS 2) Region: With minimum 800,000 and maximum 3 million inhabitants.

Operational Programme: Programme via which the Structural Funds interventions are filtered at national level, for specific domains. Documents are approved by the Commission for the purpose of implementing a Community Support Framework, comprising a coherent set of priorities with multiannual measures, and which may be implemented through recourse to one or more Funds, to one or more of the other existing financial instruments and to the EIB. An integrated operational programme is one financed by more than one Fund.

Priority Axes: Set of priorities within one Operational Program.

Regional Development: The provision of aid and other assistance to regions which are less economically developed.

Structural Funds: Financing instruments of the European Union for the member states countries.

ENDNOTES

[1]   Brussels, COM(2006) 1083/2006, COUNCIL REGULATION laying down general provisions on the European Regional Development Fund, the European Social Fund and the Cohesion Fund and repealing Regulation (EC) No. 1260/1999.

[2]   For further details visit the website www.fseromania.ro and https://actionweb.fseromania.ro/.

Chapter 12
Black Economic Empowerment, ICT, and Preferential Public Procurement in South Africa

Karunanidhi Reddy
Durban University of Technology, South Africa

Renitha Rampersad
Durban University of Technology, South Africa

ABSTRACT

Broad-based black economic empowerment has been a central part of the South African government's economic transformation strategy. The main purpose of BEE is to increase the number of black people that manage, own, and control the country's economy, and as a result, to reduce income inequalities and to contribute to economic transformation in South Africa. During apartheid in South Africa, the government procurement system favoured large, established businesses and made it difficult for newly established businesses to participate in the procurement system. This chapter gives an overview of the Black Economic Empowerment policy as a means to achieve socio-economic transformation in South Africa by providing preferences for Historically Disadvantaged Individuals (HDIs) and small businesses, when making procurement decisions. It also examines how procurement is used as a policy tool by government while simultaneously ensuring that it does not contradict the constitutional right to equality. The chapter also explores the implications of the Preferential Public Procurement Framework Act (Act 5 of 2000) and the latest procurement regulations. Finally, it discusses the use of ICT and the vital role it plays in preferential procurement in South Africa.

DOI: 10.4018/978-1-4666-2665-2.ch012

INTRODUCTION

Almost two decades have passed since a democratic government was introduced in South Africa. Whereas the apartheid system was characterized by inequality and segregation in almost every walk of life, including the social, economic and political spheres, the new government is based on integration and equality (Marais & Coetzee, 2006, pp. 111-112). The Constitution of South Africa, (Republic of South Africa, 1996) provides the basis for change in the country's social and political institutions. Hence, the term "transformative character" acknowledges the constitution's role in a period of political transition, to provide a legal framework to redress past injustices and facilitate a more just society (Liebenberg, 2010, pp. 24-25, 27). The principle of equality is one of the fundamental human rights laid down in the Constitution. However, one cannot insist on equal treatment before equality has been achieved (*President of South Africa v Hugo*, 1997(6) BCLR 708 CC pp. 728-729). The Constitution therefore provides for legislative measures designed to provide redress for historically disadvantaged individuals (Section 9[2]). The Broad-Based Black Economic Empowerment Act (BBBEE Act) (Republic of South Africa, 2003) is one such legislative measure designed to correct racial imbalances and to empower disadvantaged communities. Black Economic Empowerment (BEE) is a phenomenon taking precedence in South Africa to create and contribute towards economic transformation and to reduce income inequalities by allowing historically disadvantaged people the opportunity to own and control their own businesses and contribute towards the country's economy (Noon, 2009). One of the three elements of BEE is the use of procurement as a policy tool by government.

During the apartheid era in South Africa, the public procurement system allocated contracts to the lowest bidder unless it was clear that the organization or individual did not have the required experience to complete the contract. As a result, most government contracts were awarded to white-owned businesses. Such unfair practices made it difficult for small businesses to bid on government contracts since their costs were generally higher than larger firms. The policies during this period also discriminated against economically disadvantaged groups. The black majority in the country (because of the inequalities in income, wealth, and skills that existed between racial groups, between men and women, as well as between urban and rural areas) were not in a position to engage in formal business ventures (Beach, 2012). Since 1994, policy changes have come about that have shifted the emphasis and objectives of public procurement. Through the Constitution and the Preferential Public Procurement Framework Act (PPPF Act) (Republic of South Africa, 2000) and Preferential Procurement Regulations (Procurement Regulations) (Republic of South Africa, 2011), a framework has been created to correct the imbalances of the past through redress. Yet the promulgation of legislation alone cannot bring about the equality that is contemplated. The government also intended to use ICT to correct the imbalances mentioned, particularly through the provision of e-government services (which includes e-procurement).

The first part of this chapter examines how BEE operates. This section deals with measures that are designed to address the economic empowerment of black people in terms of business ownership. The second part analyses the implications of the PPPF Act for organs of government insofar as they may afford preferential treatment to disadvantaged businesses when making public procurement decisions. It concludes with a discussion on how ICT is used to improve and enhance the relationship between the government and the South African public.

SOUTH AFRICA DURING APARTHEID

In order to obtain a proper understanding of South Africa's attempts to provide redress for the harm caused by apartheid, one needs to understand the background of what apartheid did to South African society. Apartheid is understood to comprise a set of racially discriminating policies and forced segregation (Seekings & Nattrass, 2005, p. 18). Races were segregated socially, politically, and economically. The period between 1948 and 1994 is seen as the official period of apartheid, but such policies can be traced back to South Africa's colonial days. In the 1940s to 1950s, race was closely linked with class (Liebenberg, 2010, p. 2). Two-thirds of the population lived in rural areas. When considering the distribution of income, three broad categories were evident: rich white households at the top; Indian, coloured and urban African households in the middle; and rural African households at the bottom. This changed in the 1970s and 1980s, when class and race were no longer distinctively linked and opportunities opened up for educated black people. The income of the top 10 percent of South Africans, were on average one hundred times more than the bottom ten percent. The poor lived mostly in rural areas. They were poor because there were no members in employment or, if they were employed, it was generally in low-income jobs. Unemployment was in fact the main factor in determining overall inequality (Seekings & Nattrass, 2005, pp. 41-43; Noon, 2009, p. 617; Liebenberg, 2010, pp. 2-4).

Eighteen years have passed since the beginning of a democratic dispensation in South Africa. Whilst the apartheid system and its predecessors were characterised by segregation and unequal access to resources, the post-apartheid system is based on integration and equality (Marais & Coetzee, 2006). The South African Constitution provides for socio-economic reforms, not just to redress past injustices, but to facilitate "a restruc-turing of underlying institutional arrangements" that generates various forms of political, social and economic injustices (Liebenberg, 2010, p. 27).

In 1994, the first democratic government was elected which immediately called for major re-structuring of the economy. Amongst others, the introduction of the Black Economic Empowerment (BEE) policy, which functions as an affirmative action strategy, ensures that government supports economic empowerment and procurement practices in a sustained manner.

Government affirmative action programmes are not peculiar to South Africa. Other nations with a history of racial oppression and discrimination have also implemented affirmative action programmes to mitigate inequities resulting from oppressive legal regimes. The US Government instituted such a programme to focus on equity, justice and economic considerations (McCrudden, 2009). Affirmative action was used to address injustices against minority groups, especially African Americans. The Small Business Act of 1953 in the United States was designed to protect and assist small businesses by providing that they would receive a fair proportion of government contracts (Section 8). The expansion of set-asides for "small disadvantaged businesses" resulted in constitutional challenges on the basis that these programmes violated the Equal Protection Clause of the US Constitution. Despite these judicial setbacks, the preferential procurement programme appears to have had a definite economic impact on the communities that it aims to serve (Noon, 2009, p. 612).

Malaysia, which has experienced violence and social uprisings from economic inequalities and a racially oppressive legal regime, has established an immediate need for such programmes (Noon, 2009). Several Canadian federal and provincial schemes also link employment equity and the awarding of government contracts in an attempt to protect the minorities. Deviations on these types of linkages have increasingly been adopted in European Community countries as well (McCrudden, 2009).

For these countries, hands-on considerations such as social and economic stability have become a more serious concern than the moral aspirations of equality and justice. Just as in South Africa, each of the countries mentioned above have introduced racial preference programmes with the need for peace and social stability. In South Africa, the Black Economic Empowerment Programme has become a matter of priority to address interracial inequalities caused by apartheid.

The inequality as a result of apartheid has meant that certain individuals and communities are severely disadvantaged by inequalities in access to information and opportunity based on race and other factors. The efforts of preferential public procurement, to provide redress to the imbalances of the past, are therefore hampered, since they lack the information and the means to exercise such opportunities. The "digital divide," i.e. disparity in access to information, particularly ICTs, may deprive certain citizens from effectively participating in the economy (Kroukamp, 2005). Government could therefore bridge the divide by making such information available through the Internet.

The Right to Equality in South Africa

The formal approach to equality assumes that by treating all individuals in the same way, inequalities would be removed. Such an approach may actually reinforce such inequalities instead of redressing inequalities (Kentridge, 1996, p. 14; Reddy, 2006, p. 787). It is clear then that formal equality fails to remove the deeply entrenched patterns of inequality, particularly on the basis of race. In *President of South Africa v Hugo* (1997(6) BCLR 708 CC pp. 728-729), the Constitutional Court observed:

[A]lthough a society which affords each human being equal treatment on the basis of equal worth and freedom is our goal, we cannot achieve that goal by insisting on identical treatment in all circumstances before that goal is achieved.

Despite the transformed constitutional order in South Africa, many of the inequalities of the past still persist. As opposed to formal equality, the concept of substantive equality, takes into account the context, which includes the prevailing socio-economic conditions, and aims to redress past inequalities (Currie & De Waal, 2005, p. 233). Hence, the substantive equality approach entails an assessment of the historical context in which the equality principle is to be applied. The ideals of reconstruction and development are clearly implied in the substantive approach (Albertyn & Kentridge, 1994, p. 152). Section 9 of the South African Constitution sets out the equality principles. Section 9(2) clearly implies substantive equality by declaring: "To promote the achievement of equality, legislative and other measures designed to protect or advance persons or categories of persons disadvantaged by unfair discrimination, may be taken" (Devenish, 1999, p. 41). The PPPFA is one examples of legislative measures designed to advance historically disadvantaged groups.

In spelling out the right to equality, Section 9(3) provides that the state may not unfairly discriminate against anyone. If the government grants preferences to disadvantaged groups, will it violate the equality principle set out in Section 9? Discriminatory treatment in the past, particularly on the basis of race and gender, has resulted in the marginalisation of individuals from certain groups who were denied the privilege of engaging in public procurement. Measures of affirmative action are viewed as fair discrimination and are therefore permitted in order to eliminate historically imposed social and economic disadvantages against certain individuals (Devenish, 1999, p. 62).

It is apparent that the granting of preferences in awarding government contracts to disadvantaged groups and individuals, does not conflict with the notion of equality as espoused in the constitution. Furthermore, in terms of the Promotion of Equality and Prevention of Discrimination Act (4 of 2000), the state and all other persons have a duty and responsibility to promote equality and eliminate discrimination on the grounds of race, gender and disability (Sections 24, 28[3]). The granting of preferential procurement by the government is intended to further the aims of the Act. In addition, merely providing for legislative measures would not be enough if it ignores the inequality in access to information relating to affirmative opportunities and the technology to exploit them.

The Use of Public Procurement as a Policy Tool by Government

Bolton (2006, pp. 194-195) maintains that, as a policy tool, public procurement may be viewed as a means of "wealth redistribution" (i.e. "using procurement to channel funds to discrete categories of economic actors," for instance, disadvantaged groups in South Africa). However, from the perspective of international trade, the use of procurement as a policy tool to favour local suppliers may be viewed as a barrier to international free trade. Restrictions on the freedom of governments to use procurement as a policy tool have been introduced as a result of the promotion of free trade globally through the World Trade Organisation Government Procurement Agreement (WTO, 2012). The provision on "national treatment and non-discrimination" (Article 3) ensures that laws, regulations, procedures and practices relating to government procurement do not favour local goods or suppliers or discriminate against foreign goods or suppliers. It also encourages nations to be more transparent as far as government procurement is concerned (Article 17). As South Africa is not a member to this treaty it is not bound by these provisions. However, even if it was a member, as a

developing country it would qualify for special and differential treatment which allows the promotion of, for instance small-scale industries (Article 5). The country has, nevertheless, used procurement as a tool to achieve certain social policy objectives such as job creation, as a means to prevent discrimination and promote equality and protect the environment.

There are, however, valid arguments supporting the use of procurement as a policy tool. Arrowsmith (1995, pp. 247-248) comments that where it is properly employed, it may prove to be a useful and effective instrument. Instead of being merely a means to negotiate the "best deal," it can be used for the attainment of socio-economic goals. Bolton (2007, p. 306) admits that the use of government procurement as a policy instrument is not without controversy, but on the whole and particularly in South Africa, it can be justified.

BACKGROUND OF BLACK ECONOMIC EMPOWERMENT

Black Economic Empowerment (BEE) is an explicit South African government policy aimed at redressing past economic imbalances. For many years the apartheid structure in South Africa restricted Black (a generic term for Africans, Coloureds, and Indians) people from meaningful participation in the economy, while allowing only White South Africans full participation and business interest in the economy (Strydom, 2006).

Ramaphosa (2002; as cited by Bawa, 2005) suggests that "BEE is a moral, political, social and fundamentally economic requirement of this country's future." To support BEE objectives, several important sets of legislation have been introduced to provide new economic opportunities to disadvantaged groups. The most important initiatives have been the formulation of policies for transforming the ownership and control of particular sectors by increasing the powers of historically disadvantaged South Africans.

A highpoint of transformation is that the Private Sector in South Africa has committed itself to supporting and fast-tracking transformational developments. These companies have recognised the need for the implementation of a BEE strategy as an essential mechanism to meet the objectives as set out in the BBBEE Act, *vis a vis*, the achievement of sustainable and inclusive economic development, social stability and labour-absorbing economic growth.

Legislation Addressing Economic Inequality in South Africa

The National Small Business Act, introduced in 1996, established several institutions to support black small businesses. In 1997, government launched the public sector preferential procurement policy in terms of which government purchases were focused on supporting black small enterprise development. These procedures were regulated by the Preferential Procurement Act in 2000 (Strydom, 2005). The Competition Act of 1998 carried exemptions from the provisions on anti-competitive practices if such practices were promoting black-owned or black-controlled enterprises to become competitive. The National Empowerment Fund Act 105 of 1998 created a trust to hold equity stakes in state-owned enterprises as well as private companies on behalf of historically disadvantaged persons. The Employment Equity Act 55 of 1998 outlawed all forms of unfair discrimination in the workplace. It required employers of more than 50 people to take affirmative action in order to achieve representative employment of designated population groups in all occupations and across all organisational levels within a particular time period (Marais & Coetzee, 2006).

The Broad-Based BEE Act can be seen within the framework of several of the acts mentioned above, aimed at addressing economic inequality in South Africa. Although BEE has many components, which aim to increase the number of black people that manage, own and control the country's economy, and decrease racially based income inequalities, the core aspects of BEE are:

- Direct empowerment through the ownership and control of enterprises and assets.
- Human resources development through skills development and employment equity.
- Indirect empowerment through preferential procurement policies aimed at ensuring that black people benefit from government and private sector procurement and through the development of black owned and controlled enterprises (Hale, 2009).

The economic imperative is basically driven by the procurement chain. All state owned enterprises and government departments are legally obliged to apply BEE in their procurement activities. This means that private sector businesses that contract with government entities or departments will need to be BEE compliant in terms of certain Codes of Good Practice. These codes provide a framework for the measurement of BEE compliance across all sectors. Businesses can only become BEE compliant by measuring the BEE compliance of the other companies that they procure from. The implementation of BEE is also seen as part of good corporate governance and businesses can expose themselves to negative publicity if they are perceived as being non-BEE compliant (Hale, 2009).

BEE and Business in South Africa: Who is it Designed to Benefit?

In terms of BEE policy, state and parastatal tender practices favour companies that are owned or managed by members of previously disadvantaged communities. There is a move by the private sector to favour Small and Medium Enterprises (SMMEs), which are mostly small companies owned and run by previously disadvantaged persons. The government provides various incentives to businesses that embark on BEE ventures or which are SMMEs (Mbendi, 2011).

The BEE Act, together with the Procurement Act, have been described as the foundation acts of Government's programme in terms of using its own purchasing decisions to encourage the economic empowerment of black people. The framework created by the BEE Act provides a relatively objective measurement system through which government will be able to assess a business entity's contribution towards economic transformation relative to that of other entities.

FRAMEWORK FOR MEASUREMENT OF BEE COMPLIANCE

How is BEE Measured?

In terms of Section 9 of the Act, BEE codes of good practice provide a framework for the measurement of BBBEE compliance across all sectors. Various government departments are bound by the codes when making decisions relating to procurement, licensing, public-private partnerships, and the sale of assets (Venter & Levy, 2009, p. 238). This implies that when private enterprises wish to tender, apply for licenses, enter public-private partnerships or purchase state owned assets, they need to comply with the codes.

The Codes establish a "scorecard" system for evaluating an entity's BEE status. In terms of the scorecard, points are awarded for various identified BEE criteria, such as the proportion of the entity's equity, which is held by black persons and black women; the extent to which black persons and black women have management control over the entity; employment equity issues; preferential procurement; skills development issues and enterprise development. The higher the number of points scored by an entity in each category, the higher the BEE rating of the entity will be (Hale, 2009).

According to Labour Protect (2012), the size of a business is particularly relevant in determining the necessary levels of BEE compliance. The Codes provide for three levels of compliance based on the size of a business:

- **Exempted Micro Enterprises (EMEs):** Businesses with an annual turnover of less than R 5,000,000 (This is a new amendment. Previously, EMEs were businesses with a turnover of less than R 300,000 p.a and less than 5 staff).
- **Qualifying Small Enterprises (QSEs):** Businesses with an annual turnover of less than R 35,000,000.
- **Medium to Large Enterprises (M&Ls):** Annual turnover of more than R 35,000,000.

EMEs are exempt from BEE requirements. No matter what their ownership status (they can be 100% white owned), they are given an automatic preferential procurement rating. QSEs and M&Ls must comply with BEE if they want to do business with government (or with a business that has government contracts) and it is important to understand that their obligations may differ in some respects.

BEE consists of seven elements of company transformation: ownership, management control, employment equity, skills development, preferential procurement, enterprise development, and a residual element (DTI, 2005). In order to calculate a company's BEE status, a 'scorecard' has been developed to quantify these seven elements (Sartorius & Botha, 2008). These elements are weighted in terms of the scorecard and appear as follows: ownership, which means a percentage of shares held by black people (20 points), management and control, where directors and senior management positions are held by black people (10 points), employment equity, which means having implemented an affirmative action plan (15 points), skills development, where money is spent on up-skilling black people (15 points), preferential procurement, which means purchasing from BEE-compliant companies (20 points), enterprise development, the development of small, black-owned companies (15 points) and socio-economic development, which means social investment initiatives (5 points). A business complies with BEE by ensuring that it has sufficient points on the BEE scorecards.

From the weightings given to the various aspects of BEE in the generic scorecard the focus seems to be on direct empowerment through increased black ownership and control of enterprises and assets, increased black management at senior level, human resource development and employment equity (through the Skills Development Act and the Employment Equity Act).

A Focus on Public Procurement

In fulfilling their roles, governments need to deliver services as well as construct and maintain infrastructure for the communities that they serve. As a result, such responsibility quite often involves the purchase of goods or payments for services rendered, from the private sector. Where services were previously provided by governments themselves, the trend recently has been that governments have privatised such services, thereby increasing the use of the services of private enterprises for public sector procurement (Govender & Watermeyer, 2001, p. 1).

Procurement has been defined as a tool through which a client acquires services from a service provider through procurement documents, which define the roles and responsibilities of both the client and service provider during the delivery process (Sahle, 2002, p. 1; Rogerson, 2004, p. 180). Public procurement refers to the role of government in securing services, goods, or construction works through contracts concluded with the private sector (Govender & Watermeyer, 2001, p. 1). Sahle (2002, p. 4) observes that procurement could be

used to address and meet long-term development goals and contribute towards poverty reduction.

Since it has the potential to provide employment and business opportunities, procurement can be used by government as a policy instrument to facilitate social and economic development (Watermeyer, 2002, p. 210; as cited in Rogerson, 2004, p. 181).

THE PREFERENTIAL PROCUREMENT SYSTEM IN SOUTH AFRICA

The use of public procurement as a policy tool is specifically provided for in the South African Constitution (Republic of South Africa, 1996), which demonstrates the importance attached to the use of procurement as a tool to correct past inequalities and to uplift vulnerable groups (Bolton, 2006, p. 203, 2007, p. 39). Section 217(1) of the Constitution provides that procurement by organs of state must be fair, equitable, transparent, competitive and cost-effective. Section 217 (2) provides for preferencing policies which target persons who have been discriminated against, in allocating procurement contracts, while Section 217 (3) requires that national legislation may prescribe a framework for the implementation of such procurement policies.

"Equity" in the context of public procurement, means the "application and observance of government policies which are designed to advance persons or categories of persons disadvantaged by unfair discrimination" (Republic of South Africa, 2002, p. 8; Raga & Albrecht, 2008, pp. 794-795). Those that have been treated unfairly in the past should now be afforded the opportunity to participate in public procurement.

In 2000, South Africa passed the Preferential Procurement Policy Framework Act (PPPF Act) which established a procurement policy in terms of which preferences are granted to historically disadvantaged persons. The PPPF Act, which came into effect in 2000, is seen as one of the key tools to remedy past injustices in a country where black people were disadvantaged (Migiro, 2010, p. 1). The aim of the PPPF Act is to increase participation in public procurement by SMEs and historically disadvantaged individuals. In terms of Section 1 of the Act, organs of state have to frame their preferential procurement policy and implement it within the framework of the Act. Section 2(1) of the PPPF Act makes it clear that an organ of state "must" determine and implement its preferential procurement policy within the framework of the Act.

All organs of state are bound to use the framework as set out in the Act when engaging in public procurement (Regulation 2[2] of Procurement Regulations). The PPPF Act applies only to state organs when awarding contracts. "State organs," as defined in the PPPF Act, include a national or provincial department; a municipality; a constitutional institution (defined in the Public Finance Management Act 1 of 1999); parliament; and a provincial legislature (Regulation 1[iii]).

Although the South African Constitution (Section 217 [2]) does not make it compulsory for organs of state to grant preference in awarding contracts (it provides that they are not "prevented" from doing so), the PPPF Act does make it compulsory for state organs to do so. Section 2 (1) of the Act provides that an organ of state "must" determine and implement its preferential procurement policy.

Prior to making an invitation for tenders, a state organ has to comply with three requirements:

1. Plan for the offering of such tenders and make estimation of all costs.
2. Determine the appropriate preference point system to be used.
3. Determine whether the respective goods have been designated for local production and content (locally produced content) (Regulation 3, 2011).

Amendments to the PPPF Act that came into effect in December 2011, aim to boost local manufacturers and create more jobs in the private sector. The new Procurement Regulations allow organs of state to advertise and award tenders with the condition that only locally produced goods, services, or works, or locally manufactured goods that have more than a specified minimum threshold of local content, will be considered (Regulation 9[1]). The Procurement Regulations are intended to align the PPPF Act with provisions of the BBBEE Act on preferential procurement. This alignment emanated eight years after the BBBEE Act came into effect and four years after the Codes were gazetted (Tlhoaele, 2011).

The Preferential Points System

New Preferential Procurement Regulations have come into effect in South Africa. These new regulations are the final part of the puzzle in implementing BBBEE as anticipated in the Broad Based Black Economic Empowerment Act. This essentially means that government departments are now compelled to consider compliance with the Codes of Good Practice when evaluating tenders for government business and that all tenders must be accompanied by a valid BEE certificate (Skillsportal, 2011).

The Procurement Act (Section 2[1] [f]) requires that the contract must be awarded to the tenderer who scores the highest points in terms of the preference system. However, provision is also made for exceptional cases where certain "objective criteria" are to be considered (in addition to the preference points). This provision has been a controversial one. Hopefully, the new Procurement Regulations will add clarity to it. These regulations (Regulation 7, 2011) do permit the award of a contract to a tenderer that did not score the highest total points, provided it complies with Section 2(1)(f) of the Procurement Act. It also allows for the evaluation of tenders on functionality (Regulation 4). "Functionality" means that the tender will be measured according to certain norms relating to whether a service or commodity is designed to be more practical and useful, working or operating. These norms must be set out in the tender documents. Factors that are taken into account include: quality, reliability, viability, and durability of a service, as well as technical capacity and ability of the tenderer (Regulation 1[k] of Procurement Regulations).

A new procurement point scoring system has been established and will be used based on the BEE status level and functionality of a company. Companies with low BEE status (Level Eight) are likely to lose if bidding against companies with the highest BEE status (Level One). The 80/20 point scoring system is now increased to apply to procurement below R 1,000 000. Tenders will be evaluated in a 2-stage process: firstly, on functionality and local content, and secondly, on price and BEE status. The scoring system is applied by municipalities, state owned entities, provincial and national government departments when procuring goods and services.

The system is called the 80/20 or 90/10 for procurement value below R 1,000,000 and R 1,000,000 and over, respectively. Where the procurement value is below R 1,000,000 (80/20 system), companies will be scored against the BEE status level on a scale of 0 to 20 points, with the other 80 points being allocated for price scoring. Where the procurement value is above R 1,000,000 (90/10 system), companies will be scored against the BEE status level on a scale of 0 to 10 points, with the other 90 points being allocated for price scoring (Regulation 5 of Procurement Regulations, 2011; Tlhoaele, 2011) (see Table 1).

During apartheid, price was the significant factor in awarding public procurement contracts. The preferential procurement mechanism works within the tendering process. The evaluation of the tenders takes place by awarding certain points according to the HDI status of the contractor (Noon, 2009, p. 218). In determining the award-

Table 1. BEE status level of contributors and points awarded

B-BBEE Status Level	80/20 System for Procurement Value up to R 1000,000 Procurement Points	90/10 System for Procurement Value above R 1000,000 Procurement Points
1	20	10
2	18	9
3	16	8
4	12	5
5	8	4
6	6	3
7	4	2
8	2	1
Non-compliant contributor	0	0

Source: Based on the Preferential Procurement Regulations (Republic of South Africa, 2011, Regulations 5 and 6).

ing of such points, the attainment of two goals is considered, viz.:

1. Preference may be afforded to persons or categories of persons who were historically disadvantaged by unfair discrimination on the basis of race, gender or disability.
2. Preference may be afforded for the implementation of the Reconstruction and Development Programme (Section 2 [1][d]).

The previous regulations (2001) (Regulation 1[h]) defined a Historically Disadvantaged Individual (HDI). However, the recent regulations (2011) make no reference to HDIs. In terms of the first sub-section above, preference may therefore be granted to black people (which include African, Indian, and Coloured individuals), women, and the disabled. The Reconstruction and Development goals include the promotion of South African-owned enterprises; the creation of new jobs and the promotion of rural enterprises.

Other points are awarded according to the price that the contractor bids. Price is still the predominant factor and the majority of points are awarded on the basis of price.

A two-tier system is created depending on the value of the contract. For contracts with a Rand value between R 30 000 and R 1 million, the 80/20 scale allows for 20 points out of a hundred to be awarded for preference and the remaining 80 points are awarded for price (Section 2 (b)(ii) of PPPF Act and Regulation 5, 2011). In terms of this provision, the lowest acceptable tender scores 80 points and any other tenders which are higher in price, must score fewer points on a *pro rata* basis (Section 2[1][c]). For contracts with a Rand value of over R 1 million South African Rands, the 90/10 scale applies, with 10 points allocated for HDI status and the lowest tender scores 90 points (Section 2 [b][i] of PPPF Act and Regulation 6). Here again, any other tenders having a higher price will score fewer points on a *pro rata* basis. A contract has to be awarded to the contractor with the highest points unless other objective criteria justify the award to another contractor (Section 2[1] f).

THE CHALLENGES OF BLACK ECONOMIC EMPOWERMENT AND PREFERENTIAL PROCUREMENT

Although these processes exist, the question remains: How does BEE empower the disadvantaged? BEE was intended to transform the economy to be representative of the demographic make-up of the country. The main objective of the policy was to transfer economic power from the previously advantaged, mainly white people, to the previously disadvantaged, mainly black people. The concept of the policy itself is important to South Africa's redistribution of wealth, but has come under attack in recent years from groups representing both whites and blacks. Whites have labeled BEE 'apartheid in reverse' raising concerns

that the ANC government is out to discriminate against white South Africans. On the other hand, blacks have also become critical of BEE's intentions, raising different concerns to those of their white counterparts. The irony is that the people that BEE is supposedly helping have started raising questions as to whether the policy is truly achieving its original objective (Selaelo, 2007).

Bawa (2005) argues that, although there are strengths of BEE in the embrace of political and economic transformation in South Africa post-1994, certain challenges and criticisms exist. Interestingly, certain businesses criticise the way in which BEE has been administered, noting that the process lacks efficiency and transparency. Concern is shown over certain BEE deals which they believe have only gone through on the basis of the BEE applicant using political connections and not on the basis of merit (Bawa, 2005). The issues of "fronting" and "black diamonds" have emerged as challenges to the process of BEE, with "fronting" viewed as a criticism directed at South African business, which benefits the elite rather than the disadvantaged. It refers to situations where companies create the impression that they are complying with BBBEE priorities in order to benefit from government contracts. Many companies, desperate for BBBEE certification, often resort to dishonest measures, claiming that their secretaries, gardeners, drivers, etc., are directors. "Window dressing" often takes the form of Black people that are listed as shareholders, executives, or management, but who are unaware or uncertain of their role or participation within an enterprise (Lotheringen, 2012).

Malefane (2012) affirms that the South African Government has proposed measures, which will criminalise "fronting" and other forms of empowerment misinterpretations. According to the proposal, heads of government departments and CEOs of parastatals will have a "legal obligation" to report on the performance of their institutions in implementing BBBEE. Companies found guilty of falsifying their credentials will be dealt with, possibly through punitive measures against those found guilty of such practices.

"Black Diamonds" are seen as another challenge often related to BEE. The term "black diamonds" is used to classify the young black market and are is viewed as a product of the South African government's BEE programme that became apparent post-1994. They form around 10% of the 22 million over-18-year-old black South Africans and contribute up to 40% of the spending in this group (Goyal, 2010). There are criticisms that only the "elite few" have benefited from BEE and that the corporate sector is employing "black diamonds" in an effort to align its BEE status with its compliance with the BBBEE Act. This prevents the realization of the broad-based effect of BEE. It is apparent that BEE is not without its flaws.

Some of the challenges experienced relating to the preferential procurement system include possible conflict of interest resulting in tender board members receiving financial gain (Hill, 2007, p. 1); a lack of suitable black suppliers, resulting in fronting; poor quality of products and service delivery (mainly with inexperienced and emerging SMEs); and unfavourable pricing by SMMEs (Skae, 2006, p. 9; as cited by Migiro, 2010, p. 180). Other challenges of paying higher prices for goods due to reduced competition (as a result of preference) and inferior quality of goods and services (Watermeyer, 2000; Bolton, 2006, pp. 199-200, 2007, pp. 257-258) have also surfaced.

Despite the challenges encountered with the implementation of BEE, the government is focusing its preferential procurement policy on the development of BEE and government departments are legally bound to follow specific codes of practice in channelling their preferential procurement towards black-owned firms. The next section of this chapter will focus on preferential procurement, while the last section looks at ICT and e-government (including e-procurement) possibilities for procurement.

ICT (information and communication technology), particularly the Internet, has the potential to revolutionise government services, including preferential procurement. Due to the fact that procurement is an all-encompassing function, e-procurement solutions should encompass all procurement-bordering aspects to realise its full value. The next section concludes with a discussion on how ICT is used to improve and enhance the relationships between the government and the public in South Africa.

ICT AND PREFERENTIAL PUBLIC PROCUREMENT IN SOUTH AFRICA

Historically, ICT has been the privilege of the affluent citizens, allowing them to increase their interests. Yet the South African government has chosen to make e-government services available. E-government, which is one of the policies adopted by the South African government in order to improve service delivery, is founded on the premise that ICT tools and information are key drivers of economic and social development (Ntetha & Mostert, 2011, pp. 126-127). ICT allows companies and individuals to interact with government departments through the use of several means of communication, including desktops, laptops, cell phones, telephones and self-service stands. Tremendous improvements in ICT provide the means to send information to the "poor marginalised communities in South Africa" which can have a major impact on their lives (Mokhele & De Beer, 2007, p. 62).

Simply defined, e-procurement is the process of electronically purchasing the goods and services needed for an organization's operation. It offers a real-time platform for conducting business, while providing a significant opportunity to cut costs, increase organizational effectiveness and improve customer service (Oliviera & Amorim, 2001). An e-procurement system gives service providers the opportunity to seek procurement information online; submit tenders; and maintain and communicate information about their goods and services via the Internet. The advantages of e-governance (and in turn e-procurement) include: cost effectiveness; transparency (Singh & Sahu, 2008); curbing corruption (Wasserman & De Beer, 2004); improving access to information; improving efficiency and the ability to reach a wider section of citizens (Kroukamp, 2005; Wasserman & De Beer, 2004).

Internationally, governments have been using electronic services to reduce costs and improve on service delivery. The governments in Africa have also initiated programmes, strategies, and policies for e-government in their countries, such as the establishment of websites. Some African countries (such as South Africa – www.gov.za), have websites that function as a portal, while others (such as Kenya – http://www.e-government.go.ke/), have separate websites from e-government websites, but links to the e-government site are provided on the main government site (Onyancha, 2010, p. 34). The e-government readiness index showed that South Africa was the only African country in the top 100 countries in both 2003 and 2006 (Ngulube, 2007, p. 6). A number of government websites are in operation. For instance, the Gauteng Provincial Government Internet Portal which was opened in June 2005 in Tembisa provides online information and various services (Mphidi, 2012). Various government services, including e-procurement, are available through these websites. Government departments announce calls for tenders through their websites. Mphidi (2012) reports that of the 31 government departments, only 12 provided information on tenders on their websites.

A characteristic of disadvantaged communities, such as rural communities, is information poverty. ICT is therefore a vital link to facilitate the flow of information and knowledge to such places (Mutula & Mostert, 2010, p. 42), including information relating to public procurement opportunities and processes.

South Africa is a leader in ICT development in Africa, with a network that is 99% digital, made up of the latest technology in fixed-line,

wireless, and satellite communications. It has the most developed telecommunications network on the continent. The mobile phone industry is strength for the country (Burger, 2010; Ntetha & Mostert, 2011).

There are notable success stories of e-government in South Africa. To start with, the website of the South African government, illustrates an advanced stage of e-government, and provides the most detailed information about government services. The website provides three types of services, namely a) services for citizens; b) services for organisations; and c) services for foreign nationals. Services for citizens include information relating to birth, parenting, education and training, the youth, relationships, living with a disability, the world of work, social benefits, a place to live, transport, travel outside South Africa, moving to or visiting South Africa, sports and recreation, citizenship, dealing with the law, retirement and old age, and death. Information specific to the business community (or organisations) includes how to start an organisation or business, tax, intellectual property, import and export, permits and licences, transport, labour issues, health and safety at the workplace, and discontinuing a business. The website provides foreign nationals with information about moving to, working in, and entering South Africa (Onyancha, 2010, p. 37).

The Independent Electoral Commission (IEC) successfully developed an e-procurement system that allows for open and transparent bidding of government tenders aimed at preventing corruption. In 2004, they partnered with cell phone service providers to enable voters to Short Message Service (SMS) their identity number, and in return receive a message indicating their eligibility to vote and the voting station's details. Moreover, a satellite-enabled network made it possible for the commission to register voters; relay, collect and verify ballots; and relay results across the country. The other successful e-government project is that of the South African Revenue Services' (SARS) e-filing system which provides a way to conduct transactions related to tax returns on the Internet from government to business (G2B) (Mutula & Mostert, 2009).

The South African Government anticipates that libraries will become part of e-government on-going efforts to deliver electronic and integrated public services from a one-stop point, rather than for users to visit different government offices to obtain information.

Through e-government, the South African libraries can contribute to bridging the digital divide between the urban and rural communities where such gaps continue to widen. Libraries can also enhance their image by extending their services closer to the communities, as well as deepening democratic participation by citizens through enabling access to government held information. Libraries in South Africa can through e-government contribute to the government poverty reduction programme—the Black Economic Empowerment by enabling small and medium-sized enterprises (SMEs) to gain access to information about businesses, government opportunities, credit, etc. Through e-government, libraries can provide Internet access to the public (as they provide the hardware and software to people often free of charge), educate users on the use of e-information, assist clients in completing various government forms, assist in interpreting information retrieved from government websites to the clients, as well as helping them navigate through governments websites that are often disorganised (Berryman, 2004, p. 4; in Mutula & Mostert, 2009).

The examples highlighted above illustrate a few success stories. However, e-government projects have tended to fail because of adopting technologies without the accompanying human skills and capacities to manage, integrate and sustain them; centralizing the use of technologies by national governments without extending the benefits to intermediary institutions such as local government, parliament, civil society, etc.; not linking good governance to the broader and more inclusive democracy; high levels of digital illiteracy; and inadequate resources (Cloate, 2007; as cited in Mutula & Mostert, 2010, p. 45). Although South Africa has made significant strides in e-government, it does not seem to be leveraging the opportunities offered by such government systems.

ICT CHALLENGES FOR E-GOVERNANCE AND E-PROCUREMENT

The following challenges have been identified in respect of the delivery of e-government services in South Africa: the lack of ICT skills, particularly computer literacy skills (Mkize, 2007; Ntetha & Mostert, 2011); limited public access to Internet and other ICT technologies (United Nations, 2007). It was also noted that not all citizens have access to ICT tools or the know-how to operate them efficiently (Gosebo, 2008).

Mutula and Mostert (2010, p. 44) point out that 45 per cent of the population in South Africa is estimated to be living in rural areas, where ICT infra-structure is far less developed than in urban areas, and that PC penetration in rural areas is rather low. Inequitable access to ICTs such as personal computers, Internet and other Internet-related technologies by individuals or groups in their own country, was a challenge facing Governments in Sub-Saharan Africa (Ngulube, 2007, p. 6). Nevertheless, a study conducted by World Wide Worx indicated that South Africa was reported to have 5.3 million Internet users in 2009 (Internet World Stats, 2009).

Although South Africa has the most Internet subscribers in Africa, inequalities still exist between different groups as a result of apartheid. Surveys conducted have shown that, although there has been overall growth in the number of Internet users, these are mainly upper income earners. In terms of Internet access, black people are still disadvantaged and women are still worse off than men (Webchek, 2001, 2002; Wasserman & De Beer, 2004, p. 72).

In order to narrow the digital divide in remote, rural and disadvantaged communities, a large number of Multi-Purpose Community Centres (MPCCs) have been established by the Government. These centres offer users access to computers, Internet and fax machines, and were established with the aim of providing disadvantaged communities with access to government services, information technology and training (Mutula & Mostert, 2010, p. 42). The South African Post Office has also installed public Internet terminals in about 700 post offices throughout the country, particularly in settlements without Internet cafes and other forms of access to Internet (Department of Communications, 2008, p. 110). Geness (2004; as cited in Mutula & Mostert, 2010) points out that the delivery of services through e-government initiatives was hampered because of the lack of equal access of resources to all citizens, particularly because of the rural-urban divide. Meyer's (2007; as cited in Mutula & Mostert, 2010, p. 44) study relating to the use of MPCCs, identified the following challenges: the long distance travelled by users; lack of Internet skills; and long waiting periods and high costs of using such facilities.

The Internet must be seen, not as a catalyst for change by itself, but as one of the factors in the social arrangement, which can improve existing conditions. Hence, it is only logical from such a perspective that the Internet can bring about change only to the extent that the political and social institutions, of which it is a part, have planned or willed such change (Wasserman & De Beer, 2004, p. 67).

Hence, from the preceding discussion, one observes that inequality still exists as far as access to ICT in South Africa is concerned. Although e-government services (including procurement), increases the channels of communication for HDIs, as already indicated, there are definite challenges that are experienced, which makes it difficult to

achieve equality in access and participation in relation to government procurement. E-procurement and e-government solutions present significant potential for South Africa. The e-procurement process, however, has been slow and has not achieved the required results. This is partly due to the number of unique problems facing its implementation, i.e. a limited and monopolised supply-base, limited bandwidth, and BEE and SMME policies that complicate the feasibility of the implementation of such a solution.

FUTURE RESEARCH DIRECTIONS

A study by Watermeyer (2004) found that there was a lack of procedures both at national and provincial level to determine the effectiveness of the preferential procurement policy in assisting the individuals it was intended to assist. It is also unclear as to whether the objectives of the PPPF Act were achieved. These issues present opportunities for further research. Other research areas include the implications of the changes introduced by the 2011 Procurement Regulations, particularly the provisions relating to functionality evaluation and local content, and the increased threshold for the 80/20 points system to apply. In addition, whether the new regulations can effectively curb fronting or not, is also an area to be investigated. From an international perspective, the implications of international free trade measures for preferential procurement system in South Africa, which includes the regulations, is also a contentious issue requiring further research.

CONCLUSION

In a nutshell, the BEE strategy involves making sure government procurement supports black economic empowerment and SMMEs, as well as interventions to promote such procurement practices in the private sector by the formalisation of guidelines, codes, and partnerships and charters within the private sector.

It is clear that the objective of BEE is to increase the number of black people that manage, own, and control business enterprises and in turn, the economy. BEE links public procurement and empowerment through ownership and control of enterprises, and provides that businesses that wish to contract with organs of state need to be BEE compliant. Through the policy of preferential procurement, the South African government has used its purchasing decisions to contribute to economic transformation.

In light of the discrimination under the previous system of government in South Africa, public procurement has been used as a policy instrument for socio-economic transformation. The preference granted to disadvantaged individuals does not violate the right to equality and the principle of fairness set out in terms of Section 217 of the Constitution (Bolton, 2006, p. 213). In fact, the preference system is justified in terms of the principle of substantive equality set out in terms of Section 9 of the Constitution. Substantive equality allows for redress through legislative measures such as the PPPF Act and regulations. The PPPF Act gives effect to Section 217 by providing for a system of preferential procurement.

E-Procurement solutions have been slow in South Africa. However, they have enormous potential through a number of noticeable benefits and, in the long run, will also benefit on-line supply chain collaboration processes between companies.

BEE and preferential procurement are necessary measures in a transforming society such as South Africa. Equity is only one of the many factors taken into account in the granting of contracts by government, and should not discourage competitive businesses from participating in the tendering process.

REFERENCES

Albertyn, C., & Kentridge, J. (1994). Introduction to the right to equality in the interim constitution. *South African Journal on Human Rights, 10*(2), 149–178.

Arrowsmith, S. (1995). Public procurement as an instrument of policy and the impact of market liberalization. *The Law Quarterly Review, 111*, 235–284.

Bawa, N. (2005). New development paths for Indian business in South Africa: Evidence from Gauteng. *Africa Insight, 35*(4), 45–52.

Beach, M. (2012). *Preferential procurement policy act.* Retrieved on February 4, 2012, from http://www.ehow.com/about_6667931_preferential-procurement-policy-act.html

Bolton, P. (2006). Government procurement as a policy tool in South Africa. *Journal of Public Procurement, 6*(3), 193–217.

Bolton, P. (2007). *The law of government procurement in South Africa.* Durban, South Africa: LexisNexis Butterworths.

Currie, I., & De Waal, J. (2005). *The bill of rights handbook.* Lansdowne, South Africa: Juta & Co.

Davenport, T. R. H., & Saunders, C. (2000). *South Africa: A modern history.* Bedford, NJ: Palgrave Macmillan.

Department of Communications. (2008). *South African yearbook* 2008/2009. Retrieved on March 26, 2012, from http://www.gcis.gov.za/resource_centre/sa_info/yearbook/2009/chapter5.pdf

Devenish, G. E. (1999). *A commentary on the South African bill of rights.* Durban, South Africa: Butterworths.

DTI. (2005). *The BEE codes of good practice.* Retrieved March 2, 2012, from http://www.thedti.gov.za/bee/CODESOFGOODPRACTICE2005.htm

Geness, S. (2004). Challenges and opportunities of e-governance in South Africa. *The Electronic Library, 28*(1), 38–53.

Gosebo. (2008). *Service delivery innovation, including e-government and information management, response and comments: South African public service and administration department.* Retrieved on March 2, 2012, from http://www.dpsa.gov.za/docs/misc/hsummit/t4/presentation/social/Sld004.Htm

Govender, J. N., & Watermeyer, R. B. (2001). *Potential procurement strategies for construction industry development in the SADC region.* Unpublished Paper.

Goyal, M. (2010). Black diamonds. *Forbes India.* Retrieved on March 4, 2012, from http://www.forbes.com/2010/06/21/forbes-india-black-diamonds-middle-class-spending.html

Hale, A. (2009). *Bowman Gilfillan: BEE article for FASA.* Retrieved on March 7, 2012, from http://www.bowman.co.za/LawArticles/Law-Article~id~2132417381.asp

Hill, M. (2007). *Improved awareness needed of state procurement system – SAACE.* Retrieved March 12, 2012, from http://www.engineering-news.co.za/article.php?a_id=100101

Info Reporter, S. A. (2011). *Black economic empowerment.* Retrieved on March 4, 2011, from http://www.southafrica.info/business/trends/empowerment/bee.htm

Internet World Stats. (2009). *South Africa: Internet usage and marketing report.* Retrieved on March 26, 2012, from http://www.internetworldstats.com/af/za.htm

Islam, S., & Hassan, N. (2009). Multi-purpose community telecentres in Bangladesh: Problems and prospects. *The Electronic Library, 27*(3), 537–553. doi:10.1108/02640470910966952

Kentridge, J. (1999). Equality. In Chaskalson, M. (Ed.), *The Constitution of South Africa.* Cape Town, South Africa: Juta.

Kroukamp, H. (2005). E-governance in South Africa: Are we coping? *Acta Academia, 37*(2), 52–69.

Labour Protect. (2012). *What you need to know about BEE.* Retrieved on February 28, 2012, from http://www.labourprotect.co.za/BEE_scorecard.htm

Liebenberg, S. (2010). *Socio-economic rights: Adjudication under a transformative constitution.* Claremont, South Africa: Juta & Co.

Lotheringen, A. (2012). *What is fronting.* Retrieved on March 2, 2012, from http://southafrica.smetoolkit.org/sa/en/content/en/7694/What-is-fronting

Malefane, M. (2012). No fronting! New act to criminalise B-BEE fraud. *Sunday World.* Retrieved on March 3, 2012, from http://www.sundayworld.co.za/Feeds/SundayWorld/2012/02/12/no-fronting-new-act-to-criminalise-b-bee-fraud

Marais, F., & Coetzee, L. (2006). The determination of black ownership in companies for the purpose of black economic empowerment. *Obiter, 27*(1), 111–127.

Mbendi. (2011). *Black economic empowerment in South Africa: An overview.* Retrieved on March 16, 2011, from http://www.mbendi.com/indy/misc/blck/af/sa/p0005.htm

McCrudden, C. (2009). Social policy choices and the international and national law of government procurement: South Africa as a case study. In Corder, H. (Ed.), *Global Administrative Law.* Cape Town, South Africa: Juta & Co.

Migiro, S. O. (2010). Public sector procurement and black economic empowerment in South Africa: Challenges of preferential procurement and decentralization of the provincial tender board. *Journal of Social Development in Africa, 25*(2), 177–195.

Ministry of Finance and Public Works. (1997). *Green paper on public sector procurement reform in South Africa: A 10-point plan.* Retrieved on March 2, 2012, from http://www.polity.org.za/polity/govdocs/green_papers/procgp.html

Mkize, Z. (2007). *Public sector human resources convention.* Durban, South Africa. Retrieved on March 25, 2012, from http://www.kwazulunatal.gov.za/premier/speeches/other/19-09-2007.pdf

Mokhele, I., & De Beer, K. J. (2007). The use of information and communication technology (ICT) in e-service delivery and effective governance in South Africa. *Interim, 6*(2), 60–67.

Mphidi, H. (2012). *Digital divide and e-governance in South Africa.* Retrieved on March 2, 2012, from http://www.ais.up.ac.za/digi/docs/mphidi_paper.pdf

Mutola, S. M., & Mostert, J. (2010). Challenges and opportunities of e-governance in South Africa. *The Electronic Library, 28*(1), 38–53. doi:10.1108/02640471011023360

Ngulube, P. (2007). The nature and accessibility of e-governance in Sub Saharan Africa. *International Review of Information Ethics, 7*, 1-13. Retrieved on March 17, 2012, from http://www.i-r-i-e.net/inhalt/007/16-ngulube.pdf

Noon, C. R. (2009). The use of racial preferences in public procurement for social stability. *Public Contract Law Journal, 38*(3), 611-632. Retrieved on March 7, 2012, from http://search.proquest.com/docview/218680618?accountid=10612

Ntetha, M. A., & Mostert, B. J. (2011). Availability and utilisation of information and communication technologies for service delivery: A South African case study. *South African Journal of Library and Information Science, 77*(2), 125–137.

Oliveira, L. M. S., & Amorim, P. P. (2001). Public e-procurement. *International Financial Law Review, 10*, 43–47.

Olson, J. F. (2010). South Africa moves to a global model of corporate governance but with important national variations. *Acta Juridica: Modern Company Law for a Competitive Economy.* Retrieved on January 21, 2012, from http://search.sabinet.co.za.dutlib.dut.ac.za:2048/WebZ/images/ejour/ju_jur/ju_jur_2010_a14.pdf?sessionid=01-48548-1845022178&format=F

Onyancha, O. B. (2010). E-governance and e-governments in Africa: A webometrician's perception of the challenges, trends and issues. *Mousaion, 28*(2), 32–63.

PWC. (2011). *Corporate governance – King III report – Introduction and overview.* Retrieved on February 14, 2012, from http://www.pwc.com/za/en/king3/

Raga, K., & Albrecht, W. (2008). Determining an ethical basis for public sector procurement management: The South African local sphere of government. *Journal of Public Administration, 43*(4), 781–797.

Ramaphosa, C. (2002). Black economic empowerment: Where to now? *Sisebenza Sonke, 2*(3), 3.

Reddy, K. (2006). The horizontal application of the equality guarantees and race discrimination by the business sector. *Journal of South African Law, 4*, 783–802.

Republic of South Africa. (1996). *Constitution of South Africa act 108 of 1996.* Pretoria, South Africa: Government Printer.

Republic of South Africa. (1997). *Skills development act 97 of 1997*. Pretoria, South Africa: Government Printer.

Republic of South Africa. (1998). *Employment equity act 55 of 1998*. Pretoria, South Africa: Government Printer.

Republic of South Africa. (2000). *Preferential procurement policy framework act 5 of 2000*. Pretoria, South Africa: Government Printer.

Republic of South Africa. (2002). *General procurement guidelines*. Retrieved on March 2, 2012, from http://www.bing.com/search?q=general+procurement+-guidelines&src=IE-SearchBox&Form=IE8SRC

Republic of South Africa. (2003). *Broad-based black economic empowerment act 53 of 2003*. Pretoria, South Africa: Government Printer.

Republic of South Africa. (2011, June 8). Preferential procurement regulations. In *Government Gazette* (*Vol. 34350*). Pretoria, South Africa: Government Printer.

Retief, J. (2010). *Business day. Editor's Letter*. Cape Town, South Africa: CTP.

Rogerson, C. M. (2004). Pro-poor local economic development in South Africa: The application of public procurement. *Urban Forum, 15*(2), 180-210.

Ross, K. (2008, August 26). Time to talk on divisive race policy. *Daily News*.

Sahle, D. (2002). Procurement - A tool to address key development and social issues. *ASIST Bulletin, 14*(1&4).

Sartorius, K., & Botha, G. (2008). Black economic empowerment ownership initiatives: A Johannesburg stock exchange perspective. *Development Southern Africa, 25*(4). doi:10.1080/03768350802318530

Seekings, J., & Nattrass, N. (2005). *Class, race and inequality in South Africa*. New Haven, CT: Yale University Press. doi:10.1002/9781444395105.ch47

Selaelo, A. (2007). *South Africa: From black economic empowerment (BEE) to broad-based black economic empowerment (BBBEE)*. Retrieved on February 28, 2012, from http://www.helium.com/items/669208-south-africa-from-black-economic-empowerment-bee-to-broad-based-black-economic

Singh, A. K., & Sahu, R. (2008). Integrating internet, telephones, and call centers for delivering better quality egovernment to all citizens. *Government Information Quarterly, 25*, 477–490. doi:10.1016/j.giq.2007.01.001

Skillsportal. (2011). *BEE policy final*. Retrieved on March 7, 2012, from http://www.skillsportal.co.za/page/bee/3705033-BEE-policy-final

SouthAfrica.info. (2012). *Procurement boost for manufacturers*. Retrieved on March 2, 2012, from http://www.southafrica.info/business/economy/development/procurement-091211.htm

Strydom, P. D. F. (2005). *Black economic empowerment and small business in South Africa*. Retrieved on March 2, 2012, from http://www.sabusinesshub.co.za/section/content.php?ContentId=1381&-SectionId=23&SubsectionId=12

Tlhoaele, A. (2011a). *Understanding the new treasury procurement scoring system (2011)*. Retrieved on February 10, 2012, from http://www.beeandyourbusiness.com/new-treasury.html

Tlhoaele, A. (2011b). *BEE point system under scrutiny*. Retrieved on March 7, 2012, from http://www.skillsportal.co.za/page/bee/1026480-BEE-point-system-under-scrutiny

Tucker, C. (2003). *Summary of black economic empowerment in South Africa.* Retrieved on February 15, 2012, from http://www.bowman.co.za/LawArticles/Law-Article~id~-783041820.asp

Venter, R., Levy, A., Conradie, M., & Holtzhausen, M. (2009). *Labour relations in South Africa.* Oxford, UK: Oxford University Press.

Wasserman, H., & De Beer, A. S. (2004). E-governance and e-publicanism: Preliminary perspectives on the role of the Internet in South African democratic processes. *Communicatio, 309*(1), 64–89. doi:10.1080/02500160408537987

Watermeyer, R. (2000). The use of targeted procurement as an instrument of poverty alleviation and job creation in infrastructure projects. *Public Procurement Law Review, 9*(5), 226–250.

Watermeyer, R. B. (2004). Facilitating sustainable development through public and donor procurement regimes: Tools and techniques. *Public Procurement Law Review, 13*(1), 30.

WTO. (2012a). *Agreement on government procurement.* Retrieved on March 24, 2012, from http://www.wto.org/english/docs_e/legal_e/gpr-94_01_e.htm

WTO. (2012b). *Understanding the WTO: The agreements – Government procurement: Opening up for competition.* Retrieved on March 15, 2012 from http://www.wto.org/english/thewto_e/whatis_e/tif_e/agrm10_e.htm#govt

ADDITIONAL READING

Akafia, M. E. (2007, March-May). Public procurement systems in Africa: A regional approach to reforms. *Africagrowth Agenda*, 10-11.

Arrowsmith, S. (2010). Horizontal policies in public procurement: A taxonomy. *Journal of Public Procurement, 10*(2), 149–186.

Bolton, P. (2007). An analysis of the public procurement legislation in South Africa. *Public Procurement Law Review, 16*(1), 36.

Bolton, P. (2008). The public procurement system in South Africa: Main 6 characteristics. *Public Contract Law Journal, 37*(4), 719.

Bolton, P. (2009). Overview of the government procurement system in South Africa. In Thai, K. V. (Ed.), *International Handbook of Public Procurement* (p. 357). Boca Raton, FL: Taylor and Francis. doi:10.1201/9781420054590.ch16

Esser, I., & Dekker, A. (2008). The dynamics of corporate governance in South Africa: Broad based black economic empowerment and the enhancement of good corporate governance principles. *Journal of International Commercial Law and Technology, 3*(3), 157–169.

Frederich Ebert Foundation. (2000). *Review of business laws in Southern Africa – Part 4.* Retrieved February 3, 2012, from http://library.fes.de/fulltext/bueros/botswana/00619004.htm

Islam, S., & Hassan, N. (2009). Multi-purpose community telecentres in Bangladesh: Problems and prospects. *The Electronic Library, 27*(3), 537–553. doi:10.1108/02640470910966952

McCrudden, C. (2009). Social policy choices and the international and national law of government procurement: South Africa as a case study. In Corder, H. (Ed.), *Global Administrative Law.* Cape Town, South Africa: Juta & Co.

Ministry of Finance and Public Works. (1997). *Green paper on public sector procurement reform in South Africa: A 10-point plan.* Retrieved on March 2, 2012, from http://www.polity.org.za/polity/govdocs/green_papers/procgp.html

Moya, F. N. (2007). Transforming South Africa's corporate sector into a sustainable black powerhouse: Racial prejudices and the Lamberti debate. *Black Business Quarterly*, 114-116.

Oberholzer, D. (2011). *Preferential procurement set to reinforce BBBEE codes*. Retrieved on March 7, 2012, from http://www.fanews.co.za/article.asp?Compliance_Regulatory_~2,-General~1082,Preferential_Procurement_is_set_to_reinforce_BBBEE_Codes~11065

Pattman, R. (2008, March 23). "Blends" rare in rainbow nation. *The Tribune Herald*, p. 4.

Penfold, G., & Reyburn, P. (2008). Public procurement. In Woolman, S. (Ed.), *Constitutional Law of South Africa* (2nd ed.). Cape Town, South Africa: Juta & Co.

Plasket, C. (2006). Tendering for government contracts: Public procurement and judicial review. In Glover, G. (Ed.), *Essays in Honour of AJ Kerr*. Durban, South Africa: LexisNexis Butterworths.

Quinot, G. (2008). Worse than losing a government tender: Winning it. *Stellenbosch Law Review*, *19*(1), 68.

Retief, J. (2010). *Business day. Editor's letter*. Cape Town, South Africa: CTP.

Ross, K. (2008, August 26). Time to talk on divisive race policy. *Daily News*.

Tucker, C. (2003). *Summary of black economic empowerment in South Africa*. Retrieved on February 15, 2012, from http://www.bowman.co.za/LawArticles/Law-Article~id~-783041820.asp

Watermeyer, R. (2009). The use of targeted procurement as an instrument of poverty alleviation and job creation in infrastructure projects. *Public Procurement Law Review*, *9*, 226.

WTO. (2012a). *Agreement on government procurement*. Retrieved on March 24, 2012, from http://www.wto.org/english/docs_e/legal_e/gpr-94_01_e.htm

WTO. (2012b). *Understanding the WTO: The agreements – Government procurement: Opening up for competition*. Retrieved on March 15, 2012 from http://www.wto.org/english/thewto_e/whatis_e/tif_e/agrm10_e.htm#govt

KEY TERMS AND DEFINITIONS

Affirmative Procurement: Measures to redress inequality suffered by HDIs in government procurement opportunities.

Apartheid: Racially discriminating policies and forced segregation in terms of which Black people were restricted from full participation in the economy.

Black Economic Empowerment: A programme in terms of which the South African government grants previously disadvantaged groups' economic empowerment to provide redress for past inequalities.

Digital Divide: This refers to the disparity in access to information and ICTs, for instance, between urban and rural communities, which may deprive certain citizens from effectively participating in the economy.

E-Government: Refers to the delivery of services and information by the government by means of electronic interaction through the use of ICT, between government and the public, or between government and business.

E-Procurement: Is the process of electronically purchasing goods and services needed for an organization's or government's operation. It involves the use of ICT (including the Internet, World Wide Web, and electronic tenders).

Equality: The formal approach to equality implies that treating individuals in the same way will remove inequality. The substantive approach (Section 9[2] of the Constitution declares that "Equality implies the full and equal enjoyment of all rights and freedoms").

Equity: Refers to the government policy, which promotes equal opportunity and fair treatment in employment through the elimination of unfair discrimination and the implementation of affirmative action measures to redress inequalities and advance persons or categories of people disadvantaged by unfair discrimination.

Fronting: "Window dressing" often takes the form of Black people being listed as shareholders, executives or management in order to comply with BEE legislation, but who are unaware or uncertain of their role or participation within an enterprise.

Historically Disadvantaged Individuals (HDIs): People disadvantaged by unfair discrimination on the basis of the grounds listed in the South African Constitution, particularly, race, gender, or disability.

Information and Communication Technology (ICT): Allows companies and individuals to interact with government departments through the use of several means of communication, including desktops, laptops, cell phones, telephones, fax machines, television, radios, and self-service stands.

Preferential Public Procurement: The use of procurement as a tool by government to correct past inequalities and to uplift vulnerable groups.

Public Procurement: The process whereby the government contracts with the private sector for the supply of goods or rendering of services.

Transformation: The process of redressing past inequality and creating a more just and equitable society. One of the primary aims of the South African Constitution is the transformation of society.

Chapter 13
Public Transformation in Malaysia:
Improving Local Governance and Accountability

A.K. Siti-Nabiha
Universiti Sains Malaysia, Malaysia

Danilah Salleh
Universiti Utara Malaysi, Malaysia

ABSTRACT

Public sector governance relates to accountability, transparency, inclusiveness, and also effectiveness and efficiency of governmental organizations. Such objectives have been the intended outcome of some of the public transformation and reformation programs in Malaysia. However, even after the various improvement initiatives, there are still complaints made against public organizations, especially against local authorities regarding their lack of good governance and accountability. Thus, the question that needs to be answered is why local governance is still a problematic issue even after all the initiatives that have been implemented over the years. As such, the various challenges facing local authorities that constrains them from achieving the intended outcomes of transformation programs is discussed in this chapter. In so doing, a contextual description of the local governmental system and the contemporary reformation programs of public organizations, specifically the local authorities, are explained. In addition, the recommendations to overcome those challenges and to achieve good governance are explained in this chapter as well.

DOI: 10.4018/978-1-4666-2665-2.ch013

INTRODUCTION

Good governance can be defined as the "exercise of economic, political, and administrative authority to manage a country's affairs at all levels" (UNDP, 1997, p. 2). According to the United Nations Economic and Social Commission, good governance has eight major characteristics, which are participatory, consensus oriented, accountable, transparent, responsive, effective and efficient, equitable and inclusive, and following the rule of law. Thus, accountability is one of the main characteristics of good governance. Accountability refers to responsibility, answerability, blameworthiness, and liability of a person, group, or organization for the execution of authority and/or the fulfillment of responsibility (Gray & Jenkins, 1993; Frost, 1998).

The various public sector reformation programs in Malaysia have been initiated with the focus of ensuring good governance and better accountability of public agencies. The overall objectives of the improvement programs are to ensure better service delivery and subsequently ensuring more transparent, accountable, and inclusive and participative decision-making processes of public agencies. The intensive administrative reform programs started from late 1980s, which to a certain extent follows the philosophy of new public management with the introduction of the privatization policy and the quality work culture movement which had an emphasis on total quality management, benchmarking of services and performance based budgeting (Siti-Nabiha, 2008). However, the outcomes so far have been moderate, in the sense that the public sector in Malaysia continues to suffer from inefficiency, corruption and a host of other problems (Siddiquee, 2006). Public organisations in Malaysia, whether at the federal, state and local government levels, continued to be criticized for their lack of good governance. For example, one of the main issues that have been raised repeatedly in the Auditor-General's reports is the problem related to public procurement. As lamented by the Auditor-General in his speech in 2010:

... year in and year out, the National Audit Department has highlighted weaknesses and irregularities in public procurement at all levels, be it at the Federal, State and Local government level as well as in Statutory Bodies. Some of these weaknesses and irregularities involve serious violations of established procurement guidelines and procedures.

The same issue was raised again in April 2012 by the Auditor General in his speech, in which he notes the weaknesses in the procurement process:

If we glean the numerous audit reports, there is indeed a rather long list of what we call weaknesses in government procurement, which from the standpoint of good governance clearly indicates violation of the numerous procurement circulars and guidelines issued by the Treasury. ... One is tempted to ask why all these things happen. Where is the internal control? Where is the check and balance that is supposed to exist? What kind of monitoring was done, if there was one in the first place?

Thus, even with the various improvement programs such as the evaluation of public agencies with regards to the compliance of agencies to financial rules and procedures and use of the e-procurement system; issues pertaining to financial management and consequently good governance of public institutions have not been solved. Such weaknesses in governance have lead to Malaysian unfavorable ranking in Global Competitiveness and the 'Transparency International Corruption Perception Index.' In 2011, Malaysia was ranked 60th in Transparency International Corruption Index, an index that measures the degree to which corruption is perceived to exist among public officials and politicians. Malaysia position has worsened significantly since Malaysia was ranked 56th in 2010 and 2009 and 39th in 2005 (www.transparency.org.my). Moreover, the Global Competitiveness Report also shows a declining ranking for Malaysia, from being ranked 21st out of 134 countries in 2009 to being ranked 26th out of 139 countries in the 2010/2011 period (MPC, 2011). The downward trend is mostly due to unfavorable assessments of the institutional framework in Malaysia.

Good governance is even more crucial for the local government in Malaysia given the various competing demands and also complexities in managing local authorities due to enlargement of urban areas, higher demands from other stakeholders especially the private sector and also more discerning citizenry. The functions and responsibilities of local authorities in Malaysia are growing with the rapid rate of industrialization, trade, commerce, development of modern services and growth of town populations. These events have led to the increase in demand for urban space and urban support services which results in not only financial but also administrative burdens on local authorities. In addition, the governance issues are even more crucial in the local government given that local councilors, mayors, and presidents of local councils in Malaysia are not elected by the public but are normally political appointees.

Besides political accountability issues, it can be argued that the local government is also facing the problem of financial accountability. The most elementary form of public accountability is the requirement that local authorities give an account of their activities to the public and provide justification for what has been done throughout the year (Local Government Act, 1976). However, there are several local authorities, which are not able to produce annual financial accounts while some have inadequate annual reports that do not report the whole range of their activities. There have been accounts of audit work being affected and delayed especially when some of these local authorities were unable to produce supporting documents for expenditures that were made,

accurate accounting data and up-to-date annual accounts (The New Straits Times, 2010; www.audit.gov.my).

As governance issues and problems still persist in the Malaysian public sector, the Malaysian government continues to introduce various improvement measures and tools for public organizations. Thus, it is imperative to determine why there governance and accountability issues still persists even though there were various administrative improvements and public sector reformation programs have been implemented to improve governance and management of public institutions in Malaysia over the years. Therefore, the focus of this chapter is to discuss the challenges faced by the local government that has an impact on the governance of local authorities. This chapter also provides some recommendations on addressing these issues. However, it is imperative to first understand the context of the local government in Malaysia and the contemporary reformation programs implemented, as presented in the next section.

OVERVIEW OF THE LOCAL GOVERNMENT IN MALAYSIA

The Malaysian government structure consists of a three-tiered type of structure, which is divided into the federal, state, and local government levels. Malaysia consists of thirteen states and three Federal Territories, inheriting a British legacy and influenced by a British model in terms of local government objectives and styles (Norris, 1980; Omar, et al., 2007). In the year 2010, there were 147 local government structures which consisted of 50 city councils (municipalities) and 97 district councils. In Peninsular Malaysia, local authorities are governed by the Local Government Act, which provides a consolidated legal framework for local authorities. The East Malaysian states of Sabah and Sarawak have their own unique ordinances. The local government in Malaysia is responsible for providing and maintaining urban services that encompass fields such as public health and sanitation, waste removal and management, town planning, environmental protection and building control, general maintenance of urban infrastructure and social and economic development.

The constitution of Malaysia has specified that all areas of local government are under the power and responsibility of the state government, except in federal territories (Malaysia Constitution, Act 74: Schedule 9[2]). Thus, the state government has the power to determine the territory of the local government and also has the right to appoint the president or mayor as well as council members of the local government (Local Government Act, 1976; Omar, et al., 2007). Furthermore, the state government has direct financial power over their local authorities. The federal government interacts with the local government through the Ministry of Housing and Local Government, which exerts its influence through financial grants given to local authorities (Siti-Nabiha, 2010; Kuppusamy, 2010). As the Ministry of Housing and Local Government is responsible for coordinating and supervising local authorities, any directive from the ministry needs to be adopted by the state (Siti-Nabiha, 2010).

By law, a local government structure must consist of one Yang Di Pertua (or Mayor) with not less than eight and not more than twenty four council members (Local Government Act, 1976). Some states appoint politicians from the ruling party while others choose amongst the administrators of state services or officers of the Malaysian Administrative and Diplomatic Services. The appointments are based on either part time or full time agreements. Thus, one of the unique characteristics of the local government in Malaysia is that the councilors are political appointees and there are no local or public elections conducted to elect mayors or councilors (Siti-Nabiha, 2010).

CONTEMPORARY PUBLIC SECTOR REFORMATION PROGRAMS

There contemporary public sector improvement programs discussed in this section are the government transformation program, the implementation of e-procurement and the programs related to benchmarking and assessment of local authorities.

Government Transformation Program: Performance-Based Outcomes

To ensure accountability, transparency, and also effective and efficient services, many improvement initiatives were introduced such as the use of the Key Performance Indicators (KPIs) system in 2005 for government agencies including local authorities. However, in the beginning, the KPIs system in local authorities seemed to have been geared only towards faster service delivery. A more outcome oriented approach was then introduced under the ambit of the Government Transformation Program in 2009. The objectives of the Government Transformation Program are "to transform the government to be more effective in its delivery of services and accountable for outcomes that matter most to the Rakyat; and second, to move Malaysia forward to become an advanced, united and just society with a high standards of living for all (GTP website). In line with the intended objective of this program, the new KPIs formulated in the public agencies will emphasize on impact rather than input, on outcome rather than output.

Six National Key Result Areas (NKRAs) were identified which represent a combination of short-term priorities to address urgent citizen demands and long-term issues affecting the citizens that require immediate attention (www.pemandu. gov.my; www.mampu.gov.my). The NKRAs are reducing crime, fighting corruption, improvement of students' outcomes, improvements in the standard of living for low income groups, upgrades and improvement of rural infrastructure, and improvements in urban public transportation (GTP Annual Report, 2011). The NKRAs are headed by the respective ministers and they are held accountable for the results achieved as Key Performance Indicators (KPIs) were formulated for each NKRAs. Consequently, every ministry should have their own KPIs and the ministers' performance will be evaluated every six months. Thus, these KPIs provide a mechanism for evaluation of ministries and other government agencies.

Improving Efficiency: The Use of the E-Procurement System

To improve service delivery, transparency, and subsequently good governance, the Malaysian government introduced the e-procurement system; whereby the whole process of procurement is automated. The use of this system enables public organizations to shift from purchasing goods manually to Internet electronic based purchases from their suppliers. The benefits that were anticipated from the Internet procurement system were cost and time efficiency and also wider access to suppliers. Although suppliers need to be registered in the system, public organizations can still purchase from a company that is not registered in the e-procurement system, as long as the company is registered with the Ministry of Finance (Kalianan, et al., 2009).

However, there implementation of e-procurement system has faced some drawbacks. Kalianan et al. (2009) found that after six years of implementing the first phase of the electronic procurement system, only 50,000 out of the 120,000 suppliers that were registered with the Ministry of Finance, were registered within the system. Thus, there are still many suppliers who have not registered in the system due to the perceived high cost involved. Furthermore, even some of those who have registered are not using the system. They also found that only 6,000 suppliers are active in

utilizing the system. Hence, there are still challenges in implementing the Internet procurement system at the Federal Government level.

The implementation of e-procurement system at the local government level is also problematic. Research by Hashim (2007, 2010) on e-procurement in 21 local governments in the state of Selangor (which is one of the more economically advanced states in Malaysia) found several problematic issues relating to the implementation of e-procurement. She found that most of the local governments were not ready for e-procurement. The issues involved were the challenges in managing change, the lack of funding and also the need to implement various costly government initiatives. Furthermore, the findings of the study also revealed that ICT officers, who are mainly the IT department heads, were employed on contract basis. Hence, it was found that many of them were demotivated as even though they were in the position for over three years, they were still employed on a contract basis.

Thus, findings of the study by Hashim (2007, 2010), showed that the barriers to local government implementation of the e-procurement system are "difficulty in adjusting to change, lack of funding, complex and expensive initiatives, and rigid government bureaucracy." Other issues that hinder the e-procurement system pertain to the drawing of contracts. In addition, suppliers also have to be trained in ICT in order for the system to be successful (Mansor, 2006).

Accountability Index: Measuring Financial Management Compliance

There are several external assessments of public organizations include the local governments in Malaysia. One such assessment is the Accountability Index, an audit rating system, which was introduced by the National Audit Department in 2007 in response to the recurring problem of internal control weaknesses and non-compliance to financial laws and regulations. The introduction of the Accountability Index is in line with the 'Key Performance Indicators' system and the National Integrity Plan which aims to enhance transparency, accountability, governance and the integrity of public institutions (National Audit Department, 2008). The Accountability Index (AI) is used to measure the financial accountability of governmental agencies including local authorities in terms of compliance with financial laws and regulations (National Audit Department, 2008). As the Auditor-General (2008) states:

The AI is the first attempt to provide a structured and consistent approach to measure and compare the level of financial management compliance among Federal and State Ministries and department as well as agencies such as Federal and State Statutory Bodies, Local Authorities and Islamic Religious Councils. As a benchmarking mechanism, AI can assist the auditees to measure the progress of financial management over the years (National Audit Department, 2008, p. iii).

The ratings from one to four stars will be given to the public agencies based on the assessment made. Thus, by having accountability index, it hopes that heads of governmental agencies will be motivated to enhance their financial management through taking corrective actions and also by benchmarking their institutions with others. Consequently, government agencies are supposed to identify their weaknesses and initiate continuous improvement in their financial management as states by the Auditor-General:

By providing unbiased and objective assessments of whether public monies are responsibly and effectively managed to achieve intended results will help the government organizations achieve accountability, improve operations and still confidence among the public and stakeholders (National Audit Department, 2008, p. v).

Improvement in Service Delivery: Star Rating System for Local Authorities

The next initiative, the "Star Rating System," is targeted specifically for local councils and was introduced in 2008 by the Ministry of Housing and Local Government. This rating system grades the local councils based on their service delivery performance. The star rating system is introduced by the Ministry of Housing and Local Government to ensure that local councils perform as expected and deliver better services to the citizens. The objectives of the star rating system are to evaluate the performances of the local government in terms of service delivery, promote competitiveness, and ensure that local authorities maintain their performance after achieving good ratings. With the existence of the rating system, local agencies are expected to be more responsible and accountable in ensuring efficient and effective services.

Essentially, there are 354 indicators used in the star rating system, which covers the functions and responsibilities of local authorities. The areas of assessment are management (30%), core services (35%), customer management (15%) and community participation (20%). Initially, during the first phase of evaluation, only 47 local authorities with the status of city council and town council were assessed. During the second phase, another 51 local authorities with the status of district council were assessed. In 2008, none of the local authorities obtained a 5-star rating. However, ten local authorities managed to obtain a 4-star rating and consequently succeeded in getting not only certificates but also a special one-off fund to undertake development projects. The results were considered satisfactory as it was the first time the rating system was officially conducted. Moreover, twenty-four local authorities succeeded in obtaining a 3-star rating. Unfortunately, there was also quite a high percentage (66%) of local authorities that failed to obtain a good rating as they only managed to get 1 or 2-star ratings. This was due to the lack of good strategic and financial management and inadequate law enforcement. To date, no local authority has managed to get an exceptional 5-star rating.

Local Agenda 21: Stakeholder Participation and Consensus-Oriented Decision-Making

Since good governance also means good stakeholder participation and consensus oriented decision making (UNDP Report, 1997), there have been channels put forth to obtain public participation in local authorities. One of the initiatives that have been undertaken is the Local Agenda 21 (LA 21) program. Agenda 21 is an approach through which local communities are able to define their strategy for the community and also the action programs to be implemented. Chapter 28 of Agenda 21 clearly binds local authorities to take the lead in the implementation of sustainable development at a local level. Thus, the Malaysian government had aimed for LA 21 to be implemented in all local authorities during the 9th Malaysian Plan, that is from the year 2006 to 2010 (EPU, 2006). However, the LA 21 programs implemented in local authorities currently deals mainly with crime prevention and community projects that do not include comprehensive community engagement.

CHALLENGES OF ENSURING GOOD GOVERNANCE AND ACCOUNTABILITY FOR THE LOCAL GOVERNMENT

The primary issue of local governance in Malaysia relates to the governance structure of the local authorities. The councilors and mayors are appointed by the state government and not by citizenry. As mentioned, the councilors and in some cases even the presidents of local council are political appointees of the state government. As such, there

is the fear that local councils are more subservient to political masters rather than other stakeholders especially the main stakeholders which are the general public. This political appointment system practice consequently leads to political interference in management of local authorities especially in the enforcement activities of the local councils. One contentious issue is whether or not the public participation programs put in place has a major impact on the policy outcomes of local authorities. As mentioned earlier, the local agenda 21 program did not seem to promote or seek to obtain real participation from the public especially those pertaining to key decision-making process at the local authorities.

Another major challenge facing the local councils relates to fulfilling the demands and expectations of its stakeholders. Similar to the situations of other public sector organizations, local governments have various stakeholders with sometimes conflicting and competing demands. Thus, fulfilling the expectations or demands of one party could lead to the dissatisfaction of another group. Such situations are more complex in reality, given that councils also need to improve their financial positions, which can be achieved with the approval of rapid development and advanced industrial activities in their areas of responsibility. This however, could lead to the issue of overdevelopment. For example, the councils, in their need to improve their financial positions, might speedily approve infrastructure development projects that are not supported by the public and Non-Governmental Organizations (NGOs). Hence, it is usually the interests of the business community and political agents that takes precedence over the interests of ordinary citizens or NGOs.

The lack of accountability over major decisions made or approved by council members could be attributed to the short leadership periods at local councils. In general, the mayor or president of a local council usually has a short tenure-ship, which lasts less than two years; and many have served for less than one year (Stevens, 2006). Such short tenured leadership, which occurs not only at the local government level but also in other public organizations, leads to problems in terms of the implementation and monitoring of programs and activities. This situation is duly noted by the Auditor General:

The lack of accountability relates to failure in the implementation and monitoring stage. I believe that it is incumbent for all controlling officers to ensure that corrective actions are effectively taken and their officers and staffs are adequately trained to handle their tasks. Leadership is important. Because of staff changes, this may affect continuity of actions at the departmental/agency level and it is the responsibility of controlling officers to ensure this continuity of action (www. audit.gov.my).

The numerous changes to top leadership in councils have lead to ineffective management and impacted employees of councils and also the citizens in the areas of responsibility. More importantly, leaders frequently do not have an adequate time period during their tenures to formulate effective strategies and monitor the progress of actions taken. Some of them might not even be sufficiently committed to the implementation of initiatives or reformation programs. This lack of commitment could be because the top management of the council felt that they might not stay long at the organization and might be moved to governmental departments as has been the experience of several council leaders in some of the Malaysian states. Thus, it is unclear who should be accountable for problems concerning council projects or activities, especially when those activities extend for years or if the impact of the decisions made are felt long after the leader who approved the project has left.

Besides leadership issues, one of the key factors that influence the efficiency and effectiveness of local authorities is the availability of adequate financial resources. As expected, the lack of financial and subsequent physical capacity, limits the extent of influence and functions of the local government. Without such resources, local councils will face difficulties executing their duties as service providers and will fail to act as mediums for socio-economic growth at a local level. The enlargement of urban areas due to increasing development emphasizes the need for both adequate financial and human resources to ensure that development is managed in a healthy manner.

A lack of financial resources will have a significant impact on a local council's operations. Lack of funds also means lack of facilities such as Information Technology (IT) equipment and relevant IT expertise. For example, in one of the municipal councils, there is currently only one staff in the IT department and not enough IT facilities, which subsequently causes delays in service provisions. Adequate local government funds are vital for effective local management due to the increase in population and enlargement of urban areas that are the results of the rapid industrialization of the country.

The Malaysian government launched the Public Services Network (PSN) and Civil Service Link (CSL) about a decade ago to improve service delivery and these kinds of systems have spread widely to various other government services (Abdul-Karim, 1995), which has help to improve the speed of certain processes. However, some local authorities, especially the smaller ones that face financial constraints, are not equipped with computerized systems in their institutions. Inadequate and untrained human resources would also badly impact operations in local councils. The shortage of enforcement personnel has contributed to difficulties in enforcement activities, which has subsequently led to public dissatisfaction. For example, an area that has a population of about 70 000 people might have less than 15 enforcement officers.

Another challenge that is related to accountability in the local government is the personal reward and evaluation issue. One important criterion of a good performance measurement system is the link between staff performance and the reward and appraisal system. However, there are limited career advance opportunities in local councils. The prospect of promotion depends on the availability of posts in an organisation. Additionally, the ability of local councils to create new posts depends not only on workload and population of the area but also on its financial capacity. Thus, it is not surprising that many of the complaints and points of dissatisfaction raised by local authority personnel relate to promotion and the future prospects of their services in their respective local councils.

Compounding this issue, the lack of awareness in the general public on the scope of work, power and responsibilities of the local government has led to complaints on activities which are not under the power and jurisdiction of the local authorities or within their areas of responsibility. In addition, some of the local government's major activities involve a great deal of coordination with other agencies over which they have no control. For instance, infrastructure projects which are under federal, state, or some other governmental agency. Moreover, there are sometimes cases when the roles of local authorities are limited to only granting permits for projects without any control over major infrastructure such as main roads and electricity; which are often fundamental to the meaningful structure of plans (Mohamed Nor, 1973; Omar, et al., 2007).

RECOMMENDATIONS TO IMPROVE GOVERNANCE AND ACCOUNTABILITY

Public governance covers issues such as transparency, accountability and integrity (IFAC, 2000; as quoted by Engku Ismail, 2011). Such provisions have been the intended outcome of the transformation program. However, as mentioned, even with the numerous improvement programs and initiatives, there is still criticism regarding the government and integrity of public organizations and also of public officers. Hence, in order for the intended objectives of the transformation program to be achieved, changes pertaining to the management and governance structure of the local authorities in Malaysia needs to be undertaken.

The leadership is one of the key issues that need to be addressed as it is a vital element of sound local administration and the central point of good governance (Stein, 2008; Dewing & Russell, 2008). As mentioned before, the short tenure-ship of presidents of local councils implicates a lack of overall responsibility and ineffective overseeing of change processes. Changing of leadership also means there is insignificant accountability for the outcomes of implementation processes and decisions made by councils.

Furthermore, leadership plays a very important role in the process of change and is a major part of ensuring good organizational performance (Hill, 2006; Granger, 2009; Ballinger, 2004; Sebastian, 2007; Kungis, 2006; Mulqueen, 2005; Myers, 2001; Lee, 2000; Ryan, 2001). Thus, a longer termed tenure-ship is a precondition for greater responsibility and accountability of decisions made by local councils. The person in charge of a local council should hold the position for more than two years so that he or she will have to be accountable and responsible for the decisions made and is able to set the strategic directions of the council. A contract basis for appointment will need to be considered so that renewal of contract is based on achievement of objectives. Given that local authorities are closed organizations whereby promotion is from within, the leaders also need to motivate other employees in local authorities.

The councilors should also be from diverse parts of society, for instance, from NGOs and the general public, and not only appointed from or by those representing business communities or political interests. As Neely (1997) argues, good governance relates to good decision making and good decision-making entails stakeholder participation in the decision making process. A channel to hear the ordinary voices of citizens has to be incorporated in the decision-making processes of local councils. As such, the LA 21 program has to be undertaken more comprehensively and not done in an ad-hoc manner, not only focusing on certain issues such as crime prevention, waste management or other small community engagement programs. Citizen participation should be incorporated from the planning process to the implementation and evaluation phase especially for the determination of the strategic directions and planning of local areas. Thus, the star rating system should provide greater emphasis on incorporating rating indicators pertaining to meaningful public engagement projects. In addition, to ensure that public engagement is done seriously and local area is developed sustainably, performance indicators pertaining to sustainable development have to be considered when evaluating local authorities by using a revised star rating system.

A frequent criticism concerning public sector leadership is the lack of commitment to the fundamental principles of public service and the wellbeing of the people being assisted (New Straits Times, 2003). Thus, governance and accountability also has to be inculcated in the culture of local authorities. However, the emphasis in government organizations is mainly on managerial accountability and not governance accountability. Managerial accountability may lead to ensuring performance is in compliance to measurable outcomes rather than whether it has improved performance and enhanced justice (Dubnick, 2006). Training pertaining to inculcating pride and integrity in public service has to be conducted for all employees, management, and also councilors. The leaders and management of the councils ought to take on formal features or values such as separating of powers, check and balance, transparency, and accountability. In order for these values to be realized, the values must guide the actions of officials

throughout the system and must be imbedded in the organizational culture. Thus, methods to inculcate governance accountability rather than solely managerial accountability are needed to enhance good governance.

In order to ensure efficiency and effectiveness, the government must look seriously into fulfilling the needs of the public sector in terms of funds, staff capacities, office facilities, and IT infrastructures. Such factors could affect the competency of an agency or department since some of the complaints that are related to service delivery also relates to poor facilities. Most of the work carried out is done manually and has to go through many stages and levels of approval in local authorities. Employees should be given opportunities to rotate to other departments or agencies within their area of expertise or job function, to augment their professional development. Issues of remuneration and staff promotion, performance appraisal and related matters should be tackled before the introduction of other reformation and transformation programs (Australian Public Service Commission Report, 2003).

FUTURE RESEARCH DIRECTIONS

In depth research on the issues pertaining to governance and accountability in Malaysia are greatly needed. In view of the unique characteristics of the local authorities in Malaysia, research on how program, performance, and process accountability is achieved is required to increase effectiveness and efficiency. In addition, a major research agenda for Malaysian local councils will be on the methods to incorporate stakeholder participation in the decision-making processes of local councils. Issues such as how to reconcile the competing and sometimes diverse interests of various stakeholder groups need to be addressed as well. Other relevant research issues such as the long-term impact of the government transformation plan and a focus on managerial accountability can also be explored through longitudinal case study research.

CONCLUSION

Local councils are considered the 'hand of government' and are the closest institutions to the common public. They are the implementers and the deliverers of all government initiatives, mechanisms, and programs for the public. They provide services directly to the public and are being watched or evaluated for their effectiveness and efficiency. Hence, local authorities have to be effective and efficient in order to facilitate national growth and advance the country's competitive edge. Local authorities have the responsibility to ensure that development of their local area is done in a sustainable manner. Thus, good governance and accountability are essential components for the proper management of local authorities.

Among the main provisions for the successful existence of environmental accountability are leadership and transparency. Policies and programs that have been introduced and implemented in Malaysia are mostly based on the above provisions. However, issues and complaints from the public relating to accountability and governance of the local authorities are still continually raised. Among the various challenges faced by local authorities are political interference, lack of human resource and financial capacity and frequently changing leadership. Furthermore, the lack of dynamic organizational policies and procedures has led to the dissatisfaction of employees. Inadequate resources have led to incompetence, ineffectiveness, and service delays; while not emphasizing the role of leadership has led to the loss of an institutional sense of being and direction.

Therefore, to improve good governance, there should be a change in the local governance structure. Councilors should not be chosen based on political affiliation but should instead be from diverse stakeholders. Top management should be given longer tenure-ships to ensure accountability of decisions make and better control of implementation of projects and programs and with performance based rewards to improve management of local authority. More importantly, a comprehensive engagement with stakeholders in the decision making process is greatly needed. However, any reformation efforts will not be successful if the aspects of organizational and human factors are neglected. The concept and practice of good governance need to be inculcated in local authorities to ensure management and personnel are more responsive to the needs of citizens especially those from the disadvantage groups as this could eventually lead to a more just and equitable society.

REFERENCES

Abdul Karim, M. R. (1995). *Improving the efficiency of the public sector: A case study of Malaysia.* Paper presented at the Twelfth Meeting of Experts on the United Nations Programme in Public Administration and Finance. New York, NY.

Australia Government. (2003). *Australian public service commission report.* Canberra, Australia: Government of Australia.

Ballinger, G. A. (2004). *The impact of leadership succession on individuals in work groups.* West Lafayette, IN: Purdue University.

Cousin, M. A. (2009). *Passing the baton and letting it go: Leadership transition in a traditional AME church congregation.* Evanston, IL: Garrett-Evangelical Theological Seminary.

Denning, M. M. (2006). *Effect of leadership style on the transition from founders to professional managers: A case study of two small to medium enterprises.* Minneapolis, MN: Capella University.

Dewing, I. P., & Russell, P. O. (2008). The individualization of corporate governance: The approved persons' regime for UK financial services firms. *Accounting, Auditing & Accountability Journal, 21*(7), 978. doi:10.1108/09513570810907447

Dubnick, M. J. (2006). *Pathologies of governance reform: Promises, pervasions and perversions in the age of accountability.* Melbourne, Australia: Monash University.

Fancher, L. P. (2007). *The influence of organizational culture on the implementation of succession planning.* Francher, GA: Georgia State University.

Federal Constitution of Malaysia. (2006). *The commissioner of law revision, Malaysia under the authority of the revision of Laws act 1968.* Kuala Lumpur, Malaysia: Government of Malaysia.

Frank, H. M. (2008). Performance management practices in public sector organizations: Impact on performance. *Accounting, Auditing & Accountability Journal, 21*(3), 427. doi:10.1108/09513570810863996

Garchinsky, C. R. (2009). *Planning for the continuity of a school's vision and culture before leadership succession events.* Philadelphia, PA: Drexel University.

Granger, K. B. (2009). *The relationship between employee commitment and a change in leadership, and the leadership style that demonstrates the greatest change.* Minneapolis, MN: Capella University.

Hashim, R. (2007). *Electronic procurement project implementation issues in Selangor local government.* Shah Alam, Malaysia: University Technology Mara.

Hashim, R. (2010). Issues in electronic procurement project implementation in local government. *International Journal of Information Technology Project Management, 1*(3), 59–70. doi:10.4018/jitpm.2010070105

Hill, G. C. (2006). *On managerial succession.* College Station, TX: Texas A&M University.

IFAC. (2000). *Website.* Retrieved February 14, 2012, from www.ifac.org

Kaliannan, M., Awang, H., & Raman, M. (2009). Government purchasing: A review of e-procurement system in Malaysia. *The Journal of Knowledge Economy & Knowledge Management, 4,* 27–41.

Kaliannan, M., Awang, H., Raman, M., & Dorasamy, M. (2008). *E-procurement for the public sector: Determinants of attitude towards adoption.* Paper presented at International Conference on E-Government, ICEG 2008. New York, NY.

Kaliannan, M., & Murali, R. (2009). *E-procurement adoption in the Malaysian public sector: Organizational perspectives.* Paper presented at Service-Oriented Business Networks and Ecosystems, SOBNE 2009. New York, NY.

Kungis, J. P. (2006). *Leadership and productivity: A study of the perceptions of the non-supervisory civilian personnel at the garrison.* Minneapolis, MN: Capella University.

Kuppusamy, S. (2010). The right marriage between local government and the private sector in Malaysia? *International Journal of Institutions and Economies, 2*(2), 142–166.

Kutz, S. E. (2008). *Sensemaking for followers in leadership transition: What's going on here?* Reno, NV: University of Nevada.

Lee, S.-H. (2000). *A multidimensional view of public sector employee commitment and willingness to support productivity improvement strategies: A comparative study of public employees at the managerial-level between the United States and South Korea.* Hoboken, NJ: The State University of New Jersey.

Mandi, A. R. (2008). *A case study exploring succession planning: Supported by a quantitative analysis of governmental organizations in the Kingdom of Bahrain*. Washington, DC: The George Washington University.

Mansor, N. (2006). *Public procurement innovation in Malaysia: E-procurement*. Kuala Lumpur, Malaysia: University of Malaya. Retrieved January 18, 2012, from www.napsipag.org/PDF/E-Procurement-Malaysia.pdf

Mohamed Nor, M. A. (1973). *The role and effectiveness of the town and country planning department in national development*. Kuala Lumpur, Malaysia: University of Malaya.

Mulqueen, C. (2005). *Learning through failure: A descriptive analysis of leader behavior*. Albuquerque, NM: The University of New Mexico.

Myers, R. (2003). Ensuring ethical effectiveness. *Journal of Accountancy, 195*(2), 28–33.

National Audit Department. (2008). *Website*. Retrieved February 8, 2012, from www.audit.gov.my

Neely, A. (1998). *Measuring business performance: Why, what, and how?* London, UK: The Economist Books.

New Straits Times. (2007). *Audit standard not up to mark*. New Straits Times.

News Straits Times. (2003). *Councillors of shame*. New Straits Times.

Norris, M. W. (1980). Restructuring of local government – An assessment. *Management Review, 15*(1).

Schein, E. (1992). *Organizational culture and leadership* (2nd ed.). San Francisco, CA: Jossey-Bass.

Sebastian, M. W. (2007). *Information technology leadership perceptions and employee-centric organizational culture*. Minneapolis, MN: Walden University.

Shipman, F. B. (2007). *Formal succession planning in healthcare organizations: Meeting leadership needs in a changing American workforce*. Louisville, KY: Spalding University.

Siddiquee, N. A. (2006). Public management reform in Malaysia: Recent initiatives and experiences. *International Journal of Public Sector Management, 19*(4), 339. doi:10.1108/09513550610669185

Siti-Nabiha, A. K. (2008). New public management in Malaysia: In search of an efficient and effective service delivery. *International Journal of Management Studies, 15*, 69–90.

Siti-Nabiha, A. K. (2010). Improving the service delivery: A case study of a local authority in Malaysia. *Global Business Review, 11*(1), 65–77. doi:10.1177/097215090901100104

Stein, M. J. (2008). Beyond the boardroom: Governmental perspectives on corporate governance. *Accounting, Auditing & Accountability Journal, 21*(7), 1001. doi:10.1108/09513570810907456

Steven, A. (2006). *Malaysia's town and cities are governed by appointed mayors*. Retrieved February 5, 2012, from www.citymayors.com/government/malaysia

Stone, B., Jabbra, J. G., & Dwivedi, 0. P. (1989). *Public service accountability: A comparative perspective*. Hartford, CT: Kumarian Press.

Stutsman, K. K. (2007). *An examination of principal shortages in Florida school districts: Implications for succession planning for principal replacement*. Gainesville, FL: University of Florida.

The Local Government ACT 1976 (ACT 171) & Subsidiary Legislation as at 25 August 2005. Percetakan National Malaysia Bhd (1976).

Tischler, I. F. (2004). *How does leadership transition influence a sustained school change process? A case study*. Columbus, OH: The Ohio State University.

UNDP. (1997). *The governance policy paper*. New York, NY: UNDP.

Wheeler, M. E. (2008). *The leadership succession process in megachurches*. Philadelphia, PA: Temple University.

Yukl, G. (2002). *Leadership in organizations* (5th ed.). Upper Saddle River, NJ: Prentice Hall.

ADDITIONAL READING

Agus, A., Barker, S., & Kandampully, J. (2007). An exploratory study of service quality in the Malaysian public service sector. *International Journal of Quality & Reliability Management, 24*(2), 177. doi:10.1108/02656710710722284

Barrett, M. (2001). A stakeholder approach to responsiveness and accountability in non-profit organizations. *Social Policy Journal of New Zealand, 17*, 36–51.

Ibrahim, F. W., & Abdul Karim, M. Z. (2004). Efficiency of local governments in Malaysia and its correlates. *International Journal of Management Studies, 11*(1), 57–70.

Johl, S. K. (1993). *Accountability in the public sector in Malaysia*. (Unpublished Masters Dissertation). University of New England. Biddeford, ME.

Muttalib, M. A. (1983). *Theory of local government*. New Delhi, India: Sterling Publishers.

Omar, O., Mohammad Sharofi, I., Syed Sofian, S. I., Siti Zabedah, S., Mohd Syahrir, R., & Md Suhaimi, S., Marlina, M. L. (2007). *Public sector accounting in Malaysia*. Kuala Lumpur, Malaysia: Cengage Learning Asia.

Parker, L. D., & Guthrie, J. (1993). The Australian public sector in the 1990s: New accountability regimes in motion. *Journal of International Accounting, Auditing & Taxation, 2*(1), 59. doi:10.1016/1061-9518(93)90015-L

Siddiquee, N. A. (2008). Service delivery innovations and governance: The Malaysian experience. *Transforming Government: People. Process and Policy, 2*(3), 194.

Siddiquee, N. A. (2010). Managing for results: Lessons from public management reform in Malaysia. *International Journal of Public Sector Management, 23*(1), 38. doi:10.1108/09513551011012312

Siddiquee, N. A., & Mohamed, M. Z. (2007). Paradox of public sector reforms in Malaysia: A good governance perspective. *Public Administration Quarterly, 31*(3), 284.

Tayib, M. (1999). Financial reporting by Malaysian local authorities: A study of the needs and requirements of the users of local authority financial accounts. *International Journal of Public Sector Management, 12*(2), 103–120. doi:10.1108/09513559910263453

KEY TERMS AND DEFINITIONS

A-Star Rating System: A system that is used to evaluate the overall performance of local governments.

Electronic Procurement System: The system that enables Government agencies nationwide to procure goods and services from their suppliers electronically.

Government Transformation Program (GTP): A program that aimed to ensure government agencies will more effective in its delivery of services and accountable for outcomes.

Key Performance Indicators: Indicators that enable an organization to define and measure progress towards its strategic goals.

Local Agenda 21: It is a local government-led, community-wide, and participatory effort to establish a comprehensive action strategy for environmental protection, economic prosperity, and community well-being in the local jurisdiction or area.

One-Stop-Centres (OSCs): The centre that brings together various government agencies in the processing of development and building plan approvals.

Compilation of References

Abdul Karim, M. R. (1995). *Improving the efficiency of the public sector: A case study of Malaysia.* Paper presented at the Twelfth Meeting of Experts on the United Nations Programme in Public Administration and Finance. New York, NY.

Achterstraat, P. (2011). *Compliance review report - Procurement reform of e-procurement and e-tendering.* Retrieved from http://www.audit.nsw.gov.au/ArticleDocuments/190/03_Vol_1_2011_Compliance_Review.pdf.aspx?Embed=Y

Act 30. March 2007 No. 348. (2007) C-314/09 Strabag (2010-09-30) and C-568/08 Spijkers (2010) C-395/95 Geotronics SA v Commission (1997-04-22) E.C.R. I-2271 (1997)

Adendorff, S. A., Bothma, C., Fourie, I., & Walters, J. (2004). E-commerce and SCM. In Hugo, W. M. J., Badenhorst-Weiss, J. A., & van Biljon, E. (Eds.), *Supply Chain Management.* Pretoria, South Africa: Van Schaik.

Adler, N. (1986). *International dimensions of organizational behavior.* Boston, MA: Kent Publishing Company.

Agranoff, R. (2007). *Managing within networks: Adding value to public organizations.* Washington, DC: Georgetown University Press.

Akhdar, F. (1994). *Privatizing Saudi economy: Theory and application.* Jeddah, Saudi Arabia: Saudi Research and Publishing Co.

Akoum, I. (2009). Privatization in Saudi Arabia: Is slow beautiful? *Wiley Periodicals Inc.* Retrieved April 13, 2010, from http://www.intersince.wiley.com

Al-Ajmi, N. (2003, May 5). Saudi Arabia: The opening of a kingdom. *Arab Times Magazine.*

Albano, G., & Sparro, M. (2010). Flexible strategies for centralized public procurement. *Review of Economics and Institutions, 1*(2), 1–32. doi:10.5202/rei.v1i2.17

Albertyn, C., & Kentridge, J. (1994). Introduction to the right to equality in the interim constitution. *South African Journal on Human Rights, 10*(2), 149–178.

Al-Homeadan, A. (1996). *Factors that shape attitudes towards privatization: The case of Saudi Arabia.* (Unpublished Doctoral Dissertation). Florida Atlantic University. Boca Raton, FL.

Al-Homoud, M., & Abdalla, I. (1995). A survey of management training and development practices in the state of Kuwait. *Journal of Management Development, 14*(3), 14–25. doi:10.1108/02621719510078939

Al-Salloum, T. (1999). *Policy choice in developing countries: The case of privatization in Saudi Arabia.* (Unpublished Doctoral Dissertation). George Mason University. Fairfax, VA.

Al-Sarhan & Presly. (2001). Privatization in Saudi Arabia: An attitude survey. *Managerial Finance, 27*(10/11), 114–122. doi:10.1108/03074350110767600

Ancarani, A., & Capaldo, G. (2005). Supporting decision-making process in facilities management services procurement: A methodological approach. *Journal of Purchasing and Supply Management, 11,* 232–241. doi:10.1016/j.pursup.2005.12.004

Andersen, K. V. (2004). *E-government and public sector process rebuilding (PPR): Dilettantes, wheelbarrows, and diamonds.* Boston, MA: Kluwever Academic Publishers.

Andersen, K. V., & Henriksen, H. Z. (2006). e-Government maturity models: Extension of the Layne and Lee model. *Government Information Quarterly, 23*, 236–248. doi:10.1016/j.giq.2005.11.008

Angeles, R., & Nath, R. (2007). Business-to-business e-procurement: success factors and challenges to implementation. *Supply Chain Management: An International Journal, 12*(2), 104–115. doi:10.1108/13598540710737299

Angelopoulos, S., Kitsios, F., Kofakis, P., & Papadopoulos, T. (2010). Emerging barriers in e-government implementation. In Wimmer, M. A. (Ed.), *International Federation for Information Processing: e-Government Conference* (pp. 216–225). Lausanne, France: IEEE.

Arlbjørn, J. S., & Freytag, P. V. (2012). Public procurement vs. private purchasing: Is there any foundation for comparing and learning across the sectors? *International Journal of Public Sector Management, 25*(3), 203–220. doi:10.1108/09513551211226539

Arminas, D. (2002). Are relationships going, going, gone? *Supply Management*. Retrieved January 28, 2012, from http://www.supplymanagement.com/news/2002/are-relationships-going-going-gone/?show=recent

Arnett, S. (2011). *The NATO codification system as the foundation for eOTD and ISO standards 22745 and 8000*. Retrieved November 14, 2011, from http://www.eccma.org/2011ECCMAconf/docs/Steven%20Arnett.pdf

Arrowsmith, S. (1995). Public procurement as an instrument of policy and the impact of market liberalization. *The Law Quarterly Review, 111*, 235–284.

Arrowsmith, S. (2001). E-commerse policy and the EC procurement rules: The chasm between rhetoric and reality. In *Kluwer Law International* (pp. 1447–1477). Dordrecht, The Netherlands: Kluwer.

Arrowsmith, S. (2010). Horizontal policies in public procurement: A taxonomy. *Journal of Public Procurement, 10*(2), 149–186.

Aschoff, B., & Sofka, W. (2009). Innovation on demand – Can public procurement drive market success of innovations? *Research Policy, 38*(8), 1235–1247. doi:10.1016/j.respol.2009.06.011

Asheim, B. T., & Coenen, L. (2005). Knowledge bases and regional innovation systems: Comparing Nordic clusters. *Research Policy, 34*(8), 1173–1190. doi:10.1016/j.respol.2005.03.013

Asian Development Bank. (2010). *Technical assistance report, Republic of Indonesia: Streangthing national public procurement process*. Manila, Phillipines: Asian Development Bank.

Attorney-General's Department. (2005). *Case studies on e-procurement implementations Italy, New South Wales, New Zealand, Scotland, Western Australia*. Canberra, Australia: Australian Government. Retrieved from http://www.finance.gov.au/publications/e-procurement-research-reports/docs/Case_Studies_on_E-procurement_Implementations.pdf

Auriol, E. (2006). Corruption in procurement and public purchase. *International Journal of Industrial Organization, 24*, 867–885. doi:10.1016/j.ijindorg.2005.11.001

Australia Government. (2003). *Australian public service commission report*. Canberra, Australia: Government of Australia.

Bagliano, F. C., & Bertola, G. (2004). *Models for dynamic macroeconomics*. Oxford, UK: Oxford University Press. doi:10.1093/0199266824.001.0001

Baily, P., Farmer, D., Crocker, B., Jessop, D., & Jones, D. (2008). *Procurement principles and management*. Harlow, MA: Prentice Hall.

Baily, P., Farmer, D., Jessop, D., & Jones, D. (1994). *Purchasing principles and management*. London, UK: Gower Publishing.

Bakos, Y., & Brynjolfsson, E. (1999). Bundling information goods: Pricing, profits, and efficiency. *Management Science, 45*(12), 1613–1630. doi:10.1287/mnsc.45.12.1613

Ballinger, G. A. (2004). *The impact of leadership succession on individuals in work groups*. West Lafayette, IN: Purdue University.

Bannister, F. (2001). Dismantling the silos: extracting new value from IT investments in public administration. *Information Systems Journal, 11*(1), 65–84. doi:10.1046/j.1365-2575.2001.00094.x

Bardhan, P. (1997). Corruption and development: A review of issues. *Journal of Economic Literature, 35*(3), 1320–1346.

Barr, S. (2008, January 24). OMB, GAO to go digital on key reports. *The Washington Post.*

Basheka, B. C. (2009). Public procurement corruption and its implications on effective service delivery in Uganda: An empirical study. *International Journal of Procurement Management, 2*(4), 415–440. doi:10.1504/IJPM.2009.026072

Batchelor, C. (1999, June 17). Logistics aspires to worldly wisdom. *The Financial Times*, p. 17.

Batenburg, R. (2007). E-procurement adoption by European firms: A quantitative analysis. *Journal of Purchasing and Supply Management, 13*(3), 182–192. doi:10.1016/j.pursup.2007.09.014

Bawa, N. (2005). New development paths for Indian business in South Africa: Evidence from Gauteng. *Africa Insight, 35*(4), 45–52.

Beach, M. (2012). *Preferential procurement policy act.* Retrieved on February 4, 2012, from http://www.ehow.com/about_6667931_preferential-procurement-policy-act.html

Benson, P. (2010). Managing a data cleansing (cleaning) or cataloging project. *ECCMA.* Retrieved October 15, 2011, from http://www.eccma.org/resources/White_Papers.php#

Bertot, J. C., Jaeger, P. T., & Grimes, J. M. (2010). Using ICTs to create a culture of transparency: e-Government and social media as openness and anti-corruption tools for societies. *Government Information Quarterly, 27,* 264–271.

Betts, M., Black, P., Christensen, S., Dawson, E., Du, R., & Duncan, W. ... Gonzalez Nieto, J. (2006). Towards secure and legal e-tendering. *Journal of Information Technology in Construction, 11,* 89–102. Retrieved January 28, 2012, from http://itcon.org/cgi-bin/works/Show?2006_7

BIPSolutions. (2004). *Vault secure e-tendering document exchange service.* Retrieved January 28, 2012, from http://www.sopo.org/rtfs/vaultfaq.htm

Birks, C., Bond, S., & Radford, M. (2001). *Guide to e-procurement in the public sector: Cutting through the hype.* London, UK: Office of Government Commerce.

BIS. (2010). *Small and medium-sized enterprise (SME) statistics for the UK and regions 2009 (SME statistics).* Retrieved January 28, 2012, from http://webarchive.nationalarchives.gov.uk/+/http://stats.bis.gov.uk/ed/sme/

Blaby District Council. (2004). *Document retention and destruction procedures and guidelines.* Retrieved January 28, 2012, from http://idocs.blaby.gov.uk/external/council-democracy/dp-foi/foi-council-retention-schedule.pdf

Blackstone, E., Boganno, M., & Hakim, S. (2005). *Innovations in e-government: The thoughts of governors and mayors.* Lanham, MD: Rowman & Littlefield.

BMI. (2010). *The Saudi Arabia business forecast report. Business Monitor International.* BMI.

Boeing. (1996). *Supplier network technical data interchange (SNET-TDI).* Retrieved January 28, 2012, from http://www.boeing.com/companyoffices/doingbiz/tdi/faq.html

Bof, F., & Previtali, P. (2007). Organisational pre-conditions for e-procurement in governments: The Italian experience in the public health care sector. *The Electronic. Journal of E-Government, 5*(1), 1–10.

Bogason, P., & Toonen, T. A. J. (1998). Introduction: Networks in public administration. *Public Administration, 76*(2), 205–227. doi:10.1111/1467-9299.00098

Boldrin, M., & Canova, F. (2001). Inequality and convergence in Europe's regions: Reconsidering European regional policies. *Economic Policy, 16*(32), 207–253. doi:10.1111/1468-0327.00074

Bollerslev, T., Chou, Y. R., & Kroner, F. K. (1992). Arch modeling in finance: A review of the theory and empirical evidence. *Journal of Econometrics, 52,* 5–59. doi:10.1016/0304-4076(92)90064-X

Bolton, P. (2006). Government procurement as a policy tool in South Africa. *Journal of Public Procurement, 6*(3), 193–217.

Bolton, P. (2007). *The law of government procurement in South Africa.* Durban, South Africa: LexisNexis Butterworths.

Bonham, G., Seifert, J., & Thorson, S. (2001). *The transformational potential of e-government: The role of political leadership*. Paper presented at the 4th Pan European International Relations Conference. Kent, UK.

Bothma, C. H. (2000). *E-commerce for South African managers*. Pretoria, South Africa: Interactive Reality.

Bowerman, L. B., O'Connell, T. R., & Koehler, B. A. (2004). *Forecasting, time series, and regression: An applied approach*. Chula Vista, CA: South-Western College Publication.

Bozeman, B., & Dietz, J. S. (2001). Research policy trends in the United States: Civilian technology programs, defense technology, and the development of the national laboratories. In Laredo, P., & Mustar, P. (Eds.), *Research and Innovation Policies in the New Global Economy: An International Comparative Analysis* (pp. 47–78). Northampton, MA: Edward Elgar Publishing, Inc.

Bradley, J., & Morgenroth, E. (2004). *A study of the macroeconomic impact of the reform of EU cohesion policy*. Retrieved from http://ec.europa.eu/regional_policy/sources/docgener/studies/pdf/3cr/macro_impact.pdf

Bradley, J., & Zaleski, J. (2003). *Modeling EU accession and structural fund impacts using the new Polish HERMIN model - Report*. Retrieved from http://www.funduszestrukturalne.gov.pl/NR/rdonlyres/76D3C5FA-B01A-494C-AB9D-D31C3F624193/14808/REVISEDJ-BradleyJZaleski_HERMINPolandafterCopenhage.pdf

Brammer, S., & Walker, H. (2011). Sustainable procurement in the public sector: An international comparative study. *International Journal of Operations & Production Management*, *31*(4), 452–476. doi:10.1108/01443571111119551

Brandon-Jones, A., & Carey, S. (2010). The impact of user-perceived e-procurement quality on system and contract compliance. *International Journal of Operations & Production Management*, *31*(3), 374–396.

Bravosolution. (2008). *Government makes key cost and effective savings with innovative technology*. Retrieved January 28, 2012, from https://www.bravosolution.com/cms/news-events/press-center/08-july-2008-1/

Bravosolution. (2012). *Analyst industry reports*. Retrieved January 28, 2012, from https://www.bravosolution.com/cms/uk/resource-center/analyst-industry-reports/copy3_of_Knowledge%20Economy

Brazell, L. (2004). *Electronic signatures law and regulation: Law and regulation*. London, UK: Sweet & Maxwell.

Buchta, D., Eul, M., & Schulte-Croonenberg, H. (2010). *Strategic IT management, increase value, control performance, reduce costs*. Wiesbaden, Germany: Gabler.

Budd, L., & Hirmis, A. K. (2004). Conceptual framework for regional competitiveness. *Regional Studies*, *38*(9), 1015–1028. doi:10.1080/0034340042000292610

Building Smart. (2009). *CITE bills of quantities standard - Version 4.2*. Retrieved January 28, 2012, from http://146.87.15.57:9080/buildingSmart/CITE/standards/ascii-flat-file-members-only/cite-bills-of-quantities-standard

Building Smart. (2009). *What is BuildingSmart?* Retrieved January 28, 2012, from http://www.buildingsmart.org.uk/buildingSMART/what-is-the-iai

Building Smart. (2009). *BuildingSmart international*. Retrieved January 28, 2012, from http://www.buildingsmartalliance.org/

Building Smart. (2009). *Frequently asked questions*. Retrieved January 28, 2012, from http://buildingsmart-tech.org/implementation/faq

Cabinet Office. (1999). *Modernising government*. Retrieved January 28, 2012, from http://www.archive.official-documents.co.uk/document/cm43/4310/4310-00.htm

Cabinet Office. (2000). *Progress report against the executive summary of the modernising government white paper 1999*. Retrieved January 28, 2012, from http://archive.cabinetoffice.gov.uk/moderngov/whtpaper/summary_progress.htm#4d

Cabras, I. (2010). Use of e-procurement in local authorities' purchasing and its effects on local economies: Evidence from Cumbria, UK. *European Planning Studies*, *18*(7), 1133–1151. doi:10.1080/09654311003744209

Cabras, I. (2011). Mapping the spatial patterns of public procurement: A case study from a peripheral local authority in Northern England. *International Journal of Public Sector Management, 24*(3), 187–205. doi:10.1108/09513551111121338

Caffrey, L., Rogers, W., & Okot-Uma, O. (1999). *Government secure intranets*. London, UK: Commonwealth Secretariat.

Callois, J. M., & Aubert, F. (2007). Towards indicators of social capital for regional development issues: The case of French rural areas. *Regional Studies, 41*(6), 809–821. doi:10.1080/00343400601142720

Cañizares, E., Fernández, D., Padilla, A. J., & Ramos, A. (2001). *Competència i innovació en la nova economia*. Departament d'Indústria, Comerç i Turisme, Direcció General d'Indústria.

Capello, R. (2007). *Regional economics*. London, UK: Routledge.

Carayannis, E., & Popescu, D. (2005). Profiling a methodology for economic growth and convergence: Learning from the EU e-procurement experience for central and eastern European countries. *Technovation, 25*, 1–14. doi:10.1016/S0166-4972(03)00071-3

Carter, L., Giber, D., & Goldsmith, M. (2001). Best practices in organisation development and change: Culture, leadership, retention, performance, coaching. *Pfeiffer*. Retrieved April 8, 2010, from http://library.books24x7.com.proxy.lib.chalmers.se/

Carter, C. R., & Jennings, M. M. (2004). The role of purchasing in the socially responsible management of the supply chain: A structural equation analysis. *Journal of Business Logistics, 23*(1), 145–186. doi:10.1002/j.2158-1592.2002.tb00020.x

Carter, L., & Bélanger, F. (2005). The utilization of e-government services: Citizen trust, innovation and acceptance factors. *Information Systems Journal, 15*(1), 5–25. doi:10.1111/j.1365-2575.2005.00183.x

Carter, R. Y., & Grimm, R. (2001). Journal of public procurement under the FAU-NIGP partnership. *Journal of Public Procurement, 1*(1), 3–8.

Cartlidge, D. (2006). *New aspects of quantity surveying practice*. Oxford, UK: Elsevier Butterworth-Heinemann.

CEN. (2011). *CEN workshop on 'business interoperability interfaces on public procurement in Europe' phase 2 (WS/BII 2)*. Retrieved October 27, 2011, from http://www.cenbii.eu/about/

Chaffey, D. (2009). *e-Business and e-commerce management*. Essex, UK: Prentice Hall.

Chang, K. S. (2011). *Enhancing transparency through e-procurement*. The Republic of Korea. Retrieved from www.oecd.org/dataoecd/47/30/49311011.pdf

Chaudhry, M. A. (1992). Cauchy representation of distributions and applications to probability II. In *Proceedings of the International Symposium on Generalized Functions and their Applications*, (pp. 29-35). New York, NY: Plenum Publishing Corporation.

Chen, H., Chau, M., & Zeng, D. (2002). CI spider: A tool for competitive intelligence on the web. *Decision Support Systems, 34*, 1–17. doi:10.1016/S0167-9236(02)00002-7

Chen, S. C., & Dhillon, G. S. (2003). Interpreting dimensions of consumer trust in ecommerce. *Information Technology Management, 4*, 303–313. doi:10.1023/A:1022962631249

Chen, S., Ruikar, K., Carrillo, P., Khosrowshahi, F., & Underwood, J. (2011). *Construct IT for business, e-business in the construction industry*. Loughborough, UK: Loughborough University.

Cheung, A. (1997). The rise of privatization policies: Similar faces, diverse motives. *International Journal of Public Administration, 20*(12), 2213–2245. doi:10.1080/01900699708525293

Christensen, J., Schmidt, M., & Larsen, M. (2002). *The industrial dynamics of internet services*. Paper presented at the DRUID Summer Conference. Retrieved January 28, 2012, from http://www.druid.dk/conferences/summer2002/Papers/Christensen.pdf

Cialdini, R. B. (1993). *Influence: Science and practice* (3rd ed.). New York, NY: HarperCollins.

CITE. (2009). *What is CITE? BuildingSmart website*. Retrieved January 28, 2012, from http://www.buildingsmart.org.uk/about/cite/cite/?searchterm=CITE

Clarke, M., & Stewart, J. (1997). *Handling the wicked issues: A challenge for government.* Birmingham, UK: University of Birmingham.

Cline, R. J., & Neubig, T. S. (1999). *The sky is not falling: Why state and local revenues were not significantly impacted by the internet in 1998.* New York, NY: Ernst & Young Economics Consulting and Quantitative Analysis.

Commission Implementing Regulation. (2011). No 842/2011 of 19 August 2011 establishing standard forms for the publication of notices in the field of public procurement and repealing regulation (EC) no 1564/2005. *Official Journal of the European Union, 222*(1). Retrieved August 30, 2011 from http://eur-lex.europa.eu/LexUriServ/LexUriServ.do?uri=OJ:L:2011:222:0001:0187:EN:PDF

Consip, Q., Bertini, L., & Vidoni, A. (2009). *The electronic marketplace of the public administration – MEPA, scenario, operation and trends.* Retrieved March 9, 2011, from http://www.eng.consip.it/on-line/en/Home/ActivityandResults/ProgramfortheRationalizationof-PublicPurchases/ElectronicMarketplace/articolo613.html

Contract Journal. (2003). *Contractors urged to shun Tesco's Dutch auctions.* Retrieved January 28, 2012, from http://business.highbeam.com/410604/article-1G1-110665058/contractors-urged-shun-tesco-dutch-auctions

Cooper, P. J. (2003). *Governing by contract: Challenges and opportunities for public managers.* Washington, DC: CQ Press.

Cordesman, A. (2003). Saudi Arabia enters the twenty first century: The political, foreign policy, economic and energy dimensions. *Journal of Third World Studies, 23*(2), 248–249.

Corini, J. (2000, March). Integrating e-procurement and strategic souring. *Supply Chain Management Review, 3-7*.

Coulthard, D., & Castleman, T. (2001). Electronic procurement in government: More complicated than just good business. In *Proceedings of the 9th European Conference on Information Systems*, (pp. 999-1009). IEEE.

Cousin, M. A. (2009). *Passing the baton and letting it go: Leadership transition in a traditional AME church congregation.* Evanston, IL: Garrett-Evangelical Theological Seminary.

Crane, P. S. (1999). *Korean patterns – A royal Asiatic society-Korea.* Seoul, South Korea: Seoul Press.

Cronje, T., van Biljon, E., Naude, M., Nel, D., & Poulter. (2011). The task of purchasing and task management. In W. M. J. Hugo & J. A. Badenhorst-Weiss (Eds.), *Purchasing and Supply Management.* Pretoria, South Africa: Van Schaik.

Croom, S. R., & Brandon-Jones, A. (2005). Key issues in e-procurement: Procurement implementation and operation in the public sector. *Journal of Public Procurement, 5*(3), 367–387.

Croom, S. R., & Brandon-Jones, A. (2007). Impact of e-procurement: Experiences from implementation in the UK public sector. *Journal of Purchasing and Supply Management, 13*(4), 294–303. doi:10.1016/j.pursup.2007.09.015

Croom, S., & Johnston, R. (2003). E-service: Enhancing internal customer service through e-procurement. *International Journal of Service Industries Management, 14*(5), 539–555. doi:10.1108/09564230310500219

Currie, I., & De Waal, J. (2005). *The bill of rights handbook.* Lansdowne, South Africa: Juta & Co.

Czech Republic. (2006). *National plan for the introduction of electronic public procurement over the period 2006–2010.* Retrieved August 15, 2011, from http://kormoran.vlada.cz/usneseni/usneseni_webtest.nsf/web/cs?Open&2006&05-10

Czech Republic. (2009). *National infrastructure for electronic public procurement (NIPEZ).* Retrieved August 21, 2011, from http://www.portal-vz.cz/NIPEZ

Czech Republic. (2010). Strategy of digitization of public procurement from 2011 to 2015. *Journal of Government for the Regional and Municipal Authorities, 9*(1), 4–22.

Dacorum Borough Council. (2006). *IEG5 report.* Retrieved January 28, 2012, from www.bipsolutions.com/docstore/doc/12757.doc

Danish Act No 492 2010-05-12 in effect 2010-07-01, subsequent Complaints Board (2010)

Danziger, J. N., & Andersen, K. V. (2002). The impacts of information technology on public administration: An analysis of empirical research from the "golden age" of transformation. *International Journal of Public Administration, 25*, 591–627. doi:10.1081/PAD-120003292

Davenport, T. R. H., & Saunders, C. (2000). *South Africa: A modern history*. Bedford, NJ: Palgrave Macmillan.

Davila, A., Gupta, M., & Palmer, R. (2003). Moving procurement systems to the internet: The adoption and use of e-procurement technology models. *European Management Journal, 21*(1), 11–23. doi:10.1016/S0263-2373(02)00155-X

de Brí, F. (2009). An e-government stages of growth model based on research within the Irish revenue offices. *Electronic. Journal of E-Government, 7*(4), 219–228.

De Mente, B. (2004). *Korean business etiquette*. Singapore, Singapore: Tuttle Publishing.

De Santis, R. A. (2000). Optimal export taxes, welfare, industry concentration, and firm size: A general equilibrium analysis. *Review of International Economics, 8*(2), 319–335. doi:10.1111/1467-9396.00224

Denning, M. M. (2006). *Effect of leadership style on the transition from founders to professional managers: A case study of two small to medium enterprises*. Minneapolis, MN: Capella University.

Department of Communications. (2008). *South African yearbook* 2008/2009. Retrieved on March 26, 2012, from http://www.gcis.gov.za/resource_centre/sa_info/yearbook/2009/chapter5.pdf

DeSanctis, G., & Poole, M. S. (1994). Capturing the complexity in advanced technology use: Adaptive structuration theory. *Organization Science, 5*(2), 121–147. doi:10.1287/orsc.5.2.121

DETNI. (2004). *NICS strategic initiatives appendix B*. Retrieved January 28, 2012, from http://www.detini.gov.uk/nics_strategic_drivers.pdf

DETR. (2000). *Best value and audit commission performance indicators for 2001/2002: The gold book*. Retrieved January 28, 2012, from http://www.communities.gov.uk/archived/publications/localgovernment/bestvalueperformance

Devenish, G. E. (1999). *A commentary on the South African bill of rights*. Durban, South Africa: Butterworths.

Dewing, I. P., & Russell, P. O. (2008). The individualization of corporate governance: The approved persons' regime for UK financial services firms. *Accounting, Auditing & Accountability Journal, 21*(7), 978. doi:10.1108/09513570810907447

Dey, A., & Abowd, G. (2000). Towards a better understanding of context and context awareness. In *Proceedings of HUC*, (pp. 304-307). ACM Press.

DFP. (2009). *Central procurement directorate procurement guidance note 03/10 procurement control limits*. Retrieved January 28, 2012, from http://www.dfpni.gov.uk/index/procurement-2/cpd/cpd-policy-and-legislation/content_-_cpd_-_policy_-_procurement_guidance_notes/content_-_cpd_procurement_guidance_notes_pgn_03_-_10/pgn-03-10-26012011.pdf

Dhillon, G. S., Weerakkody, V., & Dwivedi, Y. K. (2008). Realising transformational stage e-government: A UK local authority perspective. *Electronic Government. International Journal (Toronto, Ont.), 5*(2), 162–180.

Diggs, S. N., & Roman, A. V. (2013). *Understanding and tracing accountability within the public procurement process: Interpretations, performance measurements and the possibility of developing public-private partnerships*. Public Performance & Management Review.

Dinavo, J. (1995). *Privatization in developing countries: It's impact on economic development and democracy*. London, UK: Praeger Publishers.

Dir. 07/66/EU (2010)

Dir. 07/77/EU (2010)

Dir. 2004/18/EU (2010)

Dir. 2007/66/EU (2010) Draft COM (2011)

Dir. 89/665/EU (2010)

Dir. 92/13/EU (2010)

DTI. (2005). *The BEE codes of good practice*. Retrieved March 2, 2012, from http://www.thedti.gov.za/bee/CODESOFGOODPRACTICE2005.htm

DTI. (2006). *Electronic signatures factsheet*. Retrieved January 28, 2012, from http://webarchive.nationalarchives.gov.uk/+/http://www.berr.gov.uk/files/file34339.pdf

DTI. (2009). *Electronic signatures and associated legislation*. Retrieved January 28, 2012, from http://webarchive.nationalarchives.gov.uk/+/http://www.berr.gov.uk/files/file49952.pdf

Dubnick, M. J. (2006). *Pathologies of governance reform: Promises, pervasions and perversions in the age of accountability*. Melbourne, Australia: Monash University.

Dumortier, J., & Van Eecke, P. (1999). The European draft directive on a common framework for electronic signatures. *Computer Law & Security Report, 15*(2), 106–112. doi:10.1016/S0267-3649(99)80022-3

Dunleavy, P., Margetts, H., Bastow, S., & Tinkler, J. (2006). *Digital era governance: IT corporations, the state, and e-government*. Oxford, UK: Oxford University Press.

Dunleavy, P., Margetts, H., Bastow, S., & Tinkler, J. (2006). New public management is dead: Long live digital-era governance. *Journal of Public Administration: Research and Theory, 16*(3), 467–494. doi:10.1093/jopart/mui057

Eadie, R., Millar, P., Perera, S., Heaney, G., & Barton, G. (2012). E–readiness of construction contract forms and e–tendering software. *International Journal of Procurement Management, 5*(1), 1-26. Retrieved January 28, 2012, from http://inderscience.metapress.com/content/9580t2p387mu1228/

Eadie, R., Perera, S., & Heaney, G. (2010). Identification of e-procurement drivers and barriers for UK construction organisations and ranking of these from the perspective of quantity surveyors. *Journal of Information Technology in Construction, 15*, 23-43. Retrieved January 28, 2012, from http://www.itcon.org/cgi-bin/works/Show?2010_2

Eadie, R., Perera, S., & Heaney, G. (2010). A cross discipline comparison of rankings of e-procurement drivers and barriers for UK construction organisations. *Journal of Information Technology in Construction, 15*, 217-233. Retrieved January 28, 2012, from http://www.itcon.org/cgi-bin/works/Show?2010_17

Eadie, R., Perera, S., & Heaney, G. (2011). Analysis of the use of e-procurement in the public and private sectors of the UK construction industry. *Journal of Information Technology in Construction, 16*, 669 – 686. Retrieved January 28, 2012, from http://www.itcon.org/cgi-bin/works/Show?2011_39

Eadie, R., Perera, S., Heaney, G., & Carlisle, J. (2007). Drivers and barriers to public sector e-procurement within Northern Ireland's construction industry. *Journal of Information Technology in Construction, 12*, 103-120. Retrieved January 28, 2012, from http://www.itcon.org/cgi-bin/works/Show?2007_6

eCl@ss. (2011). *Overview*. Retrieved August 30, 2011 from http://www.eclass.de/eclasscontent/standard/overview.html.en

Economides, N. (1996). The economics of networks. *International Journal of Industrial Organization, 14*(6), 673–699. doi:10.1016/0167-7187(96)01015-6

Edler, J., & Georghiou, L. (2007). Public procurement and innovation – Resurrecting the demand side. *Research Policy, 36*(7), 949–963. doi:10.1016/j.respol.2007.03.003

EFTA Court - the Icelandic E-5/98 (1999-05-12) Fagthun case (1999)

Egbu, C., Vines, M., & Tookey, J. (2004). The role of knowledge management in e-procurement initiatives for construction organisations. In *Proceedings of the ARCOM Twentieth Annual Conference 2004,* (Vol. 1, pp. 661-671). Reading, UK: Arcom.

Egeler, R., & Funk, J. (2009). Das kaufhaus des bundes – Ressortübergreifender einkauf der bundesverwaltung. The department store, the federal government - the federal government-wide purchasing. In Eßig, M., & Witt, M. (Eds.), *Öffentliche Logistik: Supply Chain Management für den öffentlichen Sektor Public Logistics: Supply Chain Management for the Public Sector*. (pp. 419–448). Berlin, Germany: Springer.

E-Quantities. (2009). *What is CITE?* Retrieved January 28, 2012, from http://www.e-quantities.com/bqfilter/cite.htm

Erridge, A., Fee, R., & McIlroy, J. (2001). *Best practice procurement: Public and private sector perspectives*. Burlington, VT: Gover Publishing Company.

Essig, M., & Batran, A. (2005). Public-private partnership: Development of long-term relationships in public procurement in Germany. *Journal of Purchasing and Supply Management, 11*(5-6), 221–231. doi:10.1016/j.pursup.2006.01.001

EU Court of Justice – the Finnish C-513/99 (J-2002-09-17) Concordia ruling and the Danish Unitron Skandinavia case C-275/98 (J 1999-11-18) (2002)

Eurlex. (2004). *European Union directive 2004/17 coordinating the procurement procedures of entities operating in the water, energy, transport and postal services sectors.* Retrieved January 28, 2012, from http://eur-lex.europa.eu/LexUriServ/LexUriServ.do?uri=CELEX:32004L0017:en:HTML

Eurlex. (2004). *European Union directive 2004/18 on the coordination of procedures for the award of public works contracts, public supply contracts and public service contracts.* Retrieved January 28, 2012, from http://eur-lex.europa.eu/LexUriServ/LexUriServ.do?uri=CELEX:32004L0018:En:HTML European Commission. (2012). *Your Europe website.* Retrieved January 28, 2012, from http://ec.europa.eu/youreurope/

Eurlex. (2011). Commission directive 2005/51/EC of 7 September 2005 amending annex XX to directive 2004/17/EC and annex VIII to directive 2004/18/EC of the European parliament and the council on public procurement. Retrieved October 27, 2011, from http://eur-lex.europa.eu/LexUriServ/LexUriServ.do?uri=OJ:L:2005:257:0127:0128:EN:PDF

Eurlex. (2011). Communication from the commission to the council, the European parliament, the European economic and social committee and the committee of the regions – Action plan for the implementation of the legal framework for electronic public procurement {SEC(2004)1639}. Retrieved August 21, 2011, from http://eurlex.europa.eu/LexUriServ/LexUriServ.do?uri=CELEX:52004DC0841:EN:HTML

Eurlex. (2011). *Directive 2004/17/EC of the European parliament and of the council coordinating the procurement procedures of entities operating in the water, energy, transport and postal services sectors.* Retrieved July 10, 2011, from http://eurlex.europa.eu/LexUriServ/LexUriServ.do?uri=OJ:L:2011:343:0077:0085:EN:PDF

Eurlex. (2011). *Directive 2004/18/EC of the European parliament and of the council of 31 March 2004 on the coordination of procedures for the award of public works contracts, public supply contracts and public service contracts.* Retrieved October 27, 2011, from http://eurlex.europa.eu/LexUriServ/LexUriServ.do?uri=OJ:L:2004:134:0114:0240:EN:PDF

Eurlex. (2011). *Directive 2009/81/EC of the European parliament and of the council of 13 July 2009 on the co-ordination of procedures for the award of certain works contracts, supply contracts and service contracts by contracting authorities or entities in the fields of defence and security, and amending directives 2004/17/EC and 2004/18/EC.* Retrieved October 17, 2011, from http://eurlex.europa.eu/LexUriServ/LexUriServ.do?uri=OJ:L:2009:216:0076:0136:EN:PDF

European Commission Directorarte. (2011). *CONSIP SPA: General info.* Retrieved, October 23, 2011, from http://www.managenergy.net/actors/1597

European Commission. (2007). *The European e-business report, a portrait of e-business in 10 sectors of the EU economy: 5th synthesis report of the e-business W@tch.* Retrieved January 28, 2012, from http://ec.europa.eu/enterprise/archives/e-business-watch/key_reports/documents/EBR06.pdf

European Commission. (2008). *Glossary: Statistical classification of products by activity (CPA).* Retrieved August 30, 2011 from http://epp.eurostat.ec.europa.eu/statistics_explained/index.php/Glossary:CPA

European Commission. (2008). Commission regulation (EC) no 213/2008 is in use since 17/09/2008. *Official Journal of the European Union.* Retrieved May 10, 2011, from http://eur-lex.europa.eu/LexUriServ/LexUriServ.do?uri=OJ:L:2008:074:0001:0375:EN:PDF

European Commission. (2009). *IDABC: The programme.* Retrieved from http://ec.europa.eu/idabc/en/chapter/3.html

European Commission. (2010). *Commission staff working document evaluation of the 2004 action plan for electronic public procurement: Accompanying document to the green paper on expanding the use of e-procurement in the EU*. Retrieved August 30, 2011 from http://www.umic.pt/images/stories/publicacoes4/Liv%20Verde%20Cont%20Publ%20Aval%202004%20Plan%20Cont%20Publi%20Electronico%20EN_2.pdf

European Commission. (2010). *ICT and e-business for an innovative and sustainable economy: 7th synthesis report of the sectoral e-business watch*. Retrieved January 28, 2012, from http://www.ebusiness-watch.org/key_reports/documents/EBR09-10.pdf

European Commission. (2010). *Interoperability solutions for European public administrations: A commission-driven EU programme (2010-2015)*. Retrieved August 21, 2011, from http://ec.europa.eu/isa/documents/isa_isa-presentation_en.pdf

European Commission. (2010). *Green paper on expanding the use of e-procurement in the EU SEC(2010) 1214*. Retrieved August 21, 2011, from http://eur-lex.europa.eu/LexUriServ/LexUriServ.do?uri=COM:2010:0571:FIN:EN:PDF

European Commission. (2011). *2010-2013 action plan for European standardisation*. Retrieved August 30, 2011, from http://ec.europa.eu/enterprise/policies/european-standards/files/standards_policy/action_plan/doc/standardisation_action_plan_en.pdf

European Commission. (2011). *Communication from the commission — Corresponding values of the thresholds of directives 2004/17/EC, 2004/18/EC and 2009/81/EC of the European parliament and of the council 2011/C 353/01 (2011)*. Retrieved January 28, 2012, from http://eur-lex.europa.eu/LexUriServ/LexUriServ.do?uri=-OJ:C:2011:353:FULL:EN:PDF

European Commission. (2011). *European standards: Policy implementation action plan for European standardisation*. Retrieved August 30, 2011 from,http://ec.europa.eu/enterprise/policies/european-standards/standardisation-policy/implementation-action-plan/index_en.htm

European Commission. (2011). *Public consultation (green paper) on expanding the use of e-procurement in the EU*. Retrieved January 28, 2012, from http://ec.europa.eu/internal_market/consultations/docs/2010/e-procurement/synthesis_en.pdf

European Committee for Standardization. (2011). *Annual report*. Retrieved December 17, 2011, from http://www.cen.eu/cen/AboutUs/AR/Pages/default.aspx

Eyob, E. (2004). E-government: Breaking the frontiers of inefficiencies in the public sector. *Electronic Government. International Journal (Toronto, Ont.)*, *1*(1), 107–114.

Falvey, R., Greenaway, D., & Yu, Z. (2007). Market size and the survival of foreign-owned firms. *The Economic Record*, *83*, 23–24. doi:10.1111/j.1475-4932.2007.00407.x

Fancher, L. P. (2007). *The influence of organizational culture on the implementation of succession planning*. Francher, GA: Georgia State University.

Fan, Y. (2000). A classification of Chinese culture. *Cross Cultural Management*, *7*(2), 3–10. doi:10.1108/13527600010797057

Federal Constitution of Malaysia. (2006). *The commissioner of law revision, Malaysia under the authority of the revision of Laws act 1968*. Kuala Lumpur, Malaysia: Government of Malaysia.

Federal eGovernment Shop. (2009). *eGovernment/eProcurement in Germany - Annual report of the European commission*. Retrieved, October 23, 2011, from http://www.kdb.bund.de/nn_1306306/SharedDocs/Aktuelles/02__kdb__subsite/2009/eGovernment.html

Federal Institute for Risk Assessment. (2011). *Procurement*. Retrieved, October 23, 2011, from http://www.bfr.bund.de/en/procurement-9810.html

Finnish Act 2010-04-30 No 321 (in force 2010-06-01) amending Act 30.3.2007/348 (2010)

Fisman, R., & Gatti, R. (2002). Decentralization and corruption: Evidence across countries. *Journal of Public Economics*, *83*(3), 325–345. doi:10.1016/S0047-2727(00)00158-4

Fogg, B. J. (1998). Persuasive computers: Perspectives and research directions. In *Proceedings of the CHI 1998 Conference on Human Factors in Computing Systems*, (pp. 225-232). Los Angeles, CA: ACM Press.

Fogg, B. J. (2002). *Persuasive technology: Using computers to change what we think and do*. San Francisco, CA: Morgan Kaufmann.

Fogg, B. J., & Nass, C. I. (1997). Silicon sycophants: The effects of computers that flatter. *International Journal of Human-Computer Studies*, *5*(46), 551–561. doi:10.1006/ijhc.1996.0104

Forrest, A. (1999). *Fifty ways towards a learning organisation*. Sterling, VA: Stylus Publishing Inc.

Forrester. (2003). ISM/Forrester report on ebusiness. *Institute for Supply Management (ISM)*. Retrieved January 28, 2012, from http://www.forrester.com/rb/Research/ismforrester_report_on_ebusiness_q1_2003/q/id/16792/t/2

Fountain, J. E. (2001). *Building the virtual state: Information technology and institutional change*. Washington, DC: Brookings Institution Press.

Fourie, M. L., & Opperman, L. (2011). *Municipal finance and accounting*. Pretoria, South Africa: Van Schaik.

Frank, H. M. (2008). Performance management practices in public sector organizations: Impact on performance. *Accounting, Auditing & Accountability Journal*, *21*(3), 427. doi:10.1108/09513570810863996

Fraser, J., Fraser, N., & McDonald, F. (2001). The impact of electronic ecommerce on purchasing in the supply chanin. In A. Erridge, R. Fee, & McIlroy (Eds.), *Best Practice Procurement: Public and Private Sector Perspectives*. Hampshire, UK: Gower Publishing.

Fratesi, U. (2008). Regional policy from a supra-regional perspective. *The Annals of Regional Science*, *42*(3), 681–703. doi:10.1007/s00168-007-0167-x

Fry, B. R., & Raadschelders, J. C. N. (2008). *Mastering public administration: From Max Weber to Dwight Waldo*. Washington, DC: CQ Press.

Garchinsky, C. R. (2009). *Planning for the continuity of a school's vision and culture before leadership succession events*. Philadelphia, PA: Drexel University.

Garvey, G. (1993). *Facing the bureaucracy: Living and dying in a public agency*. San Francisco, CA: Jossey-Bass Publishers.

Gebauer, J., Beam, C., & Segev, A. (1998). Impact of the internet on purchasing practices. *Acquisitions Review Quarterly*, *5*(2), 167–184.

Geness, S. (2004). Challenges and opportunities of e-governance in South Africa. *The Electronic Library*, *28*(1), 38–53.

Gherghinescu, O., Rinderu, P., & Iova, C. (2010). *Econometric modeling - Between relevance and simplicity*. Paper presented at 6th International Conference on Applied Business Research. Dubai, United Arab Emirates.

Gifford, D. J., & Kudrle, R. T. (2011). Antitrust approaches to dynamically competitive industries in the United States and the European Union. *Journal of Competition Law & Economics*, *7*(3), 695–731. doi:10.1093/joclec/nhr011

Gilbert, R. J., & Newbery, D. M. G. (1982). Preemptive patenting and the persistence of monopoly. *The American Economic Review*, *72*(3), 514–526.

Gil-Garcia, J. R., & Martinez-Moyano, I. J. (2007). Understanding the evolution of e-government: The influence of systems of rules on public sector dynamics. *Government Information Quarterly*, *24*, 266–290. doi:10.1016/j.giq.2006.04.005

Glover, A. (2008). *Accelerating the SME economic engine: Through transparent, simple and strategic procurement*. London, UK: HM Treasury.

Goldfinch, S. F., Gauld, R., & Herbison, P. (2009). The participation divide? E-government, political participation, and trust in government in Australia and New Zealand. *Australian Journal of Public Administration*, *68*(3), 333–350. doi:10.1111/j.1467-8500.2009.00643.x

Goolsbee, A. (2001). The implications of electronic commerce for fiscal policy (and vice versa). *The Journal of Economic Perspectives*, *15*(1), 13–24. doi:10.1257/jep.15.1.13

Goolsbee, A., & Zittrain, J. (1999). Evaluating the costs and benefits of taxing internet commerce. *National Tax Journal*, *52*(3), 413–428.

Gosebo. (2008). *Service delivery innovation, including e-government and information management, response and comments: South African public service and administration department.* Retrieved on March 2, 2012, from http://www.dpsa.gov.za/docs/misc/hsummit/t4/presentation/social/Sld004.Htm

Gottschalk, P. (2009). Maturity levels for interoperability in digital government. *Government Information Quarterly, 26,* 75–81. doi:10.1016/j.giq.2008.03.003

Govender, J. N., & Watermeyer, R. B. (2001). *Potential procurement strategies for construction industry development in the SADC region.* Unpublished Paper.

Government Gateway. (2009). *Government gateway.* Retrieved January 28, 2012, from http://www.gateway.gov.uk/

Government, H. M. (2009). *What is the government gateway?* Retrieved January 28, 2012, from http://www.direct.gov.uk/en/Diol1/DoItOnline/Doitonlinemotoring/DG_10035603

Government, H. M. (2012). *Electronic communications act 2000.* Retrieved January 28, 2012, from http://www.legislation.gov.uk/ukpga/2000/7/part/II/data.pdf

Goyal, M. (2010). Black diamonds. *Forbes India.* Retrieved on March 4, 2012, from http://www.forbes.com/2010/06/21/forbes-india-black-diamonds-middle-class-spending.html

Grace Commission. (1983). *The president's private sector survey on cost control. A Report to the President.* Washington, DC: Government Printing Office.

Granger, K. B. (2009). *The relationship between employee commitment and a change in leadership, and the leadership style that demonstrates the greatest change.* Minneapolis, MN: Capella University.

Gray, P. (2006). *The management, retention and disposal of administrative records.* Retrieved January 28, 2012, from http://www.sehd.scot.nhs.uk/mels/HDL2006_28.pdf

Gregory, , Sidak, J., & Teece, D. J. (2009). Dynamic competition in antitrust law. *Journal of Competition Law & Economics, 5*(4), 581–631. doi:10.1093/joclec/nhp024

Griffin, D., & Halpin, E. (2005). An exploratory evaluation of UK local e-government from an accountability perspective. *Electronic. Journal of E-Government, 3*(1), 13–28.

Grönlund, Å., & Horan, T. A. (2004). Introducing e-gov: History, definitions and issues. *Communications of the Association for Information Systems, 15,* 713–729.

Gunasekarana, A., McGaughey, R., Ngaic, E., & Rai, B. (2009). Impact of e-procurement: Experiences from implementation in the UK public sector. *Journal of Purchasing and Supply Management, 13,* 294–303.

GXS. (2005). *EDIFACT standards overview tutorial.* Retrieved January 28, 2012, from http://edi.gxs.com/wp-content/themes/EDI/media/Tutor_EDIFACT_GXS.pdf

Hackett, M., Robinson, I., & Stratham, G. (2007). *The aqua group guide to procurement, tendering and contract administration.* Oxford, UK: Blackwell Publishing.

Hale, A. (2009). *Bowman Gilfillan: BEE article for FASA.* Retrieved on March 7, 2012, from http://www.bowman.co.za/LawArticles/Law-Article~id~2132417381.asp

Hammer, M., & Champy, J. (1993). *Reengineering the corporation: A manifesto for business revolution.* New York, NY: Harper Business. doi:10.1016/S0007-6813(05)80064-3

Hampson, T. (2012). Fining public sector staff for data breaches 'will not work'. *UKauthorITy.* Retrieved January 28, 2012, from http://www.ukauthority.com/NewsArticle/tabid/64/Default.aspx?id=3499

Hanna, N. K. (2010). *Transforming government and building the information society: Challenges and opportunities for the developing world.* New York, NY: Springer Verlag.

Hardy, C. A., & Williams, S. P. (2008). E-government policy and practice: A theoretical and empirical exploration of public e-procurement. *Government Information Quarterly, 25,* 155–180. doi:10.1016/j.giq.2007.02.003

Hardy, C. A., & Williams, S. P. (2011). Assembling e□ government research designs: A transdisciplinary view and interactive approach. *Public Administration Review, 71*(3), 405–413. doi:10.1111/j.1540-6210.2011.02361.x

Hardy, C., & Williams, S. (2008). E-government policy and practice: A theoretical and empirical exploration of public e-procurement. *Government Information Quarterly, 25,* 155–180. doi:10.1016/j.giq.2007.02.003

Harindranath, G., Dyerson, R., & Barnes, D. (2008). ICT adoption and use in UK SMEs: A failure of initiatives? *Electronic Journal Information Systems Evaluation, 11*(2), 91 – 96. Retrieved January 28, 2012, from http://www.ejise.com

Harjumaa, M., & Oinas-Kukkonen, H. (2007). An analysis of the persuasiveness of smoking cessation web sites. In *Proceedings of the Second International Symposium on Medical Information and Communication Technology.* Oulu, Finland: University of Oulu.

Hashim, R. (2007). *Electronic procurement project implementation issues in Selangor local government.* Shah Alam, Malaysia: University Technology Mara.

Hashim, R. (2010). Issues in electronic procurement project implementation in local government. *International Journal of Information Technology Project Management, 1*(3), 59–70. doi:10.4018/jitpm.2010070105

Hawking, P., Stein, A., Wyld, D., & Forster, S. (2004). E-procurement: Is the ugly duckling actually a swan down under? *Asia Pacific Journal of Marketing and Logistics, 16*(1), 1–26. doi:10.1108/13555850410765140

Hawser, A. (2008). *Who should be liable for on-line fraud? Fighting fraud.* Retrieved January 28, 2012, from http://fightingfraud.blogspot.com/2008/10/who-should-be-liable-for-online-fraud.html

Heeks, R., & Bailur, S. (2007). Analyzing e-government research: Perspectives, philosophies, theories, methods, and practice. *Government Information Quarterly, 24,* 243–265. doi:10.1016/j.giq.2006.06.005

Heilbrunn, J. R. (2004). *Anti-corruption commissions panacea or real medicine to fight corruption?* Washington, DC: The World Bank.

Heintze, T., & Bretschneider, S. (2000). Information technology and restructuring in public organizations: Does adoption of information technology affect organizational structures, communications, and decision making? *Journal of Public Administration: Research and Theory, 10*(4), 801–829. doi:10.1093/oxfordjournals.jpart.a024292

Henriksen, H. Z., & Mahnke, V. (2005). e-Procurement adoption in the Danish public sector. *Scandinavian Journal of Economic Systems, 17*(2), 85–106.

Henriksen, H., & Mahnke, V. (2005). E-procurement adoption in the Danish public sector: The influence of economic and political rationality. *Scandinavian Journal of Information Systems, 17*(2), 85–106.

Hewson Group. (2003). *e-Government: Can it meet public expectations through a successful CRM programme?* Retrieved January 28, 2012, from http://crmguru.custhelp.com/ci/fattach/get/314/

Hill, M. (2007). *Improved awareness needed of state procurement system – SAACE.* Retrieved March 12, 2012, from http://www.engineeringnews.co.za/article.php?a_id=100101

Hill, C. (2008). *International business – Competing in the global marketplace* (7th ed.). London, UK: McGraw-Hill.

Hill, G. C. (2006). *On managerial succession.* College Station, TX: Texas A&M University.

Ho, A. (2002). Reinventing local governments and the e-government initiative. *Public Administration Review, 62*(4), 434–444. doi:10.1111/0033-3352.00197

Hofstede, G. F. (2003). *Cultural dimensions.* Retrieved from http://www.geert-hofstede.com/

Hofstede, G. F. (2001). *Culture's consequences: Comparing values, behaviours, institutions, and organizations across the nations* (2nd ed.). Thousand Oaks, CA: Sage.

Hofstede, G. F., & Bond, M. H. (1988). The Confucius connection: From cultural roots to economic growth. *Organizational Dynamics, 16,* 4–21. doi:10.1016/0090-2616(88)90009-5

Homburg, V. (2009). The social shaping of transformational government. In Weerakkody, V., Janssen, M., & Dwivedi, Y. K. (Eds.), *Handbook of Research on ICT-Enabled Transformational Government: A Global Perspective* (pp. 1–14). Hershey, PA: IGI Global. doi:10.4018/978-1-60566-390-6.ch001

Hood, C. (2007). Intellectual obsolescence and intellectual makeovers: Reflections on the tools of government after two decades. *Governance: An International Journal of Policy, Administration and Institutions, 20*(1), 127–144. doi:10.1111/j.1468-0491.2007.00347.x

Hoque, K., Kirkpatrick, I., Londsdale, C., & De Ruyter, A. (2011). Outsourcing the procurement of agency workers: The impact of vendor managed services in English social care. *Work, Employment and Society, 25*(3), 522–539. doi:10.1177/0950017011407971

Huber, B., Sweeney, E., & Smyth, A. (2004). Purchasing consortia and electronic markets – A procurement direction in integrated supply chain management. *Electronic Markets, 14*(4), 284–294. doi:10.1080/1019678041233 1311739

IAI. (2005). *IAI website*. Retrieved January 28, 2012, from http://eetd.lbl.gov/eetd-software-iai.html

IDEA. (2004). *The benefits of e-procurement*. Retrieved January 28, 2012, from http://www.idea.gov.uk/idk/aio/70780

IDEA. (2008). *e-Tendering*. Retrieved January 28, 2012, from http://www.idea.gov.uk/idk/core/page.do?pageId=82667

IFAC. (2000). *Website*. Retrieved February 14, 2012, from www.ifac.org

Info Reporter, S. A. (2011). *Black economic empowerment*. Retrieved on March 4, 2011, from http://www.southafrica.info/business/trends/empowerment/bee.htm

Information Technology Management Reform Act. (1996, January 3). *104th congress, 2nd session*. S. 1124. Washington, DC: US Congress.

International Digital Communications. (1993). *Facilities management: The nature of the opportunity*. London, UK: IDC Publishers.

International Monetary Fund. (2010). *Maldives: Public financial management*. Washington, DC: IMF.

Internet World Stats. (2009). *South Africa: Internet usage and marketing report*. Retrieved on March 26, 2012, from http://www.internetworldstats.com/af/za.htm

Irani, Z., & Love, P. (2002). Developing a frame of reference for ex-ante IT/IS investment evaluation. *European Journal of Information Systems, 11*(1), 74–82. doi:10.1057/palgrave/ejis/3000411

Irani, Z., Love, P. E. D., & Montazemi, A. (2007). E-government: Past, present and future. *European Journal of Information Systems, 16*, 103–105. doi:10.1057/palgrave.ejis.3000678

Islam, S., & Hassan, N. (2009). Multi-purpose community telecentres in Bangladesh: Problems and prospects. *The Electronic Library, 27*(3), 537–553. doi:10.1108/02640470910966952

Islington Council. (2008). *Paper-free working improves service delivery for Islington council*. Retrieved January 28, 2012, from http://www.publictechnology.net/content/18250

ISO. (2009). *ISO/TS 22745-30:2009: Industrial automation systems and integration – Open technical dictionaries and their application to master data, part 30: Identification guide representation*. Geneva, Switzerland: International Organization for Standardization.

ISO. (2009). *ISO 8000-110:2009: Data quality, part 110: Master data: Exchange of characteristic data: Syntax, semantic encoding, and conformance to data specification*. Geneva, Switzerland: International Organization for Standardization.

ISO. (2010). *ISO 22745-11:2010: Industrial automation systems and integration – Open technical dictionaries and their application to master data, part 11: Guidelines for the formulation of terminology*. Geneva, Switzerland: International Organization for Standardization.

Jae Moon, M. (2005). Procurement management in state governments: Diffusion of e-procurement practices and its determinants. *Journal of Public Procurement, 5*(1), 54–72.

Janssen, M., & Shu, W. (2008). Transformational government: Basics and key issues: A workshop. *Proceedings of ICEGOV, Cairo Egypt., 2008*, 117–122. doi:10.1145/1509096.1509120

Janssen, M., & van Veenstra, A. F. (2005). Stages of growth in e-government: An architectural approach. *The Electronic. Journal of E-Government, 3*(4), 193–200.

Jennings, D. (2001, September 6). Secure trading. *Supply Management*, 52-53.

Johnson, M. (2002). *GSA awards task to improve information security in federal agencies.* GSA #9936. Retrieved from http://www.gsa.gov/portal/content/100287

Johnston, J. M., & Romzek, B. S. (2008). Social welfare contracts as networks: The impact of network stability on management and performance. *Administration & Society*, *40*(2), 115–146. doi:10.1177/0095399707312826

Julia-Barcelo, R. (1999). Electronic contracts: A new legal framework for electronic contracts: The EU electronic commerce proposal. *Computer Law & Security Report*, *15*(3), 147–158. doi:10.1016/S0267-3649(99)80032-6

Julià-Barceló, R., & Vinje, T. (1998). Towards a European framework for digital signatures and encryption: The European commission takes a step forward for confidential and secure electronic communications. *Computer Law & Security Report*, *14*(2), 79–86.

Kahn, J. S. (1989). Culture: Demise or resurrection? *Critique of Anthropology*, *9*(2), 5–25. doi:10.1177/0308275X8900900202

Kalakota, R., Tapscott, D., & Robinson, M. (2001). *E-business 2.0: Roadmap for success* (2nd ed.). Reading, MA: Addison-Wesley Publishing Company.

Kaliannan, M., & Murali, R. (2009). *E-procurement adoption in the Malaysian public sector: Organizational perspectives.* Paper presented at Service-Oriented Business Networks and Ecosystems, SOBNE 2009. New York, NY.

Kaliannan, M., Awang, H., Raman, M., & Dorasamy, M. (2008). *E-procurement for the public sector: Determinants of attitude towards adoption.* Paper presented at International Conference on E-Government, ICEG 2008. New York, NY.

Kaliannan, M., Awang, H., & Raman, M. (2009). Government purchasing: A review of e-procurement system in Malaysia. *The Journal of Knowledge Economy & Knowledge Management*, *4*, 27–41.

Kamarck, E. C., & Nye, J. S. (Eds.). (2002). *Governance.com: Democracy in the information age.* Washington, DC: Brookings Institution Press.

Kaptein, M., & Eckles, D. (2010). Selecting effective means to any end: Futures and ethics of persuasion profiling. *Lecture Notes in Computer Science*, *6137*, 82–93. doi:10.1007/978-3-642-13226-1_10

Katok, E., & Roth, A. (2004). Adoption of electronic commerce tools in business procurement: Enhanced buying center structure and processes. *Management Science*, *50*(8), 1044–1063. doi:10.1287/mnsc.1040.0254

Katz, M. L., & Shapiro, C. (1994). Systems competition and network effects. *The Journal of Economic Perspectives*, *8*(2), 93–115. doi:10.1257/jep.8.2.93

Kejak, M., & Vavra, D. (2005). *The impact of EU structural funds on the Czech macroeconomy: Some preliminary results from the HERMIN model, report.* Prague, Czech Republic: Czech National Bank.

Kentridge, J. (1999). Equality. In Chaskalson, M. (Ed.), *The Constitution of South Africa.* Cape Town, South Africa: Juta.

Kerwin, C., & Furlong, S. (2011). *Rulemaking: How government agencies write law and make policy* (4th ed.). Washington, DC: CQ Press.

Kettinger, W., & Lee, C. C. (1995). Global measures of information service quality: A crossnational study. *Decision Sciences*, *26*(5), 569–588. doi:10.1111/j.1540-5915.1995.tb01441.x

Kettle, D. (2002). *The transformation of governance.* Baltimore, MD: Johns Hopkins University Press.

Kettle, D. (2005). *The global public management revolution* (2nd ed.). Washington, DC: Brookings Institute Press.

Khanapuri, V. B., Nayak, S., Soni, P., Sharma, S., & Soni, M. (2011). *Framework to overcome challenges of implementation of e-procurement in Indian context.* Paper presented to International Conference on Technology and Business Management. Dubai, UAE.

Kheng, C., & Al-hawamdeh, S. (2002). The adoption of electronic procurement in Singapore. *Electronic Commerce Research*, *2*(1-2), 61–73. doi:10.1023/A:1013388018056

Kim, C. S. (2007). *Kimchi and IT.* Seoul, South Korea: Ilchokak.

Kim, J., & Shunk, D. (2003). Matching indirect procurement process with different B2B e-procurement systems. *Computers in Industry*, *53*(2), 153–164. doi:10.1016/j.compind.2003.07.002

Kivijarvi, H., Hallikainen, P., & Penttinen, E. (2011). Supporting the supplier scheduling decisions in the e-invoicing implementation projects - An application of the ANP method. In *Proceedings of 44th Hawaii International Conference on System Sciences (HICSS)*, (pp. 1-12). Kauai, HI: IEEE.

Klievink, B., & Janssen, M. (2009). Realizing joined-up government - Dynamic capabilities and stage models for transformation. *Government Information Quarterly*, *26*(2), 275–284. doi:10.1016/j.giq.2008.12.007

Knudsen, D. (2003). Aligning corporate strategy, procurement strategy and e-procurement tools. *International Journal of Physical Distribution & Logistics Management*, *33*(8), 720–734. doi:10.1108/09600030310502894

Kolsaker, A. (2006). Reconceptualising e-government as a tool of governance: The UK case. *Electronic Government*, *3*(4), 347–355. doi:10.1504/EG.2006.010798

Kong, C., Li, H., & Love, P. (2001). An e-commerce system for construction material procurement. *Construction Innovation*, *1*(1), 43–54.

Kotsonis, T. (2011). A novelty is a commission draft directive on concession awards COM(2011)897, previously only dealt with in EUCJ rulings on *quasi*-procurement interpretation of EU treaty principles: Commenting on commission draft directives COM (2011) 896 and COM (2011) 895 (2010). *Public Procurement Law Report*, *20*(5), 51.

Kransdorff, A. (1998). *Corporate amnesia keeping the know-how in the company*. Oxford, UK: Butterworth-Heinemann.

Kroukamp, H. (2005). E-governance in South Africa: Are we coping? *Acta Academia*, *37*(2), 52–69.

Kumar, K., Bjorn-Anderson, N., & King, R. (1990). A cross-cultural comparison of IS designer values. *Communications of the ACM*, *33*(5), 528–538. doi:10.1145/78607.78613

Kungis, J. P. (2006). *Leadership and productivity: A study of the perceptions of the non-supervisory civilian personnel at the garrison*. Minneapolis, MN: Capella University.

Kuppusamy, S. (2010). The right marriage between local government and the private sector in Malaysia? *International Journal of Institutions and Economies*, *2*(2), 142–166.

Kurunmaki, L. (1999). Making an accounting entity: The case of the hospital in Finnish healthcare reforms. *European Accounting Review*, *8*(2), 219–237. doi:10.1080/096381899336005

Kurunmaki, L. (1999). Professional vs. financial capital in the field of health care: Struggles for the redistribution of power and control. *Accounting, Organizations and Society*, *24*(2), 95–125. doi:10.1016/S0361-3682(98)00030-0

Kutz, S. E. (2008). *Sensemaking for followers in leadership transition: What's going on here?* Reno, NV: University of Nevada.

Labour Protect. (2012). *What you need to know about BEE*. Retrieved on February 28, 2012, from http://www.labourprotect.co.za/BEE_scorecard.htm

Latham, M. (1994). *Constructing the team. Joint Government of Industry Review of Procurement and Contractual Arrangements in the UK*. London, UK: Construction Industry.

Layne, K., & Lee, J. (2001). Developing fully functional e-government: A four stage model. *Government Information Quarterly*, *18*(2), 122–136. doi:10.1016/S0740-624X(01)00066-1

Lee, J. (2010). 10 year retrospect on stage models of e-government: A qualitative metasynthesis. *Government Information Quarterly*, *27*, 220–230. doi:10.1016/j.giq.2009.12.009

Lee, M. (2010). An exploratory study on the mature level evaluation of e-procurement systems. *Journal of Public Procurement*, *10*(3), 405–427.

Lee, S.-H. (2000). *A multidimensional view of public sector employee commitment and willingness to support productivity improvement strategies: A comparative study of public employees at the managerial-level between the United States and South Korea*. Hoboken, NJ: The State University of New Jersey.

Lee, S., Xin, T., & Trimi, S. (2005). Current practices of leading e-government countries. *Communications of the ACM, 48*(10), 99–104. doi:10.1145/1089107.1089112

Leidner, D. E. (2010). Globalization, culture and information: Towards global knowledge transparency. *The Journal of Strategic Information Systems, 19*, 69–77. doi:10.1016/j.jsis.2010.02.006

Leidner, D. E., & Kayworth, T. (2006). Review: A review of culture in information systems research: Toward a theory of information technology culture conflict. *Management Information Systems Quarterly, 30*(2), 357–399.

Lenz, J. (2012). Taking dynamic signatures seriously. *Biometric Technology Today, 2011*(11–12), 9–11.

Leukel, J., & Maniatopoulos, G. (2005). A comparative analysis of product classification in public vs. private e-procurement. *The Electronic. Journal of E-Government, 3*(4), 201–212.

Li, E., & Du, T. (2005). *Advances in electronic business.* Hershey, PA: IGI Global.

Liebenberg, S. (2010). *Socio-economic rights: Adjudication under a transformative constitution.* Claremont, South Africa: Juta & Co.

Loeffler Tuggey Pauerstein Rosenthal, L. L. P. (2006). Terms of Saudi Arabia's accession to the WTO. *Middle East Policy, 13*(1), 24. doi:10.1111/j.1475-4967.2006.00235.x

Lorentziadis, P. L. (2010). Post-objective determination of weights of the evaluation factors in public procurement tenders. *European Journal of Operational Research, 200*(3), 261–267. doi:10.1016/j.ejor.2008.12.013

Lotheringen, A. (2012). *What is fronting.* Retrieved on March 2, 2012, from http://southafrica.smetoolkit.org/sa/en/content/en/7694/What-is-fronting

Lukas, A. (1999). Tax bytes: A primer on the taxation of electronic commerce. *Trade Policy Analysis, 9.*

MacManus, S. (2002). Understanding the incremental nature of e-procurement at the state and local levels. *Journal of Public procurement, 2*(1), 5-28.

Magrini, P. (2006). *Transparency in e-procurement: The Italian perspective.* Paper presented at 1st HIGH Level Seminar on E-Procurement. Naples, Italy. Retrieved from http://www.oecd.org/dataoecd/57/31/36238443.pdf

Mahmood, S. A. I. (2010). Public procurement and corruption in Bangladesh confronting the challenges and opportunities. *Journal of Public Administration and Policy Research, 2*(6), 103–111.

Malefane, M. (2012). No fronting! New act to criminalise B-BEE fraud. *Sunday World.* Retrieved on March 3, 2012, from http://www.sundayworld.co.za/Feeds/SundayWorld/2012/02/12/no-fronting-new-act-to-criminalise-b-bee-fraud

Malone, T., Yate, J., & Benjamin, R. (1987). Electronic markets and electronic hierarchies. *Communications of the ACM, 30*(6), 484–497. doi:10.1145/214762.214766

Mandi, A. R. (2008). *A case study exploring succession planning: Supported by a quantitative analysis of governmental organizations in the Kingdom of Bahrain.* Washington, DC: The George Washington University.

Mansor, N. (2006). *Public procurement innovation in Malaysia: E-procurement.* Kuala Lumpur, Malaysia: University of Malaya. Retrieved January 18, 2012, from www.napsipag.org/PDF/E-Procurement-Malaysia.pdf

Marais, F., & Coetzee, L. (2006). The determination of black ownership in companies for the purpose of black economic empowerment. *Obiter, 27*(1), 111–127.

Martin, J. (2003). *E-procurement and extranets in the UK construction industry.* Paper presented at FIG Working Week. Paris, France. Retrieved January 28, 2012, from www.fig.net/pub/fig_2003/TS_6/TS6_4_Martin.pdf

Martin, J. (2009). *2009 BCIS etendering survey report.* Retrieved January 28, 2012, from http://www.bcis.co.uk/downloads/2009_BCIS_eTendering_Survey_Report_pdf__2_.pdf

Mbendi. (2011). *Black economic empowerment in South Africa: An overview.* Retrieved on March 16, 2011, from http://www.mbendi.com/indy/misc/blck/af/sa/p0005.htm

McCrudden, C. (2004). Using public procurement to achieve social outcomes. *Natural Resources Forum, 28*(4), 257–267. doi:10.1111/j.1477-8947.2004.00099.x

McCrudden, C. (2009). Social policy choices and the international and national law of government procurement: South Africa as a case study. In Corder, H. (Ed.), *Global Administrative Law*. Cape Town, South Africa: Juta & Co.

McCue, C., & Roman, A. V. (2012). E-procurement: myth or reality? *Journal of Public Procurement, 12*(2).

McGuire, M., & Agranoff, R. (2011). The limitations of public management networks. *Public Administration, 89*(2), 265–284. doi:10.1111/j.1467-9299.2011.01917.x

McHenry, W., & Pryamonosov, D. (2010). Emerging electronic procurement in Russia's regional governments. *Journal of Public Procurement, 10*(2), 211–246.

McIntosh, G., & Sloan, B. (2001). The potential impact of electronic procurement and global sourcing within the UK construction industry. In A. Akintoye (Ed.), *Proceedings of Arcom 17th Annual Conference 2001*, (pp. 231-239). Manchester, UK: University of Salford.

McLure, C. E. (1999). *The taxation of electronic commerce: Background and proposal*. Paper presented at the Public Policy and the Internet: Taxation and Privacy. New York, NY.

McLure, C. E. (2003). The value added tax on electronic commerce in the European Union. *International Tax and Public Finance, 10*(6), 753–762. doi:10.1023/A:1026394207651

McMullan, C. (2005). *Letter to CPD: Central procurement directorate*. Belfast, Ireland: Clare House.

Merkin, R. (2006). Power distance and facework strategies. *Journal of Intercultural Communication Research, 35*, 139–160. doi:10.1080/17475750600909303

Metz, H. (1992). Saudi Arabia: A country study. *Library of Congress*. Retrieved April 15, 2010, from http://countrystudies.us/saudi-arabia/

Migiro, S. O. (2010). Public sector procurement and black economic empowerment in South Africa: Challenges of preferential procurement and decentralization of the provincial tender board. *Journal of Social Development in Africa, 25*(2), 177–195.

Milakovich, M. E. (2012). *Digital governance: New technologies for improving public service and participation*. New York, NY: Routledge.

Milward, B., & Provan, K. (2000). Governing the hollow state. *Journal of Public Administration: Research and Theory, 10*(2), 359–379. doi:10.1093/oxfordjournals.jpart.a024273

Minahan, T., & Degan, G. (2001). *Best practices in e-procuremen*. Boston, MA: Aberdeen Group. Retrieved January 28, 2012, from http://www.inkoopportal.com/inkoopportal/download/common/e-procurement_1_.pdf

Min, H., & Galle, W. (1999). Electronic commerce usage in business-to business purchasing. *International Journal of Operations & Production Management, 19*(9), 909–921. doi:10.1108/01443579910280232

Ministry of Economy and Finance. (2009). *The program for the rationalization of public authority purchases*. Retrieved October 23, 2011, from https://www.acquistinretepa.it/opencms/opencms/menu_livello_I/header/Inglese/PROGRAM

Ministry of Finance and Public Works. (1997). *Green paper on public sector procurement reform in South Africa: A 10-point plan*. Retrieved on March 2, 2012, from http://www.polity.org.za/polity/govdocs/green_papers/procgp.html

Mintrom, M. (2003). *People skills for policy analysts*. Washington, DC: Georgetown University Press.

Mkize, Z. (2007). *Public sector human resources convention*. Durban, South Africa. Retrieved on March 25, 2012, from http://www.kwazulunatal.gov.za/premier/speeches/other/19-09-2007.pdf

Moffatt, I. (1996). *Sustainable development: Principles, analysis and policies*. New York, NY: Parthenon.

Mohamed Nor, M. A. (1973). *The role and effectiveness of the town and country planning department in national development*. Kuala Lumpur, Malaysia: University of Malaya.

Mokhele, I., & De Beer, K. J. (2007). The use of information and communication technology (ICT) in e-service delivery and effective governance in South Africa. *Interim, 6*(2), 60–67.

Moon, B. J. (2004). Consumer adoption of the internet as an information search and product purchase channel: Some research hypotheses. *International Journal of Internet Marketing and Advertising, 1*(1), 104–118. doi:10.1504/IJIMA.2004.003692

Moon, M. J. (2002). The evolution of e-government among municipalities: Rhetoric or reality? *Public Administration Review, 62*(4), 424–433. doi:10.1111/0033-3352.00196

Mota, F. P. B., & Filho, R. J. (2011). Public e-procurement and the duality of technology: A comparative study in the context of Brazil and of the state of Paraiba. *Journal of Information Systems and Technology Management, 8*(2), 315–330. doi:10.4301/S1807-17752011000200003

Mota, F., & Filho, J. (2011). Public e-procurement and the duality of technology: A comparative study in the context of Brazil and the state of Paraiba. *Journal of Information Systems and Technology Management, 8*(2), 315–330. doi:10.4301/S1807-17752011000200003

Mowery, D. C. (2001). The United States national innovation system after the cold war. In Laredo, P., & Mustar, P. (Eds.), *Research and Innovation Policies in the New Global Economy: An International Comparative Analysis* (pp. 15–46). Northampton, MA: Edward Elgar Publishing, Inc.

Mphidi, H. (2012). *Digital divide and e-governance in South Africa.* Retrieved on March 2, 2012, from http://www.ais.up.ac.za/digi/docs/mphidi_paper.pdf

MRD. (2006). *National plan for the introduction of electronic public procurement over the period 2006-2010.* Prague, Czech Republic: Ministry for Regional Development of the Czech Republic.

MRD. (2011). *Strategie elektronizace zadávání veřejných zakázek pro období let 2011 až 2015* [Strategic document on electronic public procurement over the period 2011-2015]. Prague, Czech Republic: Ministry for Regional Development of the Czech Republic.

Mulqueen, C. (2005). *Learning through failure: A descriptive analysis of leader behavior.* Albuquerque, NM: The University of New Mexico.

Murray, J. G. (2009). Improving the validity of public procurement research. *International Journal of Public Sector Management, 22*(2), 91–103. doi:10.1108/09513550910934501

Mutola, S. M., & Mostert, J. (2010). Challenges and opportunities of e-governance in South Africa. *The Electronic Library, 28*(1), 38–53. doi:10.1108/02640471011023360

Myers, M. D. (1997). Qualitative research in information systems. *Management Information Systems Quarterly, 21*(2), 241–242. doi:10.2307/249422

Myers, M., & Tan, F. (2003). Beyond models of national culture in information systems research. *Advanced Topics in Global Information Management, 10*(2), 1–19.

Myers, R. (2003). Ensuring ethical effectiveness. *Journal of Accountancy, 195*(2), 28–33.

Nairn. (2000, November 1). Ripples from a quiet revolution bring net gains for manufacturing sector. *The Financial Times IT Survey,* p. 1.

Nalebuff, B. (2000). Competing against bundles. *SSRN eLibrary.* doi: 10.2139/ssrn.239684

Nalebuff, B. (2004). Bundling as an entry barrier. *The Quarterly Journal of Economics, 119*(1), 159–187. doi:10.1162/0033553047728395 51

Namenwirth, J. Z., & Weber, R. B. (1987). *Dynamics of culture.* Boston, MA: Allen & Unwin.

Nass, C. I., Steuer, J., & Tauber, E. R. (1994). Computers are social actors. In *Proceedings of the SIGCHI Conference on Human Factors in Computing Systems: Celebrating Interdependence,* (pp. 72-78). New York, NY: ACM Press.

National Archives. (2012). *Records management: Retention scheduling 5: Contractual records.* Retrieved January 28, 2012, from http://www.nationalarchives.gov.uk/documents/information-management/sched_contractual.pdf

National Audit Department. (2008). *Website.* Retrieved February 8, 2012, from www.audit.gov.my

National Performance Review. (1993). *From red tape to results: Creating a government that works better and costs less.* Washington, DC: United States Government Printing Office.

National Procurement Strategy for Local Government. (2003). *National procurement strategy for local government in England 2003-2006*. Retrieved January 28, 2012, from http://www.communities.gov.uk/publications/localgovernment/nationalprocurementstrategy

NATO. (2003). *Guide to the NATO codification system*. Retrieved April 22, 2011, from http://www.nato.int/structur/ac/135/ncs_guide/e_guide.htm

Ndou, V. (2004). E-government for developing countries: Opportunities and challenges. *The Electronic Journal of Information Systems in Developing Countries, 18*(1), 1–24.

Neef, D. (2001). *E-procurement: from strategy to implementation*. Upper Saddle River, NJ: Prentice Hall.

Neely, A. (1998). *Measuring business performance: Why, what, and how?* London, UK: The Economist Books.

Neupane, A., Soar, J., & Yong, J. (2012). *Role of public e-procurement technology to reduce corruption in government procurement*. Paper presented at the 5th International Public Procurement Conference. Seattle, WA.

New Straits Times. (2007). *Audit standard not up to mark*. New Straits Times.

News Straits Times. (2003). *Councillors of shame*. New Straits Times.

News, E. C. I. (2003). *ECI newsletter – Achieving continuous improvement and value*. Retrieved January 28, 2012, from http://www.researchandmarkets.com/reports/1530394/long_term_partnering_achieving_continuous

Ngulube, P. (2007). The nature and accessibility of e-governance in Sub Saharan Africa. *International Review of Information Ethics, 7*, 1-13. Retrieved on March 17, 2012, from http://www.i-r-i-e.net/inhalt/007/16-ngulube.pdf

NHS Purchasing and Supply Agency. (2004). *NHS PASA eAuctions pilot report*. London, UK: National Health Service.

NIFHA. (2007). *NIFHA database*. Retrieved January 28, 2012, from http://www.nifha.org/housing-association-database/

Nijkamp, P., Van der Burch, M., & Vindigni, G. (2002). A comparative institutional evaluation of public-private partnerships in Dutch urban land-use and revitalisation projects. *Urban Studies (Edinburgh, Scotland), 39*(10), 1865–1880. doi:10.1080/0042098022000002993

NJCC. (1996). *Code of practice for two stage selective tendering*. London, UK: NJCC.

Noon, C. R. (2009). The use of racial preferences in public procurement for social stability. *Public Contract Law Journal, 38*(3), 611-632. Retrieved on March 7, 2012, from http://search.proquest.com/docview/218680618?accountid=10612

Norris, M. W. (1980). Restructuring of local government – An assessment. *Management Review, 15*(1).

Ntetha, M. A., & Mostert, B. J. (2011). Availability and utilisation of information and communication technologies for service delivery: A South African case study. *South African Journal of Library and Information Science, 77*(2), 125–137.

OECD. (1999). *Defining and measuring e-commerce: A status report*. Geneva, Switzerland: OECD.

OECD. (2005). *Paris declaration on aid effectiveness*. Paris, France: OECD.

OECD. (2009). *OECD conference on empowering e-consumers strengthening consumer protection in the internet economy: Background report*. Geneva, Switzerland: OECD.

OECD. (2011). E-procurement. *Proceedings of Government at a Glance, 2011*, 152–153. OECD Publishing.

Office of Government Commerce. (2002). *A guide to e-procurement for the public sector*. London, UK: Office of Government Commerce. Retrieved from http://www.ogc.gov.uk

OGC. (2003). *Building on success*. Retrieved January 28, 2012, from http://www.ccinw.com/images/publications/OGC%20Acheiving%20Excellence%20in%20Construction.pdf

OGC. (2005). *e-Procurement in action – A guide to e-procurement for the public sector*. Retrieved January 28, 2012, from http//www.umic.pt/images/stories/publicacoes/embedded_object[1].pdf

OIG. (1997). *Audit of the office of program and integrity reviews special studies*. Retrieved January 28, 2012, from http://oig.ssa.gov/audit-office-program-and-integrity-reviews-special-studies

Oliveira, L. M. S., & Amorim, P. P. (2001). Public e-procurement. *International Financial Law Review*, *10*, 43–47.

Olson, J. F. (2010). South Africa moves to a global model of corporate governance but with important national variations. *Acta Juridica: Modern Company Law for a Competitive Economy*. Retrieved on January 21, 2012, from http://search.sabinet.co.za.dutlib.dut.ac.za:2048/WebZ/images/ejour/ju_jur/ju_jur_2010_a14.pdf?sessionid=01-48548-1845022178&format=F

Onyancha, O. B. (2010). E-governance and e-governments in Africa: A webometrician's perception of the challenges, trends and issues. *Mousaion*, *28*(2), 32–63.

Organization for Economic Co-Operation and Development. (2004). *Information technology outlook*. Paris, France: Organization for Economic Co-Operation and Development.

Organization for economic co-operation and development. (2011). *Government at a glance 2011 country note: Finland*. Retrieved from http://www.oecd.org/dataoecd/60/25/47876433.pdf

Orlikowski, W. J. (1992). The duality of technology: Rethinking the concept of technology in organizations. *Organization Science*, *3*(3), 398–427. doi:10.1287/orsc.3.3.398

Orlikowski, W. J. (2000). Using technology and constituting structures: A practice lens for studying technology in organizations. *Organization Science*, *11*(4), 404–428. doi:10.1287/orsc.11.4.404.14600

Orlikowski, W., Yates, J., Okamura, K., & Fujimoto, M. (1995). Shaping electronic communication: The meta-structuring of technology in the context of use. *Organization Science*, *6*(4), 423–444. doi:10.1287/orsc.6.4.423

Osborne, S. (2006). The new public governance: 1. *Public Management Review*, *8*(3), 377–387. doi:10.1080/14719030600853022

Padalík, M. (2009). *Software solution for codification based on NCS, eOTD and ISO 8000*. Retrieved November 26, 2009, from http://www.eccma.org/2009ECCMAconf/presentations/AURA.pdf

Palmujoki, A., Parikka-Alhola, K., & Ekroos, A. (2010). Green public procurement: Analysis of the use of environmental criteria in contracts. *Review of European Community & International Environmental Law*, *19*(2), 250–262. doi:10.1111/j.1467-9388.2010.00681.x

Panayiotou, N. A., Gayialis, S. P., & Tatsiopoulos, I. P. (2004). An e-procurement system for government purchasing. *International Journal of Production Economics*, *90*, 79–102. doi:10.1016/S0925-5273(03)00103-8

Panda, P., Sahu, G., & Gupta, P. (2010). *Promoting transparency and efficiency in public procurement: E-procurement initiatives by government of India*. Paper presented at the 7th International Conference on E-procurement (ICEG). Banglore, India.

Pan-European Public e-Procurement On-Line Project. (2011). *About PEPPOL*. Retrieved May 26, 2011, from http://www.peppol.eu/about_peppol

Pathak, R. D., Naz, R., Rahman, M. H., Smith, R. F. I., & Agarwal, K. N. (2009). E-governance to cut corruption in public service delivery: A case study of Fiji. *International Journal of Public Administration*, *32*(5), 415–437. doi:10.1080/01900690902799482

Patton, K., & McKenna, T. (2005). Scanning for competitive intelligence. *Competitive Intelligence*, *8*(2), 24–29.

Paulo, A., Bráulio, A., Tiago, O., Varajão, Q., & Eduardo, J. (2010). Electronic procurement: Dealing with supplier adoption. In Cruz-Cunha, M., Putnik, G., & Trigo, A. (Eds.), *ENTERprise Information Systems, Communications in Computer and Information Science* (*Vol. 109*, pp. 168–179). Berlin, Germany: Springer.

Pauw, J. C., Woods, G., van der Linde, G. J. A., Fourie, D., & Visser, C. B. (2009). *Managing public money: Systems from the south*. Johannesburg, South Africa: Heinemann.

Peachment, A. (1992). *The executive state: WA Inc and the constitution*. Perth, Australia: Constitutional Press.

Pearman, R. (2002). E-bidding: Who can you trust? *Contract Journal*. Retrieved January 28, 2012, from http://business.highbeam.com/410604/article-1G1-85005041/ebidding-can-you-trust

Peck, F., & Cabras, I. (2008). *Public procurement and regional development: The impact of local authority expenditure on local economies.* Paper presented to the Regional Studies Association International Conference Regions: The Dilemmas of Integration and Competition. Prague, Czech Republic.

Peck, F., & Cabras, I. (2011). The impact of local authority procurement on local economies: The case of Cumbria, North West London. *Public Policy and Administration*, *26*(3), 307–331. doi:10.1177/0952076709356859

Pena-Mora, F., & Choudary, K. (2001). Web-centric framework for secure and legally binding electronic transactions in large-scale A/E/C projects. *Journal of Computing in Civil Engineering*, *15*(4), 248–259. doi:10.1061/(ASCE)0887-3801(2001)15:4(248)

Peters, B. G. (1996). *The future of governing: Four emerging models.* Lawrence, KS: University of Kansas Press.

Pike, A., Rodríguez-Pose, A., & Tomaney, J. (2007). What kind of local and regional development and for whom? *Regional Studies*, *41*(9), 1253–1269. doi:10.1080/00343400701543355

Pinch, P. L., & Patterson, A. (2000). Public sector restructuring and regional development: The impact of compulsory competitive tendering in the UK. *Regional Studies*, *34*(3), 265–275. doi:10.1080/00343400050015104

Pomazalová, N. (2010). Possibilities of use the dynamic purchase system in the public procurement. In *The 16th International Conference The Knowledge-Based Organization*, (pp. 86-91). Sibiu, Romania: "Nicolae Bălcescu" Land Forces Academy Publishing House.

Pooler, V., Pooler, D., & Farney, S. (2004). *Global purchasing and supply management: Fulfill the vision* (2nd ed.). Boston, MA: Kluwer Academic Publishers.

Potter, C. (2000). *Trust…. not built at e-speed: Trust issues in B2B e-procurement. Price-Waterhouse Coopers Report*. London, UK: Price-Waterhouse Coopers.

Preuss, L. (2009). Addressing sustainable development through public procurement: The case of local government. *Supply Chain Management: An International Journal*, *14*(3), 213–223. doi:10.1108/13598540910954557

Pritchard, S. (2006). How can so many businesses cope without computers? *Financial Times*. Retrieved January 28, 2012, from http://www.ft.com/cms/s/1/cc145e2e-47f5-11db-a42e-0000779e2340.html

Procurement Office of the Federal Ministry of the Interior. (2011). *Electronic shopping: Procurement for the digital era.* Retrieved October 12, 2011, from http://www.bescha.bund.de/cln_100/nn_663232/sid_8010A7C909DE62ED A1D0003E313F439E/nsc_true/DE/OeffEinkauf/node.html?__nnn=true

Przymus, K. (2003). *E-procurement for a municipal government.* Retrieved January 28, 2012, from http://www.toronto.ca/inquiry/inquiry_site/cd/gg/add_pdf/77/Procurement/Electronic_Documents/Miscellaneous/Municipal_EProcurement_Study.pdf

PublicTechnology. (2004). *Next-generation Energis-supplied government secure intranet goes live.* Retrieved January 28, 2012, from http://www.publictechnology.net/content/568

PWC. (2011). *Corporate governance – King III report – Introduction and overview*. Retrieved on February 14, 2012, from http://www.pwc.com/za/en/king3/

Quah, J. S. (1999). *Combating corruption in Mongolia: Problems and prospects.* Singapore, Singapore: National University of Singapore.

Quinn, J. (1992). *Intelligent enterprise.* New York, NY: Free Press.

Radack, G. (2009). *From the eOTD to international standards for open technical dictionaries (ISO 22745) and master data quality (ISO 8000-100)*. Retrieved November 17, 2009, from http://www.eccma.org/2009ECCMAconf/presentations/GeraldRadack.pdf

Raga, K., & Albrecht, W. (2008). Determining an ethical basis for public sector procurement management: The South African local sphere of government. *Journal of Public Administration*, *43*(4), 781–797.

Raghavan, N., & Prabhu, M. (2004). Object-oriented design of a distributed agent-based framework for e-procurement. *Production Planning and Control, 15*(7), 731–741. doi:10.1080/09537280412331298229

Ramady, M. (2006, September 11). Foreign direct investment: A Saudi score sheet. *Arab News*.

Ramaphosa, C. (2002). Black economic empowerment: Where to now? *Sisebenza Sonke, 2*(3), 3.

Rankin, J., Chen, Y., & Christian, A. (2006). E-procurement in the Atlantic Canadian AEC industry. *Journal of Information Technology in Construction, 11*, 75-87. Retrieved January 28, 2012, from http://www.itcon.org/cgi-bin/works/Show?2006_6

Rawlings, J. (1998). Electronic commerce on the internet –Part 1. *Network Security, 7*, 11–14. doi:10.1016/S1353-4858(98)80010-X

Raymond, J. (2008). Benchmarking in public procurement. *Benchmarking: An International Journal, 15*(6), 782–793. doi:10.1108/14635770810915940

Records Management Society of Great Britain, Local Government Group. (2003). *General disposal guidelines for local authorities.* Retrieved January 28, 2012, from http://www.esd.org.uk/foi/records management retention guidlines for LG.pdf

Reddick, C. G., & Coggburn, J. D. (2007). E-commerce and the future of the state sales tax system: Critical issues and policy recommendations. *International Journal of Public Administration, 30*(10), 1021–1043. doi:10.1080/01900690701221373

Reddy, K. (2006). The horizontal application of the equality guarantees and race discrimination by the business sector. *Journal of South African Law, 4*, 783–802.

Reilly, D. (1999). *Secure electronic transactions: An overview.* Retrieved January 28, 2012, from http://www.davidreilly.com/topics/electronic_commerce/essays/secure_electronic_transactions.html

Reinganum, J. F. (1983). Uncertain Innovation and the persistence of monopoly. *The American Economic Review, 73*(4), 741–748.

Rejman, S. (2010). *Research program No. 907980: Applied research of integrated logistical support system technology based on automated data exchange between defense industry and MoD department.* AURA, s.r.o., Brno.

Republic of South Africa. (1996). *Constitution of South Africa act 108 of 1996.* Pretoria, South Africa: Government Printer.

Republic of South Africa. (1997). *Skills development act 97 of 1997.* Pretoria, South Africa: Government Printer.

Republic of South Africa. (1998). *Employment equity act 55 of 1998.* Pretoria, South Africa: Government Printer.

Republic of South Africa. (2000). *Preferential procurement policy framework act 5 of 2000.* Pretoria, South Africa: Government Printer.

Republic of South Africa. (2002). *General procurement guidelines.* Retrieved on March 2, 2012, from http://www.bing.com/search?q=general+procurement+-guidelines&src=IE-SearchBox&Form=IE8SRC

Republic of South Africa. (2003). *Broad-based black economic empowerment act 53 of 2003.* Pretoria, South Africa: Government Printer.

Republic of South Africa. (2011, June 8). Preferential procurement regulations. In *Government Gazette* (*Vol. 34350*). Pretoria, South Africa: Government Printer.

Retief, J. (2010). *Business day. Editor's Letter.* Cape Town, South Africa: CTP.

Ribeiro, F., & Henriques, P. (2001). How knowledge can improve e business in construction. In *Proceedings of 2nd International Postgraduate Research Conference in the Built and Human Environment.* Oxford, UK: Blackwell Publishing.

RICS. (2005). *E-tendering: RICS guidance note.* Retrieved January 28, 2012, from https://www.ricsetender-ing.com/web/RICS%20Guidance%20Note%20-%20e-Tendering.pdf

RICS. (2007). *RICS e-tendering means paper free procurement.* Retrieved January 28, 2012, from http://www.bcis.co.uk/site/scripts/news_article.aspx?newsID=73

Riggins, F., & Mitra, S. (2007). An e-evaluation framework for developing net-enabled business metrics through functionality interaction. *Journal of Organizational Computing and Electronic Commerce, 17*(2), 175–203. doi:10.1080/10919390701294129

Rinderu, P., Iova, C., Gherghinescu, O., & Neagoe-Bacanu, D. (2009). *Comparison between HRD pre-accession funds and European social fund absorption at regional level in Romania.* Paper presented at 5th International Conference on Applied Business Research. Malta, Malta.

Rogerson, C. M. (2004). Pro-poor local economic development in South Africa: The application of public procurement. *Urban Forum, 15*(2), 180-210.

Rolfstam, M. (2009). Public procurement as an innovation policy tool: The role of institutions. *Science & Public Policy, 36*(5), 349–360. doi:10.3152/030234209X442025

Roman, A. V. (2012). *Maximizing transformative impacts: Public policy and financial management through e-procurement.* Working Paper. Boca Raton, FL: Florida Atlantic University.

Roman, A. V. (2012). *The politics of bounded procurement: Purists, brokers and the politics-procurement dichotomy.* Working Paper. Boca Raton, FL: Florida Atlantic University.

Rose, N. (1999). *Powers of freedom: Reframing political thought.* Cambridge, UK: Cambridge University Press. doi:10.1017/CBO9780511488856

Rose, W. R., & Grant, G. G. (2010). Critical issues pertaining to the planning and implementation of e-government initiatives. *Government Information Quarterly, 27*, 26–33. doi:10.1016/j.giq.2009.06.002

Ross, K. (2008, August 26). Time to talk on divisive race policy. *Daily News.*

Ross, D. F. (2003). *Introduction to e-supply chain management.* Boca Raton, FL: St. Lucie Press.

Rowlinson, S., & McDermott, P. (1999). *Procurement systems.* New York, NY: E & FN Spon.

Russo, A. (2009). *Italian public administration emarketplace.* Retrieved, October 23, 2011, from http://www.epractice.eu/en/cases/mepa1

Sahle, D. (2002). Procurement - A tool to address key development and social issues. *ASIST Bulletin, 14*(1&4).

Sartorius, K., & Botha, G. (2008). Black economic empowerment ownership initiatives: A Johannesburg stock exchange perspective. *Development Southern Africa, 25*(4). doi:10.1080/03768350802318530

Sauter, V. (2005). Competitive intelligence systems: Qualitative DDS for strategic decision-making. *Business Information Review, 23*(1), 35–42.

Savas, E. S. (2000). *Privatization and public-private partnerships.* New York, NY: Chatham House.

Scanlan, M. A. (2007). Tax sensitivity in electronic commerce. *Fiscal Studies, 28*(4), 417–436. doi:10.1111/j.1475-5890.2007.00062.x

Schapper, P. R., & Veiga Malta, J. (2004). Como hacer para que el estado compre mejor. *Gobierno Digital, 3*, 16–29.

Schapper, P. R., Veiga Malta, J., & Gilbert, D. (2006). An analytical framework for the management and reform of public procurement. *Journal of Public Procurement, 6*(1), 1–26.

Schein, E. (1992). *Organizational culture and leadership* (2nd ed.). San Francisco, CA: Jossey-Bass.

Schiele, J. J., & McCue, C. P. (2011). Lean thinking and its implications for public procurement: Moving forward with assessment and implementation. *Journal of Public Procurement, 11*(2), 206–239.

Schoenherr, T., & Mabert, V. A. (2011). A comparison of online and offline procurement in B2B markets: Results from a large scale survey. *International Journal of Production Research, 49*(3), 827–846. doi:10.1080/00207540903473359

Scholl, H. J. (2005). Organizational transformation through e-government: Myth or reality? *Lecture Notes in Computer Science, 3591,* 1–11. doi:10.1007/11545156_1

Scholl, H. J. (2006). Electronic government: Information management capacity, organizational capabilities, and the sourcing mix. *Government Information Quarterly, 23*(1), 73–96. doi:10.1016/j.giq.2005.11.002

Schömann, M. (2008). *Public electronic procurement in Germany.* Retrieved May 21, 2011, from http://www.ogasun.ejgv.euskadi.net/r51-3752/es/contenidos/informacion/20_seminario_internacional/es_3seminar/adjuntos/Manfred_Schomann.pdf

Schwester, R. W. (2009). Examining the barriers to e-government adoption: Electronic. *Journal of E-Government, 7*(1), 113–122.

Sclar, E. D. (2000). *You don't always get what you pay for: The economics of privatization.* Ithaca, NY: Cornell University Press.

Sebastian, M. W. (2007). *Information technology leadership perceptions and employee-centric organizational culture.* Minneapolis, MN: Walden University.

Seekings, J., & Nattrass, N. (2005). *Class, race and inequality in South Africa.* New Haven, CT: Yale University Press. doi:10.1002/9781444395105.ch47

Selaelo, A. (2007). *South Africa: From black economic empowerment (BEE) to broad-based black economic empowerment (BBBEE).* Retrieved on February 28, 2012, from http://www.helium.com/items/669208-south-africa-from-black-economic-empowerment-bee-to-broad-based-black-economic

Shapiro, C., & Varian, H. R. (1999). *Information rules: A strategic guide to the network economy.* Boston, MA: Harvard Business Press.

Shipman, F. B. (2007). *Formal succession planning in healthcare organizations: Meeting leadership needs in a changing American workforce.* Louisville, KY: Spalding University.

Siau, K., & long, Y. (2005). Synthesizing e-government stage models-a meta-synthesis based on meta-ethnography approach. *Industrial Management & Data Systems, 105,* 443–458. doi:10.1108/02635570510592352

Siddiquee, N. A. (2006). Public management reform in Malaysia: Recent initiatives and experiences. *International Journal of Public Sector Management, 19*(4), 339. doi:10.1108/09513550610669185

SIMAP. (2010). *CPV.* Retrieved September 2, 2011 from http://simap.europa.eu/codes-and-nomenclatures/codes-cpv/codes-cpv_en.htm

SIMAP. (2011). *Information system for European public procurement.* Retrieved September 2, 2011 from http://simap.europa.eu/index_en.htm

Simon. (1965). *The shape of automation for men and management.* New York, NY: Harper & Row.

Simon, H. (1973). Applying information technology to organizational design. *Public Administration Review, 33,* 268–278. doi:10.2307/974804

Singer, M., Konstantinidis, G., Roubik, E., & Beffermann, E. (2009). Does e-procurement save the state money? *Journal of Public Procurement, 9*(1), 58–78.

Singh, A. K., & Sahu, R. (2008). Integrating internet, telephones, and call centers for delivering better quality egovernment to all citizens. *Government Information Quarterly, 25,* 477–490. doi:10.1016/j.giq.2007.01.001

Siti-Nabiha, A. K. (2008). New public management in Malaysia: In search of an efficient and effective service delivery. *International Journal of Management Studies, 15,* 69–90.

Siti-Nabiha, A. K. (2010). Improving the service delivery: A case study of a local authority in Malaysia. *Global Business Review, 11*(1), 65–77. doi:10.1177/097215090901100104

Skillsportal. (2011). *BEE policy final.* Retrieved on March 7, 2012, from http://www.skillsportal.co.za/page/bee/3705033-BEE-policy-final

Smeltzer, L., & Carr, A. (2003). Electronic reverse auctions promises, risks and conditions for success. *Industrial Marketing Management, 32*(6), 481–488. doi:10.1016/S0019-8501(02)00257-2

Smith, I. (2009). *Smart step codification phase III.* Retrieved December 12, 2010, from http://www.eccma.org/2009ECCMAconf/presentations/eOTDprocess.pdf

Smith, J. (2006). *Blogs making their impact felt. BBC Website.* Retrieved January 28, 2012, from http://news.bbc.co.uk/2/hi/technology/4976276.stm

Software, A. E. C. (2012). *Fasttrack schedule 10.* Retrieved January 28, 2012, from https://www.aecsoftware.com/

Somasundaram, R., & Damsgaard, J. (2005). Policy recommendations for electronic public procurement. *The Electronic. Journal of E-Government, 3*(3), 147–156.

Sone, J. (2011). *E-governance in central Texas: Patterns of e-gov adoption in smaller cities.* Retrieved January 28, 2012, from http://ecommons.txstate.edu/arp/381

Soufi, W. A., & Mayer, R. T. (1991). *Saudi Arabian industrial investment.* London, UK: Quorum Books.

SouthAfrica.info. (2012). *Procurement boost for manufacturers.* Retrieved on March 2, 2012, from http://www.southafrica.info/business/economy/development/procurement-091211.htm

Spalde, C., Sullivan, F., de Lusignan, S., & Madeley, J. (2006). e-Prescribing, efficiency, quality: Lessons from the computerization of UK family practice. *Journal of the American Medical Informatics Association, 13*(5), 470–475. doi:10.1197/jamia.M2041

Standstill and injunctions – C-81/98 "Alcatel" – (Dir. 06/77 amended) Dir. 89/665/EC (2010)

Stein, M. J. (2008). Beyond the boardroom: Governmental perspectives on corporate governance. *Accounting, Auditing & Accountability Journal, 21*(7), 1001. doi:10.1108/09513570810907456

Steven, A. (2006). *Malaysia's town and cities are governed by appointed mayors.* Retrieved February 5, 2012, from www.citymayors.com/government/malaysia

Stewart, G. K. (2005). *Introduction to applied econometrics.* London, UK: Thomson Brooks.

Stone, B., Jabbra, J. G., & Dwivedi, 0. P. (1989). *Public service accountability: A comparative perspective.* Hartford, CT: Kumarian Press.

Strydom, P. D. F. (2005). *Black economic empowerment and small business in South Africa.* Retrieved on March 2, 2012, from http://www.sabusinesshub.co.za/section/content.php?ContentId=1381&SectionId=23&SubsectionId=12

Stutsman, K. K. (2007). *An examination of principal shortages in Florida school districts: Implications for succession planning for principal replacement.* Gainesville, FL: University of Florida.

Sun, S., Zhao, J., & Wang, H. (2012). An agent based approach for exception handling in e-procurement management. *Expert Systems with Applications, 39*(1), 1174–1182. doi:10.1016/j.eswa.2011.07.121

Svensson, J., Trommel, W., & Lantink, T. (2008). Re-employment services in the Netherlands: A comparative study of bureaucratic, market and network forms of organization. *Public Administration Review, 68*(3), 505–515. doi:10.1111/j.1540-6210.2008.00886.x

Talero, E. (2001). *Electronic government procurement, concepts and country experiences.* Washington, DC: The World Bank.

Taylor, F. W. (1967). *The principles of scientific management.* New York, NY: Norton.

Teich, J., Wallenius, H., Wallenius, J., & Koppius, O. (2004). Emerging multiple issue e-auctions. *European Journal of Operational Research, 159*(1), 1–16. doi:10.1016/j.ejor.2003.05.001

Thai, K. V. (2001). Public procurement re-examined. *Journal of Public Procurement, 1*(1), 9–50.

The Local Government ACT 1976 (ACT 171) & Subsidiary Legislation as at 25 August 2005. Percetakan National Malaysia Bhd (1976).

Thoren, C. (2004). The procurement of usable and accessible software. *Information Access in the Information Society, 3*(1), 102–106.

Tindsley, G., & Stephenson, P. (2008). E-tendering process within construction: A UK perspective. *Tsinghua Science and Technology, 13*(1), 273–278. doi:10.1016/S1007-0214(08)70161-5

Tischler, I. F. (2004). *How does leadership transition influence a sustained school change process? A case study.* Columbus, OH: The Ohio State University.

Tlhoaele, A. (2011). *Understanding the new treasury procurement scoring system (2011).* Retrieved on February 10, 2012, from http://www.beeandyourbusiness.com/new-treasury.html

Tlhoaele, A. (2011). *BEE point system under scrutiny.* Retrieved on March 7, 2012, from http://www.skillsportal.co.za/page/bee/1026480-BEE-point-system-under-scrutiny

Tödtling, F., & Trippl, M. (2005). One size fits all? Towards a differentiated regional innovation policy approach. *Research Policy, 34*(8), 1203–1219.

Torres, L., Pina, N., & Royo, S. (2005). e-government and the transformation of public administrations in EU countries. *Online Information Review, 29*(5), 531–553. doi:10.1108/14684520510628918

Tran, Q., Huang, D., Liu, B., & Ekram, H. (2011). A construction enterprise's readiness level in implementing e-procurement: A system engineering assessment model. *Systems Engineering Procedia, 2,* 131-141. Retrieved January 28, 2012, from http://www.sciencedirect.com/science/article/pii/S2211381911001056

TSO. (2006). *Public contracts regulations 2006.* Retrieved January 28, 2012, from http://www.opsi.gov.uk/si/si2006/uksi_20060005_en.pdf

TSO. (2009). *Public contracts (amendment) regulations 2009.* Retrieved January 28, 2012, from http://www.legislation.gov.uk/uksi/2009/2992/contents/made

Tucker, C. (2003). *Summary of black economic empowerment in South Africa.* Retrieved on February 15, 2012, from http://www.bowman.co.za/LawArticles/Law-Article~id~-783041820.asp

Tuunanen, T., Peffers, K., Gengler, C., Hui, W., & Virtanen, V. (2006). Developing feature sets for geographically diverse external end users: A call for value-based preference modelling. *Journal of Information Technology Theory & Application, 8*(2), 42–51.

UKonline. (2003). *UK online annual report 2003.* Retrieved January 28, 2012, from http://collection.europarchive.org/tna/20040722012352/http://e-government.cabinetoffice.gov.uk/MediaCentre/NewOnSiteArticle/fs/en?CONTENT_ID=4006060&chk=rIWVHj

UNDP. (1997). *The governance policy paper.* New York, NY: UNDP.

UNECE. (2008). *UNEDIFACT draft directory.* Retrieved January 28, 2012, from http://www.unece.org/trade/untdid/welcome.htm

United Nations. (2001). *Using the UNSPSC: Why coding and classifying products is critical to success in electronic commerce.* United Nations Standard Products and Services Code White Paper. Retrieved September 2, 2011, from http://www.unspsc.org/documentation.asp

United Nations. (2010). *E-government survey 2010: Leveraging e-government at a time of financial and economic crisis.* New York, NY: United Nations.

United States Government Accountability Office. (2005). Competitive sourcing: Greater emphasis needed on increasing efficiency and improving performance. *Journal of Public Procurement, 5*(3), 401–441.

Vaidya, K., Sajeev, A. S., & Callender, G. (2006). Critical factors that influence e-procurement implementation success in the public sector. *Journal of Public Procurement, 6*(1), 70–99.

Van Slyke, D. M. (2007). Agents or stewards: Using theory to understand the government-nonprofit social service contracting relationship. *Journal of Public Administration: Research and Theory, 17*(2), 157–187. doi:10.1093/jopart/mul012

Van Veenstra, A. F., Klievink, B., & Janssen, M. (2011). Barriers and impediments to transformational government: Insights from literature and practice. *Electronic Government. International Journal (Toronto, Ont.), 8*(2/3), 226–241.

Varian, H. R. (1985). Price discrimination and social welfare. *The American Economic Review, 75*(4), 870–875.

Varian, H. R. (2001). High-technology industries and market structure. In *Proceedings* (pp. 65–101). Kansas City, MO: Federal Reserve Bank of Kansas City.

Varney, M. (2011). E-procurement- Current law and future challenges. *ERA-Forum, 12*(2), 185-204.

Venter, R., Levy, A., Conradie, M., & Holtzhausen, M. (2009). *Labour relations in South Africa.* Oxford, UK: Oxford University Press.

Vernon, M. (1999, March 24). Livelier image for a low-profile task. *The Financial Times,* p. 16.

Walker, H., & Brammer, S. (2009). Sustainable procurement in the United Kingdom public sector. *Supply Chain Management: An International Journal, 14*(2), 128–137. doi:10.1108/13598540910941993

Walker, H., & Harland, C. (2007). e-Procurement in the United Nations: Influences, issues and impact. *International Journal of Operations & Production Management, 28*(9), 831–857. doi:10.1108/01443570810895276

Walsham, G. (1993). *Interpreting information systems in organization*. New York, NY: John Wiley.

Walsham, G. (2002). Cross-cultural software production and use: a structurational analysis. *Management Information Systems Quarterly, 26*(4), 359–380. doi:10.2307/4132313

Wamuziri, S., & Seywright, A. (2005). Procurement of construction projects in local government. *Municipal Engineer, 158*(2), 145. doi:10.1680/muen.2005.158.2.145

Wang, M. (2007). Do the regulations on electronic signatures facilitate international electronic commerce? A critical review. *Computer Law & Security Report, 23*(1), 32–41. doi:10.1016/j.clsr.2006.09.006

Wang, Y., Chang, C., & Heng, M. (2004). The levels of information technology adoption, business network, and strategic position model for evaluating supply chain integration. *Journal of Electronic Commerce Research, 5*(2), 85–98.

Wasserman, H., & De Beer, A. S. (2004). E-governance and e-publicanism: Preliminary perspectives on the role of the Internet in South African democratic processes. *Communicatio, 309*(1), 64–89. doi:10.1080/02500160408537987

Watermeyer, R. (2000). The use of targeted procurement as an instrument of poverty alleviation and job creation in infrastructure projects. *Public Procurement Law Review, 9*(5), 226–250.

Watermeyer, R. B. (2004). Facilitating sustainable development through public and donor procurement regimes: Tools and techniques. *Public Procurement Law Review, 13*(1), 30.

Weerakkody, V., & Dhillon, G. (2008). Moving from e-government to t-government: A study of process re-engineering challenges in a UK local authority context. *International Journal of Electronic Government Research, 4*(4), 1–16. doi:10.4018/jegr.2008100101

Weerakkody, V., Janssen, M., & Dwivedi, Y. (2011). Transformational change and business process re-engineering (BPR): Lessons from the British and Dutch public sector. *Government Information Quarterly, 28*(3), 320–328. doi:10.1016/j.giq.2010.07.010

West, D. (2001). *e-Government and the transformation of public sector delivery*. Paper presented at the Annual Meeting of the American Political Science Association. San Francisco, CA.

Westcott, T., & Mayer, P. (2002). Electronic tendering: is it delivering? A UK and European perspective. In *Proceedings of RICS Foundation Construction and Building Research Conference – COBRA 2002*. Nottingham, UK: Nottingham Trent University.

West, D. (2004). e-Government and the transformation of service delivery and citizen attitudes. *Public Administration Review, 64*(1), 15–27. doi:10.1111/j.1540-6210.2004.00343.x

West, D. M. (2005). *Digital government: Technology and public sector performance*. Princeton, NJ: Princeton University Press.

Wheeler, M. E. (2008). *The leadership succession process in megachurches*. Philadelphia, PA: Temple University.

Williams, C., & Lynnes, R. (2002). e-Business without the commerce. In *Proceedings of the Water Environment Federation*, (pp. 298-303). WEF/AWWA.

Williams, R. (2007). Briefing: The public contracts regulations 2006. In *Proceedings of the Institution of Civil Engineers Management Procurement and Law*, (pp. 45-49). Retrieved January 28, 2012, from http://www.icevirtuallibrary.com/content/article/10.1680/mpal.2007.160.2.45

Winston, N., & Eastaway, M. P. (2008). Sustainable housing in the urban context: International sustainable development indicator sets and housing. *Social Indicators Research, 87*(2), 211–221. doi:10.1007/s11205-007-9165-8

Wiseman, A. E. (2000). *The internet economy: Access, taxes, and market structure*. Washington, DC: Brookings Institution Press.

Wong, C., & Sloan, B. (2004). Use of ICT for e-procurement in the UK construction industry: A survey of SMES readiness. In F. Khosrowshami (Ed.), *Proceedings of ARCOM Twentieth Annual Conference 2004*, (Vol. 1, pp. 620-628). Reading, UK: Arcom.

World Bank. (2004). *Strategic electronic government procurement – Strategic overview an introduction for executives.* New York, NY: World Bank Institute.

World Trade Organisation. (1996). *Government procurement agreement: Agreement on government procurement.* New York, NY: WTO.

Wright, B. (1999). Electronic signatures: Making electronic signatures a reality. *Computer Law & Security Report, 15*(6), 401–402. doi:10.1016/S0267-3649(99)80090-9

Wright, B. E., Moynihan, D. P., & Pandey, S. K. (2011). Pulling the levers: Transformational leadership, public service motivation, and mission valence. *Public Administration Review, 72*(2).

Wright, J. N. (1996). Creating a quality culture. *Journal of General Management, 21*(3), 19–29.

WTO. (1994). *The Uruguay round final act annex 4 in legal texts: The WTO agreements.* Retrieved January 28, 2012, from http://www.wto.org/english/docs_e/legal_e/final_e.htm

WTO. (2011). *The WTO regime on government procurement: Challenge and reform.* Cambridge, UK: Cambridge University Press.

WTO. (2012). *Agreement on government procurement.* Retrieved on March 24, 2012, from http://www.wto.org/english/docs_e/legal_e/gpr-94_01_e.htm

WTO. (2012). *Understanding the WTO: The agreements – Government procurement: Opening up for competition.* Retrieved on March 15, 2012 from http://www.wto.org/english/thewto_e/whatis_e/tif_e/agrm10_e.htm#govt

Xu, M. (2007). *Managing strategic intelligence: Techniques and technologies.* Hershey, PA: IGI Global. doi:10.4018/978-1-59904-243-5

Yukl, G. (2002). *Leadership in organizations* (5th ed.). Upper Saddle River, NJ: Prentice Hall.

Yum, J. O. (1988). The impact of Confucianism on interpersonal relationships and communication patterns in East Asia. *Communication Monographs, 55*(4), 374–388. doi:10.1080/03637758809376178

Zhang, H., & Yang, J. (2011). *Research on application of e-tender in China.* Paper presented to International Conference on Internet Technology and Applications (iTAP). New York, NY.

About the Contributors

Nataša Pomazalová is an Assistant Professor at University of Defense in the Czech Republic. Her main research areas are e-government and e-public procurement. She is on the international editorial board of *Journal of E-Government Studies and Best Practices* and has acted as reviewer and adviser for national and international journals and academic conferences. She is active member of several national and international research projects.

* * *

Fareed Alyagout graduated at King Fahd University of Petroleum and Minerals with a BSc degree in Mechanical Engineering and Master Degree in Business Administration, also completed PhD Degree at University of Science in Malaysia. In a career spanning more than 25 years in the Power and Desalination Sector, he served the Saudi Electricity Company and Saline Water Conversion Corporation before assuming his present position as President of National Power Company since 2003. He is a Board Member in National Power Company, Jubail Energy Company, and Industrial Gases Company, also as a Technical Advisor for Al-Zamil Group Holding Company. He is active in various social activities, Executive Director for Al Basar International Foundation (World Health Organization programs for blindness prevention in Asia and Africa), board member for Isra University in Pakistan, and board member for Makkah Ophthalmology College in Sudan. He is also an Adjunct Professor in University Malaysia Pahang.

Nirmala Dorasamy is Senior Lecturer in the Department of Public Management and Economics at the Durban University of Technology. She lectures in the undergraduate and postgraduate programmes at DUT, PALAMA, and Department of Defence. She is on the editorial committee for international journals (*Journal of Business Management and Economics* and *African Journal of Business Management*) and a local journal (REBOC). She has been involved in a collaborative study with the Swinburne University of Technology in Australia and the American University in Cairo. She has been a keynote speaker and session chair at international conferences, while also presenting the conference communiqué. Her research area of focus is ethics and public sector management. She has co-authored textbooks for senior secondary learners.

Robert Eadie is the Course Director for MEng/BEng Hons Civil Engineering at the University of Ulster. He holds a PhD in Art Design and the Built Environment with the topic "Being e-Procurement in Construction." His research focuses on procurement and pedagogy. He spent 20 years in industry prior to moving into research, implementing e-procurement within a government department, and sitting on the Northern Ireland Civil Service e-Procurement Strategy Working Group. He represents Engineers Ireland at the professional college, which lobbies government, and is also an examiner for Chartered Status in the industry.

Modest Fluvià is Professor of Economics at the Universitat de Girona and Visiting Professor at ESADE Business School (Universitat Ramon Llull), both in Catalonia (Spain). He holds a M. Phil. from Oxford University (1989) and a Ph.D. from the Universitat de Barcelona (1983). He has taught at the Universitat de Barcelona and ESADE Business School. His research has focused particularly on industrial economics, agriculture, and tourism. He has published his research in books and international scientific journals, such as Tourism Management and Tourism Economics.

Oana Gherghinescu graduated in Economics at University of Craiova, Romania, in 2002. She continued her studies in the same field and earned a PhD in Economics, as well. Currently, she is appointed as Senior Lecturer by the Faculty of Economics and Business Administration, University of Craiova. Her teaching and research interests are focused on project management, monetary policies, and structural funds absorption. Ms. Gherghinescu coordinated over 10 large-scale projects, was deeply involved in several assessment exercises for the European Commission, and/or national projects/programmes. In addition, Ms. Gherghinescu set-up a successful private consultancy company in order to validate her theoretical knowledge.

Oldřich Hájek completed his Ph.D studies at University of Ostrava in Environmental Geography in 2008. Recently, he is Director of the Department of Regional Development, Public Administration and Law at Tomas Bata University in Zlin. His research interest is focused on various aspects of development at different geographical scales. He is co-author of the book *Cohesion Policy in Broader Relations* (with Jiří Novosák, in Czech only), and author of the book *Regional Disparities and Regional Policy: The Czech Republic in the Programming Period 2007-2013* (in Czech only). He participated in several projects focused on elaboration of strategic development documents for the City of Zlín and Zlín Region. Oldřich Hájek was the Head of Strategic Department at Zlín Region in 2007-2010.

Sami Halonen is a PhD student at the Department of Information Processing Science at the University of Oulu, Finland. He did his Masters in Software Business comparing Korean and Finnish companies. He studied in and worked in South Korea for two and a half years.

George Heaney is Professor of Construction at the University of Ulster and Director of Constructing Excellence in Northern Ireland. His work blends between academic enterprise and applied research in construction management involving such topics as procurement, project performance, and supply chain integration. With colleagues, he has published widely and presented at conferences and seminars. His academic enterprise activities keep him close to industry and link him into a UK-wide network on construction improvement.

Kai Krüger is Doctor Juris University of Oslo 1973, Associate Professor at Scandinavian Institute of Maritime Law 1967-1972, Professor at Law Faculty at University of Bergen since 1973 (Emeritus from 2010) and Faculty Dean (1993-1995). His professional activities are focused on private law, maritime law, contract and consumer law, European Union/European Economic Area law, public contract law/ procurement law, intellectual property law, construction and fabrication works contracts. He has been member of Norwegian Society of Science and Letters (1990), Consumer Sales Complaint Board (1978-1992) and Norwegian Procurement Complaint Board (from 2003), and member of Construction Works Disputes Expert Panel (from 1978).

Jiří Machů graduated at Tomas Bata University in Zlín in 2010 in Public Administration and Regional Development. Recently, he is going to complete his Ph.D studies in Management and Economics at Tomas Bata University in Zlín. His research interest is oriented towards various aspects of development at different geographical scales, with a special focus on public procurement. He is author of several research articles and studies focused on public procurement. He participated in several projects focused on elaboration of strategic development documents for the City of Zlín and Zlín Region.

Jiří Novosák completed his Ph.D studies at University of Ostrava in Environmental Geography in 2009. Recently, he is Senior Lecturer at Tomas Bata University in Zlín. His research interest is focused on various aspects of development at different geographical scales. He is co-editor of the book *Migration, Development, and Environment* published by Cambridge Scholar Publishing in 2008 and co-author of the books *Shaping the Development of Developing Countries, Cohesion Policy in Broader Relations* (in Czech only) and *Evaluation of Brownfields Development Potential* (in Czech only). He participated in several projects focused on elaboration of strategic development documents for the City of Zlín and Zlín Region.

Srinath Perera is the Chair and Professor of Construction Economics at Northumbria University with research interests in e-business, construction innovation, risk and value management, sustainability evaluation techniques, whole life costing, carbon estimating. He has over 20 years' experience in academia and industry and has worked as a chartered quantity surveyor and consultant project manager. He has published extensively and presented papers in the broader areas of construction informatics, construction economics, and quantity surveying. He has served as external examiner for several PhD and construction-related programmes in both UK and Ireland. He is a coordinator of the CIB task group TG83: e-business in construction (www.construction-ebusiness.org).

Teppo Räisänen is a Principal Lecturer at the School of Business and Information Management at the Oulu University of Applied Sciences. He has a PhD in Information Systems. He has published more than 20 peer-reviewed articles including publications in *International Journal on Computer Science and Information Systems*, *Journal of Healthcare Information Systems and Informatics*, Hawaii International Conference on Systems Science, and *Journal of Healthcare Information Management*. He has 10 years of working experience with printed media, digital media, and social media.

Renitha Rampersad is Senior Lecturer in the Department of Public Relations Management in the Faculty of Management Sciences at the Durban University of Technology in South Africa. She has a Doctor of Philosophy in Communication Science and her specialist research areas are transformation in business, ethical business practices, transformation, and consumer protection in South Africa, corporate social investment and HIV/AIDS, intercultural communication and work integrated learning in South Africa. She has published her research in local and international peer-reviewed journals and books and has presented at both national and international conferences, including collaborative writings on both a national and international level. She is a member of public relations and communication associations and is a reviewer for national and international journals.

Karunanidhi Reddy is Head of the Applied Law Department, Faculty of Management Sciences, at the Durban University of Technology, South Africa. His specialist research areas focus on law and business and include BEE and socio-economic transformation, ethical business practices, transformation and consumer protection in South Africa, the right to equality, discrimination, and implications for business, and international trade law and development in Africa. He has published in local and international peer-reviewed journals and presented at both national and international conferences. He has been editor of the *Faculty Research Journal* and is a reviewer for national and international journals.

Stanislav Rejman started in AURA Company at the beginning of the year 2009. He became a member of the team engaged in standardization and cataloging projects. He also led the team that developed an Informational System (IS) for cataloging according eOTD. Nowadays, he works as a manager for support of the data quality compliant with ISO 8000 and ISO 22754. He is very experienced in the field of development, implementation, service, and support of enterprise IS (ERP, CRM). In years 1991-2008, he worked as a project manager on comprehensive implementations of ERP systems, e.g. for company Vodafone. He also managed authorized training centres for Microsoft and IBM. Stanislav Rejman graduated from Technical University of Brno, specialization of technical cybernetics, measurement, and automatic control systems.

Paul Rinderu started his academic career in 1990 and is currently a Professor at the University of Craiova, Romania. He earned a PhD in Biomechanics and another one in International Economics. Complementary to teaching duties, he performs research activities on econometric modeling, structural funds absorption, and quality management. Mr. Rinderu is strongly involved in implementing various projects financed by different donors, until now leading over 10 large-scale projects and being involved in over 20 EuropeAid field missions in Algeria, Bosnia and Herzegovina, Kosovo, Serbia, Syria, etc. He is also member of different professional organizations and boards in this specific field of interest.

Alexandru V. Roman is a Ph.D. Candidate, School of Public Administration, Florida Atlantic University, Boca Raton, Florida, USA. He holds a Master's degree in Business Administration from State University of New York Institute of Technology and a Master's degree in Economics from State University of New York at Albany. His research focuses on public corruption, public procurement, and e-government. He has authored or co-authored articles that have appeared in journals such as *Public Performance and Management Review*, *Administrative Theory and Praxis*, and *Journal of Public Procurement*.

Danilah Salleh is currently doing her PhD at Universiti Sains Malaysia. She obtained her MSc in Engineering Business Management from Warwick University, United Kingdom, and Bachelor Degree in Accounting from University Teknologi Mara, Malaysia. She is now a Senior Lecturer at Universiti Utara Malaysia (UUM) and has taught a number of courses at UUM like Public Sector Accounting and Financial and Management Accounting. She has experience in the area of manufacturing as she worked as Production, Planning, and Control Assistant at Procurement Department in Epson Precision Johor, and has experience in banking. Her area of specialization is in qualitative and case study research and also in management accounting dealing with organizational and accounting change and in public sector accounting.

A.K. Siti-Nabiha is currently an Associate Professor and Program Manager for Doctor of Business Administration at the Graduate School of Business, Universiti Sains Malaysia. Her area of specialisation is in qualitative and case study research in management accounting dealing with organisational and accounting change specifically with changes in organisational performance measurement and systems of accountability both in the public and private sectors. She obtained her PhD in accounting from University of Manchester, United Kingdom, and MBA from Saint Louis University, USA. She has published research articles in both international and national journals and has also published two books. She taught accounting and finance courses at Universiti Utara Malaysia and University Sains Malaysia at both the undergraduate and postgraduate levels. She has also conducted workshops and training programs for universities in the ASEAN region and also for organisations in the private sector.

Joshua M. Steinfeld is a doctoral student of public administration at Florida Atlantic University's School of Public Administration. His research interests include public procurement, finance, budgeting, public policy, and international relations. He earned a Bachelor of Science in Business Administration at Boston University, a Master of Professional Studies in Organizational Leadership at University of Denver, and a Master of Science in Finance at Johns Hopkins University. Professional accolades include a successful career trading commodity future derivatives, representing a significant portion of global volume dealing in electronically traded products such as equity futures, precious metals, energy, and soft commodities.

Khi V. Thai is Professor and Director, School of Public Administration, and also Interim Director, School of Criminology and Criminal Justice, Florida Atlantic University. His expertise is in public budgeting, financial management, and public procurement. He authored or co-authored over 100 refereed journal articles, book chapters, books, technical reports, and has been editing three academic journals. Most recently, he has provided technical assistance to the South Florida Water Management District, the Government of Sierra Leone, Uganda, Bulgaria, Columbia, United Nations, USAID, and the Federal Government of Canada in the area of procurement reforms, procurement integrity, and international procurement. He is the founder of the Public Procurement Research Center in 1999, and served as its director until 2007. In 2004, Professor Thai initiated the International Public Procurement Conference, which has become the largest international conference in the field of public procurement in the world.

Ricard Rigall-I-Torrent teaches Economics at the Universitat de Girona, in Catalonia (Spain). He holds an MSc in Economics from the London School of Economics and a Ph.D. from the Universitat de Girona. His research has focused on economic analysis of tourism and culture, local provision of public goods, and teaching methods for teaching economics. He has published his research in books and international journals, such as *Tourism Management, Tourism Economics, Journal of Forecasting,* and *International Review of Economics Education.*

Demetra Lupu Visanescu graduated Higher Education Studies in Economics. After earning her BSc she continued training in the field and earned the Ph.D. in Accounting. She carried out an ardent activity in the public procurement domain since 2001. In addition, she actively participated in the implementation of several projects financed from structural funds. She possesses good knowledge on theoretical aspects and in particular on practicalities of implementation of public procurement through electronic means. Acquired knowledge, especially through practical work carried out in the field of public procurement, allows her to conduct training activities in this specific field of interest.

Sean Watts is Asian Management and Entrepreneurship Professor and Chair of Business and Economics at Yonsei, Korea's premier private university. He studied a BSc, three MBA programs, nuclear medicine, practiced medicine, and fell in love with business and education. He is Canadian, consulted with various organizations in Asia from Fortune 500s to CIA and United Nations, and enjoys helping small entrepreneurial ventures. He has worked with 128 countries and helped develop the world's largest manufacturer of computer chips—Applied Materials from $200 million to over $1 billion in one year.

Index

CPSIA information can be obtained at www.ICGtesting.com
Printed in the USA
BVOW052027061112

304851BV00007B/14/P